A Charismatic Companion to

THE ONE YEAR™ BIBLE

Creation House
Lake Mary, Florida

Printed in the United States of America
Library of Congress Catalog Card Number: 90-55272
International Standard Book Number: 0-88419-274-1

Creation House
Strang Communications Company
600 Rinehart Road
Lake Mary, FL 32746
(407) 333-0600

This book is dedicated to all who abide in Christ and allow His Word to abide in them—His true disciples.

Contents

Introduction

As a pastor pioneering a church in 1987, I discovered that most of my parishioners were not spending daily time in the Bible. And I knew they wouldn't grow as much as they could just from listening to my sermons. They needed a *daily diet* of God's Word.

It seemed that few were reading the Bible each day, and even fewer had ever read the entire Bible, because they had no plan. They also had no one to help them understand what they were reading. So I promised my congregation that, if they would read through the Bible with me in the next year using a daily guide, I would write a commentary to explain the portions. And I would pass out the commentary for each week at church on Sunday.

Little did I realize the task to which I had committed myself! But at the end of the year I knew it was worth the effort: I could see the spiritual growth in the lives of those who read through the Bible with me. They had a good working knowledge of the history of the Old and New Testaments. They knew the Bible stories and the important characters. They had a balanced understanding of the character of God. They had grown closer to Him. They were more dedicated and faithful. They knew who they were in Christ. They had learned to walk by faith.

So I want to welcome you to the first day of the best year of *your* life. I am thrilled that you've decided to read through the Bible with me during the next 365 days. And I can assure you that indeed this will be your best year yet as you draw closer to God through the daily reading of His Word.

There's nothing else on earth like the Bible. In numbers alone, it has sold more copies than any other book. It was written over a period of fifteen hundred years by more than forty different authors on three continents in three different languages. Yet it is completely harmonious in its numerous themes. Appropriately enough, it was the very *first* book to be printed on a printing press. And it has since been published in more languages than any other book in history.

The Bible is a *supernatural* book. It contains the accounts of hundreds of miraculous events, and there is no other volume that comes close to its distinct divine inspiration. Its ancient pages contain numerous detailed predictions that have all come to pass and hundreds more that will be fulfilled in the future. No other book is nearly as reliable a guide to what will happen in years to come.

The Bible is by far the most *interesting* book in the world. It contains history, law, prophecy, poetry, parables, allegories and the biographies, diaries and personal correspondence of some of the most fascinating people who ever lived. Most important, the Bible reveals God to us and His plan for every person. Because of that, no book has changed the lives of more people. Your life will likewise be deeply affected in the next twelve months!

This daily commentary follows the same plan as the *One Year Bible* published by Tyndale, so you may find it helpful to purchase a copy and read from it. I recommend the New American Standard Bible, which I use personally and quote throughout this book.

Following this plan, you will be reading portions from the Old and New Testaments each day, as well as from Psalms and Proverbs. I suggest you read the commentary after *first* reading the corresponding Scripture passage. There are some cases when you may want to read my commentary first, such as in books that are more difficult to understand or during the first day of a new book when I provide some historical background. *But this commentary will never replace the Bible, so use it only to supplement what the Holy Spirit is showing you during your time of reading the Scriptures.*

You'll need approximately a half hour per day to read the Scriptures and the commentary, depending on your reading speed. That may seem like a lot of time, but it will be well worth it. If your idea of daily Bible reading is to read one verse from a Scripture calendar, this book is not for you! I wrote it for the person who is hungry to know God better. You will be even more enriched if you investigate the various cross-references I list within the text.

This commentary is every bit as imperfect as I am, and I am certainly open to kind, constructive criticism. My desire is not to bore you with catalogues of facts and dates, but to encourage you every day, to help you understand what you're reading and to help you grow spiritually. May God bless you as you read His holy Word during the next 365 days!

Finally, I want to thank those wonderful people whose assistance has been invaluable during the preparation of the manuscript. They are Debbie Aiello, LaVerne Kirkwood (my wonderful mother), Ron (Barnabas) Miles, Virginia Steppling, Paul Stidham, Wayne and Addie Stidham and, most important, my wife, Rebecca. God has used them all, and I don't know what I would have done without each one.

David S. Kirkwood
January 1989

JANUARY 1

GENESIS 1:1-2:25

Jesus said in Mark 11:23, "Whoever says to this mountain, 'Be taken up and cast into the sea,' and does not doubt in his heart, but believes that what he says is going to happen, it shall be granted him." Here at the beginning of the Bible, God was demonstrating what Jesus said would work for *us*.

Notice that nine times the words "Then God said" are found in these first two chapters of Genesis. The writer of the book of Hebrews told us, "By faith we understand that the worlds were prepared by the *word of God*" (11:3, italics mine). Not only do we have faith that God created the world, but we also see that God spoke the creation into existence. According to Jesus, we, too, can speak "our world" into existence. Words that are believed in our hearts and spoken with our mouths can accomplish what seems impossible.

That's why it's so important that we have our hearts filled with God's Word—so that, as we speak it in faith, God's promises may come to pass in our lives. In fact, if you're saved, you activated this principle in the first few moments of your salvation. Romans 10:9-10 says "that if you *confess with your mouth* Jesus as Lord, and *believe in your heart* that God raised Him from the dead, you shall be saved; for with the heart man *believes*, resulting in righteousness, and with the mouth he *confesses*, resulting in salvation" (italics mine). Purpose today that you will believe and speak only what agrees with God's Word.

We also learn in this passage that we can address more than one person as God. Notice Genesis 1:26: "Then God said, 'Let *Us* make man in *Our* image, according to *Our* likeness' " (italics mine). The majority of the Old Testament was originally written in the Hebrew language, and the word in this verse that is translated "God" is the Hebrew word *Elohim*. It can be literally translated "Gods." We know from the rest of the Bible that there are three persons who can be addressed as God: the Father, the Son and the Holy Spirit. Jesus taught us that we should make our requests to the Father in His name (see John 16:23).

We also see that God gave Adam certain authority. God told him to fill the earth and subdue it, to rule over the fish, the birds and every living thing.

Many believe that Adam lost his authority to Satan when he sinned. It's a common misconception among religious people that God is running everything in the world today. God *is* sovereign, and His plans *will* come to pass, but it's also clear that Satan is ruling the world's system. That's why he's called "the god of this world" in 2 Corinthians 4:4.

When Satan tempted Jesus in the wilderness, he showed Him "all the kingdoms of the world in a moment of time" (Luke 4:5). And then he said to Jesus, "I will give you all this domain and its glory; *for it has been handed over to me, and I give it to whomever I wish*" (Luke 4:6, italics mine). Jesus didn't refute him. Satan, his demons and the human race are responsible for all the evil in the world today, not God. In the New Testament we will learn that on the cross Jesus rendered "powerless him who had the power of death, that is the devil" (Heb. 2:14). *Satan has no authority over those who believe in Jesus.*

Finally, we see that God made it easy for Adam and Eve. He didn't tell them, "Don't commit adultery," because there was no one with whom to commit adultery. He didn't tell them, "Don't steal," because there was no reason to steal. With only two people in the world, if something was stolen, it would be pretty obvious who the thief was! However, God did tell them there was one tree from which they shouldn't eat (though it was among many trees from which they could eat). As free moral agents, Adam and Eve had to be tested to see if they could be trusted to obey. They failed the test by their disobedience, as all of us since them have failed God's test by our own disobedience. So we all need a Savior. Thanks be to God for sending us a Savior!

MATTHEW 1:1-2:12

The only detail of Jesus' genealogy we need to remember now is that He was a descendant of Abraham, Isaac, Jacob (same as Israel), Judah and eventually David. This listing in Matthew is Jesus' genealogy through Joseph, not Mary, so in one sense it's irrelevant, because Joseph was not Jesus' father. God was. Jesus' genealogy through Mary is listed in Luke's Gospel. Both Mary and Joseph were descendants of David, but Mary was descended from David's son Nathan, whereas Joseph was descended through David's son Solomon.

We read that Joseph, upon discovering that his fiancee was pregnant, desired to put Mary away secretly. Then an engagement was legally binding and could be broken only by divorce. We witness Joseph's godly character and true love for Mary; he wanted to "disengage" her secretly, not wishing to disgrace her because of her alleged unfaithfulness to him. Further, he, like Mary, would have to face the ridicule of people who knew she was pregnant before they were married. Also notice that he had no sexual relationship with her until after the birth of Jesus, so truly the prophecy was fulfilled that a virgin would bear a Son (see Is. 7:14).

Notice also that the wise men didn't visit Jesus when He was a newborn, but probably when He was closer to two years old. They visited Him in a house, but we know Jesus was born in a stable or a cave and that He was laid in a feeding trough right after His birth. Tomorrow we will discover another clue that affirms the wise men arrived approximately two years after Jesus was born.

PSALM 1:1-6

We'll read about this theme throughout the Bible: it pays to serve God! Only those who meditate in God's Word can be compared to a tree planted by streams of water. In a dry land like Israel, this example has great significance. It means that our source of life and strength never dries up, and we're ready for whatever adversity the devil may bring.

PROVERBS 1:1-6

It doesn't matter how wise we already are; as we read through the Proverbs, we will become wiser.

JANUARY 2

GENESIS 3:1-4:26

Adam and Eve, like every person since them, had a choice. They could obey or disobey God. Satan initiated their disobedience by using the same methods he uses today. First, he convinced Eve to doubt the consequences of her sin. He said, "You surely shall not die!" in direct contradiction to what God had said (3:4). Today, many people listen to Satan's lies, believing, for example, that no person will go to hell to suffer eternally.

Second, Satan influenced Eve to doubt God's true character. He told her that God didn't want them to eat from the tree because God wanted to withhold something good from them, the knowledge of good and evil. Again today, many people have a distorted view of God's character. They think God gave commandments to spoil their fun, when in reality He gave us commandments to enhance our lives.

Third, Satan mixed a lot of truth with his lies. He told them that in the day they ate of the fruit, their eyes would be opened, and they would be like God, knowing good and evil. (All those statements are obviously true from examining the rest of the text.) The same technique is used by various cults today. If you wanted to poison a dog, you wouldn't just feed him poison; you would sprinkle poison on a steak. We should be very careful that what we listen to in spiritual matters can be proved by many scriptures.

The fundamental error of Adam and Eve was that they doubted God's word. Satan will do all he can to deceive us into doubting God's word. But it is impossible for God to lie (see Titus 1:2).

Although God had said that Adam and Eve would die in the day they ate of the fruit, it's obvious they didn't die physically. They died spiritually. The New Testament teaches that human beings are tripartite in their nature. They are composed of three parts: spirit, soul and body (see 1 Thess. 5:23). You are a spirit who has a soul (mind, emotions, intellect) and lives in a body. Your spirit and soul are eternal. When your body ceases to function, your spirit and soul will leave your body and go to heaven if you're saved. Your spirit is the part of you that is born again. Before you were born again, your spirit was dead in relationship to God, just as Adam's and Eve's spirits became on the day they sinned.

Being dead spiritually means being separated from God. It means having the nature of Satan in your spirit. But when your spirit is reborn, you become alive spiritually, one spirit with Jesus Christ (see 1 Cor. 6:17). You actually become a child of God and receive His nature.

Today we also read the first promise of the Messiah's coming to save humanity. He is spoken of in Genesis 3:15 as the "seed" of "the woman" and the One who would some day crush the serpent's head.

In chapter 4 we read about Cain and Abel. The book of Hebrews reveals that God accepted Abel's offering and not Cain's because Abel came to God in faith (see Heb. 11:4). It really wasn't *what* he brought but *how* he brought it that pleased the Lord. God had already killed an animal and clothed Adam and Eve in the skins, so perhaps Abel acted on that knowledge. Or possibly God had already taught them the Old Testament principle of animal sacrifice (representative of Christ's ultimate sacrifice on the cross). Regardless, Cain became the first murderer, showing clearly that Satan's nature had flooded his spirit, and he paid the consequences.

MATTHEW 2:13-3:6

Today we discover the second evidence that the wise men visited Jesus when He was about two years old. Herod had all the male children of Bethlehem and its environs murdered who were "from *two years old and under*, according to the time which he had ascertained" from the wise men (v. 16, italics mine).

God protected Jesus, Joseph and Mary by forewarning them of impending events, not by changing those events. If we stay in fellowship with the Lord, He'll show us things to come as well, either for our protection or so we can be ready for approaching adversity. God loves all His children!

John's baptism was somewhat similar to Christian baptism, yet in many ways different. His symbolized repentance and the washing away of sin, but that's where the similarities end. When we're baptized as Christians, it symbolizes our complete identification with Christ. Going under the water signifies the death of our old self with Christ and our burial. When we come out of the water, it symbolizes our new self that, like Christ, has risen from the dead. We have passed from spiritual death to spiritual life and are new creations in Christ Jesus (see 2 Cor. 5:17). Our sins have been washed away!

PSALM 2:1-12

This is a prophetic messianic psalm, pointing toward the time described in Revelation 20. At that time Jesus will have been ruling the world from Mount Zion in Jerusalem for one thousand years, and Satan will be released from prison to deceive the nations once more. He will gather the nations together for war against Christ, and they will all be destroyed when fire falls from heaven (see Rev. 20:7-10). However, this psalm has application to any who are fighting God's plan (see Acts 4:25-26). Clearly, Jesus is speaking in verses 7-9 (see Heb. 1:5).

PROVERBS 1:7-9

This short section tells us that a person really knows nothing at all until he has a fear, or reverence, for almighty God.

JANUARY 3

GENESIS 5:1-7:24

We don't need to spend all our time trying to understand details of Scripture that offer us little help on the path of spiritual growth. If God thinks something is important, He'll emphasize it throughout the Bible. He wants us to grow spiritually so we can reach the world with the gospel. But figuring out where Cain got his wife will not help us lead someone else to Jesus.

One of those once-mentioned, minor details is found in today's reading. Who are the sons of God who took wives for themselves from the daughters of men in chapter 6? Two theories are offered. One says that the sons of God were the godly descendants of Seth and that the daughters of men were ungodly descendants of Cain. The other states that the sons of God were fallen angels and that the daughters of men were just that—daughters of men. Their sexual relationships produced races of giants. Believe it or not, the second theory probably has more scriptural evidence to support it. As I stated previously, however, neither theory is going to help us grow spiritually.

The important concept from today's

reading is this: God is holy, and where His mercy ends, His judgment begins. Anything that we can learn about God's character will help us. And while the Bible says that God is love (see 1 John 4:8), it also says He is a consuming fire (see Heb. 12:29). Paul wrote in Romans 11:22, "Behold then the *kindness* and *severity* of God" (italics mine).

God saved the few righteous people on the earth from judgment. The New Testament teaches that we who are trusting in Jesus are not destined for wrath (see 1 Thess. 5:9). So there is no need to be fearful when we read in the book of Revelation about the terrible things that are going to happen on the earth soon. We won't be here.

A few facts about the ark, the animals and the water might be helpful to quiet skeptics who say the story of the flood is just a myth. The ark was about 450 feet long by 75 feet wide. That means it was six times as long as it was wide, which is the exact proportion of modern naval vessels. The total animal population would not have exceeded thirty-five thousand vertebrates with the average size of a sheep. Approximately 150 boxcars could have carried them all, and the ark had a capacity of at least 520 boxcars! It wasn't until 1884 that a larger boat was built.

Could the whole earth have been covered with water? Today there is enough water on the earth to cover it entirely to a depth of two miles! Surely an omnipotent God could have caused such a flood.

MATTHEW 3:7-4:11

John the Baptist was quite a "fire and brimstone" preacher, wasn't he? In no uncertain terms, he informed the Jews that their salvation wasn't guaranteed just because they were descendants of Abraham. Too many people today think their salvation is sure because they had a grandfather who was a preacher or because their parents are Christians. But the truth is this: God has no grandchildren, just children, and we must come to Him on our own, through Jesus Christ. And if we're truly born again, our lives will reveal it. There will be "fruit in keeping with [our] repentance" (3:8). *People who say they are born again but whose lives are no different from those of the unregenerate are just fooling themselves.*

Jesus was baptized to identify with humanity, not because He needed to repent or have His sins washed away. He was sinless. At this time we also see a beautiful picture of the trinity: the *Spirit* descended in the form of a dove; the *Father* said, "This is My beloved Son" (3:17); and the *Son* came up out of the water.

The Scripture teaches that Jesus was tempted in all ways just as we are (see Heb. 4:15), so the temptation in the wilderness was not the only time Jesus was enticed. Because He was the Son of God, it's hard for us to understand that He could be tempted, but we must remember that He was also 100 percent man. This passage further makes it plain that *it is not a sin to be tempted.* We can expect temptations to come for the rest of our lives, and we should view them as tests to be passed. Apparently, because the "first Adam" was tested, so, too, the "second Adam" (see 1 Cor. 15:45) had to be tested. Thank God, Jesus passed every test!

Satan tempted Jesus in the same manner he will tempt us. First, he tried to make Jesus doubt who He was. Satan said to Him, "*If* You are the Son of God..." (4:3, italics mine). The devil tries to make Christians doubt who they are as well. According to God's Word, we are children of God, temples of the Holy Spirit, more than conquerors and forgiven of all our past sins. Hallelujah!

Don't let the devil talk you out of it!

Second, Satan took the Scriptures out of context, attempting to influence Jesus to act foolishly and jump from the pinnacle of the temple. You can make the Bible say anything you want it to say by pulling out isolated verses. We need to know the whole Bible, not just small portions. This is the chief reason people are lured into the cults. They don't know enough of the Bible, so they're easily deceived by cult leaders who can quote a few verses.

Third, Satan tempted Jesus to take a shortcut to what He knew He would eventually possess anyway. Some day all the kingdoms of this world will belong to Jesus, and He will reign for a thousand years. Satan was offering them to Jesus right then—if Jesus would only bow down before him. Jesus took God's way to His ultimate destiny—the way of the cross. We, too, must not give in to temptations to take compromising shortcuts. His promises will surely come to pass, so let us hold fast in our faith.

PSALM 3:1-8

Like many of the psalms written by David, this one tells us the exact trial he was facing at the time. It will be a few months before we read the story of David's fleeing for his life from his own son Absalom (the occasion of this particular psalm).

David began this psalm by talking about his trouble, but he ended by talking about how God was going to deliver him. Here is a secret for getting our prayers answered. We may certainly start by talking about the problem, but we need to finish by expressing our faith in God for the answer. Jesus said that anything we ask in prayer, *believing*, we shall receive (see Matt. 21:22).

PROVERBS 1:10-19

Here we read of a principle found from the beginning to the end of the Bible: we reap what we sow. In the months ahead, we'll see example after example of this principle.

JANUARY 4

GENESIS 8:1-10:32

We're reading today about one of our relatives, for all of us are descended from the patriarch Noah.

Noah and his family were actually inside the ark for a little over one year. What a test of his faith and patience that must have been! I just hope for his sake that all the animals on board spent the year in hibernation!

After the waters receded, God made a great promise: as long as the earth remains, seedtime and harvest, cold and heat, summer and winter, and day and night will not cease. Most people miss the one condition on this promise: "while the earth remains." Some day God is going to make a new earth, which is spoken of in the last two chapters of the book of Revelation. Then this promise will no longer be in force. At that time, "there shall no longer be any night; and they shall not have need of the light of a lamp nor the light of the sun, because the Lord God shall illumine them" (Rev. 22:5).

God also promised that He would never again destroy every living thing by a flood, and He created the rainbow as a sign of His pledge. With our scientific minds, we would say that God created the principle of the refraction of light. We can imagine how Noah and his family would be tempted to fear the next time there was a good thunderstorm, as well as what a comfort it was for them to see a rainbow. Likewise, when the rain begins to fall in our own lives, it's a good time to renew our faith by looking once again at God's promises.

The first ten chapters of Genesis cover a time span of about two thousand years. So, of necessity, many details of certain events are left out. The story of Noah's sin of drunkenness and his cursing of Canaan, for example, leaves a key question unanswered: what was so evil about Ham's seeing his father naked? Some commentators suggest that the Hebrew language here implies homosexuality.

Why was Ham's son Canaan cursed as a result? Possibly he played a part in Ham's sin. Or perhaps this wasn't really a curse placed on Canaan, but a foreshadowing of what would happen to the descendants of Canaan, who were cursed for their own wickedness. Again, too many details are absent for us to know for certain.

The important revelation is that Noah's prophecy came to pass. Canaan's descendants became servants to Shem's and Japheth's offspring. The people of Israel were all descendants of Shem, and they invaded and dispossessed the people of Canaan's land according to God's plan. (We'll read about that in the book of Joshua.) God has also "enlarged Japheth," as Noah said. The descendants of Japheth make up the Indo-European peoples, which would include most North and South Americans, most Europeans and many South Asians.

The records of Noah's descendants in chapter 10 may seem boring, but they're significant. We'll read some of these tribal names later on and see that they help Bible scholars better understand end-time events. Some key names for us to keep in mind are Japheth's sons Magog, Tubal and Meshech (see Ezek. 38:2), as well as Ham's son Canaan, who became the father of the Jebusites, the Amorites and the Girgashites. Again, those were the nations that Joshua and the people of Israel dispossessed in "Canaan's land."

MATTHEW 4:12-25

We learn today that the very first word of Jesus' first sermon was "Repent!" Repentance is the starting place in a relationship with God. "To repent" means to see and understand that you have been heading in the wrong direction and to make a decision to go the other way.

Matthew left out some details that Luke included concerning the calling of Peter and Andrew (see Luke 5:1-11). When we read in Luke's Gospel of Peter's seeing a miraculous catch of fish right before his eyes, it's easy to understand why he immediately left everything to follow Jesus.

People ask today, "How can I know if God is calling me into the ministry?" I always tell them, "Don't worry. If God has called you, He knows how to get your attention and make His direction clear." However, *all* of us are called to be fishers of men in some capacity.

The threefold earthly ministry of Christ is summed up beautifully in verses 23-24. Jesus was teaching, preaching and healing. We will discuss this at greater length later, but suffice it to say that Jesus was multi-gifted. (That's an understatement!) Today some are anointed to *preach* the gospel, some are gifted to *teach* the Word of God and some are anointed to *heal* the sick. We need all the different ministries. Together they reflect the true ministry of Christ.

PSALM 4:1-8

Keep in mind that the psalms were originally set to music and sung, just as we sing choruses today. In the Hebrew language they were even more beautiful. The New Testament says that we should teach and admonish one another with "psalms and hymns and spiritual songs, singing with thankfulness in your hearts to God" (Col. 3:16). One of the best places to obey this scripture daily is while taking a shower! Why not turn your humdrum shower time into a festival of praise?

PROVERBS 1:20-23

Do you ever wonder how people can be so deaf and blind to the reality of God's ways? As this passage so aptly tells us, God's wisdom is readily available to all.

JANUARY 5

GENESIS 11:1-13:4

The tower of Babel was a supreme monument of rebellion against God. It was quite possibly being built as a center for heathen worship of the heavens. The people literally said, "Let us build for ourselves...a tower whose *top [is] heaven*" (italics mine; the words "will reach" in the NASB are in italics, indicating they were added by the translators and not included in the original text). God confounded their plans by confusing their language and scattering them over the earth. More than five thousand languages and dialects are used in the world today, although many of those have probably evolved since the tower of Babel. We also assume that after this incident the various races of mankind evolved from the small inbreeding groups of the next few generations, as it is well-established that genetic variations take place quickly under such circumstances.

We see in Genesis 11 that Abram (later to be renamed Abraham) was descended from Noah's son Shem. The modern word *Semitic* is derived from his name and literally means "descended from Shem." You've probably heard the term *anti-Semitic* as well; it describes someone who is prejudiced against Jews. (Technically, however, Jews aren't the only Semitic people. The Arabs are also Semites.)

Abram became the father of Isaac, and Isaac became the father of Jacob, who was renamed Israel. All the people of the nation of Israel descended from his twelve sons. One of those was named Judah, from which the modern word *Jew* is derived. Jesus was a descendant of Judah.

Abram traveled with his father and wife from Ur of the Chaldeans to Haran, which was close to the modern border between Syria and Turkey. It was there that the Lord spoke to Abram the great promises that have all come true. The final promise found in Genesis 12:3 is still being fulfilled at this very minute! God said that in Abram all the families of the earth would be blessed. God was speaking of the day when Jesus would die for the sins of all humanity. Jesus told us to take the gospel to *all* the nations (literally, "families") of the earth (Matt. 28:19). And as they hear and accept, God's promise to Abraham is coming to pass. *Can you see that God's ultimate purpose in calling Abram was to bless all mankind through Jesus Christ? God was planning for your salvation more than four thousand years ago!*

Abram traveled to the land of Canaan (remember that Canaan was a son of Noah's son Ham), and there God promised He would give his descendants that land, which would be roughly the territory of modern Israel. That pledge wasn't fulfilled for about six hundred years, when God delivered the people of Israel from Egypt and brought them into the promised land.

Abram kept traveling south to the Negev and, because of famine, continued south into Egypt (although the Bible is silent about whether God directed him that way). But there he made a blunder. He was afraid the Egyptians would kill him because they would desire his beautiful sixty-five-year-old wife. Sarai lived to be 127, which means that to us she would have looked like someone in her 30s. Abram told the Egyptians that Sarai was his sister, which was partly true, because she was his half-sister.

God mercifully delivered Abram, even in his deceitfulness and fear. So Abram traveled back to the altar he had built near Bethel (not far from Jerusalem) and "called on the name of the Lord" (13:4). Probably he was repenting for what he'd done in Egypt!

MATTHEW 5:1-26

The beatitudes (vv. 3-12), as they're called, have been interpreted in numerous ways. I prefer to look at them as the blessed steps of conversion and spiritual growth. Others look at them differently, so everyone must decide for himself.

Step one: Realize you are spiritually poor and have a vacuum only God can fill. Step two: Mourn over your past sins, and repent. Step three: Humble yourself to admit your need for a Savior, and receive Him! (The word translated "gentle" in v. 5, or "meek" in the King James Version, can also be translated "humble.") Step four: Hunger and thirst to be holy and Christlike. Step five: Grow in true love, showing mercy as you have been shown mercy. Step six: Purify your heart and motives. Step seven: Grow to be one who helps others make their peace with God by leading them to Christ. Step eight: Grow to where you are willing to suffer persecution for the sake of the gospel.

We are the salt of the earth—what preserves it and gives it its flavor! We're also the light of the world, bringing glory to God as people see our changed lives!

Thank God that our righteousness surpasses that of the Pharisees (v. 20), as we have had the righteousness of Christ imputed to us (see 2 Cor. 5:21)! The Lord laid our sins on Jesus and placed Jesus' righteousness on us.

Jesus made clear our course of action when we know that a relationship with a brother or sister in God's family is hurt. We are to go to the person and work for reconciliation. How many Christians wouldn't dare visit a certain church because their relationship with a person in that congregation is not right? Jesus didn't say to avoid such people, but to go to them, because *if your relationship with a brother isn't right, your relationship with God isn't right!* That's why Jesus said first to go and be reconciled to your brother, then present your offering at the altar. He didn't say it would be easy; He just said to do it.

We read in verse 25 that we are on the way to standing before the judge. That's what this life is—a journey to the great Judge. Thank God that those of us who have believed in Jesus have made our peace with Him already.

PSALM 5:1-12

There was a time in my Christian walk when I couldn't understand why the book of Psalms was in the Bible. But after I had been through some difficulties similar to David's, I understood. What great encouragement and comfort they offer in time of test and trial! Maybe you can relate to this psalm if you've ever had people spread lies about you. (If that's happening to you right now, it also helps to know that there are true things they could tell about you [if they knew them] that would make you look even worse. Thank God they don't know the truth!)

PROVERBS 1:24-28

Unheeded warnings offer no help after calamity has come.

JANUARY 6

GENESIS 13:5-15:21

Today we read of the parting of Abram and his nephew Lot. Their life-style was very much like that of the Arab Bedouins who live in Israel today, moving their tents from one place to another, looking for water and pasture for their livestock. Both Abram and Lot were very rich, even by today's standards. Abram could muster an army of 318 men, all of whom worked for him (see 14:14). Because the land could not sustain both of their herds, Abram unselfishly worked out an agreement with his nephew. Lot made the mistake of moving his tents near Sodom, which would soon be destroyed by the Lord.

By chapter 14, Lot was living in Sodom, and he and his household had been taken captive by the invading armies of Chedorlaomer and his three allies. *It is always a mistake to join with godless people* (see 2 Cor. 6:14-18). Unfortunately, it seems Lot was a slow learner. After his rescue he moved right back into Sodom.

After Abram's valiant rescue of Lot, he gave a tithe of the spoils to Melchizedek, priest of God Most High. Many teach that it was here that the principle of tithing was instituted. However, archaeological excavations of Ur of the Chaldeans (Abram's hometown) reveal that *even the people of Ur gave tithes to support their temple and its worship of heathen deities*. So tithing existed long before Abram and may have been practiced by the earliest patriarchs.

Who was Melchizedek? Nobody really knows. He was simply called "priest of God Most High" (*El Elyon*). Some think Melchizedek was the pre-incarnate Christ. Certainly the book of Hebrews indicates that he serves as a type of Christ, and we'll discuss the subject more when we read that New Testament book.

Although Abram was childless, God promised him that one of his descendants would be his heir and that he would have as many descendants as there are stars in heaven. According to Paul, all of us who believe in Jesus have become "Abraham's offspring" (Gal. 3:29). So we can look at ourselves as one of those stars Abram was gazing at that night!

The strange ceremony in which God and Abram participated was not so strange to Abram. He understood easily that God was making a covenant with him, the most solemn, binding agreement between two persons. To break a covenant meant facing a death sentence (see also Jer. 34:18-20). Covenants are still practiced by some cultures today, but the closest comparable ceremony in our culture is the wedding with its vows.

Once again God promised that He would give Abram's descendants the land of Canaan, but this time He revealed more exact information. Abram's descendants would be enslaved in a foreign nation for four hundred years. But God promised to judge that nation and bring out His people with many possessions. This was fulfilled about six hundred years later, when God delivered the people of Israel from Egypt by great judgments. And true to His word, they came out "with silver and gold" (see Ps. 105:37).

Why would it take so long before it

came to pass? The answer is found in 15:16: "for the iniquity of the Amorite is not yet complete."

God knew that the sinful path of the Amorites was taking them deeper into decadence, and it would eventually descend to the point where He would bring judgment. It is essential that we understand this. *God brought the people of Israel from Egypt to possess Canaan's land because of the wickedness of the Canaanites.* God is fair. He wasn't playing a game of favorites. In fact, the people of Israel eventually lost the land to foreigners because of their own sinfulness.

MATTHEW 5:27-48

Here Jesus taught that sin is not just an outward action, but a condition of the heart. What difference is there between a man who commits adultery and one who fantasizes about it all day long? Both are sinners. What difference is there between a murderer and a man who hates so much that he would murder if he could get away with it? Both are sinners. So many religious people think they're righteous because they're outwardly holy, yet inwardly they're horrible sinners. That's why we all need to be born again—because we all need a new inner nature. Once we make Christ our Lord and Savior, we become brand-new creatures (see 2 Cor. 5:17).

Jesus was not teaching self-mutilation in verses 29-30. He was speaking hyperbolically (exaggeration for effect) to make the point that hell is such a terrible place that it would be worth cutting off your hand to stay out of it.

In Jesus' day divorce was easy and commonplace. Moses had permitted divorce under the Law because of the hardness of the people's hearts, and many in Christ's day were taking Moses' words as an "any reason" license for a quick divorce. What's the difference between adultery and a man who has divorced his wife because he has found a more attractive sex partner? None.

The test of true spirituality is how we love. It's easy to love those who love us, but it's difficult to love those who mistreat us. When we do, however, we're manifesting the true character of God, who causes the sun to shine on the evil and the good and sends rain upon the righteous and the unrighteous. (In Jesus' society, rain didn't have the negative connotation it holds for many of us. Farmers need sun and rain, and both are looked on as a blessing from God.)

PSALM 6:1-10

Notice how once again David ended his prayer with a confession of his faith in God's deliverance. Quit saying, "I wonder if the Lord heard my prayer." Start saying like David, "The Lord has heard my supplication, the Lord receives my prayer" (v. 9).

PROVERBS 1:29-33

As one preacher said, "Sometimes the worst judgment the Lord can give us is to just let us have our own way."

JANUARY 7

GENESIS 16:1-18:19

Today we learn a little more of the strange customs that existed in Abram's day. If a wife could produce no heir for her husband, she could give her slave girl to him, and the resulting child would become hers. Such an agreement could even be written into the marriage contract.

What Abram and Sarai did is what we call "taking things into your own hands." But God doesn't need help in fulfilling His promises. And when we take things into our own hands, we make a mess of things, just as Abram and Sarai did. The ensuing animosity between Sarai and Hagar is not surprising at all.

Hagar's son Ishmael became the progenitor of the Arabs. To this day both Arabs and Jews worship at Abraham's tomb, tracing their roots to him. (The Arabs believe that God told Abraham to sacrifice Ishmael, not Isaac, in the story recorded in Genesis 22. And because Ishmael was the older son, they believe the promised land belongs to them, not the Jews.) God's description of Ishmael and his descendants in 16:12 seems accurate even to this day, as we hear frequent reports of Arab terrorists and of the constant conflict between Arabs and Jews. And to think it all started with Abram and Sarai's taking things into their own hands.

In chapter 17 God spoke again—twenty-four years after He originally spoke to Abram in Haran. This time God changed Abram's name to Abraham, which means "father of a multitude." The book of Romans, commenting on this incident, tells us that God "calls into being that which does not exist" (Rom. 4:17). Once again we see God displaying the principle of Mark 11:23: words spoken in faith from the heart come to pass! Sarai also received a name change, to Sarah, which means "princess."

At the same time, God instituted the covenant sign of circumcision. It had been practiced before by various tribes, and it usually signified the beginning of adult status. To Abraham and his household, it meant they were marked as God's own.

Notice that God said circumcision was to be performed on the eighth day of a child's life. Medical authorities have since discovered that a baby's blood has the highest clotting factor on the eighth day of its life. Not only that, but studies have also proved that women whose husbands are circumcised have *much* less chance of contracting cervical cancer. God knows what He's doing!

We read in chapters 17-18 of incidents in which both Abraham and Sarah laughed at the thought of having a child in their old age. Sarah's laugh was clearly a laugh of doubt, but many commentators think Abraham's laugh was one of faith. Possibly Abraham was laughing at how funny it would be for two old people to have a son! Yet nothing is too difficult for the Lord, and He assured the aged couple that within one year the promise would come to pass.

If we truly believe God's promises, we should be full of joy because we're certain of their fulfillment. Unfortunately, too many Christians are "Sarah laughers" rather than "Abraham laughers." They, like Sarah, have more faith in the way things look than in what God has promised.

Who were Abraham's three visitors in chapter 18? We assume that two were angels and one was the Lord (see 19:1). After visiting Abraham, they went off to visit Sodom.

MATTHEW 6:1-24

Jesus' teaching on the subject of holiness during His Sermon on the Mount was radically different from any other teaching of His day. Time and again He emphasized that true holiness is determined by inward motivations, not necessarily outward actions. We can easily test our motives by doing exactly what Jesus said here: giving in secret. If we're doing good deeds to be seen by men, we have no reward with God because our motives are all wrong. How many pastors have had members of their congregations hand them checks that were "too big" to put in the collection plate? How many Christians lead different lives at home from what they show at church?

Directly before Jesus taught His disciples the Lord's prayer, He told them specifically not to use meaningless repetition when they prayed. So it's doubtful He intended for this prayer to be repeated over and over. Jesus said, "Pray, then, *in this way*" (italics mine). So the form of this prayer is a good one to follow.

We pray to our heavenly Father as His children. We begin by worshipping and praising Him. We ask first for His kingdom to be established according to His will, and then for our own needs. We forgive those who have wronged us and ask forgiveness for our wrongs against God. We ask also for His protection.

Jesus also warned about the "deceitfulness of riches"; they promise happiness but bring no lasting satisfaction. We cannot serve God *and* money (mammon), but Jesus didn't say we couldn't serve God and *have* money. The important thing is that Jesus is Lord over our lives *and money*, not money the lord over Jesus and our lives. Are we living to get or living to give?

PSALM 7:1-17

Christians sometimes find it difficult to understand how David could pray for God to judge his enemies. We must realize that, if God didn't do something, David would be killed by his enemies. If we have enemies, they're usually people with whom we've had some disagreement, not people who are out to kill us. I'm sure that, if we had the kind of enemies David had, we would pray the same way.

PROVERBS 2:1-5

This is a great promise for those of us who want true wisdom and knowledge of God. But it's clear these blessings won't come to the casual observer—only to the diligent seeker. Jesus said that if we abide in His word we are truly His disciples (see John 8:31).

JANUARY 8

GENESIS 18:20-19:38

When God said that the sin of Sodom and Gomorrah was "exceedingly grave," it seems an understatement in light of Sodom's reception of the two visiting angels in Genesis 19. Here was a whole city of homosexuals who desired sex with the two visitors. (These angels appeared to look like men, as they often do.) What's amazing is that God restrained His wrath for such a long time against this wicked place. Truly God's mercy is incredible!

What is possibly even more amazing is that God agreed to spare the whole city if He could find just ten righteous people living there. Abraham must have thought that God could find at least ten, as he knew that his nephew Lot, Lot's wife and their two daughters and husbands-to-be lived in Sodom. Surely there were four other righteous people there besides them.

But there weren't, and God destroyed the cities. But He didn't do anything until He had rescued Lot and his family.

Unlike many biblical cities, the remains of Sodom and Gomorrah cannot be seen today. They're probably under the south end of the Dead Sea, whose level has risen since the judgment. However, archaeologists have discovered that around 2050 B.C., a violent explosion occurred in that area, during which red-hot salt and sulfur were hurled into the air. It truly did rain "fire and brimstone" on Sodom and Gomorrah.

Why did Lot's wife turn into a pillar of salt for looking back? It's possible that what is really meant is that she "turned back," just as people have rushed back into their burning homes to save some "important" item and have perished in the blaze (see Jesus' comments in Luke 17:31-32). Regardless, the angel did tell them, "Don't look behind you."

Lot's two daughters "took things into their own hands" and committed incest to become the mothers of the Moabites and the Ammonites. Keep those names in mind, because we'll read about their subsequent history in the months ahead. Both nations caused the people of Israel considerable problems and still do today. However, one descendant of Moab by the name of Ruth became part of the lineage of Jesus.

MATTHEW 6:25-7:14

With a heavenly Father as caring as ours, we have no reason to worry about anything. Our problem is that we don't always trust Him as we should. This portion of Scripture is a good one to memorize or turn to frequently when we're tempted to be worrisome. Peter wrote, "Casting all your anxiety upon Him, because He cares for you" (1 Pet. 5:7). We should be seeking first His kingdom (6:33) rather than seeking what this world has to offer.

We are commanded not to judge, but we'll read tomorrow that we can and should inspect fruit. So what does it mean to judge another? First, we should realize that we never know the whole story. You've probably had people form opinions of you based on imperfect knowledge. We may see someone sin, but we might not see him repent an hour later. We might see people overcome with anger, but we have no idea what they've been enduring all their lives. We should always believe the best about people until we know the worst. And even then we should still show them mercy, just as God has shown us mercy.

Second, we, unlike God, never know what's in a person's heart. People can do right things for the wrong reasons and wrong things for the right reasons. Let's leave that kind of judgment to God alone.

Third, none of us has a right to point out someone else's faults when we have so many ourselves. When we criticize others, we show what a high opinion we have of ourselves.

What a tremendous promise Jesus gave us in this passage! His theology of prayer was far superior to that of modern theologians who say that when we ask, God might say yes, no or give us the opposite of what we request. Like any good father, God loves to give His children good gifts.

Jesus said that the entire ethical teachings of the Law of Moses and the prophets are summed up in the saying "Do unto others as you would have them do unto you." If we want to simplify our walk of holiness, we should just follow this simple rule. Then we'll always do what is pleasing to the Lord. Couples who follow this rule have heaven-made marriages. Church members who follow it have wonderful fellowship. Business people who obey this rule have prospering companies.

PSALM 8:1-9

Truly, the majesty of God is revealed in His creation. Have you ever, like David, gazed at the stars and stood in awe of the greatness of God? Have you ever looked down at the earth from up in a jet and marveled at the love of God? How majestic is His name in all the earth!

PROVERBS 2:6-15

The wisest thing a person can do is obey God.

JANUARY 9

GENESIS 20:1-22:24

Once again Abraham pulled the stunt he used in Egypt twenty-five years before, saying Sarah was his sister. He was still afraid he would be killed because of her beauty. This is surprising to us, as Sarah was now about ninety years old! Some think, however, that because she was given the ability to bear a child at that age, her body was rejuvenated, and she therefore looked much younger than she actually was. (And quite possibly Abraham, at age one hundred, had a little rejuvenation as well!)

Regardless, it becomes clear that Abraham was far from perfect. He should have trusted that God would protect him, because the promise that he and his wife would be parents had not yet been fulfilled. But once again the Lord mercifully straightened out the situation. We must remember that the Lord showed Abraham mercy in these situations not only for his sake, but also for the sake of us who would believe in the coming "seed" of Abraham, Jesus Christ.

Finally, twenty-five years after God's original promise, Isaac (whose name means "laughter") was born. When he was weaned, Abraham held a great feast, and Ishmael (who was now about sixteen years old) mocked his half-brother. The New Testament says that he "persecuted" Isaac (Gal. 4:29). God directed Abraham to listen to Sarah, and at her request, Hagar and Ishmael were sent off. What a heartbreak it must have been to Abraham to send his older son away. But he was paying the price for doubting God before and taking things into his own hands. God mercifully provided for Hagar and Ishmael, however, and today his many descendants (as God promised) live all over the Middle East.

It is clear from the story of the testing of Abraham in Genesis 22 that God wants nothing to come before Him in our lives. Too few Christians realize this, but God does test His children, just as all good parents evaluate their children to see if they can be given greater responsibilities. Adam was the first man to be tested, and he obviously failed his first trial. Many Scripture passages refer to God's testings, and we will read in the months ahead about the various means God uses. Sometimes He'll test us as He did Abraham: by telling us to do something very difficult or to give up something very dear to us. God wants to use us, but He can only use those He can trust. "He who is faithful in a very little thing is faithful also in much" (Luke 16:10). Let us be determined to be found faithful!

God never intended that Abraham would actually kill his son, and He planned from the start to stop Abraham at the last minute if he followed through.

Notice that Abraham said to his servant in verse 5, "Stay here with the donkey, and I and the lad will go yonder; and *we will worship and return to you*" (italics mine). It's obvious that Abraham believed God would keep His promise that his descendants would be named through Isaac. The book of Hebrews tells us that Abraham believed that, after he killed his son and offered him up on the altar, God would raise him from the dead (see Heb. 11:17-19).

Why did God say in verse 12, "Now *I know* that you fear God" (italics mine)? Doesn't God know everything in advance? Certainly, but until this test, Abraham's faith had never faced so great a challenge. In that sense God "found out" what was in Abraham's heart at that moment in time.

Although this story reveals to us how much Abraham loved God, it reminds us even more of how much God loves the world, because He gave His only begotten Son for us. The place where Abraham almost offered up Isaac is thought to be only a few hundred yards from where Christ was crucified. Truly Abraham's words "God will provide for Himself the lamb" had greater significance than he and Isaac imagined.

After Abraham's testing, the Lord solemnly reiterated the promises of His covenant, and we once again hear of God's ultimate purpose in choosing Abraham—to bring blessing to all the earth through one of Abraham's descendants. *This is the predominant theme of the whole Bible.*

MATTHEW 7:15-29

We learned yesterday that we're not to judge, but we read today that we are to be fruit inspectors. We should beware of false prophets. Though some insist that prophets no longer exist, the Bible clearly teaches that for as long as the saints need perfecting there will be those who are called to the ministry of the prophet (see Eph. 4:11-13).

Those of us who believe Jesus is still calling prophets must be heedful of Jesus' admonition. Just because people prophesy, perform miracles or cast out demons does not prove they're sent from God. (The Antichrist will come with many false wonders and miracles.) We should inspect the fruit of their lives and ministries. Are people being drawn to Christ? Does this prophet lead a holy life? Jesus was teaching here that there will not only be false prophets, but false Christians as well. They, too, can be known by their fruits. But we must not get unbalanced. (Jesus did all the things spoken of here that He Himself said don't guarantee salvation: He prophesied, performed miracles and cast out demons.) The false prophets and Christians that Jesus spoke of were those "who practice lawlessness" (v. 23).

The example of the man who built his house on the rock and the man who built his house on the sand is applicable to every human being. Notice that the storms of life came to both men, but the man who was the "doer" of the Word of the Lord stood fast. Being doers of God's Word doesn't mean that trials won't come our way. But it does mean we won't be swept or blown away when they come. The wisest thing any man, woman or child can do is obey God's Word.

PSALM 9:1-12

David knew God and walked with Him. Again and again we will hear David affirming the justice, righteousness, compassion and greatness of God. We should be praising God not just in church but, like David, all the time.

PROVERBS 2:16-22

Israel's history attests to the truthfulness of verses 21-22: "For the upright will live in the land, and the blameless will remain in it; but the wicked will be cut off from the land, and the treacherous will be uprooted from it." The wicked Canaanites were uprooted from their land by Israel, and when Israel became as wicked as the Canaanites, they, too, were uprooted by the Assyrians and Babylonians. Keep that in mind as we study the historical books of the Bible.

JANUARY 10

GENESIS 23:1-24:51

Sarah lived to a ripe old age of 127 when Abraham was about 137 and Isaac was about 37. (Can you believe that Abraham remarried after her death and had more children?) Sarah was buried in a cave in Hebron, where later Abraham, Isaac, Jacob, Leah and Rebekah were all buried as well. The site can still be visited, and Jews and Arabs both worship there.

Abraham's taking on the responsibility of finding a wife for his thirty-seven-year-old son may seem strange to our modern minds. However, marriages were always arranged by the parents in Abraham's time, and this custom is still practiced in some places in the Middle East. When you think about it, who is the most qualified to find a lifelong mate for another person? The parents already have experience in marriage. They know many other married people. They know the qualities to look for in a prospective mate. And they know their son or daughter well. Our modern system of two people falling in love and making their own choices has been proven to work only 50 percent of the time. Two people in love are usually blind to each other's faults, and they usually have no experience on which to base their choice, either. I have always told single people that, before they're engaged to "Mr. Right" or "Miss Right," they should ask their parents and closest friends if they think they are making the right choice. "In abundance of counselors there is victory" (Prov. 11:14).

Abraham didn't want Isaac to marry one of the heathen women in Canaan's land where he lived, so he made his servant place his hand under his thigh (a custom similar to our placing our hand on the Bible in court) and take an oath that he would go to Abraham's home country to find a wife for Isaac. Any believer who marries an unbeliever is bound to have trouble with his new "father-in-law," the devil!

Abraham's servant made the five-hundred-mile journey back to Mesopotamia with ten camels loaded with gifts for Isaac's future bride and her family. When he arrived, he "put out a fleece" before the Lord to determine His will. (Under the New Covenant, however, we have the Holy Spirit living inside us to guide us.) God worked it out that Rebekah, who was Isaac's second cousin, arrived on the scene and, in fulfillment of the servant's prayer, watered his ten camels. That would have been quite a task, as one camel can drink thirty gallons of water! The rest is history.

Notice in verse 35 that Abraham's servant said the Lord had made his master rich and had "given him flocks and herds, and silver and gold, and servants and maids, and camels and donkeys." We know that Abraham was prosperous, but we also know that God came first in his life. (He was willing to give up his son in obedience to God.) *God is not opposed to our having money as long as He has our hearts.* And if He has our hearts, He has control over our money as well.

MATTHEW 8:1-17

Before Jesus heals this leper, He first corrects his theology. The leper, like some Christians today, believed that Jesus could heal him, but was uncertain if Jesus would heal him. Jesus, who "is the same yesterday, today and forever" (Heb. 13:8) said, "I am willing!" He is just as willing to heal us today.

PSALM 9:13-20

Ultimately, God's judgment will come upon all nations and men. In the meantime, we must trust that God knows what He's doing, even if we're tempted to feel forgotten. When it seems that God is slow, we must remind ourselves that a thousand years is like one day to the Lord (see 2 Pet. 3:8).

PROVERBS 3:1-6

When very old people are asked for the secret to long life, inevitably there will be one who says: "Fast women and a cigar and two shots of whiskey a day!" According to what we read, however—and according to medical authorities—that's not so. Keeping God's commandments adds years to our lives. On the other hand, every cigarette a person smokes costs 14.4 minutes of life.

JANUARY 11

GENESIS 24:52-26:16

The story of Isaac and Rebekah reminds us that our heavenly Father, like Abraham, is looking for a bride for His Son. The church, as the bride of Christ, has yet to see her betrothed, but the day is coming when she, like Rebekah, will see Him face to face. When that day arrives, a wonderful wedding feast is planned!

After Sarah's death, Abraham remarried and had even more children. He finally died at age 175. His first son, Ishmael, had twelve sons, just as God promised (see Gen. 17:20).

After twenty years of marriage Isaac and Rebekah had twin boys in answer to prayer: Esau, the elder, and Jacob. God had told Rebekah that two nations were in her womb and that the older would serve the younger. Esau became the father of the Edomites, of whom we will read many more times; Jacob became the father of the Israelites. Esau liked to hunt in the fields, and Jacob liked to live in tents. Isaac loved Esau; Rebekah loved Jacob. Picking favorites like that was a mistake, as anyone can tell you who has grown up in the same kind of family.

Our modern minds don't understand the story of Esau's selling his birthright. That belonged to the firstborn, but obviously it could be sold or given away. Having the birthright meant having the position as head of the family and all the blessings that would go along with it, as well as receiving a double inheritance of the estate. We can hardly praise Jacob for his "smooth move," but the Scripture greatly condemns Esau for "despising his birthright." The book of Hebrews warns us that "there [should] be no immoral or godless person like Esau, who sold his own birthright for a single meal" (Heb. 12:16).

When Isaac settled in Gerar, Philistine territory, the Lord (mercifully) appeared to him and confirmed that the promises of the covenant of Abraham were now his. The Messiah would come from his lineage.

Isaac also displayed the weakness of his father, bluffing that his wife was his sister. Once again God mercifully intervened, and Isaac began to prosper under God's blessings. But he still had a few lessons to learn.

MATTHEW 8:18-34

To be a follower of Jesus back in His time, a person had to do just that—follow Jesus, as He traveled almost constantly. We have it easier today, since we can usually stay in one place and still be a follower of Jesus. He was simply reminding these two men who said they would follow Him that there would be a price for keeping their commitment. Jesus had no place to lay His head because He was always on the move, and they had no time to wait for someone's funeral. Jesus had a mission to fulfill. The message to us is plain: *Nothing should come between us and following Jesus.*

Jesus was at Peter's home in Capernaum, located right on the shores of the Sea of Galilee. That sea could be better called a lake, as it's only about seven miles wide and fourteen miles long. The local topography makes it subject to sudden, violent storms that can turn the calm waters into a choppy sea in a very short time. Can you imagine the awe the disciples felt as the raging winds and stormy sea were perfectly subdued in an instant by Jesus' command? Probably, Jesus here demonstrated the gift of special faith, listed as one of the nine gifts of the Spirit in 1 Corinthians 12:1-10.

The Bible says that Jesus came to destroy the works of the devil (see 1 John 3:8). Even the devil himself knows that he's doomed, and apparently these demons knew that a time was coming when they, too, would be tormented (v. 29). We also suppose that demons would prefer habitation in animals if they can't find habitation in a human being, since these demons asked to be permitted to enter the swine. In people and animals, demons have their widest range of expression in the physical realm.

Isn't it a shame that the people of the region of the Gerasenes, after witnessing this great miracle, asked Jesus to leave? And then we see the true character of God in Jesus, as He politely departed at their request.

PSALM 10:1-15

The people of God have often asked why God doesn't do something to the wicked for their deeds. He will, but He will show them a great deal of mercy first, giving them plenty of time to change their ways (see 2 Pet. 3:8-9).

PROVERBS 3:7-8

Obedience not only lengthens one's life, but it also guarantees a healthier life along the way. God promised Israel that if they would obey Him, He would take sickness from their midst (see Ex. 23:25-26).

JANUARY 12

GENESIS 26:17-27:46

No one fully understands the ritual of the "giving of the blessing" practiced by some of the patriarchs near the end of their lives. The giving of the blessing was considered an important determination of events in the future lives of descendants. Probably it was a manifestation of the gift of prophecy and the word of wisdom. But how could God use Isaac to deliver a prophecy to Jacob when Isaac thought that he was delivering it to Esau?

We must remember that God's plan always comes to pass, regardless of how men work against it or just botch it up. One time God used a donkey to deliver a message to a prophet (see Num. 22), so it's no problem for Him to use a deceived old man to speak His plan unknowingly. (In the New Testament, an unsaved high priest prophesied concerning Christ and didn't even realize it. See John 11:49-52.) God had said even before Jacob and Esau were born that the older would serve the younger (25:23).

The New Testament gives us very little help in understanding this story. The book of Hebrews tells us that "by faith Isaac blessed Jacob and Esau, even regarding things to come" (Heb. 11:20).

There is no need to lie and cheat to bring God's purposes to pass either. Some justify Rebekah and Jacob's deceitfulness with the argument that Isaac was about to bless the wrong son. But even if Isaac was about to make a mistake, Rebekah and Jacob did not need to contrive and carry out their plan. It was God's problem, not theirs.

The consequences of their sin were grave. Jacob the tent-dweller had to flee for his life into exile, and *his mother, Rebekah, would never see him again*. Jacob would reap exactly what he had sown. Why would God choose such a deceitful man as Jacob to receive the blessings of Abraham and Isaac? Because God doesn't make His choices based on our works. God chooses based on His own grace. (Esau would have been no better choice anyway, based on his works as we read of them in 25:34, 26:34-35 and 27:41.) Both men were sinners, and both needed a Savior.

God has likewise chosen you and me, not because of our works (which would send us straight to hell), but because of His grace. Incidentally, although Isaac had thought that the day of his death was drawing near, he lived at least another forty years after this event.

MATTHEW 9:1-17

One spiritual principle demonstrated in this story of the healing of the paralytic in Capernaum is that forgiveness of sin and healing of sickness are provisions of the cross. Jesus first told this man that his sins were forgiven, and then He told him to rise and take up his bed. The Bible teaches that Jesus not only bore our sins in His body on the cross, but also our sickness and diseases (see Is. 53:4 [margin], with Matt. 8:17). Those twin truths are referred to as the "full gospel."

On the same day that we discuss God's choosing of an imperfect man named Jacob, we also read of God's choosing of another imperfect man named Matthew. (He wrote this Gospel.) As a general rule, tax collectors in Jesus' day were extremely dishonest and hated by most of the Jews. Jesus spoke of tax collectors as being in the same category as harlots.

The Pharisees, who were extremely devout keepers of the letter of the law, objected that Jesus was spending time with tax collectors and other sinners. Jesus' reply was classic: "I did not come to call the righteous, but sinners" (v. 13). It is quite possible that Jesus had a note of sarcasm in His voice when He spoke those words. His real meaning may have been more like, "I didn't come to call people to repentance who *think* they're so righteous that they need no changing, but people *who realize they're sinners*." We have already read that our righteousness must surpass that of the Pharisees if we're to enter the kingdom of heaven (see 5:20).

Jesus' words in verses 15-17 can be interpreted in a number of ways, all of which make sense. One view is that Jesus was finding "new receptacles" (the tax gatherers and sinners) to fill with His teaching and revelation, because the "old receptacles" (the scribes and Pharisees) couldn't handle it. To this day much of Jesus' "new wine" is more than some "old wineskins" can handle! Are you a fresh wineskin?

PSALM 10:16-18

PROVERBS 3:9-10

We are simply stewards of all that God has entrusted to us. For us to withhold what rightfully belongs to Him is poor stewardship indeed. Notice that it is only those who are trustworthy to whom God promises an abundance. Stingy Christians have no rights to such blessings.

JANUARY 13

GENESIS 28:1-29:35

Rebekah sent her favorite son, Jacob, away for "a few days" (v. 44) until Esau's anger subsided, but it turned out that he was gone for twenty years! She would never see him again.

Both Isaac and Rebekah didn't want Jacob to marry one of the Canaanite women, so they sent him off to her brother Laban in Paddan-aram, from which she had come more than sixty years before to marry Isaac. On the long journey there (about five hundred miles), Jacob had a vision in his sleep. And during that vision he received the promises of Abraham and Isaac. In his seed all the families of the earth would be blessed, because Jesus would be one of his descendants. God didn't choose Jacob because of his holiness. God chose Jacob because *He was thinking of you and me*, that we might have a Savior.

This was the beginning of Jacob's walk with God. He had some lessons yet to learn. But he made a vow that if the Lord would be with him, keep him safe and bring him back to the promised land, the Lord would be his God, and he would give a tenth of his income to the Lord. Jacob knew that tithing was required by God, and this was hundreds of years before the Law of Moses stated such.

When Jacob finally arrived in his mother's hometown, he met his cousin Rachel for the first time and quickly fell in love with her. He wasn't in much of a bargaining position, though, to purchase her as his bride (a custom still practiced in parts of the Middle East). So he struck a bargain of seven years of labor in return for the hand of Rachel. His love was so great that the time quickly flew by.

But this is when Jacob the deceiver was deceived. Just as he had impersonated his brother seven years before with his mother's blessing, now Leah impersonated her sister with her father's blessing. Jacob truly reaped what he had sown. Now he had to work another seven years for Uncle Laban and live with two wives for many years to come.

God never forbade polygamy in the Old Testament, but He never endorsed it, either. (God gave Adam *one* wife.) All the patriarchs who had more than one wife had trouble because of it, including Jacob. Later, the Law forbade a man to marry his wife's sister while the first wife was still living.

We can't help but ask how Jacob could have unknowingly married and spent his wedding night with the wrong woman. No doubt during the wedding ceremony Leah had a veil covering her face. In fact, Jacob had probably never seen Rachel or Leah without veils. Later on, either the lights were turned down low or Jacob drank too much wine at the wedding dinner or Leah kept her veil on. We don't know. We'll have to ask Jacob when we get to heaven.

The Bible says that Jacob loved Rachel more than Leah, which we can understand. It would be difficult to love someone who impersonated your fiancee and tricked you into marrying her. But Jacob loved Leah enough to have seven children by her. One of them was Judah, of whom Jesus was a descendant.

MATTHEW 9:18-38

It's sad that some Christians believe the healing ministry of Jesus has ceased, especially when there are so many scriptural examples of people whom Christ healed to build our faith. Praise God that "Jesus Christ is the same yesterday and today, yes and forever" (Heb. 13:8)!

Jesus indicated it was the faith of the woman with the hemorrhage and the faith of the two blind men that brought their healings. In the more detailed account of the raising of the synagogue official's daughter in Mark's Gospel, we will see that it was his faith that brought his daughter back to life. It is our faith that brings God's will to pass in our lives, not our hopes. Hope always leaves room for failure. Hope always says "maybe." Faith means being convinced, absolutely certain. I'm not hoping that I'll *be* saved; I'm believing that I *am* saved. It's so important that we know what God has said, because faith comes from hearing His promises (see Rom. 10:17). Conversely, if we don't know what God has promised, we have no basis for faith. All we can do is hope.

Why did Jesus say that the synagogue official's daughter was only sleeping? Possibly He was calling into being that which does not exist (see Rom. 4:17). Or possibly the girl was actually sleeping, having passed from death to sleep by that time.

When Jesus made the statement that the harvest is plentiful, there were only about 200 million people living on planet Earth. Today there are twenty-five times that many, or about *5 billion people* (1988 figures). Truly the harvest is even more plentiful than ever before, and the need for workers is much greater than ever before. Pray that the Lord will send more laborers, adding, "Lord, send me!"

PSALM 11:1-7

Here is a scripture affirming that God tests the righteous and the wicked (v. 5). We should be ever aware that the Lord's eyes are always upon us. I have noticed that my children are much more obedient when they're aware of my presence. If we remember that God is watching and testing us, we, too, will be much more obedient.

PROVERBS 3:11-12

God loves His children, and He disciplines them in the same way that good parents discipline their kids. First, He disciplines us *by His Word*. If we obey His Word, we don't have to be concerned with further discipline. But if we won't listen to His Word, we'll be "spanked" in one way or another. Sometimes it comes through sickness (see 1 Cor. 11:30; however, sickness does not always indicate God's discipline). Sometimes it comes through some calamity. We'll read in future weeks of many cases of God's loving discipline.

If you're suffering in some way, you should make sure you haven't opened the door through disobedience. If you have, you can close the door by confessing your sin and repenting (see 1 John 1:9). However, many fine, obedient Christians are suffering only because they don't know their rights and privileges in Christ, and the devil is having a carnival with their lives. We will discuss the subject further when we come to the appropriate passages.

JANUARY 14

GENESIS 30:1-31:16

Today we're reminded of the strange custom practiced first by Abraham and Sarah, and now by Isaac and Rachel. If a wife could not bear children for her husband, she could give him her maidservant, and the resulting child would be hers. (Actually, this custom isn't so strange in light of all the cases of surrogate motherhood in our society.) The pregnant maidservant would actually give birth to her child sitting on her mistress's knees.

The strife between Rachel and Leah dragged on for years as they competed for their husband's love. Finally, barren Rachel bore a son who would be very special; his name was Joseph. But now Jacob had four "wives," and the complications can only be imagined. The strife carried down to their children and climaxed when the eleven brothers sold Joseph into slavery. How much better it is to have one wife!

Jacob had been gone from his parents for fourteen years now, and he longed to go back. He had served Laban all that time, and all he had to show for it in wages were his two wives, his two concubines and his children. But shrewd Laban had gotten rich in the meantime. So Jacob worked out a new deal, and this time he had some bargaining power, as Laban knew he was about to lose a good man. All the black sheep and the speckled and spotted goats would become Jacob's. (They probably were the most unusual. You've no doubt heard the expression "He's the black sheep of the family.")

I don't know of anyone who has been able to explain adequately Jacob's methods of increasing his portion of the flocks. There is no scientific basis for what he did. It may have been God's supernatural blessing, and quite possibly Jacob was acting in faith on what God had told him to do. Regardless, we should take comfort in knowing that no matter how terrible our boss might be, God can still bless us. *He* is our source, not our employer! After six more years of working for his Uncle Laban, Jacob became a very rich man, and Laban and his sons were no longer as friendly toward the one they took advantage of for fourteen years. Now it was Laban's turn to reap what he had sown.

It had been twenty years since Jacob left home; now God commanded him to return. Even Rachel and Leah, Laban's own daughters, heartily agreed their father had not done right. They were ready to go with Jacob back to the promised land.

MATTHEW 10:1-25

Jesus' twelve disciples were an unlikely lot to become founding fathers of the world's greatest institution. Four of them were unschooled fishermen, one was a dishonest tax collector, and one was a right-wing revolutionary (Simon the Zealot). God can use anybody, which means there's hope for you and me!

Jesus told them to preach that the long-awaited kingdom was at hand and to heal the sick, raise the dead and cleanse the lepers. The Lord's methods of reaching the lost haven't changed during the church age, as witnessed in the book of Acts. God is still sending out supernaturally equipped men and women to reach the lost.

Jesus also told His disciples that if a certain city didn't receive them they were to shake the dust off their feet as a sign against it. God doesn't want us to waste our time trying to reach unreceptive people when there are some who have not yet had even a single opportunity to hear the gospel. Why should anyone hear the gospel twice until everyone has heard it once?

Jesus informed the twelve that life would be no bed of roses as they traveled from city to city. He promised they would experience incredible hatred and intense persecution. Some would be betrayed even by their own family members. We, too, can expect to experience persecution and hatred as we take a stand for Jesus, even from family members. But there is no price too great to pay for knowing and serving Jesus. One thing is certain: we will never win anyone to Christ—be it friends, enemies or family—by compromising our stand for Him.

PSALM 12:1-8

God hates lying and every form of deception. Some people are certain they never lie, but they have categorized lying into "white lies" and "black lies." The Bible makes no such distinction. David wrote of those who speak with "flattering lips"; flattery is a form of lying. The compliments we pass out should be sincere, not designed to take advantage of another person.

PROVERBS 3:13-15

We need to be more concerned with gaining wisdom than gaining anything else. There is no better place to seek wisdom than in the Bible. Christians who are "too busy" to study the Word of God are indeed too busy.

JANUARY 15

GENESIS 31:17-32:12

Although God had told Jacob to depart for the land of his relatives, he still didn't fully trust in God. He was afraid that, if he told Laban he was leaving, Laban would take Rachel and Leah from him by force, not allowing them to go. So he departed secretly, and when Laban discovered what had happened, he journeyed *275 miles* to catch up with them. We can hardly blame Laban for wanting to kiss his daughters and grandchildren good-bye, but we can hardly blame Jacob for fearing Laban, either. He understood Laban's character only too well. However, God worked it out for both of them by warning Laban not to speak good or bad to Jacob. As in most arguments, there was right and wrong on both sides.

Unknown to Jacob, Rachel had stolen her father's household idols before their departure. According to archaeological discoveries from that region and time, the person possessing the household idols held proof of ownership to the estate. Rachel was trying to ensure that, when Laban died, her husband would be rightful owner of all that was Laban's, even at the expense of Laban's sons. Her actions were obviously wrong, and the idols were eventually buried at Shechem.

Jacob was still in the learning process and was still reaping the consequences of his sin of twenty years ago. For now he had to face his brother, Esau, from whom he had stolen the birthright and blessing. He sent messengers ahead to let Esau know he was coming, and his messengers returned to tell him Esau was coming to meet him with four hundred men. God didn't tell him what Esau's attitude would be, and Jacob expected the worst. God has a way of bringing us to repentance, even if it takes twenty years for us to face the consequences of our disobedience. Jacob prayed fervently and reminded God of His promises to him. What a difference there is between this prayer and the prayer he prayed twenty years ago on his way to Paddan-aram! Jacob was maturing in his time of trial. Difficulties do have a way of drawing us closer to God, don't they?

MATTHEW 10:26-11:6

The greatness of God's love is further revealed in the first New Testament verses we read today. God knows when every sparrow falls to the ground. He knows the exact number of hairs on our heads. *Jesus says that we have value.* This is contrary to so much of what is taught today. We can feel good about ourselves, because we're loved by God and have great value in His sight. God, like all good parents, doesn't want His children to be full of pride, but He does want us to have a good self-image. He doesn't want us hanging our heads all the time and confessing that we are poor, no-good, worthless sinners. We're special, because we're God's own children. *If you hate yourself, you're hating someone whom God loves.*

Jesus knew well that the consequences of His coming would not always be nice and peaceful. There would be strife and division, even among family members. However, He warned that no one should turn his back on Him just to "keep the peace." We must love Him more than anyone else and be willing to "carry our cross"—that is, be willing to suffer and die if need be for our faith in Him. Everything done for Christ's cause will be rewarded. No good deed goes unnoticed before Him.

Even John the Baptist, Christ's forerunner, had doubts about Jesus. Possibly John thought that Jesus would come in judgment (which He will some day). Jesus' proofs of His messiahship were the supernatural signs and wonders He performed. If Jesus was not the Messiah, who is? Nobody else comes close to His qualifications!

PSALM 13:1-6

Here is another beautiful example of a prayer that begins with a complaint but ends in joyful faith. We should not be focusing on the problem but on the promises God has made. Sometimes rejoicing has to be done in faith, because in the natural there's nothing to rejoice about. But if we're trusting God, there's always something to be happy about. God's Word works!

PROVERBS 3:16-18

We learned before that applying God's wisdom extends our life span, but now we read of two other benefits: riches and honor. God is not opposed to our having money as long as it doesn't have us. And God is not opposed to our having honor as long as we stay humble and give Him the glory.

JANUARY 16

GENESIS 32:13-34:31

The story of Jacob's wrestling with the angel (see Hos. 12:3-4) is difficult to understand. Angels can appear as men, as we've already seen, so a wrestling match is possible. But what was an angel doing wrestling with a man? Why did they wrestle all night? It's clear that Jacob desired God's blessing and His assurance that his encounter with

Esau would go well. No doubt he was also wrestling with his conscience, and at the end of the match Jacob was a new man with a new name, Israel.

The next morning he had to face Esau. We have to wonder if Esau's original intentions were good, since he came with four hundred men, or if his intentions became good in answer to Jacob's prayer. Or maybe his intentions became good as he saw Jacob off in the distance, bowing to the ground seven times. Regardless, we do see the fulfillment of what Isaac had said to Esau twenty years before: "and your brother you shall serve; but it shall come about when you become restless, that you shall break his yoke from your neck" (27:40).

Jacob was completely surprised and greatly relieved by his brother's gracious reception. And it's evident that Esau had been greatly blessed during the past twenty years as well in spite of his distress when his blessing was stolen. Jacob's crisis was over, and the lesson had been learned.

Esau asked Jacob to journey with him to Seir, but Jacob made an excuse: "I've got all these women and children to slow me down, so you go ahead. We'll travel at our own pace and meet you in Seir." Jacob really had no intention of going to Seir, which was south and not part of the promised land. He was heading toward Shechem, which was west and in the territory of Canaan's land. Apparently he was still wary of his brother. When Jacob arrived in Shechem, he kept his vow of twenty years before (see 28:20-22) and erected an altar to the God who had brought him safely home. He called it El-Elohe-Israel: God, the God of Israel. The Lord was no longer just "the God of Abraham and Isaac," but now finally He was also the God of Israel.

The rape of Dinah by Shechem the Hivite gives us a picture of the moral condition of the tribes living in Canaan's land during this time. But the reprisal of Jacob's sons also gives us an idea of their own poor spiritual condition. Other incidents we have yet to read about will erase all doubt that Jacob's sons were anything but a pathetic bunch of rogues (with the exception of Joseph). Remember that Jacob was now around ninety years old, and he had just started really to walk with God. So his sons had been raised without the benefit of a spiritual father to teach them the ways of God or set the right example before them. Simeon and Levi were clearly wrong in their vindictiveness, as we know that the Bible says, "Never take your own revenge, beloved, but leave room for the wrath of God, for it is written, Vengeance is Mine, I will repay, says the Lord" (Rom. 12:19). Their treacherous acts of murder had far-reaching consequences for them, as we'll read in Genesis 49. Their brothers, who participated in the looting of the city, were guilty as well. We assume that Joseph, the youngest, took no part in his brothers' crimes.

MATTHEW 11:7-30

When Jesus said that he who is least in the kingdom of heaven is greater than John the Baptist, after saying there was no one born of women who was greater than John the Baptist, we have to wonder what He meant. The only acceptable explanation is that those who make it to heaven will be greater than John in terms of their privileges and blessing. They will not be greater because of what they do for God but because of what God does for them.

Jesus' words here concerning the kingdom of heaven's suffering violence and violent men taking it by force have been interpreted in various ways. Some prefer the viewpoint that He was speaking of the Zealots (those Jews who were trying to establish the kingdom of God by overthrowing the Roman domination of their country). God's kingdom will never come as a result of political action or violence. Another interpretation is that God's kingdom is open only to those who possess an "I don't take no for an answer" type of faith and not to casual inquirers.

Jesus began His reproach of the unrepentant cities by comparing the people to children playing in the marketplace. No matter how God tried to reach these people, through John or Jesus, they couldn't be reached. They had an excuse no matter what. Jesus' reproach of Chorazin, Bethsaida and Capernaum, where He performed the majority of His miracles, demonstrates that "from everyone who has been given much shall much be required" (Luke 12:48). We have already read the story of what happened to Sodom, and we'll eventually read what happened to Tyre and Sidon. Jesus was actually saying that the people in Chorazin, Bethsaida and Capernaum had harder hearts than the people of Sodom, Tyre and Sidon! If the people of those cities had seen Jesus' miracles, He said, they would have repented.

But there were those who were receptive in Jesus' day. They were "babes," as Jesus called them in verse 25. They were discovering that Jesus gave them true rest by relieving them of their burden of guilt and sin. Jesus' yoke is easy, and His burden is light. If you are overburdened in your work for Jesus, you're taking on more than He has given you to carry.

PSALM 14:1-7

David spoke here of the utter depravity of unregenerate mankind. The Bible says that all people have sinned and fallen short of the glory of God (see Rom. 3:23) and that all unsaved people have a sinful nature residing in their spirits. Thank God that we have now been made righteous through Jesus Christ! This psalm doesn't apply to those of us who have been born again. We are doing good. We are seeking after God. We are no longer corrupt.

PROVERBS 3:19-20

JANUARY 17

GENESIS 35:1-36:43

It seems that God was now calling the household of Jacob to repentance and a renewed relationship with Him. The Lord told Jacob to move to Bethel, where He had appeared to him originally when he fled from Esau. Jacob told his household to put away their foreign gods, to purify themselves (they needed purifying, didn't they?) and to change their garments. It was time for a fresh start and a new consecration to the Lord. The Lord again appeared to Jacob after his consecration and reaffirmed His covenant with him. Thank God that no matter how far a person might stray from Him, there is always a way back through His forgiveness.

As they traveled on, nearing Bethlehem, Rachel died giving birth to Jacob's twelfth son, Benjamin. Remember that, when Rachel stole Laban's household idols and Laban accused Jacob, Jacob said, "The one with whom you find your gods shall not live" (Gen. 31:32). Although Rachel was not discovered at that time, she indeed suffered an untimely death. She was buried just a few miles from where Jesus was born in Bethlehem, and her tomb can be visited today. Incidentally, the apostle Paul was descended from the tribe of Benjamin.

Although Jacob had tried to bring a reformation to his household, we see almost immediately that his sons experienced little true change. Reuben, Jacob's firstborn son, lay with Jacob's concubine Bilhah, by whom Jacob's sons Dan and Naphtali had been born. Some say that by this act Reuben forfeited the birthright and blessing, which also passed by Simeon and Levi (the second and third born) for their murderous acts we read about yesterday. Finally it rested on Judah, Jacob's fourth son, from whom Jesus was descended. (However, we'll soon see that Judah was no saint, either.) Some say that Joseph naturally had the birthright, as he was the oldest son of Jacob's intended first wife, Rachel. Regardless, Reuben, Levi and Simeon all later paid the consequences for their sin, which we will read about at the end of Genesis.

MATTHEW 12:1-21

Today we learn the difference between what is called the "spirit of the law" and the "letter of the law." The Pharisees were experts at keeping the letter of the law. They knew God had commanded that no work should be done on the Sabbath, so they had lists of what would be considered work and what would not. They followed their interpretations of God's law stringently.

On the other hand, Jesus understood the spirit of the law. That is, He understood the reason God had given certain rules. He knew that God gave the commandment for not working on the Sabbath because we need a holy day of rest. Mark's Gospel records that Jesus said, "The Sabbath was made for man, and not man for the Sabbath" (Mark 2:27). God always has a reason for His commandments. He is *always* motivated by His love for us. He doesn't intend that our lives be a drudgery of keeping endless lists of dos and don'ts. His commandments were given to enhance our lives.

We also have the example of Jesus' healing a man with a withered hand on the Sabbath. The Pharisees considered it unlawful to heal on the Sabbath, so healing must have fallen into their "work" category. But Jesus knew it was lawful to do good on the Sabbath. And He reaffirmed the value of people in God's sight by making a comparison between rescuing a sheep from a pit and healing a man.

Unfortunately, some Christians fall into the same trap as the Pharisees. I remember once meeting a man who wouldn't shave on Sundays lest he break the Sabbath. That wouldn't have been so bad, but he was the church organist. Every Sunday morning, it looked as if a hobo was playing the organ!

We must not forget that God also intended the Sabbath to be kept holy. It wasn't to be a day to skip church and go to the lake. It should be a day of celebration and also a day of concentration on God. How much more spiritual growth might take place if Christians devoted one entire day each week to concentration on the Lord? To some, Sunday is a day to go to church and then watch television the rest of the day. Of course, we are to serve the Lord every day of the week.

PSALM 15:1-5

One mark of a godly person is that "he swears to his own hurt, and does not change" (v. 4). That means he's a man of his word, even if it costs him because he spoke too quickly. How difficult it is to find men and women of their word these days.

PROVERBS 3:21-26

Today we are commanded not to fear (v. 25). Fear is really the exact opposite of faith, yet it's just like faith in many respects. Fear could be defined as "faith in Satan." The only time God's Word would create fear in people is when they aren't obeying it. Other than that, God's Word always brings peace and joy. But Satan's word never brings peace or joy. It carries with it anxiety and torment. So we can tell if we're believing God or Satan just by our inward feelings. If we're experiencing worry or fear, we're believing Satan's lies (unless we're in disobedience, of course). If our "sleep [is] sweet" (v. 24), we're trusting the Lord.

JANUARY 18

GENESIS 37:1-38:30

Today we begin the amazing story of Joseph, to which twelve chapters of Genesis are devoted. We will see that Joseph is one of the most Christlike characters from the Old Testament.

We've already learned what kind of people Joseph's brothers were, so it's no wonder that Joseph brought back a bad report of them to Jacob (v. 2). He could hardly have brought back a good report of those rogues! To complicate matters, Jacob, who had a favorite wife and who was raised by parents who had favorite sons, now had a favorite son himself: Joseph. His brothers resented that, understandably.

Joseph was more of a prophet than a politician when he related his dreams to his family. However, if Joseph's brothers had better understood the character of God, who has no favorite children, they would have realized that, if Joseph was going to be exalted over them, it was for *their* benefit and blessing. And that's how it turned out to be, as we'll see.

Reuben redeemed himself a little in the story of the plot against Joseph, but the other ten sons were heartless and quite depraved. How similar this story is to Christ's, who was sold by his own for thirty pieces of silver!

The story of Judah and Tamar could be right from a modern soap opera. What's amazing is that from their relationship was born Perez, who was in the lineage of Jesus. Maybe that's why this story is recorded in Scripture. When Judah told his second son to take his sister-in-law as his wife after the death of her husband, it was in keeping with the custom of the day. If a man died childless, his brother was required to raise heirs to him by his widow. The law later stipulated that exact practice (see Deut. 25:5), and believe it or not, the custom is still practiced in some parts of the world today. I'm sure Judah had a red face when Tamar, whom he had condemned as a harlot, revealed that she was pregnant by him. Talk about putting your foot in your mouth!

I'm reminded of the story of the woman who was caught in the act of adultery in John 8. Her accusers wanted to stone her, but Jesus told them, "He who is without sin among you, let him be the first to throw a stone." We should be very careful in condemning others when we ourselves have been just as guilty before God.

MATTHEW 12:22-45

The unpardonable sin of which Jesus spoke in these verses has long been a subject of debate. Let's examine the passage closely. The Pharisees were saying that Jesus was using Satan's power to perform His signs. In other words, they were calling the work of the Holy

Spirit the work of the devil. Possibly what Jesus meant is that, when people's hearts are so hard that they can see a miracle by the Holy Spirit's power and call it the work of the devil, there is no forgiveness for them. A human heart could get no harder than that. Jesus had already said that the people of certain cities in which He had performed many miracles had harder hearts than the people of Sodom. We know that the people of Sodom reached a place where forgiveness was no longer offered to them, and the people to whom Jesus was referring had reached the same place.

Jesus specifically said that He would spend three days and three nights in the heart of the earth, just as Jonah spent three days and nights in the belly of the sea monster. Jesus' spirit did not go to heaven to be with the Father immediately after His death. Some argue that His spirit did go to heaven immediately, and Jesus was only referring to His body. However, Jesus plainly said to Mary when He appeared to her *after* His resurrection, "I have not yet ascended to the Father" (John 20:17).

So what happened to Jesus' spirit after He died? Jesus told the thief on the cross, "Today you shall be with Me in Paradise" (Luke 23:43). We'll study this subject further in future lessons, but there is substantial biblical evidence that old covenant saints who died did not go to heaven, but rather to a place called "paradise," which was located in the heart of the earth. Jesus spent three days there before He ascended to His Father.

Once again we read of Jesus' condemnations of those who had rejected Him. The men of Nineveh, who repented at Jonah's preaching, and the Queen of the South, who came to hear Solomon's wisdom (two stories we have yet to read in the Old Testament), will condemn Christ's listeners at the judgment. The generation of Jesus' day, just like ours, was going from bad to worse. But thank God that, for people who serve Him, things are getting better and better!

PSALM 16:1-11

Speaking of Jesus' going to the heart of the earth, today's psalm adds supporting evidence for that event. According to both Peter and Paul, it was Jesus who was speaking in the latter part of this psalm (see Acts 2:22-32; 13:32-37). God did not abandon Jesus' soul to Sheol or allow His body to undergo decay. The Hebrew word *Sheol* and the Greek word *Hades* both refer to the same place. Sheol/Hades was divided into two compartments: paradise and the place of torment. We will look into this subject more fully when we read Luke 16:19-31.

PROVERBS 3:27-32

Verse 32 of this passage literally says, "His private counsel is with the upright." God wants to be in close fellowship with us, but we must "draw near to God and He will draw near to [us]" (James 4:8).

JANUARY 19

GENESIS 39:1-41:16

One lesson we can learn from Joseph's story is that, no matter what kind of unfortunate circumstances we face, God is able to bless and deliver us. Joseph was sold as a slave to an Egyptian officer named Potiphar, but God was with him, and he became prosperous (v. 2). Even after Joseph was framed by Potiphar's amorous wife, the Lord blessed and prospered him in jail. (I doubt that any of Joseph's brothers would have resisted that woman's daily advances. Joseph was in a class by himself in comparison to the rest of his family.) God is able to grant us favor in other people's eyes, just as He did for Joseph. But how many of us would have given up and rotted away in that jail? *Joseph's key to success was that he was faithful in whatever circumstance he found himself.*

It must have been God who gave the chief cupbearer and the chief baker their dreams. They were given primarily for Joseph's benefit, because God was planning to give Pharaoh a dream in two years that Joseph would interpret for him. It must have been a trial for Joseph to be supernaturally used of God to interpret those dreams, yet still be confined to prison month after month. Why didn't God deliver him sooner? We don't know. But no doubt Joseph matured spiritually during his trials. One thing is certain—people who suffer tribulation have a unique opportunity to learn perseverance and develop character (see Rom. 5:3-4). Sometimes God's way up is down first. Joseph would soon be the second in command over all of Egypt. Powerful people are apt to be better leaders if they have suffered under powerful people.

When God's time arrived, everything was in place for the exaltation of Joseph. Even before he had heard Pharaoh's dream or interpreted it, he was already giving the credit and glory to God. This is the day he had been waiting for!

MATTHEW 12:46-13:23

The parable of the sower is the key parable to understanding all the others according to Mark 4:13. In this parable, the sower doesn't change, nor does the seed. This really could be called the parable of the soils, because the soil is what changes. The soil, of course, represents the hearts of people and their varying receptivity to God's Word. Any time I preach the Word of God, I can look out over the congregation and see those four different soils represented.

Some people's hearts, like the soil alongside of the road, have been hardened. They can't be helped until their hearts are somehow softened. Some people's hearts, like the rocky soil, receive the Word at first, but as soon as something they experience or see contradicts the Word, they give up. Jesus said that persecution and affliction arise because of the Word's being sown. If you're sowing God's Word in your heart, Satan is going to do all he can to get you to doubt or to discourage you.

Still others are like the soil that has also received thorn seeds. They listen to God's Word, but they also listen to anything and everything that would make them doubt it. They have their priorities all wrong, getting wrapped up in the cares of this life. They're rarely in church, and making money is very important to them.

Then there are those who are like the good soil. They're receptive. They hold fast to the Word, even when a flood comes to wash the seed away, because they know God can't lie. They have their priorities right, putting God before everything else in their lives. They produce fruit for the kingdom of God.

Although it seems as if Jesus is purposely not wanting certain people to understand His message (from reading vv. 10-15), we must remember that anyone could become one of Jesus' disciples, get with the "in crowd" and hear the explanation to His parables. Jesus just wasn't handing out spiritual truths to casual observers. He even told us: "Do not throw your pearls before swine" (Matt. 7:6).

PSALM 17:1-15

David acknowledged that God had tried his heart and tested him (v. 3). We'll read similar statements from the lips of other great men of God. Let us determine to pass whatever test we're facing. If life brought no difficulties, there would be no need to trust God, would there? We have already read quite a few of David's psalms, and have you noticed that he was a man who faced many trials? But he was also a man of great faith. Great victories mean great battles. Great faith means great trials.

PROVERBS 3:33-35

Have you ever claimed this promise that God blesses the dwelling of the righteous?

JANUARY 20

GENESIS 41:17-42:17

God had revealed His divine destiny to Joseph when he was about seventeen years old, but it was thirteen years before he was exalted in Egypt. It wasn't exactly thirteen years of joyful bliss, either! Sometimes before God can work through us, He must work in us. If Joseph has ever read the New Testament in heaven, I'll bet his favorite verse is Romans 8:28: "And we know that God causes all things to work together for good to those who love God, to those who are called according to His purpose." Psalm 105:19, speaking of the story of Joseph, says that "the word of the Lord tested him." Although the Scriptures don't record it, we can be sure that Joseph had his doubts and fears, that he was just as human as you and I. We're blessed to have a record of his life, because God has not changed since then, so we have a better idea of how He'll deal with us. Joseph's story should inspire our confidence that the Lord is not through with us yet. He has a divine destiny for all of us, and we must trust Him; He knows what He's doing.

Apparently, the seven-year famine ravaged the entire known world. Of course, that was pretty much limited to what we call the Middle East today. With no food in Canaan, Jacob had to do something, and he had no choice but to send his sons to buy grain in Egypt. Remember that the ten brothers hadn't seen Joseph in about twenty-one years. He was just a teenager when they sold him into slavery. So when they arrived, they bowed down before him in unknowing fulfillment of the dream God gave him more than twenty years before.

Why didn't Joseph immediately reveal his true identity to his brothers? Some think he wanted to get back at them and make them suffer. (He could have had them killed on the spot, though, if he'd wanted.) Others who believe Joseph was above that think he simply wanted to bring his brothers to a place of repentance. The second view is probably the best. His ten brothers needed some repentance. When Joseph accused them of being spies, they said, "We are all sons of one man; we are honest men" (42:11). What must have been going through Joseph's mind when he heard that statement?

Jacob didn't allow Benjamin, his youngest and only remaining son born of Rachel, to travel to Egypt with his other sons. But now Joseph required them to prove their honesty by returning to Canaan's land and bringing Benjamin back for him to see. (Perhaps Joseph rightly assumed that Benjamin had now become his father's favorite son, and he wondered how his brothers had been treating him.)

Just as God brought Jacob to a place of repentance after twenty years of being away from his brother, Esau, now the Lord was bringing Joseph's brothers to repentance after twenty years of being away from Joseph. God may take His time by our reckoning, but He's a great teacher.

MATTHEW 13:24-46

Jesus' parables are not open to any other interpretation when the interpretation is given by Jesus, as in the case of the parable of the tares and wheat. It's clear that God allows the devil to sow his tares right among God's wheat, but the time is coming when there will be a separation of the wheat and tares. Those who don't believe in a literal hell of fire should read this parable.

We are offered no such explanations of the other parables we read today. These are open for intelligent interpretation. The parable of the mustard seed and the parable of the leaven probably have similar meanings. Although the kingdom of God started small with Jesus and a few of His followers, eventually it will cover the earth. We know that some day there will be no other kingdom. The mustard seed is a minuscule seed that grows into a large bush, and a little leaven (yeast) permeates the whole lump of dough.

The parables of the hidden treasure and the costly pearl probably have similar meanings as well. There is nothing that can compare in value to having a part in God's kingdom, and it would be worth giving up everything and anything to obtain it. Some think that the man who finds the treasure in the field and the merchant seeking fine pearls should be compared to Jesus, who gave up His life to possess the church, which is represented by the treasure buried in the field and the costly pearl. Both interpretations are good.

PSALM 18:1-15

This psalm was spoken by David on the day of his great deliverance from Saul, which we'll read about in the book of 1 Samuel. It's good to read a psalm that was written after a victory rather than during a great trial. We can say along with David, "The Lord is my rock and my fortress and my deliverer." Do you know Him as your stability, your protector and the one who rescues you from your troubles?

PROVERBS 4:1-6

Apparently Solomon's father, David, took time to instruct his son and impress upon him the importance of gaining wisdom. How many Christian fathers are taking time with their children to do the same?

JANUARY 21

GENESIS 42:18-43:34

God's plan to bring Joseph's brothers to repentance was working. When Joseph detained Simeon, allowing his other nine brothers to return to Canaan, they said to one another, "Truly we are guilty concerning our brother, because we saw the distress of his soul when he pleaded with us, yet we would not listen; therefore this distress has come upon us" (42:21). They realized they were reaping what they had sown. When they returned to Egypt the second time to buy more grain, they were clearly afraid they would become slaves (43:18). Now they were getting a taste of how Joseph felt when they sold him into slavery.

Why was Simeon detained rather than one of the other brothers? Possibly because he had been the ringleader in the plot against Joseph. He may well have been detained in the same prison in which Joseph had spent time after he was framed by Potiphar's wife.

When Joseph saw Benjamin, he was moved to tears, since he had not seen his little brother in more than twenty-one years. Benjamin was only a baby then. Remember that Benjamin was his only "full brother" (born of Rachel), while the other ten were half-brothers. They were seated for dinner with Joseph, in order from oldest to youngest, and we read that "the men looked at one another in astonishment" (43;33). They must have wondered how Joseph knew their ages! Benjamin received a portion that was five times bigger than the rest. Why? Possibly Joseph wanted to see the reaction of the other brothers. Would they be jealous of Benjamin as they had been of him? Had these men truly come to a place of repentance?

MATTHEW 13:47-14:12

The people of Jesus' hometown of Nazareth took offense at Him because they knew Him only from *before* He was baptized in the Holy Spirit. Jesus, just like Joseph, entered into His ministry at age thirty, and He performed no signs or wonders and displayed no supernatural ability to teach until then. Of course, Jesus must have been known as a good, upright man, as He never sinned. But they could hardly believe that it was the same person. As a result of their unbelief Jesus didn't perform many miracles in Nazareth. They just couldn't believe He was actually the anointed Son of God, because they knew Him as the carpenter's son.

Luke's Gospel goes into greater detail on what happened in Nazareth, so we'll wait until then to discuss it further. But just as Jesus had trouble being received by His own people, so many times we, too, have trouble being received by our own. They know us only from before we were born again and can hardly believe that God has changed us into new creations. But over a process of time they begin to see and believe. Let's be careful to keep a good testimony before them.

Incidentally, it's obvious from the evidence in verses 55 and 56 that Mary had other children after Jesus was born.

PSALM 18:16-36

David sounded like the apostle Paul, who said, "I can do all things *through Him who strengthens me*" (Phil. 4:13, italics mine). Both Paul and David were positive men, because their God was a big God. When you compare what's coming out of your mouth today with what David said, do you wonder if your God is too small?

PROVERBS 4:7-10

JANUARY 22

GENESIS 44:1-45:28

This account of Joseph and his brothers is one of the most moving stories in the Bible, and today it reaches its emotional climax. We have no doubt that the ten brothers were all brought to a place of repentance as we read of their saying to Joseph, "What can we speak? And how can we justify ourselves? *God has found out the iniquity of your servants;* behold, we are my lord's slaves" (44:16, italics mine). They fully expected to become slaves, just as Joseph had become a slave when they sold him for twenty pieces of silver.

Nat 322.45

Delta 383.10

Here we learn a valuable spiritual principle. Once these men confessed their sin and repented, they were forgiven, and God's blessings came immediately. No doubt if they had not repented, they would have had to face punishment. Likewise, once we have asked for forgiveness of our sins and repented, God does not hold our sin against us or punish us. Of course, many times we have to face the natural consequences of our sin, but if God has forgiven us, He is not holding anything against us (see 1 John 1:9). Praise God!

Joseph, in recognizing God's overruling hand in his life, was able to forgive his brothers completely for their cruelty to him twenty-two years before. Jesus taught us that we're to forgive those who wrong us because we have been forgiven our offenses against God. We must trust God, like Joseph, that *no person can really do us harm.* If God allows harm to come to us, it is ultimately for our good and the good of others. It takes faith to believe that, doesn't it? In Joseph's case, God allowed his brothers to harm him for *his* good and for *their* ultimate good (after their repentance, of course). Most of all, God allowed it for *our* good. By preserving the family of Jacob from starving in Canaan, the "seed of Abraham and Isaac" was preserved, thus ensuring the eventual coming of the Messiah. God was thinking of you way back then.

Obviously, Joseph is a beautiful type of Christ. He was a beloved son. He was sent by his father to his brothers. He was hated by them and sold for pieces of silver. He was severely tempted. He was "killed" and "came back to life" as far as his father was concerned. He freely forgave his offenders and provided a "new home" for them in a place that was a "paradise" by comparison to where they had been living.

MATTHEW 14:13-36

At the news of John the Baptist's death, Jesus withdrew to a lonely place by Himself. It's good for us to follow His example, to take time to be by ourselves, to think about where we've come from and where we're going. So many of us are caught up in the fast pace of day-to-day living and never pause for a moment of reflection, never stop to clear our minds or seek a new perspective. God is calling us to come away from the hustle, to spend time fellowshipping with Him.

When Jesus "fed the five thousand," He really fed a minimum of twenty thousand people, because they only counted *men* who were present. If every man brought his wife, and if each couple had two children, there were at least twenty thousand people fed, all with five loaves and two fish. One liberal "scholar" said that they had very large loaves of bread in those days. They must have been quite large for each one to have fed four thousand people! Beyond that, the Gospel of John tells us that the five loaves and two fish were carried by one young boy. They were his lunch. That "educated scholar" forgot to do his homework. The little boy must have been pretty strong to carry five such loaves of bread plus two whales! He must have had quite an appetite as well!

We laugh that the disciples thought they were seeing a ghost when they saw Jesus walking toward them on the water. But what would you think if you were out on a boat at night and saw a person walking toward you on the water? This story would have been great to catch on film! Peter, always ready to say something stupid, said to the Lord, "Lord, if it is You, command me to come to You on the water."

I've always wondered what his logic was in making such a statement. (What if it was really a ghost and not Jesus, and the ghost said, "Come"?) Maybe Peter really did believe it was Jesus and just wanted an excuse to walk on the water. Regardless, he and the disciples learned a good lesson about faith during Peter's escapade. Peter was literally "walking by faith" as he made his way toward Jesus. But when he began to look at the wind and waves (the circumstances), he doubted that it was possible to do what he was doing. He immediately began to sink. We, too, begin to sink when we doubt God's Word. Contrary circumstances will tempt us to doubt. But as long as we keep our eyes on the Word, we can do the impossible. Jesus said, "All things are possible to him who believes" (Mark 9:23). However, I wouldn't recommend trying to walk on water, as Jesus only gave that promise to Peter! Find the promises in Scripture that apply to all of us, and stand on them in faith until they come to pass in your life.

Verse 36 says, "And they began to entreat Him that they might just touch the fringe of His cloak; and as many as touched it were cured." Apparently, the tangible healing power with which Jesus was anointed even saturated His clothes. This reminds us of the story in Acts 19, where we read that the apostle Paul was also anointed by God with a tangible healing anointing. In that case, it saturated his clothes as well. The Scripture says that "handkerchiefs or aprons were even carried from his body to the sick, and the diseases left them and the evil spirits went out" (Acts 19:12). Remember that the woman with the hemorrhage in Matthew 9 just touched the fringe of Jesus' cloak, and she felt an immediate healing in her body.

PSALM 18:37-50

David said that his Lord lives (v. 46). Does your Lord live? If He does, He is working in your life and circumstances. We may not be involved in actual physical conflict like David, but all of us face difficulties at times and feel as if we're in battle. Let's shout at those times, "My Lord lives!" and trust Him to come to our rescue.

PROVERBS 4:11-13

JANUARY 23

GENESIS 46:1-47:31

Jacob's family consisted of about seventy persons when they went down to Egypt, and during the next four hundred years they multiplied to more than three million! Some say that God had a good reason for moving Jacob's household from Canaan to Egypt. Since the Egyptians loathed shepherds (46:34), the Israelites' occupation as shepherds was a natural barrier to intermarriage. If they had stayed in Canaan, they may very well have intermarried with the Canaanites, eventually losing their identity. But in Egypt they remained a separate and distinct people.

Israel's clan settled in the section of Egypt called Goshen. That name is important to remember as we'll soon see. Egypt in those days was not the square land mass you see on modern maps. Its border basically surrounded the Nile River, its delta and its flood region, as the rest of the land was unusable desert.

Joseph's wise plan of conservation for seven years paid off for Pharaoh and the people of Egypt, who would have starved otherwise during the famine. Joseph enjoyed seventeen years of being with his father before the latter died at age 147. Remember that Joseph had been separated from his father for as many as twenty-two years while God was preparing him to become the prime minister of

Egypt to ensure the survival of Jacob's family. So God made it up to him. Whatever sacrifice God calls us to make for the sake of His purposes, we can be sure He will make it up to us as well (see Mark 4:29-30).

MATTHEW 15:1-28

The Pharisees, like many modern religious leaders, were great ones to emphasize their traditions above the Word of God. Any time someone responds to a spiritual question with the answer "Because this is how we've always done it," watch out! You're listening to a Pharisee. Traditions in themselves are not bad as long as they're based on God's Word. Every church ought to practice the traditions of the Lord's supper and baptism. The danger comes when men *disregard* the Word of God in favor of traditions that actually transgress the Word. This is what Jesus was condemning. The Pharisees had invalidated the commandment of honoring parents with a loophole that said a man didn't have to assist his elderly parents financially—as long as he gave the money to support the Pharisees. They were also more concerned about having ceremoniously clean hands than they were about having a truly clean heart (vv. 10-20).

Opinions differ over the true interpretation of how Jesus treated the Syrophoenician woman. I'll give you my opinion. First, she was a Canaanite, a nationality you should know about by now. The Jews of Jesus' day were some of the most bigoted people who have ever lived. They looked upon themselves as the people God had specially chosen to bless rather than as the people God had specially chosen to bring blessing to all peoples. If you weren't a Jew, they had a term to describe you: a dog.

Jesus' statements to this woman were so out of character for Him, based on the rest of His life's story in the Bible. He had already healed some who were not Jewish. Remember the centurion's son? (The centurion was a Roman.) In Luke 17 Jesus healed a Samaritan leper. So why did Jesus speak this way to this poor Syrophoenician woman? I have to believe that this story was placed directly after Jesus' rebuke of the Pharisees for a reason: He was imitating the way a typical Pharisee would speak. I believe He was speaking facetiously when He said, "I was sent only to the lost sheep of the house of Israel" (v. 24), because He ministered to many non-Jewish people. Besides, we know Jesus was sent to die for the whole human race.

We think sometimes that Jesus spoke in a monotone voice, using no figures of speech, but that's not true. We've already heard Jesus use the figures of speech we call simile and hyperbole. Why is it so hard to think that Jesus, like us, sometimes spoke facetiously, especially when we read the end of this story and find the lady's daughter *was* delivered? If Jesus was seriously saying God sent Him only for Jews, and if He really believed that non-Jews were dogs, He should never have delivered this woman's daughter.

So there you have it. Even if you don't agree with me, you can't let this story deter your faith in the goodness of God. If you believe that Jesus was completely serious here, your faith should really grow. Why? Because to you, this story teaches that even if Jesus doesn't approve of you, He'll still heal you!

PSALM 19:1-14

The apostle Paul said in his letter to the Romans that all men are without excuse before God, because "since the creation of the world His invisible attributes, His eternal power and divine nature, have been clearly seen, being understood through what has been made"

(Rom. 1:20). Anyone can look up at the stars at night and see that there's a wonderful Creator. But that's only the first revelation of God. We can only *begin* to know Him through the creation. The second step is through His Word. That's why David, after speaking of God's great creation, devoted the second part of this psalm to extolling the Word of God. Aren't you glad you have the Bible, and not just the sun, stars and mountains to reveal God to you?

PROVERBS 4:14-19

You have just read one of my favorite proverbs: "The path of the righteous is like the light of dawn, that shines brighter and brighter until the full day." For we who have had the righteousness of Christ imputed to us, this proverb means that God has laid out a path before us. That path gets brighter and brighter. Or we could say that our lives get better and better as long as we stay on that path. Make this your positive confession: "My life is getting better and better as I follow God's path for my life!"

JANUARY 24

GENESIS 48:1-49:33

We come now to the final chapter of Jacob's colorful life story, and we read that near the end of his life he practiced what had also been practiced by his father, Isaac. I assume that this is the gift of prophecy working together with the word of wisdom (see 1 Cor. 12). Jacob (Israel) took Joseph's two sons as his own and prophesied that from the younger of the two, Ephraim, would come a multitude of nations. He also indicated that the tribe of Ephraim would become greater than the tribe of Manasseh, which, of course, came true. So Ephraim and Manasseh became half tribes in Israel, and Joseph's name did not carry on as one of the twelve tribes. Eventually the tribe of Reuben would disappear, and the tribe of Simeon would be absorbed into Judah and Benjamin.

Then Jacob gathered his sons together to tell them "what shall befall you in the days to come" (49:1). His prophecies aren't completely clear to us, but then they weren't spoken to us, either. Much of what he said referred to the time when the twelve tribes would possess Canaan in about 380 years. Reuben was told he would not have preeminence because he went in to his father's concubine (see Gen. 35:22). Simeon and Levi, who massacred the men of Shechem (see Gen. 34:25-30), would be scattered in Israel. As stated before, Simeon was absorbed into Judah and Benjamin. Levi was dispersed among all the tribes of Israel as the priestly tribe.

Judah would be the kingly tribe (49:10) from which David was descended, as were all the other kings of Judah. The most outstanding "king of the Jews," of course, would be Jesus, who is called in the book of Revelation *"the Lion that is from the tribe of Judah"* (Rev. 5:5, italics mine).

MATTHEW 15:29-16:12

This time we can be certain that Jesus fed at least sixteen thousand if we count women and children. If Jesus' followers back in His day were like His followers in our day, the majority of them were women. So He may very well have fed thirty thousand for all we know. Notice that they picked up seven baskets full of leftovers after their lunch. To me this says three things. First, God delights in giving us an abundance. Jesus provided more than they needed. Second,

God does not want us to be wasteful. They picked up the leftovers. And third, God doesn't want us to foul His creation. They cleaned up after they were done.

Jesus said that an evil and adulterous generation seeks after a sign. However, we must take what He said in context. Jesus was performing all kinds of signs all the time, but He didn't perform one here at the Pharisees' request. Why not? Because they were testing Him (16:1). This was a case of evil men with hardened hearts wanting Jesus to prove Himself immediately. The Bible says that no one should put God to a test. However, it isn't wrong for us as believers to want to see signs and wonders. We're told in 1 Corinthians to covet the gifts of the Spirit. So our motivation is different from that of the Pharisees. We want God to be glorified. We're not challenging God to "prove Himself."

The incident between Jesus and His disciples in verses 6-12 rings a message that we need to hear loud and clear: God can do it again! When we look back and see how God has provided for us before, and when we think of what He has brought us through already, what makes us ever think He won't do it again? He hasn't changed since the last time He healed or rescued us!

PSALM 20:1-9

Talk about a faith-filled prayer! David made at least seven positive statements in this short psalm. Let's not be guilty of just reading these Spirit-given prayers. Let's meditate on them and compare our prayers with them to see if we're praying like David—with expectancy.

PROVERBS 4:20-27

Speaking of meditating on God's Word, it's clear that the son of the man who wrote the psalm we just read felt that meditation was of utmost importance. Solomon said that the benefits of meditation are *life and health* (4:22). We usually associate meditation with other religions, but the Bible states over and over that meditation in God's Word should be practiced by all of us. We shouldn't just read God's Word; we should feed on it.

JANUARY 25

GENESIS 50:1-EXODUS 2:10

Today we finish our first book of the Bible, Genesis. We have covered the history of about 2,250 years. I hope you read it many more times before Jesus returns. You will find that the Bible never gets old to you. No matter how many times you read it, the Holy Spirit can still teach you more from its pages. I hope you're forming a daily habit now that will last for the rest of your life.

When Jacob died, the ten brothers were fearful that Joseph might still be holding a grudge against them after thirty years. So they told Joseph that right before Jacob died, he instructed them to tell Joseph to be sure to forgive them. This may or may not have been true. However, Joseph had long before forgiven, and his classic response was so gracious: *"You meant evil against me, but God meant it for good"* (50:20, italics mine).

Joseph, near his own death at age 110, made the sons of Israel swear that they would carry his bones out of Egypt at the Exodus. The book of Hebrews tells us that "by faith Joseph, when he was dying, made mention of the exodus of the sons of Israel, and gave orders concerning his bones" (Heb. 11:22). Joseph trusted that God would keep His word to Abraham, Isaac and Jacob—that one day the sons of Israel would go up and possess the land of Canaan. He wanted his bones to go with them. They did, about 330 years later. Joseph died about 1,800 years before Jesus was born.

The book of Exodus is every bit as good as Genesis. It covers the history of Israel for about 431 years. We know that Joseph lived in Egypt 61 years after his family came from Canaan. No doubt those years, and the immediate years that followed, were wonderful times for the people of Israel. But sometime later their situation changed, as a new Pharaoh arose who "did not know Joseph" (50:8). It must have been quite a long time later, because Israel had multiplied to where the Pharaoh could say, "The people of the sons of Israel are *more and mightier than we*" (1:9, italics mine). So the oppression must have begun at least three hundred years after Jacob and his family arrived from Canaan.

We learn a valuable lesson about civil disobedience from the Hebrew midwives Shiphrah and Puah. God wants us to obey the governmental authorities. The apostle Paul made this very clear in Romans 13:1-8. However, if the government dictates that we must disobey God, we should *disobey the government*. The Hebrew midwives did this, and God blessed them for it.

During a time when all male babies of Israel were supposed to be drowned in the Nile by Pharaoh's decree, Pharaoh's daughter paid Moses' mother to nurse her own baby. Isn't that just like God? The book of Hebrews states that "by faith Moses, when he was born, was hidden for three months by his parents, because they saw he was a beautiful child; and they were not afraid of the king's edict" (Heb. 11:23). So we know that Moses' mother didn't put Moses in that basket along the Nile out of fear, but because of faith. She was trusting God to intervene somehow. I doubt she ever dreamed the dictator's own daughter would pay her to raise her son. We know that she reared Moses until he was weaned, which would have been until he was about two or three years old.

MATTHEW 16:13-17:9

The rock on which Jesus would build His church was not Peter but the revelation that Jesus was the Christ, the Son of the living God. With that revelation a person enters the kingdom of God and becomes a part of Christ's body, the church. That's how Jesus builds His church. (The Greek word for *Peter* is *petros*, meaning "a stone." The Greek word for *rock* in verse 18 is *petra*, which means "a large stone" or "bedrock.") Interestingly, the district of Caesarea Philippi, where Jesus made this statement that the gates of hell would not prevail against His church, has a cave that was known as the "gates of hell." It had long been a place of demon worship and child sacrifices. Jesus always had a way of making His point unforgettable.

Peter was no doubt completely sincere in rebuking Jesus for His announcement of His crucifixion, but he was sincerely wrong. When Jesus called Peter "Satan," it probably rattled the listening disciples, so Jesus explained Himself in the next few verses. He made it clear that His followers would have to deny themselves. But He promised that, if they would quit seeking after their own interests and start seeking after God's, they would discover true fulfillment and life. On the other hand, if they continued seeking after their own interests, they would eventually be disappointed, finding only emptiness. Are you seeking after your own interests or God's? That's a question we all must answer.

When Jesus said there were some standing there who would not taste death until they saw the Son of Man coming in His kingdom, His words were fulfilled in the next few verses. Peter, James and John saw how Jesus will look when He comes in glory. His face will shine like the sun, and His garments will be as white as light. Praise God! We'll read this same story in Mark and Luke's Gospel accounts and will say more about it then.

PSALM 21:1-13

The way that David spoke of God is so different from the way some Christians speak of Him. David said, "Thou hast given him his heart's desire, and Thou hast not withheld the request of his lips. For Thou dost meet him with the blessings of good things." If some of us had written this psalm, it would have said something like, "Thou *hast* withheld his heart's desire, and Thou *hast* withheld the request of his lips to teach him some lesson. For Thou dost *not* meet him with the blessings of good things, lest he become proud." Let us never forget that God is a good God and that as our Father He loves us dearly. He loves to give us good gifts (see Matt. 7:11).

PROVERBS 5:1-6

JANUARY 26

EXODUS 2:11-3:22

Moses represents so many of us who are completely sincere and want to bring about justice, but who go about it in our own strength and make a mess of things. Moses murdered an Egyptian, which was obviously not God's way of doing things, and the result was that Moses became a fugitive for forty years. Apparently Moses already had a premonition that God was going to use him to deliver the children of Israel out of Egypt. The New Testament, commenting on this story, says: "And when he saw one of them being treated unjustly, he defended him and took vengeance for the oppressed by striking down the Egyptian. And he supposed that his brethren understood that God was granting them deliverance through him; but they did not understand" (Acts 7:24-25). So Moses knew that God was going to use him, but he took things into his own hands and missed God's timing.

Forty years later, when the Lord appeared to Moses in the burning bush, the once impatient Moses had now become Moses the hesitant excuse-giver. He was eighty years old, and God told him that the time had come to fulfill His six-hundred-year-old promise to Abraham.

Notice that the Lord already knew Pharaoh would turn down Moses' request, but He still told him to go and make his request. Why? Because God is merciful and just. He was giving Pharaoh a chance to do the right thing without any compulsion. This way God would be justified, and Pharaoh would be without excuse. God wants us to take the message of the gospel to everyone, yet He well knows that not everyone will receive it. But once they've heard it, they won't be able to stand before God at their judgment and say they never heard the truth.

Also notice that God promised Moses that the children of Israel would come out of Egypt not as poor slaves but as prosperous people. Not necessarily. God didn't prosper the Israelites to satisfy their selfish desires, though, because soon Moses was taking up a collection for the construction of the tabernacle. God never blesses us to keep all the blessing to ourselves. He blesses us to make us a blessing to Him and others.

MATTHEW 17:10-27

Malachi, the final prophet of the Old Testament, had prophesied that God would send Elijah "before the coming of the great and terrible day of the Lord" (Mal. 4:5). Jesus indicated that John the Baptist, who came "in the spirit and power of Elijah" (Luke 1:17), partially fulfilled Malachi's prophecy. But Jesus also said the prophecy still had future fulfillment. Some think that Elijah will be one of the two witnesses of the book of Revelation (see Rev. 11:3). However, Jesus said that Elijah will come and "restore all things." This is hardly the ministry of the two witnesses of Revelation. Could it be that the Lord will, in these last days, anoint some person with "the spirit and power of Elijah" and that his ministry will restore the church to the power and simplicity of the book of Acts? It sounds almost too good to be true. One thing is certain: the church today needs to be restored to the pattern found in the book of Acts. We need more of the Holy Spirit's work and less of men's ideas.

Concerning the story of the man with the demon-possessed son, we know that Jesus had already given the apostles authority over all demons (see Matt. 10:1). So why did they fail to bring deliverance to this boy? Very plainly they failed because of their lack of faith (v. 20). That's why Jesus, after hearing of their failure, said, "O *unbelieving* and perverted generation, how long shall I be with you? How long shall I put up with you?" (17:17, italics mine).

This teaches us a valuable lesson. We, too, have been given authority over Satan and demons (see Mark 16:17). But our authority doesn't work automatically just because we have it. We must have faith in order to bring deliverance to others or even to ourselves. The Bible says that we resist the devil by faith (see 1 Pet. 5:8-9), and that means not being moved by what we see or hear or feel. It means trusting in the Word of God alone and disregarding all contrary evidence.

Verse 21 mentions that this kind of demon could only come out through prayer and fasting. The NASB marginal note indicates that this verse is not found in many ancient manuscripts, which means it's questionable whether Jesus actually said these words. But if Jesus actually spoke verse 21, we need an explanation. Prayer and fasting cannot increase the authority God has already given. However, by spending time in prayer and fasting, we could actually increase our faith in the authority God has given us.

The two-drachma tax spoken of here was an annual tax paid by all Jews over twenty for the upkeep of the temple. Jesus made the point to Peter that the kings of the earth always exempt their sons from paying taxes. So Jesus, as the Son of God, should have been exempt from paying the temple tax, as it was God's temple. Regardless, I'm sure Peter had a great time going fishing that day! Peter found that the fish had a "stater" in its mouth, which would be equal to four drachmas, exactly enough to pay his and Jesus' tax. Today you can eat what is called "St. Peter's fish" near the Sea of Galilee.

PSALM 22:1-18

This psalm is clearly messianic, since Jesus Himself quoted the first verse as He was dying on the cross (see Matt. 27:46). We get a better understanding of Jesus' feelings on the cross as we read this psalm. He cried out, "My God, My God, why hast Thou forsaken Me?" Did God really forsake Him, or did He just feel forsaken? We know God did not forsake Jesus forever, because God raised Him from the dead after three days, and He is now seated at His Father's right hand. And in one sense Jesus was never forsaken by God, because on the cross He was fulfilling God's plan. However, in another sense Jesus was forsaken. The Bible says that Jesus bore our sins in His body on the cross (see 1 Pet. 2:24). He took upon Himself the iniquity of us all (see Is. 53:6). He was condemned in our place and took our guilt. In that state He felt just like a sinner, cut off from His Father, facing God's terrible wrath.

Notice how closely this psalm corresponds to Jesus' experience on the cross. The psalmist spoke of how the mockers gathered around him in verse 7. Verse 16 says, "They pierced my hands and my feet." And to think this psalm was written hundreds of years before crucifixion was even invented as a form of capital punishment! Verse 18 says, "They divide my garments among them, and for my clothing they cast lots." Clearly David was under the inspiration of the Holy Spirit as he penned his psalms.

PROVERBS 5:7-14

JANUARY 27

EXODUS 4:1-5:21

Moses' reluctance to obey the Lord is typical of many people God calls to do a job for Him. They, too, have struggled with obedience. They, too, have learned that God accepts no excuses and that He sometimes chooses the most unlikely candidates for His ministry. In our weakness His power is perfected (see 2 Cor. 12:9). And Moses was equipped with supernatural power to make his message believable, first to Israel, then to Pharaoh.

On the way back to Egypt, the Lord informed Moses that He would harden Pharaoh's heart so that he would not let Israel go. This is hard for us to understand unless we read ahead in the story to see what actually happened. God hardened Pharaoh's heart only after Pharaoh had first hardened it himself.

A verse in the New Testament is similar (speaking of those who follow the Antichrist): "And for this reason God will send upon them a deluding influence so that they might believe what is false, in order that they all may be judged who did not believe the truth, but took pleasure in wickedness" (2 Thess. 2:11-12). But notice that these are people who already had an opportunity to believe the truth and took pleasure in wickedness instead. God is not in the business of hardening hearts or sending deluding influences upon sincere, receptive people who have not had ample opportunity to receive the truth. God is *always* fair. Remember that the previous Pharaoh had decreed the mass murder of tens of thousands of Hebrew children. He was the "Hitler" of Egypt. The Pharaoh of Moses' day didn't display much concern for human rights, either!

Moses the excuse-giver almost totally

blew it when he didn't circumcise his first-born son, and in so doing he actually broke covenant with God (see Gen. 17:14). Possibly Moses was struck with some grave illness, and he quickly instructed his Midianite wife to perform the circumcision. Incidentally, Moses' wife was a descendant of Abraham through his wife Keturah (see Gen. 25:1).

Moses soon got a taste of what his life would be like for the next forty years as the people of Israel began their grumblings against him. He would hear them complain many more times before his ministry was fulfilled. This time, as every time hereafter, the people of Israel doubted God because of momentary affliction. It didn't *look* as if things were getting better, as God had promised. But if God has spoken, His word will surely come to pass—maybe not as soon as we would like, *but it will surely come to pass.*

MATTHEW 18:1-22

Jesus said that unless we're converted and become like children, we shall never see the kingdom of heaven. What did He mean? There are two answers that are both satisfactory. Possibly Jesus was referring to the fact that children are spiritually alive. When we speak of a person being spiritually dead or spiritually alive, we are referring to the condition of his spirit, or his "inward man" (2 Cor. 4:16). The Christian world is divided on this issue. Many feel that children are born with "original sin" in their spirits, which they inherited from Adam.

We must believe that Jesus was speaking hyperbolically when He told us to cut off our hand or foot if it causes us to stumble. The point is that hell is such a terrible place that it would be worth cutting off your hand or plucking out your eye to stay out of it.

Jesus plainly outlined the structure for church discipline in verses 15-17. If a brother sins against us, we are to go to him *in private* and gently confront him. If we do that in a spirit of meekness, nine times out of ten the offender will immediately repent. The point is that we're not to publicize the sin committed. On the other hand, we are not just to keep quiet about it and harbor a grudge for the next thirty years. God wants us to have open communication with our brothers and sisters. That's why Jesus said that if we remember that our brother has something against us, we should leave our gift at the altar and go to the offended person to work for reconciliation (see Matt. 5:23-24).

There are only two times when you should be the first person to go to a brother with whom your relationship is not right: when he has offended you and when you've offended him!

In verses 18-19 we get an intimation of the authority the church has been given as Christ's body on this earth. Clearly, verse 18 in this context applies to church discipline. But verse 19 is a tremendous prayer promise: "If two of you agree on earth about anything that they may ask, it shall be done for them by My Father who is in heaven." This further amplifies God's desire for unity in our relationships with the other members of the body of Christ.

Finally, on the same subject, Jesus said that we must forgive a brother who has offended us for as many as 490 times! Once again He was using hyperbole to make His point: there should be no limit to our forgiveness, just as there's no limit to His.

PSALM 22:19-31

We learned yesterday that this psalm speaks prophetically of the crucifixion of Jesus. This second half that we read today probably speaks of the worldwide redemption that will come to pass as a result of Christ's suffering. Some day, "*all the families of the nations* will worship before" the Lord (v. 27, italics mine). God's promise to Abraham that all the families of the earth would be blessed through his seed was simply being reaffirmed here by David. God's plan hasn't changed. God loves *every* member of *every* family (race, tribe, ethnic group) of the earth. Let us work to help accomplish God's purpose!

PROVERBS 5:15-21

This whole chapter in Proverbs has been devoted to warnings against fornication and adultery. Sex outside the bonds of marriage is a sin—no ifs, ands or buts. Being engaged to someone does not make premarital sex OK, either. The Bible is clear on this subject. It isn't open for debate. Adulterers and fornicators are going to hell unless they repent and make Jesus their Lord (see 1 Cor. 6:9-11).

JANUARY 28

EXODUS 5:22-7:24

Poor Moses was caught between God and men. God wasn't working as fast as Moses would have liked, and the people had lost faith in him. All pastors can relate to Moses' trials and should thank God that they don't have a congregation of over two million people as he did. Moses complained to God that the sons of Israel were no longer listening to him, so how could the Lord expect Pharaoh to listen to him? Mercifully, God once again informed Moses that His deliverance would not take place without "great judgments" on Egypt. God had told Abraham the same thing about six hundred years before.

Moses' first sign, his rod changing into a serpent, had little success in convincing Pharaoh, as Pharaoh's sorcerers imitated the sign with their magic. This incident reveals how advanced the Egyptians were in their satanic religion and worship. (We know that the Antichrist will come with many false signs and wonders, too. See 2 Thess. 2:9.) And even as Moses' serpent swallowed all their serpents, Pharaoh hardened his heart.

Can you imagine seeing a wide river of water suddenly turn into a river of blood? Not only the Nile, but practically all the available water in Egypt was suddenly turned to blood. Picture yourself sitting in your bathtub, and suddenly the water turns to blood. Imagine drawing blood from the well in your yard. That's what happened in Egypt, yet Pharaoh was unmoved because his magicians duplicated the miracle. Some theologians don't believe the Nile actually turned to blood; they think this story is just a fable. They don't realize it, but they're demonstrating the same hard-heartedness as Pharaoh. Nothing is too difficult for the Lord. If you want to see a bigger miracle than the Nile's changing into blood, just look in the mirror!

Notice that, although Pharaoh's magicians could sometimes duplicate God's judgments, *they could not stop them.*

MATTHEW 18:23-19:12

The parable of the unforgiving servant is truly a masterpiece of Jesus' teaching ministry. The servant owed his master the equivalent of about $50 million and was completely forgiven. It was a debt impossible to repay. This represents, of course, the mountain of sins of which God has freely forgiven us.

The servant had a fellow servant who owed him "one hundred denarii" (18:28). That would be equivalent to about one hundred days' wages in Jesus' time, so think of it as two-fifths, or 40 percent, of your annual salary. If you make $25,000 a year, the debt for you would be $10,000. That's pretty substantial, isn't it? When we think of the wrongs that have been done us, some of them may look quite large, too. But by comparison to our wrongs against the Lord, they're nothing. That's why we should freely forgive those who wrong us—because we've been forgiven infinitely more by God.

If we don't forgive our brother from our hearts, Jesus promised that we will be turned over to the tormentors. That doesn't mean we'll go to hell; it just indicates that by harboring unforgiveness, we open the door to the devil and his demons in our lives. Under the old covenant, when God wanted to discipline His people, He would turn them over to their physical enemies. Under the new covenant, God sometimes disciplines His children by turning them over to their spiritual enemies (Satan and demons) to bring them to repentance (see 1 Cor. 5:1-5).

In Jesus' day, there were two schools of thought among Jewish teachers about Moses' laws of divorce. Moses permitted divorce if a man "found some indecency" in his wife (see Deut. 24:1). The question was, what constituted an "indecency"? As usual, there were the liberals and the conservatives. The liberals said that a man could divorce his wife for any reason at all. If he didn't like how she cooked his eggs in the morning, he could divorce her for that "indecency." The conservatives said that Moses was speaking only of sexual misconduct. Jesus made it plain that He was on the side of the conservatives. God joins two people together, and He expects them to stay together. (More about divorce when we look at 1 Cor. 7.) If you have already been divorced, God's forgiveness is offered, of course. You haven't committed the unpardonable sin. If you're contemplating a divorce, you should see your pastor.

The "indecency" the liberals were finding in their wives probably had nothing to do with how they cooked their eggs in the morning. It was more likely that they found more attractive sexual partners and divorced their wives to pursue them. That kind of divorce is obviously no different from adultery.

Their next question, "Why then did Moses command to give her a certificate of divorce and send her away?" revealed their misunderstanding of the spirit of the law. Moses never *commanded* divorce; he *permitted* it. In Moses' day, a man could divorce his wife *verbally*, and that was it. Moses said that the woman should be given a *legal document* from her husband stating that he divorced her, thus allowing her remarriage. This protected the divorced Hebrew women (who had remarried) from ex-husbands who had *verbally* divorced them. They could not be accused of adultery by their ex-husbands when they remarried.

Divorce was commonplace in Jesus' day, and apparently the disciples were shocked at Jesus' hard-line view. If it was as He said, maybe it was better never to marry at all! Jesus replied that in some cases God calls men to a single life for the sake of the kingdom of God. The apostle Paul taught that to remain single takes a special gift from God and that single people have certain advantages over married persons in their ability to devote their lives to the Lord (see 1 Cor. 7).

PSALM 23:1-6

Psalm 22 revealed Jesus as the suffering servant on the cross—His past ministry. Psalm 23 reveals Jesus as the good shepherd—His present ministry. Psalm 24 reveals Him as the ruling king over all the earth—His future ministry! Psalm 23 is probably the best-known and most-loved of all the psalms.

Just imagine yourself as the little sheep that is lying down in green pastures and being led beside quiet waters. You have nothing to fear in the dark valleys of life. Your shepherd has promised never to leave you or forsake you. He may not eliminate all your enemies right now, but He will prepare a feast for you in their presence. You have an abundant supply so that your cup overflows. Goodness and loving-kindness will follow you all the days of your life. What more could you want?

PROVERBS 5:22-23

JANUARY 29

EXODUS 7:25-9:35

The second plague (of frogs) was somewhat worse than the first, and we'll see that the nine plagues became increasingly severe as Pharaoh continued to harden his heart. Even in God's judgments, we see His mercy displayed. God did not start by killing all the firstborn in Egypt. After each plague, Pharaoh could have honestly repented and avoided the following plagues. Notice also that the magicians of Egypt couldn't stop the frogs. All they could do was add to the problem by producing more frogs!

The third and fourth plagues of gnats and flies could not be reproduced by the magicians. Then even *they* tried to convince Pharaoh to soften his heart.

Notice also that God made a separation between His people in the land of Goshen and the people of Egypt. God's people never have to worry about suffering the wrath of God along with the wicked. This is probably the best supportive argument that the church will be raptured from the earth *before* the seven-year tribulation period spoken of in the book of Revelation and elsewhere. God has not destined us for wrath (1 Thess. 5:9)! He made the same division during the fifth plague, in which all the Egyptian livestock died of pestilence. Pharaoh saw that none of the Israelite livestock died, but still he hardened his heart.

Next came the plague of boils, and then the plague of hail. By this time, some of the Egyptians heeded the word of the Lord and brought in their servants and surviving livestock from the fields, lest they be killed by the hail. Once again, there was no hail on Goshen.

It has been observed that each of those plagues God sent made a mockery of a certain Egyptian god. They had a god of the Nile, a frog-goddess named Hekt, a sacred bull god, a cow goddess, a god of the atmosphere, a god to protect Egypt from locusts, and a sun-god named Ra. God is bigger than the devil and all his false gods.

MATTHEW 19:13-30

I love to read how Jesus treated little children. He wasn't too busy or too important to take time to minister to them. May God help us that we never see ourselves as too important to take time for children. To a large extent, children's sense of worth stems directly from the amount of time their parents spend with them. There's no such thing as "quality time" and "nonquality time," as some parents want to believe. *Any and all* time that parents spend with their children is quality time. *Children learn what they live.*

The story of the rich young ruler raises

some important questions. If someone came to you and asked, "What shall I do to obtain eternal life?" what would you say? I would say to believe in Jesus as Savior, and make Him your Lord. But before people can believe in Jesus as Savior, they must first believe that they *need* a Savior. In other words, they must realize that they are sinners. This rich young ruler thought he was a pretty good person, even after Jesus told him directly that no one is good but God alone (v. 17). The man claimed to have kept the commandments Jesus listed in verses 18-19. However, he was still a sinner who needed a Savior, as revealed by Jesus' final test. This young man loved money more than God. If Jesus told you to sell everything you owned, would you do it? If you wouldn't, Jesus is not your Lord.

Jesus then made the startling statement that it's easier for a camel to go through the eye of a needle than for a rich man to enter the kingdom of God. Why? Because to many rich people, money is their god, and you cannot serve God and money (see Matt. 6:24). You can serve God and have money, as witnessed by various rich people in the Bible, but you had better hold your money loosely! Paul wrote to Timothy to "instruct those who are rich in this present world...to be rich in good works, to be generous and ready to share, storing up for themselves the treasure of a good foundation for the future" (1 Tim. 6:17-19).

Those who have proved trustworthy with the use of money will be entrusted with more money. If this rich young ruler had given as Jesus told him, he would have received back many times more according to the word of the Lord in verse 29. But notice that Jesus didn't tell that to the rich young ruler. He told it to the disciples here only after they had already made great material sacrifices. If Jesus had been a typical preacher like me, He would have run after the rich young ruler and said, "Wait! Come back! If you give everything up, I guarantee you'll get much more in return!" When we constantly tell people about the promised return to try to motivate them to give, they sometimes give for the wrong reason—to get more. We should give to God because we want to obey Him, regardless of whether we ever get a financial return. Is Jesus your Lord, or is He just a good investment?

PSALM 24:1-10

This psalm may well be speaking prophetically of the time when Jesus returns and comes to Jerusalem to set up His millennial (a thousand years) kingdom. And truly the present gates of Jerusalem are "ancient" (vv. 7,9), being about five hundred years old. Or it is possible that this psalm was sung by David as the ark of the covenant was brought to Jerusalem after its capture and return by the Philistines (see 2 Sam. 6:12). At that time, David danced before the Lord with all his might.

PROVERBS 6:1-5

Becoming "surety for your neighbor" would be the equivalent of co-signing a loan for somebody. That is usually a foolish mistake. If you've done it, try to get out of it as soon as possible.

JANUARY 30

EXODUS 10:1-12:13

The threat of a plague of locusts brought even Pharaoh's servants to entreat him to let Israel go. We can imagine the situation in Egypt by now. They exclaimed to Pharaoh, "Do you not realize that Egypt is destroyed?" (10:7). Swarms of locusts are not uncommon in some parts of the Middle East, including Palestine. When they come, nothing green is left. Modern swarms have been known to cover four hundred square miles!

After the three days of darkness, there was only one judgment left: the death of all the firstborn of Egypt. (Remember that after three hours of darkness, God's firstborn Son, Jesus, died as well. But He died for our sins, so that judgment would not fall on us.)

True to His promise to Abraham, God brought forth the people of Israel with "many possessions" (Gen. 15:14). Israel plundered the Egyptians. Some ask, "Is this fair?" We must keep in mind that Israel was only now being paid for years of unpaid slave labor. Egypt was just reaping what it had sown.

My favorite verse today is 11:7. After God told Moses that all the firstborn of Egypt would die, He said, "But against any of the sons of Israel a dog shall not even bark...that you may understand how the Lord makes a distinction between Egypt and Israel." There is a vast difference between how the Lord treats His people and how He treats those who aren't His. Does God love you? He loves you so much that He doesn't even like dogs barking at you!

The feast of the Passover, which was instituted that day, was rich in obvious symbolism. Jesus Himself was called the "Lamb of God who takes away the sin of the world!" (John 1:29). The Passover lamb had to be a male without blemish, representing Christ's sinless life. They were to take some of the blood of the lamb and put it on the doorposts of their houses so the destroying angel would pass over them. We, too, have been protected and delivered through the shed blood of Jesus, but only as we apply it by faith. They ate the lamb, symbolizing to us that "Christ our Passover" (1 Cor. 5:7) now lives within us, and we are now members of His body. They were to eat the Passover in haste, signifying the imminent wrath of God and the need to receive Christ *now*. Notice that God changed their calendar as well: "This month shall be the beginning of months for you" (12:2). Once a person receives Christ, life begins again.

The unleavened bread was to remind them of their hasty departure, because the bread did not have time to rise. Leaven represents sin in the Bible; therefore, eating bread before it had time to be leavened symbolizes how God saved us before sin utterly ran its course in our lives, taking us to hell in the end, "fully leavened." The people were to eat only unleavened bread for seven days after the Passover. This represents the fact that once a person has received Christ, he is no longer to practice sin.

The bitter herbs they were commanded to eat were to remind them of the bitterness of their lives as slaves in Egypt. Can you see what a wonderful time the Passover feast would be for generations, as children asked their parents what everything represented? Most important, we must remember that Jesus was crucified during the Passover festival.

MATTHEW 20:1-28

The parable of the laborers in the vineyard speaks plainly of God's loving generosity and fairness. Some have interpreted the parable to mean that no matter at what age we're saved, and no matter what we did before the time of our conversion, we'll all have the same reward: eternal life in heaven. This is no doubt true and may well be the correct interpretation. However, the Bible plainly teaches that there will be various rewards in heaven based on each person's faithfulness. So possibly the parable speaks of the fairness with which those rewards will be passed out. They won't be based on the amount of time spent in service, because those who came to Christ at an early age would have a definite advantage. Rather, the rewards will be based on our faithfulness to work during the time we had the opportunity. Those of us who have served the Lord for many years shouldn't be jealous when we see God bless someone who has served the devil for years but who finally joins the family of God.

Many thought that Jesus was at the brink of establishing the long-awaited kingdom, and no doubt the mother of James and John was one of them. She asked preferment for her sons: to sit at His right and left hands in His kingdom. Jesus had already promised that they would be sitting on thrones during His future reign (see 19:28). Now He asked them if they were able to drink the cup He was about to drink. They probably had no idea what Jesus was talking about, but they still said yes. Jesus was speaking of His death on the cross. I have news for James and John; the seat to the left of Jesus is already taken by God the Father. And those who wish to be great in the kingdom of God must become servants, not lords.

PSALM 25:1-15

This psalm, like a number of them, is acrostic. That is, each new line of the psalm begins with the next consecutive letter in the Hebrew alphabet. Don't you wish you could read Hebrew now? Why don't you make verses 4-5 your prayer today?

Once again, notice David's expression of his faith. He said: "For He *will* pluck my feet out of the net" (v. 15, italics mine). All of us at times feel caught in a net. You may be like me; as I'm writing this very sentence, a circumstance exists that makes me feel caught. But I know that faith-filled words have power, because Jesus said they do. And so I boldly declare that God will pluck my feet out of the net!

PROVERBS 6:6-11

It takes more than faith to guarantee that all your needs will be supplied. It takes a willingness to work hard, plan ahead and save for the future. Most of all, it takes application of God-given wisdom.

JANUARY 31

EXODUS 12:14-13:16

Unfortunately, some of us have a very unbalanced view of God, looking at Him as hyperjudgmental at the expense of His great mercy and love. But others look at God as hyperloving, negating His judgmental side and concluding that anything they consider "negative" must be the work of the devil and not of God. It takes an examination of the whole Bible to have a truly balanced view of God's character.

Today we read of God's judgment on Egypt, of *His* killing all the firstborn. It wasn't the devil who killed them. The Scripture plainly says that it was God (see 12:23,29). This is the same God who sends people to hell. Some Christians cringe at such a statement. They argue, "How could a loving God send people to hell?" The answer is simple. God *is* loving, but He's also holy. In His love He has offered the free gift of salvation for all who will believe in Jesus. In His holiness He chooses to punish those who reject His free gift.

Some Christians will say that God doesn't send anyone to hell—they send themselves. That's a nice way to try to make God "look better," but God doesn't need our help to cover His "faults." He doesn't have any faults to cover! Yes, people in a sense "send themselves to hell" by their own choice, but God is the One who created heaven and hell, and He's the One who decides to which they will go.

No one knows exactly how many people were involved in the Exodus. We read that there were 600,000 Israelite men (age twenty and over), so estimates range from 2 to 5 million people. From now on in our study I will be assuming that there were 3.5 million. If they marched fifty people across, the line would stretch for forty miles! If they marched at two and a half miles per hour, it would take them sixteen hours to pass the same point! The estimated dates given for the Exodus range from 1445 B.C. to 1290 B.C.

Notice that God said no bones of the Passover lamb were to be broken. Remember that none of Jesus' bones was broken on the cross, because He died sooner than the two criminals with whom He was crucified. The legs of the criminals were broken to speed their death by asphyxiation.

Notice also that God instituted an ordinance that all the firstborn males in Israel belonged to Him. If it was a firstborn male of one of their livestock, they must sacrifice it to the Lord. If it was a firstborn son, they must "redeem" him, or "buy him back," from the Lord by making an offering. (That's why Mary and Joseph offered either a pair of turtledoves or two young pigeons in the temple after the birth of Jesus. See Luke 2:22-24.) God didn't want the people of Israel to forget how He killed all the firstborn in Egypt to bring about their deliverance. As they sacrificed all the firstborn of their herds and flocks and redeemed their firstborn sons from generation to generation, children would ask why. (You can always count on children to ask that.) Pity the child who asks why, and his father says, "I don't know, but this is what we've always done." That child is a potential Pharisee.

MATTHEW 20:29-21:22

Those two blind men whom Jesus healed demonstrated persevering faith. Their friends told them to be quiet, but they just cried out louder, "Lord, have mercy on us" (20:31). People will always try to discourage us from trusting that God is good and that He will heal us. But we must keep our eyes on Jesus, knowing He hasn't changed at all since He walked this earth. This scripture says that Jesus was *moved with compassion* when He healed the two blind men. That means He healed them because He loved them. Has His love waned? Has His compassion diminished? No, a thousand times no! If He healed those two blind men who came to Him in faith, He will heal you and me if we cry out to Him in faith!

Jesus made His triumphal entry into Jerusalem on a donkey, fulfilling Zechariah's prophecy (see Zech. 9:9). It was close to the time of the Passover feast, and Jerusalem was crowded with visiting Jews from many places. Jesus and the disciples had to lodge in Bethany each night, about two miles from Jerusalem. Each day they would travel over the Mount of Olives, through (or nearby) the Garden of Gethsemane and into Jerusalem.

Today in the New Testament we have revealed to us more than just one part of Jesus' character. We've already witnessed His great love in the healing of the two blind men. Now we see Him in His holiness, casting out the moneychangers from the temple. Just picture that in your mind! John's Gospel tells us Jesus drove them out with a whip (although John's account may well have been of an earlier cleansing incident). He must have been quite angry. Some think Jesus was displaying supernatural strength in this incident, somewhat like the Old Testament character Samson. We certainly must wonder why they didn't restrain Him, as it was one man against probably a hundred or more others.

Jesus didn't restrain the children who were crying out in the temple, "Hosanna to the Son of David" (21:15). He didn't believe that praise should be done silently. Have you ever been to a football game? When the home team scores a touchdown, the fans jump and celebrate. If you have real praise in your heart, it can't help but come out your mouth.

The incident of the cursing of the fig tree is recorded in more detail in Mark's Gospel, so we'll look at it further then. But don't be bothered by the fact that Jesus was angry at a fig tree. He was just using the opportunity to teach a valuable spiritual principle: words spoken in faith from our hearts have creative power. Some may want to argue with that, but they'll have to argue with Jesus, because *He* said it.

No one has fully plumbed the depths of this scripture, because no one yet has become fully grown in faith. But let's not join the ranks of the doubters of these words of Jesus. On the other hand, let's not join the ranks of the extremists who try to have faith for things not promised to them in God's Word. We can move mountains with faith-filled words if our words are based upon God's Word.

PSALM 25:16-22

PROVERBS 6:12-15

What a warning for deceivers and strife-spreaders! Their calamity comes suddenly, not gradually, and there is no healing for them.

FEBRUARY 1

EXODUS 13:17-15:18

The Israelites moved south or southeast in their exodus, avoiding the land of the Philistines. God knew they weren't yet ready for war. I'm glad God treats us the same way. He never takes us through more than we can handle. If you're going through some difficulties, God knows you have the faith and patience to endure, *because He won't allow you to be tempted beyond what you are able to handle* (see 1 Cor. 10:13).

Did you notice that the Israelites carried Joseph's bones with them? This is an example of someone's faith working 330 years after his death!

When the people of Israel saw the chariots of Pharaoh in hot pursuit, their hearts filled with fear. Jesus said that out of the abundance of the heart the mouth speaks. *That's why we need to have our hearts filled with God's Word: so we can speak it out of our mouths in times of trial.* The Israelites had no real concept of God's character or they never would have been afraid of Pharaoh. God had brought ten plagues upon Egypt to deliver them, so why would He abandon them now? In fact, in a roundabout way, God "inspired" Pharaoh to pursue Israel. God said He would harden Pharaoh's heart *so that he would chase after the*

Israelites (see 14:4), and then He would be glorified in the deliverance. Yet the Israelites were preparing to die!

Believe it or not, some modern scholars try to convince us that the Israelites passed through the Sea of Reeds, where the water was only a few inches deep. If that were the case, however, God did an even greater miracle than we know: He drowned the entire Egyptian army in ankle-deep water!

This story represents much New Testament truth. After we have been delivered out of the kingdom of darkness (Egypt) by the blood of our "Passover Lamb," we should be immediately baptized in water according to Christ's atonement. By the time we're baptized, we should realize that the power of the enemy over our lives has been broken completely. Satan no longer has authority over us. When we read this story of the Israelites' gazing at the dead Egyptian bodies along the shore, we should remember that Satan is "all washed up"!

MATTHEW 21:23-46

The parable of the two sons has a great moral. We would usually say it's "Talk is cheap" or "Actions speak louder than words." But this parable has a deeper significance because it deals with our relationship to God. There are plenty of religious people today who take pride in having a Bible and going to church. They may have certain Bible verses memorized. (They might even read this commentary every day!) But the important question is, are they *obeying* God?

The chief priests and the Pharisees understood that Jesus was talking about them in the parable of the landowner, but they probably didn't fully understand its significance (see v. 41). However, Jesus told them plainly that the kingdom of God would be taken away from them and given to a nation producing fruit. He was speaking either of His rejection by the Jewish *leaders* and His acceptance by tax-gatherers and harlots, or of His rejection by the Jews and acceptance by the Gentiles. I lean toward the first possibility, since that was the message of the preceding parable of the two sons.

PSALM 26:1-12

In this psalm David prayed for vindication. Only those who have done right and walked with integrity can pray such a prayer, and it appears David met those qualifications. Before we pray such a prayer, we need first to examine ourselves and ask the Lord, as David did, to examine us. We might discover that we're simply reaping what we've sown and that praying for the vindication of our righteousness would be a waste of time. It wouldn't have done Jacob any good to pray for vindication when Laban tricked him into marrying the wrong woman! He was just reaping his harvest.

PROVERBS 6:16-19

If someone had asked you before today to make a list of the things God hates most, what would your list have looked like? Would pride have been at the top? Would "spreading strife among brothers" even have been on it? Did you notice that lying is on God's list twice?

FEBRUARY 2

EXODUS 15:19-17:17

The 3.5 million people of Israel were working their way down the western edge of the Sinai Peninsula, which is nothing but desert. After three days, the water they had brought with them was gone, and they were one big group of thirsty people! Finally they arrived at the oasis of Marah, and the people ran to the water's edge to drink their fill. But, alas, the water was undrinkable! Of course, it was then Pastor Moses' fault for bringing them out of Egypt, where the former slaves had plenty to drink. *But we read that God actually brought them* to that place to test them (see v. 25). They obviously failed the test. *They didn't trust the God who had already performed at least twelve major miracles in the past few months.*

In spite of that, God provided water by making the bitter waters sweet. In addition, He promised that if they would obey Him from now on, they wouldn't have to be concerned with the diseases of the Egyptians. Health was a part of their covenant with God. If the new covenant, which is called a "better covenant" in Hebrews 8:6, is actually better, *it must include healing for our bodies*. By the time this year is over you won't have a doubt about it.

There's not much food in the desert, either, and a few days later Pastor Moses and Assistant Pastor Aaron heard more grumblings. The Lord once again had a solution, but He tied it into another test for the Israelites (see v. 4). He was going to send some quail for dinner that evening and provide bread each morning after the evaporation of the dew. But here was the test: each person was to gather only an omer of manna. They weren't permitted to save any leftovers for the next day or it would become foul. On the sixth day of the week they were to gather two omers per person so they would have some for the Sabbath. (It wouldn't become foul on the Sabbath.) And they were *not* to go out looking for manna on the Sabbath, because there wouldn't be any.

Did they pass this test of simple-to-obey instructions? No way. Some people tried to keep leftovers, displaying a lack of faith that there would be a provision the next morning. Some people went out looking for manna on the Sabbath, showing they hadn't collected twice as much on the sixth day, possibly fearing it would go foul. Now think about this: God planned for them to eat manna for maybe a few months as they traveled to the promised land. But it became their food for forty years.

Every day we need "fresh manna" from the Lord too. Jesus said, "Man shall not live on bread alone, but on every word that proceeds out of the mouth of God" (Matt. 4:4). Our manna is our feeding on God's Word. We need it *every day*. Trying to live on last Sunday's sermon is like trying to live on yesterday's manna.

Next it was no water again. The people needed something with which to wash down their miracle manna! More grumblings and more doubt ensued. Once again the Lord provided by producing water from a rock. This time we read that the people actually *tested the Lord* by saying, "Is the Lord among us, or not?" (17:7). You would think that by now they would have figured out that God was going to take care of them, *even if He did sometimes let them get to a place where they were tempted to doubt*.

God has promised to supply all our needs. Sometimes He will allow our faith to be tested, but if we hold fast He always comes through. As much as we don't like to admit it, there are some things God can teach us in times of adversity that we would never learn in times of prosperity. *One of them is how to trust Him.*

MATTHEW 22:1-33

The parable of the marriage feast was spoken by Jesus directly after He announced that the kingdom of God would be taken away from the nonrepentant Jewish leaders and given to repentant sinners (or possibly taken from the Jews and given to the Gentiles; see 21:31,43). This parable carries that same message, and Jesus may even have predicted the destruction of Jerusalem in verse 8. The perplexing question that arises concerns this man who was *at the wedding feast* yet had no "wedding clothes" (v. 13). The parable ends with the moral: "For many are called, but few are chosen" (v. 14).

Let's work backward through the parable. The final statement, or moral, is probably the moral for the *entire* parable and doesn't just apply to the one wedding guest who was found without wedding clothes. It literally says, "For many are *invited*, but few chosen" (italics mine). Truly many were invited to the wedding feast, including all Jews in Jesus' day. But they "paid no attention" (v. 5) to their invitation, so others, no matter what their moral standing, were chosen. According to how you interpret this parable, those who were gathered from the highways and byways represent either tax-gatherers and harlots or all the Gentiles.

In Jesus' day, wealthy people provided special robes for their wedding guests. The wedding robes here probably represent "the robes of righteousness" that are given only by God. If we come to God in our *own* righteousness we will be cast out. But if we come to Him through the righteousness of Christ, we have a right to sit at His table!

Next we read how the Herodians and Pharisees tried to trap Jesus in what He said. If Jesus endorsed paying the poll-tax to Caesar, He would be looked upon as a traitor by many of the Jews. But if He endorsed *not* paying the tax, they could report Him to the governor (see Luke 20:20). Jesus had the perfect answer: "Render to Caesar the things that are Caesar's; and to God the things that are God's." He saw no conflict between paying taxes and also paying tithes.

The Sadducees' attempted entrapment was no more successful. They didn't believe there would ever be a resurrection. (That's why they were "sad, you see!") But the Bible teaches that one day *all* people who have ever lived will experience a bodily resurrection. We'll read about it in the books of Daniel, John and Revelation.

We learn from Jesus' response that there will be no marriage after the resurrection or in heaven. For those of us who are enjoying the blessings of a good marriage now, this is sad news. Possibly the reason there will be no marriage in heaven is that, once there, we will experience the transparency and closeness with all fellow believers that we enjoy now only with our spouses. But nobody really knows.

PSALM 27:1-6

This time I counted about twelve "positive confessions" spoken by David. If the Lord truly is our light and salvation, whom should we fear? Nobody! If the Lord is our defense, whom should we dread? No one! If there's someone you fear, ask God to help you look at that relationship in the light of these verses.

PROVERBS 6:20-26

FEBRUARY 3

EXODUS 17:8-19:15

We learn from Israel's battle with the Amalekites that once we have been delivered from "Egypt" (the world) we can expect the enemy to attack before long. According to Deuteronomy 25:18 the Amalekites attacked the "stragglers at [the] rear" when they "were faint and weary." It is vitally important that all Christians, especially new ones, stay close to the rest of the people of God. Satan sets his eyes on those who show signs of weariness and begin to fall to the rear. Beware when you find yourself saying, "I'm just so tired of going to church. I think I'll just excuse myself from the next service." You're now marked by Satan. Every pastor has seen such people in a weakened condition fall under satanic attack.

We also learn that our battles are really won in prayer and not on the battlefield. Whenever Moses' hands were raised to the Lord, Israel prevailed. Thank God for prayer warriors who spend time each day praying for the saints! They're the unknowns who win the victories in their prayer closets.

Notice that God didn't appoint a committee when He wanted to deliver His people. He called *one man* to do the task (Moses), and then He called another man (Aaron) to assist him. *God calls a pastor to lead a flock, and He calls lay people to assist the pastor in getting the job done.* Too many pastors are overloaded with work because no one is willing to share the load, thinking it's the pastor's job to do it all. That's one reason many pastors have heart attacks or quit the ministry. It's easy to point the finger of condemnation at a person who has left the ministry, but I wonder sometimes who will get the blame for it on judgment day. Are you helping your pastor get the job done, or are you expecting him to do it all "since he gets paid to do it"?

Three months after the Exodus the people arrived at Mount Sinai, also known as Mount Horeb, where the Lord had appeared to Moses in the burning bush. There God made another promise: if the people of Israel would keep His covenant, He would make them a kingdom of priests. They promised wholeheartedly to obey the Lord, but we'll read soon that it wasn't long before they were worshipping a golden calf. Consequently, they never became a kingdom of priests. (However, God did choose the Levites to be the priestly tribe.)

MATTHEW 22:34-23:12

We read yesterday that the Pharisees, Herodians and Sadducees tried to manipulate Jesus into saying something that would discredit Him. Today we read that the Pharisees gave it one last try, but their final attempt was useless as well. No one could argue with Jesus about what was the great commandment of the Law. They were probably hoping He would say something besides what He did. Jesus also stumped them with His question about David. Apparently they accepted the concept of a human messiah but not a divine one. I love verse 46: "Nor did anyone dare from that day on to ask Him another question."

Chapter 23 is devoted almost completely to exposing the religious leaders of Jesus' day. (How true His descriptions are of many *modern* religious leaders!) Their main fault was that they were in the ministry not to serve but to be served. They performed all their good deeds only to be applauded by men. They loved the respectful greetings they received, the chief seats they sat in and the great titles bestowed on them. All of us need to examine our motives for what we do. If we act differently in church from how we act at home, something is wrong. A good way to test our motives is to do something for someone secretly. That way we'll know if our goodness stems only from a desire to have other people see how nice we are.

PSALM 27:7-14

I love the final verse of this psalm: "Wait for the Lord; be strong, and let your heart take courage; yes, wait for the Lord." Let that sink in. No matter what you're going through, if you will take this advice David offers, things will turn out fine. Notice that twice he mentions waiting for the Lord. God doesn't always operate His business according to our timetables. When our faith is tested, we need to be patient and keep on trusting God's promises. He cannot lie!

PROVERBS 6:27-35

FEBRUARY 4

EXODUS 19:16-21:21

It must have been quite a sight to see the Lord descend upon Mount Sinai. Everybody who saw it was trembling; even the mountain itself shook. All the people of Israel heard the voice of God as He spoke the Ten Commandments. They saw the smoke and lightning and heard the thunder, finally requesting that God just speak to Moses from then on. He could pass on what God had said! Moses indicated that this was another test, according to 20:20. Exactly what the test was we don't know. Possibly it was God's commandment that no one should come near the mountain, or possibly it was the Ten Commandments themselves.

What did God mean when He said He would visit the iniquity of the fathers on the children to the third and fourth generations of those who hated Him (see 20:5)? First, He couldn't mean (as some seem to think) that He punishes children for sins their parents commit. Everyone knows that's unfair, and God Himself condemns and forbids that practice (see Deut. 24:16, Ezek. 18:132). So what did God mean?

We know that parents can easily pass their sins down to their children by wrong example. And then those children pass the same unholy traits to *their* children. God holds parents accountable for what they teach their kids. Possibly God was saying here that He is so holy that He will hold parents accountable for four generations' worth of filtered-down sin if they set the wrong example. That's sobering!

Taking God's name in vain is more than simply using it in conjunction with a swear word. In Exodus 15:26 God revealed one of His names as "Jehovah-rapha," or "the Lord your healer." *Thus, when we don't look to the Lord as our healer, we're actually taking His name in vain.* God also revealed Himself to Abraham as "Jehovah-jireh," or "the Lord our provider." So when we don't trust the Lord to provide for us, we are again, in a sense, taking His name in vain.

The first commandment that comes with a promise is the fourth one. God promised that if people will honor their father and mother, their days will be prolonged. That doesn't apply to just *children* honoring their parents but to anyone who has parents.

God said not to murder, but He later differentiated between premeditated murder and accidental killing. We must also remember God Himself instituted capital punishment and at times commanded His people to go to war, so we need a balanced viewpoint on this subject.

To covet doesn't mean simply to have a desire. It means to lust after something and to desire it enviously. I might admire my friend's new car, but I'm not coveting it. If I like it enough, I might even go buy one just like it, but still I haven't coveted. However, when I'm jealous and envious of someone else's possession and begin to lose sleep over it, *then* I'm coveting.

Notice God commanded that when the Israelites built an altar for their sacrifices, they were to build it from *uncut* stones. If they built it with cut stones it would be profaned before the Lord. Probably the Lord was trying to get across to them that they could do nothing to approach Him by their works. If they built an altar from nicely cut stones they might think God was accepting their sacrifices because of the beauty of their craftsmanship. *We come to God only because of His grace, not because of anything we've done.*

When we read of the ordinances for the treatment of slaves, remember that God wasn't talking about the kind of slavery with which most of us are acquainted. The cruel practices of the slavery our country allowed were altogether different from the slavery we're reading about.

First, this was *voluntary* slavery. Moses was talking about buying a *fellow Hebrew* as a slave. Nobody was taking anybody away from his family to force him to be a slave. Further, this slavery could last for a maximum of six years. In some cases, however, when the seventh year arrived, the year of freedom, some slaves would *desire to remain slaves* because they loved their masters (v. 5). Also notice that slaves were not treated as inferior people. What about the statement concerning fathers' *selling* their daughters as slaves? *All* fathers sold their daughters either as wives or, in some cases, as concubines or secondary wives (remember Laban). And female slaves or concubines were to be treated completely fairly, or else the girl could go back to her father.

Finally, we read some of the crimes that were capital offenses. Murder, kidnapping and, believe it or not, cursing or striking parents brought the death penalty. We'd have a lot of dead teenagers if this code were enforced in our society! *But it makes God's view of parent-child relationships clear. Children should respect and obey their parents.*

MATTHEW 23:13-39

What a chapter! Jesus didn't mince words in today's passage. Seven times He called the scribes and Pharisees hypocrites. Five times He called them blind. Once He called them fools. And once He called them a brood of vipers! Again we see that the basic sin of the scribes and Pharisees was that while they looked clean on the outside, they were dirty on the inside. They were truly hypocrites and were justly condemned by Jesus.

Jesus even informed them that He was going to send prophets and wise men to them, and He knew they would persecute and kill them. So why did He send them? So that the religious leaders would be without excuse on judgment day. Don't ever judge a pastor or missionary by how many people he reaches. The idea that a missionary or pastor is out of God's will simply because of low numbers is totally unscriptural. *Sometimes God sends messengers to people whom He knows will be unreceptive.*

This passage reveals to us once again the dual character of Jesus. He was stern yet compassionate. Right after He rebuked the religious leaders He lamented over Jerusalem. His love was so great. He simply wanted to bless the people of Jerusalem, just as a mother hen gathers her chicks under her wings, but they rejected Him. Jesus wasn't having a pity party for Himself because of His rejection; He was feeling sorry for them because they missed His blessings. Now all that remained for them was judgment, which would come in the form of a Roman army to destroy their city in about forty years.

PSALM 28:1-9

Notice again how David started by acknowledging the problem and making his requests, then ended by confessing his faith in God. In verse 2 he was asking God to hear his supplication. But by verse 6 he was praising God because God had heard. The whole prayer takes only about thirty seconds to pray. *It doesn't take long to connect with heaven.*

PROVERBS 7:1-5

FEBRUARY 5

EXODUS 21:22-23:13

Today we continue reading "the civil laws" given to govern the people of Israel. One thing that stands out above all else is the fairness of these laws. Something in the heart of every person yearns for justice. In our society it often seems that the criminal is more protected than the victim. Not so in what we read today.

First, we see again how fairly slaves were treated. If a man struck his slave in the eye and blinded him, or if he knocked out a tooth, the slave could go free immediately.

Every detail of fairness was worked through in these laws. For example, if a man had an ox that hurt another man's ox so that it died, the law said they were to sell the live ox, divide the money equally and divide the dead ox as well. If the killer ox had been known to gore other oxen previously, and its owner had not confined it, however, he had to pay the other man full price for the dead ox, which then became fully his. You can't get any fairer than that.

All the other laws concerning property rights were just as fair. If a thief was breaking into someone's house and was struck so that he died, there was no guilt on the part of the man who killed the thief. He was acting in self-defense. Everyone knows that's fair. Yet many times in our society someone has shot a thief breaking into his house, only to be sued for damages by the thief. I once read of a man who tried to commit suicide by jumping from a building but instead landed on a pedestrian. The pedestrian was killed, and the man who tried to commit suicide lived. He then sued the estate of the dead pedestrian for preventing his suicide! It sounds unbelievable, but it really happened.

Notice God's great compassion for orphans and widows. God promised that the wife and children of anybody who oppressed them would themselves become widows and orphans.

God also has special compassion for the poor. The Israelites were not permitted to lend money at interest to the poor or to keep a poor man's cloak overnight as a pledge to repay a loan. Every seventh year they were to let the land rest and lie fallow so that the poor could go out into the fields and eat their fill. On the other hand, God commanded that no person should show partiality to a poor man when he had a dispute. God is fair and demands fairness from His people!

We also read that God's desire for us to do good to our enemies began here in the Old Testament. "If you see the donkey of one who hates you lying helpless under its load, you shall refrain from leaving it to him, you shall surely release it with him" (23:5).

Finally, we read God's purpose in instituting the Sabbath. He wants all people to rest and refresh themselves. All these laws may seem tedious to read, but they help us better understand God's character. Aren't you glad that He is who He is?

MATTHEW 24:1-28

Here we read the beginning of what is called the Olivet Discourse. While in the temple area of Jerusalem, Jesus predicted that a day was coming when not one stone of the temple would be left upon another. That was an amazing statement, as it took forty-six years to build the temple. Later, on the Mount of Olives, the disciples asked Jesus three questions. They knew that only in a war would the temple ever be destroyed. There would have to be an invading army. If Jesus told you that a foreign country would invade the United States, wouldn't you want to know when? So the disciples asked when the temple would be destroyed and what would be the sign of His coming and of the end of the age.

Apparently Matthew, unlike Luke, didn't record Jesus' answer to their first question. We'll look closely at Luke's version when we come to it. Interpretations vary, but I believe (for now at least!) that all of Jesus' response in Matthew's account was in answer to the questions about His coming and the end of the age. If not, then only through verse 13 could be considered an answer concerning when Jerusalem would be destroyed, because in verse 14 Jesus was clearly talking about the end.

The "abomination of desolation... spoken of through Daniel the prophet" (v. 15) speaks of the time when the Antichrist sets himself up in the temple (which, incidentally, has yet to be rebuilt) in Jerusalem and proclaims that he is God. We'll study this more when we read the book of Daniel (for now, see 2 Thess. 2:4). If you believe as I and many Christians do, there's no reason to be concerned about the Antichrist because the church will be raptured before the tribulation period, when the Antichrist comes to power. However, there will be many people born again during the tribulation, including many Jews living in Jerusalem. They will benefit greatly by Jesus' words here concerning what to do. At that time many false christs will arise and even perform signs and wonders to deceive God's elect. But if people know what Jesus said here, then they won't be deceived. When Jesus comes back at the end of the tribulation period, it will be like a lightning flash.

PSALM 29:1-11

Have you ever sat and enjoyed a powerful thunderstorm? When I see great trees bend in the wind, watch the lightning flash and hear the crack of nearby thunder, it makes me think of God. Apparently storms had the same effect on David. The Bible teaches that we can learn something about what God is like by looking at creation. The thunderstorm reveals His power, His majesty and His awesomeness. David compared the thunder to God's voice, and it's interesting that when God spoke audibly to Jesus from heaven (see John 12:28), many of those who heard it thought it had thundered.

PROVERBS 7:6-23

What a picture the Scripture paints for us today of the folly of a man enticed by an adulteress! No one can accuse the Bible of beating around the bush when it comes to sensitive topics. This man is compared to an ox going to slaughter. The Bible speaks of the *passing pleasures* of sin. Sin *can* be pleasurable for a short while, but eventually the sinner must face the consequences.

FEBRUARY 6

EXODUS 23:14-25:40

God said that the Israelites should celebrate the three feasts before Him each year: Passover, Pentecost and the Feast of Tabernacles. Remember that Jesus was crucified during Passover, and the Holy Spirit fell upon the people in the upper room during Pentecost (see Acts 2). Isn't our God wonderful? He actually *commanded* the people to celebrate feasts.

Once again God promises health to Israel if they will obey. He also promises that there will be no one miscarrying or barren among them! Christians can claim these promises as well, because we know that we have a better covenant with God than Israel (Heb. 8:6)!

Understanding the reason for some of the commandments we read today is more difficult, however. God said to never offer the blood of a sacrifice with leavened bread. The blood of the sacrifices represented the precious blood of Christ, and leaven always represents sin. Of course, Jesus' blood and sin don't mix. Then God said they should not let any fat from any feast remain until the next morning. Perhaps this represents the fact that Christ's body was taken from the cross before sunset. Why did God say they weren't to boil a baby animal in the milk of its mother? Some say that was a pagan practice of the Canaanites, who believed it would increase fertility. Others say that God considered it cruel. We can't know for certain.

Remember that God was not being unfair in promising Israel He would drive their enemies from the land of Canaan. He was using Israel as a tool of His judgment on the wicked inhabitants of Canaan. That's why He told Israel to make no covenants with the Canaanites and not allow them to live in the land—lest Israel be influenced to sin.

When Moses was on Mount Sinai for forty days, he was given the plans for the tabernacle and all its furnishings. The detailed instructions may seem boring, but according to the book of Hebrews God was explaining to Moses how to make a replica of what already existed in heaven. Beyond that, the tabernacle was rich in new covenant symbolism. Three main pieces are listed in what we read today: the ark of the covenant, the table of showbread and the golden lampstand. God told Moses to take up an offering from the people. Remember that they had plundered the Egyptians when they left. Whenever God blesses us, He never intends for us to keep it all to ourselves.

The ark of the covenant was basically a rectangular gold box about four feet long and two-and-a-half feet wide and high. It had rings on all four corners of its base in which to insert poles by which to carry it. On its top was the mercy seat, which had two large, golden angels with outstretched wings facing each other. It was on this mercy seat that God would speak to Moses. The ark probably represented Christ; there God met man, and atonement for sins was made each year. The ark of the covenant was lost in 586 B.C. when King Nebuchadnezzar destroyed Jerusalem. Some say Jeremiah hid it and believe that it will be discovered soon.

The table of showbread was a golden table, its top being about three feet long and a foot-and-a-half wide. On top of the table the "bread of the Presence" was laid fresh each Sabbath. There were twelve loaves, which were eaten only by the priests. There are many possible interpretations of what the showbread represents. In my opinion the showbread also represents Christ, the living Word of God, the bread from heaven. He Himself broke bread at the last supper and said it represented His body. It may also represent the written Word of God. Jesus said that "man shall not live on bread alone, but on every word that proceeds out of the mouth of God" (Matt. 4:4).

If you've ever seen a Jewish menorah, you have a pretty good idea what the golden lampstand looked like. It had one central shaft with three branches coming from each side. I believe this lampstand points once again to Christ, the light of the world. The books of Isaiah and Revelation speak of the sevenfold Spirit of God that rested upon Jesus (see Is. 11:2), so the lampstand may very well also represent the Holy Spirit.

MATTHEW 24:29-51

When Jesus returns at the end of the great tribulation period, His angels will gather the elect from the "four winds, from one end of the sky to the other" (v. 31). What are His elect doing up in the sky? We must remember that we will be with Jesus in heaven *already* when He returns to earth. The rapture takes place seven years before the tribulation ends. (We will study this in great detail when we read the book of Daniel.) But it is *we who will be gathered* to return with Jesus to set up His kingdom on earth, where He will reign for one thousand years. Notice that Jesus went on to compare that time with the time of Noah. Then it was the unrighteous who were taken off the earth, and the righteous remained. When we return with Jesus, I believe the unrighteous will again be taken off the earth while the righteous will remain. (Read verses 39-41 closely.)

The point of the rest of the chapter, as well as most of the next chapter, is that we should stay alert, because no one knows when Jesus will return. Again, this passage is not speaking of the rapture of the church but rather the second advent of Christ after the great tribulation. When you begin to study the end times, however, you will find that there are almost as many interpretations as there are interpreters. I'm certainly not going to be dogmatic in this study. The important thing is, are you ready to meet God? The second most important question is, are others around you ready to meet God? Many end-time details have little significance in personal spiritual growth. Jesus wants to find us doing His will *whenever* He comes.

PSALM 30:1-12

Don't ever forget verse 5 of today's psalm: "For His anger is but for a moment, His favor is for a lifetime; weeping may last for the night, but a shout of joy comes in the morning." All God's children have experienced the discipline of their loving heavenly Father (see Heb. 12:8). It isn't fun to be disciplined, but after the "spanking" God pours His favor upon us. Don't think that God has been holding a grudge against you for years. More than anything else, He loves us. When we're disciplined by Him, it's because He loves us and wants us to share in His holiness (see Heb. 12:10).

PROVERBS 7:24-27

FEBRUARY 7

EXODUS 26:1-27:21

I know, I know. You're not real excited about what you've read today. To be honest, the next three days in the book of Exodus are going to be a little tedious. This is where many well-intentioned "through the whole Bible" readers stumble and quit. They think that the rest of the Old Testament is going to be as boring as today's reading. But that's not so. Hang in there, and it will get better. I guarantee it.

Today's reading is not without spiritual application. Everything about the tabernacle and its furnishings points to Jesus and His redemptive work. The tabernacle was designed so that it could be carried from place to place as Israel traveled through the wilderness. Basically, the whole thing was a tent within a tent, except the outer tent was just four walls of curtains about seven feet high. Those outer curtains defined the borders of the *tabernacle court*, which was a large, open area about 150 feet by 75 feet. Within the court sat the second tent, the tabernacle itself. (Actually it was a room of gold-covered wooden walls within a tent.) It contained the holy place and the holy of holies, in which the ark of the covenant sat. The two holy places were separated by a curtain.

It was this curtain that was ripped from top to bottom when Jesus cried out, "It is finished!" The book of Hebrews tells us the separating curtain represented Jesus' flesh (Heb. 10:20). We now have access into the holy of holies through the blood of Christ!

The big tent, or outer court, had no roof, but the tabernacle itself did. Therefore, the tabernacle would have been dark inside, except that it was lighted by the six-branched golden lampstand of which we read yesterday. It stood in the holy place along with the table of showbread, but only the high priest could enter into the holy of holies, and that but once a year. We'll discuss the significance of all this later, but remember that the tabernacle and its furnishings are all copies of what exists in heaven.

In chapter 27 we read of the bronze altar, which sat within the outer court directly in front of the tabernacle. This is where all the sacrifices were made. It was about seven feet square and five feet high, large enough for burning bulls and sheep. Of course, all the animal sacrifices pointed to Christ's ultimate sacrifice on the cross. When an Israelite brought an animal to be slain to atone for his sins, he saw a picture of something completely innocent dying for the sins of someone completely guilty.

MATTHEW 25:1-20

The parable of the ten virgins and the parable of the talents both have basically the same meaning: be faithful and stay ready. In Jesus' day weddings were carried out somewhat differently from today's customs. First, a man had to pay money to his bride's father to "purchase" her. A good woman cost a lot of money! There are still places in the Middle East where men must purchase their brides. In some areas the bride prices have gone sky high because the discovery of oil has brought lots of money into the local economy!

Once the purchase price was worked out, the man and woman were "engaged." The engagement was so binding that it could be broken only by divorce. That's what Joseph was planning to do with Mary when he discovered she was pregnant. (He was going to divorce her quietly because otherwise, as a supposed *adulteress*, she could be stoned to death.)

The wedding itself was an elaborate occasion. Bride and bridegroom were dressed like a queen and king. The bridegroom would leave his home and walk to the home of his bride. From there he would take her back to his home in a wedding procession, and the wedding guests would light their way through the darkened streets with oil lamps. The ten virgins in this story were either stationed at the bride's home, waiting for the bridegroom to arrive, or at his house, waiting for both bride and bridegroom to arrive. The point is that five of them weren't ready. They had their lamps but no oil to keep them lit. By the time they had purchased oil the wedding feast was already in progress, and they could not gain entrance.

There's some danger in trying to find significance in every detail of every parable (e.g. what the oil represents, whether there's any meaning to the number of virgins and why the five didn't *share* their oil). The point is obvious. There is going to be a great wedding feast, and you don't want to miss it. Make sure your lamp is lit and you have plenty of reserve oil. That is, make sure you're saved and you persevere in the faith.

Concerning the parable of the talents, true Christians all have a desire to spread the good news of Jesus Christ. Truly, the first gift we receive from God is the hearing of the gospel. If we're faithful to share it, more "talents," or gifts and responsibilities, are given to us. Have you been faithful with the "one talent" God has given you?

PSALM 31:1-8

You probably expect me to say something about David's faith as expressed in his prayer. Well, I'm not going to say anything about it, even though this psalm is another fine example of David's expressing his confidence in the midst of trial. I won't point out to you verses 3 and 4, which are exceptionally strong positive confessions. Neither will I call your attention to verse 7, where David said he would rejoice and be glad even though times were hard. No, I'm not going to do it. I'll just allow you to glean whatever truth you can from this reading!

PROVERBS 8:1-11

FEBRUARY 8

EXODUS 28:1-43

Today we read that Moses' brother Aaron and his four sons were chosen to minister as priests in the tabernacle. They had to wear the proper clothing and follow God's instruction for ministry or they would die. (Later on two of Aaron's sons offered "strange fire" to the Lord and forfeited their lives. See Num. 3:4.) This chapter deals primarily with Aaron's garments, which were rich in symbolism.

First Aaron wore a blue robe, which had bells and pomegranates attached to its hem. This was so Aaron could be heard as he ministered in the tabernacle. If the bells stopped tinkling, those outside would know that the high priest had done something wrong and fallen dead in the holy of holies. Tradition says the Jews actually tied a rope to the high priest's ankle before he went into the holy of holies so that if he died they could drag him out!

On top of the robe was an ephod, which would be something like an apron, with the names of the twelve tribes engraved on an onyx stone set in gold on the shoulder straps. Attached to the front of the ephod was the breastplate, which was about ten inches square and had twelve precious stones in four rows, each with the name of one of the twelve tribes written on it.

It's clear that Aaron was representing *all* of Israel in his ministry. This would be somewhat equivalent to a pastor's wearing a shirt with the names of everyone in his church written on it! Notice the breastplate was over Aaron's heart. He also wore a turban that had a gold headplate with the inscription "Holy to the Lord." Aaron was a type of our high priest, the Lord Jesus Christ, who entered into the heavenly holy of holies with His blood, having obtained eternal redemption for us.

MATTHEW 25:31-26:13

This judgment we read about today is usually considered to be one that will occur at the end of the seven-year tribulation and is referred to as "the judgment of the nations." Opinions differ from there on. Some say this is the final judgment, and *each individual* will be either a "sheep" or a "goat." Those who treated Christ's brothers in a compassionate way will enter eternal life, and those who showed Christ's brothers no compassion will go to eternal punishment. Certainly the Bible teaches that true Christians will display love for fellow Christians, or Jesus' brothers (see 1 John 3:14; James 2:14-16).

Others look upon this judgment as a separation of *different nations* based on how they treated Jewish believers in Israel during the tribulation. Those nations that had compassion will be permitted to enter into the millennial reign of Christ. Those that didn't will be removed from the earth.

I side with the first interpretation, but I see some validity in the second. Maybe they're both right! I don't think this is the *final judgment*, as the book of Revelation speaks of "the great white throne judgment," where even those who have died are judged (see Rev. 20:12-15). Again, let's not get sidetracked. No matter what the correct interpretation, if you were to stand in this judgment, how would you fare? Is it evident that you're a Christian by the way you treat Christians in less-fortunate circumstances than yourself?

Now we have come to the time of *two days* before the Passover feast. There is some debate about exactly when Jesus ate the Passover meal with the disciples. Matthew, Mark and Luke make it seem as if Jesus and His disciples ate the Passover meal when everyone else did—the same day all the lambs were slain. But John makes it clear that Jesus' final meal with the disciples happened *before* the Passover, so that *Jesus was crucified the same hour that all the Passover lambs were being slain* (see John 18:28). That is much more than ironic—it's overwhelmingly and perfectly symbolic.

Jesus said that the woman who poured precious ointment on His head would be remembered for what she did as the gospel was preached around the world. His prediction has certainly come true. It was just fulfilled one more time as you read about it!

PSALM 31:9-18

David encouraged himself in this particular trial by saying to the Lord: "Thou art my God" (v. 14). That's really all we need to know and believe in times of difficulty. If the Lord is our God, we can be confident that everything is going to turn out according to His perfect will. We sometimes complicate things by learning all the rules of faith and how to trust God, when all we really need to say is, "Thou art my God!" If He is, you haven't a thing to worry about!

PROVERBS 8:12-13

FEBRUARY 9

EXODUS 29:1-30:10

Aaron and his sons had to go through an elaborate ordination ceremony. The one aspect of it that stands out above all others is that animal sacrifices were made on their behalf. It was very clear to Aaron and his sons that they weren't priests because of anything they had done but rather in spite of what they had done. They were priests because of God's grace. Notice that they placed their hands on the heads of the sacrifices, symbolically transferring their guilt to the animals. Moses also had to sprinkle some of the blood of the sacrifices on Aaron and his garments and on the altar itself. *Everything was made holy through the blood.*

I can't claim to understand all the details and symbolism of the ordination ceremony, but the major symbolisms are obvious. (I never worry about what I don't understand; I just try to apply what I do!) Notice also that the priests *ate* part of the animal sacrifice. This probably is representative of Christ's coming to live inside us by the Holy Spirit. The New Testament teaches that all who believe in Jesus are priests unto God and have a right to come to Him themselves, with no other mediator than Jesus.

Moses also received instructions about the altar of incense. This was about eighteen inches square and was the final piece of furniture actually in the tabernacle. It sat in the holy place right in front of the curtain that divided the two holy places.

It is interesting that there were *three* "doorways" in the tabernacle and its court, and they were all *in a row*. There was only one entrance into the court, on the east side. As you walked through it, directly in front of you would be the bronze altar of sacrifice. It stood directly between you and the tabernacle, where the presence of God was. The meaning is clear. To approach God, sacrifice must first be made for our sins. *There is no other way.* Once you got past the *bronze altar*, you would come directly to the *bronze laver*, of which we will read tomorrow. Aaron and his sons were required to wash their hands and feet there before entering the holy place or before offering any sacrifices. Again, the symbolism seems to point to the regeneration of the Holy Spirit or else the washing of the water of the Word of God (see Eph. 5:26).

The point is, once sacrifice has been made, you must have your mind washed, or renewed, with the Word of God if you want to get nearer to Him! Once past the bronze laver, you could walk into the tabernacle through the second "door" and into the holy place. Once in the holy place, to your right would be the table of showbread, and to your left would be the golden lampstand. Directly in front of you would be the altar of incense.

The incense represents prayer and worship rising to God (see Rev. 5:8; 8:3-4). Again the point seems to be that if you want to get closer to the Lord, you must partake of the bread of God's Word (the showbread), be illuminated by the Holy Spirit (the lampstand) and enter into prayer and worship to the Lord. Only then can a person enter into the holy of holies and commune with God.

MATTHEW 26:14-46

Whether or not Jesus and His disciples actually ate the Passover meal on the day of the Passover feast, this incident is still filled with incredible symbolism. It was here that the ordinance of the Lord's supper was instituted. I'm sure you can now see the similarities between the Passover meal and the Lord's supper. *The first Lord's supper was a Passover meal!* The bread Jesus ate *had* to have been unleavened, which represented His body, broken for us, and His sinlessness (leaven almost always represents sin). The wine was symbolic of His blood, shed by our Passover Lamb (see 1 Cor. 5:7).

When Jesus prayed that, if it were possible, to let "this cup pass from Me" (26:39), He was probably speaking of the cup of God's wrath which He would experience. God said in Jeremiah 25:15: "Take this cup of the wine of wrath from My hand." Remember that Jesus was about to take upon Himself all the sins and guilt of the world and suffer the ultimate penalty of death by crucifixion. It's no wonder He recoiled from the thought. But, praise God, He also prayed: "Not as I will, but as thou wilt." Jesus *willingly* went to the cross because of His great love for humanity.

PSALM 31:19-24

David finishes this beautiful psalm with the admonition to "Be strong, and let your heart take courage." Remember that he was still in the midst of his trial. We, too, need to continually remind ourselves to be strong and take courage, because God cannot fail. If you're going through some difficulty right now, just say out loud to yourself, "Be strong, and let your heart take courage." Keep saying it until you feel that courage rise up within you. When it does, there will be a smile on your face!

PROVERBS 8:14-26

Today we read a promise that with wisdom come riches and honor and enduring wealth (v. 18). And that personified wisdom wants to endow those who love her with wealth, that she might fill their treasuries (v. 21). Isn't it a shame that some unsaved people use legitimate wisdom to prosper while some Christians just remain poor? God promised us that if we lack wisdom we should ask in faith from Him, and He will give it to us (James 1:5). God is not opposed to our having money; He is opposed to greed and covetousness. God wants His children to prosper, just as any good parent wants his children to prosper. It may not come overnight, but it will come by faith, patience, obedience and wisdom.

FEBRUARY 10

EXODUS 30:11-31:18

Don't forget that Moses received all of these instructions during his forty days on Mount Sinai. The Lord told him that whenever they took a census of the people he was to collect a half-shekel from each person over age twenty "as a ransom." It appears the Lord wanted Israel to remember they were not their own, but now belonged to Him. The New Testament says that we, too, are not our own but have been bought with a price. In a sense we were put up on the auction block with both Jesus and the devil bidding, and Jesus paid the highest price! Let us never forget that we are now God's property. He owns us, our money and possessions, our time and our future.

This man Bezalel is the first person of whom the Bible speaks as being filled with the Spirit. He was specially gifted for craftsmanship to build the tabernacle and its furnishings. Notice that God gifts people to also do things other than preach or teach. The New Testament speaks of the "gifts of...helps" (1 Cor. 12:28), and Bezalel and Oholiab could be the first examples of men anointed for that type of ministry. Thank God for those in the body of Christ today who recognize their special anointing to help in such practical areas. We need more of them.

Keeping the Sabbath was considered so serious by the Lord that breaking it was punishable by death. This may seem harsh, but who are we to criticize the Lord? Although we're not under the Law, it seems to me that if God considered this to be so important, we should be taking it more seriously than we do. We should all have a day of rest and refreshing in which to celebrate God's goodness and worship Him corporately. When Christian families go on vacation, they should find a church to attend. This impresses the children with the importance of regular church attendance and honoring the Lord before all else. If you're out camping in the woods and it's impossible to go to church, have your own little church service. If the husband, who is supposed to be the head and spiritual leader, is too carnal to take such a responsibility, his wife should take the initiative.

MATTHEW 26:47-68

When Jesus was arrested in the garden, He stated that He could pray to His Father and immediately twelve legions of angels would be at His disposal. One legion would be six thousand, so twelve legions would be seventy-two thousand angels! I bring this to your attention for two reasons. First, it indicates once again that Jesus went to the cross by His own volition and was not in any way forced or pressured by the Father. Second, those seventy-two thousand angels are still around, because angels don't die. The Bible says angels are "ministering spirits, sent out to render service for the sake of those who will inherit salvation" (Heb. 1:14). To put it simply, that means angels are here to help you!

When Jesus declared He was indeed the Son of God at His mock trial before the chief priests and Sanhedrin, the high priest tore his robes. This seems strange to us, but it was a custom of their day that had been practiced for at least a couple of thousand years. When people tore their clothes, it indicated a strong emotion of alarm concerning a present situation. In this case it was Jesus' supposed blasphemy that stirred up the high priest so much he tore his robe. Isn't it amazing that people could become so evil that *they would actually accuse God of blasphemy?* Once the verdict was pronounced, they spit in Jesus' face. After that they somehow covered His eyes and beat Him, which is ten times worse than just being beaten, because you have no idea when and where to expect a punch. At least if you can see a blow coming you can prepare for it. That's why they said in verse 68: "Prophesy to us, You Christ; who is the one who hit You?" Remember that Peter had been watching all this from a distance.

PSALM 32:1-11

When we try to hide our sins, we will feel just as David did in this psalm. But when we confess them, we'll experience the cleansing, healing forgiveness that David also experienced. God promises to forgive us and cleanse us when we confess our wrongs (1 John 1:9). You may have a confession to make that you have been holding in for a long time. Don't carry the guilt any longer. Confess it and receive complete forgiveness.

PROVERBS 8:27-31

FEBRUARY 11

EXODUS 32:1-33:23

This has to be one of the greatest passages in Exodus. The people of Israel hadn't forgotten about all that God had done for them. They just got tired of waiting for Moses to come down from the mountain after he had been there almost six weeks. Notice that after Aaron made the golden calf he said, "This is your god, O Israel, *who brought you up from the land of Egypt... Tomorrow shall be a feast to the Lord*" (32:4-5, italics mine). But the people had no excuse, because they had already heard the Ten Commandments spoken by the audible voice of God about forty days before. The *second* thing God had told them was that they should not make any idols or any likeness of what was in heaven above or on the earth beneath (see Ex. 20:4); yet now they were offering sacrifices to a golden calf. Their worship ended with wild feasting and sexual immorality (see 32:6).

The ensuing conversation between God and Moses was almost comical. Notice what God said to Moses: "*Your* people, whom *you* brought up from the land of Egypt..." (32:7, italics mine). But Moses' reply to the Lord was: "Why doth Thine anger burn against *Thy* people whom *Thou* hast brought out from the land of Egypt...?" (32:11, italics mine). It seems as if neither wanted to claim responsibility!

Then comes one of the greatest examples of intercessory prayer that we have in the Bible. Nobody fully comprehends everything about this incident, but we can make some interesting observations. First, Moses saved the lives of all the Israelites by his prayer. *Because of what he said, God changed His mind.* I know that sounds wrong, but we just read those exact words in verse 14. Is there more to this story? I think so. I believe we're reading a classic example of the struggle between the holiness of God and the mercy of God. (I say "struggle" for lack of a better way to put it.) God takes no pleasure in the death of the wicked (see Ezek. 18:23,32). Yet in order for God to be holy, just and moral, He *must* mete out punishments to deserving offenders. However, He takes no pleasure in it, just as no parent *enjoys* spanking his children.

Why did God say in verse 10 to Moses, "Now then let Me alone, that My anger may burn against them"? *Is it because God actually wanted Moses to intercede for the people so that He would have an "excuse" not to destroy Israel?* I know that sounds simplistic, but God could have said not a word to Moses and just destroyed Israel. But when God said, "Let Me alone, *that* My anger may burn" (italics mine), I think Moses' ears pricked up, because he *now realized he could change the situation.*

Moses' argument that God had promised Abraham, Isaac and Jacob that He would bring their descendants into the promised land wasn't really valid. God had already told Moses that He would make a new nation from Moses, who was a descendant of Abraham, Isaac and Jacob. I think God didn't really want to destroy Israel, but He had to because of His holiness and His Law—unless He could find an "excuse" not to. That excuse was simply that someone had *asked* Him not to. I may be wrong, but for more amazing reading on this subject, read Ezekiel 22. In verses 30 and 31 God Himself said, "And I searched for a man among them who should build up the wall and stand in the gap before Me for the land, that I should not destroy it; but I found no one. Thus I have poured out

My indignation on them." The implication is that if God could have found someone to intercede, His judgment could have been at least forestalled. Can we forestall God's judgment on our nation? I have to say absolutely yes.

Did you notice how Aaron lied when he was questioned by Moses about how the golden calf came into being? He put all the blame on the people and made it sound as if the calf came from the fire supernaturally, when he had fashioned it. Apparently Moses later discovered the truth of what had happened because he is the author of the book of Exodus.

When Moses and Joshua arrived at the Israelite camp, things were so out of control that drastic action had to be taken. Some versions of the Scripture indicate the people were involved in nude dancing along with their idolatrous worship. Three thousand of the ringleaders were slain by the Levites, and order was restored. Three thousand may sound like a lot, but remember we're talking about 3.5 million people who deserved judgment. God was actually quite merciful.

Moses' true character shines in this story. He prayed that God would not destroy Israel and turned down the opportunity to have a new nation named after him. (If God made the same offer to many pastors today when they were having trouble with their congregations, they would say, "Lord, let 'em have it, and start with the deacons!") And Moses wasn't satisfied with having God spare their lives. He interceded a *second time* for God to forgive the people; if not, then Moses requested that God blot his name from His book! As a result, God did forgive them, yet not without some discipline first (see 32:35), and He renewed His promise to bring them into the promised land. However, He declared that His presence would not go with them any longer until Moses prayed again, and God granted Moses his third request! Moses' fourth request was granted as well. He asked to see God's glory, and God Himself walked by and allowed Moses to see His back. Does God answer prayer? You'd better believe it!

MATTHEW 26:69-27:14

After Peter watched Jesus' trial and then witnessed His being spit upon and beaten, he decided it was best not to identify himself with Jesus any longer. Just as Jesus had foretold, Peter then denied Jesus three times. *The wonderful part of this story is that within two months' time Peter had completely turned around and was used of God mightily* (as recorded in the book of Acts). This is another testimony to the love and forgiveness of God. If you have ever disappointed the Lord, don't feel He has rejected you. *Even if you've denied knowing Him when questioned, God can and will restore you.*

Jesus was detained overnight, probably at Caiaphas's house. In Jerusalem today you can visit the supposed site of Caiaphas's house and actually go into the "pit" where Jesus was kept that night. It is a dark cave with a hole at the top, adjacent to a torture chamber. To visit it is to feel some of the immense loneliness Jesus must have felt the night of His betrayal and trial.

Judas felt remorse for what he had done, but most commentators don't believe he truly repented. He certainly didn't receive forgiveness by faith, or else he wouldn't have hung himself. Luke recorded in the book of Acts that Judas bought a field with the thirty pieces of silver. We read today that this is true in the sense that the field was bought with Judas's money, so he was actually the owner, though dead.

The Jews were not permitted to execute any person without the governor's permission because Israel was under

Roman domination at that time. Therefore, Jesus had to be presented before Pilate, the Roman procurator.

PSALM 33:1-11

I feel so sorry for Christians who have never had the blessing of experiencing true scriptural worship. If you think singing three hymns that nobody understands is true worship, you're sadly mistaken. God wants us to express our own praise to Him *from our hearts*. Yet I've been in "worship services" where half the people didn't even sing and the other half sang something they didn't understand. Today we read that God wants us to *shout* before Him. If you've never done that, I encourage you to obey the Bible! There is something about shouting for joy before the Lord that is absolutely exhilarating!

PROVERBS 8:32-36

FEBRUARY 12

EXODUS 34:1-35:9

Verses 6 and 7 of chapter 34 contain a beautiful description of God's full character, spoken by God Himself. He is first of all *compassionate, gracious, slow to anger and abounding in lovingkindness and truth*. He forgives iniquity, transgression and sin. So there you have God's great love. But there's still more. Finally God says that He will by no means leave the guilty unpunished. He is also a great judge who is holy and just. Don't ever become imbalanced in your understanding of God's character. Many get into the ditch of misunderstanding on one side or the other, but we need to stay right in the middle of the road.

Once again, at Moses' intercession, God renewed His covenant with Israel. Moses was up on Mount Sinai another forty days. Why forty *more* days? Nobody knows for certain. I think God was testing the people of Israel again. Last time they got impatient waiting for Moses on the mountain. Would they pull the same stunt again? To me this makes it very clear that if we fail one of God's tests, we get to take it over again!

Have you ever had a key chain that glows in the dark? I have one, and in order for it to glow in the dark I have to hold it up against a light for a few seconds to "charge it up." This is similar to what happened to Moses' face. We don't have all the details, but we do know that Moses saw the "shekinah" glory of God as he spoke with Him on the mountain and in the meeting tent. Somehow it "charged" Moses' face to glow with the same glory.

The final chapters of Exodus are dedicated to the carrying out of all the instructions Moses received concerning the tabernacle, its furnishings and the priestly garments. But don't be concerned; it will take us only the next three days to finish the book.

MATTHEW 27:15-31

Gentile Pilate turned out to be more righteous than the Jewish leaders and the people of Jerusalem. His wife was given a dream *from the Lord* that Jesus was innocent, and she warned her husband. It appears Pilate thought he could get out of his predicament of having to condemn Jesus by offering the Jews a choice of whom he would release—Jesus or a known murderer and insurrectionist named Barabbas. Surely the people, when offered such a choice, would vote for the release of Jesus. But instead they shouted for Barabbas's release. What a picture of the purpose of Christ's life in this one incident: Jesus the innocent was condemned, and because of it the guilty one was pardoned and went free. *Barabbas represents you and me.*

When Pilate asked the crowd what evil Christ had done, they could make no accusation and only shouted "Crucify Him!" The mob was so out of control a riot was about to start, so Pilate granted their request, but only after symbolically washing his hands in front of them and declaring that he was innocent of Jesus' blood. Their reply: "His blood be on us and on our children!" (v. 25). In a sense they cursed themselves, and about thirty-seven years later they and their children perished at the hands of the Romans, who destroyed Jerusalem in A.D. 70.

According to John's Gospel Pilate had Jesus whipped thirty-nine times in hopes of saving Him from crucifixion by convincing the Jews that He had suffered enough. The Roman scourge was similar to what we call a cat-o'-nine-tails: a whip with many lashes. The Roman version had small, sharp bone fragments or pieces of metal attached to the ends so that the whip actually ripped the flesh off its victim each time a lash was given. After Jesus was whipped He was brought in front of the mob once again, who, *even after seeing His lacerated back, still demanded that He be crucified.*

PSALM 33:12-22

I hope you aren't reading these psalms too quickly. If you have a little more time, spend it meditating on what you have just read. Notice that the psalmist said the Lord keeps us alive in famine (v. 19). Troubles may come, but the Lord delivers us from them. Sometimes we're guilty of trying to believe that famines will never come in our lives. God hasn't promised us that. But we can trust Him to keep us alive when they do come. *We aren't exempt from troubles and trials, but we are promised deliverance!*

PROVERBS 9:1-6

FEBRUARY 13

EXODUS 35:10-36:38

If you don't have a basic picture of the tabernacle and its court and furnishings, I encourage you to go back and read the commentary of Exodus 25-28. Such an understanding is important.

Most of the material wealth of Israel was in the form of jewelry, as there were no banks in which they could keep their money. (Without paper money, their economy was no doubt much more stable than ours.) The prosperous Israelites, who had been poor slaves just a few months before, gave willingly to support the work of the tabernacle. In fact, they gave so willingly that Moses had to tell them to stop giving! (Every pastor dreams of such a thing.)

The boards that we read about today were actually the portable pieces of the walls of the tabernacle. The structure was covered with a tent roof which was in turn covered with porpoise skins, possibly for preservation and waterproofing. This was a special place, as the holy presence of God would rest there.

MATTHEW 27:32-66

Right before the Roman soldiers hammered the nails through Jesus' hands and feet, they offered Him wine mingled with gall. This would have relieved the pain of the nails ripping through His flesh considerably, but Jesus refused it after taking a sip. He was willing to suffer to the *full extent* of what you and I deserved. It's amazing to me that people can hear the story of Jesus' crucifixion without having their hearts broken enough to receive Him as Savior. *His love is so great.*

Jesus died on the cross after only a few hours, even though crucified people usually survived for days. This gives us an idea of how terribly Jesus had been abused by the Roman soldiers. Also, don't forget that He had already received thirty-nine lashes, which was enough to kill some who received them. We know that Jesus was on the cross for at least three hours, and possibly six. He died at three o'clock in the afternoon.

Matthew's Gospel seems to be directed toward Jewish readers, so his account contains many references to Old Testament prophecies that Jesus fulfilled. Today's reading contains five direct Old Testament references, four from Psalm 22 and one from Psalm 69. It had been prophesied that Jesus would be offered wine mixed with gall, that lots would be cast for His clothing (Jesus hung *naked* on the cross) and that Jesus would be mocked by the spectators. Jesus Himself directed the onlookers to His prophetic connection to Psalm 22 when He quoted the first verse: "My God, My God, why hast Thou forsaken Me?"

It was on the cross that Jesus "became sin" (2 Cor. 5:21), or, as some say, He became a "sin offering." First Peter 2:24 clearly states that Jesus bore our sins in His body on the cross. Of course, no one at the time, not even the apostles or Jesus' mother, understood why He had to die. It would take revelation from the Holy Spirit and from Jesus Himself, after His resurrection, before anyone knew the real meaning of what had transpired.

Immediately after Jesus died the curtain in the temple was ripped in half from top to bottom. This was not the curtain in the tabernacle that we've been reading about in Exodus. The tabernacle was eventually replaced by a permanent temple, which was replaced by another temple, which was replaced by another temple (the last one was built by Herod). However, it had the same design as the tabernacle, with a holy place and a holy of holies. The curtain we read about here was the curtain that divided the two holy places. The significance is obvious. Jesus has paved the way for every person to have access to God. He is the only One who can grant access to the Father. *Also, the temple of God changed locations that day. A few days later, born-again men and women became the temples of the Holy Spirit. Now you and I are the holy of holies.*

I'm glad the chief priests and Pharisees decided to make Jesus' grave as secure as possible with Pilate's help because that makes Jesus' resurrection even more believable. Nobody came by one night and stole His body! Guards were posted, and they even put a seal on the stone to make sure there was no chance that someone could come by and steal the body.

PSALM 34:1-10

We already know that Jesus had at least seventy-two thousand angels at His disposal, and today we read that all people who fear the Lord have angels encamped about them. Those angels aren't just spectators; they are there to rescue us. Can you think of any time when some angels might have been involved in saving your life? Verse 10 is a wonderful promise: "They who seek the Lord shall not be in want of any good thing." I'm claiming that one right now!

PROVERBS 9:7-8

It's a waste of time to try to correct some people. How about you? Do others recognize that you're open to constructive criticism?

FEBRUARY 14

EXODUS 37:1-38:31

Today we read of the actual construction of the tabernacle and its court and furnishings. There isn't much new information here. We're given the total cost of the project, but it is by ancient measures. If we convert the cost to modern equivalents, just the silver and gold would be worth about $27 million! Does that give you an idea of how much God prospered those poor Israelite slaves during their deliverance?

This tabernacle would be used for 324 to 479 years (depending on which date you accept for the Exodus) and would be the focal point of Israel's worship until Solomon built a temple for the Lord in Jerusalem.

The ark of the covenant, which sat in the holy of holies, would soon contain a sample of manna, the two tablets of stone on which were written the Ten Commandments and Aaron's rod that budded, all of which we'll read later. This must have been a *very* heavy box, since it was covered with gold inside and out.

Tomorrow we'll finish the book of Exodus, and then you will have completed two Old Testament books and one New Testament book. Don't you feel good about yourself? You should!

MATTHEW 28:1-20

There's no doubt that Jesus spoke some of His most significant words *after* His resurrection in order to impress upon the disciples' minds the task that was before them. *And there's no doubt that Matthew ended his Gospel with what he considered to be Jesus' most important post-resurrection words to impress upon the minds of his readers the task that lies before them.* Jesus wants us all to be involved in the process of making disciples. But you won't ever reach the point where you can make a disciple unless you *first are a disciple yourself.*

There's a difference between being a disciple of Christ and just being born again. *All disciples of Christ have been born again, but not all who are born again are disciples.* To be born again costs you nothing because the price was paid in full by Jesus on the cross. *But there's a cost to being a disciple of Jesus.* It could cost you your life!

I've discovered at least five requirements people must meet before they can be considered disciples. We'll read four of them in Luke and John. But all of them together can be summed up in one requirement: radical commitment to Jesus. The first requirement, which we just read, indicates that disciples are *learning*; the end result is that they're obeying Jesus' commands. That disqualifies many born-again people from calling themselves disciples. For example, if you're lax in your church attendance and your study of God's Word, I guarantee that you are *not* a disciple of Jesus Christ.

Also notice that Jesus wants disciples to be made of *all* nations. The word translated "nations" is the Greek word *ethnos*. From it we derive our modern word *ethnic*. It could be better translated "families," "tribes" or "ethnic groups." The United States is made up of many ethnic groups, some of which have no witnessing church to reach them with the gospel. Some countries, such as India (which contains one-sixth of the world's population), can be divided into thirty-five hundred different groups! It has been estimated that there are as many as twenty-three thousand different "ethnoses" in the world today, of which twelve thousand have no church within their culture to reach them. *Evangelism is the supreme task of the church, and it should be the one thing that is being concentrated on more than anything else.* When the church gets involved in reaching the world as it should, there won't be time for bickering anymore.

PSALM 34:11-22

Isn't this a great psalm? Today we read the recipe for many good days of life: keep your tongue from evil and your lips from speaking deceitfully. Depart from evil, do good and pursue peace. That's simple enough.

The main message of today's reading is that although the righteous have troubles, God delivers them every time. This is a good, balanced statement found in verse 19. Walking by faith doesn't mean we won't have troubles. Satan, this world and our flesh will fight us every step of the way. Life is full of difficulties, but as we trust in the Lord we gain complete victory every time. Those of us who walk by faith smile at the future!

PROVERBS 9:9-10

FEBRUARY 15

EXODUS 39:1-40:38

Finally the tabernacle was completed, and everything was set up and put in its proper place as God had commanded. It had been about one year since the Exodus. The most interesting part of today's reading is when the glory-cloud rested upon and filled the tabernacle. That cloud was continually present for the next forty years, and by it God led the Israelites through the wilderness. As long as the cloud remained over the tabernacle, the people of Israel stayed put. But when it moved, the people packed up and followed it. It appeared as a cloud by day and as fire by night. It must have been quite a sight! Evidently Moses *attempted* to gain entrance to the tent of meeting but couldn't because of the cloud. About three hundred years later, when Solomon dedicated his temple to the Lord, the same thing happened. The whole temple was filled with a cloud, and the Bible says that the "priests could not stand to minister" (2 Chron. 5:13-14). In modern terminology we would say they were "slain in the Spirit"!

Truly now God was dwelling *with* them, right in their very midst. If this incident fills you with awe, don't forget that God dwells *in you. We are now His temple.* Maybe we should be taking better care of our temples, don't you think?

MARK 1:1-28

Mark's Gospel is the shortest of the four, and unlike Matthew it was written to non-Jewish readers. It contains very little information not in Matthew, Luke and John, yet Mark's unique style presents Jesus in a light the other writers don't. You're going to love it!

Not all Jews were completely exclusionary, and from time to time certain Gentiles would convert to Judaism. When they did, they had to be circumcised if they were male and then baptized by immersion. It represented a washing away of sins and a new life. (When Christians are baptized, it means all that and more. See my comments on Matt. 3.) This is why John's baptism was so significant. For a Jew to be baptized, just like a pagan proselyte, he had to humble himself. These folks who were baptized by John were for the most part sincere Jews who were truly repenting to prepare themselves for the coming of the Messiah. Incidentally, they weren't *sprinkled* with a few drops of water; they went down under the water. That's how Jesus was baptized as well. There is no precedent for infant sprinkling in the New Testament. They were all immersed after having believed.

Notice that right after Jesus was baptized the Holy Spirit *led* Him into the wilderness (desert). Here we see another scriptural example of God's testings. Sometimes He will lead us into difficult situations as well, but only for our good. God wants to use us to bless others, but we must prove ourselves faithful first. May you and I pass every test!

Peter, Andrew, James and John didn't leave their nets to follow Jesus for some mysterious reason. Luke gives us more details of the story. Jesus performed the miracle of a great catch of fish right before their eyes that day (see Luke 5:1-11). It was convincing enough for them to leave everything and follow the "miracle man."

Isn't it amazing that this demon in the man of Capernaum couldn't resist showing off his knowledge that Jesus was the Son of God? *Showing off is a trait of the devil.* We should beware when we say or do anything to impress others.

PSALM 35:1-16

I don't see any ethical problems with this psalm as some commentators do. They contend that it conflicts with Jesus' teaching to "turn the other cheek." However, when Jesus said that we should turn the other cheek, He was referring to when we are persecuted for His cause. Read it and see. But if some evil person tries to murder me, I'm going to defend myself. It's clear from this psalm that *David's life was at stake*. If you were in his situation, facing the incredibly evil people David described here, I'm sure you would pray the same way.

PROVERBS 9:11-12

Wisdom adds days and years to our lives!

FEBRUARY 16

LEVITICUS 1:1-3:17

The book of Leviticus was written by Moses. Israel remained camped at the foot of Mount Sinai while Moses probably wrote the majority of this book. It contains many laws regarding the sacrificial system, the duties of the priests, and civil, religious and dietary laws. In it God also reveals principles of hygiene and sanitation and information concerning how diseases are spread that "modern man" didn't discover for another thirty-five hundred years! This is a supernatural book, just like the other sixty-five books of the Bible.

There were five different kinds of offerings a person could bring to the tabernacle. Not enough information is given so that we can say with confidence what each particular offering represented. However, four of the offerings have in common the idea that sinful man can only approach a holy God by means of a blood sacrifice. Such sacrifice was found in many ancient religions even before Moses' time, probably because the whole idea originally came by revelation from God to Adam and Eve. (Remember that

God covered their nakedness with *animal skins*. Also, Abel, their son, brought to God an animal sacrifice.) No doubt the revelation of the animal sacrifice was passed down from generation to generation, even though its meaning became perverted. It is still practiced by pagans the world over, but its significance is usually antibiblical (i.e., it is thought that the worshipper is buying favor from his god or feeding his god with the sacrifice). In the Scriptures, the blood sacrifice always points to Christ—the innocent dying for the guilty.

Today we read of the first three offerings: the burnt offering, the grain offering and the peace offering. All these are classified as "sweet savor" offerings, whereas the other two offerings, the sin and guilt offerings, are not spoken of as creating a "soothing aroma" to the Lord (1:9,17; 2:2,9; etc.). So we say that three of these offerings are for *maintaining* fellowship with the Lord and two are for *restoring broken fellowship* with the Lord.

When *we* come to the Lord in prayer, we don't always come with the same kind of prayer. Sometimes we come to Him with a prayer of confession, sometimes with a prayer of thanksgiving, sometimes with a prayer of dedication and so on. Just as Israel had different rules to follow for each kind of offering, so we must follow different rules for different kinds of prayer. The prayer of dedication always ends with "if it be Thy will." The prayer of faith never ends with those words, however, because it can only be prayed when the will of God is known.

We read first of the burnt offering. It was the only offering in which the *entire* animal was burned (except its hide). Some think it was a token of the offerer's *dedication* to God, and some say it was given simply out of appreciation to God. There is obviously an element of atonement in this sacrifice (see v. 4). Depending on the wealth of the person making the offering, he could bring an expensive bull, a mid-priced goat or an inexpensive bird.

The grain offering was usually offered along with an animal sacrifice. Its significance is not known, but it's obvious the offerer was giving something of value to the Lord. It cost him. Only a small part of it was actually burned on the altar. The rest was eaten by Aaron and his sons. No leaven was permitted in the grain offering. As stated before, leaven usually represents sin. Why there could be no honey, I don't know. Salt could be representative of preservation against corruption. God's covenant will be preserved, hence "the salt of the covenant" (2:13).

Finally, the peace offering was made as a thanksgiving to God. In this case the *offerer* ate part of the sacrifice. Possibly this speaks of the personal blessing experienced when one worships and thanks the Lord. Again, no one understands all the significance of these offerings. If it were important the Lord would have made it more plain for us.

MARK 1:29-2:12

We'll be reading many things we already read in Matthew's Gospel, but it won't hurt us. However, as a general rule I won't comment on passages that are the same as in Matthew unless I can add something new.

Some preachers argue that Jesus healed people only to prove His deity. They claim that healing is no longer for today, since His deity was well-established two thousand years ago. But verses 41 and 43-44 suggest otherwise. If Jesus was healing people only to establish His deity, why did He order this leper whom He had healed not to tell anyone? Jesus' healings *did* prove His deity, but His motivation was compassion (see v. 41). His compassion has not waned!

The reason Jesus told this man not to tell anybody about his healing was that He didn't want the extra advertisement. Because this man didn't do what the Lord said, Jesus could no longer enter a city publicly but had to remain in the unpopulated areas. Yet still people were coming to Him from everywhere. A few days later Jesus quietly entered Capernaum again, and as soon as He was discovered a crowd gathered. Before long the house was packed, and even the doors and windows were blocked with listeners. That's when the four men arrived with their paralyzed friend on a stretcher.

Notice that before Jesus healed the man the Bible says He *saw their faith.* How can you see faith? By a person's actions. I can tell when you have faith that a chair will support you when I see you sit down on it. Notice also that Jesus saw *their* faith. It's obvious that all five of them had faith, because they went to such great lengths to get to Jesus. They climbed up on the roof, dug a hole through it and lowered their friend with ropes. (Incidentally, the roof was flat.)

Some say only the four walking men had faith, but I say no. How many paralyzed people would let you carry them up on a roof, cut a hole through that roof and then lower them down through the hole? In addition, when Jesus told this man to rise and walk, he did it. The average doubting believer would have said, "Now, Jesus, I'd love to get up and walk—that's what I came here for. But You'll have to heal me first before I can do that!" *Faith is acting upon God's Word.*

Once a country church in the Midwest was having a special prayer meeting for rain because the congregation was comprised mostly of farmers and it hadn't rained in several weeks. One little boy had so much faith he brought an umbrella to church with him, even after his parents tried to discourage him. It rained, but it was because that little boy *believed. Faith prepares to see the promise come to pass.* Faith doesn't take no for an answer and never gives up.

PSALM 35:17-28

David said in today's reading that the Lord "delights in the prosperity of His servant" (v. 27). If God delights in the prosperity of His servants, how much more He delights in the prosperity of His own *children.*

PROVERBS 9:13-18

The first nine chapters of Proverbs can almost be considered an introduction to the whole book. Beginning tomorrow with chapter 10, it really starts getting good, with hundreds of proverbs and wise sayings. By the time we get through them all you won't believe how much wiser you've grown!

FEBRUARY 17

LEVITICUS 4:1-5:19

Today we read of the "nonsweet savor offerings," the sin and guilt offerings. These are offerings an Israelite would make to the Lord when he was out of fellowship with Him and wanted it to be restored. It's difficult to understand the difference between the two, but it seems the sin offering was for unintentional sins and a person's sinful nature, whereas the trespass offering was for specific sins.

All these offerings had a standard ritual. The offering was brought to the tabernacle, where the offerer laid his hands on its head. This signified a transfer of his guilt to the animal. The animal was slain, and its blood was then sprinkled against the altar (except in the case of the sin offering, where the blood was sprinkled on the altar of incense). Part of the sacrifice was burned on the altar and part was eaten by the priests, except in the case of the burnt offering, which was completely burned, and the peace offering, of which part was shared by priests *and* worshippers. In the case of the sin offering, part of the animal was burned "outside the camp where the ashes are poured out" (4:12).

We know without any doubt that this pointed to Christ's dying *outside* the walls of Jerusalem. Hebrews 13:11-12 says, "For the bodies of those animals whose blood is brought into the holy place by the high priest as an offering for sin, are burned outside the camp. Therefore Jesus also, that He might sanctify the people through His own blood, suffered outside the gate."

Although we may not understand all the symbolism involved with these sacrifices, the main meaning is crystal clear: sinful people cannot approach God unless their sin is dealt with. The only way it can be dealt with, other than by the death of the people themselves, is by the death of an innocent substitute. All these sacrifices pointed to Jesus. Aren't you glad you're living under the new covenant? When we sin, all that's required of us is to repent and ask forgiveness, because the ultimate sacrifice, God's Lamb, has already been slain (see 1 John 1:9).

MARK 2:13-3:6

Today's reading deals primarily with the true interpretation of the law. When the law said Israelites were to be separate from the Gentiles (see Lev. 20:22-26), the scribes and Pharisees used it to justify their exclusiveness and holier-than-thou attitude. But Jesus *ate* with tax-gatherers and sinners. God meant that we shouldn't *participate* in the sins of sinful people, not that we shouldn't try to help them out of their sin. Jesus put it beautifully when He said, "It is not those who are healthy who need a physician, but those who are sick" (2:17). When Jesus spent time with sinners, He was trying to help sick people.

When the law forbade working on the Sabbath, the Pharisees added their own definitions about what work was and took offense that Jesus and the disciples were "working" on the Sabbath by picking some heads of grain. However, that wasn't God's intention. He made the Sabbath because of His *love for man.* The Pharisees had turned it into a day to dread.

PSALM 36:1-12

We all know God loves us, but most of us could use more revelation concerning *how much* He loves us. Paul prayed for the Ephesian Christians that they would know the "love of Christ which surpasses knowledge" (Eph. 3:19). David said that the Lord's lovingkindness extends to the heavens, and His faithfulness reaches to the skies.

PROVERBS 10:1-2

We will learn that the Proverbs predict the future in many cases. For example, today we read that "ill-gotten gains do not profit." We all know that they may profit for a while, but ultimately they fail. *Anything* done in an underhanded manner ultimately backfires.

FEBRUARY 18

LEVITICUS 6:1-7:27

When I read of all the priests' duties regarding the various offerings, and when I read about the portions of the sacrifices that were allotted to the priests, I'm reminded that the only reason for the priests' existence was that the people were sinful. If the people were perfect, there would have been no need for priests. It helps those of us who are ministers to realize that if the people in our churches were perfect, we would be out of a job! (On the other hand, according to the apostle Paul, this passage also teaches us that ministers should make their living from their ministry. See 1 Cor. 9:14.)

Mature lay persons who have leadership positions in the church should realize that as well. They will have to put up with imperfect people. Some will be grumblers. Some will be unfaithful. Some will be just plain flaky. But God loves those people so much He gave them pastors and mature lay leaders to help them grow! You know, God is actually putting up with all of us!

Much of what we read today has little application to New Testament believers. However, all of these instructions are related symbolically to what Jesus has done for us. For example, in 6:25 God said the sin offering was *holy* to the Lord. In 6:29 God said it was *most holy*. Anything it touched became holy. Jesus was our sin offering. Even though Jesus "became sin" (2 Cor. 5:21) on the cross, *He was not a sinner and did not become sinful on the cross*. He was personally holy before the cross, during it and after it. But He did take on Himself the guilt of all our sin.

Also notice that the fire on the altar of sacrifice was to be kept burning always. The people of Israel had that continual reminder that their sins could always be atoned for. God's fire of forgiveness never goes out. You can't sin so much that the fire would ever be smothered!

You may have some questions about "clean" and "unclean" things and people at this point, but we'll discuss them later in our study of Leviticus. For now I'll just say that Moses was speaking of things and people as being *ceremonially* clean and unclean.

MARK 3:7-30

When we read that Jesus withdrew to the sea (see v. 7), it means the Sea of Galilee. I think of it as a lake, because it's only seven miles wide and fourteen miles long.

People were coming from long distances to see Jesus. Look in the back of your Bible at one of the maps that details where Jesus traveled. Try to locate the cities of Tyre, Sidon and Jerusalem; the regions of Judea, Galilee and Idumea; and the Sea of Galilee and Jordan River—all spoken of in verses 7-8. Then you'll have an idea of how far people were traveling to see the Lord. According to my calculations, some came from points as far as 120 miles away. That may not sound like very far these days, but this was eighteen hundred years before the automobile or airplane. People walked or at best rode a donkey.

We see here that Jesus healed the multitudes, and He also cast out demons. This type of exorcism was so powerful and so much a part of the ministry of Jesus that the scribes who had come down from Jerusalem charged that He was casting out demons by Beelzebul, the ruler of the demons. The scribes themselves acknowledged Jesus' irresistible power and authority over every demonic force and over every sickness.

Paul wrote to the Philippians that Jesus had been exalted to the right hand of the Father and that at the name of Jesus "every knee should bow, of those who are in heaven, and on earth, and under the earth, and that every tongue should confess that Jesus Christ is Lord..." (Phil. 2:10). We see in verse 11 that the demons, when confronted with the power and authority, cried out, "You are the Son of God!" What a sight it will be at the last judgment when every creature that has ever lived will acknowledge that Jesus Christ is Lord!

For a discussion on blaspheming the Holy Spirit, see my comments on Matthew 12:25-32 (unless you can still remember what I said!).

PSALM 37:1-11

In my opinion this is one of David's masterpieces. We have already read quite a few psalms where David complained of evil people who had slandered him and were trying to destroy him. This psalm was written not in the midst of one of those trials, but looking back at the outcome of those trials. If you ever find yourself being taken advantage of by evil people, this is the psalm you want to memorize.

Some Christians quote the portion of this psalm that says, "He will give you the desires of your heart." It's fine to quote the promise, but don't forget about the conditions. If you don't meet them, this promise doesn't apply to you. We are required first to trust in the Lord and do good. Then we must cultivate faithfulness and delight ourselves in the Lord. Finally we must commit our way to the Lord, and *only then* can we expect that He will give us the desires of our hearts. If you do all that and *the* "desire of your heart" is to have a $10,000 diamond necklace or a Rolls Royce, you've missed it somewhere.

The point of this psalm is to encourage us to not get upset about evil people who prosper. Their day is coming. They will have to answer to God.

PROVERBS 10:3-4

Here is a promise that God will always see to it that we are fed. We learn that hard work is a condition to prosperity. God doesn't bless laziness.

FEBRUARY 19

LEVITICUS 7:28-9:6

I know you're probably not thrilled with Leviticus so far. But hang tough. Don't forget you're reading the actual words of God. And we will find some applications to our lives in this book.

We don't know exactly what the "Urim and Thummim" were (8:8), other than that they were used to determine God's will in certain decisions (see Num. 27:21; 1 Sam. 28:6). Whatever they were, they fell into disuse after the rise of the Old Testament prophets. They were kept in Aaron's fancy breastpiece.

Under the new covenant we have the Holy Spirit within our spirits to guide us. Most of the time He doesn't lead us by an audible voice but by "impressions" in our hearts. How do I know I'm called to the ministry? Not because I heard the audible voice of God calling me, but because of an inward conviction. How do I know I'm supposed to go to the mission field? Because of an inward conviction. How do you know you're supposed to teach Sunday school or bake a pie for one of your neighbors? You will feel good about it in your spirit. You'll have a "leading" and a desire to do it.

Why did Moses put some blood from the sacrifice of the ram of ordination on Aaron and his sons' right ear lobes, right thumbs and right big toes? Because God told him to! Why did God tell him to? Nobody knows, but some guess that it signified that the priests' ears were to be consecrated to hear God's word, their hands were to be consecrated to do God's will and their feet were to be consecrated to follow God's ways.

This long ordination and anointing ceremony for Moses, Aaron, Aaron's sons and the people of Israel might seem boring to you and me, but wait until you read the grand finale tomorrow! The impression I'm left with after today's reading is that God is holy and meticulous, and we should solemnly obey whatever He says to do. And as much as I personally dislike ceremony, I must admit that maybe God isn't as informal as some of us like to think!

MARK 3:31-4:25

Isn't it wonderful to know that you are a brother or sister of the Lord Jesus Christ? For the most part the Bible states only that God has sons. This is probably because back in Jesus' day only sons had privileges as far as the family was concerned. But the Bible clearly says that in Christ there is neither male nor female (see Gal. 3:28), so women have the same rank before God as men.

We have already read the parable of the sower and the soils in Matthew's Gospel, but let me point out a few things I didn't mention earlier. First, just because we get the Word of God in our hearts does not mean that Satan can't steal it. In verse 15 the Greek actually says, "Satan comes and takes away the word which has been sown *in their hearts*." Sometimes we tell people that they just need to get God's Word in them, but that's not completely true. They need to get God's Word in them and then *keep it there until it grows roots, sprouts and eventually produces fruit.*

Also, this parable makes very clear what we should beware of in our spiritual lives, because our spiritual growth is completely dependent on the Word of God in our hearts. First, we should watch out for Satan, who will try to steal the Word. How does he do it? By bringing circumstances into our lives that look contradictory to what Scripture says; by bringing negative statements from "friends" and relatives that can lead us to doubt what God has said; by tempting us not to have a daily time in the Bible.

Second, we should beware of "the worries of the world." Have you noticed how you tend to feel after you watch the litany of sin and disaster on the evening news? If we keep meditating on that stuff we'll find the Word of God being choked in our lives.

Third, we should beware of "the deceitfulness of riches." When we dream of owning some new possession and then finally buy it, we usually discover that dreaming was more fun than actually owning it. That's how riches deceive us. They promise happiness but don't deliver. And if we get all caught up in chasing after more "things," the Word of God will be choked, and we won't produce any fruit. *God's Word has to take first place in our lives.*

PSALM 37:12-29

Don't you love this psalm? Look again at verse 13, speaking of how God views the wicked person who plots against the righteous: "The Lord laughs at him; for He sees his day is coming." Did you realize the Lord laughs? Even if it looks as though the wicked are doing better than the righteous, that's only temporary. God doesn't play just one inning; He plays until He wins, and His victories are eternal!

I love verse 24 too, speaking of the righteous man: "When he falls, he shall not be hurled headlong; because the Lord is the One who holds his hand." Sometimes righteous people make mistakes and fall, but the Lord will pick them up if they let Him.

PROVERBS 10:5

Some Christians, including myself at one time, think it's wrong to have a savings account. But according to this proverb it's wise to save up some extra during good times so you're prepared for not-so-good times whenever they come. (Most people experience at least a few of those times in their lives.)

FEBRUARY 20

LEVITICUS 9:7-10:20

Didn't I tell you this long ceremony had a grand finale that was spectacular? When Moses and Aaron came out of the tent of meeting to bless the people, the glory of the Lord appeared, and fire came "out from before the Lord" and consumed the offering on the altar! I wonder where that fire actually came from? It may have jumped out of that glory that appeared; it may have come shooting out of the holy of holies; or else it just fell from heaven. Whatever the case, when it happened, the people shouted and fell on their faces.

Unfortunately, tragedy followed shortly thereafter. Two of Aaron's sons offered "strange fire" before the Lord and were consumed by fire that came from the presence of the Lord. God made a pretty clear statement of what He thinks of men coming to Him on their own terms, didn't He? People try that all the time with the Lord, but they aren't consumed instantly because God shows them mercy in their ignorance. But Nadab and Abihu were without excuse. They had the full revelation of God and how He must be approached, yet they didn't treat Him as holy. Are you getting a better picture of the holiness of God? Aren't you glad you're saved from His wrath by the blood of Christ (see 1 Thess. 5:9)?

Poor Aaron and his remaining sons weren't even permitted to go outside the tabernacle court, because according to God's original commandment the priests were not permitted to leave the area for seven days during their ordination. Plus, if they touched a dead body, they would become ceremonially unclean. So their distant relatives had to bury Nadab and Abihu. Moses told the three remaining priests never to drink strong drink or wine when they came to minister, so one possible inference is that Nadab and Abihu had been drinking before this incident.

MARK 4:26-5:20

The parable of the seed that we read today wasn't recorded in Matthew. It seems to teach us that God already had planned how His kingdom would increase. It started by Jesus' planting seeds of God's Word, and those seeds would continually reproduce until eventually the harvest would arrive. That harvest has yet to come, but it will at the end of the age.

The parable of the mustard seed is similar. The kingdom of God started small but has now grown to include millions. The birds nesting in its branches represent some corruption in the church, or quite possibly they don't represent anything.

When Jesus decided to cross the Sea of Galilee in the evening, He said, "Let us go over to the other side" (4:35). Notice He didn't say, "Let's go halfway and sink." Jesus said they were going to the other side, so the disciples should have had faith that they would make it, no matter what befell them. Isn't this a good picture of life? We are traveling to "the other side," but Satan tries to defeat us along the way. When he does, we should rebuke him by faith and continue our journey. If Jesus says something, *it's true!* No matter how much our circumstances tempt us to doubt, we should speak in faith.

Do you sometimes feel as if your boat is sinking and you're facing insurmountable odds? Rise up in faith and speak what God has said to the circumstance! Keep rowing! Your calm is straight ahead.

Once the madman of the Gerasenes was delivered, he wanted so much to accompany Jesus on His journeys. But Jesus said no. Jesus commanded some people to follow Him, and now here was a man whom Jesus forbade to follow Him. My point is that we all have to do what God tells *us* to do individually. And we shouldn't judge others if God has given them a different calling. I think ministers are more guilty of this than anyone. I hear pastors always talking about how "the local church" is what God is saying to the body of Christ today. I hear evangelists say pastors aren't involved enough in soul-winning. I hear missionaries say everyone who stays in the United States is missing God's direction. God is saying different things to different people. He may tell you to attend a big church, and He might tell someone else to attend a small one. All Christians wonder, *Why doesn't everybody in this city attend my church?* They all think their church is the best! We need to keep our noses out of other people's business and walk in love.

PSALM 37:30-40

God is our strength in time of trouble (v. 39), but that's only true for Christians who believe it. The Bible says we should "be strong in the Lord, and in the strength of *His* might" (Eph. 6:10, italics mine). Too many times we try to go it alone, when all along the Lord is waiting to carry our burden and give us strength. If you haven't experienced that yet, you're missing out on a great blessing. This is not some kind of psychology; this is fact. God wants to be our strength in times of trouble.

PROVERBS 10:6-7

FEBRUARY 21

LEVITICUS 11:1-12:8

Today we read some interesting instructions concerning what the people of Israel were and were not permitted to eat. The big question most of us have is why? Did God give these rules for a reason? Some suggest that God made all these rules so the people would have a better chance of breaking them and therefore would have a better chance of realizing they were sinners who needed a Savior. However, as I read how Israel failed to keep just the Ten Commandments, I don't think they needed any more rules to make their sin plain. I believe God's rules are always motivated by love for people. In other words, it was *best* for Israel that they obey these dietary laws, and today we have at least some understanding of why.

God spoke these dietary commands long before there was any such thing as refrigeration, and food would spoil quickly in the warm climate of the Middle East. Beyond that, we know that some animals were more likely than others to be carriers of disease. For example, Israel was forbidden to eat pork. (That means no ham or bacon for breakfast!) We know that pork is especially susceptible to carrying disease and that if it's inadequately cooked it can harbor trichinosis. There's an old British saying that pork should be eaten only in the months that have an "r" in them—that is, the cold months. Pigs are hosts to numerous parasites. *Vermin and birds of prey* (see 11:13-19) are also more likely to be disease-carriers. Even today, *shellfish* (see 11:12) often cause food poisoning and intestinal inflammation. Incidentally, under the new covenant Jesus declared all foods clean (see Mark 7:19). The New Testament teaches that "everything created by God is good, and nothing is to be rejected, if it is received with gratitude; for it is sanctified by means of the word of God and prayer" (1 Tim. 4:4-5). This is another reason we have a "better covenant" (Heb. 8:6).

God declared any person who touched the carcass of a dead animal to be unclean, and He required that person to wash his clothes. We will read in the book of Numbers that if a person touched a dead human body he was required to *bathe himself* and wash his clothes.

Do you realize that only in the last two hundred years has humanity had any knowledge of infectious diseases and how they spread? Nobody knew anything about germs until the nineteenth century. In 1846 an obstetrician noted that during one year in his Vienna hospital 451 new mothers died from blood poisoning in one ward, whereas in another ward only ninety died. What was the difference between the two wards? In the one where the 451 mothers died, *doctors* had delivered the babies. In the other ward, where ninety mothers had died, midwives had delivered the babies. This fine doctor, Ignaz Semmelweiss, suggested a logical reason for the discrepancy in results. The doctors were teaching anatomy in the morgue each morning, dissecting dead bodies, and then *delivering babies in the afternoons*. They wouldn't even wash their hands in between, because nobody had ever heard of infectious disease! Doctor Semmelweiss was ridiculed by his peers for suggesting they were "carrying something invisible" from the morgue to the delivery rooms. He eventually died in an insane asylum! But the people of Israel were protected from infectious disease thirty-four hundred years earlier! Now tell me the Bible isn't inspired by God!

As for chapter 12, I don't understand why a woman would be considered unclean after delivering a baby. Most commentators say that she was only ceremonially unclean. However, in the back of my mind I have to wonder if there wasn't some good medical reason. It took mankind thirty-four hundred years to learn the principles of infectious disease, so perhaps there's something we don't yet know about childbirth.

MARK 5:21-43

I'm glad this poor woman with the hemorrhage hadn't heard some of the negative sermons preached against "positive confession." Notice in verse 28 that as she was working her way to Jesus she was *saying*, "If I just touch His garments, I shall get well." When we believe something in our hearts, it will come out our mouths. As Jesus said, out of the abundance of the heart the mouth speaks (see Matt. 12:34-35). That's why we must fill our hearts with God's Word; positive confessions will be the natural result. It's easy to tell who believes God's

Word and who doesn't—just listen to what they say.

Notice that Jesus *felt* healing power flow forth from His body. It was transferable through cloth, as I have discussed previously.

Also notice that it was in response to Jairus's *faith* that Jesus brought his daughter back to life. Jesus said to him, "Do not be afraid any longer, only believe." If we're afraid, we're not believing. Fear and faith are opposites. However, it is possible to have faith in your heart but have doubts and fears come into your mind. In fact, it's normal for that to happen. Any time I try to trust God according to His promises, doubts always assail my mind. But as I keep on believing in my heart, the promise comes to pass. *Faith is of the heart* (see Rom. 10:10).

Christians need to learn the difference between the heart and head, or I could say between the spirit and the mind. When we have faith in our *hearts*, Satan will bring doubts to our *minds*. But we're OK as long as we don't allow those doubts to drop down into our hearts Faith is an interesting thing. It's a fight against the devil and doubts. However, it's also a rest on God's promise. How blessed is the person who trusts the Lord!

PSALM 38:1-22

This psalm was written by David when he was experiencing the discipline of the Lord. Now don't be as foolish as some Christians. God only disciplines *disobedient* people. (Some Christians will say they don't know why God is disciplining them, but that's absurd.) It is obvious that David was experiencing sickness (v. 3). When illness attacks, Christians should do a quick check on their lives. Are they harboring unforgiveness? How have they been treating their loved ones? Have they ripped off someone? If they know of some disobedience, they should repent and ask forgiveness, then pray for healing and receive it by faith in God's Word. If they don't know of any disobedience, they should realize their sickness is an attack of the devil and trust God for healing.

We can tell that David was really suffering during the time he penned this psalm. But we also know that God's "anger is but for a moment, [but] His favor is for a lifetime" (Ps. 30:5). God disciplines us for the same reason any good parent disciplines his children: because He wants us to turn out right.

PROVERBS 10:8-9

No one ever "gets away with it." Sooner or later sin is discovered. God sees to it, because He is the great judge of the universe.

FEBRUARY 22

LEVITICUS 13:1-59

What we read today makes more sense when we understand (as stated yesterday) that humanity had no knowledge of infectious disease until the nineteenth century. But thirty-four hundred years earlier God gave Israel instructions in how to prevent the spread of infectious disease by quarantine. Today we read of various skin diseases, one of which is leprosy, although it probably was somewhat different from the modern disease of the same name. If a person was pronounced unclean after inspection by the priest, he had to live "outside the camp." And whenever he came near others he was required to cry out, "Unclean! Unclean!" so they wouldn't come in contact with him.

This gives us a balanced view of God and His healing power. As Christians we don't deny the existence of sickness as some cults do. Also, we don't disregard the natural laws of health and sanitation. For example, if I know that one of my daughter's friends has the flu, I don't allow her to go play with that friend. I know some Christians who would send their children and just "believe God." To me that borders on testing God. He has given us brains and expects us to use them.

Unfortunately, we aren't given more information about why a person might develop one of these conditions described today. Did he open the door through disobedience? Very possibly. God had promised about a year prior to this that He would take sickness from their midst if they would be diligent to obey (see Ex. 23:25). We'll read tomorrow that the leprosy spoken of was something a person could be healed of, and then that person could be restored to a normal life.

MARK 6:1-29

Jesus' listeners in His hometown of Nazareth had obviously heard the reports of His miracles throughout Galilee. They also experienced firsthand His tremendous anointing to teach. But they were astonished because they remembered Him from just a few years before when He seemed no more than a carpenter's son. They couldn't believe He was the Son of God. (In Luke's Gospel we discover that Jesus tried to convince the people of Nazareth of that fact during His sermon there.) Their unbelief hindered Jesus from doing any major miracles in Nazareth. However, He did heal a few people with minor ailments.

If people's unbelief hindered *Jesus* from getting people healed, people's unbelief is also going to hinder you and me from getting people healed. You can't get a person saved who won't believe in Jesus, can you? Neither can you get a person healed who won't believe that Jesus will heal him.

Notice that verse 5 says Jesus *could* do no miracle there. It doesn't say He *wouldn't*. Unbelief is what hindered Him. What's the cure for unbelief? Hearing the Word of God. So Jesus then "was going around the villages teaching" (v. 6).

Jesus sent out the twelve to preach repentance, to heal by anointing the sick with oil and to cast out demons. He forewarned them that in some towns they would not be received, but He sent them anyway.

I used to wonder why John the Baptist would tell *pagan* Herod that it was unlawful for him to be married to his brother's wife. Now I know. Herod was Jewish, and therefore He was supposed to be under the Law. So it *was* unlawful for him. Herodias had divorced Herod's half-brother Philip in order to marry him. (Believe it or not, Philip and Herod were *uncles* of Herodias.) Of course, as already stated, there's no difference between adultery and divorcing your spouse because you've found someone you like better. Incidentally, Herod and Herodias were eventually deposed and banished to Gaul.

PSALM 39:1-13

Here is another psalm written by David when under God's discipline. It's obvious that his suffering had moved him to contemplate his transient life and to think about those things that are of real value (see vv. 4-6,11). Suffering has a way of making you think and making you repent!

PROVERBS 10:10

FEBRUARY 23

LEVITICUS 14:1-57

The law of leprosy'' we've been reading about for the past three days raises many questions. It's obvious the general term here translated ''leprosy'' is not the leprosy of which we speak in our day because even a garment or house could become leprous. The term must have referred to a kind of mildew or rot in such cases unless this was some kind of phenomenon that no longer exists.

The law for cleansing a leper indicates that the condition was brought on by sin, as the cleansed person had to present a sin offering, guilt offering, burnt offering and grain offering in order to be restored. The main point is that *healing from sickness was wrought by atonement.* An animal had to die.

MARK 6:30-56

When the apostles returned from their first preaching assignment, they and Jesus were so mobbed by the people they didn't even have time to eat. Jesus realized they needed to rest for a while. (Most preachers can appreciate that.) So they hopped in a small boat and headed across the Sea of Galilee. They didn't get much time to rest, though, as the crowds saw them leave and ran ahead to meet them on the other side.

I marvel at Jesus at this point. If I had been Him, I would have screamed, gotten back in the boat and spent the next few days out in the middle of the lake! But the Scripture says when Jesus saw the multitudes (from whom He had been trying to get away), *He felt compassion for them* because they were like sheep without a shepherd. So He fed them spiritually with His teaching, and then He fed them physically by multiplying fish and loaves. Meeting spiritual needs is always more important than taking care of physical needs, but physical needs are still important.

After supper, Jesus put His disciples back in the boat to take a short trip across the Sea of Galilee. Then He sent the multitude away. The Bible says Jesus bid them farewell. We always picture Jesus preaching a sermon or working some miracle, but can you picture Him standing along the shore of Galilee, waving good-bye to the people as they left His outdoor restaurant?

The disciples didn't make very good progress in their short journey across the Sea of Galilee. They departed in the evening, and by about four o' clock in the morning they were still rowing against contrary winds. From the high hills that surround the lake, you can see practically the whole surface, and Jesus saw the disciples straining at the oars. This is the part we don't want to miss. The Bible says Jesus came to them, walking on the water, and ''*He intended to pass by them*'' (italics mine). This short statement reveals the ''gentlemanly'' quality of the Lord. He doesn't get involved in our affairs unless we ask Him.

This story is also a perfect picture of the majority of Christians. We live our lives ''straining at the oars,'' and Jesus just walks on by because we've made up our minds that *we* can make it on our own. But observe what happened when Jesus stepped into the boat. Immediately the winds stopped. Are you tired of straining at the oars? Do you want the winds to stop blowing? Invite Jesus into your boat!

PSALM 40:1-10

According to Hebrews 10:4-10, at least part of today's psalm is prophetic. It was Jesus speaking in verses 6-8. The writer of Hebrews comments that this section of Scripture indicates it was impossible for the blood of bulls and goats to take away sin, and that those sacrifices only pointed to Christ. It would be worth your while to read those few verses in Hebrews.

PROVERBS 10:11-12

If we truly love people, we won't want to expose their faults but will rather hide them. Are you a gossiper or a lover?

FEBRUARY 24

LEVITICUS 15:1-16:28

The "discharge" spoken of in the first fifteen verses of chapter 15 could be referring to numerous kinds of discharges, such as pus from infected tissue. Again we assume the law was given for sterilization to prevent the spreading of infection. These instructions could have saved multitudes of lives during the spread of the bubonic plague, which killed millions in every great civilization from 430 B.C. until the beginning of our century. The disease causes swelling in the lymph glands, which then drain infectious pus. In the 1300s more than one-fourth of Europe's population was wiped out by bubonic plague. Between 1894 and 1914 as many as ten million died from it in India alone!

If people had followed the instructions of these fifteen verses, millions would never have died. But they had no knowledge of how infectious disease spread, and when a person in a hospital died of bubonic plague, they would take the corpse off the bed and, without even changing the sheets, lay down the next person! Those who cared for the sick didn't even know to wash their hands and so helped to spread the dreaded disease. But thousands of years earlier God had said, "Every bed on which the person with the discharge lies becomes unclean. Anyone, moreover, who touches his bed shall wash his clothes and bathe in water and be unclean until evening" (vv. 4-5).

The next few verses, which deal with a man having a seminal emission, certainly are not trying to teach that sex is sinful. Again it seems that strict regard to cleanliness in all sexual matters was a safeguard to health. No offering was required in this case, probably because this is a natural function of the body. A man just became ceremonially unclean until sunset. The same would be true for a woman during menstruation.

Chapter 16 deals with instructions for the annual Day of Atonement, which is also known as Yom Kippur. It occurs in October and was the only day that the high priest could enter into the holy of holies to sprinkle blood on the mercy seat. When this ceremony was completed, Israel was reconciled to God for another year. Aaron first had to make sacrifice for his own sins before he could offer sacrifice for the people's sins. Jesus, the high priest of the new covenant, did not need to offer sacrifice for His sins because He was sinless. He entered the heavenly holy of holies not year after year but once, and not with the blood of bulls or goats but with His own blood, to obtain an eternal redemption for us.

Of the two goats used in this ceremony, one was sacrificed and one was not. The one not sacrificed was the scapegoat. Aaron would lay his hands on it and confess the sins of the congregation. Then that goat would be led off to be released in the wilderness. *The people of Israel thus had a visible sign that their sins were being taken away and forgotten.*

MARK 7:1-23

After reading all those tedious rules regarding the washing of unclean things, it's surprising that the scribes and Pharisees would want to add any more regulations concerning washing pots and pitchers and cups and eating with impure hands. But they did! They had all kinds of traditions they followed at the neglect of the true commandments. Jesus called their traditions "the precepts of men." (What do you think Jesus would say about some churches that are steeped in tradition today?) The Pharisees considered themselves to be holy because they were outwardly clean. Jesus said, however, that holiness is determined by what's on the inside of a person. There are plenty of folks who are clean on the outside but dirty on the inside. They need to be born again.

Did you catch verse 19, which says that Jesus declared all foods clean? Don't listen to any preacher or Christian who says that we should be following the dietary laws of Leviticus today. That's hogwash. However, it's not a bad idea to wash your hands before you eat, take a bath once in a while and avoid touching dead animals!

PSALM 40:11-17

David finished his prayer with the request, "Do not delay, O my God!" Sometimes the Lord doesn't work as fast as we would like. I'm sure you've felt that way. But we all need to learn to trust God. If there were no waiting period, no faith would be required, right? According to the book of Hebrews, it is through *faith and patience* that we inherit the promises (see Heb. 6:12).

PROVERBS 10:13-14

FEBRUARY 25

LEVITICUS 16:29-18:30

Every sacrifice brought to the tabernacle was representative of Christ, who shed His blood for the remission of our sins. In our reading today we learn that God not only required the blood of sacrificial animals to be poured out but also the blood of all animals that were killed. The Israelites were forbidden to eat meat "with the blood," because "the life of the flesh is in the blood" (17:11), and God said that He had given it to them on the altar to make atonement for their souls. In other words, it was the blood that God accepted as a ransom to pay the price for their sins. Blood is representative of life, and when the blood had been poured out it was proof that death had taken place. So under the old covenant the blood of *all* animals was considered sacred because it represented God's system of atonement.

Chapter 18 reveals the moral condition of the Egyptians, from whom the Israelites had just departed, and the Canaanites, whom the Israelites were about to expel from the promised land. Both Egyptians and Canaanites had degenerated to the place where incest, adultery, homosexuality, bestiality and child-sacrifice were common practices. It's important that you keep those facts in mind as you read about Israel's conquest of Canaan. If you don't, you might be tempted to think God was unfair in His treatment of the Canaanites. God used Israel as a tool of His judgment upon this wicked group of people to whom He had shown mercy for hundreds of years. Eventually, believe it or not, *Israel would become worse than the wicked people they dispossessed.*

MARK 7:24-8:10

For an explanation of the story of the Syrophoenician woman, see my comments on Matthew 15:21-28.

The deaf and partially dumb man whom Jesus healed is a beautiful example of one of the varied healing methods used by Jesus. In this case He placed His fingers in the man's ears, touched the man's tongue with His saliva, looked up toward heaven and with a deep sigh said, "Be opened!" (7:34). Immediately the man was healed. Can you imagine the expression on the man's face right then?

This was the only time Jesus ministered in that manner. He did use His saliva to perform healing in two other cases, but in two different ways. Tomorrow we'll read where He spit *directly* into a blind man's eyes. And in John's Gospel we'll read of how Jesus made clay from His saliva, rubbed it in a blind man's eyes and then told him to go wash it off. People get upset when some ministers lay hands on people for their healing. What would they think if those ministers starting spitting on blind people? Jesus doesn't fit into anyone's little box.

Again may I point out that after Jesus healed this man He told him not to tell anyone what had happened. *Jesus healed people because He loved them.* If Jesus still loves people, which He does, He's still healing them.

To add fuel to my fire, notice why Jesus fed the four thousand. He said, "I feel compassion for the multitude because they have remained with Me now three days, and have nothing to eat" (8:2). He didn't say, "I feel like this would be a good time to prove My deity, so I think I'll multiply some food." *Jesus' primary motivation was His compassion for people in need.* And Jesus is just as compassionate today, because the Bible says He "is the same yesterday and today, yes and forever" (Heb. 13:8).

PSALM 41:1-13

The wonderful promise in the first few verses of this psalm is that a person who considers the poor will be helped by the Lord in time of trouble. This is one of the major themes found in the Bible: we reap what we sow. If we show others mercy, we will be shown mercy. David even observed that those who consider the poor are restored to health by God (see v. 3).

The Bible speaks of giving tithes *and offerings*. The Israelites gave more than just tithes. In fact, every third year they were required to give a second tithe, of which a portion would go to the needy. Many of us need to take God's concern for the poor more seriously. Of course, God doesn't want us supporting lazy people, but He does want us to help those who are *truly poor*. In those cases we need to be led by the Holy Spirit.

PROVERBS 10:15-16

Many of the proverbs are simply true, unfortunate observations of how things really are. It's true that rich people's money is their fortress—that is, their money affords them some protection. But money doesn't protect anyone from God's wrath, from calamity or from sickness. Their "fortress" is in their imagination (see Prov. 18:11). And, unfortunately, poverty ruins many people. It drives some deep into sin. But it doesn't have to. It *can* drive people to God if they'll let it, as it did in the case of the prodigal son (Luke 15:11-32).

FEBRUARY 26

LEVITICUS 19:1-20:21

I always enjoy reading these "sundry laws," as they reveal God's character to us in a different way. For example, wasn't that an interesting law about not reaping the harvest in the corners of their fields so the poor could have part of the harvest? God is so wise, because in this case *the poor would have to work if they wanted to eat*. There's nothing more counterproductive for society, or more demeaning to the less fortunate, than giving them free handouts month after month.

The commandment to love others as ourselves wasn't just a new covenant law, as some suppose. We read it today. Israelites were not permitted to hate their countrymen, bear a grudge or take their own vengeance. They could rebuke their neighbor, but only from a loving motivation. How many of us need repair in those areas? To hold a grudge against a fellow Christian is a serious offense. If you find yourself continually thinking angry thoughts toward certain other believers, you need to examine your heart. You may have to deal with unforgiveness. Of course, everyone has been mistreated at some time or other, and no doubt the devil will bring those things to our minds from time to time. That's not unforgiveness. It's only unforgiveness when we *dwell* on those thoughts or *act* upon them.

In 19:23-25 God commanded that when the Israelites came into Canaan's land and planted fruit trees, they were not permitted to pick the fruit until the fourth year. This practice greatly increased chances for heavy crops in the years thereafter.

Why did the Lord command the men never to round off the side growth of their beards? Probably it was a practice of the Canaanites and played some part in their pagan religion. The Canaanites also practiced making cuts in their bodies for the dead. (In Hawaii the native people used to pluck out one of their eyes and knock out their teeth as an expression of mourning for a lost family member.) And the people were actually throwing live babies into fires as an act of worship to the false god Molech. We cringe at the thought, but in our society millions of babies have been ripped to pieces by suction tubes while still alive in the womb. It's probably happening just a few miles from your home every day. Those babies are being offered up to a god called "selfishness." So our perverted society is not much better than the one in Canaan.

God commanded that the young should revere the elderly because He knew the tendency of sinful man is just the opposite. All children should "reverence" their parents, according to 19:3.

MARK 8:11-38

While crossing the Sea of Galilee, Jesus warned His disciples to beware of the leaven of Herod and the Pharisees. He was speaking figuratively of the teaching, hypocrisy and life-styles of those people. We'll read many examples in John's Gospel where Jesus spoke figuratively and His listeners tried to interpret what He said literally. Here is one example. The disciples thought Jesus was referring to the fact that they had forgotten to take enough bread on their trip across the lake. They had only one small loaf. (Doesn't it make you feel better that the disciples, even being *with* Jesus, could forget to take care of certain details?) They had forgotten that

Jesus had already multiplied bread twice before. Many times we also forget how God has provided before and doubt if He will provide for us now. God hasn't changed since the last time He came through for you!

Some have used this incident of Jesus' healing the blind man as an argument against those of us who believe that when praying in faith, a person need only pray *once*. However, nothing is said here of Jesus *praying twice*. He simply *laid His hands on the man twice*.

Jesus again made a call of discipleship to the multitudes. To be His followers they had to deny themselves and "take up a cross." However, Jesus promises true fulfillment to those who are willing to pay the price, but only emptiness to those who aren't. *Have you experienced the fulfillment of paying the price to be a true disciple of Jesus?* Or do you hide your Christianity because you're ashamed of Jesus and what He has said? If you do, Jesus will be ashamed of you when He comes (v. 38).

PSALM 42:1-11

Did you notice that several times in this psalm David encouraged himself? He said in verse 5 and in verse 11: "Why are you in despair, O my soul?... Hope in God, for I shall yet praise Him." Sometimes we need to speak to our souls (minds and emotions) and tell them to get in line with God's Word. Our minds may tell us to quit, or that God has forsaken us, but in our hearts we know that couldn't be true. That's the time we should allow our hearts to speak up and say, "Now, soul, things might appear bad. The eyes and ears might be sending you negative messages. But we have something more trustworthy than the eyes and ears. We already know how this situation is going to turn out, because we have God's Word on the subject. Repent of your doubting, you poor soul, and let's get together and rejoice!"

PROVERBS 10:17

A spiritual person is open to constructive criticism and has a teachable spirit.

FEBRUARY 27

LEVITICUS 20:22-22:16

I know today's reading is not very interesting, but this is as bad as it gets! Hang in there.

Today's section deals primarily with the requirements of the priests, the descendants of Aaron. They were not permitted to defile themselves by touching dead bodies, other than in the case of their immediate families. They could not marry a widow, a divorced woman or a nonvirgin. Only the priests' immediate families could eat the priests' portion of the sacrifices. Only priests without physical defects could minister in the tabernacle. Any defilement meant that they could have no contact with the holy things. The high priest had even stricter requirements.

Beyond all this, the people of Israel were required to bring only flawless sacrifices, as they represented the sinless Christ. I think the point of today's reading is that God deserves the best. Nothing else is worthy of Him. Are you giving Him your best?

MARK 9:1-29

Won't it be nice to talk with Moses and Elijah and other great Bible characters when we get to heaven? Then we can ask them all the details the Bible leaves out. Peter, James and John had the opportunity to talk with Moses and Elijah, but James and John were too overwhelmed to speak, and Peter was too confused to say anything intelligent.

After Jesus' transfiguration, He told the three disciples not to tell anyone about the experience until after He had risen from the dead. Peter spoke of that experience many years later in his second epistle: "For we did not follow cleverly devised tales when we made known to you the power and coming of our Lord Jesus Christ, but we were eyewitnesses of His majesty. For when He received honor and glory from God the Father, such an utterance as this was made to Him by the Majestic Glory, 'This is My beloved Son with whom I am well-pleased'—and we ourselves heard this utterance made from heaven when we were with Him on the holy mountain" (2 Pet. 1:16-18).

We've already read the story of the man with the demon-possessed son in Matthew, but Mark gives us more details. Jesus was obviously angry or greatly disappointed when He learned that His disciples failed to bring deliverance to this boy. He had already given them authority to cast out demons, and they had done it successfully. But this time they failed. The boy's father didn't possess much faith, as evidenced by his desperate cry to Jesus: "If You can do *anything*, take pity on us and help us!" (italics mine). Jesus said in reply, "If you can!"

There are various interpretations of what Jesus meant. Possibly He was just repeating in surprise what the boy's father had said. In other words, Jesus was saying, "*If* I can? Of course I can, because all things are possible to him who believes! And I believe!" Another possibility is that Jesus was placing the responsibility on the boy's father to have faith for his son's deliverance. The man then admitted he was struggling to believe and still had doubts. Regardless, Jesus cast out the deaf and dumb spirit.

The disciples later asked Jesus why they failed. Matthew's account records the reason as unbelief, whereas Mark's version indicates that it was a failure to pray and fast. Very possibly Jesus gave both reasons. To cast out this demon may have taken more faith than the disciples were used to exercising, so it would have been necessary to spend time in prayer and fasting to increase their faith. Prayer and fasting couldn't increase the authority they possessed, but it could increase their faith in that authority if they meditated on Jesus' promises to them. *The point is that God-given authority doesn't just automatically work because we possess it. We must have faith in that authority.* Any time we deal with Satan or demons, we must realize that our fight is one of faith.

PSALM 43:1-5

Once again we find David encouraging himself.

PROVERBS 10:18

The reason the slanderer is a fool is that his slander always comes back to him, and eventually people discover his true character.

FEBRUARY 28

LEVITICUS 22:17-23:44

You're probably happy we will be finishing the book of Leviticus in three more days! (By then we'll be a little more than one-sixth of the way through the entire Bible!) However, the next few days in Leviticus will be better than the last few, I guarantee you. The next *two books* in the Old Testament have their dry times as well, but they also have a number of good stories you will learn from and enjoy reading. After that the Old Testament covers hundreds of years of stories that will bless your socks off. We're already reading the Psalms and Proverbs, and we'll also be reading the books of the prophets, which I'm sure will bolster our faith and help us to grow. The books of the Bible written to new covenant believers are the various New Testament letters written by some of the apostles. They are by far the most applicable to our lives.

As I mentioned yesterday, God expected the best from His people, so He required flawless animals for sacrifices. When we read some of the prophets, we'll discover that when Israel began to backslide they started bringing God imperfect animals. Some were blind, maimed or otherwise flawed. We should constantly stay on the watch to make sure we're giving God our best. It is a sure sign of backsliding when we reserve the best for ourselves and give God only second best.

Chapter 23 lists all the religious festivals instituted by the Lord. It may seem as if Israel spent a lot of their time partying, but let's examine them closer. First they were to celebrate the weekly Sabbath. It began on Friday at sundown and lasted until Saturday at sundown.

Second was the Feast of Passover, which occurred in either March or April. It was a one-day event celebrating God's deliverance of Israel out of Egypt. Third, in conjunction with the Passover Feast, was the Feast of Unleavened Bread. From the night of the Passover, Israel was not permitted to eat any leavened bread for seven days. It probably represented the fact that once we have been redeemed by the blood of God's Lamb we should no longer participate in sin.

Fourth was the Feast of the Firstfruits. It probably occurred three days after the Passover, so that it too would be included in the Feast of Unleavened Bread. We think it represented the resurrection of Jesus three days after His crucifixion, as He was the "firstfruits" of all of those who will be resurrected (see 1 Cor. 15:23). This would be somewhat equivalent to our Easter.

Fifth was the Feast of Pentecost, which came exactly fifty days after the Feast of the Firstfruits. It would have occurred in June. On that day the church was born in Jerusalem. At the Feast of the Firstfruits the people were commanded to wave a *sheaf of grain* before the Lord. However, at the Feast of Pentecost they were required to bring *loaves of bread* to wave before the Lord. The symbolism is obvious. The sheaf of grain represented Christ in His resurrection. (A dead grain is planted, yet it produces a live grain.) The loaves represent the church, made up of many "resurrected grains."

Sixth was the Feast of Trumpets, which would have been celebrated at the end of September on our calendar. It announced the coming of the Day of Atonement, which came ten days later, in October. Finally was the Feast of Booths, or Tabernacles, when Israel would live in little makeshift tents for eight days to remind them of how God brought them through the wilderness after their deliverance from Egypt. It took place five days after the Day of Atonement. Thus, these feasts basically were celebrated one right after another in two sets: one in the spring and one in the fall (except for Pentecost, celebrated in the summer).

It's good to have a basic understanding of the feasts to help us as we read the New Testament. Jesus participated in all of them during His earthly life. We'll read in John's Gospel that He went up to Jerusalem to the Feast of Booths. During that feast the Jews would take water from the pool of Siloam and pour it out in remembrance of how God provided water from a rock in the wilderness. (We have already read that story in Exodus.) It was on the last day of that feast that Jesus proclaimed if any were thirsty, they should come to Him and drink, and out from them would flow rivers of living water (see John 7:2, 37-38).

MARK 9:30-10:12

It should make every pastor feel better to know that Jesus had to deal with strife and immaturity in His little church of twelve parishioners. These men were actually arguing over who was the greatest! When Jesus asked them what they were discussing, they were all silent, since they already knew how Jesus viewed self-aggrandizement. In God's kingdom the greatest person is the servant.

Jesus sure gave a good plug for Sunday school teachers (who normally take a back seat in the church hierarchy) when He said, "Whoever receives one child like this in My name is receiving Me... And whoever causes one of these little ones who believe to stumble, it would be better for him if, with a heavy millstone hung around his neck, he had been cast into the sea" (9:37,42). In Jesus' eyes, children are important members of God's kingdom! Sunday school teachers should know how vitally important their task is, and parents should solemnly consider their responsibilities to raise their children in the "discipline and instruction of the Lord" (Eph. 6:4).

Since I've twice explained Jesus' words about cutting your hand off and plucking your eye out, I won't go into them again. However, Jesus spoke in this passage of people's being cast *bodily* into hell. This hell is the Hebrew word *Gehenna* and is synonymous with "the lake of fire and brimstone" spoken of in Revelation 20:10. When an unsaved person dies during this present age, his body decays, but his spirit goes to Hades, the place of torment. At the end of this age all those people will be bodily resurrected and then stand before the great white throne of judgment. After that they will be cast into *Gehenna*, which refers to the Hinnom Valley, located right outside Jerusalem, where the trash of a large garbage dump burned continually. Worms fed unceasingly on the rotting garbage. The implication is clear: a person who rejects God's grace will become God's garbage.

I have to admit I don't know what Jesus meant when He said that everyone will be salted with fire. Since this statement directly follows His warnings of the fires of hell, I'm inclined to think the fire of which He spoke here is the same. Some suggest that it means God permits every person to go through fiery trials to cause us to seek Him. I have to agree that all people experience various trials in their lives, and in many cases those trials have stirred them to seek God. And most Christians have found that spiritual growth takes place in times of trial. The trial itself doesn't cause us to grow, but it causes us to draw closer to God through prayer and trusting His Word.

For an explanation of Jesus' teaching on divorce, please refer to my comments on Matthew 19:1-9.

PSALM 44:1-8

In this psalm the writer encouraged his own faith by remembering the great things God had done in the past. The psalmist reminded himself that he should not trust in his sword or bow, but that his victory would come through the Lord (vv. 6-7). We, too, should be careful that we're not relying on ourselves but putting our confidence in the Lord. We do what is possible and trust God to do the *impossible.*

PROVERBS 10:19

The less you talk, the less you'll sin!

FEBRUARY 29

If this is leap year, today you get a day off from my commentary but not a day off from God's Word! Read whatever you'd like in the Scriptures today.

MARCH 1

LEVITICUS 24:1-25:46

This man who blasphemed the name of the Lord must have been a degenerate of the worst kind. Just think of all the miracles he had seen in the past two years; yet he still blasphemed God. He deserved death, and that's what the Lord commanded. His punishment was an object lesson for all Israel. God is holy, and His name should only be spoken reverently.

God's instructions concerning a Sabbath rest for the land are interesting. It's good for the future crops if the land is permitted to "rest." But the Lord had a higher purpose than soil revitalization. He was thinking of the poor who would be permitted to gather freely all that grew of its own accord during that seventh year. And according to Deuteronomy 31:10-13, it was not God's intention that the people of Israel be idle for that year, but that they would use their free time to learn God's law and teach His commandments to their children. God even promised to bless the harvest of the sixth year so they would have a full supply until the harvest of the ninth year (see 25:21).

After a period of forty-nine years would come the year of Jubilee. If an Israelite had been forced to sell his land, when the fiftieth year arrived, he got it back. So if a person fell on hard times, he was guaranteed another chance at least once, and maybe twice, in his lifetime. Also, the original owner always had the "right of redemption." That is, if he sold his land, he had the right to buy it back at a fair price based on the price for which he had sold it and the number of years left until the Jubilee.

This system would prevent wealthy people from becoming wealthier (at others' expense) by amassing a lot of land. In Third-World agricultural countries today, the landowners are wealthy, and everyone else (the peasants) works for slave wages. With God's system of the year of Jubilee, that could never happen.

Unfortunately, the people of Israel never kept this law even once. They remained in Canaan's land for 490 years until God judged them for their apostasy by removing them to Babylon. God told them they would be in Babylon for seventy years while the land in Canaan rested, thus making up for the seventy neglected seventh-year Sabbaths.

All Hebrew slaves (who had sold themselves as slaves for economic reasons) would go free after six years of service or at the year of Jubilee. Foreign slaves could be kept for a lifetime, however, and even bequeathed as part of an inheritance. This was a form of God's judgment on the surrounding wicked nations. Yet even those slaves had to be treated fairly by Israel.

MARK 10:13-31

Can you picture Jesus holding children in His arms? Do you think He was smiling? I'm sure He was. The disciples tried to prevent the children from coming to Him, probably because they felt He was too important to waste time on children. But that's not how Jesus felt; *He wasn't too important for anybody.* How about you? Are there people who you feel are below you? Are there some with whom you just can't be bothered? If so, *repent.*

For an explanation of the story of the rich young ruler, see my comments on Matthew 19:16-30.

We must be careful not to misapply Jesus' promise of the hundredfold return to the giving of money in an offering. That would be making Jesus say something He didn't. Peter just said that he and the other disciples had left *everything* to follow Jesus—their businesses, families and homes. That was quite a price to pay. But for those who sacrifice all for the sake of spreading the gospel, Jesus promised *them* a hundredfold return. And those who qualify cannot dictate when their promised return will come. Jesus only said it would come "in the present age" (v. 30). And notice that He also promised them *persecutions* along with their hundredfold return!

PSALM 44:9-26

This section of Psalm 44 is very difficult to interpret. Obviously the Israeli army had suffered a great defeat. We can immediately think of scriptural examples of such times, but in those cases God was using the foreign army as a tool of His judgment upon sinful Israel. In this case, the psalmist claimed they had not sinned (see vv. 17-18). As was Job, the psalmist was bewildered about why God had permitted these terrible circumstances. One thing is certain: God's character is consistent throughout the Bible. He is not a Dr. Jekyll and Mr. Hyde.

So why did God allow His people to suffer? That question has been asked for centuries. First of all, the devil and his people hate God's people. Throughout history, persecution has come. Jesus promised it. The list of Christian martyrs numbers in the millions, and God permitted every death. Some say those martyrs didn't have enough faith or they would have "believed" their way to deliverance. That's foolish. All the original apostles were martyred, except for possibly John and, of course, Judas Iscariot. Some say that God *couldn't* have delivered them because Satan is the god of this world, so God has no control. That is equally foolish in light of all the people God delivered from martyrdom in the Bible when He chose to do so. *Nobody has the full picture*, but we can be certain God had His purposes. One day Jesus will reign over this world, and there will be no more unrighteousness. In the meantime, we can simply trust God.

PROVERBS 10:20-21

MARCH 2

LEVITICUS 25:47-27:13

When I read the blessings of obedience and the curses of disobedience listed in today's section, I conclude that it pays to obey, and it costs to disobey! Actually, what God spoke here was prophecy, because Israel did reach a point where all these promised judgments came upon them. Notice that God promised the land would enjoy its Sabbaths when the Israelites were deported to another country for their disobedience (26:34). But, most important, notice how God promised that if they would humble themselves and repent, He would forgive and eventually restore them. That He did.

Chapter 27 deals with the valuations of men, animals, houses and fields. A person could dedicate such things to the Lord, and he would give to God an equivalent amount of money. I don't think anyone fully understands everything in this chapter, so don't worry about it.

MARK 10:32-52

We read that, as Jesus journeyed to Jerusalem, His followers were amazed and fearful. Everyone was aware that if Jesus went to Jerusalem, His life would be in danger. So Jesus made it plain that He knew exactly what He was doing, and He predicted He would be delivered up to be crucified. But James and John didn't believe it. They thought, probably like the rest, that if Jesus was going to Jerusalem with His life in danger, it must be the time when He would set up His kingdom. That's what they had been waiting for! No more Romans! So James and John immediately asked if they could be the number two and three men in the new kingdom. Jesus then asked if they were willing to drink the drink He would drink and be baptized as He would be baptized.

I have to wonder if Jesus was just playing along with them in their complete ignorance. Jesus was speaking of His suffering and crucifixion. Little did they know that the kingdom they were expecting wouldn't arrive for at least two thousand years!

When the other apostles heard of James and John's request, they didn't like it. Quite possibly they were *all* hoping to be Jesus' right-hand man in the new kingdom. But Jesus said that any person who wants to be great in the kingdom must become a servant to all. *The way up is down.*

Speaking of servanthood, Jesus preached what He practiced. In the next few verses, we see Him saying to blind Bartimaeus, "What do you want Me to do for you?" That's the second time in today's reading where Jesus asks that question (vv. 36, 51). *Jesus, certainly the greatest in the kingdom, loved to serve and proclaimed that He did not come to be served, but to serve* (v. 45). What would you say if Jesus stood before you right now and asked, "What do you want Me to do for *you*?" All of us could immediately think of some request. Why don't you make that request right now? Jesus hasn't changed. He loves you every bit as much as Bartimaeus and James and John. He's waiting to hear your request!

When Jesus called for Bartimaeus to come to Him, the Bible says that Bartimaeus, "casting aside his cloak," jumped up. We can tell he had faith, because even when his friends tried to discourage him, he still cried out for Jesus to have mercy on him. And when Jesus called him, he didn't gradually get in the mood to go to Jesus, but rather he *jumped up*. Faith can be seen in action.

I read once that in Jesus' day, blind people wore a certain kind of cloak so others would recognize they were blind. If that's true, when Bartimaeus cast aside his cloak, it was another strong indication of his faith in Jesus. *He prepared to be blessed!* Are you expecting and preparing to be blessed?

PSALM 45:1-17

This psalm is a wedding hymn, and from a symbolic interpretation, it alludes to the future wedding of King Jesus to His bride, the church. The writer of Hebrews quotes verses 6-7 of this psalm in reference to Jesus, so this psalm is clearly messianic (see Heb. 1:8-9). The book of Revelation speaks of the "marriage of the Lamb" to a bride who "has made herself ready" and who is clothed in robes of righteousness (see Rev. 19:7-9). You might read this psalm again from the standpoint that the king spoken of is Jesus and the bride is the church. Then you'll get an idea of what a royal wedding ceremony we have to look forward to!

PROVERBS 10:22

How can anyone argue with this proverb? God wants to supply all our needs abundantly. That includes spiritual, physical and emotional needs.

MARCH 3

LEVITICUS 27:14-NUMBERS 1:54

Today we finish Leviticus. The last section continues to deal with the valuation of certain things a person might dedicate to the Lord. For example, if he dedicated a field to the Lord, it was no longer his field, but the Lord's. From then on, it became the priests' property. However, the original owner could buy it back, but he had to pay the valuation plus another 20 percent. Realize that the Israelites didn't tithe their paychecks; they tithed on any and every increase. For example, a man would give a tenth of his newborn flocks to the Lord. However, he could buy back his tithed flocks if he paid the determined valuation plus another 20 percent. I always chuckle inwardly when I hear someone say God is not that concerned about what we do with our money. Tell that to the people under the old covenant!

The book of Numbers covers Israel's history as the people wandered in the desert for thirty-eight years. At the beginning of this book, there were 603,550 men in Israel twenty years old and upward. But by the end of this book, all but three would be dead. The overwhelming majority never possessed their rightful inheritance because of fear and disobedience.

We can learn many spiritual lessons from the book of Numbers. The apostle Paul, writing about the history of Israel, said, "Now these things happened to them as an example, and they were written for our instruction, upon whom the ends of the ages have come" (1 Cor. 10:11). Israel was obviously a type of the church: delivered from the kingdom of darkness (Egypt), baptized in water (the crossing of the Red Sea), healed of sickness and disease, tested in the wilderness, fed by the Word of God (manna) and drinking from a rock that Paul said represented Christ (1 Cor. 10:4).

Specifically, Israel in the book of Numbers represents the church full of unbelief and not coming into her full inheritance. Yet Joshua and Caleb, who were the clear minority, represent the part of the church that trusts the promises of God and fights the adversary by faith until the full inheritance is received. By the end of Numbers, you'll have to decide if you're going to be a doubting Israelite who will spend your life "wandering in the desert" or a faith-filled Joshua or Caleb who will receive what God has promised.

You've probably figured out already how the book of Numbers got its name.

God wanted a census of men fit for military duty. Every tribe was included except the Levites, who were in charge of the tabernacle. The next census, taken thirty-eight years later, gave an official count of 1,820 fewer men. Unbelieving Israel did not grow numerically in the desert as they did in Egypt.

MARK 11:1-26

Jesus finally made His triumphal entry into Jerusalem. As I mentioned yesterday, most of Jesus' followers thought this would mark the beginning of the Messiah's reign spoken of by the prophets. So they gave Him a grand welcome, spreading their garments and leafy branches on the road before Him. But Jesus' crucifixion was just a few days away.

The next morning, on the way back to Jerusalem, Jesus cursed the fig tree. Many think that tree represented Israel, which should have been producing spiritual fruit but was barren. Israel was therefore cursed by God. This interpretation may well be true, but the Bible doesn't say.

The following day, Jesus and His disciples are again making the journey from Bethany to Jerusalem. Peter notices that the fig tree has withered from the roots up. Jesus then makes one of His most astonishing statements: "Truly I say to you, whoever says to this mountain, 'Be taken up and cast into the sea,' and does not doubt in his heart, but believes that what he says is going to happen, it shall be granted him." Many commentators avoid commenting on this amazing statement. They often try to explain it away. I believe however, *Jesus meant what He said and said what He meant.* If we speak with our mouths that which we believe in our hearts, it will come to pass. It doesn't work just because someone *speaks*; it doesn't work if someone simply *believes*; it doesn't work if someone only *hopes*. What Jesus taught will work if someone both believes in his heart and speaks with his mouth. Jesus prefaced this amazing statement with the admonition to "have faith in God." If it is true that our faith-filled words carry so much power, it's no wonder He wants us to have faith in God.

When we come right down to it, everyone has faith in his heart—faith in God or faith in the devil. I call faith in the devil fear. If you don't have faith in God, then you'll have fear in your heart. And if you have fear in your heart, whenever you speak those fears from your mouth, you are actually setting in motion a spiritual principle that will work against you. Some people say that this spiritual principle can't work in a negative sense. Jesus, however, just demonstrated that it *can* work in a negative way. When He cursed the fig tree, His words brought death!

If you are one of those persons who continually says, "My grandmother died of cancer when she was forty-two, my mother died of cancer when she was thirty-nine and I'll probably be dead before I reach age forty," then you need to hear what Jesus is saying. *You need to have faith in God!* God said that He would grant you a long life (Ps. 91:16)! But if you keep believing and saying that you are going to die by the time you are forty, you probably will! Start saying only what agrees with God's Word. If your words don't agree with God's Word, then you are speaking what the Bible calls "an evil report."

It is absolutely amazing to witness the changes that occur in people's lives when they begin speaking God's Word from their mouths. Good things start happening! Quit cursing yourself and start believing and saying what God says! You may not notice immediate change in your circumstances, but remember that it took twenty-four hours before Peter noticed what had happened to the fig tree.

Also notice verse 24. When praying, we are to believe that we receive *when we pray*. Too many only want to believe after they see the answer to their prayer. But that's not faith. In the world they say, "Seeing is believing." In God's kingdom, we can say *believing is seeing* (see Heb. 11:1).

PSALM 46:1-11

God is "a very present help in trouble" (v. 1). When difficulties or trials come, we can hide in His care and know we are safe. When we feel as if we can't go on, we can rely on Him to be our strength. Too many Christians are doing things in their own strength and abilities. Why does God live inside us—just to be a spiritual hitchhiker? No, He is there to help us in every situation.

PROVERBS 10:23

MARCH 4

NUMBERS 2:1-3:51

From the number of fighting-age men we can estimate the total population of Israel to be over three million. Yet God took care of them for *forty years in a desert!* Someone calculated that it would have taken fifty railway boxcars of manna each day to feed such a multitude, plus at least twelve million gallons of water! Their camp would have been an area of at least one hundred square miles (ten miles by ten miles)!

God had a specific order in which the tribes were to camp around the tabernacle. The Levites, chosen to carry out all the duties related to the tabernacle, camped in three groups in very close proximity around it. The other ten tribes, plus the half-tribes of Ephraim and Manasseh, camped beyond the Levites in a huge circle according to God's direction—either north, south, east or west. Notice that the Lord's tabernacle was always at the center.

God had originally said that all the firstborn sons of Israel belonged to Him, because He had spared them during the killing of all the firstborn in Egypt. Apparently, it was the Lord's intention that all the firstborn of Israel would be set apart for special service to Him (see Ex. 13:2). But because of repeated sin, God's plan was altered. Now He said He would trade all the firstborn of Israel for all the descendants of Levi. Remember that it was the Levites who were "on the Lord's side" during the incident of the golden calf.

MARK 11:27-12:17

Jesus concluded His great statement about mountain-moving faith with a commandment to forgive anyone who has wronged us. We have no right, Jesus said, to expect God to forgive us if we don't forgive others. This is an example of an even larger spiritual principle: *God treats us as we treat others.* We will reap what we sow. If you want God to treat you better, start treating others better!

Jesus' parable of the vine-growers reveals God's view of the majority of Jewish leaders in that day. God expected fruit from His vineyard, but none was received. He continually sent prophets and wise men to the Jews, but each one was persecuted or martyred. Finally God sent His Son, whom they would soon kill as well. Then God would "destroy the vine-growers, and...give the vineyard to others" (12:9).

PSALM 47:1-9

This psalm is clearly prophetic, speaking of the time when God will reign over all the earth. The Lord will descend His throne with a shout and the sound of a trumpet (v. 5). Truly that is something to clap our hands over and shout about, as the psalmist says in verse 1.

PROVERBS 10:24-25

Here is a good "positive confession" to make: "The desire of the righteous *will* be granted" (v. 24, italics mine). And because God has made me righteous by the blood of Christ, my desire will be granted. Quit saying, "I wonder if God hears my prayers?"

MARCH 5

NUMBERS 4:1-5:31

Today we read the different duties of the three divisions of Levi. The Kohathites transported the sacred tabernacle furniture after the priests had covered it. The Gershonites carried the curtains and coverings of the tabernacle. The Merarites had charge of the various pieces of framework. Altogether, they made up 8,580 men who had to be thirty years of age or older to perform the work of the tabernacle. Jesus entered His ministry at age thirty as well.

The test for adultery in chapter 5 may sound at first like a superstitious rite. Some commentators have suggested it worked by psychological suggestion, or that the herb drink caused a miscarriage if the woman was pregnant. If, however, it worked only by causing a miscarriage, it would have never detected an adulterous woman who was not pregnant! No, this was a test given by God Himself, and it worked because of His supernatural power. The point is that God knows when we sin, and people will bear their punishment unless they receive God's mercy through His ordained plan. For Israel, it was through the sacrifices (which represented Christ). For us, it is through Christ Himself.

MARK 12:18-37

According to Jesus, the greatest commandment is to love God, and the second greatest is to love your neighbor as yourself. Those are not part of the Ten Commandments given through Moses, yet they fulfill everything the moral law has to say. If we love God and our neighbor, we won't steal, lie and so on. The apostle Paul said love is the fulfillment of the law (see Rom. 13:10). I'm so glad that we who are under the new covenant have only two commandments to follow.

PSALM 48:1-14

This could very well be another prophetic psalm speaking of the time when Jesus will rule the earth from Mount Zion in Jerusalem. (Mount Zion, Zion and Jerusalem are practically synonymous in the Bible.) However, as with many prophecies, this psalm could have a double meaning. (Bible scholars refer to that as "the law of double reference.") It may well have been written after God's deliverance of Jerusalem as recorded in 2 Chronicles 20, which could explain the verses concerning the kings who passed by together and were terrified (vv. 4-6).

PROVERBS 10:26

You may never have had vinegar in your teeth, but we all know that lazy people leave a "bad taste in our mouths." Having smoke in your eyes is no fun, either! God *wants* us to rest at times, but He never intended anyone to be lazy. *We should work hard and then rest.*

MARCH 6

NUMBERS 6:1-7:89

Chapter 6 deals with the law of the Nazarite vow. The word *Nazarite* is derived from the Hebrew word that means "to dedicate." The person who took the vow of the Nazarite was specially dedicating himself to the Lord for a predetermined period of time. His vow was not required but was completely voluntary and could last for as long as a lifetime. In the Old Testament, we know that Samson was a Nazarite. It seems the prophet Samuel also became one. In the New Testament, John the Baptist, who "drank no wine or liquor" (Luke 1:15), could have taken the Nazarite vow.

We can't be sure of the symbolism behind the prohibitions under which Nazarites lived, but my opinion is that they were simply a way for people to prove their dedication to God. It was a sacrifice to give up drinking any grape products. (They didn't have much else to drink.) It was a humiliation for a man to have long hair. And if people were willing to not even attend a close relative's funeral, they clearly loved God more than anyone. *We also should consider the Lord more important than earthly pleasures, people's approval and our own loved ones.*

In chapter 7 we read what seems to be a repetitious list of the dedication offerings of the twelve tribes for the tabernacle (this is the second-longest chapter in the Bible). However, it blesses me to know that the Lord knows how much each one of us gives to His work. Both chapters we read today deal with dedication and sacrifice to the Lord. We should ask ourselves, "What does it cost me to serve the Lord?" I'm afraid that many Christians would say that it costs them nothing. Is your only sacrifice to God what you put in the offering plate on Sunday morning or attendance in church that takes up an hour of "your time"? Is He speaking to you to give up some of the legitimate pleasures of life to serve Him more fully? *The only way we can prove our love for God is by obedience.* If you were put on trial for loving God, would there be enough evidence to convict you? What has it cost you *this week* to serve God?

MARK 12:38-13:13

It's interesting that after reading those passages in Numbers concerning self-dedication to the Lord, we would also read today the story of the widow's mite. Again the question is, *are we really sacrificing anything to serve the Lord?* For some people it is as easy for them to pay their tithes as it is for me to buy a piece of bubblegum. What if the Lord told you to sell your new car, buy a used one and send the extra money to a missionary? Would you do it? What if He told you not to buy a new dress when you wanted one but to give the money to someone else who needs basic clothes? Would you? What if the Lord told you to quit watching your favorite TV show each week and spend that time praying for the lost? Would you?

Did you notice the price that Jesus said would be paid by some for His cause?

Some will be arrested; some will be delivered up to the courts; some will be flogged; and some will be hated by their children or parents and turned over by them for execution!

PSALM 49:1-20

It sounds as if people had the same false values three thousand years ago that they do today. Money and prestige were real marks of success. But the psalmist wrote that nobody "can take it with him." I agree. I've never seen a U-Haul trailer in a funeral procession!

PROVERBS 10:27-28

MARCH 7

NUMBERS 8:1-9:23

We read in 8:24 that the Levites could begin service at age twenty-five. Two days ago, we read that the entrance age was thirty. But Jewish tradition teaches there was a five-year apprenticeship before they entered into full service at age thirty.

In chapter 9 Israel celebrated its second Passover. The first they had celebrated in Egypt.

Once again we read of the glory cloud that continually rested on the tabernacle. It appeared like a cloud in the day and like fire at night, so the people always had a visible sign the Lord was with them. When the cloud moved, they moved. When it remained, they remained. Notice that God didn't speak audibly to Israel and say, "Now it's time to move on, so everybody get up! We're heading north today!" The people just kept their eyes on the cloud. They had no prior warning of when it would move. And when it started moving, they had no idea where it would lead them or how far it would go.

Under the new covenant, God leads us in a somewhat similar way. We can't expect to hear an audible voice, either. We can only follow the peace in our hearts. Wherever it leads us, we must go. We have no prior warning; we must stay constantly alert. And we must walk by faith, because God doesn't always give us the whole picture from the beginning, but leads us one step at a time.

MARK 13:14-37

The "abomination of desolation" spoken of by the prophet Daniel and referred to here by Jesus is the Antichrist. His "desolation" will be when he sets himself up in the temple in Jerusalem and proclaims he is God. That incident will occur at the middle of the seven-year tribulation period and will mark the beginning of the "great tribulation" period. When that event happens, the *believing* Jews and others who are living in Jerusalem and the surrounding area will be glad for what we've read today. They will know to run for their lives immediately. Jesus predicted an ensuing terrible time of tribulation such as the world has never witnessed. You can imagine how horrible it will be if it will top every holocaust that has yet occurred. In fact, Jesus said that unless those days were shortened, no life would survive its horror! (We'll read more about it in the book of Revelation.) However, there is no need for alarm, because the church will be raptured to heaven before then.

At the end of the tribulation, the sun will be darkened, the moon won't give off any light (of course) and the stars will be falling from the heavens. Then Jesus will return to destroy the armies of the Antichrist and set up His millennial kingdom. When Jesus warned His listeners to stay alert, He really wasn't referring to us but to those who will be on the earth at the time of His second coming. However, the same principle holds for those of us who are looking forward to the rapture of the church. We don't know when it will be. In fact, we'll have much less warning. At least those who will be on the earth right before the second coming can read what we've read today and have some idea when to expect Him.

The first difference between the rapture and the second coming is that they will be separated by at least seven years (some will argue three-and-a-half). Also, at the rapture, Jesus will never touch the earth; we'll rise to meet Him in the air, and He'll take us back to heaven with Him. At the second coming, however, Jesus will descend upon the Mount of Olives and stay for one thousand years! At that time, we'll come back with Him to help set up and administrate His kingdom. I want to be very cautious when I teach about the end times, because there are so many varying opinions in the body of Christ. However, what I have just given to you is accepted by many, if not most, evangelical Christians.

PSALM 50:1-23

This psalm wasn't just *inspired* by the Spirit; it contains actual words spoken by God (from verse 5 on). He seems to have been reproving Israel for their false view of the sacrifices they were offering. He didn't need their animal sacrifices; He wanted them to offer sacrifices of thanksgiving from their hearts, not just go through rituals.

God also warned the wicked man who slanders his own brother. The Lord said that because He delays judgment, the wicked think they're getting away with their sins. But that's not the case. God has only been showing them mercy to give them time to repent. But the time for judgment is coming soon.

PROVERBS 10:29-30

MARCH 8

NUMBERS 10:1-11:23

It's nice to be back into some stories again instead of more laws! The people of Israel had been gone from Egypt now for one year and one month. And once again they had the nerve to grumble and complain, so the Lord became angry and sent fire that consumed the outskirts of the camp. When Moses prayed, God stopped the fire—but the people complained again. This time they were tired of the manna they had been eating for the last twelve months for breakfast, lunch and dinner. They used to eat fish, melons, cucumbers, onions and garlic in Egypt, and they wanted to go back. They seemed to forget about making bricks in Egypt and having their babies thrown into the Nile! And they forgot where they were headed: to the promised land that "flows with milk and honey."

Poor Moses complained to God that the burden of all these crybabies was too much for him to handle. In answer, God gave him seventy "assistant pastors" and promised that Israel would have plenty of meat to eat the next day. In fact, He would give them enough meat for a month—so much that manna would taste good again. If there were three and a half million people, and each one ate a pound of meat per day, God would be promising to provide a total of 54,250 tons of meat. If one cow weighed 900 pounds, 54,250 tons would be more than one hundred thousand cows! Even Moses doubted God could do it. But I love the Lord's response: "Is the Lord's power limited?" (11:23). If God could provide meat for three-and-a-half million Israelites, do you think He can pay your electric bill?

MARK 14:1-21

The woman who poured the vial of costly perfume over Jesus' head was severely criticized by some of the disciples. To be honest, I think I would have reacted the same way. That perfume was worth at least three hundred denarii. One denarius was equivalent to a day's wages, so that perfume was worth *one and one-fifth of a year's salary.* If you make $20,000 a year, to you that perfume was worth $24,000. But Jesus didn't rebuke her and said she had actually done a good thing. John's Gospel reveals that the woman was Mary and the one who complained was Judas Iscariot, who really wasn't concerned about the poor. Rather, he was angry because he used to steal money from Jesus' money box (see John 12:2-6).

We should be careful in criticizing people who use their money for the Lord, even if we don't agree with how they spend it. If one person feels led to buy pads for pews, that's between him and God. If another person feels led to buy a jet for an evangelist, that is between him and the Lord. If someone feels led to give money to derelicts on Skid Row, that's between him and the Lord. If another person gives his money to overseas missions, that's between him and the Lord. It's not our place to judge what other Christians do with their money based on what God has told us to do with *our* money.

PSALM 51:1-19

This psalm was written by David after he had committed adultery with Bathsheba. We'll read about it in the book of 2 Samuel. It's a tragic story, but God forgave him after his repentance and prayer of confession. If David, the great king of Israel, could commit adultery and have his lover's husband killed, and then God forgave him, what could you do that God wouldn't forgive? I'm not saying this to encourage you to sin! But all of us do fall, and when that happens, I don't want you to be duped by the devil into thinking you have gone beyond God's mercy.

PROVERBS 10:31-32

MARCH 9

NUMBERS 11:24-13:33

When God anointed the seventy elders with the Holy Spirit in order to assist Moses, they all prophesied (see 11:25). It was a sign to them that the Holy Spirit was upon them. These men only prophesied once, but new covenant believers who are baptized in the Holy Spirit can speak in other tongues any time they desire (1 Cor. 14:14-19). Under the new covenant, every person who is born again has the Holy Spirit *within* him.

Just as God promised, He sent meat for the Israelites in the form of quail. We read that He sent so many that the person who gathered the least collected ten homers. According to the marginal note in my Bible, one homer was about eleven bushels. So the person who gathered the least gathered 110 bushels of quail. If only the men over age nineteen gathered the quail, and if ten quail could fit in a bushel, then Israel gathered at least 660 million quail! That's a lot of birds! And this was the second time God had provided meat by sending quail.

This story illustrates a perfect balance on the subject of biblical prosperity. God provided an abundance for the people of Israel. But some became greedy, hoarding up more than they could ever carry with them. God then sent a plague that killed the greedy ones. The moral is that God is not opposed to our being prosperous, but He *is* opposed to our being greedy.

Moses had already displayed great humility and selflessness. We read today that he was unconcerned when God anointed the seventy others with the Holy Spirit (though Joshua was jealous for his sake). Moses never wanted his job in the first place, and he wasn't threatened when God used others in positions of authority.

Now Moses' own brother Aaron and sister Miriam challenged his authority and questioned his marriage to a Cushite woman (possibly she was a black woman from Ethiopia). Moses apparently didn't even defend himself, but the Lord certainly did. We assume Miriam and not Aaron was stricken with leprosy because she was the instigator. Moses, displaying a Christlike spirit, prayed that Miriam be healed. God said that He would heal her, but only after Miriam had suffered outside the camp as a leper for seven days.

When God told Moses to send spies into the promised land, it wasn't so they could decide whether they could overcome the inhabitants. It was only so they could have a better idea of the topography and the size of the cities, as well as what the people were like, so they would be better prepared to take the land. But of the twelve spies who scouted in Canaan for forty days, ten came to the conclusion that it would be *impossible* for Israel to take possession of the land. They made what we call a "bad confession." That is, what they said contradicted God. Joshua and Caleb made "positive confessions" based *not* on what they had seen but on what God said. As a result, Joshua and Caleb would be the only men over age nineteen ever to live in the promised land. The rest would wander in the wilderness and die within thirty-eight years.

MARK 14:22-52

Some Christians argue that the communion elements *actually become* the body and blood of Jesus, because Jesus said of the bread, "This is My body," and of the wine, "This is My blood" (vv. 22,24). However, I personally find it hard to believe that Jesus meant those statements literally, because He was in His body when He said them. So if the elements weren't really Christ's body and blood when He instituted the Lord's supper, why would the elements actually be His body and blood when *we* observe it? Jesus spoke symbolically numerous times before this, and it makes sense to take this statement symbolically as well.

All the disciples fled for their lives, just as Jesus predicted, but Peter followed behind at a distance. Who was the young man who left his linen covering behind as he fled naked? Nobody knows, but some think it was Mark, the writer of this Gospel.

PSALM 52:1-9

Here is another psalm written by David when he was going through a trial. This time he was running for his life from wicked King Saul, of whom we will read when we get to the book of 1 Samuel. David was not moved by his present situation but trusted that God would deliver him. Notice how he ended this psalm with praise and thanksgiving. The prayer of faith always ends on a positive note. If you are presently facing a trial, dig into the Word of God to see what the outcome is going to be. Then believe it and start rejoicing! It is so wonderful to know that the victory is at hand!

PROVERBS 11:1-3

God expects fairness and integrity in our dealings with others (vv. 1,3). He will humble those who exalt themselves, and to those who humble themselves He will give wisdom. To be humble doesn't mean you go around staring at the floor all the time. It means you don't have an unrealistic opinion of yourself, you admit when you're wrong and you look out not just for your own interests, but also for the interests of others.

MARCH 10

NUMBERS 14:1-15:16

Today's story is about a classic crisis in Moses' ministry. A lesser person would have encouraged God to go ahead and destroy the people for their rebellion, but not Moses. He prayed for them even though the majority wanted to kill Moses, Aaron, Caleb and Joshua and appoint a leader who would take them back to Egypt. God had performed many mighty miracles to bring them to where they were, and yet they actually accused Him of bringing them into Canaan so that they would be killed by the Canaanites!

Moses reminded the Lord of how kind He is by quoting what He had said about Himself. And once again it seems that God granted Moses' request because He really didn't want to destroy Israel, but He had no reason to spare them unless someone asked Him.

God pronounced judgment. The people had forfeited their right to enter the promised land. Every person who was at least twenty years old would be dead within thirty-eight years, except Joshua and Caleb. In a very short time, the ten spies who brought back the evil report would die in a plague.

The people were understandably saddened by God's pronouncement and rebelled again, deciding to go ahead immediately to possess the land. But it was impossible for them to go by faith, because they no longer had a promise to stand on. They acted *presumptuously* and were defeated badly in their first and last battles.

Many Christians today make the same mistake of acting presumptuously. For example, it's fine for a married couple to pray that God will give them children. But it would be presumptuous to pray that they not have any children for three years even without using birth control, or to "trust" that God will give them first a boy and then two girls. Before we believe God for anything, we need to be certain that what we're praying for is His will.

MARK 14:53-72

Jesus' trial before the seventy-one-member Sanhedrin was probably held late at night so it could be done in a more secretive manner. If they had arrested Him when He was teaching or healing in the temple, there might have been a riot. Jesus' trial was a mockery of justice, and Jesus didn't even defend Himself against their inconsistent accusations. The high priest was no doubt relieved that there could be an end to the absurd time of testimony once Jesus declared who He was. After judgment was pronounced against Him, they mocked Him, spat on Him, blindfolded Him and beat Him. That the spiritual leaders of Israel actually spat upon and struck God's Son is hard to fathom, isn't it?

Again we read of Peter's denial of the Lord. At least Peter had the courage to stay near Jesus. The other disciples were nowhere to be found. The third time Peter denied Jesus, he began to curse and swear. And this is the man who would become a great leader in the church in Jerusalem!

PSALM 53:1-6

According to what we read today, atheists are fools (v. 1). I have to agree in light of the wealth of evidence for the existence of God. *It takes much more faith to believe there is no God than to believe there is.* When we look at creation, we know there must be a Creator. It's the same as when I look at my wristwatch and know there must be a watchmaker. It would take a lot of faith to believe my watch just "happened." I don't have enough faith to be an atheist. *People have to throw away their intelligence to believe God doesn't exist.*

PROVERBS 11:4

MARCH 11

NUMBERS 15:17-16:40

It may seem harsh that a man would be stoned to death for gathering wood on the Sabbath. But God had already stated plainly on several occasions the law of keeping the Sabbath and the penalty for violations. God means what He says.

Chapter 16 brings us to an even harsher judgment on rebellion. Korah, a Levite, along with 250 others, complained of Aaron's monopoly on the priesthood. Dathan and Abiram said that Moses had exalted himself and was not a man of his word because he hadn't brought them into the promised land yet. Both these rebellions were really directed toward God Himself, who had called both Moses and Aaron. *And this time even Moses lost his patience.* God planned to consume the entire congregation, but Moses interceded for the people again, and only the instigators were destroyed.

In his epistle the apostle Jude warned the church that there were people right in their midst who were no different from Korah. He said they were "*grumblers, finding fault, following after their own lusts; they speak arrogantly, flattering people for the sake of gaining an advantage*" (Jude 16, italics mine). I've met a few people like that in the church!

It's difficult to believe, but we'll read tomorrow that *the Israelites actually blamed Moses and Aaron for the death of those people*. Is it any wonder that God desired to put an end to all of them? People who wonder how a loving God could send people to hell should read this story. God only sends the wicked to hell. And He has provided a way whereby *any* person can receive forgiveness and not have to pay for his sins. Thanks be to God for the gift of His Son, Jesus Christ!

MARK 15:1-47

Jesus was detained overnight while the members of the Sanhedrin slept. The next morning, because they had no authority to execute anyone, they had to take Jesus before Pilate, the Roman governor of Judea. They knew well that

Pilate would not condemn Jesus for blasphemy, so they brought the charge of treason against Him. Even Pilate tried to change the Jews' attitude toward Jesus, but it was a lost cause. Incidentally, it is believed that Pilate committed suicide later on in his life.

Jesus was then turned over to some soldiers to be crucified, who first wanted to have their "fun" with Him. Their further mockery and beating transpired at a place called "the Pavement" (John 19:13). Today in Jerusalem, visitors can stand on the Pavement, discovered in the early 1900s under a convent built on the site. One stone actually has a board scratched on it on which the Roman soldiers played a game called "King."

Pilate was surprised to discover that Jesus was dead after being on the cross only six hours. Many survived for days. But Jesus was half dead before He even got there. The Jews didn't want anyone hanging on a cross during the Sabbath, so they had the legs of the two criminals broken to speed their death by asphyxiation. To stay alive on the cross, a person had to push himself up by the nails in his feet to get a breath of air. With broken legs that was impossible. Jesus' legs weren't broken because He was already dead. But not for long!

PSALM 54:1-7

This is one of the shortest psalms written by David, and the reason may have been that he was once again on the run from King Saul. The prayer took less than thirty seconds to pray, but it got the job done!

Notice how this prayer progresses. First David asked God to act on his behalf (vv. 1-3). Then he confessed that the Lord *would* deliver him (vv. 4-5). Finally, he thanked God that he *was delivered* and stated that his eyes *looked* with satisfaction on his enemies (vv. 6-7). That's how our prayers for help should progress as well.

PROVERBS 11:5-6

MARCH 12

NUMBERS 16:41-18:32

It's hard for me to believe that the Israelites could grumble at Moses again after what they had just seen happen to Korah. But they did, and 14,700 more people died before the plague was stopped by Aaron's running through the congregation with an incense censer, drawing a line between the dead and living.

God mercifully performed yet another sign to quell the rebellion against Aaron and Moses. There seems still to have been some doubt about God's choosing Aaron to be high priest and the Levites as ministers. So God caused Aaron's dead almond rod to blossom and produce ripe almonds overnight. *Still the people complained.* I don't know how the Lord ever put up with them; I lose my patience just reading about their grumbling and complaining!

God had a plan to provide for the needs of the priests and the Levites by giving the priests parts of the sacrifices and by giving the Levites the tithe of Israel. However, the Levites were commanded to tithe the tithe which they received and give it to the priests.

MARK 16:1-20

Mark is the only Gospel writer who recorded Jesus' words concerning the five signs that would accompany believers. But what Jesus said lines up perfectly with what actually happened in the book of Acts. The believers cast out demons, spoke in tongues and laid hands on sick people and healed them. Those signs still accompany new covenant believers, because Jesus never said they were only for first-century Christians.

The only example of "picking up serpents" that we have in the book of Acts is when Paul was bitten by a poisonous snake on the island of Malta (see Acts 28:1-5). It should have killed him, but he shook it off and suffered no harm. Some have interpreted Jesus' words to mean that God wants us to have snake-handling church services, but that's foolish. It falls into the category of tempting God. We have no record in the book of Acts of someone's drinking a poison and not suffering any harm, but once again let me say that we should not tempt God. If someone does try to poison us, we have the right to claim that it won't hurt us!

PSALM 55:1-23

My favorite verse in this psalm is 22: "Cast your burden upon the Lord, and He will sustain you." Our problem is that we try to carry our burdens ourselves. For that reason, God cannot work on them. If we have them, He doesn't. It takes faith to cast our cares on Him, but how much better it is to be carefree than to be weighed down with worries! Worry is just another word for *doubting*.

PROVERBS 11:7

MARCH 13

NUMBERS 19:1-20:29

If you're wondering why God made such a big deal about what to do if someone touched a corpse, remember that during the plague of Numbers 16, at least 14,700 people had died. No doubt thousands of people had been defiled by contact with the dead bodies. Also remember that in a forty-year period, at least one million people died in the wilderness. They had a lot of funerals during those years! And each time someone died it was a reminder of the penalty of their disobedience. I assume God was concerned about the spread of infectious disease, or else the uncleanliness was only symbolic because of the association of sin with death. The main point that we should concern ourselves with is that God provided a way for an unclean person to become clean again, and it was through an atonement. The New Testament says that before we were born again, we had been defiled by spiritual death and were unclean as well. But through the atoning sacrifice of Jesus, we who were unclean are now clean. Praise God!

The forty years of wandering in the desert were almost over, and we see that the surviving Israelites weren't much different from their predecessors. God led them to a place where there was no water, and the grumbling began again. God then graciously provided water, but Moses disobeyed God by striking the designated rock rather than speaking to it. On top of that, Moses seemed to take credit for the miracle when he said, "Listen now, you rebels; shall *we* bring forth water for you out of this rock?" (20:10, italics mine). God said that Moses didn't treat Him as holy before the people. Therefore, he would not enter the promised land. However, we've already read in Matthew and Mark that Moses visited the promised land about fourteen hundred years later, when he appeared on the Mount of Transfiguration with Jesus!

We also read that the Edomites, who were descended from Jacob's brother Esau and thus "brothers" with the Israelites (20:14), would not allow Israel to pass through their territory. That made the Israelites take a fifty-mile detour through the hot desert. Sometimes when our brothers will not cooperate with God's plan, it means taking detours to God's will, but that shouldn't stop us from obeying. Don't blame your lack of spiritual growth on an uncooperative husband or wife or friends or parents. Use those obstacles as stepping stones, not stumbling blocks.

LUKE 1:1-25

Today we begin my favorite Gospel. Luke was a doctor, and God used him to write this Gospel and the book of Acts, so we have to believe God is not against doctors as some extremists would want us to believe. Yes, God is in the healing business, and He can heal without any doctor assisting Him, but He's not opposed to doctors. Doctors can't really heal anyone anyway; they can only help in the healing process God created.

Luke says he researched everything carefully, gathering his facts from those who were eyewitnesses to Jesus' life. Remember that Luke was not one of the twelve original apostles and probably was not born again until after Christ's resurrection. He wrote this book about twenty-five to thirty years later.

We've already read all the details of the tabernacle built in the wilderness. Later on, Solomon built a temple patterned after that tabernacle; it was destroyed by Nebuchadnezzar approximately 587 years before Christ. About seventy years later, the temple was rebuilt, and it was eventually improved upon by Herod in Jesus' time. That was the temple in which Zacharias ministered.

By Jesus' day, there were thousands of descendants of Aaron, of course, and they took turns fulfilling the priestly duties in the temple. This occasion of Zacharias's going into the holy place to burn incense was a once-in-a-lifetime event. I'm sure he was nervous, but he must have been really shocked to meet an angel whom no one had seen since Daniel's time, five hundred years before! The last revelation God had given Israel was about four hundred years before through the prophet Malachi, and now Gabriel informed Zacharias that the Elijah promised by Malachi (see Mal. 4:5) was about to arrive on the scene, and he would be Zacharias's son! Of course, John the Baptist was not actually Elijah, but he came in Elijah's spirit and power (see v. 17).

Zacharias spoke words of doubt, and so he is divinely disciplined by being made mute for nine months. It is better to say nothing at all than to speak words of doubt!

PSALM 56:1-13

David was no different from you or me in his struggle to fight the fight of faith. The situation didn't look good from his viewpoint, but he encouraged himself to trust the Lord. Twice he asked himself the question, "What can man do to me?" He admitted that he had been afraid, but he declared he was trusting God and therefore would not be afraid any longer. Likewise we will be tempted many times to doubt and be afraid. We also should declare our faith in the Lord's promises.

PROVERBS 11:8

We've already read at least one incident where this proverb was proved true. Israel was delivered out of the Red Sea and replaced by the Egyptians, who drowned there. Notice again that this proverb doesn't promise righteous people won't have any troubles. It just promises that when they do have trouble, they will be delivered. Praise the Lord!

MARCH 14

NUMBERS 21:1-22:20

God's people go through trials at two different times: when they're obeying Him and when they're not. That is why it's *not* a good idea to try to determine if you're in God's will by circumstances. We can only determine God's will by His written Word and by His spoken word in our hearts. Satan sends difficulties when we're following the Lord, and God will allow difficulties in order to get our attention when we're not listening to Him. The first thing we should do when trouble comes is to examine ourselves to make sure we are obeying the Lord.

In today's case of the fiery serpents, Israel's trouble clearly came as a result of disobedience. But just *two verses* before, the Israelites were experiencing trouble because they *were* following God's leading. God had led them once again to a place where they would have to trust Him to supply water. At that point they should have lifted their hands to the Lord and said: "We praise You, God! You have always provided for us before, and You aren't going to let us down this time!" But they grumbled instead of trusting, and that's when God sent the serpents to bring them to repentance.

When they did confess their sin, the Lord commanded Moses to fashion a bronze serpent and put it on a pole. If anyone was bitten by a snake, he could look to the snake on the pole and be healed. You no doubt have seen that the medical profession uses the symbol of the snake on the pole for its emblem. I've actually heard Christians say that proves the medical profession is of the devil! They didn't realize it was right out of the Bible!

That snake on a pole was clearly a type of Christ on the cross. Jesus Himself said, "And as Moses lifted up the serpent in the wilderness, even so must the Son of Man be lifted up; that whoever believes may in Him have eternal life" (John 3:14-15). The question is, why was it a snake on a pole rather than a lamb or some other more common symbol of Christ? Probably because Jesus "became sin" (2 Cor. 5:21) on the cross. Anyone who has "been bitten" by sin can look to Jesus the Savior and be cleansed of the venom of spiritual death that resides within.

After victories against Sihon, king of the Amorites, and Og, king of Bashan, Israel was within sight of the promised land just across the Jordan River. They were now in the territory of the Moabites, descendants of Lot by incest with one of his daughters. Their king, Balak, along with all the Moabites, dreaded what they knew was about to happen to them. They decided to hire a well-known but mysterious prophet named Balaam, who lived four hundred miles to the north, to curse the Israelites. The Lord tells Balaam not to curse Israel because they are blessed by Him, so Balaam tells them he can't take the job. Balak then sends a larger delegation and offers Balaam as much money as he desires, but Balaam tells them he cannot disobey the Lord. Balaam hopes that the Lord will change

His mind, and asks them to stay overnight while he asks the Lord again. From here on, it depends on what version of the Bible you read that determines what God said to Balaam. Some versions indicate that God said it was all right for Balaam to go with them as long as he only spoke what God told him to speak. Other versions indicate God said that if the men came back again, then it would be all right if Balaam went along with them. The second interpretation seems to be the best. We will read tomorrow that God gets angry at Balaam for going with the delegation from Moab. The New Testament indicates that Balaam wanted the money they offered (see 2 Pet. 2:15; Jude 11).

LUKE 1:26-56

Christ had to be born of a virgin, of course, because He existed long before Mary or anyone else. The baby in Mary's womb was not a new person but One who had always existed. According to the angel Gabriel, that child would fulfill the promise to David that one of his descendants would sit on the throne of Israel forever (see 2 Sam. 7:12-13), and He would also fulfill God's promise through Isaiah that the Messiah's kingdom would have no end (see Is. 9:6-7)! Mary didn't doubt Gabriel's word as Zacharias had done.

Many pseudo-intelligent people scoff at the idea of a virgin birth, saying that it would be impossible. But there must be at least ten thousand miracles associated with the conception and development of *every* baby, so what's the big deal if God adds one more miracle by having a baby conceived without the aid of a father's sperm? *Nothing is too difficult for the Lord*, just as Gabriel said.

PSALM 57:1-11

What is so amazing is that these encouraging psalms were written by a man who was undergoing severe trials! While the average person would be writing his will and picking hymns to be sung at his funeral, David was confessing his trust that God would deliver him. Anyone who says he will sing and awaken the dawn has control over his circumstances! Are you awakening the dawn, or is it awakening you? Take charge of your circumstances by faith!

PROVERBS 11:9-11

MARCH 15

NUMBERS 22:21-23:30

If God was angry at Balaam for going with the Moabite delegation, then it must have been (as stated yesterday) that God had told him to go only if the men came to him once again with their request. Or very possibly it wasn't the fact that Balaam went that displeased God, but *his motive for going,* which was to get rich. 2 Peter 2:15-16 says that Balaam loved the wages of unrighteousness. He was in it for the money.

When Balaam's donkey spoke to him, I think we have the first biblical example of "speaking in unknown tongues." As far as I know, Hebrew is a foreign language to donkeys! Balaam was so incensed by his sore foot that he responded to his donkey's question before he realized his donkey was speaking! Many people scoff at the idea that a donkey could actually talk, but once again I must say that nothing is too hard for the Lord. If New Testament believers can speak in languages they've never learned, why can't an Old Testament donkey speak in a language he has never learned?

Once Balaam realized the seriousness of his offense, he offered to turn back, which I think indicates that he knew all along he wasn't supposed to be going. God permitted him to continue, however, and true to the Lord's character, He turned bad into good for Israel. We read today that twice Israel received divine prophetic blessings from Balaam's lips.

This story reminds me of what a pastor friend of mine who lives in Haiti once told me. Haiti is a stronghold for voodoo religion, which holds the people under fear of being cursed by the voodoo priests. My friend told me the curses actually do work—*except on Christians*. "If God is for us, who is against us?" (Rom. 8:31).

LUKE 1:57-80

Both Zacharias and Mary, who had no training in how to prophesy, were used marvelously to do just that. We should be very careful that the Holy Spirit is giving us the unction to prophesy rather than just our own desire motivating us. Only the Lord knows the number of prophecies spoken in churches that are only man-made utterances. If God wants you to prophesy, you will sense the Spirit "pushing it through," and you will find it difficult *not* to prophesy. Many people who prophesy are just sensing what God is saying to them personally, and they interpret it as what God wants them to say to everyone else. Other people think they have to be worked up into a frenzy or some ecstatic state before they can prophesy, but that doesn't seem to have been the case with Zacharias or Mary—or Balaam's donkey!

PSALM 58:1-11

We all love to see a movie where good triumphs over evil in the end. We can praise God that in His plan, good ultimately *will* triumph over evil. That doesn't always happen as soon as we'd like, however, because God shows mercy to evil people, giving them time to repent. We should never doubt God's justice just because He is slow to anger. The day of judgment is coming. Just make sure you're ready yourself.

PROVERBS 11:12-13

Anytime someone says to you, "Now don't tell anyone you heard this from me, but I heard...," you're listening to a tale-bearer. Because we reap what we sow, sooner or later that person will be the subject of someone else's tales.

MARCH 16

NUMBERS 24:1-25:18

For the third time we read that Balaam blessed Israel. Balak is infuriated by it, exclaiming that he will not pay for such sorry service! Although Balaam was mightily used of God, he regrets that he has missed a golden opportunity to make a lot of money. According to Revelation 2:14, Balaam "kept teaching Balak to put a stumbling block before the sons of Israel, to eat things sacrificed to idols, and to commit acts of immorality." Apparently Balaam advised Balak that if he could get Israel to sin, God would judge them Himself. So he advised Balak to have the Moabite women invite the men of Israel to their pagan worship services, which included immoral sexual practices. That they did, and to an extent Balaam's plan worked. We read in chapter 25 that Israel began to play the harlot with the daughters of Moab. Judgment fell, and before the plague ended twenty-four thousand were dead. We will read later that Balaam was subsequently killed by Israel in battle (see 31:8).

Not only did the New Testament writers John and Peter have something to say about the greedy Balaam, but Jude did too: "Woe to them! For they have gone the way of Cain, *and for pay they have rushed headlong into the error of Balaam*, and perished in the rebellion of Korah" (v. 11, italics mine). You can see why we need to know the Old Testament in order to understand the New.

LUKE 2:1-35

When Caesar made his proclamation of a census, Joseph and Mary had no choice but to make the sixty-five-mile journey from Nazareth to Bethlehem to register in Joseph's hometown. The Greek word translated "inn" is the word *kataluma*, which really doesn't describe an inn or hotel as we know it. It refers to a temporary shelter where overflow crowds would sleep during times such as Passover, when masses of people would come to Jerusalem. (There probably was no innkeeper.) For this reason, many believe Jesus was born in the spring, near the time of the Passover, because Jerusalem and nearby Bethlehem would have had *katalumas* erected to accommodate all of the pilgrims. Also, we know that during Passover there would have been numerous shepherds keeping watch over their flocks on the nearby hills, since thousands of lambs would be needed for Passover sacrifices.

More than likely, Jesus was born out in the open, in a stable or in a shepherd's cave near Bethlehem. He was laid in a feeding trough for a cradle. I think you can see it was not a pretty picture; an animal stall isn't exactly the best place for a mother to deliver. Unlike the Christmas cards in which the wise men, shepherds and animals all smile serenely at the warm golden glow from the cradle, the true scene would have been enough to make you weep. Jesus suffered rejection at His birth, during His life and at His death.

Jesus was circumcised according to the law on the eighth day of His life. I'm sure Mary hurt for Jesus as He cried out under the priest's flint knife. She had little idea that just thirty-three years later she would see her Son's blood flow again as He hung from the cross.

It is clear that Joseph and Mary were not wealthy people, because they were only able to offer the poor family's pair of turtledoves or pigeons when they presented baby Jesus at the temple. God had commanded in the twelfth chapter of Leviticus that the mother of a newborn son should bring a one-year-old lamb for a burnt offering, plus a young pigeon or turtledove for a sin offering. But if she couldn't afford a lamb, then she could substitute a pigeon or turtledove. However, within about two years, when the wise men arrived with their gifts, Joseph and Mary suddenly became very prosperous. They probably needed the money to sustain them in Egypt when they were hiding from Herod.

The short story of Simeon, who knew supernaturally that Jesus was the Messiah, indicates there were some spiritual people living at that time who were looking for the promised Christ. It was then just as it is now: sincere people seek for God, and hypocritical religious people profess to know God but deny Him by their deeds.

PSALM 59:1-17

Have you noticed how David expressed his faith in every trial? If he were alive today, he would no doubt be criticized as "one of those positive confession preachers"! The same could be said for Joshua and Caleb. Personally, I would rather be criticized along with Joshua, Caleb and David than perish in the wilderness with the critics! The occasion of this psalm was when David's life *was in danger from all quarters*. Yet he said he would sing joyfully of God's lovingkindness. How could he be so happy? Because he already knew the outcome: God would deliver him from all his afflictions. He reminds me of Paul and Silas, who were singing praises to God at midnight while they were chained to the wall in a prison (see Acts 16:22-30). If you have faith, you can smile at adversity! Check out your faith today when you look in the mirror.

PROVERBS 11:14

It's good to seek guidance as long as it comes from people who know God. When the twelve spies trekked into Canaan, the majority brought back a bad report and brought ruin to all who listened to them. Make sure *your* counselors are full of faith.

MARCH 17

NUMBERS 26:1-51

It had been about thirty-eight years from the first census of Numbers 1, and we know that at least 1.2 million people died during that time due to God's judgment upon their sin. God had kept His word. The purpose of this census seems to have been for the fair division of the land Israel was about to inherit.

LUKE 2:36-52

Luke is the only Gospel writer who tells us anything about Jesus' childhood. Many have wondered what Jesus was like during His younger years, but we have to trust that if God wanted us to know more, He would have told us more. From this little excerpt in Luke, we know Jesus was not an average child but showed signs of great maturity and spirituality even at a young age. No doubt His parents never had any trouble with Him, except in this case where His hunger to learn kept Him in Jerusalem after the Passover. He was not rebellious during His teenage years, didn't spend any time sowing wild oats as a young man and lived His life in *perfect* accordance with the laws of Moses. Of course, Jesus never performed any miracles until age thirty and had no special anointing to preach or teach until then, either. He was probably known in Nazareth as a very, very good man.

PSALM 60:1-12

Here we read an urgent cry for help against Israel's enemies Moab, Edom and Philistia. We know this prayer was answered according to God's promise in verse 8 and the faith expressed in verse 12: "Through God we shall do valiantly, and it is He who will tread down our adversaries." That's another positive confession that we should all be saying.

PROVERBS 11:15

Remember that "going surety" would be the equivalent of our co-signing a loan.

MARCH 18

NUMBERS 26:52-28:15

If you have thought God was a male chauvinist, now you know better. Those daughters of Zelophehad wanted to share in the land that was being doled out to everyone else. Their father had died without having any sons, and it looked as if their family would inherit no land because of it. But God plainly said to Moses, "The daughters of Zelophehad are right in their statements," and He enacted a new law to settle all future controversies of this nature. My point is that *God wants women to receive their inheritance just as much as men.*

It was almost time for Moses to die (he was 120 years old), and God allowed him to see the promised land even though he couldn't enter it. The Lord designated Joshua, who had been working closely with Moses for the past forty years, as Israel's new leader. Notice that Moses laid his hands on Joshua at his "ordination service." This was not an empty ritual but an actual transfer of God's anointing. Joshua would need supernatural ability for the task that lay before him.

LUKE 3:1-22

John the Baptist's statement that his listeners needed to bring forth fruits in keeping with their repentance certainly applies to all of us. If we have truly repented of something, we will turn away from it with God's help.

I have seen so many Christians come forward at dedication services, ask God's forgiveness, but there is no change in their behavior. If we have truly repented, then we should bring forth the fruits of our repentance! If we make a quality decision to obey God, no demon can stop us. Our primary problem is that we don't really believe that Jesus has set us free from the power of sin. The New Testament teaches that *we don't have to sin anymore, because the power of sin has been broken over our lives!* Jesus was speaking of the power of sin when He said: "If therefore the Son shall make you free, you shall be free indeed." We are no longer slaves to sin, and once you believe that in your heart, bad habits are a thing of the past. Once you believe it, you are free of the daily condemnation of constant sin. Jesus is not only your Savior but your deliverer from sin!

PSALM 61:1-8

Sometimes as we read through the psalms, we come to the Hebrew word *Selah* in the text. It is thought that the word means we're to pause at that point, or that possibly there was an instrumental interlude at that place. When we read the word as we have today, we should stop to reflect for a few moments. *The psalms were not meant to be read in a hurry.* Instead, we should meditate upon them, and allow them to cause faith to rise up within us. If you obeyed the "selah" today, you would have imagined yourself like a little chick sheltered under its mother's wings, taking refuge from the cold winds of life!

PROVERBS 11:16-17

The reason a merciful man does himself good is that people who sow mercy reap mercy. *When you are mistreated or ignored, look on that situation as an opportunity to store up some mercy for yourself!*

MARCH 19

NUMBERS 28:16-29:40

Today's reading was not particularly interesting, but it was essential information for old covenant Israelites. We have already discussed the feasts and their significance in the commentary on Leviticus 23, so you can refer back to that to refresh your memory. They all anticipated the atoning work of Jesus Christ.

LUKE 3:23-38

Today's genealogy of Jesus was through Mary. Matthew's listing was Jesus' genealogy through Joseph, who (of course) was not really Jesus' father.

PSALM 62:1-12

You can just feel the strength of David's inward conviction that the Lord was his Rock as you read this psalm. Notice that David spoke to his soul (mind) and told it to wait in silence for God. When our souls want to dwell on thoughts of doubt, we need to do the same. David's mind was screaming at him to be *reasonable* and quit trusting in God. But he was determined to hold fast in faith. Let's follow his example and not give in to doubts. Hold fast! Darkness comes before the dawn!

PROVERBS 11:18-19

MARCH 20

NUMBERS 30:1-31:54

Chapter 30 deals with the law of vows. All vows that were made were binding, except in the case of an unmarried woman, whose vow could be annulled by her father, and a married woman, whose vow could be annulled by her husband. If anything, this chapter should emphasize the seriousness of keeping our word and always telling the truth.

In chapter 31, God commanded Israel to take vengeance on the Midianites. It seems the words *Midianites* and *Moabites* are used interchangeably in these passages. The Midianites were the ones who enticed the men of Israel to participate in the immoral worship of Baal at the advice of the apostate prophet Balaam (see 31:16). Those people were extremely wicked and deserved exactly what they got, or God would not have executed such severe judgment. Balaam himself was killed during the battle (see 31:8).

After the battle, the spoils were divided. One five-hundredth of the armies' portion went to the priests, and one-fiftieth of the people's portion went to the Levites. *God never blesses us so we can keep all the blessing to ourselves.* We should never forget to give back the Lord's portion.

LUKE 4:1-30

Before Jesus entered into His public ministry, two things took place. First, the Holy Spirit descended upon Him in bodily form like a dove. *Before any Christian enters into ministry for the Lord, he too needs to be baptized in the Holy Spirit.*

Second, He had to be tested. Notice that it was the *Holy Spirit* who led Him into the wilderness to be tempted by the devil (see 4:1). Every believer will go through times of testing. This is especially true of those who enter full-time ministry. God only promotes those He can trust. If we prove ourselves faithful in small things, then the Lord knows He can trust us with bigger things. Of course, Jesus passed His forty days of testing with flying colors!

For a discussion of the specific temptations Jesus experienced, please see my comments on Matthew 4:1-11.

We have already read in Mark's Gospel that Jesus encountered unbelief in His hometown of Nazareth and so could not do any miracles there except for healing a few people with minor ailments. Luke's Gospel gives us more details and helps us to understand Jesus' ministry. Jesus read a text from Isaiah that actually spoke of Himself and how He was anointed by the Holy Spirit for supernatural ministry. According to Isaiah, Jesus was anointed to preach, to bring deliverance and to heal; that (of course) is what we see Him doing throughout Scripture. He wanted the people to believe that He was God's anointed so they could receive all the blessings He had to offer them. Unfortunately, very few believed His message, and Jesus was hindered by their lack of faith.

The same is true for us today. All we can do is tell people the good news that Jesus will save, deliver and heal them. If they refuse to believe it, we are hindered.

We know Jesus had already performed quite a few miracles in Capernaum before this, and the news had traveled to Nazareth, only about twenty miles away. The people had been waiting to see their "hometown boy turned miracle-worker" perform some tricks for them—not with expectancy, but with skepticism. Jesus told them a prophet is not without honor except in His hometown, and then He proved His point with two biblical examples of prophets' helping Gentile people. (We will read both of these stories when we get to 1 Kings.)

We have no record of Jesus' performing any miracle prior to His baptism and the testing in the wilderness. Yet when Jesus emerges from the wilderness He returns to Galilee in the power of the Spirit (Luke 4:14).

The apostle Paul records that the Lord once said to him, "My grace is sufficient for you, for power is perfected in weakness" (2 Cor. 12:9). It is in times of testing that we learn our limitations and the power of God available to us when we trust in His ability.

God always uses broken vessels through which to pour out His power. He doesn't anoint those with power who cannot sympathize with those who are in need of it. The writer of Hebrews said, "For we do not have a high priest who cannot sympathize with our weaknesses, but one who has been tempted in all things as we are, yet without sin" (Heb. 4:15).

Jesus' listeners, who had spoken so highly of Him at the beginning of His sermon, were now ready to throw Him off a nearby cliff. Why? Probably because they didn't like hearing how God passed up Israelites to bless Gentiles. (Sometimes God's people are more heathen than the heathen, aren't they?) You can visit that cliff in Nazareth today, and I can guarantee you that if someone threw you from it, as one little boy exclaimed, "it would kill you *constantly*!" But Jesus escaped supernaturally.

PSALM 63:1-11

I had never seen *how much faith* David had in his trials until I read through the Psalms for this commentary. It is amazing to me. David said by faith that "those who seek my life, to destroy it...will be delivered over to the power of the sword." If this psalm was referring to the time when David was fleeing from King Saul, what David said came to pass. Saul died by the sword. David was obviously not one who just praised God in church, but all the time. How about you? *Do you lift up your hands to God even during times of trial?* Paul said we should "rejoice in the Lord always" (Phil. 4:4).

PROVERBS 11:20-21

Because I don't comment on some of the proverbs doesn't mean they aren't important. It probably just means the proverb is self-explanatory and needs no comment. One of those times is today.

MARCH 21

NUMBERS 32:1-33:39

Moses' initial concern with the Gadites' and Reubenites' request to settle on the east side of the Jordan was that they would *discourage* the other people of Israel. According to Moses, that's what had happened forty years before, when ten of the twelve spies brought back an evil report; they discouraged the people who believed them, and consequently they *all* perished in the wilderness. *What a serious offense it is to discourage fellow members of the body of Christ from entering into what God has promised them!* May God have mercy on all the so-called ministers who have discouraged sincere Christians. Even if we conduct a service that is geared to get folks to repent, after they repent they should be encouraged to know that God has forgiven them and the future is brighter than ever.

The Gadites, Reubenites and half-tribe of Manasseh worked out a deal with Moses and so possessed the land on the east side of the Jordan. Their decision to occupy what was not really part of the promised land would later prove to be a bad one. We'll read in the book of Joshua how it almost caused civil war between east and west. On top of that, about five hundred years later, when God permitted Assyria to conquer Israel for its apostasy, the first tribes to be carried into captivity were Gad, Reuben and Manasseh. Compromise always has its price.

LUKE 4:31-5:11

Those who make fun of Christians who rebuke sicknesses are making fun of Jesus, who rebuked the fever in Peter's mother-in-law. Some will say, "But that was Jesus who rebuked the fever; He was the Son of God." But didn't Jesus Himself say that we who believe in Him would do the same works He did (see John 14:12)? And didn't Jesus say we could speak to mountains and make them move? If we really believe something, we will talk as if we believe it.

Jesus doesn't heal just "big" sicknesses or diseases either. He doesn't heal only blindness, deafness, lameness and cancer; He also heals colds, sore throats, earaches and fevers. *Anything that qualifies as sickness qualifies for healing by the Lord.*

The Lake of Gennesaret, the Sea of Chinnereth and the Sea of Galilee are all the same body of water. What you called it all depended on your standpoint.

(Some good folks from Texas, when asked what country they're from, always reply, "Texas!" They have a little different perspective from the rest of us.)

The story of Peter's catching all the fish demonstrates several spiritual principles. First, *it always pays to trust the words of Jesus in spite of what circumstances might be saying*. Peter and his companions had worked all night and had not caught any fish. The reason they worked all night is because they knew from experience that night was the time to catch the fish they were after. Now it was day. They were tired and ready to go home after an unprofitable night's work. Plus, they had already washed their nets. However, their obedience to Jesus paid off!

Second, the experience demonstrated to Peter, who would soon be fishing for men, that *Jesus knew where the fish were*. We should always get Jesus' plan for evangelizing certain areas instead of just working our own programs. The Holy Spirit has been given to help us do that job.

Third, *if we give to God, He will give back to us abundantly*. It was Peter's boat that Jesus had borrowed, and it was Peter's boat that was filled with fish.

Fourth, *God loves to prosper us*. The boats were sinking, and the nets were breaking with blessing! I believe God will give us wisdom to succeed in our jobs as well.

PSALM 64:1-10

We, like David, sometimes have to encourage ourselves that God is righteous and that it does ultimately pay to obey Him, even though we are tempted to doubt as we see evil plans temporarily succeed. If it looks as if evil people are winning now, don't worry about it. Their day is coming! Pray that they will open their hearts to Jesus before then.

PROVERBS 11:22

MARCH 22

NUMBERS 33:40-35:34

Today we read again that God was driving the Canaanites from their land because of their gross sin. God told the Israelites to destroy all the idols and high places in the land. Those were the places where babies were thrown alive into fires, and where gross sexual immoralities took place mixed with pagan worship. The Lord said that if the Israelites didn't remove them, they would become thorns in the Israelites' sides and pricks in their eyes.

Unfortunately, some Christians have been taught that Canaan is a type of heaven—our promised land. Canaan *doesn't* represent heaven, because there will be no battles to be fought there! Canaan represents the rights and privileges we have in Christ that we must possess by faith in God's promises. It wasn't easy for Israel to possess its inheritance, and it didn't happen overnight. We, too, must fight the devil and his demons, the world, the flesh and sometimes even unbelieving Christians if we're going to possess what is rightfully ours through the blood of Christ. Many Christians spend their entire lives wandering in the desert. Their walk with God consists of taking short "vacations" back to Egypt and then repenting out in the desert another time! God wants us to get beyond that stage. *Get out of the desert, stay out of Egypt and start entering the promised land.*

In chapter 34 we read of the borders of the land God was giving Israel. Those would be roughly the borders of modern Israel (including the so-called occupied West Bank), except that today the countries of Jordan and Syria occupy the east bank of the Jordan, which was then possessed by Reuben, Gad and Manasseh. You probably have a map in the back of your Bible that shows this division.

The Levites were not given any inheritance of land, but rather forty-eight cities with pasturage. This was so the Levites would be scattered throughout all of Israel. They were to somewhat fill the role of modern-day pastors. Of those forty-eight cities, God designated six which would be "cities of refuge." If a person accidentally killed another person, he could flee to one of those cities and be guaranteed a fair trial. Apparently the ancient people would enter into covenants with each other, which guaranteed that if someone killed him, his covenant partner was bound to revenge the death. Such arrangements offered a degree of protection for the average person. The manslayer's only guarantee of safety was if he remained within the borders of one of the cities of refuge until the death of the high priest. If he was caught outside the borders by the "blood avenger," then the "blood avenger" could kill him. After the death of the high priest he could return to his original home.

At a trial, a person could not be put to death based on the testimony of just one witness. God commanded that there be at least two witnesses, which may sound like fundamental justice to you and me, but it was probably revolutionary jurisprudence at the time! God also commanded the death sentence for murderers.

LUKE 5:12-28

We have already read both of these healing stories in Matthew and Mark, so there's not much new that I can say. Luke makes one statement that Matthew and Mark don't, however: great multitudes were coming to *hear Jesus and to be healed* of their sicknesses (v. 15). Many Christians attend every healing meeting they can, hoping that they will be healed by Jesus, when what they should be doing first is *listening to the words of Jesus*. Listen to what Jesus has said about how to receive healing. Most times, people must hear first if they are to be healed. Once you've heard God's Word and your faith has grown, you won't need to rely upon someone else's prayers to receive from God. You'll know that the Lord will hear and answer your prayers as fast as any evangelist's.

There are a number of cults that call themselves Christian but deny that Jesus was *God in the flesh*. They will admit Jesus was the *s*on of God (small s), but not that He was the *S*on of God (capital S, indicating deity). That is heresy. Throughout the Bible, Jesus' standing as fully God is clearly established. Today we read that He forgave sins, and even the Pharisees and scribes realized that because only God Himself has that power, Jesus was claiming to be God (see vv. 20-24).

PSALM 65:1-13

Isn't it amazing that people can view the marvel of creation daily but still deny the existence of God? David did a beautiful job under the Holy Spirit's inspiration of describing how great and wondrous God's creation is. Everything works together in a delicate balance, and even the growing of grain is a miracle beyond our understanding.

PROVERBS 11:23

MARCH 23

NUMBERS 36:1-DEUTERONOMY 1:46

The final chapter of Numbers deals with the resolution of one more legal dispute concerning the land. God had already decreed that if a man died with no sons, his land would be inherited by his daughters, as in the case of Zelophehad. Some of the Israelites from the Zelophehad's tribe realized, however, that if Zelophehad's daughters married men from other tribes, their tribe (Manasseh) would lose some of its land when Zelophehad's daughter's sons inherited it. So a second decree was made saying that Zelophehad's daughters (or any other women in similar circumstances) may only marry men from their own tribe. That way, the apportioned pieces of land would remain with tribes to which they originally belonged.

All this is rather irrelevant today, but it demonstrates that *God is completely fair*. Also, the incident gives us a glimpse of the somewhat limited unity between the tribes of Israel. They were willing to work together to conquer the inhabitants of Canaan, yet they still maintained strong tribal allegiance. Later we'll read of a split in the kingdom and years of civil war. In this passage, we see some of the seeds of disunity being sown.

Deuteronomy is the last of the five books written by Moses, which together are referred to as the Pentateuch. Deuteronomy could be subtitled "Moses' Last Words." It is his final sermon, addressed to the children of the disobedient (and now dead) Israelites who failed to possess their inheritance. In it he repeats many laws we've already heard. But remember he was speaking to a new generation. Moses knew God better than anyone in his era and was no doubt one of the greatest men of God in all history. The date of the events of Deuteronomy is approximately 1260 B.C.

As Moses recounted the events of forty years prior, he gave some fresh details. For example, the idea of spying out the land came from the people, not God, as we would have thought from the account in Numbers (see 1:22).

Also, God told Moses that Joshua would be the one to lead the people into their inheritance, so Moses should encourage him (see 1:38). We need more people to *encourage* the leaders of the church. Ministers don't need their fellow Christians to discourage them—they have the world and the devil to do that! The Bible says we all should encourage one another day by day (see Heb. 3:13). *Are you an encourager or a discourager?*

LUKE 5:29-6:11

Israel was under Roman domination during the time of Jesus. Roman officials sold the right to collect taxes in a certain area to the highest bidder, who would then be the chief tax collector. However, the tax collectors would charge a rate that greatly exceeded what Rome required, pocketing the difference and thus earning a very good living. They were looked upon as cheats and traitors by the average Jew.

Before you condemn the Pharisees for criticizing Jesus, consider how you would react if you saw Jesus go into a gay bar and have a meal with a group of homosexuals. That might bring it into better perspective. Jesus came to rescue sinners. The only way to do that is to talk with them. The only way to talk with them is to be with them. The only way to be with them is to go where they are. God never commanded sinners to go to church! He commanded saints to go to the sinners!

For an explanation of new wine in old

wineskins, please see my comments on Matthew 9:15-17.

You may have wondered why Jesus and the disciples were going through someone else's fields and eating his grain. Isn't that stealing? No, not according to the law of Moses. (It would be under our law, of course.) In Deuteronomy 23:25 we will read this commandment: "When you enter your neighbor's standing grain, then you may pluck the heads with your hand, but you shall not wield a sickle in your neighbor's standing grain." Notice that the Pharisees were only angry that Jesus was picking the heads of wheat on the Sabbath, and not that He was stealing someone else's wheat! Jesus obeyed the law completely and never transgressed even the most insignificant requirement.

PSALM 66:1-20

What an encouraging psalm this one is! In verse 10 the psalmist said, "For Thou hast tried us, O God; Thou hast refined us as silver is refined." How is silver refined? It's heated up, which causes the impurities to rise to the top, where they're scraped off, leaving behind purer silver. So, too, in our lives, when trying circumstances "heat us up" and the impurities rise to the surface, God scrapes them off, leaving behind a purer, more holy vessel. If you look back over your Christian life, you'll see you grew the most spiritually during times of trial. Trials cause us to dig into and trust God's Word and draw closer to Him.

PROVERBS 11:24-26

Do you want increase? Then scatter. Do you want to be prosperous? Be generous. Do you want less? Hoard what you have. Do you want to be poor? Be stingy. God's ways sure are different from man's, aren't they?

MARCH 24

DEUTERONOMY 2:1-3:29

It is interesting that God had not only decreed that *Israel* would possess the land of Canaan, but He had chosen territories for other nations as well. Paul said in one of his sermons in Athens, "[God] made from one, every nation of mankind to live on all the face of the earth, having determined their appointed times, and *the boundaries of their habitation*, that they should seek God..." (Acts 17:26-27, italics mine). Nobody fully understands God's sovereignty, but we have no doubt that God has always had His hand in history, which is truly "His story."

History is really determined by humanity's response to God. In Jeremiah 18:7-10, God said, "At one moment I might speak concerning a nation or concerning a kingdom to uproot, to pull down, or to destroy it; if that nation against which I have spoken turns from its evil, I will relent concerning the calamity I planned to bring on it. Or at another moment I might speak concerning a nation or concerning a kingdom to build up or to plant it; if it does evil in My sight by not obeying My voice, then I will think better of the good with which I had promised to bless it."

Moses also said God had hardened the spirit of Sihon, king of Heshbon, and made his heart obstinate. This no doubt was the same as in the case of Pharaoh of Egypt. God does not harden the hearts of sincere, God-seeking people. To further His purposes, God sometimes hardens those whose hearts are already beyond repentance.

LUKE 6:12-38

I must believe that Jesus' sermons were relevant to the people to whom He was speaking. Although there isn't much in the Gospels about it, Jesus' followers *must have been receiving a lot of persecution*. I say that so you can better understand the next few verses, which have been so misunderstood because they have been taken out of context.

Jesus said, "But woe to you who are rich, for you are receiving your comfort in full" (v. 24). I, like you, have most of the comforts that the majority of Americans enjoy. By worldwide standards, we're rich. Was Jesus saying woe to us? If so, He was also saying woe to Abraham, Isaac, Jacob, David, Solomon, Job, Hezekiah and a host of other wealthy yet godly Bible characters. No, Jesus was acknowledging that many had decided *not* to follow Him because they didn't want to experience the financial hardships they knew would result (they might lose their jobs, would have to repent of certain business practices, etc). Jesus was saying *woe* to them. I say woe to anyone who lets anything stand in the way of following Jesus!

When Jesus said, "Woe to you who laugh now," He wasn't saying that it is wrong for us to have a good time or tell a joke. He was referring to those who were laughing at His followers.

Jesus' statements regarding turning the other cheek and so on are extraordinary. They apply to *believers who are being persecuted for their faith*. If some thief tries to rob me of my TV, I'm not going to offer him my stereo also. But if the persecution against Christians gets so out of hand that a non-Christian comes to my home and demands my TV *because I am a Christian* and he knows the law will not prosecute him, I'll tell him: "These possessions are meaningless to me, and if by giving them to you I can soften your heart to accept my Savior, then I give them to you freely. God bless you!"

You may think persecution against Christians could never get that bad, but it can, and it has. According to the book of Hebrews, some of the early Christians "accepted joyfully the seizure of [their] property" (Heb. 10:34). In the book of Revelation we're told that in the end times, unless a person takes the mark of the beast, which guarantees his damnation, he won't be able to buy or sell anything!

Jesus' sermon is an absolute masterpiece worthy of hours of meditation. In my opinion, the most important sentence would be verse 31: "And just as you want people to treat you, treat them in the same way." Our relationships would improve dramatically if we would do just that.

PSALM 67:1-7

According to verse 7, God blesses us so that all the ends of the earth may fear Him. This is a good motivation for wanting to be blessed of God—that others might recognize that God is alive and blesses those who follow Him. I love to tell unbelievers about the goodness of God in my life!

PROVERBS 11:27

MARCH 25

DEUTERONOMY 4:1-49

Some people have questioned how God could be love (see 1 John 4:8) and how Moses could say that God is a jealous God (see 4:24) when Paul taught that *love is not jealous* (see 1 Cor. 13:4). A key verse that gives the answer is 2 Corinthians 11:2, where Paul said, "For I am jealous for you with a *godly jealousy*" (italics mine). Godly jealousy is the unselfish kind of jealousy parents have for their children. I want my children to be closer to my wife and me than anyone else, because I know that's best for them. In the same way, God is jealous for us.

In this sermon Moses prophesied exactly what would happen to Israel in the future. In verses 25-30, he forewarned that they would remain long in the land, but then they would turn away from God and serve idols. Consequently, God would scatter them to other nations, where they would repent, and then God would restore them. *That's exactly what came to pass about five hundred years later*, and we'll read all about it in a few months.

LUKE 6:39-7:10

Jesus' example of taking a speck out of someone else's eye while you have a log in yours must have caused His listeners to chuckle. His observation is so true of human nature. I've found that the people who are most critical of others usually have the *least right to be critical* because they have so many faults themselves. If fault-finders would turn their searchlight on themselves, they would turn it off permanently! Of course, there is a difference between *constructive* criticism and *destructive* criticism. Constructive criticism is *offered*; destructive criticism is *given*. When I am offered *constructive* criticism, I receive it, and I thank God for the person who offered it. He is still my good friend. When I am given *destructive* criticism, I resist it, and I hope I don't see that person for a while! I have a hard time receiving criticism from people who have logs in their eyes!

Jesus also said we can tell what's in a person's heart by what comes out of his mouth. A person full of hatred speaks hatred; a person full of love speaks love. What's coming out of your mouth?

Many Christians are not building their house on the rock of Christ even though they attend church two or three times a week. The only people who are truly building their lives on the rock are those who *hear and obey* God's Word. *The trials of life come to us all, but only the "doers of the Word" are able to weather the storms.*

This centurion who requested that Jesus heal his slave (or possibly his son) certainly demonstrated great faith. He believed that Jesus didn't have to be physically present in order for his son to be healed, but that Jesus only had to speak the word. God wants our faith to grow to the point where we will believe that the pastor doesn't have to lay hands upon us in order to be healed. He wants us to believe that any of us can make our requests to the Lord ourselves, and that God will hear and answer our prayers. God has no favorite children, and He will hear and answer your prayers as fast as anyone else's!

PSALM 68:1-18

At least part of this psalm spoke prophetically of the Lord Jesus. According to the book of Ephesians, verse 18 refers to what happened after Christ's resurrection. Possibly the "captives" spoken of here that He "led captive" were all those who had died in faith and who were waiting in paradise (in the heart of the earth) for Jesus to take them to heaven. The gifts that He gave (also spoken of in verse 18) were the ministry gifts of apostles, prophets, evangelists, pastors and teachers, according to Ephesians 4:11. Did you know that your pastor was a gift to you from Jesus?

PROVERBS 11:28

MARCH 26

DEUTERONOMY 5:1-6:25

All of this is easy to understand, isn't it? I like it when things are spelled out so black is black and white is white. If there is one theme in what we have read today, and if there is one theme in the whole book of Deuteronomy, it is this: "Obey God and be blessed. Disobey God and be cursed." We have already heard the Ten Commandments when we read Exodus 20, but today we get another interesting glimpse of the Lord's heart. In verse 29 of chapter 5 we read God Himself saying: "Oh that they had such a heart in them, that they would fear Me, and keep all My commandments always, that it may be well with them and with their sons forever!" Can you see that God *longs* for people to listen to Him so that they will be blessed? God has given us commandments that will make our lives better, because He loves us. If we obey God, the blessings naturally come. Even unsaved people who follow God's principles in a limited way naturally experience the blessings of obedience. *When we don't listen to God, we hurt ourselves.*

Notice that the responsibility for teaching children the Word of God is not given to Sunday school teachers. According to 6:7, parents are responsible to *diligently* teach their children the ways of God. Many Christian parents miss out on God's best, however, because they don't live the same at home as they do in church, and the children easily recognize the hypocrisy and are turned off to Christianity. I think that a child raised by ungodly, non-Christian parents has a better chance that he will wind up serving Jesus than a child raised by lukewarm or hypocritical Christian parents. Raising children is no easy task in our corrupt society, and the highest priority for Christian parents should be to make sure that they are diligently training their children. When it is done half-heartedly, chances are slim that the children will follow God.

God also warned the Israelites that once they became prosperous, they should not forget Him. Prosperity is a great blessing, but it can easily become a curse if it causes a person to be less dedicated to the Lord. Jesus spoke of how the "deceitfulness of riches" could choke God's Word in a person's life. Be careful that when you start making more money, your church attendance, daily prayer, and study and devotion to the Lord don't begin to wane. I've seen it happen numerous times to good Christians.

LUKE 7:11-35

The death of this widow's only son wasn't sad just because of the personal loss of a son, but also because she would now have no means of survival. She didn't have social security to fall back on, so if Jesus had not raised her son from the dead, she was more than likely guaranteed a life of poverty. Does God have feelings? We have just read that Jesus "felt compassion" for this widow. He hurts for hurting people. He doesn't just sympathize with them. He will do something to change their circumstances!

Could you imagine being at a funeral and seeing the dead person get up out of his coffin and speak? That would have a tendency to shake up the funeral attendees! It's no wonder that after Jesus performed this miracle, "fear gripped them all, and they began glorifying God" (v. 16).

While in prison, John the Baptist apparently began to doubt that Jesus was the Messiah, since the long-awaited kingdom had not yet been established. Jesus reassured him by sending back report of His fulfilling the messianic prophecies of Isaiah—His preaching, His healing and His miracles. John would have recognized Jesus' quotations from Isaiah immediately, because he knew that he himself had fulfilled prophecy found in Isaiah 40 (see John 1:23).

PSALM 68:19-35

Verse 19 is a good one to memorize: "Blessed be the Lord, who daily bears our burden...." We need to let the Lord bear our burdens and not try to bear them ourselves. Why don't you just cast all your cares on Him right now and let Him work out those things you're worrying about? You'll feel ten pounds lighter!

PROVERBS 11:29-31

When Solomon speaks of "troubling your own house," he is not speaking of a house of bricks and mortar. He is speaking of a person's family and relatives. Possibly what Solomon is saying here is that when it comes time for inheritances to be passed out, the person who has caused trouble in his family will get nothing.

MARCH 27

DEUTERONOMY 7:1-8:20

Do you remember God's earlier statement that He would visit the iniquity of the fathers on the children to the third and fourth generations of those who hated Him? I assume He meant He holds people accountable for sins they pass down through example to their children, who pass them on to their children, and so on. Today we read a similar statement, but notice it says nothing about God's punishing people for their parents' or grandparents' sins: "The Lord your God, He is God, the faithful God, who keeps His covenant and His lovingkindness to a thousandth generation with those who love Him and keep His commandments; but repays those who hate Him to their faces, to destroy them; He will not delay with him who hates Him, He will repay him to his face" (7:9-10). Only the *guilty person* is repaid, not his children or grandchildren.

If Israel obeyed, God would bless them in every area of life that was significant to them. He promised that no one would be barren. He promised that no one's cattle would be barren (7:14)! Now, if God loved Israel enough to heal their cattle of barrenness, don't you think He loves us, His children, enough so that none of us will be barren as well? Absolutely yes.

God also promised that He would remove from them all sickness (7:15)! If we have a better covenant established on better promises (Heb. 8:6), then healing *must* be included in our new covenant, or else it's not better than the old one. Thank God that healing *is* a part of our covenant. Of course, Israel had to *obey* God to walk in divine health. We do too. We can't expect God's best unless we are giving Him our best.

In chapter 8 Moses plainly said God had been testing Israel for forty years in order to know what was in their hearts, whether or not they would obey His commandments (8:2). God uses various methods to test. One way He tested Israel, according to 8:3, is that He let them go hungry. He wanted Israel to know that "man does not live by bread alone, but man lives by everything that proceeds out of the mouth of the Lord" (8:3). God wants us to be completely dependent on Him, looking to Him as our source for everything. God disciplines us just as a father disciplines his son (8:5). He is dedicated to our spiritual growth, and it's much easier if we cooperate with His plan! The whole purpose of God's testings is to *do good for us in the end* (8:16)!

Finally, may I say that this chapter reaffirms the fact that God wants to abundantly prosper His own, as long as it doesn't distract them from serving Him. We must never forget that God gives "the power to make wealth" (8:18). I fear for Christians who talk about how much money *they* have made.

LUKE 7:36-8:3

The question is, how could this sinful woman wet Jesus' feet with her tears, wipe them with her hair, and then kiss His feet and anoint them with perfume? She was standing *behind* Him while He was eating a meal at a table. The answer is that in Jesus' day, people ate their meals *lying down*, propped up on one arm, and feeding themselves from food at a center table with their free hand. (Thus the expression: "They reclined at table....") So it was very easy for this woman to do what the Bible said she did!

Notice that Jesus didn't stop this woman from worshipping Him. He was God, and God should be worshipped. There's no way Jesus could have just been a "good man." A mere good man wouldn't let someone worship him. Jesus was either God or a terrible person, and we know which of those is true.

Simon the Pharisee had not extended the common courtesy of having Jesus' feet washed when He entered his house. (That was always done in Jesus' day, as people's sandaled feet became quite dirty walking on unpaved streets.) Nor did Simon offer Jesus the common greeting kiss or anoint His head with oil. Once again, God can tell what is in our hearts by our actions. This "sinful woman," who probably was a harlot, expressed her great love and reverence for Jesus. She had been forgiven of much, and her faith was what saved her. *People who know they have been forgiven by God act like it. They are grateful and want to serve Him for the rest of their lives.*

Jesus' ministry was and is supported by individual donations from people who love Him (8:3). *God's ministry goes on because people who love Him give money to see that it continues.*

PSALM 69:1-18

This is another psalm that contains prophecies concerning Christ's ministry and crucifixion. Verse 9 says, "For zeal for Thy house has consumed me." According to John 2:17, this scripture was fulfilled by Jesus when He cast the moneychangers from the temple.

PROVERBS 12:1

Wise people receive constructive criticism. Fools don't.

MARCH 28

DEUTERONOMY 9:1-10:22

If we haven't understood before, God couldn't have made it clearer than He does today. It wasn't because of Israel's righteousness that God was bringing them into the promised land, but because of the present inhabitants' wickedness (see 9:4-5). And believe me, *these nations had to be incredibly wicked for God to take such severe measures against them.*

There's not much to explain about today's portion of Moses' great sermon, but I hope you're enjoying it as much as I am. Everything he says today you should remember from previous readings, because it's just a recap of forty years of history in the desert.

LUKE 8:4-21

We have already read the parable of the sower in both Matthew and Mark. Luke adds one little significant phrase. Speaking of the person who represents the "good ground," Jesus said that person has an "honest and good heart." The condition of the heart determines if people will receive Jesus into their lives. We should never hesitate to share the gospel just because it appears they have hard hearts. God's Word can *change* hearts. I have seen people who seemingly were hard-shell cases who have wept with repentance at the hearing of the gospel. And I have seen people who seemed so soft and kind vehemently resist the message of God's love through Christ. The gospel is really what will reveal what is in a person's heart. The writer of the book of Hebrews said that the Word of God is like a two-edged sword, which is able to cut to the point of division between a person's soul and spirit (Heb. 4:12). Many people have soft souls but hard spirits, and other people have hard souls but soft spirits!

Once we know the truth, it is our responsibility to share it with others, rather than "putting our lamp under a bushel." If we hear and receive God's Word, more revelation will be given to us. But if we refuse to listen to God's initial revelation, we will lose even what we think we already possess (see v. 18).

PSALM 69:19-36

I'm sure you picked out the messianic prophecies in this portion of Psalm 69. In verse 21, the psalmist said he was given gall and vinegar, just as Christ was when on the cross (see Matt. 27:34). He said in verse 26 that they had persecuted "him whom Thou Thyself hast smitten." Truly this was the case during Jesus' crucifixion, as He bore upon Himself the sins of the world, and therefore the wrath of God. Why did the Holy Spirit hide these messianic prophecies in psalms written by David while he was going through trials? Possibly because God was hiding His plan from the devil. According to 1 Corinthians 2:8, if the devil and his demons had known what was actually being accomplished on the cross, they would never have inspired men to crucify Jesus. Satan didn't realize it, but he played right into God's hands. The very thing he thought would defeat God's plan actually helped to accomplish it!

PROVERBS 12:2-3

MARCH 29

DEUTERONOMY 11:1-12:32

Moses told the people that the land they were about to inherit was not like the land of Egypt, where they had to water their crops "with their feet." He was referring to the use of waterwheels, which were used to pump water from the Nile to irrigate crops. God said that Canaan was a land well-watered with rains, and as long as the people walked in obedience, their crops would always be watered. Again and again we see the theme: "Obey God and be blessed. Disobey God and be cursed."

The Lord never wanted Israel to forget His commandments, so He told them to impress His words on their hearts and souls (see 11:18). He also said they should bind them as a sign on their hands and as frontals on their foreheads. If you've ever seen an Orthodox Jew during his time of ritualistic prayer, you've seen him actually bind a box called a *phylactery* on his wrist and forehead; it contains verses from Exodus and Deuteronomy. God further instructed Israel to write His words on the doorposts of their houses, and Orthodox Jews, right beside their doors, nail a small, thin box called a *mezuzah*, which contains the words of Deuteronomy 6:4-9 and 11:13-21.

You can see how the use of phylacteries and mezuzahs could easily become a meaningless tradition, which it has. I once sat beside an Orthodox Jew on a long flight and watched him go through his ritualistic prayers. I asked him what it was he was praying as he read from his prayer book, and he said he didn't know because he didn't understand Hebrew! Before I get too critical of the Jews, let me ask: How many Christians always keep a ritualistic copy of the Bible on their coffee tables? God wants His Word *in our hearts*.

God also said He would establish a place where Israelites could bring their tithes, offerings and sacrifices once they were in the promised land. At first, that place was Shiloh, where the tabernacle was set up for several hundred years. Shiloh is an important name to remember. After that, God's designated place became Jerusalem, once Solomon built the great temple there. Because the Levites were scattered throughout Israel, each Israelite town would have had one Levite in their locality who would have been considered "the Levite within their gates" (12:12,18). Each Levite would be supported by the people of his region, because Levites were not given any land like everyone else. At the Feast of Tabernacles (during harvest time), all Israel would travel to God's designated place with "their Levite" and eat part of their tithe during the feast. The extra grain would have then been placed in the "storehouses" located in the temple area (see Mal. 3:10). That extra grain was used to sustain all the Levites.

LUKE 8:22-39

We've read twice before the stories of Jesus' calming the Sea of Galilee and delivering the demon-possessed man who was from the country of the Gerasenes.

Are there demon-possessed people today? Yes, because the same demons of Jesus' day are still around today. In our country, most obviously demon-possessed people get locked away in institutions. Occasionally we hear of someone who hears voices that command him to kill people and so on. Those kinds of people are no doubt demon-possessed. In more primitive countries I've seen demon-possessed people walking completely naked through public areas, with long, twisted hair and filthy bodies. If they get violent, they're normally kept in a cage or tied to a tree like an animal.

No Christian could be demon-possessed, because the Holy Spirit lives in the believer's spirit. However, there is little doubt that Christians can be *demon-oppressed* if they permit it. Being demon-oppressed means the demon does not live inside a person's spirit, but has invaded the soul (mind) or is influencing the thought life. All Christians are attacked periodically in their thoughts by evil spirits who bring doubts, temptations and evil thoughts. We should not entertain those thoughts or allow ourselves to dwell on them but *immediately rebuke them in the name of Jesus* and *replace them with thoughts that are in line with God's Word. Satan has no authority over us unless we give it to him.* Every one of us will have to learn to resist him by faith and obedience to God's Word!

PSALM 70:1-5

This is obviously a prayer of desperation. David exhorts all who seek God (as he was doing in this prayer) to rejoice, be glad and praise God. If you're going through a time of trouble, why don't you stop right now and have a rejoicing session? Show God your faith in His delivering power!

PROVERBS 12:4

MARCH 30

DEUTERONOMY 13:1-15:23

Today we read of another means whereby God might test us. We have to believe that it was the devil who gave him his power to perform a false sign or wonder. However, God said it was a test. In other words, God will evaluate His people when Satan tempts them. Any time we experience one of Satan's temptations, God is watching us to test our obedience. Also remember that God has promised He will not allow us to be tempted beyond what we are able to resist, and that with every temptation, He provides a way of escape (see 1 Cor. 10:13).

God told the Israelites that if anyone—their best friend, their children or even their spouse—tried to influence them to serve other gods, that person should be reported and then stoned to death. Serving God must come before even friends and family. The point of capital punishment is made clear in 13:11. It brings fear to people and deters crime. The only thing that restrains unregenerate people from committing crimes is the fear of being caught. You might say, "But what about good, moral people?" They, too, are motivated by their fear of getting caught. However, their fear is being caught by their other "good, moral friends"! Their moral conduct is determined by the crowd with which they associate. On the other hand, a true Christian's moral conduct is motivated by an inward desire to do right and by the fear of God.

Moses once again restated the law of tithing. Every year, each Israelite brought a tenth of his increase of crops and animals to God's designated place (Shiloh, and later Jerusalem) and rejoiced before God in a sacrificial feast with his family, servants and Levites. Of course, there was no way for them to eat all the tithe in a few meals. The remainder was stored away to sustain the Levites all year long. Every third year, what was known as a "second tithe," according to many *Jewish* commentators, was distributed to the poor, widows, orphans and Levites within one's own town. So the people of Israel gave more than just 10 percent of their increase, yet they were permitted to eat a portion of it themselves. They also gave additional offerings to the Lord.

Some interpret the commands of chapter 15 as God's prohibition of any debt longer than seven years. But no one was mortgaging homes back then. These were simply person-to-person loans, given to help out someone who was struggling financially. Although it's always best to be debt-free, it's not wrong for a new covenant believer to have a thirty-year mortgage based on these verses.

Normally, loans would be paid back within a year at harvest time. It was then that a debtor would have the money to pay back his debts. This seven-year mark was not a *remission* of debts—that only happened at the year of Jubilee. This seven-year mark only allowed an extension of one more year for the debtor to pay back his debts. Looking at chapter 15, I think you can understand the temptation that would face people who lent money when the seventh year was drawing near. They would be inclined not to lend money to a hurting friend. It was a good test of their love and faith, because God promised to bless them for their generosity (see 15:10).

LUKE 8:40-9:6

Here we read of two healings already described in Matthew's and Mark's Gospels. In both cases the healings were done in response to the individuals' faith. *In fact, the majority of specific cases of healings performed by Jesus were in response to someone's faith.* It was the minority of cases that would fall under the category of "gifts of healing"—cases in which an individual could be healed without faith. Even atheists have been healed through the manifestation of "gifts of healings." And if the majority of people healed under Christ's earthly ministry were healed by faith, the majority of people who are healed today are going to be healed by faith. Don't wait around for an evangelist whom God uses in special gifts of the Spirit to come through your town in order get your healing! Your evangelist or "special gift of healing" may never come! However, you need to realize that your healing has already come two thousand years ago! By Jesus' stripes you were healed (1 Pet. 2:24). *If Jairus and this woman with the issue of blood can receive healing by faith, so can you.*

Jesus told His disciples to go out and minister from city to city, taking nothing with them. They would have to learn to trust God for their daily needs. Later, Jesus asked them, "When I sent you out without purse and bag and sandals, you did not lack anything, did you?" Their response was, "No, nothing" (Luke 22:35). They were taken care of as they walked in faith, as is everyone who walks by faith.

PSALM 71:1-24

You can almost observe the psalmist's faith grow as you read through this psalm. By the end, he was speaking of what *did* happen (past tense), and it's the same thing he had prayed *to* happen (present tense) just moments before! (Compare v. 13 with v. 24.) Faith "calls into being that which does not exist" (Rom. 4:17). If we believe that we receive when we pray (see Mark 11:24), we will call things into existence as well!

PROVERBS 12:5-7

MARCH 31

DEUTERONOMY 16:1-17:20

We read once again of the three major feasts celebrated by Israel: Passover, Pentecost and Booths. Jesus, of course, faithfully attended all these throughout His earthly life.

We read in chapter 17 that when a person had gone to serve other gods, on the testimony of two or three witnesses he should be stoned to death. Requiring two witnesses ensures justice, as both witnesses can be questioned separately and at length to determine if they have conspired to invent their story. The witnesses were also required to throw the first stones, which would be a further guarantee that true justice prevailed. It would take some *very* evil people to falsely accuse someone and then look into his eyes as they threw the first stones at him. Remember what Jesus said to the men who had caught a woman in the act of adultery? "He who is without sin among you, *let him be the first to throw a stone at her*" (John 8:7, italics mine).

It was God's intention that Israel always remain a theocracy, but He knew they would eventually want to have a king like their neighboring nations did. So He permitted it, and the first king was Saul. God also foresaw the downfall of David's son Solomon, who had no excuse, because God said in verses 16-17 that the king should never multiply horses or wives for himself. Solomon did both, and his seven hundred wives and three hundred concubines turned his heart from God (see 1 Kin. 10:25-11:4). Solomon himself realized in his old age that one wife was best (Eccl. 9:9).

LUKE 9:7-27

The Bible says Herod "kept trying to see" Jesus (v. 9). You would have thought that Jesus would take special time to accommodate this great political figure, but He didn't. Jesus took time to minister to little children, but He gave no special privilege to King Herod.

The feeding of the five thousand was no doubt a stupendous miracle. It demonstrates God's desire to abundantly meet our needs. Usually God uses more natural means to supply our needs, such as giving us a job or giving us wisdom, but I'm glad to know that if there is no "natural way" to supply my needs, God is not limited, and He can use supernatural means to help us!

We need to meditate on Jesus' words about losing and gaining our lives. The Lord was saying that the person who lives for selfish desires finds only emptiness, and loses the chance to experience life the way God intended. The person who lives for God and His desires will find fulfillment and true life as God planned. The apostle Paul said: "For to me, to live is Christ, and to die is gain" (Phil. 1:21). I've heard some preachers say, "Let Christ into your life!" That's good if they're speaking to non-Christians. But Christians already have Jesus inside them and need to let Him *out*, not in! *Is Christ living through you?*

PSALM 72:1-20

This psalm was written by Solomon. Under his reign, Israel experienced its "golden age," and this prayer may have had a lot to do with the years of prosperity and peace. All of us should be praying for "kings and all who are in authority, in order that we might lead a tranquil and quiet life in all godliness and dignity" (1 Tim. 2:2).

PROVERBS 12:8-9

The Proverbs are full of interesting comparisons, as in verse 9 today. Of course, it would be best to be highly esteemed *and* well-off, but that's rare! It always helps to look at the bright side of your circumstances. One consolation we *always* have is that our circumstances could be worse!

APRIL 1

DEUTERONOMY 18:1-20:20

A clearer idea of how bad things really were in Canaan is presented in chapter 18. The inhabitants were not only throwing their children into fires, but they were also involved in divination, witchcraft, sorcery and spiritism.

Moses promised that God would raise up a prophet like himself, and we know now that he was speaking of the Lord Jesus Christ. Because of this prophecy, the priests and Levites from Jerusalem asked John the Baptist if he were "the Prophet" (see John 1:21). John responded that he was not. Jesus Himself said in John 5:46, "For if you believed Moses, you would believe Me; for he wrote of Me." The apostle Peter also quoted from this promise, and he had no doubts that Jesus was the prophet of whom Moses had spoken (see Acts 3:22-23).

We read one new twist on the Law today concerning the person found guilty of perjury (deliberately giving false testimony while under oath). The perjurer's sentence was to be the same as the defendant would have received had he been found guilty. You can't get any fairer than that.

We also get a revelation of God's great mercy, as He instructed Israel to offer terms of peace to cities that were not in the Canaanite nations. However, Israel was *not* to offer terms of peace to the cities of Canaan. Why? Those cities were past the point of receiving God's mercy and were about to be judged.

LUKE 9:28-50

Isn't it amazing that in the Old Testament, we read about Moses' giving a sermon around 1260 B.C., and now, in the New Testament, about thirteen hundred years later, we read about Moses' talking with Jesus on a mountain? Is there life after death? I'm sure Moses believed in it! I wonder what He was doing all those years?

When Jesus came down from the mountain, He was met by the father of the demon-possessed boy. We have already read this story twice, but let me point out that when Jesus commanded the boy to be brought to Him, almost immediately the boy began to have violent convulsions. You may never have to cast out a demon, but we can learn from this story that *the devil puts on his biggest show when he knows he's in trouble.* Demons try their hardest at the end! *If it seems the devil is trying hard to defeat you, take courage, because that's a good sign your complete victory is near!*

PSALM 73:1-28

This honest psalmist, like most of us, asked the age-old question, "Why do the wicked prosper?" He even began to doubt God's justice and wondered if it was worthwhile to serve God. However, the answer lies in verse 17, when the writer said he perceived "their end." At death, every person must stand before God. It is then that the wicked are ultimately repaid and the righteous are ultimately rewarded.

PROVERBS 12:10

APRIL 2

DEUTERONOMY 21:1-22:30

You're probably beginning to realize that we're reading about a barbaric time period, but all those laws were relevant to the people of that time.

God permitted men to have more than one wife under the old covenant, but He never endorsed it. He created only one woman for Adam, and that standard is clearly the best. Every major character in the Bible who had more than one wife had trouble. Naturally there would be jealousy between wives, and naturally the man would love one of his wives more than the others.

Regardless, according to what we read today, a man had to show complete fairness to his sons of different wives. The firstborn, even if born of an "unloved wife" (that phrase sounds terrible, doesn't it?), was to receive twice what the other sons received.

The punishment of a rebellious son may sound harsh, but for the parents to actually deliver their son over to death would indicate the child was incorrigible. They had to proclaim at the gates of the city that he was stubborn, rebellious, disobedient, a glutton and a drunkard. *I guarantee that after this happened once, there would be a lot of obedient teenagers in the city.*

God forbade men to wear women's clothes, and vice versa. That doesn't mean women can't wear women's pants. But God *is* against the common practice of transvestites, and apparently they existed even back then.

The laws of sexual morality don't leave anything to guesswork. This first law, where a man accused his wife of not being a virgin when he married her, helped to prevent a man from taking a wife only to fulfill carnal desires and then get rid of her by falsely accusing her. A blood-stained sheet from the wedding bed is still used as proof of a woman's virginity in some places in the Middle East.

LUKE 9:51-10:12

It's hard to believe Jesus' disciples had no better grasp of God's character than to think Jesus would want them to call down fire from heaven on the Samaritans because they didn't receive them. God is longsuffering toward obstinate people, as I'm sure you realize from reading the Old Testament. *Isn't it amazing that you better understand God's character than James and John did at that point in their lives?* And to think that those men went on to write a few books of the New Testament! They were the same disciples who had asked to sit at Jesus' right and left hand in His kingdom, and who had just been involved in an argument over who was the greatest. They really grew spiritually after Jesus' resurrection, *and that means there's hope for me and you!*

Jesus' requirements for discipleship were exacting. To "be a follower of Jesus," a person had to literally follow Jesus from place to place. (Jesus was "going along the road" as He made all these statements in 9:58-62.) Today we don't have to keep moving from place to place to be disciples, but we should be willing to pay whatever price it *does* take. If you had been living in Jesus' day, would you have followed Him from town to town in order to learn from Him? *Don't tell me you would if any old excuse can keep you from going to church.*

Some say that the man who requested to first go bury his father was actually waiting for his father to die so that he could receive his inheritance. If his father was already dead, there was nothing more important for this man to do but "go and proclaim everywhere the kingdom of God" as Jesus had commanded him. It is too late for dead people to repent and believe the gospel. We need to get the message out to as many of the living as we can before it is too late for them too.

PSALM 74:1-23

This is a difficult psalm to interpret, because we don't know the exact occasion of its writing. The psalmist spoke of the temple's being destroyed, so the occasion could have been the destruction by Nebuchadnezzar in 586 B.C. or another of the desecrations the temple suffered (spoken prophetically). Regardless, the fall of the temple had occurred because of God's judgment on Israel (v. 1). Still, the psalmist knew God's deliverance would come. Even when *we're* disciplined by the Lord, we should remind ourselves that His anger is for a moment, but His favor is for a lifetime.

PROVERBS 12:11

APRIL 3

DEUTERONOMY 23:1-25:19

We read today that no one who was emasculated or castrated could enter the assembly of the Lord. This seems to be a strange commandment; one reason for it might be that castration and emasculation were practiced by the Canaanites to prove their devotion to their gods. God was saying He abhors that perverted practice. Also, no one of illegitimate birth could enter the Lord's assembly. That doesn't mean God hates those born illegitimately, because it is no fault of their own, but that God condemns the fornication and adultery that produce illegitimate babies.

God also said no Ammonite or Moabite should enter His assembly. But under the new covenant, we are commanded to love even our enemies. We must realize that no one was born again under the old covenant. Yes, people were saved by faith, but they never had the Holy Spirit living inside them, and they were never given a new nature. We who are born again, however, have the "love of God...poured out within our hearts through the Holy Spirit" (Rom. 5:5), and we therefore have a supernatural ability to love as God loves.

We have already read passages concerning Old Testament slavery before today, and I have endeavored to point out that the slavery which God permitted was much more humane than what we think of when we think of "slavery." Today we read an interesting commandment in 23:15 that almost catches us by surprise, but which I believe reveals God's attitude about slavery in a wonderful way: "You *shall not* hand over to his master a slave who has escaped from his master to you" (italics mine). God is probably referring to slaves who had escaped from foreign countries.

In 24:16, God forbade Israel from punishing any person for his parent's or children's sins. It seems odd that God would have to mention such fundamental concepts of justice, but Israel obviously needed to hear it. The concepts that seem universal to us are actually foreign in many societies that have not yet been influenced by the Bible.

You probably realize now why Jesus was whipped *thirty-nine times* before He was crucified. God permitted a punishment of forty lashes, but the Jews always gave thirty-nine just in case there was a miscount! The apostle Paul received thirty-nine lashes on *five separate occasions* (see 2 Cor. 11:24).

The custom of marrying a dead brother's wife to preserve his name in Israel seems strange to us. (Just imagine having to marry one of your brothers-in-law or sisters-in-law!) But the purpose was to keep the land from changing hands to a different family as a result of a sonless man's death. We'll need to remember this concept when we read the book of Ruth, who was a *Moabitess* and is listed in Jesus' genealogy. (Remember what we read about Moabites today in 23:3. Ruth's story gives us a better understanding of God's feelings toward Moabites.)

LUKE 10:13-37

According to Jesus, Satan was once in heaven before he fell (see 10:18). The Bible doesn't say exactly what happened, but we'll read in Isaiah 14 and Ezekiel 28 that Satan was proud because of his beauty. He tried to exalt himself above God and was consequently cast down from heaven to earth. Praise God that we have been given authority to "tread upon serpents and scorpions, and over all the power of the enemy" (v. 19), and therefore should not be afraid of Satan or any of his demons! *They are no match for us who have been given the authority to use the name of Jesus.*

Jesus was not telling the lawyer of whom we read today that he could be saved by his good works. Jesus knew that before a person could receive Him as Savior, he first had to see himself as a sinner. No one has ever completely kept the commandment the lawyer quoted. Even as he quoted it, his heart was condemning him, because he tried to justify himself by asking, "And who is my neighbor?" In his thinking, his neighbors certainly didn't include Samaritans—people whom most Jews despised. Jesus finished His story by asking, "Which of these three do you think proved to be a neighbor to the man who fell into the robbers' hands?" Notice that the prejudiced lawyer wouldn't even say, "The Samaritan," but rather, "The one who showed mercy toward him." Our neighbor is anyone in need whose path we cross. *Anyone prejudiced against others is breaking this great commandment.*

One other aspect of this story is that the Samaritan is a type of Jesus. He found us "bleeding and dying by the Jericho road," as one gospel song puts it, and "He poured in the oil and the wine!" The fact that the Samaritan found the man "half-dead" could represent the fact that most people are "half-dead," that is, physically alive but spiritually dead. The priest and Levite represent the law's inability to save us. The Lord Jesus, just as the Samaritan, felt compassion for us and bandaged up our wounds, pouring oil and wine on them, possibly representing the new birth and the baptism of the Holy Spirit. He then brought us to the inn and paid the full price for our care and preservation.

PSALM 75:1-10

We read in verse 6, "For not from the east, nor from the west, nor from the desert comes exaltation." God is the one who exalts, and if we humble ourselves as servants, He will promote us.

PROVERBS 12:12-14

APRIL 4

DEUTERONOMY 26:1-27:26

Thankfulness should characterize every Christian. How many times do we take for granted what God has done for us? This was one reason God commanded the Israelites to bring their firstfruits as an offering—to acknowledge that their blessing came from God, and to thank Him for it. Most of us give thanks before we eat a meal, but are we truly thankful in our hearts, or are we just following a ritual? *We should be thanking God all the time for His blessings.*

Notice that after an Israelite brought his "second tithe" during the third year, he was to pray a prescribed prayer to the Lord. That prayer included the final words: "Look down from Thy holy habitation, from heaven, and *bless Thy people Israel,* and the ground which Thou hast given us..." (26:25, italics mine). Once we bring our tithe to God, we should ask and expect a blessing in return.

LUKE 10:38-11:13

Only Luke records the story of Mary and Martha, and it contains a sermon in a nutshell about ordering our priorities. I would have thought Jesus would have nicely corrected Mary, reminding her she shouldn't be so selfish and should be helping her sister, Martha, with the preparations. But not so. Mary wanted to be with Jesus, which rightfully should take precedence over any distractions. You may have to cut something out of your schedule to read God's Word every day, but Jesus says the same thing about you that He did Mary: "Mary has chosen the good part, which shall not be taken away from her" (10:42).

In chapter 11, Jesus was once again teaching fundamentals of prayer, just as He taught during the Sermon on the Mount that we read in Matthew's Gospel. Jesus was no different from traveling teachers in the church today; He taught the same things over and over again to different crowds. We need to grow beyond the stage of praying only the "Lord's prayer." However, this short prayer does reveal foundational truths concerning prayer (see my comments on Matt. 6:9-13).

The story Jesus told in the verses following the Lord's prayer have been misinterpreted by some to mean we can get our prayers answered only if we keep on repeating the same requests. But the friend who is awakened represents everything that God isn't. He asks not to be bothered. He's cranky. He was sleeping. How could that be God? We know clearly from Scripture that the Lord loves to answer our requests.

Jesus said that the man received his request because of his "persistence." My marginal note says that another translation would be "shamelessness," which is much closer to the original Greek in this passage. *The man received because he had the nerve to ask.* In other words, he had faith that his friend would grant his request, so he shamelessly woke him up and asked him. And it worked! Jesus' point was that if faith works to get our requests from unwilling people, *how much more* will it work to get our requests from a very willing God! That's why Jesus finished off this story by declaring, "Ask, and *it shall* be given to you; seek, and you *shall* find; knock, and *it shall* be opened to you" (11:9, italics mine). You can't get more positive than that, can you? The Bible says, "Let us therefore come boldly unto the throne of grace, that we may obtain mercy, and find grace to help in time of need" (Heb. 4:16, KJV).

Jesus finishes His teaching with even more assuring promises that we will get that for which we ask. God is good! He doesn't mind being compared to an earthly father, as long as we realize that He is a thousand times better than the best father on earth!

PSALM 76:1-12

This psalm praises God for the deliverance of Jerusalem from an invading army. Possibly the occasion was when, in one night, God's angel struck down 185,000 Assyrians who had assembled to take Jerusalem. We'll read that faith-building story in Isaiah 36-37. God is still our deliverer, and we need to expect not defeat, but victory. *What are you expecting?*

PROVERBS 12:15-17

APRIL 5

DEUTERONOMY 28:1-68

I don't know how God could have made a stronger statement that *it pays* to obey Him, and it costs to disobey.

Keep in mind that because God keeps His promises, this chapter is prophetic. Israel experienced every curse spoken of here—down to the last jot and tittle. Assyria and Babylon would eventually come against Israel and deport the Hebrews to their lands. Families would be broken apart. Sickness and disease would spread. Poverty would plague them. Some would even try to sell themselves as slaves in Egypt, but because of the glut of slaves, there would be no buyers. Some would resort to cannibalism to survive their enemies' sieges. You would think the threat of these curses would be enough to ensure everyone's complete obedience! But it wasn't.

Think of our situation today. The promise of eternity in hell for nonbelievers ought to be enough to bring them to repentance. But in too many cases, it is not. That reveals the incredible evil in the human heart.

LUKE 11:14-36

If you've been delivered from a demon, there is no reason to fear that it can get back into you (or your life) unless you *allow* it. Notice that this expelled demon returned and found "the house" (possibly the man's life, or soul or spirit) "swept and in order" (v. 25). The man was clean of any demons, but there was nothing in his life to fill the void. The man should have filled himself with God's Word so that he could have resisted the evil spirit when it returned.

If you had a problem before with demonic oppression, or even possession, you can be sure the demon will come back sometime and try to regain foothold in your life. *Now* is the time to get ready. Purpose that you are going to keep your mind on God's Word, and determine to be fully obedient so the demon can gain no entrance. Sickness is many times the same way. If you have been healed of some sickness or disease, don't be surprised if the symptoms come back upon you sometime. When they come, don't accept them! *Resist the devil by believing and quoting what God has said until the symptoms go away.*

In verses 27-28, we read of the first person who wanted to give undue prominence to Jesus' mother, Mary. This lady shouted out, "Blessed is the womb that bore You, and the breasts at which You nursed." But Jesus said, "On the contrary, blessed are those who hear the word of God, and observe it."

In verse 32, Jesus authenticated the book of Jonah, which some regard as only a tall tale of a man's being swallowed by a fish. But God, the One who created both people and fish, is certainly powerful enough to have a man swallowed by a fish and survive.

Jesus' statement about the eye's being the lamp of the body is somewhat difficult for us to interpret. *But the point is that we should be extremely cautious about what we listen to and look at.* Those who spend time looking at pornographic pictures fill themselves with darkness. Those who allow words of doubt and unbelief to pass through their eyes or ears are going to find their spirits affected.

PSALM 77:1-20

If you have ever had doubtful thoughts assail your mind, you can identify with the psalmist's words today. He was under some extremely stressful circumstances and had sunk to the point that he questioned God's love for him (see vv. 8-9). But he didn't remain in that low state. He acknowledged that God never changes, and he began to meditate on what God had done in the past. Surely God would do it again.

PROVERBS 12:18

This is a great proverb. Our words should heal, not cut.

APRIL 6

DEUTERONOMY 29:1-30:20

Chapter 29 ends with these words: "The secret things belong to the Lord our God, but the things revealed belong to us and to our sons forever" (v. 29). It's good to know that God has some secrets and that we're only responsible for what He has revealed. Don't ever expect to understand everything. Even the apostle Paul said, "For now we see in a mirror dimly...now I know in part" (1 Cor. 13:12). Some day we *will* have more complete understanding, but for now we must be satisfied with what the Lord has willed for us to know.

Chapter 30 is a bright spot among the solemn chapters that go before it, as God promises restoration after judgment and repentance. When the Israelites who were in Babylonian captivity came to repentance after seventy years in exile, God restored them to the promised land. (We'll read all about it in the coming months.)

God said to Israel what He says to all people today: He has set before us life and death, blessing and cursing. He even *commands* us to choose life and blessing. But He still allows us to make the choice ourselves.

LUKE 11:37-12:7

Jesus was kind, but He wasn't always *socially* polite. He had been invited to a Pharisee's home for lunch, and you would think there would have been a better time and place to pronounce woe upon and rebuke the Pharisees!

We're all potential modern Pharisees, so it's worth our time to listen to Christ's criticisms of them and then examine ourselves. First, the Pharisees looked clean on the outside, but on the inside they were dirty. Many Christians are filled with jealousy, unforgiveness or lust and need a good cleanup. Of course, we're all tempted to be jealous, to not forgive and to lust. The important thing is that we don't allow those sins to *get hold of us*. If you're struggling with something you can't seem to get free of, go see your pastor or someone else who is spiritually mature enough to know how to help you. Most problems of that sort begin in the mind and can be ended only by making a determination to control your thought-life. It will be difficult at first, but bad thinking habits can be overcome through practice. In *some* extreme cases, deliverance will have to be administered.

Second, the Pharisees majored on minors; they neglected important matters and emphasized trivial ones. Christians and churches can easily fall into the same trap, and often do. They will spend all their effort on some insignificant biblical facts, become wrapped up in some new doctrine or argue over certain verses while the people in the world around them are perishing. We need to place importance on what God says is important without neglecting the minor things, either.

Third, the Pharisees loved power, praise and prestige. Their lives were for show. We should live our lives to please God, and not to impress men. It's easy to tell which we're doing if we compare how we act in private with how we act in church.

In 12:4-7, we learn that we should *fear* God, but that we should also trust in His great love for us and realize our great worth in His eyes. We need a healthy balance. The person who has a great fear of God but doesn't realize His great love is always under condemnation. Yet the person who knows how much God loves him but fails to have much fear of God is usually not too holy.

PSALM 78:1-31

I can't tell you how happy I am that you remember all that the psalmist was speaking about. Aren't you glad that you're reading through the whole Bible and learning so much?

PROVERBS 12:19-20

Deceitful people may prosper for a while, but not forever. Those who always speak the truth may suffer for it *temporarily*, but they will be established forever and experience joy always!

APRIL 7

DEUTERONOMY 31:1-32:27

Moses exhorted Joshua and the people not to be afraid, because God would go before them and drive out the wicked nations of Canaan. Fear is one of the greatest enemies of God's people, robbing them of faith and opening the door for Satan. When fear comes to our minds, we need to resist it by faith in God's promises. Paul said that God has not given us *a spirit of fear*, but of power and love and discipline (2 Tim. 1:7).

We also read today one of the saddest portions of Scripture. God told Moses that He knew Israel would turn away from Him and serve other gods, and thus He would have to judge them. Notice that God said Israel would turn away *after they became prosperous* (see 31:20). More money and possessions should draw us *closer* to God, since we have more to thank Him for and to give away to spread the gospel. Unfortunately, money often has the opposite effect. Beware, when God blesses you enough to buy a boat, that you don't skip church in the summer months because you're out on the lake. *You would be better off poor.*

We're always reading of Israel's turning to serve other gods. We might complacently say that could never happen to us. How many of us are going to become Buddhists or devil-worshippers? The Bible teaches, however, that any time we allow something to take a more important place in our lives than God, we are committing idolatry. A television set, making money or the pursuit of success can become idols. The apostle John ended his first epistle with this sentence: "Little children, guard yourselves from idols" (1 John 5:21). If there is *one* verse we American Christians need to heed, that's it.

LUKE 12:8-34

For an explanation of the sin of blasphemy against the Holy Spirit, please see my comments on Matthew 12:25-32.

The man who asked Jesus to tell his brother to divide the family inheritance with him was not necessarily greedy, but he had the potential to easily become greedy. I think we can all sympathize with him if he had been cheated out of his rightful inheritance by his brother. But we don't know all the details, so it is impossible to know if he was in the right or in the wrong. Regardless of whether the man who asked for Jesus' help was being treated right or wrong, gaining a family inheritance is not worth losing your salvation. As Jesus said, life is much more than possessions (see v. 15). The parable of the rich man was told to illustrate that point. His life was a waste because he was not "rich toward God."

If you died tonight, would you be satisfied? Could you look back and say, "My life counted. I lived to serve God. My efforts continue to bring blessing to others, even though I'm gone"? We should examine our hearts and ask, What do I own that I worry about someone stealing? Maybe you should give it away! *God wants our hearts in heaven.*

PSALM 78:32-55

I love this particular psalm, because it helps us gain a deeper understanding of God's character. We read in verses 38, 40-41: "Often He *restrained* His anger, and did not arouse all His wrath....How often they rebelled against Him in the wilderness, and *grieved* Him in the desert! And again and again they *tempted* God, and *pained* the Holy One of Israel" (italics mine). Obviously, God is not a robot, but experiences emotions very similar to ours. Like earthly parents, God sometimes seems to wrestle with whether or not He should discipline His children. He hates to see them cry, but He knows they need correction if they're going to turn out right. Just because we appear to get away with repeated sin for a while does not mean God approves. The delay is an indication of God's mercy!

PROVERBS 12:21-23

APRIL 8

DEUTERONOMY 32:28-52

Today we continue reading the song Moses was commanded to teach Israel so that God would have a witness against them when they turned from Him. This song speaks of Israel's past, present and depressing future, but notice that God promised eventual deliverance from the enemies He would use to judge them.

We also read that Moses' life was just about over. God's punishment of not permitting Moses to enter the promised land may seem harsh to us, but we trust that Moses went to a better place than Canaan after his death!

LUKE 12:35-59

We can't know for certain the significance of every detail of Jesus' word picture, but let's not miss the obvious message. *Let's live as if the rapture is going to occur momentarily.*

Are there degrees of punishment in hell? Verses 47-48 seem to suggest there are. On the other side of the coin, even we Christians are going to stand before

Christ's judgment seat some day to give an account of what we've done as Christians. There we will receive praise or condemnation from Jesus and be rewarded for our deeds (see 2 Cor. 5:10). The same principle that applies to the unsaved also applies to us: "From everyone who has been given much shall much be required" (v. 48). *Don't ever forget that this life is simply a preparation for the next.* Thank God that complete pardon is offered to us in Christ, but God wants us to do more than be forgiven and keep on sinning! He wants us to have victory over sin in our lives, and He has promised us the power to do it (see John 8:31-36).

Jesus did not mean in verses 51-53 that He wanted to bring division to families, because it's clear He died for everyone and desires all men to be saved (see 1 Tim. 2:4). Probably Jesus was saying that as a result of His coming, it was inevitable that families would be divided, as has proved to be the case. *No matter what our families say, we should serve God with all of our heart.*

PSALM 78:56-64

PROVERBS 12:24

If you're looking for an easy way to succeed, forget it! God endorses hard work.

APRIL 9

DEUTERONOMY 33:1-29

Just as we read how Jacob, near the end of his life, blessed his twelve sons in the final part of Genesis, today we read of Moses, near the end of his life, blessing the tribes of Israel in the final part of Deuteronomy. We assume that this must have been the gift of prophecy working with the gift of the word of wisdom.

In verse 24, Moses said, "Asher... may he dip his foot in oil." Some Christians have interpreted this as a promise that oil will be discovered in the land of Asher, which was in the northwestern section of Israel—enough to have invested several million dollars and actually started drilling. At the time of this writing, no oil has been discovered, and I would hate to invest money on such a vague prophecy! God may just as well have meant that Asher's territory would be blessed with the oil of many olive trees.

LUKE 13:1-21

Notice that Jesus used two contemporary tragedies to warn His listeners of future judgments. Not that God caused the two tragedies, but He had permitted them. And Jesus implied that those who died were deserving of their fate. The survivors were equally deserving, but they were still receiving mercy and being given time to repent. He made the same point in the parable of the fig tree (vv. 6-9). Jerusalem, and all of Israel, are comparable to the fruitless fig tree. God had been looking for fruit and found none, but He was still allowing time for repentance. However, time was running out. Judgment was impending.

Is Satan responsible for sickness? He is according to this story of the woman with the spirit of infirmity. Jesus said, "Satan has bound [her] for eighteen long years" (v. 16). God, on the other hand, wants you to be healed. That is why Jesus bore your sickness and carried your diseases (Matt. 8:17)! Believe that you receive healing according to Mark 11:23-24!

For explanation of the parable of the mustard seed and leaven, please see my comments on Matthew 13:31-33.

PSALM 78:65-72

PROVERBS 12:25

There is no way to encourage folks who won't believe God's word. Let's be people who have a "good word" with which to encourage others weighed down by anxiety. The Bible is filled with such good words.

APRIL 10

DEUTERONOMY 34:1-JOSHUA 2:24

Today you have completed the Pentateuch. That's quite an accomplishment! According to my surveys, the large majority of born-again people have never done that.

Moses had an unusual funeral: God performed the ceremony. Nobody knows why, but many think it was so that there would never be a shrine built at his tomb, which undoubtedly would have happened if anyone had known the place of his burial. Although Moses was not permitted to enter the promised land, he did eventually stand in Canaan when he appeared with Elijah on the Mount of Transfiguration with Jesus. Moses died when he was 120 years old, and we read that "his eye was not dim, nor his vigor abated" (34:7). When you walk with God, old age doesn't have to be a time to dread!

Now we come to the wonderful book of Joshua. The date is somewhere between 1400 and 1240 B.C. Joshua had been appointed by God to be Moses' successor. He had been Moses' right-hand man for forty years and was one of the two spies who brought back a good report from Canaan. If you think you're too old for God to use you, keep in mind that Joshua was probably in his *nineties* at the beginning of this book.

What was Joshua's divine formula for success? It is found in 1:8: "This book of the law shall not depart from your mouth, but you shall meditate on it day and night, so that you may be careful to do according to all that is written in it; for *then you will make your way prosperous, and then you will have success*" (italics mine). That formula will work for you and me, too. Jesus said that the person who hears and does His words will be safe when the storms of life come (Matt. 7:24-27). The apostle James wrote that the "doers of the word" are blessed (James 1:22-25).

When the two spies whom Joshua sent across the Jordan came to Jericho, they providentially wound up at the home of a harlot named Rahab. She later married an Israelite named Salmon and eventually became the great, great grandmother of David! That means she was in the lineage of Christ!

Keep in mind that God never condoned Rahab's harlotry or even her lying to protect the spies. She was about to get saved and would later learn the holy ways of the Lord. Her story clearly illustrates the truth that salvation is by faith, and not by works. Rahab *believed* in Israel's God, and she acted on the spies' promise of protection and deliverance by hanging a scarlet thread from her window. (Many see the scarlet thread as a type of the blood of Christ.)

Like all true believers, Rahab immediately became a little evangelist. That's one good way to tell if people have really been saved—they have a concern for their lost friends. The writer of the book of Hebrews tells us that "by faith Rahab the harlot did not perish along with those who were disobedient, after she had welcomed the spies in peace" (Heb. 11:31).

LUKE 13:22-14:6

Truly the way to salvation is through a "narrow door." Jesus is the only "true door" to God's mercy, yet people have fashioned many doors by which they attempt to gain a righteous standing before God. Those of whom Jesus was speaking here were trusting that *their acquaintance* with Jesus would be sufficient for obtaining eternal life. But knowing *about* Jesus is not the same as knowing Him. The difference is revealed by a person's deeds. Notice that the Lord said, "Depart from Me, *all you evildoers*" (13:27, italics mine). So many know about Jesus and even faithfully attend church. Yet they deny they actually know Him by their daily deeds.

Doesn't Jesus' lament over Jerusalem reveal His great love for people? He wasn't feeling sorry for Himself, but for the people of Jerusalem.

In chapter 14, Jesus healed a man of dropsy. It was unlikely that this diseased man would have been invited to eat at a chief Pharisee's house. Perhaps he was invited only to see if Jesus would heal on the Sabbath. Afterward no one could debate Jesus' logic: if it is lawful to rescue an animal on the Sabbath day, certainly it is lawful to rescue a man from sickness.

PSALM 79:1-13

The occasion of this psalm may well have been the destruction of Jerusalem in about 586 B.C. by Babylon. It was a case of God's judgment on apostate Israel, so we know this psalmist's prayer was not immediately answered. This was a case of praying when it was too late! The captivity in Babylon would last seventy years. I wonder how many people will be fervently praying during their first few minutes in hell?

PROVERBS 12:26

APRIL 11

JOSHUA 3:1-4:24

God used Moses to split the Red Sea, and today we read that He used Joshua to stop the flow of the flooded Jordan River. When you think about it, Joshua's miracle may have been greater than Moses'. At the Red Sea, all God had to do was split a section down the middle and form two dams. Here at the Jordan, God had to either "freeze" the entire river upstream to stop its flow or somehow pile up the water for a number of hours. Incidentally, this particular spot on the Jordan was the same section where Jesus was baptized by John the Baptist.

Notice that it wasn't *until* the priests (who were carrying the ark of the covenant) got their feet wet in the Jordan that the river stopped flowing. Faith without works is dead (James 2:17). Immediately after they came up from the dry riverbed, the river returned to its normal flooded stage. God was not one moment early or one moment late in His timing of this miracle! We need to have faith in God's timing as well. He is always running on time!

LUKE 14:7-35

At more elaborate banquets in Jesus' day, there were always certain "seats of honor," just as we normally have a head table at modern banquets. At that particular meal attended by lawyers and Pharisees, Jesus noticed how those "men of God" were vying to sit in the places of honor. Because of Christianity's influence, almost everyone in our society knows that it looks bad to exalt yourself. But we work out more subtle ways to exalt ourselves. We would never think of sitting in some honored seat unless we were asked. However, we don't hesitate to "casually" mention how much money we have, or what important person we know, or how God has used us so gloriously! Jesus' lesson is still true for us: if we exalt ourselves, we will be humbled. If we humble ourselves, we'll be exalted.

Jesus touched another sensitive nerve when He instructed the host to invite the poor, crippled and blind to his next dinner. Preparing a meal for friends or relatives is a sacrifice, but chances are we'll get our day of rest when they return the favor. God wants us to do kind deeds for people who *can't pay us back*.

I believe that in all three discipleship requirements named in verses 25-35, Jesus was speaking hyperbolically—using exaggeration to make a point. Surely Jesus doesn't want us to *hate* our parents, spouse, brothers and sisters and children. But Jesus was strongly saying that we have to love Him more than anyone to qualify as His disciples. Our love for others should seem almost like hate in comparison to our love for Jesus.

Neither did Jesus mean that we literally need to carry a cross to be His disciples. Carrying a cross is symbolic of two things: carrying a burden and taking a path that leads to death. Do you carry a burden for people who don't know the Lord? If you do, your actions will show it. However, I've noticed, as most pastors have, that when a missionary speaker is announced for the next service, attendance is way down. Second, are you on the path that leads to death? I'm speaking of death to your own selfish wants, death to worry about what others are thinking of you and death to giving in to the desires of the flesh.

Jesus doesn't necessarily want us to give away all our possessions, either (v. 33). If we did, where would we live? Where would we sleep? How would we get to work? What would we wear? No, I think Jesus meant that *no possession can dominate the affections of a true disciple*.

Let's take a look at our lives and see if we measure up. Is there some person, possession or desire that has a hold on you? If the Lord told you to give it away, would it be a struggle? Or is He first in your life?

PSALM 80:1-19

This psalm is similar to the one we read yesterday. Israel was experiencing the Lord's judgment for its sin. After Solomon's reign, the nation was split into two separate kingdoms, north and south. The ten northern tribes became Israel, and the tribes of Judah and Benjamin to the south became known as Judah. The north was more evil than the south, and consequently it was judged much earlier, as God permitted the Assyrians to come and deport Israel. About 130 years later, Judah fell to the Babylonians. The occasion of this psalm was probably after the deportation of the northern kingdom but before the fall of Judah.

PROVERBS 12:27-28

APRIL 12

JOSHUA 5:1-7:15

Today we read another example of God's perfect timing. As soon as Israel crossed over the Jordan and ate some of the produce of the promised land, the manna, which had sustained the people for almost forty years, ceased to appear. There was plenty of food in Canaan, so there was no longer any need for God's miraculous provision. God has promised to supply our needs too. If that requires a miracle, God will perform one. But if not, we shouldn't be expecting one. Jesus didn't feed people every day by multiplying fish and bread. Most times, He and His followers bought their food at the market.

The conquest of Jericho contains a number of helpful spiritual principles. The first is that we can never be led by circumstances. In 6:1, we read that Jericho was tightly shut. That means all the doors, or gates, into the city were closed. In those days, a city's walls were its primary means of defense. What would have happened if Joshua had prayed: "Lord, if it is not your will for us to take Jericho, just shut all the doors"? We should be led only by the word of God, whether it is the written Word of God in the Bible or the spoken word of God in our hearts by the Holy Spirit.

I heard a preacher say once, "You can always tell you are in God's will if everything is easy." If that were true, however, the apostle Paul would have spent his whole ministry out of God's will, since he faced difficulties everywhere he went.

The second lesson is found in God's statement to Joshua before the great battle: "See, I *have given* Jericho into your hand" (6:2, italics mine). The same God who called Abraham "a father of many nations" even when Abraham was childless is the God who "calleth those things which be not as though they were" (Rom. 4:17, KJV). *If God says something is going to happen, it is as good as happened!* That's why we are supposed to "believe that [we] have received" when we pray (Mark 11:24).

God's instructions for taking the city seem strange. All I can think is that the Israelites were being tested once again to see if they would completely trust God. So the Israeli army circled Jericho once each day for six days and seven times on the seventh day. The Jerichoites were probably casting insults at the Israelites each day when they circled the city. But God's people experienced the reward of those who walk by faith and possessed the city with supernatural help. Notice that God required them to shout *before the walls fell*. That's faith in action! Anyone can shout *after* the walls have fallen!

After the city is burned with fire, Joshua speaks a curse upon the man who will rebuild it: "...with the loss of his first-born he shall lay its foundation, and with the loss of his youngest son he shall set up its gates" (6:26). We will read how this curse actually came to pass four hundred years later in 1 Kings 16:34.

After the great victory at Jericho, Israel suffered a devastating defeat at Ai. As always, the problem was not with God. God had said that all the silver and gold of Jericho was to be put in His treasury, so Achan's sin was actually stealing what belonged to God (according to Malachi 3:8).

LUKE 15:1-32

Luke 15 contains three stories that all teach the same lesson: God delights in showing mercy to undeserving, sinful people. They had a party when you got saved!

The story of the prodigal son is last, probably because it best illustrates what Jesus wants *us* to understand. The older brother resented the way their father had treated the younger brother so mercifully; he felt he deserved better treatment for his better behavior. He was no different from the Pharisees who grumbled that Jesus ate with sinners. If they had been truly spiritual, they would have been glad that God was showing mercy to sinful people. Let's be careful never to allow a Pharisaic attitude to rob us of true Christlikeness.

What I like best about this story is the great love displayed by the father. Notice that he saw his son coming even when he was a long distance away. Then he *ran* to him, *embraced* him and *kissed* him. He didn't even wait for his son's confession! Finally, he threw a big party for him. We should never think that we have to talk God into saving us or forgiving us when we sin. He is ready and waiting to see our first sign of repentance and faith.

PSALM 81:1-16

PROVERBS 13:1

APRIL 13

JOSHUA 7:16-9:2

Keep in mind that Achan was responsible for the death of thirty-six Israeli soldiers. He knew full well that what he had done was wrong, as indicated by the fact that he hid the stolen booty. Why did Israel stone Achan's entire family for his sin? It's not entirely clear that they did. In 7:25, my Bible reads, "And all Israel stoned them with stones," but in the margin it indicates that "them" should be literally translated "him." We have already read God's law that stated no child should be punished for his father's sins. God only said to burn the offender and all that belonged to him (7:15). If all of Achan's family *was* stoned, they must have all been knowledgeable of the crime and old enough to be held accountable as accomplices.

After the sin was dealt with, blessing and victory could return to Israel. This concept applies to us as well. When we suffer calamity, we should first check on ourselves to make certain we have not opened the door through disobedience.

LUKE 16:1-18

The story of the unrighteous steward is difficult to interpret. This steward was apparently in charge of "accounts receivable" for his master. He had been abusing his stewardship, involved in some form of embezzlement. When he was called on the carpet, he knew he would lose his job. What should he do? He formulated a plan so that his master's creditors would take care of him after he was fired.

The problem in interpreting the story is with what Jesus said in verse 9: "And I say to you, make friends for yourselves by means of the mammon of unrighteousness; that when it fails, they may receive you into the eternal dwellings." I believe Jesus was being sarcastic when He said to "make friends by the means of unrighteous mammon." Certainly God would not want us to *buy* our friends or cheat anyone as did this unfaithful steward. Further, what could Jesus have meant by "they may receive you into the eternal dwellings"? There are only two eternal dwelling places, heaven and hell. Cheating someone out of money can't ensure a place in heaven! That's why I believe verse 9 was spoken sarcastically. However, from there through verse 13, it all makes sense and certainly contradicts the message of verse 9 if it is *not* a sarcastic statement.

This story illustrates the fact that "he who is faithful in a very little thing is faithful also in much; and he who is unrighteous in a very little thing is unrighteous also in much" (v. 10). The story is told of a man who owned a dry-cleaning business and who, before hiring a new worker, would have him work for one day. During that day, the owner would place a quarter in the pocket of a pair of trousers that were to be cleaned by his new worker. If the worker brought the quarter to his new employer, he was hired permanently. If he didn't, he was fired at the end of the day. If the new worker couldn't be trusted with someone else's quarter, he couldn't be trusted to run the shop when the owner wasn't around.

Jesus went on to say that one of the first areas in which God will test us is money. If we can't be trusted to pay our tithes and to be good stewards of God's money, God knows He can't trust us in other areas, either. The main moral is summed up in verse 13: "You cannot serve God and mammon."

PSALM 82:1-8

PROVERBS 13:2-3

We are advised many times in the Proverbs to guard our lips. *Those who speak whatever comes to their minds regret it later.*

APRIL 14

JOSHUA 9:3-10:43

Today we read of Joshua's making a major blunder. The people of Gibeon, living in Canaan (a few miles from Jerusalem) and marked for judgment, realized they were doomed after they heard the report of Israel's successes in battle. So they worked out a shrewd plan to deceive Israel into making a covenant with them. They would be slaves for the rest of their lives, but at least they would live. Their deception worked only because Joshua and the other leaders didn't bother to seek the Lord's counsel.

Here is a good lesson for us to learn. *Things aren't always as they appear to be. People who appear to have good intentions may in truth be selfishly ambitious.* That's why we need to seek the Lord's counsel even when everything appears fine. Unless we learn to be led by the Holy Spirit, we become easy prey to selfish and designing people.

Notice the Gibeonites had confidence the Israelites would keep their word even when they discovered they had been deceived. The Israelites knew that God expected them to keep their word at all times. Apparently the covenant agreement included a military alliance, so when five other kings of Canaan attacked the Gibeonites a short time later, Israel was bound to come to their aid.

During this battle, Joshua commanded the sun to stand still, and it did for an entire day! This may sound hard to believe, but it was no problem for God. Of course, Joshua had no knowledge that the earth was revolving around the sun. From his standpoint, it was the sun that moved across the sky each day. I read an article in the January 8, 1972, edition of the *Pittsburgh Press* that told of some astronauts and scientists in Green Belt,

Maryland, who used a large computer to research the position of the sun, moon and planets across the centuries. They didn't want to send up a satellite and have it bump into something! They found there were twenty-four hours missing in elapsed time in space! One of the "religious fellows" pulled out his Bible and showed the scientists what we have just read. The missing day had been found!

LUKE 16:19-17:10

The story of the rich man and Lazarus does not teach that poor people go to heaven and rich people go to hell. Lazarus was a believer, and the rich man obviously was not.

This story may have been true and not just another parable (Jesus mentioned the poor man by name). If it was true, it provides the bulk of the evidence for the belief that old covenant saints did not go to heaven, but rather to a place called "paradise" or "Abraham's bosom." It was located very close to "the place of torment," yet separated from it by a great chasm (see v. 26). Together, "paradise" and "the place of torment" made up the place called "Hades," or the Old Testament word *Sheol*. Apparently the people in "the place of torment" were able to see across the chasm into "paradise" (v. 23).

The rich man recognized that it was too late for him and that his brothers would share his fate. Isn't it amazing that a person who could be so uncompassionate on earth could become so concerned for others once in hell? It must be a horrible place.

The apostles, like most of us, desired more faith. But faith doesn't come by praying for it, but by hearing God's Word. Jesus told them that only a little faith can cause a tree to be uprooted and planted in the sea. And more important than having great faith is being obedient to God (see vv. 7-10). Actually, obedience is faith in action. You wouldn't obey if you didn't believe. That's why faith and obedience go hand in hand. If you say you have faith in God's Word but don't obey His commandments, you're fooling yourself.

PSALM 83:1-18

Asaph prays for deliverance, but not just for the sake of deliverance. He desires that God would be glorified through it. This was not some sort of psychology he was trying to use on God to get his prayers answered. He genuinely wanted God to be magnified through His display of power. This should ultimately be the motivation for all our prayers. It is fine to desire to be healed, but let us desire even more that God would receive glory for it! If we desire prosperity or success, let it be for the Lord's glory!

PROVERBS 13:4

APRIL 15

JOSHUA 11:1-12:24

Yesterday, if you didn't realize it, we read about Joshua's conquering a good portion of southern Palestine. Today we read of his victories against the alliance of kings of northern Palestine.

Verse 11:20 says that "it was of the Lord to harden their hearts, to meet Israel in battle in order that he might utterly destroy them." Here again is a case of God's hardening hearts. But realize that these Canaanites had been given years of opportunity to repent, and they hardened their own hearts. Sometimes, to bring His purposes to pass, God hardened the hearts of people whose hearts were already so hard that they were beyond mercy. This was the case earlier in Egypt, and now also in Canaan.

At the end of chapter 12, Joshua had supreme military command in the promised land. However, there would still be years of "mopping up" operations. But Canaan had been subdued to the point where the land could be divided between the tribes.

LUKE 17:11-37

Under levitical law, lepers were forbidden to come in contact with nonleprous people due to contagion. Whenever lepers were in public places, they had to cry out, "Unclean! Unclean!" It was a terrible way to live, so as we would expect, lepers hung out together. Their disease was enough to break down traditional racial barriers between Jews and Samaritans, as in the case of these ten lepers whom Jesus encountered. At least one was a Samaritan.

These ten men had to believe that by the time they arrived for the priests' inspection (as also prescribed by levitical law) they would be cleansed. And they had to obey Jesus' command to go and show themselves to the priests. That was no easy task, as *it meant a journey of possibly fifty miles to Jerusalem on foot.* I wonder how far they had traveled before they noticed they were cleansed? In my opinion, the Samaritan who returned to give thanks to Jesus displayed more faith than the rest, because I doubt if the Jewish priests would have shown him the courtesy of a lawful inspection. He was not one of them!

This story also illustrates that healing doesn't always come instantaneously. Sometimes it is gradual. If we have faith, we will be willing to persevere for as long as it takes. If we "believe that we receive when we pray" (Mark 11:24), then it will make no difference to us when the manifestation comes. As far as we are concerned, we have already received by faith the answer to our prayer, not because we feel or see it, but because God's Word says so!

When Jesus spoke in verses 22-36 of His second coming, He was not referring to the rapture of the church. When the rapture hits, there won't be any opportunity to decide about whether to go into your house to retrieve your goods (see v. 31)! You'll be changed in the "twinkling of an eye" (1 Cor. 15:52), and you'll be gone! Jesus was referring here to the time of His second coming at the end of the tribulation. As in Noah's time and the destruction of Sodom and Gomorrah, judgment came and removed the unrighteous from the earth, while the righteous were protected. So it will be when Jesus comes in His mighty wrath and sets up His kingdom on the earth.

PSALM 84:1-12

How blessed is the man who trusts in God! The Lord is a sun (He shines warmth and light) and a shield (He protects us). He gives grace (undeserved favor) and glory (He lifts us up). "No good thing does He withhold from those who walk uprightly" (v. 11).

PROVERBS 13:5-6

APRIL 16

JOSHUA 13:1-14:15

You might want to turn to the back of your Bible and look at a map showing how Canaan was divided among the twelve tribes. I'm warning you in advance that we're going to be reading some dry information in the next few days, the description of those tribal boundaries. Do like me: read quickly! And don't feel guilty, because the boundaries are of no importance to new covenant believers.

Caleb, you'll recall, was the only spy besides Joshua who brought back a good report. Only he and Joshua, because of their faith, had survived forty years in the wilderness. I can hardly wait to meet Caleb in heaven! At eighty-five years old, he was still looking for a mountain to climb and capture for the glory of God! He didn't get older, he got better! His story is a wonderful example of God's blessings on an elderly man who has fully followed Him.

LUKE 18:1-17

In verses 1-8 is another prayer parable that has been greatly misunderstood. Jesus was not teaching that we should bombard God with our requests until we wear Him out, as this widow did with the unjust judge. God cannot be compared to such a person who neither fears God nor respects others (see v. 4). Jesus' point was that if an *unjust* judge gave justice to this widow, *how much more will God, a righteous judge, bring about justice to His own who are requesting it.* Unlike the unjust judge, God will bring justice *speedily* to His own (v. 8).

We can ask with confidence for anything God has promised in His Word. However, praying for an end to persecution doesn't fall into that category, because we are not promised exemption from persecution. Sure, we can pray about it, but it's a prayer of hope, not faith. From many biblical examples, we know God sometimes permits it and sometimes doesn't. There are times when He delivered His people from death (Daniel in the lion's den), and there are times He didn't deliver them from death (Stephen, the first martyr of the church).

I can't think of a clearer example of salvation by faith than the story of the Pharisee and the publican (tax-gatherer). The sinful tax-gatherer was truly repentant, asked for mercy and got it. He left the temple *justified,* which means "just-as-if-I'd never sinned"! The Pharisee, proud of his holiness, left the temple unsaved, because he was trusting in his good works to save him. One good way to determine if a person is truly saved is to ask, "If you were to stand before God, and He asked why He should let you into heaven, what would you say?" A true Christian will talk only about how Jesus died for his sins and provided assurance of eternal life.

PSALM 85:1-13

Those who truly know God's character are always filled with optimism, just like this psalmist. Even though he was experiencing God's discipline, he knew that, as always, God would forgive and restore.

PROVERBS 13:7-8

We have all met poor people who pretend to be wealthy and wealthy people who pretend to be poor. Both rich and poor are concerned about what others think of them. In that respect, they have the same problem. Beyond that, money has the potential to create a lot of problems. So why are we striving so hard to get rich?

APRIL 17

JOSHUA 15:1-63

If you look in your Bible's map section, you can see where the borders of the tribe of Judah were positioned. At the time of the writing of the book of Joshua, Jerusalem had not been taken from the Jebusites. Later on, we'll read in the book of 2 Samuel that David, of the tribe of Judah, eventually conquered the city and made it the capital of Israel.

LUKE 18:18-43

For a discussion of the rich young ruler, see my comments on Matthew 19:16-26.

The reason Jesus said that it is easier for a camel to go through the eye of a needle than for a rich man to enter the kingdom of heaven is because in many cases (but not all) rich people are completely consumed with making money. It occupies their thoughts day and night. Money is truly their god. It has control of their lives. The problem with the rich young ruler was that money was his god. Just as Jesus said, you can't serve God and money. That tells us that it is not a sin for us to have money. It is only a sin for money to have us.

Anytime we read a story in the Gospels about Jesus' healing someone, we should realize it was recorded for a reason: to inspire us to trust God, just as did the person of whom we're reading. God loves you just as much as He loved blind Bartimaeus. However, keep in mind that there were plenty of other blind people like Bartimaeus who never were healed by Jesus. There is no doubt that God loved them as much as He did Bartimaeus. So why weren't they healed? Because they didn't have the faith of Bartimaeus. Bartimaeus would not be discouraged, and he persevered until he got what he was after. In that sense, his healing didn't come instantaneously. Our faith will often be tested as well, but if we hold fast, determined never to give in to defeat, there is no doubt that God will keep His Word to us.

PSALM 86:1-17

In verse 14, David said, "Arrogant men have risen up against me, and a band of violent men have sought my life, and they have not set Thee before them." The next verse reveals that David understood *why* God had not dealt with those men just yet: "But Thou, O Lord, art a God merciful and gracious, slow to anger and abundant in lovingkindness and truth" (v. 15). All of us have had to endure others' arrogance and hatred while God shows them mercy, giving them opportunity to repent. Those are good times to exercise the love and forgiveness God has placed in our hearts.

PROVERBS 13:9-10

"Through presumption comes nothing but strife" (v. 10). Have you ever assumed something that you later found was untrue? All of us have. That's why it is so important to communicate when we have a relationship problem with someone. To avoid talking about the dividing issue only generates more strife. But when we communicate openly, there can be no presumptions, and the devil cannot fill our minds with his lies.

APRIL 18

JOSHUA 16:1-18:28

Although Israel was in the promised land and had won many victories, we see them falling short of all God intended. Reuben, Gad and the half tribe of Manasseh had compromised and settled in the land east of the Jordan. Judah had possessed its inheritance but failed to drive the Jebusites from Jerusalem (see 15:63). Ephraim possessed its portion, but did not drive the Canaanites from Gezer (see 16:10). Manasseh lacked faith to drive out all the Canaanites in its territory because they "had chariots of iron" (17:16). And today we read that the seven remaining tribes also procrastinated in taking their inheritance.

Such failure is so representative of many Christians today! Few of us even have the faith to enter into our rights and privileges in Christ. Too many spend their Christian lives out in the "wilderness." And even those who enter in leave small "unconquered areas" in their lives for years. Some continue to be fearful of Satan and allow him foothold in their territory. We need to heed Joshua: "How long will you put off entering to take possession of the land which the Lord, the God of your fathers, has given you?" (18:3). Let's go for it all!

LUKE 19:1-27

The Jericho where Jesus met Zaccheus was the same Jericho that had been destroyed by Joshua about thirteen hundred years earlier. Isn't it great to be able to read the New Testament with the foundation of an Old Testament knowledge?

Jesus declared that salvation had come to Zaccheus that day, not because of his works, but because of his faith that Jesus was the Christ. However, *his works of repentance proved his faith.*

Incidentally, there is no "doctrine of making restitution" (after our conversion to Christ) stated in the Bible. Zaccheus is the only example in the Gospels of making restitution for past sins. All of us will have to do what we feel the Lord is saying to us. However, we must be careful not to open the door to a spirit of condemnation that deceives us into thinking we must right every wrong that we ever committed before our salvation. That would be impossible. On the other hand, if I have *recently wronged someone as a Christian*, I certainly should go and ask his forgiveness (see Matt. 5:23-24).

All those who were traveling with Jesus thought He was about to establish the long-awaited kingdom of God. He had already told His apostles that He would be scourged and crucified, but His statements were incomprehensible to them. So Jesus told them a parable to let them in on God's plan. What were they to do after His ascension? *They were to make a profit for God's kingdom.* (And you thought the church was a nonprofit organization!) Everyone who produces such a spiritual profit will get a reward (or some kind of authority) when Christ returns.

Notice that though the one who produced no profit received no reward, it doesn't say he was cast in hell because of it. The apostle Paul taught that some will suffer loss of reward at Christ's judgment seat, but will still be saved (see 1 Cor. 3:12-15). Are you making a profit for God's kingdom?

PSALM 87:1-7

Zion is the mountain on which the city of Jerusalem sits. So the words *Zion* and *Jerusalem* are almost synonymous. This psalm must be prophetic, as it speaks of enemies of Israel being inhabitants of the holy city: Egyptians, Babylonians, Philistines and so on. Some day Jerusalem will be the capital of the world, with Jesus Himself ruling there.

PROVERBS 13:11

APRIL 19

JOSHUA 19:1-20:9

The division of the land of which we are reading took place at Shiloh, where the tabernacle was set up and would remain for about four hundred years.

Simeon, the smallest tribe at the last census, was given part of Judah's territory, which was apparently too large for Judah alone. Back in Genesis 49, Jacob had cursed the anger of Simeon and Levi, because they had slaughtered the men of Shechem after their sister had been raped by the king's son. Jacob said of Simeon and Levi in his prophecy, "I will disperse them in Jacob, and scatter them in Israel" (Gen. 49:7). It may be that in today's passage we see the complete fulfillment of that prophecy. Levi, as the priestly tribe, received no inheritance of land but was allotted forty-eight cities scattered throughout Israel. Now Simeon, living in Judah's land, became absorbed by Judah.

In chapter 20, we read of the designation of six "cities of refuge" in which a manslayer (not a murderer) could flee to escape the wrath of the "blood avenger." Three were located east of the Jordan, and three to the west. They were chosen in locations that were in the upper, middle and lower portions of Israel, so that a manslayer anywhere in Israel could easily get to one. Under the old covenant, whenever the high priest died, the manslayer was permitted to return to his home. Under the new covenant, our High Priest is Jesus (see Heb. 4:14). When He died, we were released from our bondage as well!

LUKE 19:28-48

Jesus made His triumphal entry into Jerusalem riding on a donkey in direct fulfillment of Zechariah 9:9: "Rejoice greatly, O daughter of Zion! Shout in triumph, O daughter of Jerusalem! Behold, your king is coming to you; He is just and endowed with salvation, humble, and mounted on a donkey, even on a colt, the foal of a donkey." The crowds were shouting from Psalm 118:26: "Blessed is the King who comes in the name of the Lord!" They were correct in applying this scripture to Jesus. And Jesus would state a few days later that He was the rejected stone of Psalm 118:22 (see Luke 20:17).

The Mount of Olives sits directly beside Jerusalem. It was probably from there, looking across the Kidron Valley, that Jesus wept over the city. Picturing Jesus weeping over Jerusalem gives you a little deeper revelation of the Lord's character, doesn't it? While weeping, Jesus predicted the destruction of Jerusalem in about thirty-seven years by the Roman army. God would use the Romans as a tool of His divine judgment upon Israel for its rejection of the Messiah.

I have read the ancient historian Josephus's eyewitness account of the destruction of Jerusalem. Jerusalem was besieged by Titus during the Passover, when Jews were gathered from all over Israel. The siege lasted for months, so that no one could get in or out of the city. Thousands died of starvation, and those who went out at night to gather food were caught and crucified near the city walls each day. By the time Jerusalem fell, more than *one million Jews had died*. No wonder Jesus wept.

PSALM 88:1-18

This is by far the darkest of all the psalms. It's one of the few that finishes without a happy ending or a statement of faith. However, the fact that the psalmist was praying indicates he still had hope that God would deliver him. Keep in mind that the writer knew he was suffering God's discipline (vv. 7,16).

PROVERBS 13:12-14

APRIL 20

JOSHUA 21:1-22:20

I like the final verse of chapter 21: "Not one of the good promises which the Lord had made to the house of Israel failed; all came to pass." We know it is *impossible* for God to lie (see Titus 1:2). If we aren't experiencing what He has promised, the problem is not with the sending end.

Three days ago we read the proverb that said, "Through presumption comes nothing but strife" (Prov. 13:10), and today and tomorrow we read a perfect illustration of that truth. The two-and-a-half tribes on the eastern side of the Jordan built an altar like the one at Shiloh. When the report reached the tribes on the western side, they assumed the eastern tribes were rebelling against the Lord. I'm glad they decided to communicate before they made their declaration of war! We'll have to wait for tomorrow to learn the outcome.

LUKE 20:1-26

We read the parable of the vine-growers in Matthew and Mark, but may I also point out from this parable the danger of looking for significance in every detail of every parable. Look at what the owner of the vineyard (God) said after his servants (the prophets) had all been beaten or killed by the vine-growers (Israel): "What shall I do? I will send my beloved son; perhaps they will respect him" (v. 13). Does that mean God really thought His Son would be well-received? No, God knew Jesus would be rejected and crucified on the cross. That's why it's dangerous to assign significance to every detail of every parable. We should just look for the obvious symbolism and leave the little details alone.

The Bible teaches that we should be subject to the ruling authorities, unless, of course, the ruling authorities dictate that we should disobey God. Paying taxes is not contrary to God's law. God established human government, and it takes taxes to run a government. Paul made these things clear in Romans 13:6-7.

PSALM 89:1-13

At times I have had difficulty praising God for very long—not because He wasn't worthy, but because there's no one with whom to compare Him! As the psalmist said, "Who is like Thee, O mighty Lord?" (vs. 8). It almost seems that the English language is inadequate to do God justice.

PROVERBS 13:15-16

APRIL 21

JOSHUA 22:21-23:16

Today we learn that the "altar of offense" was really an "altar of witness." It just goes to show that we can easily pass judgment on people by observing their deeds and not realize that their motives are pure. The Israelites discovered that the truth was the exact opposite of what they had thought. That's why Jesus said we should not pass judgment.

Joshua, near his death, gave his final admonition to Israel to stay true to the Lord. He warned them never to intermarry with the other nations or to have any close association with them, lest they be dragged down by sin. Likewise, any Christian who marries a non-Christian is heading for misery, and any Christian who has a close association with unbelievers is going to be tempted to draw back from God. Of course, we must befriend unbelievers and try to reach them for the Lord. But for Christians to develop *close* friendships with non-Christians is spiritually dangerous (see 2 Cor. 6:15-18).

LUKE 20:27-47

We read recently about the law of marrying a deceased brother's wife if he had had no children (see Deut. 25:5). That was the law to which the Sadducees were referring when they questioned Jesus. Of course, their illustration was ridiculous—seven brothers who all died successively without children. They were trying to make the doctrine of the afterlife ridiculous. Those poor Sadducees believed that when you were dead, you had no spiritual existence. But Jesus testified that Abraham, Isaac and Jacob were alive and well in heaven at the time of Moses (see v. 37).

Jesus also stumped them with His question about David's prophesying about the Messiah. They hadn't recognized the scriptural concept of a *divine* Messiah; their Messiah was to be only human. Jesus, of course, was 100 percent man and 100 percent God.

Because Jesus again asserted that the religious leaders would receive greater condemnation, we must assume that there are going to be degrees of punishment in hell, just as there are degrees of reward in heaven.

PSALM 89:14-37

Although no one is seated on the throne of David presently, God said that He would establish David's seed and throne *forever* (see vv. 29, 36). We understand now that Jesus is the "seed" to whom the psalmist was referring, and He *will* someday sit on the throne of David forever. Jesus was a direct descendant of David through both his mother and Joseph.

PROVERBS 13:17-19

APRIL 22

JOSHUA 24:1-33

I think you got an idea of what lay ahead for the nation of Israel as we read in 24:31, "And Israel served the Lord all the days of Joshua and all the days of the elders who survived Joshua." The implication is that after the time of those elders, Israel *ceased* following the Lord. In only one generation, Israel was back to serving other gods. The people of Joshua's generation *failed* to pass on their spiritual heritage to their children.

Christian parents today need to work harder than ever to be certain their children are raised in the nurture and admonition of the Lord. We must be very careful with whom we allow our children to be friends, realizing that they are going to be greatly influenced by those with whom they consistently associate. There should be no higher earthly priority than to raise our children for God. There probably is no greater challenge.

LUKE 21:1-28

The story of the widow's mite divulges an important spiritual truth: the amount of our sacrifice is not measured by how much we give to God, but by how much we have *left* after we've given. Giving out of our surplus really takes no sacrifice at all. Such gifts don't impress God. God is impressed by sacrificial giving, and for many people, they don't have to give much for it to be considered sacrificial. This widow was one of those. Notice Jesus didn't discourage her from giving sacrificially, because He knew that this woman would be rewarded.

Both Matthew and Mark recorded Jesus' Olivet discourse, but Luke included some information the other Gospel writers left out, concentrating on Jesus' response to the question about the destruction of the temple. In verses 12-24, Jesus told the disciples that they would be persecuted and delivered to synagogues and prisons. Before the end of Acts 6, *all* twelve apostles had spent a night in jail and stood trial before the Sanhedrin, and Peter and John had spent two nights in jail and been on trial twice! In both cases, just as Jesus promised, the apostles received supernatural utterance and wisdom that none of their opponents could resist or refute (see v. 5).

Just as Jesus promised, almost all the twelve were martyred for their faith. In some cases, they were apparently betrayed by their own friends or families (see v. 16). All were hated during their ministries (see v. 17). Isn't it amazing that Jesus could tell them they would be killed, but yet *not a hair on their heads would perish* (see v. 18)? That's further evidence of the resurrection of our bodies at the end of the age.

In verse 20 Jesus warns that when they see Jerusalem surrounded by armies, they should know that her desolation is at hand. It was in A.D. 66 that Rome sent a general named Cestius to crush a Jewish revolt. He surrounded Jerusalem for six months of siege, and then withdrew for some unknown reason. It was after Cestius's withdrawal that all the Christians left Jerusalem. Within a short time, there would be no opportunity to get out alive. When Jerusalem fell to Titus in A.D. 70, Christians were not killed in the holocaust! They had been forewarned forty years before.

Finally, Jesus said the Jews would be led captive into all the nations, and Jerusalem would be trampled underfoot by the Gentiles until the times of the Gentiles would be fulfilled (see v. 24). After the Roman conquest under Titus in A.D. 70, the Jews *were* led captive into all nations and still reside in many countries of the world. Jerusalem has been trampled underfoot by Gentiles for centuries—by Romans, Byzantines, Persians, Arabs, Frenchmen, Germans, Turks and the British. Finally, Israel repossessed Jerusalem from Jordan in 1967 during the Six-Day War. It looks as if "the times of the Gentiles" are almost over!

From verses 24 to 25, we pass through the church age and into the tribulation period. At the end of seven years, Jesus will return (see v. 27)!

PSALM 89:38-52

If anything, this psalm should keep us walking in the fear of the Lord by reminding us how miserable it is to be under His discipline! The writer of Hebrews said, "All discipline for the moment seems not to be joyful, but sorrowful; yet to those who have been trained by it, afterwards it yields the peaceful fruit of righteousness" (Heb. 12:11).

PROVERBS 13:20-23

We should be careful whom we are following, because we will become just like them (see v. 20).

APRIL 23

JUDGES 1:1-2:9

Welcome to the book of Judges, which recounts the history of twelve successive leaders whom God raised up to deliver Israel from its enemies after Joshua's death. We will cover more than three hundred years of Israel's history and will learn of God's mercies in ways yet unseen. You'll see that if ever the saying "History repeats itself" were true, it was true for the Israelites. Over and over again, they turned from God, were overpowered by their enemies and then repentantly cried out for God to deliver them, which He always did. We'll also read how God used some very imperfect people to establish His purposes, and it will strengthen our understanding of how God responds to our faith in spite of our faults. We're going to be blessed!

Today we read of the various Israelite tribes that failed to drive out the inhabitants of their territories completely. The Canaanites who were permitted to remain became "thorns in their sides," just as God had forewarned. God also predicted that the Canaanite gods would become snares to Israel.

This picture of Israel is representative of Christians, who although they are saved, fail to overcome the world, the flesh and the devil in their lives and consequently experience the troubles of which God has forewarned. Once we're transferred from the kingdom of darkness into the kingdom of God, we need to go to work immediately on renewing our minds and working out the rest of our salvation (see Rom. 12:2; Phil. 2:12). Let's not be satisfied with just obtaining our "fire insurance." Let's press on to take *all* of our inheritance!

Joshua died at age 110, having lived an interesting and colorful life. You'll get to meet him personally some day!

LUKE 21:29-22:13

You and I will be off the earth by the time of Christ's return. Jesus said that "this generation will not pass away until all things take place" (v. 32). Obviously, He couldn't have meant the generation that was living when He spoke those words, because they're all dead, and those things have not yet taken place. Either He meant all those things would come to pass in one generation, or, as my Bible's marginal note indicates, the word *generation* could be translated "race." That would indicate that the Jewish race (or possibly the Christian "race") would not pass away until all those things took place. Truly, it is nothing short of a miracle that the Jewish race and culture still exist in the world today, in light of all the persecution they have received through the centuries.

Satan entered into Judas, but it was

only because Judas *allowed* Satan to enter. Satan cannot enter a person indiscriminately. Judas betrayed Jesus because he opened the door to Satan, and Satan motivated him. Don't forget that Judas was with Jesus for three years. No doubt he had healed the sick, cast out demons and preached the gospel right along with the other apostles. He didn't have any noticeable evil tendencies to the degree that the other apostles suspected him of being Christ's predicted betrayer (see Matt. 26:22).

We know from John's Gospel, however, that Judas had at least one major character flaw: he loved money and used to steal from Jesus' money box (see John 12:6). It was through that flaw that Satan got into Judas's life. *He betrayed Jesus because he saw an opportunity to make a good sum of money.* It's hard to imagine, but that's what can happen to people who love money more than God. Now you understand better why Jesus said, "You can't serve God and money." Judas had heard Him say it many times, but it fell on deaf ears. Paul wrote, "For the love of money is a root of all sorts of evil, and some by longing for it have wandered away from the faith, and pierced themselves with many a pang" (1 Tim. 6:10).

PSALMS 90:1-91:16

Psalm 90 was written by Moses, and it gives us a little better idea how he must have felt as he wandered in the desert with the Israelites. Remember that he witnessed more than one million funerals during those forty long years.

Psalm 91 is an all-time favorite of a lot of Christians. I don't know of any psalm that can bolster your faith as much as this one.

PROVERBS 13:24-25

So much for the modern theory of the harms of spanking children! Don't be brainwashed (or I should say "braindirtied") by so-called experts. And when you spank children for disobedience, do it on their rear. That's true "childrearing"!

APRIL 24

JUDGES 2:10-3:31

As long as Israel had a strong spiritual leader, the people faithfully served the Lord. But as soon as that leader died, they returned to idolatry. Isn't it sad that even Christians so easily fall away from God when their favorite TV evangelist goes off the air or their pastor is replaced? We all need leaders to follow, but our eyes should be on Jesus and not on some man. If your standard of measurement is other Christians, you're probably backsliding, because those other Christians are probably measuring themselves by you!

Because of Israel's apostasy, God said He would *not* drive out the remaining inhabitants of the promised land, in order to test Israel by them (see 2:22; 3:4). In other words, God *permitted* a temptation for the Israelites. *He didn't tempt them, but He did allow them to be tempted.* In the same way, God never tempts us (see James 1:13), but He does allow us to be tempted. However, He has promised that we will never be tempted beyond what we are able to resist (see 1 Cor. 10:13). Thus, no Christian can ever truthfully say, "The devil made me do it!"

How were the remaining Canaanite nations a test? God had commanded Israel never to intermarry with the Canaanites and never to serve the Canaanites' gods.

By allowing some of the Canaanites to remain, the Israelites were faced with a choice they wouldn't have had otherwise. We read in 3:5-6, "And the sons of Israel lived among the Canaanites, the Hittites, the Amorites, the Perizzites, the Hivites, and the Jebusites; and they took their daughters for themselves as wives, and gave their own daughters to their sons, and served their gods." They failed God's test. Consequently, God gave them over to serve Cushanrishathaim, king of Mesopotamia for eight years.

Under the old covenant, God disciplined the Israelites by turning them over to their physical enemies. Under the new covenant, God disciplines us in a variety of ways, sometimes even by turning the unrepentant over to their spiritual enemies (Matt. 18:21-35; 1 Cor. 5:4-5; 11:28-32; 1 Tim. 1:20). If we judge ourselves and confess our sins, however, He won't have to discipline us (see 1 Cor. 11:31; 1 John 1:9).

LUKE 22:14-34

Today we read about an incident we have not seen in any other Gospel. Jesus told Peter that Satan had demanded (or, as my Bible's marginal note says, "obtained by asking") permission to sift Peter like wheat. In this one verse, we get a glimpse of a subject about which we would all like to know more. We want to be careful not to build major doctrines on one or two verses. However, we also don't want to ignore portions of Scripture, like this one, that offer insight yet raise questions too. Does Satan have access to God? Apparently he did in this case. It reminds us of the story of Job, which we'll read in a few months.

What was the sifting Peter endured? From the context of these verses, it probably was his experience of denying the Lord three times after he promised he would never do such a thing. When the realization of what he had done hit him, he wept bitter tears. It was not until after Jesus' resurrection that Peter would "turn again" (v. 32) and be able to "strengthen his brothers" as Jesus commanded him. In the end, Peter was a better man for it, because he had to evaluate his heart, and he experienced the cleansing, restoring forgiveness of Jesus.

PSALMS 92:1-93:5

Don't these psalms lift you up? They're so positive! Read them slowly, and let them sink in. If you don't feel better, check your pulse to see if you're still alive! The last few verses of Psalm 92 promise that the righteous person will flourish like a palm tree and grow like a cedar in Lebanon. Both of those trees display a stately majesty. Even in old age, the righteous will still bear fruit and be full of sap and very green!

Psalm 93 speaks of the majesty, strength, holiness and steadfastness of God. Like the earth itself, which shall not be moved, God's throne is established from the beginning of time.

PROVERBS 14:1-2

APRIL 25

JUDGES 4:1-5:31

So far we have read through three cycles of sin, oppression, repentance and deliverance. In this third cycle, God used two women to bring deliverance to His people. Israel's march down Mount Tabor into the valley of Megiddo was the nation's step of faith, and God responded in a miraculous way. Suddenly, there was a cloudburst, and the river Kishon, which normally is a quiet brook, turned into a raging torrent. According to 5:20-21, the river itself swept away some of Sisera's army. In the resulting confusion, Israel easily defeated its enemy. "And the land was undisturbed for forty years" (5:31).

LUKE 22:35-53

The first time Jesus sent out His disciples, He told them to take no extra money, no knapsack and not even a second pair of sandals. They had to walk by faith, trusting their needs would be supplied on their way. This time, however, Jesus instructed them to take along extra provisions, and even to take along a sword (see v. 36). Why such a complete change of instructions? The answer is probably found in the next verse, in which Jesus said He would be classed among criminals. In other words, the receptive climate the apostles had previously experienced in their ministries would no longer exist. When they first traveled into a town and announced they had been sent by Jesus, more often than not they found a good number of receptive people. But now, because Jesus was about to gain the reputation of a crucified criminal, it wouldn't be so easy for His associates to find warm welcomes.

PSALM 94:1-23

Once again, we see that God shows mercy to evil people to give them time to repent. Eventually His judgment does come, but it always takes longer than we want it to—*except when we ourselves are being judged.*

PROVERBS 14:3-4

Verse 4 contains a good business principle. No profits come without effort. If you don't have an ox, you don't have to bother cleaning up his manger. But you also don't enjoy the profits that can come with owning an ox.

APRIL 26

JUDGES 6:1-40

It seems that God is always choosing unlikely characters to fulfill His plans. Today we read that Gideon, a very unlikely candidate, was given the task of overthrowing the Midianites. Gideon himself felt completely unqualified until he began to see himself as God saw him.

Gideon reminds me of so many of us who have a poor self-image even though God has made us special people. His Word declares that we are His own sons (see Gal. 3:26) who are dearly loved (see John 17:23). We are new creations in Christ (see 2 Cor. 5:17) and have been made more than conquerors (see Rom. 8:37). We can do all things through Christ who strengthens us (see Phil. 4:13), and our bodies are temples of the Holy Spirit (see 1 Cor. 6:19). If you really believe all that, there's no way you can have a poor self-image!

Gideon, even after seeing an angel of the Lord and his offering consumed by fire, was still timid about following God's instructions to tear down the altar of Baal. So he obeyed God at night (which is better than not obeying God at all)! The local Baal worshippers were enraged when they discovered their altar had been destroyed, but Gideon was spared by his father's good sense: if Baal was angry about it, let *him* punish Gideon.

God's patience with Gideon is amazing. Look at what Gideon prays before his encounter with the Midianites: "If Thou wilt deliver Israel through me, *as Thou hast spoken...*" (vs. 36, italics mine). That's doubt and unbelief if I ever heard it! But God shows him mercy and confirms His promise to Gideon by the miracle of the wet fleece. Even Gideon knows that he is getting close to tempting God, but he makes one more request for God to reverse the miracle the following night. This time the fleece is dry and the ground is wet. I think any of us would have been convinced of God's will by then!

Whatever you do, don't try "putting out a fleece." Under the new covenant, we have the Holy Spirit to guide us by an *inward witness*. If you need direction, pray until you have peace about what God wants you to do. Don't be praying, "Lord, if You want me to marry that certain person, please have it be a cloudy day tomorrow!" The devil might send some clouds so that you marry that person and have to live with a dark cloud hanging over you for the rest of your life!

LUKE 22:54-23:12

Can you imagine how Peter must have felt when the cock crowed and his eyes met the Lord's? Peter didn't just feel bad; he was completely ashamed of himself and went outside to weep bitterly. The tough fisherman from Galilee was being "sifted like wheat" just as Jesus had predicted (22:31).

The charge against Jesus before the Sanhedrin was blasphemy. (They found *God* guilty of claiming to be divine.) Of course, the Roman Pilate would never condemn a man for being a religious fanatic, but the Sanhedrin had no authority to execute Jesus without a sentence from the governor. So their charge before Pilate was treason. Pilate tried to pass the buck to Herod, but to no avail. Eventually all those people—the Sanhedrin, Pilate, Herod, the soldiers who mocked Christ and the crowd that cried for His crucifixion—had to stand before Jesus' judgment.

PSALMS 95:1-96:13

Praise the Lord! God wants us to sing, shout and kneel before Him in our worship. Our worship to Him should come from the heart.

PROVERBS 14:5-6

APRIL 27

JUDGES 7:1-8:17

God wanted it to be very clear to Israel that He was the one who delivered them from the Midianites, so He purposely stacked the odds against Israel. That's a good lesson for us to learn as well. When God allows circumstances to stack up against us to the point where deliverance seems impossible, it may be so we'll know that when deliverance comes, it was God who delivered us and nobody else.

Did you notice whom God first eliminated from Gideon's army? *The fearful.* Twenty-two thousand Israelites didn't have faith that God could bring victory (see 7:3). Once again, the believers among God's people were in the minority. I imagine the fearful ones felt no shame but probably mocked those who had stayed to fight. Can't you hear their criticisms? "They are going to defeat a million Midianites? They should open their eyes to reality!" We should never be ashamed that we are in the minority if we are trusting God's promises. I would rather be a winner who is part of the minority than a loser who is part of the majority!

The second test God had Gideon perform to eliminate part of his "oversized" army was to look at the way each man got his drink of water. There's been a lot of speculation about the significance of this test, but one possibility is that it had *no* special significance. The Bible just doesn't say. Nine thousand, seven hundred men were eliminated as a result, and Gideon was left with three hundred.

I am so blessed in reading Gideon's story, because God was so merciful to Gideon's fears. God knew that Gideon still had some doubts, so God told him to sneak into the Midianite camp and listen to a conversation between two soldiers. Once again, God's promise of victory was confirmed.

LUKE 23:13-43

There are few other passages that reveal the depths of Jesus' love more than Luke's record of Jesus' journey through Jerusalem to Golgotha. Following Him were many women who were weeping in their sorrow for Him. Jesus, unconcerned about Himself, told them to weep for themselves and for their children because of what would eventually befall them. This was another prediction of the future holocaust in Jerusalem and a foreshadowing of the judgment of the entire world at His return. Even on the cross, Jesus' concern was for His mother (see John 19:26-27) and for the soldiers who were dividing His garments (see Luke 23:34). He answered none of His revilers but felt only sorrow for them. *His love is amazing.*

PSALMS 97:1-98:9

Can you imagine seeing an entire mountain melt "like wax at the presence of the Lord" (97:5)? That's how powerful the Lord's presence is! What really amazes me is that God has made us able to "stand in the presence of His glory blameless with great joy" (Jude 24)!

PROVERBS 14:7-8

We become like those with whom we associate. If you don't want to be foolish, don't spend your time with fools.

APRIL 28

JUDGES 8:18-9:21

Gideon displayed great Christlikeness when he turned down the opportunity to become king over Israel. Every opportunity for exaltation is not from the Lord, *especially when it puts us in a place that only God should have*. Gideon recognized this opportunity was not from the Lord.

Gideon did make a few mistakes, however. One was his request of gold from Israel and then fashioning it into an ephod, which became an idol to the people. Second, he married many wives and thus became the father of seventy-two sons. A truly wise man will have only one wife, even in societies where polygamy is permitted. Any man in the Bible who had more than one wife had family troubles as a result. As we read today, after Gideon's death, his son Abimelech, with the support of the people of the cities of Shechem and Beth-millo, murdered all the rest of Gideon's sons with the exception of one.

Jotham, Gideon's surviving innocent son, used a parable to tell his brothers' murderers that they would reap what they had sown. Proverbs 17:13 says, "He who returns evil for good, evil will not depart from his house." Don't cheat by reading ahead, but I'm sure you've figured out that Jotham's words came to pass. God showed those wicked people mercy for three years, and then He set in motion their doom.

LUKE 23:44-24:12

Based on other existing graves from Jesus' time, His gravestone was probably cut in the shape of a large wheel, about four to six feet in diameter. It hadn't been rolled away so Jesus could get out, but so the women and the apostles could get in!

The women were the first to announce the good news of Jesus' resurrection, and the "spiritual" apostles didn't believe them! At least Peter and John (see John 20:2-8) had the curiosity to run to the tomb and investigate for themselves.

Because we know the end of the story, it's difficult for us to see things from the apostles' standpoint. But as far as they were concerned, Jesus was dead and gone for good. All their dreams for the kingdom were crushed. The last three years of their lives seemed pointless. Can you imagine how Peter felt? He had denied the Lord three times, and that was the last time he had seen Jesus alive. It seems that he, more than any other apostle besides John, hoped that Mary's report was true. That may be why he ran to the tomb himself.

PSALM 99:1-9

PROVERBS 14:9-10

The deepest emotions of our hearts cannot be felt by anyone but ourselves. That's another reason it's so good to know the Lord: He knows us better than we know ourselves. He understands!

APRIL 29

JUDGES 9:22-10:18

In today's reading from Judges 9, the evil Abimelech and Shechemites all got what they deserved. Could they have repented and not suffered judgment? Yes. In fact, God gave them three years to repent. If we don't repent of our sins, we, too, will reap what we've sown. God guarantees it (see Gal. 6:7).

In chapter 10, we read of another cycle of Israel's history of sin, oppression, repentance and deliverance. God used the Philistines and Ammonites to discipline His people. When the Israelites cried out to the Lord for deliverance, *He told them to cry out to the gods they had been serving!* So they put away their idols and once again began to serve the Lord, and we read that God "could bear the misery of Israel no longer" (10:16). Isn't that a wonderful way of expressing God's great love for His people? He took no enjoyment from watching them suffer. I'm sure that in your spirit, you are developing a balanced understanding of the "kindness and severity of God" (Rom. 11:22).

LUKE 24:13-53

Today we finish the last of the "synoptic" Gospels, so-called because all three are so similar. You will soon see that John's Gospel is quite different.

Jesus isn't a liar. But He did *pretend* to have no knowledge of His own crucifixion and resurrection when He spoke with the two disciples on the road to Emmaus. In addition, when they approached the village, "He acted as though He would go farther" (v. 28). It almost sounds as if Jesus was enjoying playing a trick on these disciples for a time, intending that they would recognize Him only at the appropriate moment.

I would love to have been there when Jesus gave His Bible lesson to those two disciples, pointing out all the scriptures that spoke of Himself in the Old Testament. Jesus no doubt explained Psalm 22, Isaiah 53 and a host of other messianic passages. We read that Jesus began with Moses (the Pentateuch) and then went through all the prophets. He must have even pointed out how Jonah's experience of being three days and nights in the fish's belly prefigured His three days and nights in the heart of the earth.

At dinner that evening, "their eyes were opened" (v. 31), and they recognized Jesus. Possibly, as Jesus broke the bread, they saw the nailprints in His hands! Can you imagine the look on their faces at the realization that this was Jesus, and then seeing Him suddenly disappear?

Back in Jerusalem (seven miles away), when Jesus suddenly stood in the midst of those in the upper room, I'm sure they just about swallowed their Adam's apples! They thought they were seeing a spirit, but Jesus let them touch Him and watch Him eat some fish. *True Christians believe in the bodily resurrection of Jesus.* (A number of cults teach that Jesus was only resurrected spiritually.)

Note that the first word of Jesus' commission was *repentance* (v. 47). There can be no salvation without it. Repentance means a turning from sin. Our modern phrase "Accept Jesus as your Savior" is nowhere to be found in the Bible. *God wants people to repent and make Jesus Christ their Lord*, as well as trusting Him as their Savior. We should be careful not to neglect telling people about the need for repentance.

Along with the commission, Jesus promised to endue the disciples with power for the task. All they had to do was wait in Jerusalem until the Holy Spirit came. We'll read about that in the book of Acts.

PSALM 100:1-5

Serve the Lord with gladness," we read today. Yet many of us serve Him reluctantly and halfheartedly. The word *enthusiasm* is derived from two Greek words, one meaning "God" and the other meaning "within." So *enthusiasm* really means "having God within you"! That's why Christians should be the world's most enthusiastic people! If you've lost the joy of serving Jesus, repent and stir yourself up! You ought to be having the time of your life!

PROVERBS 14:11-12

APRIL 30

JUDGES 11:1-12:15

So far in the book of Judges, God had used a variety of people, including a young coward, to deliver His people from oppression. Now He used Jephthah, the rejected son of a harlot. Are you getting the point? What are your excuses for why the Lord can't use you? We'll have them all eliminated by the end of this book!

Jephthah, like a lot of Christians, failed

to realize that God blesses us simply because of His grace. We don't have to make vows to "twist His arm" to make Him work for us. When you think about Jephthah's vow, it's a ridiculous deal and reveals even further his lack of understanding of God's character. He was saying in effect: "God, if You'll give me victory, I'll give You a goat!" (As in many places in the world today, people and animals lived under one roof, but in separate rooms.) No doubt he was expecting such an animal to come out of the house first. Jephthah was relating to God as the Canaanites related to their gods.

He certainly never expected his daughter would be the first to greet him when he returned, and he was overwhelmed with grief when she did. Did Jephthah actually offer his own daughter as a burnt offering? The Scripture is unclear. If he did, *it was in no way endorsed by the Lord*. Child sacrifices were forbidden under the law. If he didn't, it may be she was "offered up to the Lord" by living a life of perpetual virginity and working in the Lord's service at the tabernacle in Shiloh.

Jephthah wasn't as tactful as Gideon in dealing with the Ephraimites, and confrontation was inevitable. When the civil war ended, forty-two thousand men of Ephraim were dead, and the storm clouds for a national split were gathering in Israel.

JOHN 1:1-28

The synoptic Gospels were probably all available for reference when the apostle John wrote his account around A.D. 90. However, about 90 percent of his Gospel can't be found in any of the other three. John was writing to people whom he assumed already had a fair knowledge of the Lord (see 1:16). That's probably why this Gospel is the favorite of most Christians. John was one of the "inner circle" of three, along with his brother James and Peter. Quite possibly, he knew Jesus better than any other person of his day. And if it weren't for his Gospel, we wouldn't know Jesus nearly as well as we do.

John's Gospel contains certain vital truths. For example, the very first verse teaches us that Jesus was God. The second and third verses reveal that Jesus has existed from eternity and was involved in the creation of the universe. Only Jesus can offer eternal life, and that life brings "light" into our spirits, driving out the darkness that was there before (see 1:4). Those who have believed in Him have been made children of God who can truthfully say they have been born of God (see 1:12-13). I'm sorry to say that those precious truths have been memorized only as cold theological facts by too many Christians. Think of it! We are God's kids!

When the priests and Levites visited John the Baptist to learn his biblical identity, they asked him three questions. Was he the Christ? Elijah? The Prophet? They were looking for one or all of those based on Old Testament promises. The Christ was foretold throughout the Old Testament. The Prophet was predicted by Moses in Deuteronomy 18:15: "The Lord your God will raise up for you a prophet like me from among you, from your countrymen, you shall listen to him." We know, of course, that Jesus was that Prophet. God also had promised in the last few verses of Malachi, the last book of the Old Testament, that He would send Elijah before the coming of the "great and terrible day of the Lord" (Mal. 4:5). John the Baptist fulfilled that prophecy at least in part, although *he himself didn't realize it*. All he knew was that he was fulfilling some verses in Isaiah (see 1:23), preparing the way for the ministry of the Lord Jesus.

PSALM 101:1-8

David certainly had good intentions to follow God fully, and he sounds like the kind of person we need in our government. Martin Luther spoke of this psalm as "a mirror for magistrates." Christians have been criticized lately for bringing "moral issues" into the political limelight, but I would rather have a person in office who has resolved to follow God in all matters than people who think they are God.

PROVERBS 14:13-14

MAY 1

JUDGES 13:1-14:20

So far in the book of Judges we have covered more than 250 years of Israel's sad history. We've read about some colorful characters, but none compares with Samson. There's no doubt that Samson was specially chosen by God to perform a certain task. However, God never violates a person's free will, and even a God-called minister who is used to perform miracles can choose to follow sin. Ministers have no special gifts to live what they preach.

Samson's life is hard to interpret, and commentators are divided on a number of issues. We must not forget, however, that Samson was called of God to be under the Nazarite vow all his life. According to Numbers 6 a Nazarite was not permitted to eat grapes or raisins or to drink grape juice, wine or strong drink. He was also forbidden to cut his hair or to touch any corpse.

We have to assume that Samson was led of the Lord to seek his wife from the Philistines, according to 14:4. God at least *allowed* it to bring His purposes to pass. (Philistia was not one of the nations with whom Israel was forbidden to intermarry.)

At times throughout his life we see Samson displaying an enormous supernatural strength. The first time was when Samson killed a vicious lion with his bare hands on the way to visit his fiancee. Most artists have portrayed Samson as a muscle-man, but however big his muscles were, there's no way he could have performed his feats of strength without supernatural ability.

I assume that when the Spirit of God came upon Samson, and he killed thirty men of the Philistine city of Ashkelon in order to have thirty garments to give to the wedding guests who tricked him, the city of Ashkelon was particularly deserving of punishment. Again, it's hard to know what was commissioned by the Lord and what was permitted.

Some commentators say that Samson was at fault because of his disobedience to his parents. They didn't want him to take a Philistine wife. However, the text plainly says that Samson's parents "did not know that it was of the Lord" (14:4).

Others interpret the incident when the lion attacked Samson as a sign from the Lord that Samson was stepping out of God's will by attempting to marry a Philistine girl. But the Bible doesn't say that, and God protected him from the lion even when he was supposedly out of God's will.

Others point out that Samson broke his Nazarite vow when he touched the corpse of the lion, but as I understand it the Nazarite was only forbidden to touch a *human* corpse (see Num. 6).

Some say that Samson broke his Nazarite vow of abstinence from wine at his own wedding feast, but the Bible says nothing of what Samson drank at that time. I'm inclined to think that up until this point, *Samson has done nothing out of God's will.*

Finally, Samson goes back to his father's house, and his wife is given by her father to Samson's "best man." Probably, Samson had never consummated his marriage.

JOHN 1:29-51

John, more than any other Gospel writer, gives us insight into the purpose of Christ's coming. Today's first verse declares Jesus to be "the Lamb of God who takes away the sin of the world." Having read the Pentateuch, you understand exactly what that means.

Apparently during Jesus' first conversation with Peter, He changed his name from Simon to Peter. *Simon* means "reed," a tall grass with hollow stalks; *Peter* means "rock." At his first encounter with Jesus, he was changed from a reed to a rock!

When a person truly encounters Jesus, his self-image is radically changed. It doesn't matter what you were before your salvation. You may have been a loser, but the Lord says you're a winner. You may have felt unloved, but the Lord says you are dearly loved. You may have felt weak, but the Lord says He is your strength. You may have felt a lack of ability, but the Lord says you can do all things through Him. You may have been sick, but the Lord says He is your healer. You may have been poor, but the Lord says He is your provider. I could go on and on, but my point is that God wants us to see ourselves as He does. Whether you realize it or not, you are *wonderful*. Start believing it and acting like it!

PSALM 102:1-28

Once again we read the prayer of a person who, along with others, was suffering God's discipline (see v. 10). The occasion of its writing was obviously some invasion of Jerusalem. According to Hebrews 1:10-12, at least part of this psalm was addressed to the Lord Jesus (vv. 25-27). For that reason some regard this psalm as entirely messianic, foretelling Christ's feelings on the cross. If this psalm *is* entirely messianic, we have another perfect example of "the law of double reference." The psalmist said that now God's time had arrived to have compassion on Zion (see v. 13), meaning not just that God's judgment was almost finished, but also that when Jesus died on the cross, it was God's greatest display of love and compassion for His people.

PROVERBS 14:15-16

Unfortunately, some Christians will naively believe anything, because we've been taught that doubting is wrong. However, it's wrong only to doubt *God's words*. It's always wise to use caution when believing the words of other people, including those in the ministry. Trust is something that should be earned.

MAY 2

JUDGES 15:1-16:31

You need to go out and treat yourself today, because you have read one-third of the entire Bible. Congratulations!

Let me say again that the details of Samson's life are foggy, but the Holy Spirit has given us that which is important.

Samson decided to visit his wife, who lived with her parents. This may seem strange to us, but such marriage agreements existed in those days. It was during that visit that Samson discovered that his wife had been given to his best man. Samson vowed revenge on the Philistines.

The Lord helped Samson to get revenge in order to bring judgment upon the Philistines. I don't know how Samson could have caught three hundred foxes and set the Philistine fields aflame by tying torches to the foxes' tails without God's help!

They blamed Samson's father-in-law and his daughter and consequently burned them alive. Remember, the Philistines had previously threatened to do just that when Samson's fiancee wouldn't tell them the answer to the riddle. Unfortunately, she suffered the very fate that she tried to escape. When Samson heard of their treacherous act, he "struck them ruthlessly with a great slaughter" (15:8). No doubt, Samson became public enemy number one.

Samson is willingly apprehended by his fellow Israelites and delivered to the Philistines. Once again the Spirit of the Lord anoints him and he kills a thousand men with a donkey's jawbone.

Judges 15 ends by informing us that Samson judged Israel for twenty years. That probably indicates there is a great space of time between this chapter and the next—chapter 16 may have begun twenty years later.

Samson's great weakness was women, and although commentators disagree about what Samson did right or wrong, there is *no doubt* he was out of the Lord's will when he had sex with a prostitute in Gaza. However, he may very well have been led of the Lord to go to Gaza, because once again the anointing came upon him to pull down the city gates and carry them thirty-eight miles and up a mountain that rose more than three thousand feet.

How could God use Samson after he had just committed an immoral act? This is difficult for us to understand. But God's gifts and callings are "irrevocable" (Rom. 11:29). Ministers are only *stewards* of God's grace. Samson in Gaza was no different from an evangelist who is led to preach in a certain city but while there falls into adultery, yet still preaches anointed sermons and sees people get saved. Although God will not take away the gift or calling He has given to a person, if that person persists in sin, God will judge. Samson was shown mercy in the case of the prostitute of Gaza, but his unbridled lust eventually brought his downfall.

We realize, of course, that Samson's strength was not in his hair, but that his long hair was a sign of his lifetime separation to God under the Nazarite vow. With his hair shaved off, his special relationship with God was also severed, and God would not anoint him with strength to escape the consequences of his sin. The man of God whose downfall had come through the lust of his eyes now had his eyes gouged out by the Philistines.

While in prison Samson had time to reflect on his life and apparently came to a place of repentance and reconsecration. Once more God anointed him with strength, and it seems that Samson fulfilled the ministry to which God had called him—to begin to deliver Israel from the Philistines (see 13:5). Most of the great Philistine leaders were probably killed in the collapse of the pillared temple.

We can learn many lessons from Samson's life, but I only want to point to one in conclusion. When two people live together out of wedlock, both usually think they are loved by the other. But they're just using each other, because where there is no marriage commitment between people having a sexual relationship, there is no real love. They should get ready for heartache. Samson thought Delilah loved him. How wrong he was!

JOHN 2:1-25

If Jesus changed water into wine, how could anyone say it's a sin to drink alcohol? I used to think that myself—until I learned that the wine in Jesus' day was so low in alcoholic content that it wouldn't even be considered an alcoholic beverage by modern standards. For a person to get drunk on wine in Jesus' day, he had to consume several gallons. Any degree of intoxication is a sin, so we cannot justify drinking modern wines just because Jesus changed water into slightly fermented grape juice at a wedding feast. Every Christian should avoid even the appearance of evil.

The cleansing of the temple we read about today was not the same incident recorded in the other Gospels; this event occurred at the beginning of Jesus' ministry, while the other occurred near the end of His life. In this case Jesus actually made the scourge of cords with which He drove out the moneychangers. Why wasn't Jesus arrested for disorderly conduct? Possibly because everyone knew that what was going on was wrong, but no one before was brave enough to do anything about it. There's nothing wrong with exchanging money or selling animals, but those folks had turned God's temple into a discount store. Three years later when Jesus cleansed the temple again, He accused them of making God's temple into a den of thieves. So we assume those people were ripping off their customers—Jews who had come to worship God. *They were using the Lord to make dishonest gain.*

How little Jesus' audience realized the truth of His statement about the temple's being destroyed and rebuilt in three days! Jesus' body was even more a temple of God than Herod's great house of worship.

PSALM 103:1-22

I hope that by now you are convinced that it is God's will for us to be healed. Not only must we believe that God wants us to be healed, we must know how to receive healing.

Jesus said that we are to believe that we receive when we pray (Mark 11:24). If we believe that we receive something when we pray, then we will talk and act like we have received it. If you are having difficulty receiving what you know God has promised, spend extra time meditating on Mark 11:23-24.

PROVERBS 14:17-19

MAY 3

JUDGES 17:1-18:31

Get ready for some pretty depressing chapters in Israel's history. These last pages of the book of Judges have one key theme, found in 17:6: "In those days there was no king in Israel; every man did what was right in his own eyes." The story of Micah's idolatry is a perfect illustration, and that's probably why the Holy Spirit had it preserved for us to read.

In making silver idols, Micah's mother certainly revealed how far she was from understanding the ways of the Lord, since crafting any graven image was a transgression of the second commandment. The same was true of Micah when he consecrated one of his sons to be a priest in a shrine he had built for those and other idols. Talk about starting your own religion! To make matters worse, Micah hired a passing Levite to become his personal priest and thought the Lord would bless him for it!

The actions of the Danites further show that everybody was doing what was right in his own eyes. However, the tabernacle was still set up at Shiloh (see 18:31), so we know there was some small remnant who had a true knowledge of the Lord.

If that story seems hard to believe, just look at many liberal churches today. When people neglect the true revelation of God, it's amazing what they will come up with to replace it.

JOHN 3:1-21

The Gospel of John is full of Jesus' spiritual sayings that His confused listeners tried to interpret literally. Such was the case in this story of Jesus' conversation with Nicodemus. Nicodemus had no idea how a person could be born again, but Jesus explained He was talking about a spiritual rebirth, not a physical one. Every person is actually a spirit who has a soul and who lives in a body. It is the spirit that needs to be regenerated by the Holy Spirit, because it is spiritually dead. That person then has a brand new nature. As the Bible puts it, Jesus comes to live inside!

Jesus said that just as you can't see the wind but you can see the effects of it (see v. 8), so, too, do the effects of spiritual rebirth show up on the outside. If the leaves aren't rustling, the wind isn't blowing.

What did Jesus mean when he said, "Unless one is born of *water* and the Spirit, he cannot enter into the kingdom of God" (v. 5, italics mine)? Most think that water is symbolic of the Word of God. The Word is what gives us faith to believe in Jesus. Ephesians 5:25-26 says, "Christ also loved the church and gave Himself up for her; that He might sanctify her, having cleansed her by *the washing of water with the word*" (italics mine).

As Jesus described it, God's plan of salvation is very simple. We are only required to believe in Jesus (see v. 16)—to believe that He is the Son of God and that He was raised from the dead. If we believe that, we will act differently. If He is the Son of God and if He is still alive, we must obey Him!

Why don't all people believe the gospel when they hear it? Because they love darkness (see v. 19). That is, they know that if they believe in Jesus they will have to stop sinning, and they don't want to. It all boils down to the condition of their heart.

PSALM 104:1-23

Isn't this a great psalm extolling the wonders of God's creation? Isn't it sad that so often we're too busy to take time and marvel? If your prayer life is suffering, maybe you should take a walk in the woods and view what God has done. Or take a walk outside at night and gaze at the stars. God is great, and God is good!

PROVERBS 14:20-21

Verse 20 is another commentary on the way things normally are, but verse 21 states a moral truth about how things should be. People tend to love the rich more than the poor, but only because most are out for what they can get. God wants us to show no partiality; our love for others should be based on our Christ-like character, not on potential personal profits.

MAY 4

JUDGES 19:1-20:48

And you thought the spiritual decline in Israel looked bad in yesterday's reading! Today's story is the ultimate example of how far Israel had fallen since the days of Joshua. It's inconceivable that such a rape and murder could have occurred, much less have been condoned by anyone else, in his day. It's also hard to believe that you can read such things in the Bible, but there they are.

Once the civil war over this offense began, we have to wonder why God permitted the allied tribes to lose so many men and, in fact, even instructed them to go to battle (see 20:23). We can only conclude that the whole thing was being used by God as judgment on *all* tribes, and especially Benjamin. It wasn't until the third day of battle that the Lord began to fight on behalf of the allied tribes. When it was over, almost the entire tribe of Benjamin had been annihilated.

JOHN 3:22-4:3

John the Baptist had a good attitude didn't he? He recognized that Jesus would increase but he would decrease. That would be a good prayer for us—that Jesus would increase and we would decrease. We should be a reflection *of* Christ rather than a reflection *on* Him.

We see the obvious correlation between faith and obedience in John's statement in 3:36: "He who *believes* in the Son has eternal life; but he who does not *obey* the Son shall not see life, but the wrath of God abides on him" (italics mine). *Believing ones are obedient ones.*

What is eternal life? Most Christians think it means they are going to live forever, but everyone is going to live forever whether they are saved or not. So in that sense everyone has eternal life. The Greek word translated "life" in 3:36 is the word *zoe* (zoe-ay). *Zoe* is the supernatural life of God that is imparted to our spirits when we are born again. That life replaces the death that is in our spirits prior to being saved. We read in John 1:4, speaking of Jesus, "In Him was life [zoe], and the life [zoe] was the light of men." That "life" enlightens our spirits. It's difficult to describe, but I'm sure you realize that something happened inside you when you were saved! That was *zoe*, and it's still there! Keep your eyes alert for the many more verses in John that speak of "life" or "eternal life."

PSALM 104:24-35

PROVERBS 14:22-24

God is not opposed to Christians having money. The writer says "the crown of the wise is their riches." The main purpose for which God blesses the wise with riches is to support the advancement of the kingdom of God.

MAY 5

JUDGES 21:1-RUTH 1:22

If you thought the last two days' readings in the book of Judges were depressing, today's outdoes them both. Keep in mind that the theme of Judges is that "every man did what was right in his own eyes." We read that phrase in 17:6 and again in the final verse of the entire book.

By the end of the civil war every person of the tribe of Benjamin had been slaughtered except for six hundred fighting men who had found refuge in the wilderness. A total of sixty-five thousand Israelites had died. The allied tribes were very sad, because in the heat of their initial anger they had all sworn never to permit their daughters to marry men from Benjamin. Therefore the tribe of Benjamin was doomed to extinction once the six hundred died.

Their solution baffles me, but once again, "Every man was doing what was right in his own eyes." The book of Judges is a revelation of what happens when people turn from serving God and become a law unto themselves: the result is confusion, suffering and a breakdown of normal society. The pattern has been repeated hundreds of times through the centuries—in fact, we can see it happening in our own society today.

Praise God that the book of Ruth has an entirely different story to tell! It's also set during the time of the judges, yet we'll see that God was still working His plan of redemption for the human race, and there were still godly people living while the rest of the nation slipped into apostasy.

The Bible doesn't say why there was famine in Israel, but in light of what we know of the times it's not difficult to guess. Neither do we know if Elimelech was right or wrong to migrate to the land of Moab on the eastern side of the Dead Sea. But he was leaving his inheritance, and he died shortly after arriving in Moab.

When Naomi decided to return to Israel, her argument to her daughters-in-law that they should stay in Moab would seem strange if we didn't understand the custom of a man's marrying his dead brother's wife to raise up offspring in his name. Naomi told Orpah and Ruth that even if she married that day, it would be years before they could marry her new sons!

Naomi had probably been witnessing to Orpah and Ruth for years, and now Ruth wanted to remain close to her "spiritual mother" and meet other people of the God of Israel. Her promise of devotion is beautiful: "For where you go, I will go, and where you lodge, I will lodge. Your people shall be my people, and your God, my God....Thus may the Lord do to me, and worse, if anything but death parts you and me" (vv. 16-17). I have to think that her love for the Lord had the greatest influence on her decision. And I'm glad to say the story has a happy ending for both Naomi and Ruth. (No reading ahead now!)

JOHN 4:4-42

Although the majority of Jews were prejudiced against Samaritans in Jesus' day, He loved them unreservedly. This story of the woman at the well of Samaria beautifully illustrates our Lord's concern for all the different people of the world.

The woman may very well have been an outcast herself, as we find her drawing water from the well at noon. Most often, women would draw their water when it was cooler, in the morning or evening, and spend some time discussing the local gossip. But this woman had come alone. *Jesus took time for a woman who was hated by the Jewish race, had suffered the rejection of divorce five times, was very possibly an outcast among her own people and was now living with a man immorally.* What a lesson we can learn from Jesus' love! The church also should show no bigotry. We should be against divorce but not against divorced people. The church should hate immorality but not immoral people.

Notice the beautiful way Jesus witnessed to this Samaritan woman. He didn't start by asking if she was interested in God. Instead He caught her attention by His love. She was shocked that He, a Jew, would even speak to her. We, too, should first get the attention of unsaved people by our love.

Second, He captured her interest by talking about something she could understand, comparing it to something of which she had no knowledge (i.e., "water" with "living water"). We can often direct a conversation about natural things to spiritual issues by making comparisons.

Third, Jesus sparked a desire for what He had to offer. The woman was asking for living water before she even knew what it was! We need to speak and live so that people want what we have even before they know what it is!

What was the living water of which Jesus spoke? He was referring to the Holy Spirit who comes to live inside us when we are spiritually reborn. He is the "well of water springing up to eternal life" (Greek *zoe*) (v. 14). Once we have taken a drink of that living water, our inward thirst is satisfied.

All through the Gospel of John, Jesus spoke on a spiritual plane, and His listeners tried to interpret what He said from a natural perspective. This Samaritan woman was one of them! But she eventually understood and not only believed in the Lord, but also became the first evangelist to Samaria.

What does it mean to worship "in spirit and truth" (v. 23)? I believe it means to worship God from our hearts (spirits) and with sincerity (in truth). So much of our worship is done insincerely from our heads. We need to grow to the place where we don't have to be stimulated by a fired-up worship leader to get in the mood to worship God.

Jesus told the disciples He had a hunger to do God's will (see v. 34). I hope you have sensed that hunger in your spirit as well. Jesus in you is longing to minister to people through you. The feeling you get after you have done God's will is better than the feeling you get after you've eaten a T-bone steak!

PSALM 105:1-15

PROVERBS 14:25

MAY 6

RUTH 2:1-4:22

When Naomi and Ruth returned to Bethlehem, they had nothing, but thankfully God had made provision for the poor in the Law of Moses. We have already read in Leviticus 19:9-10: "Now when you reap the harvest of your land, you shall not reap to the very corners of your field, neither shall you gather the gleanings of your harvest...you shall leave them for the needy and for the stranger." So Ruth went out to gather the gleanings (what was missed by the reapers) and ended up in the field of Boaz, a cousin of Ruth's dead husband, according to Jewish historians. Little did Ruth realized that this was the beginning of a love story that would play a part in the greatest love story of all time! Eventually one of Ruth's descendants, Joseph, would become Jesus' earthly father in the same town of Bethlehem.

As you've read, this story has a totally happy ending. Ruth married Boaz, her kinsman-redeemer, and she and Naomi were provided for until death. Ruth had a child who became the grandfather of David. Notice also that in this story Boaz is a type of Christ, who had mercy on us when we were destitute and who redeemed us. We have now become His Gentile bride.

JOHN 4:43-54

John is the only Gospel writer to record this healing of the nobleman's son. Jesus was back in Cana of Galilee, where He had changed the water into wine. A royal official, having learned that Jesus was there, traveled from Capernaum to request that Jesus heal his son. When Jesus said, "Unless you people see signs and wonders, you simply will not believe" (v. 48), He was probably indicating that the report of the water changing into wine was what sparked faith in this man to come to Jesus.

When Jesus told the nobleman to go his way because his son lived, the Bible says that he believed the word of Jesus and went. But if we examine the story closely, we see more evidence of the man's faith. He probably could have returned home that same day because it was only about one o'clock in the afternoon, and Capernaum was only about fifteen miles from Cana. But there was no need for him to rush home to see how his son was doing. He believed, so it was not until the next day that he arrived. Remember that his son had been dying. *This man rested in Jesus' promise.*

If we are believing God, we also don't need to be in a hurry or check to see "if" God's Word is working. Faith acts as if the desire has already come to pass.

PSALM 105:16-36

Aren't you happy that you understand all the incidents of which the psalmist speaks in this psalm?

PROVERBS 14:26-27

MAY 7

1 SAMUEL 1:1-2:21

The two books of Samuel are all about the prophet Samuel and the first two kings of Israel, Saul and David. We're going to read stories that you might remember from your childhood Sunday school classes, such as the story of David and Goliath. We will join David in the trials during which he wrote some of the anointed psalms we have already read. You're going to love these books, because they contain stories that cover a time period of about one hundred years.

The events in these books follow the time of the judges. So the tabernacle was still set up at Shiloh where it had been for the past four hundred years. It was there that Elkanah would travel year after year with his two wives to offer sacrifices to the Lord. We have yet to read an example of a man who had more than one wife and didn't have trouble as a result. Elkanah was no exception. One wife, Peninnah, gave him sons and daughters, while Hannah remained barren. Peninnah would provoke Hannah bitterly because of it, and also possibly because she realized their husband loved Hannah the most. But the Lord had closed Hannah's womb. The result was that Hannah made a vow to the Lord. Hannah rose from her prayer with joy (see 1:18), which certainly was an indication of her faith. If we have faith when we pray, we will also rise from prayer with a smile.

Samuel was probably weaned at about age three, and then he was taken by his mother to stay with Eli the priest at Shiloh. What a heartbreaking task that must have been for Hannah, but she was determined to keep her vow.

Although Eli was the high priest of Israel, like too many ministers he failed at the job of raising his sons to fear the Lord. Why he failed, we don't know. But his failure makes me realize there's more to raising children successfully than just making sure they're in church every Sunday. In Eli's day there was only one "church," and he spent practically every day there! His sons worked with him there. Perhaps they became cynical about the things of God when they saw the hypocrisy of the Israelites. Perhaps their father was so busy that he failed to spend time with his sons, or maybe he simply failed to train them properly. We'll read tomorrow that in some ways Eli's sons were only imitating their father's example.

Our reading today ends on a good note. God gave Hannah three more sons and two daughters. *You can't outgive God.* Whatever we give Him, He always makes it up to us.

JOHN 5:1-23

This story of the crippled man at the pool of Bethesda is a beautiful example of the "gift of healing." Jesus healed people primarily by two methods: by inspiring them to believe and be healed by their faith, and by the ministry of gifts of healings.

Gifts of healings operate as the Spirit wills (1 Cor. 12:1-11). They can work on behalf of people who have little or no faith at all. Such healings are completely the work of God. Notice that it was not this man's faith in Jesus which brought about his healing. When questioned by the Jews, the formerly crippled man didn't know who it was who had commanded him to take up his pallet and walk! It couldn't have been his faith in Jesus that healed him.

This incident took place at the Pool of Bethesda, which I always imagined to be a shallow wading pool until I visited the (supposed) excavations of it in Jerusalem. To my surprise it was actually a reservoir more than twenty feet deep! If that was the pool these sick people were waiting for an angel to stir up, it would have taken some faith for crippled or blind people to jump in, because if they didn't get healed, they may very well have drowned!

Jesus later told the man He had healed that he should sin no more so that nothing worse would befall him (see v. 14). The clear implication is that if the man sinned, he could open the door to something worse than his previous sickness. We, too, can open the door to sickness through sin and need to examine ourselves when sickness attacks. Of course, not all sickness comes as a result of sin. At times it comes only because Satan hates you. Every person will have to seek God for himself in these instances.

PSALM 105:37-45

When God brought Israel out of Egypt He not only prospered them with the Egyptians' silver and gold, but He granted them divine health as well. We read today that "among His tribes there was not one who stumbled" (v. 37).

PROVERBS 14:28-29

We always regret it when we lose our temper. Have you ever said you were going to give someone a piece of your mind? My mother-in-law says, "You better not give them a piece of your mind. You might need all of it someday!"

MAY 8

1 SAMUEL 2:22-4:22

The judgment on the house of Eli was not just because of the sin of Eli's two sons but also because of Eli's own sin. According to 2:29 Eli was just as guilty of taking the best portions of the sacrifices, which belonged to the Lord. We read that he had honored his sons above the Lord, which probably means he had allowed them to get away with their sacrilege with his full knowledge. And Eli benefited from his sons' taking the best of the offerings, because God accused him of getting fat from eating them (see 2:29). When he died, Eli must have been very fat, because he broke his neck by falling from a chair (see 4:18). What an example of being destroyed by your own sin!

We read a verse today that is right from the lips of God and that I want you to remember always. God said in 2:30, "For those who honor Me I will honor, and those who despise Me will be lightly esteemed." What does it mean to honor God? It means to obey Him, trust Him and give Him the glory when He uses us. But don't forget the negative part of that promise. Eli had despised God by serving his own interests above God's, so he was lightly esteemed. God promised that the priesthood would not continue through Eli's house.

Young Samuel obviously heard the audible voice of God and also saw Him in visions (see 3:4-8,10,15,21). Of course, God has not promised to speak to us in an audible voice, so we shouldn't be seeking such manifestations. If they come, fine, but if not, that's fine too. However, God *has* promised to guide us. He does that primarily through an inward witness.

It's sad that the Israelites thought they would be ensured victory over the Philistines if they took the ark of the covenant with them into battle. They were trying to use it as a good-luck charm. But it obviously didn't work, and the city of Shiloh was destroyed. Today you can visit the pile of stones that remain (see Jer. 7:12-15).

JOHN 5:24-47

When Jesus promised that everyone who believes will not come into judgment but will have passed out of death into life, He was speaking of spiritual death and life. We are spiritually alive, and our spirits now have a new nature in them. We have become actual children of God. Think about that!

Eventually every person who ever died is going to be bodily resurrected. That is, the elements that used to make up their bodies will be reformed to make new bodies, and their spirits, which never died, will once again be reunited with their bodies. God made the first man out of dirt, so it will be no problem for Him to make a few billion more. If we study other scriptures about the resurrection that will take place, we discover that not everyone will be resurrected at the same time. At the rapture of the church, all those who have died in Christ will experience a resurrection and will then have glorified bodies, as Christ has now. It won't be until *the end* of the millennial reign of Christ when the unrighteous will be resurrected to stand at the final judgment (see Rev. 20:5).

Jesus' argument before the Jews who hated Him was so honest and pure. He pointed out that there was so much evidence for His divinity that there really was no argument against Him. John the Baptist, Jesus' own miracles, God the Father and the entire Old Testament pointed to Jesus as the Christ. *A person would have to not want to see it in order not to see it.*

Why didn't they receive Him? Because they were more concerned with what others would think than with what God thought (see v. 44). Isn't that the main reason people won't believe in Jesus today? They'll go to certain churches as long as it's socially acceptable. I guarantee that once you become a born-again Christian, people are going to think you're strange. But we don't ever want it to be socially acceptable to be born again, because then everyone would fake being saved.

PSALM 106:1-12

PROVERBS 14:30-31

Verse 30 has been proved to be scientifically true. People who live under stress open the door to sickness. Thank God that no matter how stressful our circumstances, we can cast our cares on our loving heavenly Father (see 1 Pet. 5:7).

MAY 9

1 SAMUEL 5:1-7:17

Even though God had used the Philistines as a means of judgment upon Israel, that didn't mean the Philistines themselves were not once again ripe for their own judgment. Sometimes we're tempted to think that all God did in the Old Testament was send His judgment constantly, but we must realize we're covering hundreds of years of history over a few pages.

Notice that God didn't judge the Philistines without first giving them opportunity to repent. Twice when the ark of the covenant was in the house of the Philistine god Dagon, the priests found the statue of Dagon fallen on his face before the ark. You would think they would have gotten the message and said to themselves, The God of Israel is obviously more powerful than our god, and He's trying to persuade us to serve Him, so let's do it! But no, they just moved the ark out of Dagon's house! And that is when we see the judgment of the tumors coming upon the various cities in which the ark was located. Even then you would think they would have repented and turned to God, but their solution was just to get rid of the ark.

It took seven months of plagues and tumors before the Philistines returned the ark, and when they did, God still revealed Himself through a miracle. They placed the ark on a cart and yoked it to two milch cows who had never had yokes on them. After taking their calves away from them, the Philistines watched as the two cows miraculously pulled the cart together toward Israel. They would have been expected to head in the direction of their calves! Through this sign the Philistines had no doubt (and no more excuse) that it was the God of Israel who had judged them.

One sad note at the end of chapter 6 is the death of 50,070 Israelites (the NIV says 70) who looked into the ark. Their sin was equivalent to entering into the holy of holies in the tabernacle. God must be treated with respect.

I sometimes think we need a good dose of God's holiness. I cringe when I see how disrespectful some Christians are toward God. For example, when we come together in church to worship Him corporately, you can count on the same people to come in late every time. Would you be late for an appointment with the president of the country? Why not? Because he is important. So how can we justify our disrespect for God? Our actions reveal our attitudes toward God.

What a difference it made in battle

against their enemies when the Israelites truly repented and sought the Lord. The Philistines were easily defeated with the Lord's help.

JOHN 6:1-21

In this fourth account of the feeding of the five thousand, John includes one significant point the other Gospel writers left out: Jesus *tested* Philip by asking him where they could buy enough food to feed the multitude (see v. 6). Would he say, Nothing is impossible with You, Jesus! Or would he say, It's crazy to think we could ever feed all these people! When you see a problem arising, do you see doom and gloom, or do you see another opportunity for God to move on your behalf? Jesus is evaluating your faith too!

One other detail John includes is that at that time, Jesus' followers were desiring to take Him forcefully and make Him king (see v. 15). They were blind to their need of a *spiritual* deliverer and were looking only for a *political* deliverer. They didn't realize that their need for freedom from the kingdom of Satan was more necessary than their need to be delivered from the Romans. We Christians should be careful not to fall into that same trap. Although it's important that we as responsible citizens be involved in our government, we should realize that good government and good societies stem from good people. Our greatest battle is not against corruption in government but against the corruption that has invaded all people's spirits and holds them in bondage. When people change, government and society change.

One final, unique detail we read today when Jesus walked on the water is that when He stepped into the boat, they were immediately arriving at land. All thirteen men and a boat were instantly transported for as much as a couple of miles! We'll read in the book of Acts how God transported Philip the evangelist in the same way.

PSALM 106:13-31

PROVERBS 14:32-33

MAY 10

1 SAMUEL 8:1-9:27

It is so sad to read that a man with as much integrity as Samuel didn't succeed in raising his sons to be of the same character—just like Eli. Their stories serve as a warning to us. It was Samuel who appointed his sons as judges over Israel, not God. And Samuel made the same mistake that other men of God have made since then. They love their sons so much that they try to pass on their own ministries to them. Yet the sons can never fill their fathers' shoes unless they go through the same trials and training their fathers endured. All parents need to beware. We work so hard to give our children everything we didn't have as children, but as a result our children never enjoy what we did have—like the joy of dreaming or working toward a goal.

Obviously it wasn't God's perfect will that Israel have a king like other nations. But God judged them by giving them what they wanted. In effect He was saying, "So you want a king? O.K., I'll give you one, and you'll learn a lesson!" As God said through His prophet Hosea years later, "I gave you a king in My anger, and took him away in My wrath" (Hos. 13:11). Sometimes the worst judgment God can give us is to let us have our own way.

God Himself said to Samuel, "They have not rejected you, but they have rejected Me from being king over them" (8:7). If I had been God, I would have rejected them right then, but God is purely unselfish. He only wanted to be their king because He knew that would be best for them. He even warned them of the price they would have to pay if they wanted a king, but they would not be persuaded even by God!

Keep in mind as the story of Saul's kingship unfolds that he started as a selfless, humble person. When first respectfully spoken of by Samuel, Saul replied, "Am I not a Benjamite, of the smallest of the tribes of Israel?" (Remember that only six hundred men of Benjamin were still alive at the end of the book of Judges.) "And my family the least of all the families of the tribe of Benjamin? Why then do you speak to me in this way?" (9:21). Saul was saying he was least worthy of any man in Israel to be spoken of so respectfully. But God chooses the foolish things to confound the wise, as we have learned from His choices of the judges before Samuel and Saul.

JOHN 6:22-42

Not all of Jesus' followers were believers. They liked the free fast food (see v. 26)! Jesus said they should follow Him because they believed He was the Son of God. The free food could only temporarily help their bodies, but by receiving Jesus, the spiritual "manna," their spirits could be forever changed. When Jesus claimed He had come from heaven, the Jews took offense again because they recognized only the natural and the physical. Jesus' body didn't come from heaven—that came from His mother, Mary. But His spirit, which always existed from eternity past, came down from heaven and was "clothed in flesh."

PSALM 106:32-48

Up to this point in Psalm 106 everything was history as far as our reading Israel's story was concerned. But today we read of the dreaded future when Israel would actually degenerate to become worse than the Canaanites they had displaced. These people of God would resort to throwing their children into the fire to appease the gods whom they now served. We have already read of temporary judgments, where God allowed a foreign nation to oppress Israel *in* their land. But things would get worse, and we will eventually see how God sent a foreign nation to uproot and deport Israel *from* the promised land. It was during that exile that this psalmist wrote (see v. 47).

PROVERBS 14:34-35

How true we know verse 34 to be! When a nation serves the Lord, it results in exaltation. We have seen in our time nations that used to serve God slip into apostasy and fall from their exalted position in the world. It seems to be happening to our nation even now.

MAY 11

1 SAMUEL 10:1-11:15

Samuel poured a flask of oil on Saul's head, symbolizing the anointing of the Holy Spirit that would rest upon him to be king of Israel. Notice that Saul had no special training we know of, had no natural leadership abilities and had never expected to obtain a great position, yet

God chose him. All he had going for him was his good looks (see 9:2).

When Saul returned to his home, in his humility (and possibly for fear that he would be thought insane) he didn't even tell his uncle all that Samuel said about his becoming king. Later at the assembly at Mizpah, when Saul was publicly chosen by lot to be king, he was hiding. It took a word of knowledge through a prophet to discover his whereabouts. Finally, when certain "worthless men" complained about the choice of "Saul the nobody," Saul did not exercise his right to imprison such rebellious ones, but kept quiet. He was truly a humble person.

I point this out so you'll remember Saul's fine character as we see him change. Later he will try to murder the innocent and display an ungodly selfishness and jealousy.

JOHN 6:43-71

When Jesus said that no one could come to Him without being drawn by the Father (v. 44), He was not saying that God draws some and does not draw others. God draws *everyone* to Jesus. That is why He has revealed Himself to *every* man through creation. That is why He has commissioned us to take the gospel to *every* person.

Jesus was saying in verse 44 that God is the initiator of our salvation—it was planned, consummated and made known to us only because of His love for us. God even put within every person the hunger that only Jesus can satisfy. All we can do is respond in faith!

Jesus said that He is the "bread of life" (v. 48). In speaking of His body and blood as food and drink, He was again revealing spiritual truth, but His listeners became even more confused—perhaps willfully at this point. Yet to the Jews, who were forbidden to eat anything "with the blood" (see Lev. 17:10-14), Jesus' statement about drinking His blood had to be startling. Drinking Jesus' blood, however, is symbolic of taking His life into our spirits, and it was through His blood that atonement was made for our sins.

Jesus Himself later told His disciples that the words He had spoken are "spirit and are life" (v. 63). Although Peter didn't fully understand, at least he realized that only Jesus had life-giving words (see v. 68). Because of this belief, Peter and the disciples had come to believe that Jesus was the Messiah (see v. 69).

PSALM 107:1-43

This is one of my favorite psalms because it so beautifully illustrates the love and mercy of God. We read of four examples of people who got into trouble, and in two cases their trouble was because of their own sin (see vv. 11, 17). Yet when they cried to the Lord, He delivered them. We should never think the Lord won't help us just because it's our own fault we get into trouble. He is so good and so merciful.

PROVERBS 15:1-3

When people raise their voices against us, if we will respond with a gentle answer, most times they will immediately quiet down. They'll be ashamed that they're so out of control when we're so under control.

MAY 12

1 SAMUEL 12:1-13:22

Saul made a grave mistake when he assumed the priestly office and offered sacrifices rather than waiting for Samuel. Saul was neither called nor anointed to minister as a priest, and in so doing he dishonored the Lord. When Samuel arrived, he prophetically informed Saul that because of his disobedience, his kingship would not be established forever over Israel as it would have been otherwise (13:13-14). It may sound like a harsh judgment, but it had no immediate effect on Saul. It didn't mean he couldn't continue to be king. In fact, he remained king for about thirty-two more years (if we accept the NASB rendering of the incomplete text of 13:1; other translations vary). When God said He would seek for a man after His own heart, it was ten years before that man was even born. His name, of course, was David.

JOHN 7:1-29

Remember that the Feast of Booths (or Tabernacles) was the October/November celebration in which all the men of Israel would live in little booths for eight days commemorating their ancestors' wanderings in the wilderness. This was the feast Jesus' brothers urged Him to attend. (Yes, Mary did have other children after Jesus.)

Jesus' arguments with the Jews were pretty self-explanatory. Isn't it amazing that people could have full knowledge of Jesus' miracles, hear His teaching and see Him with their own eyes yet not believe in Him? They were saying the same things about Jesus then that people are saying today. What it comes down to is the condition of a person's heart. Those who are pure of heart will believe. It's not that others can't believe, but that they don't want to believe.

PSALM 108:1-13

Could you tell that this psalm was written by David without reading the credits at the beginning? It should be apparent, once we read the final confession: "Through God we shall do valiantly; and it is He who will tread down our adversaries." That's faith! David was so certain, even when things didn't look good, because he was standing on the promises of God that he had quoted in verses 7-9. When we recite God's promises, it helps our faith to grow as well. Make a habit of saying what God says.

PROVERBS 15:4

MAY 13

1 SAMUEL 13:23-14:52

Today we're introduced to Jonathan, the brave son of Saul. He shines as one of the most Christlike characters of the Old Testament, and through his faith Israel defeated the Philistine army as you just read. What can we learn from this story? Notice that God didn't act until someone had faith and acted first. Many times we think we're waiting on God, but He is actually waiting on us. He has already made His will known by giving His promises, and now it's our move. Don't try to believe God's Word. Just act on it. That is believing.

Saul made one foolish mistake in his overzealousness, placing his army under an oath that they wouldn't eat anything until the battle was finished. When Jonathan innocently broke the oath, we wonder why they took the whole thing so seriously. But do you remember in Joshua's day when Achan unlawfully kept some of the spoil that was "under the ban" in the war against Jericho? As a result of his disobedience, thirty-six Israelite soldiers had died in battle at Ai. It's no wonder that Saul and the rest of the Israelite army took this incident so seriously.

Saul was so true to his word that he was actually going to kill his son, but Jonathan was rescued by the Israelite soldiers, who thankfully saw no justice in Jonathan's execution. The fault actually belonged to Saul, who had given this foolish order in the first place. But God didn't punish him for it, and in fact He continued to use Saul mightily in battle to deliver Israel (see 14:47-48).

JOHN 7:30-53

At the Feast of Tabernacles each day the priest would get water from the Pool of Siloam in Jerusalem and pour it out at the altar of the temple. It was with this ceremony as a backdrop that Jesus uttered, "If any man is thirsty, let him come to Me and drink. He who believes in Me, as the Scripture said, 'From his innermost being shall flow rivers of living water' " (vv. 37-38). The water was representative of the Holy Spirit, as it also was in Jesus' statement to the woman at the well of Samaria. He had spoken to her of believing in Him and having a "well of water springing up to eternal life" residing within (John 4:14).

Those two scriptures illustrate a beautiful comparison between being born of the Spirit and being filled with (or baptized in) the Spirit. The first experience is when people are born again and the Holy Spirit comes into their spirit and gives them life (*zoe*). It is primarily for their personal benefit. But when people are baptized in the Holy Spirit, the experience is not just for their own benefit but also for the benefit of others. Notice the difference between the two experiences. One is "a well of water springing up to eternal life," and the other speaks of "rivers of living water" flowing from a person's "innermost being." The baptism in the Holy Spirit empowers us to be witnesses to the world.

The arguments surrounding Jesus haven't changed in two thousand years, have they? For example, look at verse 48: "No one of the rulers or Pharisees has believed in Him, has he?" People today will say, "My pastor or priest has never talked about being born again or making Jesus my personal Savior and Lord. So it must not be important or valid." They blindly follow their blind leaders. When people say to me, "You've just been brainwashed," I remind them that isn't the case. I have changed my beliefs. I don't believe what the blind leaders used to teach me in the liberal church I attended. My opponents are actually the ones who are brainwashed. They believe what they've been told since they were children, having never bothered to read the Bible for themselves lest their views be challenged!

PSALM 109:1-31

This is the strongest cry for vengeance that I can think of in the Bible. Apparently some of David's friends had completely betrayed him, and his great hurt is evident. He actually prayed for the death of his opponent (see v. 9). I don't think David's prayer comes up to the mark of loving our enemies or praying for those who persecute us as Jesus commanded. At least David wasn't taking his own vengeance but was leaving it up to God. However, to say that

David was "out of line" takes away the possibility of the Holy Spirit's inspiration, and we believe these are not just prayers, but prayers inspired by the Holy Spirit. My opinion is that David was inspired to pray this prayer against extremely wicked people who deserved death (see v. 16).

PROVERBS 15:5-7

Another promise of prosperity!

MAY 14

1 SAMUEL 15:1-16:23

Today we see the beginning of Saul's change of character. After his victory over the Amalekites, he set up a monument to himself. That doesn't sound like the humble man we read about a few pages ago. Furthermore, he disobeyed the word of the Lord by allowing Agag, king of Amalek, to live, as well as many of the sheep and oxen.

Sometimes I hear Christians misuse verse 15:22 to say that God wants only our obedience, so we don't need to make any sacrifices for Him. However, sometimes obeying God does involve making sacrifices! In that case obedience and sacrifice go hand in hand.

Why did Saul sin? Because he feared the people (see 15:24). You can't go very far with God if you're afraid of people. God told Saul that he will lose his kingship. When Samuel refused to travel with him, Saul's longing to be honored is evident in his reply: "...please honor me now before the elders of my people and before Israel, and go back with me..." (v. 30). Saul has changed from a humble servant of God to an image-conscious, self-interested fearer of man. Apparently Samuel grieved for months over Saul, and when God told Samuel to anoint a new king, Saul's character had degenerated to the point where Samuel feared Saul would kill him if he found out.

We read a beautiful verse in chapter 16. Samuel thought for sure that the next king would be Jesse's son Eliab. But the Lord said, "Do not look at his appearance or at the height of his stature...for God sees not as man sees, for man looks at the outward appearance, but the Lord looks at the heart" (v. 7). A lot of pretty people have ugly hearts. We should always be conscious that the Lord knows exactly what's in our hearts. We can hide it from others but not from Him.

When "the Lord departed from Saul" and "an evil spirit from God terrorized him," it doesn't mean God actually sent an evil spirit. It means God permitted an evil spirit to terrorize Saul as a means of discipline. However, whenever David played his harp, the evil spirit would depart. (Here was a manifestation of God's mercy.) That ought to tell us something about the importance of the music to which we listen. Music is an invention of God, but the devil has perverted it. When you grow spiritually, you realize more and more how true that is. Music can bring the peace of God or it can bring the dark suggestions and confusion of Satan. It is obvious that evil spirits don't like God's kind of music. They flee when they hear it!

JOHN 8:1-20

What a great story this is of the woman caught in adultery! But where was the other party? I wonder why he got away. This incident gives us insight into the chauvinistic character of the scribes and Pharisees.

They thought they had Jesus. If He

didn't say the woman should be stoned, they could prove He couldn't be from God, because the Law commanded her stoning. If He did say she should be stoned, He would get in trouble with the Roman authorities, who gave no such authority to the Jews. Only God could have the wisdom Jesus displayed. We have to wonder what Jesus wrote with His finger on the ground. Some think it was the names of all the scribes' and Pharisees' lovers.

Can you imagine how the woman felt? She had expected to feel rocks crushing her body, but now all she felt was the warmth of His great love.

What lesson does this story hold for us? Simply that we have no right to condemn others in light of our own sins. People who criticize all the time are blind and proud. And those who are the most critical often have the least right to be critical.

Jesus once again spoke symbolically of Himself by saying He is the light of the world (see v. 12). During the Feast of Tabernacles, which had just ended the day prior, four great candelabras were lit at dusk representing the pillar of fire that led Israel through the wilderness. That pillar of fire actually symbolized Jesus, who brings light to the darkness of this world and guides us on our journey through life.

PSALM 110:1-7

This is definitely a messianic psalm, and portions of it are quoted a number of times in the New Testament as referring to Jesus. God said to Him after His resurrection, "Sit at My right hand, until I make Thine enemies a footstool for Thy feet" (v. 1). And it was God who declared that Jesus was the high priest of the new covenant, "according to the order of Melchizedek" (v. 4). Essentially this psalm speaks of the time when Jesus will rule the earth during His millennial reign from Mount Zion (see v. 2).

PROVERBS 15:8-10

MAY 15

1 SAMUEL 17:1-18:4

If a cubit is equal to about eighteen inches, Goliath was more than nine feet tall! Any football team in America would love to have Goliath playing for it.

David displayed such an amazing degree of faith that I believe he had been given the gift of "special faith" (see 1 Cor. 12:9). He recognized that the Lord delivered him from "the paw of the lion and from the paw of the bear" (17:37). When the gift of special faith comes upon you, you can't doubt. However, the principles of faith are always the same. David said what he believed (see 17:46-47), and he acted on his faith.

To fell the giant, David used a sling which was just two strings attached to a pouch. David swung the sling around and around then released one string at the precise moment, which in turn released the stone. Can you imagine the chances of that rock's being thrown so accurately that it hit Goliath "right between the eyes"? And that it was traveling fast enough to "sink" into Goliath's forehead so that it killed him? There must have been a few angels adjusting the direction of the projectile and increasing its velocity somewhat along the way! The point is that we can do all things *through Christ* who strengthens us (see Phil. 4:13). All things are possible to him who believes (see Mark 9:23).

David and Saul's son Jonathan became close friends, and they entered into a covenant with one another. Part of the ritual was the exchanging of clothes and weapons. It meant they would always support and defend one another—and one another's descendants. Bear that in mind, as we will read of how years later David kept his covenant by helping one of Jonathan's descendants. And we'll read how Jonathan defied even his own father to keep his covenant with David.

JOHN 8:21-30

PSALM 111:1-10

I love these psalms! I hope you aren't just skimming over them. We should be reading them the way we eat good chocolate—slowly, savoring every luscious moment! You should feel something warming up inside you or a refreshing in your spirit, or else you're reading too quickly.

PROVERBS 15:11

God knows our every motivation and thought. That's something to think about!

MAY 16

1 SAMUEL 18:5-19:24

Today we read the beginning of the end for Saul. His downfall started by allowing jealousy to invade his heart. This is a great warning to you and me. We will often be tempted to jealousy, but we must not allow it to get hold of us. Instead we must learn to be content and thankful for how God has blessed us. Jealousy is a killer!

Once again we have good evidence that the "evil spirit from God" was really an evil spirit from Satan that was permitted by God. If the evil spirit was truly *from* God, why did it motivate Saul to try to kill David, who was already chosen of God to be the next king of Israel? No doubt Saul opened the door wider for this spirit to oppress him when he allowed jealousy to grip his heart.

Notice that David had the same humility Saul first displayed when he was becoming king of Israel. When Saul promised his daughter Merab to David in marriage, David replied, "Who am I, and what is my life or my father's family in Israel, that I should be the king's son-in-law?" (18:18). David's life is a good example of the biblical promise that he who humbles himself shall be exalted (see 1 Pet. 5:6).

Isn't it neat that the very thing Satan tried to use to get David killed was the same thing God used to exalt David? Saul wanted David to die in battle, but David never lost a fight! If we trust God, we can be certain He will turn hell's stumbling blocks into heaven's stepping stones! God "causes all things to work together for good" for us (Rom. 8:28).

Today we read of a few of the trials during which David composed his psalms. We skim over these stories without realizing that David came very close to death on several occasions. Three times Saul threw his spear at David from close range! Once David's house was being watched by Saul's spies with the intention of killing him when he came out, but David escaped.

Two questions are usually raised concerning today's reading. First, why did David have a "household idol" in his house (see 19:13)? The "idol" was probably just a statue. It is quite clear that David served the Lord and not some false god.

Second, how could Saul, who had turned into such an evil person, be used of God to prophesy (see 19:23)? But if God used Balaam's donkey to prophesy, certainly He is powerful enough to use a jealous king. God can stop the enemy any way He chooses.

JOHN 8:31-59

In this section we read a fundamental truth that if known by the church would revolutionize what we do. As Jesus spoke the words of His claim to divinity, many of the Jews believed in Him (see v. 30). But Jesus was not satisfied that they would just believe in Him. He wanted more. So He turned and said to "those Jews who had believed in Him, 'If you abide in My word, then you are truly disciples of Mine; and you shall know the truth, and the truth shall make you free' " (vv. 31-32). There is no doubt that a person can believe in Jesus yet not be a disciple of Jesus. Jesus wants all believers to become disciples, and the requirement for discipleship is to abide in His Word. That means more than just believing that Jesus is the Son of God. It means more than just knowing the promises. It means more than just reading the Bible every day. It means knowing and believing and obeying all that Jesus has said. It is not enough to know promises of prosperity. Being a disciple means taking up our cross daily and following Him. It means to love Him above all else. Most important, are you a disciple or just a believer?

Why are so many Christians still bound by old habits? Why do they still struggle with sin constantly? The answer is quite simple: they aren't yet disciples of Jesus Christ. His disciples know the truth and the truth sets them free. Only those who abide in Jesus' Word can be free from slavery to sin.

Notice that Jesus told these religious Jews that their father was Satan (see v. 44). Spiritually speaking that's true of all who have not been born again. They are more or less ruled by evil spirits whether they realize it or not. Once we are born again, God becomes the Father of our spirits, and we take on His nature. That's why Paul said that if any person is in Christ, he has become a new creature (see 2 Cor. 5:17).

Jesus also promised that those who keep His Word will never taste death. His listeners thought He was speaking of physical death, but we realize He was speaking of spiritual death, of which the end result is the "second death"—being cast into the lake of fire (see Rev. 20:14).

Jesus clearly claimed to be God when He said, "Before Abraham was born, I am." "I AM" was the name that God told Moses to call Him in the book of Exodus (see Ex. 3:14). The Jews recognized this and consequently tried to stone Jesus right then. But Jesus escaped, probably by transporting supernaturally out of the temple (see your marginal note on v. 59)!

PSALM 112:1-10

Wealth and riches are in the house of the righteous (v. 3). Notice that it also says that the righteous man is a giver (vv. 5,9). Don't claim verse 3 without obeying verses 5 and 9!

PROVERBS 15:12-14

A wise person seeks constructive criticism. Others can see faults to which we're blind. Have you ever asked your closest friend or your spouse if there is any area in which you need improvement? If someone says, "Oh, you need no improvement," be careful! Do you know any perfect people?

MAY 17

1 SAMUEL 20:1-21:15

Jonathan shines like a star in this unfolding drama. He would have been the natural heir to his father's throne, yet he had no ambition to be king. Although he knew that God had chosen David to be his father's successor, he didn't display a hint of jealousy. He simply had submitted himself to the will of God.

The covenant to which David and Jonathan agreed specifically included both of their descendants (see 20:15-16,42). Normally when a new dynasty of kings began, all the former dynasty's relatives and descendants would be killed, eliminating any possibility of the old dynasty's regaining the throne. Because of this covenant Jonathan had nothing to fear as far as his descendants were concerned, because David had his trust in God. God was exalting him to be king, so God would maintain and protect him as king. He had no worries of a coup by the former dynasty.

David and Jonathan's kissing each other may seem a little strange. However, in many other cultures of the world it's completely acceptable for men to kiss other men on the cheek. The love that David and Jonathan had for one another was that of pure friendship expressed in the manner of their culture.

Jesus made reference to this story of David's eating the consecrated bread of which we read today (see Matt. 12:1-5). Remember that in the holy place of the tabernacle were kept the twelve loaves of the Bread of Presence. It was removed weekly to be replaced with new loaves, and the old loaves were to be eaten only by the priests. The Pharisees condemned Jesus and His disciples because they were picking and eating grain on the Sabbath, so Jesus applied David's story to His situation. David, the future king of Israel, was fleeing for his life, so certainly it was all right for him to eat the consecrated bread. By the same token, Jesus, the King of kings, had nothing to eat, so it was all right for Him and His disciples to pick and eat grain on the Sabbath. May the Lord help us to understand the difference between the letter of the law and the spirit of the law!

JOHN 9:1-41

Notice that this healing was not the result of the man's faith. He did not come seeking Jesus, but rather Jesus just happened to pass by him, and the disciples asked their question. However, the man did have to display obedience by going to the pool of Siloam to wash the clay from his eyes. That wasn't easy for a blind man to do.

Don't you love the conversation between the healed man and the Pharisees? He could offer no deep theological dissertation to refute them, but he did have quite a testimony! No one can argue with your testimony either. Many times the best witness is just telling what a difference Jesus has made in your life. Unfortunately, those evil Pharisees would not believe even though an irrefutable miracle had taken place, and the poor man was kicked out of their conference. People won't always want to listen to your testimony, either, but thank God for the ones who will.

PSALMS 113:1-114:8

Psalm 113 contains a promise for wives who have not been able to have children. We also see a promise for poor people in verse 7. God cannot lie! Believe what He says, and He'll make His Word good in your life!

PROVERBS 15:15-17

Our attitude during adversity makes all the difference in the world. If we're trusting God, we'll have joy and peace. Complaining never helps or changes the situation, so we might as well just rejoice and trust the Lord.

MAY 18

1 SAMUEL 22:1-23:29

David's entire family was in danger of being taken hostage or even killed by Saul. He takes his elderly parents to Moab for their safety since David was part Moabite through his great-grandmother Ruth.

Saul ruthlessly ordered the slaughter of all the priests, women and children of Nob for their supposed conspiracy with David against him. Could this be the same humble man who hid when his name was chosen to be king of Israel? Power had completely corrupted him.

David would spend many months running from Saul, and through his experiences God would prepare him to be king. He would have first-hand knowledge of how power can destroy and of the evil ends of unbridled jealousy. He would grow strong in faith from continually having to trust God for everything. And as we'll read tomorrow, he would have his integrity tested a number of times as God allowed him the opportunity to get revenge.

Did you know you have been enrolled in "God's school of life"? He is preparing you for future responsibilities as well. None of us will ever graduate, but we want to make sure we continue to pass to the next grade! How are you doing?

JOHN 10:1-21

To a people familiar with shepherding, Jesus' shepherd and sheep analogies were easily understandable. But those of us who don't know much about shepherding can sometimes miss the significance of what He was saying.

First, sheep know their shepherd's voice. When several different flocks are grazing in one area or drinking at one well, it appears that the shepherds would never be able to sort out which sheep belong to which shepherd. However, all the shepherds need do is call their sheep, and the flocks immediately divide and follow their respective shepherds. If a stranger calls them, they will not be fooled into following him. In the same way when we first heard Jesus calling us, we instinctively knew that it was Him, and we know His voice now when He calls us or gives us instruction.

Second, when a shepherd gathered his flock for the night, he would build a fence out of stones with a small opening in one part of the wall. After all the sheep were within the wall the shepherd himself would lie down across the opening for the night, thus actually becoming "the door of the sheepfold." Truly Jesus is the only way we can gain entrance into God's sheepfold.

Third, the good shepherd sincerely cared for his sheep, whereas robbers were only interested in killing the sheep to make a profit. The shepherd spent day and night with the sheep for months. At times he had to protect them from wolves and even lions and bears (as David did) at the obvious risk of his own life. A temporary or hireling shepherd would run at the first sign of trouble. The "hireling" was representative of the scribes and Pharisees, who had no real concern for the people. But Jesus gave His life for us! He is completely devoted to our well-being.

Who were the "other sheep" that were

not of "this fold" (v. 16)? No doubt Jesus was speaking about the Gentiles who would believe in Him. (That's you and me. He was thinking about us even then!)

PSALM 115:1-18

Another faith-building, encouraging psalm! God is your help and your shield (see v. 11). Is He helping you? Many Christians, if they were honest, would have to say no (except that God is helping them get to heaven). Too many of us are relying on ourselves and not on the Lord, but He wants to help us in everything we do. Make that a positive confession until it sinks into your heart: "God is my help and my shield!" Doesn't it feel good to say it?

PROVERBS 15:18-19

Would you rather travel on a hedge of thorns or on a highway? Being lazy is like trying to travel on that hedge—you get nowhere fast! But just a change of attitude can mean the difference between pain or progress.

MAY 19

1 SAMUEL 24:1-25:44

David was allowed the perfect opportunity to get revenge against Saul, but he refused to stretch out his hand against the man whom God had called to be king. David knew that revenge was the Lord's job, and so as long as God was showing Saul mercy, David showed him the same. We are commanded to do likewise. Jesus said that we should be merciful just as our heavenly Father is merciful (see Luke 6:36).

David's treatment of Nabal has raised the eyebrows of some casual readers, but when we look closely at the whole story, most questions are answered. First, David and his band of six hundred men had provided Nabal's flock of three thousand sheep and one thousand goats protection for months. The shepherds were appreciative of David's service and recognized that his kindness should surely be returned (see 25:15-16). Apparently this wasn't Nabal's first display of ingratitude, as one of his servants didn't hesitate to call him a "worthless man" in front of Abigail, Nabal's own wife (see 25:17)! Abigail described her husband to David using the same words (see 25:25). The Bible plainly says that Nabal was "harsh and evil in his dealings" (25:3). He was a drunkard (see 25:36). David claimed that Nabal had returned him evil for good (25:21). Finally, Nabal knew (or at least should have known) that David was the future king of Israel (his wife knew it). For that reason alone he should have shown David more respect. To put it simply, when Nabal died, no one cried.

David knew better than to take revenge against Nabal, but his anger got the best of him. Fortunately Abigail interceded, and was able to cool David's temper. David praises Abigail for stopping him from "avenging himself by his own hand" (25:33). In other words, David knew that revenge was the Lord's responsibility, not his.

JOHN 10:22-42

PSALM 116:1-19

The old-covenant author of this psalm had a wonderful revelation of the goodness of God. God hears our prayers (see v. 1); He is gracious and compassionate (see v. 5); He deals bountifully with us (see v. 7); He rescues us (see v. 8); He extends benefits toward us (see v. 12). Even our death is precious in His sight (see v. 15)! What more could we ask for?

PROVERBS 15:20-21

MAY 20

1 SAMUEL 26:1-28:25

David knew God well enough to know that sooner or later Saul would reap what he had sown. David wasn't about to be the one to repay Saul, but he was sure that eventually God would either kill Saul, allow him to be killed in battle or simply have him die and face his judgment.

David finally grew tired of running from Saul in the wilderness of Judah so he decided to live in Philistine territory. Once again David had to lie for self-preservation. I have to wonder why David was able to trust God so strongly for revenge against and protection from Saul, but yet he couldn't trust God enough to simply remain in the Judean wilderness. It seems obvious that David entered a stage of doubt at this time. He said in 27:1, "Now I will perish one day by the hand of Saul." God had promised David that he would one day be the king, and now he was saying Saul would kill him sooner or later. It was then that David moved to Philistine territory and found himself in a position where he had to lie.

King Achish believed David's lies and as a result trusted him enough to actually take him and his band with the Philistine armies to attack Israel! Can you see the predicament David had gotten himself into? We find him traveling with the Philistines to attack his own nation. We'll have to wait until tomorrow to see the end result of David's doubt.

There is some debate about whether the medium Saul consulted brought up the deceased prophet Samuel or just an evil spirit impersonating Samuel. I believe God actually allowed Samuel's spirit to come from "Abraham's bosom" (or "paradise") to speak with Saul. Notice that when this medium saw Samuel coming out of the earth, she cried out for fear (see 28:12). She wasn't used to such a real manifestation! Second, notice that what Samuel said was exactly in line with God's word, and what he predicted came to pass—Saul and his sons were dead the next day.

Incidentally, this passage gives further evidence that old-covenant saints did not go to heaven when they died, but to the center of the earth—to Hades, which was divided into two compartments, "the place of torment" and "paradise." Samuel came up "out of the earth" (28:13). That's where he was. Jesus emptied paradise when He was raised from the dead and took all those saints with Him to heaven.

JOHN 11:1-53

Jesus was not saying that God was glorified by Lazarus's sickness in verse 4. He meant that the end result of this sickness would not be death but the glorifying of God when Lazarus was raised from the dead. Occasionally you run across a sick person who uses John 11:4 to say that his sickness is for God's glory. The only way God gets glory out of sickness is when He heals the afflicted person. Only Satan gets glory from sickness.

Why did Jesus weep if He knew that Lazarus would be raised from the dead? No one knows for certain. Since Jesus was the most compassionate Person to ever walk the face of the earth, possibly He wept because He was among other weeping people. Paul wrote that we should weep with those who weep (Rom. 12:15). But my best guess is that Jesus wept for Lazarus because He knew Lazarus was going to have to come back to this sinful world after spending four glorious days in paradise.

Don't you wish you could have been there to witness the resurrection of Lazarus? He probably didn't come walking out of the grave, because he was wrapped up in cloths like a mummy. (His legs were probably wrapped together, and he certainly couldn't have seen where he was going with his head wrapped!) That's why Jesus said, "Unbind him, and let him go" (v. 44).

Lazarus is a good representation of new Christians—freshly raised from the dead (the old life) but still bound in grave clothes (old thinking-patterns and habits, etc.). They need someone to take the time to unbind them and let them go. We need to show baby Christians some mercy and give them time to grow up. Too often we expect them to be full-grown Christians in one week's time. We also need to take care of them and be responsible for them. They usually can't make it on their own and need a more mature Christian to disciple them.

Caiaphas prophesied without even realizing it (see v. 51), so such a thing must be possible. I can think of a number of times when people have prophesied to me without being aware of it.

PSALM 117:1-2

Welcome to the shortest psalm in the Bible. This may be a short one, but it's good! It's also helpful preparation for Psalm 119, the longest psalm, which will take us ten days to read.

PROVERBS 15:22-23

Thinking about a major change or move? Get advice from those who have already done what you're considering. You'll be glad you did.

MAY 21

1 SAMUEL 29:1-31:13

If David, as a result of his doubt and deception, had ended up fighting his own countrymen, it would have put a real damper on his future kingship! Fortunately the other Philistine kings were not as trusting as Achish, and David and his men were forced to turn back. But that's when David suffered the consequences of his missteps.

He must have realized, as he surveyed his burned-out city and heard the murmurings of his men against him, that it would have been better for him to have stayed in Israel and trusted God for protection from Saul. Now is when we read that David "strengthened himself in the Lord" (30:6). It probably means he got back into fellowship with the Lord and repented of his doubt. God sometimes helps us to avoid future big mistakes by allowing us to make present little mistakes.

The day David defeated the Amalekites was a day of great deliverance for David, as we read that not much later (just as David had once predicted), Saul was killed in battle. He finally reaped what he had sown.

JOHN 11:54-12:19

These next nine chapters of John's Gospel cover about ten days. Only John recorded so much detail of Jesus' final words to His disciples.

Six days before the Passover Jesus journeyed secretly to Bethany, about two miles from Jerusalem, to the home of Lazarus, Martha and Mary. That's where Mary anointed Jesus with expensive ointment that, as I mentioned before, was worth over a year's average salary in Jesus' day. That's when Judas sinfully questioned what Mary had done, stating that the money could have been used to help poor people.

Judas wasn't concerned about the poor. All he saw was a lost opportunity to gain personal wealth. Things aren't always as they appear to be, are they? God knows the hearts of men. Judas was a lover of money, and for that reason he betrayed Jesus for thirty pieces of silver.

PSALM 118:1-18

This sure sounds like one of David's psalms, although he isn't given the credit as its author. Whoever it was, he certainly knew God. He said that the Lord had disciplined him severely but had not given him over to death (see v. 18). Sometimes God's discipline is severe, but only because it's for our ultimate good. If we want to avoid discipline, all we need do is obey! Whether we're in the midst of discipline or not, we always know the Lord is for us (see v. 6) and that it's always best to trust in Him (see vv. 8-9). Where is your trust? God wants us to trust Him for more than salvation. He wants us to trust Him for everything.

PROVERBS 15:24-26

MAY 22

2 SAMUEL 1:1-2:11

This Amalekite's story of Saul's death is somewhat different from what we read yesterday in 1 Samuel. Possibly the man was lying, hoping to receive honor from David as the one responsible for killing Saul. In that case he misunderstood David's character and paid with his life. If this Amalekite was telling the truth and had actually killed Saul, Saul's suicide attempt must have failed, and this Amalekite finished him off.

We can't help but admire David's reaction at the news of Saul's death. His eulogy was gracious, and he made no mention of the dark side of Saul's character, speaking only of the good Saul accomplished during his reign. We also should talk about the good in people rather than the bad. (Everybody has a good and a bad side!)

I don't know why God allowed Jonathan to be slain along with his father. I'm sure it was for the ultimate good of Israel and for Jonathan, but the Bible offers no explanation. In such cases all we can do is trust in the Lord's wisdom and goodness.

Finally, many years after God's original promise, David became king. He had been through many tests and was now ready to be used to bring God's purposes to pass in Israel. As usual, when God begins to work His plan, Satan immediately tries to counteract it. In this case Satan worked to bring division to Israel, and he temporarily succeeded by establishing Ish-bosheth as king over the northern tribes. Certainly one of Satan's most effective strategies in thwarting God's plan is to bring disunity and strife between God's people. We can't put all the blame on Satan for the disunity that exists today in the body of Christ, because Satan can only bring disunity where Christians allow him to do so. Since God is now working to bring the final harvest into the kingdom, let's guard ourselves from Satan's ploy. Let's determine that we're going to work together to spread the gospel and not allow disagreements to divide us!

JOHN 12:20-50

When we weren't following Jesus but were following sin, it was like walking in darkness. We fell down a lot and were bruised. We had no idea where we were going. But now we're walking where there is light and we can see the way. Aren't you glad you're walking in the light? I am!

For people to come to Jesus they must reach a place of dissatisfaction with their lives. As long as they love the status quo, they will never experience God's life or eternal life (see v. 25). People who are going through difficulties are generally more receptive to the gospel than those who are not facing trials. I know a Christian man who has started a suicide hotline ministry, and he is reaching many people for the Lord who call at the brink of committing suicide. They have reached the point of really hating their lives, and thank God that someone is there to help them find a life they can love!

Jesus promised that if He were lifted up, He would draw all people to Himself. God is drawing every person to Himself. He's not forcing them to come, but He is drawing them.

PSALM 118:19-29

We read another messianic promise that I imagine you noticed in verse 22, which Jesus quoted as referring to Himself. He was the stone the builders rejected but that became the chief cornerstone. One verse later we read a phrase that we sing many times: "This is the day which the Lord has made; let us rejoice and be glad in it" (v. 24). The psalmist was not referring to one twenty-four hour period but to the day of walking in all the blessings the "chief cornerstone" has brought to us.

PROVERBS 15:27-28

MAY 23

2 SAMUEL 2:12-3:39

If there is one lesson that stands out above all others to me today, it's simply this: just because God calls a person to do a task doesn't mean that everything will fall into place or be easy. David was in God's perfect will as king of all Israel, yet there were many difficulties. In fact, from the onset most of Israel opposed him. Only the tribe of Judah was supportive. As we read today, it took two years and a civil war before David became king over *all* Israel. If God calls you to do a task for Him, you can expect that the devil will put up as many roadblocks as he can. But if we persevere in faith, the victory is guaranteed!

Most of today's storyline is self-explanatory. One lesson we can learn is that it isn't always right to defend our own relatives. If they're in the wrong, we should stay on the side that's right. Above all else we must serve God. He is our most important relative—our spiritual Father!

David, like most great monarchs of his time, took a number of wives. We read today that he had six while living in Hebron (see 3:2-5). That was a mistake, and we will soon read of his problems with polygamy.

JOHN 13:1-30

John said that it was the devil who put the idea into Judas's heart to betray Jesus (see v. 2). Notice that it doesn't say the devil *made* Judas betray Jesus. Judas listened to Satan and acted on Satan's suggestion. It could very well have been any other disciple, but Judas was open to the idea. He saw an opportunity to make some money, and the devil used that temptation to lead Judas astray.

One of the most amazing stories in Scripture is this one of Jesus washing men's feet. Can you imagine that? Jesus said that the greatest one is the servant of all, so we should expect that Jesus, who is the greatest, would be an extraordinary servant. It's His true nature. If He were physically with you right now, it would be His nature to wash your feet. Would you let Him? Or would you protest in pride like Peter? Having your feet washed by someone else is a humbling experience. It wouldn't have been quite as bad for the disciples, because in their day foot-washing was a common courtesy extended to guests. (People wore only sandals and traveled on dusty roads that were used by animals as well as people. Washing feet was essential!) Usually, however, it was done by household servants. Are you getting a revelation of Jesus' humility? *He is wonderful.*

The point Jesus was making with His foot-washing was that we should be serving one another in true humility. Too often we aspire to positions of power in the body of Christ when we should be seeking opportunities to serve one another unselfishly.

How could John have been reclining on Jesus' breast at the supper table (see v. 23)? They were eating lying down (on their sides) around a center table, which was commonly done then. Each person would be lying on a couch propped up on one arm and feeding himself with the other. John was at one of the places directly beside Jesus, and he leaned back on Jesus' breast for a short time to converse with Him. Apparently his was a secret question that not all the disciples heard (see v. 28).

PSALM 119:1-16

This psalm (the longest in the Bible) is broken up into twenty-two eight-verse sections. The headings of each section are successive letters in the Hebrew alphabet, and every verse begins with the same Hebrew letter as the section head. You can see how much we miss when reading the English translation. You will also notice that almost every verse mentions something about God's Word. This psalmist recognized the importance of knowing, meditating upon and obeying Scripture.

PROVERBS 15:29-30

MAY 24

2 SAMUEL 4:1-6:23

The two murderers of Ish-bosheth certainly had misread David's character. Although Ish-bosheth had been David's chief enemy, David was not at all happy that he was dead. Apparently David knew more about the murderers than we have recorded in the Bible, because he stated that Ish-bosheth was a righteous man in comparison to them (see 4:11). I assume David acted in complete justice in decreeing the death sentence for those two men.

Did you notice how David won his second war of chapter 5 against the Philistines? He wasn't supposed to attack until he heard "the sound of marching in the tops of the balsam trees" (5:24). I can only guess that God opened David's ears to hear into the spiritual realm, and he heard the sound of angels marching before him! Angels are out there, you know. There are some that are constantly camped around *you* (see Ps. 34:7).

God had specifically said that the ark of the covenant was only to be transported on poles, on the shoulders of the Levites. But David at first had it transported in a new cart. During the journey from Baale-judah to Jerusalem the cart apparently came to a rough place, and the ark almost fell off. A man named Uzzah reached out to steady the ark, and when he touched it, he fell dead for his irreverence. We shouldn't question God about this man's death; we should just accept the story for what it says. Yes, God is love, but He's also holy. The things of God should be handled with reverence.

David's first wife (and Saul's daughter) "despised David in her heart" as she witnessed his dancing before the Lord with all his might when the ark was brought into Jerusalem (see 6:16). If you ever despise anyone who is more on-fire for God than you are, watch out! Michal was judged with barrenness. David didn't care what anyone thought about his excitement for the Lord. He was a person after God's own heart. How about you?

JOHN 13:31-14:14

We have already read the requirements that qualify one to be a disciple of Jesus (see Luke 14:25-33; John 8:31-32). What's the distinguishing mark of a true disciple? Love for other disciples. The word for "love" here is the Greek word *agapeo*. It speaks of a love that is given freely and is not based on the merits of the receiver but on the character of the giver. Most of what people call "love" in the world is really only selfishness. Even many Christian marriages are based on a love that says, I love you *because*.... And when there's no longer any "because," the "love" stops. God's love says, I love you no matter what! I've noticed that some believers do not display much love for true disciples, branding them as "ultraspiritual."

Verse 14:3 is one of the two references to the rapture of the church that we have in the Gospels. The other reference is also found in John's Gospel (see 14:18).

What did Jesus mean when He said that those who believe in Him would do the same works as He did and greater works (see 14:12)? Most seem to think the "greater works" are the works of getting people born again and baptized in the Holy Spirit. Truly those are greater miracles than even raising someone from the dead.

As far as believers doing "the same works" Jesus did, some think Jesus was referring to the whole body of Christ corporately doing the same works as He did. Some say it means each of us should be doing the same works as Jesus, yet some preachers who say that aren't coming anywhere close to doing the same works Jesus did. In fact, even the original apostles never performed certain miracles that Jesus did (e.g., multiplying food). The large majority of the miracles recorded in the book of Acts were done by apostles or evangelists, not ordinary believers. Possibly Jesus' statement will have its complete fulfillment some time in the future. We know that the nine gifts of the Spirit are referred to as "the powers of the age to come" (Heb. 6:5), which must be referring to the millennium. This is not to say that miracles and gifts of the Spirit are not for today, but that not all believers (if we examine all the Scripture on the subject) should expect to walk on water, raise the dead and multiply food. Jesus has promised that *all* believers can cast out demons and lay hands on the sick (see Mark 16:17-18).

PSALM 119:17-32

Every answer to every human problem can be found in God's Word. It should hold first place in our lives.

PROVERBS 15:31-32

These proverbs mean that we should listen to our pastor's sermons! And your pastor's sermons should sometimes contain some "reproof" (see 2 Tim. 4:2).

MAY 25

2 SAMUEL 7:1-8:18

Today we read an excellent example of what I have mentioned before as "the law of double reference," when a word from God has two meanings composed of an initial fulfillment and also an ultimate fulfillment. When David planned to build a "house" for God, God told him that it was not for him to build but for one of his descendants or his "seed" (see 7:12). We will read how David's son Solomon did build a beautiful temple for the Lord, initially fulfilling God's promise. But the scripture was ultimately fulfilled in Jesus Christ, who built a "true house" for God.

We are that house—the church (see 1 Cor. 3:9; 2 Cor. 6:16; Heb. 3:6). And it is the throne of Jesus Christ that shall be established forever as God promised. (The Davidic dynasty no longer exists in Israel, but it will continue perpetually through David's descendant Jesus.) God also promised that this "seed" whom He would raise up would be a son to Him, and that He (God) would be a father to him (the seed). How true this was when applied to Jesus! In fact, the writer of Hebrews quotes this promise as referring to Jesus (see Heb. 1:5), so there's no doubt this passage is messianic. Remember that the angel Gabriel said to Mary concerning Jesus, "He will be great, and will be called the Son of the Most High; and the Lord God will give him the throne of His father David...and His kingdom will have no end" (Luke 1:32-33).

God further said that when the "seed" committed iniquity, He would "correct him with the rod of men and the strokes of the sons of men" (7:14). We know that Jesus never committed sin, but we also know He "became sin" on the cross (see 2 Cor. 5:21). Jesus was whipped thirty-nine times as part of His "punishment." Can you see the two meanings of these verses? Isn't God clever?

Under David's righteous rule Israel once again rose to ascendancy among the surrounding nations, overcoming all her enemies. God blesses obedience, and Israel's victories and defeats in battle were her spiritual barometers. This is not to say that the righteous don't face difficulties and tests, but they do win their battles, whereas the unrighteous sink lower and lower. God will bless your obedience as well! He is a "rewarder of those who seek Him" (Heb. 11:6).

JOHN 14:15-31

What a beautiful portion of Scripture this is! Jesus promised to send the Holy Spirit to be our Helper. The Greek word for "helper" is *paracletos*, which means "someone called alongside to help." I wonder how many of us truly rely on the help of the Holy

Spirit, who lives inside all of us who are born again? I'm certain we all need improvement in this area. The Holy Spirit wants to help in everything we do (as long as it isn't contrary to God's will, of course). Jesus said He wants to teach us all things (see v. 26). He also will bring to our remembrance what Jesus said. That was especially important for the apostles who would write the Gospels.

Jesus also promised that the Holy Spirit would be with us forever (see v. 16). Some Christians are fearful of losing the Holy Spirit when they sin, but that's not possible according to Jesus' promise.

When Jesus said that He would be in us and we in Him (see v. 20) and that He and the Father would make their abode with us (see v. 23), He obviously wasn't talking on a physical plane. Jesus and the Father are in us through the indwelling Holy Spirit. We're not physically "in Christ," but because our spirits are joined with the Holy Spirit, we are spiritually part of Christ. This is an amazing revelation of which no one has yet plumbed the depths!

Have you noticed how much more spiritual revelation John offers in comparison to the other Gospel writers? The Gospel of John is a great preparation for the epistles to the New Testament churches.

Do you have God's peace? Jesus promised it to us, but it must be received by faith. It is up to us not to allow our hearts to be troubled or fearful. If Jesus said we don't have to be troubled or fearful in our hearts, then we don't!

PSALM 119:33-48

PROVERBS 15:33

MAY 26

2 SAMUEL 9:1-11:27

David kept his covenant with Jonathan, even though Jonathan had been dead for years, by showing kindness to his son Mephibosheth. Poor Mephibosheth had apparently been fed lies about David for years and thought David would surely have him killed when he was summoned. What a surprise for him! Within a few minutes he was extremely wealthy and being treated like one of David's own sons. Mephibosheth is a good representation of so many of us who at one time had a perverted idea of what God is like. You may have thought He was out to get you and that He didn't like you, but one day you discovered that He *loves* you. That was a great day!

Commentators differ on how much Bathsheba should be blamed for committing adultery with David. I don't think we have reason to believe, as portrayed in some Hollywood movies, that Bathsheba intentionally seduced David. We read in 11:1-2 that Bathsheba was bathing within view from David's roof at the time "when kings go out to battle." So I assume Bathsheba figured that David was not in his residence, although we can't be certain. Possibly she was bathing in an open inner courtyard that could only be seen from the vantage of David's roof. Regardless, there is no doubt that Bathsheba was just as much guilty of adultery as David. She didn't have to do it even though David was the king. She could have resisted.

Notice sin's downward spiral path. First, David saw Bathsheba. That was apparently by accident. He could have stopped looking, but he lusted after her. He then inquired who she was and found out she was married and not "fair game" to become David's seventh wife. (You'd think he would have been satisfied with six women from which to choose.) David didn't have to call Bathsheba to come to him, but he did. Once she was pregnant David could have repented, but he conspired to cover his sin by having Bathsheba's husband murdered.

Do you see how his sin grew progressively worse? We should realize that the time to beat sin is now. And the only way out is repentance. Hiding our sin only leads to more sin. Furthermore, it's impossible to hide sin from God; only from people can it be hidden. But think about it: David tried to hide his sin from God, but eventually everyone in his kingdom knew of it, and every person who has ever read the Bible for the past three thousand years knows about it!

JOHN 15:1-27

Today I'm going to have the same problem that I know I'll have when we start reading the epistles: there is much rich spiritual truth that I would like to comment on, but I don't have enough space. I trust that you're relying on the Holy Spirit to point out what I don't.

Commentators differ about the true meaning of Jesus' statement in verse 2. Some say those branches that will be taken away represent unsaved people, but Jesus said they were branches that were "in Him," so they must be saved people. Some say this verse proves that a saved person can go to hell. But it doesn't say anything about hell, and it could refer to physical death, which the Bible teaches is a possible judgment for sinful believers (see Acts 5:1-10; 1 Cor. 11:29-32). There's no doubt, however, that it refers to some type of judgment.

Jesus also said that those branches that bear fruit will be pruned in order that they might bear more fruit. But to the unlearned observer pruning looks as if it would produce less fruit. Have you ever experienced the pruning of our heavenly Father? Ultimately, because of God's workings, you bear more fruit for the kingdom of God. This is a wonderful revelation, and it needs to be taught more often.

The key to bearing much fruit for the Lord is simply abiding in Jesus the vine. Like a branch on a vine we must be completely dependent on Jesus as our source for everything. We must trust His words, obey His commands, fellowship with Him all the time and put Him first in our lives. Abiding in Him could be considered an equivalent to being a true disciple (see v. 8). Those who do abide in Him will witness many answers to their prayers (see vv. 7-8). And only those who know God's Word can pray effectively.

The unsaved person in Jesus' comparison is found in verse 6. He does not abide in Jesus at all and is "thrown away" and cast into the fire.

I can't emphasize enough the importance of Jesus' commandment for us to love one another. I'm so glad He didn't command us to always *agree* with one another! We can disagree without being disagreeable. If we love one another, we will respect one another's opinions. We will not spread gossip or expose a person's faults. We will not harbor grudges. We will try to work together for the sake of the kingdom of God.

Jesus gave us the commandment to love one another. It was not just a suggestion or a "helpful hint from heaven." Why did Jesus stress the importance of loving each other? Because He knew that if we didn't love each other, His whole plan would be ruined. The world would never hear the gospel. I'm convinced that the more we can get the leaders in the body of Christ to love one another the better we'll be able to accomplish the great commission.

Finally, we shouldn't be surprised

when the world hates us (see v. 18). Jesus promised it would happen, and that's one promise you won't have to claim by faith! We are redeemed from hell but we're not exempt from suffering persecution. When you're persecuted by the world, it's a sign you're doing something right! Remember that they *killed* Jesus.

PSALM 119:49-64

PROVERBS 16:1-3

People can do the right things for the wrong reasons. We should never judge anyone else's motives, but we should certainly examine our own as God does (see v. 2). It's easy to fool yourself into thinking you have pure motives when you really don't. Why not have an "examination period" during your time of prayer today?

MAY 27

2 SAMUEL 12:1-31

David was not only an adulterer and then a murderer, but finally a hypocrite as well. His anger burned against the imaginary rich man in Nathan's parable, and he pronounced a judgment of death and fourfold restitution upon him. In reality he was deciding his own judgment. You can imagine his embarrassment when Nathan exclaimed, "You are the man!" David would reap exactly what he had sown.

The question is raised: "Didn't God say that a child should never be punished for his parents' sins?" Yes, He did, but we must remember that when a baby dies, it's the parents who suffer, not the child. The child goes immediately to heaven and is truly much better off there than here on earth. When God said that no child shall be punished for his parents' sins, He was referring to the idea that God would afflict some child with a lifelong disease because of sins committed by his parents. Death is the greatest blessing for those who go to heaven. But the death of a child is a terrible loss for the parents who are left behind.

David prayed and fasted earnestly that his baby would not die, hoping the Lord would change His mind. But the Lord did not. It never hurts to pray as long as there's hope, but in order to pray the prayer of faith you *must* have a promise on which to stand. David had no such promise. In fact, he was praying *against* the promise that his child would die. He was praying in hope, not faith.

Why is this sordid story recorded in the Bible? It serves as a warning to all of us. We must be constantly vigilant against temptation lest we pay the dire consequences of falling into sin's trap. If a God-fearing man like David could fall, you and I are equally or even more vulnerable. Beware! Run from temptation! And if you fall into it, confess it, don't cover it!

The comfort we have at the death of any Christian is just as David said: "I shall go to him, but he will not return to me" (v. 23). Thank God that all Christian departures from this world are only temporary separations!

When David defeated the Ammonites, we read that he "brought out the people who were in it, and set them under saws, sharp iron instruments, and iron axes, and made them pass through the brick-kiln" (v. 31). This may sound like sadistic torture, but at least one of my commentaries says that the Hebrew text could easily be translated to mean that David put the Ammonite captives into hard labor with saws, axes and so on and made them work to make bricks. That would certainly be a more acceptable reading (the NIV translates it such).

JOHN 16:1-33

Isn't it amazing that Jesus told His disciples it was to their advantage that He go away (see v. 7)? That's a real compliment to the Holy Spirit. Think about it—if Jesus were physically present on the earth, He would be limited in where He could be at any given time. But through the Holy Spirit Jesus can be with us *all*. Because the Holy Spirit and Jesus have identical natures, having the Holy Spirit is just like having Jesus all the time!

Here is the true test of whether we're experiencing the blessings of having the Holy Spirit within us: is our fellowship with Him as exciting as if Jesus were physically present all the time? If it is, we're experiencing the Holy Spirit the way God intended. But I think most of us have room to grow in that area. Think of it: God is with you and in you! That's incredible! Let's work on becoming more conscious of the Holy Spirit's presence in our lives.

Jesus plainly said that He had more which He wanted to tell the disciples, but they weren't ready to receive it yet. The Holy Spirit, however, would pick up where He left off (see vv. 12-13). That's precisely why we have the epistles to the churches in the Bible. They are every bit as God-inspired as the Gospels. Some Christians have made the great mistake of placing higher authority or more importance on the Gospels because they contain the words of Jesus, whereas the epistles contain only the "words of men." That is entirely incorrect.

It would be good to memorize the prayer promise of verses 23-24. You can't expect to have your prayers answered if you don't know the promises upon which you are standing. This promise of answered prayer is obviously given for the age of the new covenant believers. In that day Jesus said His listeners would not be making their requests to Him, but to the Father in Jesus' name. Only through Jesus do we have rightful access to the Father.

PSALM 119:65-80

Before I was afflicted I went astray, but now I keep Thy word" (v. 67). God can use affliction to teach us to obey His Word. He is a good Father and will discipline us when we need it.

PROVERBS 16:4-5

Verse 4 is a difficult one to interpret. We must remember that God didn't make wicked people wicked. He makes all men free moral agents, and thus there is the possibility that they will become wicked. Those who choose wickedness will face God's predetermined judgment.

MAY 28

2 SAMUEL 13:1-39

Today we begin to see the fulfillment of Nathan's prophecy of God's judgment upon David. David said the rich man should pay fourfold for his sin. So far David had lost two children, and he would lose two more before the story was over.

After three years of Absalom's exile, David longed to see him. Unknown to David the stage was being set for a conspiracy by Absalom to overthrow his own father's throne.

JOHN 17:1-26

Chapter 17 has been titled "the high-priestly prayer of Jesus." It is full of deep revelation, much of which I am not qualified to comment on. However, I do want to bring to your attention several key passages. First, notice that three times Jesus prayed for His disciples and us as well that we might be unified (see vv. 11,21,23). Only if we work together can we ever hope to accomplish the great commission. Why is unity so important? Because it will result in the world's knowing the gospel (see vv. 21,23). God wants us to be one to the same extent that He and Jesus are one (see v. 21)! So we still have a long way to go.

Did you know that God loves you as much as He loves Jesus? That's what Jesus said He wants the world to know in verse 23, yet many Christians don't even know it yet! God has no favorite children.

Not only does God love unselfishly, but He has also placed His love in each of us, giving us the ability to love as He does (see v. 26). You might know some people of whom you would say, I just can't love that person, or, I just can't forgive that person. But God's love in you can love or forgive that person! Quit trying to love in your own power

PSALM 119:81-96

"If Thy law had not been my delight, then I would have perished in my affliction" (v. 92). I can say "Amen" to that! Christians who are not rooted and grounded in God's Word are washed away by their afflictions. But those who cling to the promises will endure any trial. That's why I'm so glad you're going through the Bible with me. I know you're growing and are better prepared for life's journey.

PROVERBS 16:6-7

Every verse in the Bible must be taken in context with the rest of the Bible. Verse 7 is not saying that if you have enemies, you're not pleasing to the Lord. Jesus had a lot of enemies. So did Israel even when the people were walking righteously. If people are pleasing to the Lord, I guarantee they will have enemies, but God will not allow their enemies to triumph over them. To that degree their enemies are at peace with them, but notice they are still enemies.

MAY 29

2 SAMUEL 14:1-15:22

As you read about Joab's plan, could you see how David was reaping *exactly* what he had sown? He now had the same problem with Absalom that God had faced with David when he had Uriah murdered. David had deserved death. If God pardoned him with no punishment, He would be accused of injustice. But God didn't want David to die because of His love for him.

David's solution was only partial forgiveness. Absalom was allowed to return, but he was not permitted to see his father. Obviously David was still struggling between love and justice. Absalom's own father had rejected him for apparently no good reason because Absalom viewed his revenge against Amnon as perfectly justified. So Absalom launched his conspiracy with the help of David's trusted counselor Ahithophel (who was Bathsheba's grandfather). His coup was successful, except that King David escaped with his life from Jerusalem. Apparently the majority of the population of Jerusalem was still supportive of David.

JOHN 18:1-24

Only John records that Jesus' captors were slain in the spirit when Jesus said, "I am *He*" (v.6). (The word *He* is italicized, indicating it was not part of the original text.) There must have been some kind of supernatural power present for the Roman guards to fall down.

John is also the only Gospel writer who records all of Jesus' "I ams." He said: "I am the bread of life" (6:35); "I am the light of the world" (8:12); "I am the door of the sheep" (10:7); "I am the good shepherd" (10:11); "I am the Son of God" (10:36); "I am the resurrection and the life" (11:25); "I am the way, and the truth, and the life" (14:6); and "I am the true vine" (15:1). Jesus is all of those, and we need to get to know Him in all those ways.

PSALM 119:97-112

According to verse 100 we can gain wisdom from obeying God's Word that even elderly people haven't learned during their entire lives. God's Word is a light to our path and a lamp to our feet (see v. 105). That's a good analogy, don't you think?

PROVERBS 16:8-9

MAY 30

2 SAMUEL 15:23-16:23

I have to admire David's faith in God and his resignation to the will of God as he was fleeing from Jerusalem. He had simply placed himself in the hands of God. Surely he recognized he was enduring discipline for his sin with Bathsheba. Even when being cursed by Shimei, a descendant of Saul, David didn't take revenge, allowing room for the possibility that God had told Shimei to curse him. We, too, need to let the Lord fight our battles for us.

It's important that you remember the names of the various characters in this story, because we will be reading about most of them again in the next few days. Ahithophel was David's most trusted counselor and also Bathsheba's grandfather. He completely betrayed David by conspiring with Absalom. Hushai was another of David's trusted counselors, who feigned loyalty to Absalom in order to work as a spy in Absalom's court and thwart his plans against David. Ziba was the servant of Mephibosheth (Jonathan's crippled son to whom David had shown great kindness). He saw the opportunity to profit by betraying his master. He lied to David about Mephibosheth's supposed disloyalty to David.

At Ahithophel's advice, Absalom had sex with David's concubines in a tent on his roof. This was designed to prove to the Israelites that Absalom had made himself odious to his father and thus there was no possibility of reconciliation between them. It was also a fulfillment of God's promise of judgment to David through Nathan (see 12:11-12).

JOHN 18:25-19:22

When Pilate asked the Jews for the formal accusation they were making against Jesus, they were really unprepared. They simply replied that they wouldn't have brought Him in unless He was an evildoer. So Pilate, unaware that they wanted the death penalty for Christ, instructed them to judge Him themselves. Under Roman law the Jews were forbidden to execute anyone. (If they had executed Jesus themselves, they would have done it by stoning Him. So according to verse 32 Jesus was accurate in His prediction that He would die by hanging on a cross, the Roman method of capital punishment. See John 12:32-33.)

Notice that Pilate declared Jesus innocent three times (see 18:38; 19:4,6), yet he bowed to the pressure of the Jews. He hoped that after scourging Jesus they would be satisfied that He had suffered enough punishment, yet they still insisted on crucifixion. Pilate caved in to their threat that if he released a man who claimed to be a king, they would report him to Caesar as an accomplice to a conspiracy. It seems Pilate attempted to gain some revenge by having the sign placed on Jesus' cross that read "King of the Jews"—a humiliation to them but ironically the absolute truth. Jesus was their King and will some day reign from the very city in which He was crucified!

PSALM 119:113-128

We all should evaluate whether we have the high regard for God's Word that this psalmist did. I'm sure most of us have room to grow.

PROVERBS 16:10-11

In biblical times people bought many commodities based on weight, just as we do today. However, their scales were much more primitive than ours, adjusted by stones hanging in a bag on one end of a balance. It was easy to cheat someone. But God was concerned about "all the weights of the bag" (v. 11), and He is just as concerned today that we be honest in all our dealings.

MAY 31

2 SAMUEL 17:1-29

Ahithophel's counsel was actually better than Hushai's, but the Lord is able to thwart the counsel of the ungodly, and that's what He did in order that Absalom might fall. It also resulted in Ahithophel's committing suicide.

JOHN 19:23-42

We assume that "the disciple whom Jesus loved" (v. 26) was John, the author of this Gospel. Isn't it amazing that Jesus, even while in agony on the cross, arranged for his mother to be taken care of by John? Apparently Joseph was dead by this time.

Notice that Nicodemus and Joseph of Arimathea wrapped Jesus' body in linen cloths along with myrrh and aloes of about one hundred pounds weight (see v. 39). Jesus' body looked like a mummy. When Peter and John later ran to the tomb to see if Jesus had truly been resurrected, all they saw was a hollow shell of the mummy wrappings! They had no doubt that Jesus was alive. If His body had simply been stolen, the wrappings would have been either unwrapped or missing.

PSALM 119:129-152

PROVERBS 16:12-13

JUNE 1

2 SAMUEL 18:1-19:10

David found himself in a terrible predicament. He had to go to battle against his son to preserve his own life. And at the news of Absalom's death, what could he do? How could he rejoice in such a victory? It brought only sorrow, compounded by the fact that David knew this tragedy was a portion of God's judgment on him. To make matters worse, his sorrow almost created a political disaster, narrowly averted through the counsel of Joab. How David's heart must have been torn, having to be joyful the day his son died!

JOHN 20:1-31

I love the little details John reports in his account of the resurrection. As stated yesterday, Peter and John would have seen a hollow case of mummy wrappings when they peered into the tomb. But the face cloth (a cloth that would have been laid over the unwrapped face of Jesus) was not where it should have been. When Jesus' spirit came back into His body, He apparently then passed right through the linen wrappings and lifted off the face cloth, rolled it up neatly and laid it aside. No wonder the Bible says that when they saw, they believed (see 20:8)! There was no possible alternate explanation to what happened. Jesus hadn't been unconscious and then revived. No one had stolen the body. Jesus had come back to life and passed through the one-hundred-pound wrappings supernaturally.

After three days of being dead and then being resurrected just a short time, Jesus still had not ascended to His Father (see v. 17). So where was His spirit while His body was dead? As I have mentioned before, it was in "paradise," in the heart of the earth. Keep in mind that Hades was divided into two compartments, the place of torment and paradise. I'm not saying that Jesus suffered the torments of the damned. He told the one thief on the cross that they would be together that same day in paradise (see Luke 23:43).

When Jesus first appeared to the disciples after His resurrection, He breathed on them and said, "Receive the Holy Spirit" (v. 22). However, the disciples were not baptized in the Holy Spirit until about fifty days later on the day of Pentecost. Once again we see that there are two distinct works of the Holy Spirit. When we are born again, the Holy Spirit comes to live inside of us. The baptism in the Holy Spirit then allows us to be "clothed with power from on high" (Luke 24:49) so that we can reach the world with the gospel.

Then Jesus told them that if they would forgive the sins of any, their sins would be forgiven them; and if they would retain the sins of any, they would be retained (see v. 23). This is a difficult verse to interpret, but I think He probably meant that they were to carry the message of forgiveness to everyone. Whoever accepted it would be forgiven, and whoever didn't would not.

My favorite portion of today's reading is when Jesus said to Mary, "But go to My brethren, and say to them, 'I ascend to My Father and your Father, and My God and your God' " (v. 17). Praise God! Up until then God was not the Father of the disciples. But now God is our Father, not just our God, and Jesus is our brother.

PSALM 119:153-76

PROVERBS 16:14-15

JUNE 2

2 SAMUEL 19:11-20:13

You can understand the political dilemma in which David found himself. He was once again the king of a nation of people who the day before were uniting to overthrow him. Most of the people had turned their hearts back toward David, but his own tribe of Judah had not yet sent in its vote of confidence. So David made a move to prove his goodwill toward Judah by promoting Amasa, the commander of Absalom's army, to be his own commander-in-chief, replacing Joab. It was a poor decision that David would later regret, but it did win the tribe of Judah back to him.

We don't know exactly how long David's exile lasted, but based on some scriptural evidence it must have been at least several weeks, and possibly more than a month. David graciously pardoned Shimei for cursing him when he was fleeing from Absalom. (It's a good idea to be careful whom you talk against, because that person may someday be your boss!) David also learned the truth about Mephibosheth and hastily decided to divide the inheritance between him and his deceitful servant, Ziba. Oh, how the tables can turn!

Amazingly, a division between Judah and the northern tribes resulted because of petty jealousy over the king, and Sheba led the ten tribes in revolt against David. In the ensuing war Joab jealously murdered his replacement, Amasa (a member of his own family). Joab was a ruthless man who had only his own interests at heart. This was his second act of cold-blooded murder, as we read previously of his killing Abner, who may also have looked like a threat to him (see 3:26-28). David would not forget it, and one day Joab would be repaid for his treachery.

JOHN 21:1-25

Jesus' nature hadn't changed one bit since His death and resurrection—He was still a wonderful servant. Did you notice how He took the time to prepare breakfast for the disciples when they came to Him along the Sea of Galilee? True spirituality is measured by servanthood.

There still needed to be a work done in Peter's heart, and after breakfast Jesus asked him a probing question: "Do you love Me more than these?" In most of our modern translations it appears that Jesus asked Peter the same question three times, but actually He didn't. The first two times, Jesus asked Peter if he loved Him using the Greek word *agapeo* for "love." The final time, He used the Greek word *phileo,* which is also translated "love." *Phileo* means "to love as a friend loves." *Phileo* says, "I love you because of…." *Agapeo* means "to love unselfishly." It's the kind of love God has for us, based not on the merit of the receiver but on the character of the giver.

Jesus said, "Peter, do you love Me unselfishly?"

Peter replied resignedly, "Yes, Lord, You know I only love You as a friend. I'm not willing to make a sacrifice for You yet."

Jesus asked the same question the second time, and Peter gave the same response. The third time, Jesus said to Peter, "Do you even love Me as a friend?" (Possibly Peter had not yet spoken to Jesus about his three denials of Him.)

The Scripture says that this time Peter was grieved because Jesus was questioning if he had even *phileo* for Him. Peter replied, "Lord, you know all things;

You know that I love you as a friend" (vv. 15-17).

Can you see what a difference this passage makes when we compare Greek with English? Notice that regardless of Peter's response, Jesus still called him to fulfill a ministry (i.e., "Feed my lambs"). How about you? Do you have *phileo* or *agapeo* for God? God wants to be more than just your friend. He wants to be your Lord.

PSALM 120:1-7

Here is a prayer for deliverance from slanderous and deceitful people. When the psalmist said that he was sojourning in Meshech and dwelling in the tents of Kedar, he was simply saying he was dwelling among the ungodly. God's people will always seek for peace (see v. 7).

PROVERBS 16:16-17

JUNE 3

2 SAMUEL 20:14-22:20

What a strange story we read today! After three years of famine, David asked the Lord for the reason. The Lord told him it was because Saul and his family had killed some of the Gibeonites. Do you remember who they were? They were Amorites who had come to Joshua pretending to be from some far country and tricked Israel into entering a covenant with them (see Josh. 9:3-27). The covenant was binding from generation to generation, but Saul, among his other evil deeds, had broken the covenant.

We should never allow stories like this one to alarm us, because we understand enough of God's character to "fill in the blanks." We know that God is always just. Remember that the famine didn't come just because of Saul, but also because of "his bloody house" (21:1), which would mean Saul's sons and grandsons. Saul had already received what he deserved, and no doubt these seven men had murdered some Gibeonites and therefore also deserved to die. They probably should have been put to death a long time before this, but Israel hedged on its righteous duty to carry out the law. So God allowed a famine to drive David and Israel to a place where they would see to it that justice was meted out.

ACTS 1:1-26

Technically, we could say that we have finally just begun the New Testament. Why? Because the four Gospel accounts all took place under the old covenant. We have just entered what Bible scholars call the "church age."

The book of Acts was written by Luke, the doctor, who did a thorough and accurate job of recording the history of the early church, especially the ministry of Peter and the apostle Paul. It covers a period of at least thirty years. The purpose for preserving the historical account of the early church is simple: so that each generation of Christians will not deviate from the pattern God laid down for the early church.

It is still God's intention that the same methods be followed to make disciples of all nations. As we read through this wonderful book, I encourage you to compare your Christian experience with that of the first believers. One message stands out above all others in this book: God's church is reaching out to the world with the gospel. A congregation that is doing nothing to help reach all the nations of the world is not a true New Testament church.

According to 1:1, Luke's first account was a record of "all that Jesus began to do and teach." In this book we will read of how Jesus, who promised to build His church, used people full of the Holy Spirit to continue His work. Under the new covenant the church is the "body of Christ." That's not just a catchy saying but a vital truth. Jesus lives in each of us who is born again, and we should be wholly dependent on Him to work through us to build the church. As individual believers we should be asking for and expecting the Holy Spirit's help to make us effective witnesses for Christ.

The aid of the Holy Spirit is so essential that Jesus commanded His disciples not to leave Jerusalem until they were baptized in the Holy Spirit. Jesus did not begin His ministry until He was baptized in the Holy Spirit, and the same pattern should apply to us. Jesus said, "As the Father has sent Me, I also send you" (John 20:21). He had a supernatural ministry, and so should the church. It is no wonder that the church across the world today is growing most rapidly among Christians who believe in and receive the baptism in the Holy Spirit, because without the Holy Spirit the church has no power.

God's plan was for the disciples to witness in "Jerusalem, and in all Judea and Samaria, and even to the remotest part of the earth" (v. 8). Many Christians and even pastors use this verse as an excuse. They say, "I must first reach my 'Jerusalem' before I can move out to 'Judea' and 'Samaria,' and then to the remotest part of the earth." But they're misreading what Jesus said. He did not say, "First Jerusalem, then Judea and Samaria, and then the remote places." God loves the people in the remote places just as much as He loves the people in Jerusalem. It's unfair for the people in the remote places to have to wait until the people in Jerusalem first hear the gospel.

Today is the last time in New Testament history that you'll read of anyone determining God's will by drawing lots or any similar manner. The disciples probably chose Judas's replacement that way because they were not yet baptized in the Holy Spirit. Under the new covenant we are to seek direction from Him. Unfortunately, many Christians seek direction from God in every way other than the way God promised (i.e., they seek to determine His will through "signs" and "coincidences").

Some commentators point out that the name of the disciple they chose is never mentioned again in the book of Acts, supposedly proving that God wasn't involved in their selection process. However, a number of the other eleven apostles are never mentioned again either, yet Jesus *personally* chose them.

PSALM 121:1-8

Aren't you glad God never sleeps or slumbers (see v. 4)? That means there's no reason for us to stay awake late at night worrying. Give your cares to the Lord before you go to bed, and let Him work on them while you sleep! By the way, this tremendous psalm contains at least eleven promises. Can you find them all?

PROVERBS 16:18

This verse states one of the major themes of the entire Bible.

JUNE 4

2 SAMUEL 22:21-23:23

You probably wondered how David could so boldly declare his righteousness in 22:21-25 in light of his adultery with Bathsheba. But notice that this psalm was written before that ever happened (see 22:1). To see how David felt after he had so grievously sinned, read Psalm 51. Besides that, after David confessed his sin to the Lord, he was righteous once again.

This psalm we have just read is a celebration of God's faithful deliverance in David's life. David had learned to rely on the Lord for everything, and that's why this psalm is so full of positive statements. He knew that God was his lamp (see 22:29) and that with God's help nothing was impossible (see 22:30). He had experienced God's protection and His stability (see 22:31-33). He had learned that God would give him strength (see 22:35, 40). David knew God! It took perseverance through many trials, but it was worth it. If we will draw close to the Lord and continually act on His Word, we too will grow. More than likely there are situations in your life right now that God could use to help you grow—if you will apply His Word.

The listing of David's mighty men in chapter 23 almost sounds far-fetched. How could one man kill eight hundred men by himself (see 23:8)? How could a man kill a lion in a pit on a snowy day (see 23:20)? The secret of their strength was not that they lifted weights every day, but that they trusted God. All things are possible to him who believes!

ACTS 2:1-47

God gave the disciples the Holy Spirit so they *could take the gospel to all* ethnos—all peoples, tribes and tongues. As those 120 disciples spoke supernaturally in languages they had never learned, they knew they were speaking in the languages of people somewhere in the world whom God loved and wanted to reach with the gospel. I think that we charismatic Christians as a whole have unfortunately missed God's point when it comes to understanding the baptism in the Holy Spirit. We place so much emphasis on the tongues, when the tongues are given to point us toward the world that is dying without Christ. If you are baptized in the Holy Spirit, every time you speak in tongues it should make you realize that God wants to reach people who are not like you. I encourage you to get involved in God's plan to reach the world in any way you can.

This supernatural outpouring could not have occurred during a more strategic time than during the Feast of Pentecost, when Jews were visiting Jerusalem from all over the known world. At least fifteen different nationalities were present to witness that great event, and no doubt they spread the word of it when they returned to their own countries. Also notice that then, as now, some of the witnesses made fun of speaking in tongues and tried to explain it away.

Peter's sermon was a masterpiece, obviously inspired by the Holy Spirit, proving that Jesus was the Christ and that the Scriptures had predicted His resurrection. Notice that Peter never asked anyone to "invite Jesus into your heart" or "accept Jesus as Savior." His formula for salvation was simple: repent and be baptized. There is no salvation without repentance. When you repent, you change your belief about who Jesus was and is; you begin to trust that He is the

Messiah. You also turn from your sin and from then on follow and obey Jesus, who is now your Lord.

Notice also the four-fold emphasis of the early church—they were devoted to the apostles' teaching, to fellowship, to the breaking of bread and to prayer. Modern disciples of Jesus Christ are devoted to those same things. "Breaking of bread" could be referring to taking the Lord's supper together or just to eating their meals together (see v. 46). Remember that Jesus said the mark of true disciples will be their love for one another (see John 13:35). That love will be manifested in practical ways, just as we read how the early disciples shared everything they owned with one another (see v. 44). Believers who are not disciples of Christ are stingy with their possessions and not concerned much about the needs of others.

PSALM 122:1-9

If any city in the world needs prayer for peace, Jerusalem is that city! When we pray for the peace of Jerusalem, we're actually praying for God's kingdom to come. Why? Simply because there will be no peace in Jerusalem until the Prince of Peace reigns from that city.

PROVERBS 16:19-20

Blessed is he who trusts in the Lord!" All I can say is amen!

JUNE 5

2 SAMUEL 23:24-24:25

I'm sure you have some questions about this story! It's a difficult one to interpret.

First, we know that God was angry with all of Israel for their sin (see 24:1). Therefore I can say with certainty that this was not a punishment against Israel because of David's sin, as he seemed to think (see 24:17). God was disciplining the entire nation, and by the time the plague was checked seventy thousand Israelites were dead.

What did David's census have to do with all this? Why was it wrong for him to count the people of Israel? Some suggest that David's motivation was one of pride, and that Joab, detecting David's vainglory, tried to persuade him not to have the census taken (see 24:3). Or possibly David's sin was one of doubt. Notice he had only the eligible fighting men of Israel and Judah numbered (see 24:9). Maybe he was taking stock to see if he had enough of an army to be ensured victory in battle. If so, his faith was no longer in the Lord. Beyond these things, God had commanded Israel through Moses, "When you take a census of the sons of Israel to number them, then each one of them shall give a ransom for himself to the Lord, when you number them, that there may be no plague among them when you number them" (Ex. 30:12). Each Israelite was commanded to give a contribution during a census, but there is no record of such a collection during this census. Possibly that act of disobedience was the "straw that broke the camel's back," and God's wrath was unleashed against Israel.

Notice that even in the pestilence God showed mercy and restrained His full wrath in response to David's entreaty (see 24:25). At the end of the story David built an altar on the site where Solomon would later build his great temple. In David's time it was just outside the city of Jerusalem, but by Jesus' time it was inside the expanded city walls.

ACTS 3:1-26

This healing came about because Peter was anointed by the Holy Spirit with a special gift of healing (see 1 Cor. 12:1-11). Possibly the gift of special faith was in operation as well, because it would take more than ordinary faith to grab a crippled person by the arm, lift him up and expect him to stand and walk. (If you don't believe me, just try it sometime!) One preacher said: "This man asked for alms, but he got legs!" Praise God! The miracle happened not only for the crippled man's sake, but also for the benefit of all the people who would be attracted to the gospel. As a result of one miracle and one sermon, five thousand men came to believe in Jesus (see 4:4)! That isn't even counting the women and children! At this point in the church's history, we know the Jerusalem church had at least 8,120 members, and it was only a few days old.

Peter's tremendous sermon (delivered with the help of the Holy Spirit) concluded with a quotation from Genesis in which God told Abraham that in his seed all the families (tribes or culture groups) of the earth would be blessed. We know, of course, that the seed was Jesus. In Revelation 5:9 we read of a future scene in heaven where the Lord is worshipped with a new song: "Worthy art Thou...for Thou wast slain, and didst purchase for God with Thy blood men from every tribe and tongue and people and nation." God's plan from the time of Abraham was to purchase people from every group of people on the earth.

Are you a part of bringing God's plan to pass? Some ethnologists estimate that although there are about two hundred nations in the world today, there are as many as twenty-three thousand different culture groups. Twelve thousand of them have no witnessing church within their culture. The major thrust of the church in these last days will be to take the gospel to those unreached groups.

PSALM 123:1-4

There is no better place to be than the place where you have to look to God as your source.

PROVERBS 16:21-23

JUNE 6

1 KINGS 1:1-53

Welcome to the books of 1 and 2 Kings! We will cover about four hundred years by the time we complete both books. We'll read of David's final days and of Solomon's golden age. We'll also read of the division of Israel into two separate nations: Israel (the ten northern tribes) and Judah (the tribes of Judah and Benjamin). Judah would always have a descendant of David on its throne, whereas Israel would have a number of different dynasties. Judah would have a few good kings, but Israel would have all bad kings. In the end, Israel would be deported to Assyria, and about 136 years later Judah would be deported to Babylon—both because of their apostasy. We'll watch Israel decline from a God-blessed, prosperous, world-renowned, unified nation to a God-cursed, divided, poverty-stricken group of slaves. The overall message shouts to us loud and clear: obey God and be blessed! Disobey God and face the consequences! Finally, we'll read about the lives of two amazing prophets, Elijah and Elisha. You're going to love these books!

ACTS 4:1-37

Remember that Jesus told His disciples they would be delivered up to the courts and synagogues, and that when it happened they shouldn't concern themselves with planning a defense, because the Holy Spirit would give them words that none of their opponents could refute (see Matt. 10:17-20). Today we read one fulfillment of Jesus' promise. Notice that just prior to Peter's defense before the Sanhedrin he was filled with the Holy Spirit (see v. 8). So as you read Peter's speech, realize that it's just as if you're reading prophecy. Peter's hearers marveled (see v. 13) because this "uneducated and untrained" man had spoken with such eloquence, power and confidence. It was God speaking to them through Peter, and they didn't even realize it.

Isn't it amazing that every member of the Sanhedrin knew that a forty-year-old man who had been crippled since birth had been healed totally, yet not one of them came to believe in Jesus as a result? Some people's hearts are so hard they can't be reached.

Notice that when Peter and John returned from the Sanhedrin, they went to their companions and had a prayer meeting. Also notice that one person didn't lead them in prayer while the rest were quiet. They all prayed together at the same time! Both ways of praying are scriptural. God is big enough to hear everybody's prayers all at once!

Also notice how they knew that without God's help they were helpless in witnessing (see vv. 29-30). We should have the same attitude. God is the one who gives us opportunities to share with others. And the Holy Spirit will give us just the right words to draw them to Christ. Have you ever been witnessing to someone and found yourself saying something you didn't intend to say, or quoting Scripture you didn't know you could quote? That's the Holy Spirit working through you!

The early believers were not just believers in Jesus but were true disciples. How do I know? Because of their love for one another. Those early disciples held everything they owned in common, and there was therefore *not one needy person among them* (see v. 34). They weren't all millionaires, but each person's needs were met. That is prosperity!

God was even leading some of them to sell land and houses. Personally, I think that means that people who had land they weren't using or more than one home were selling those things to bring the proceeds to the apostles.

PSALM 124:1-8

If you've ever been in a place where you had to rely on God's help, you can relate to this psalm, because there is no doubt the Lord delivered you. If you're in one of those situations presently, say with this psalmist: "Our help is in the name of the Lord, who made heaven and earth" (v. 8). The implication is that if God can make heaven and earth, He can make a way out of your problem.

PROVERBS 16:24

Yes! Thank God for people who speak pleasant words!

JUNE 7

1 KINGS 2:1-3:3

David was about to die so he gave Solomon some final instructions concerning what to do after he was gone. Specifically, he was to have Joab and Shimei killed because of their crimes and the potential threat they posed to his reign. Solomon had his half-brother Adonijah executed for the same reason, because of his request to have Abishag, David's beautiful "bed-warmer," as his wife. This was a threat to Solomon's reign since the possession of a king's harem was a claim to the throne. (Remember what Absalom did when David fled from him? He immediately had sexual relations with David's concubines.)

Solomon also dismissed Abiathar as priest because he had joined with Adonijah in his attempt to exalt himself as king. This fulfilled God's word to Eli that his descendants would not always possess the priesthood.

Solomon's first wife was a daughter of Pharaoh, and the Bible calls it a "marriage alliance." Modern people have little understanding of such arrangements, but I think we can all understand that if one king would marry another king's daughter, there was little chance of war between those two nations for a while.

ACTS 5:1-42

Ananias and Sapphira's sin was lying to the Holy Spirit. Peter plainly stated that they didn't have to sell their property, and once it was sold, they didn't have to give all the proceeds to the church. However, they publicly declared that they were giving the full amount when they were actually keeping a portion for themselves. That's hypocrisy. So God made an example out of them, and it brought fear upon the whole church.

Peter knew supernaturally the true condition of their hearts; this is an example of a manifestation of the gift of a "word of knowledge." The "word of wisdom" is similar, except that it deals with future events (see 1 Cor. 12:1-11).

What surprises me in this story is that no one ran and told Ananias's wife what had happened to her husband. She didn't even get to attend his funeral. And three hours after Ananias died (see v. 7), the church was still in session. Sapphira died as well, and the poor guys who had buried Ananias got back just in time to pick Sapphira off the floor to bury her. Can you imagine what it was like when that congregation went home that day? People might have asked them, "What happened in church today?"

"Oh, we had two hypocrites fall dead during the offering!" Yikes!

God is love, but He is also holy. I'm sure Ananias and Sapphira went to heaven, but they lost their potential reward for serving God on the earth.

I'm sure you noticed that the revival in Jerusalem included many healings, particularly through Peter's ministry. Jesus plainly said that one of the signs that would follow believers is that they would lay hands on the sick and they would recover (see Mark 16:18).

Gamaliel's counsel was wise. If something is of God, it can't be stopped. Notice that after the apostles were flogged, it didn't defeat them but caused them to rejoice! They were thankful to be considered worthy to suffer for Jesus' cause. Carnal Christians can't understand the apostles' reaction to their flogging because their own relationship with Jesus is one-sided—they only want Jesus to serve them. Have you noticed that in most Christian bookstores the majority of books deal with self-fulfillment? If someone ever wrote a book titled *How to Sweat, Bleed and Die for Jesus Christ*,

I doubt it would be a best-seller. (I suppose that's why I titled this book *Your Best Year Yet*.)

PSALM 125:1-5

I like the first part of this psalm. When we trust in God, we're like Mount Zion, which cannot be moved. We can't stand on more solid ground than God's promises.

PROVERBS 16:25

Most people think the way to heaven is through good deeds, but they are sadly mistaken. That is a way that "seems right to man" but ends in death. This is a good verse to memorize for future witnessing opportunities.

JUNE 8

1 KINGS 3:4-4:34

Solomon's request for wisdom above anything else is the best Old Testament example I can think of that demonstrates the New Testament principle, "Seek first His kingdom...and all these things shall be added to you" (Matt. 6:33). Because Solomon's greatest desire was to be equipped to serve, God promised him all the things that *most* people are seeking above all else: money, long life and honor. The only people God can trust with those things are people who want to serve. Otherwise they would use those things to hurt other people. If your primary motivation is to serve others, you have a great life ahead of you. If it's to gain money, honor or to live a long time, get ready to learn some hard lessons.

I know you noticed it, but I just can't help mentioning it: isn't the wisdom Solomon demonstrated in the case of the two harlots amazing? You probably said to yourself, *I would never have thought of that!* But you would have, too, if God had given you the wisdom.

The good news is that God has promised us wisdom, but it has to be prayed for in faith (see James 1:5-8). Don't just ask for wisdom; ask for it, receive it and act upon it.

How wise was Solomon? There has never been another man wiser except for Jesus Himself. Remember that we have been reading Solomon's proverbs every day for the past five months. Praise God that Solomon's God-given wisdom can rub off on us!

ACTS 6:1-15

Speaking of wisdom, thank God the apostles had the wisdom not to neglect the preaching of the Word of God in order to wait on tables. The seven men they chose to oversee the food ministry were probably the first people to fill the office of "deacon." The Greek word translated "deacon" actually means "a servant."

Notice that the apostles "laid their hands upon" those first deacons when they set them apart for service. Laying on of hands is not some empty ritual but a point of contact to release an anointing into the life of the person. One of the seven was named Stephen and one was named Philip. We soon read that they became changed men after the apostles laid hands on them.

Another principle is demonstrated here as well. Stephen was faithful to serve in whatever way he could, and God promoted him for his faithfulness. Too often, young ministers want to preach to the multitudes, yet they're not willing to do the mundane chores of service for God.

We should be willing to do anything for the Lord, and then He'll promote us as we remain faithful.

PSALM 126:1-6

We will read the story of how Nebuchadnezzar deported the Jews of Jerusalem to Babylon about 550 years before Christ. After seventy years in exile, God worked it out so they could return and rebuild Jerusalem. This psalm was probably written in reference to that time.

PROVERBS 16:26-27

A hungry stomach is a wonderful cure for laziness.

JUNE 9

1 KINGS 5:1-6:38

I think you can tell that Solomon's temple was an impressive piece of architecture. It was about ninety feet long, thirty feet wide and forty-five feet high. The whole thing was covered with gold! In 1925 the Illinois Society of Architects estimated that the total construction cost for the temple and its accessories would have been about $87 billion (by 1925 standards)! But if you think a gold-covered temple is elaborate, realize that someday you'll live in a city where the streets are paved with gold (see Rev. 21:21)!

Solomon's temple is no longer in Jerusalem, but what is known today as the Western Wall (or "wailing wall") may possibly have stones in it that were part of a support platform for Solomon's temple. Many Jews pray there today. Now the gold-topped Muslim Mosque of Omar sits on the site where the temple used to be. We know from Jesus' promises that the temple will be rebuilt before the middle of the tribulation period.

Under the modern city of Jerusalem the quarries from which Solomon dug his stones can still be visited. It's a marvel to see the amount of work that was done to carve out those huge stones, all without modern equipment.

The temple had the basic design of the tabernacle of Moses, with a holy place and a holy of holies, where the ark of the covenant would be kept. This temple was twice as long and twice as wide as Moses' tabernacle. Against the outside walls, three stories of rooms were built. This beautiful building would be destroyed about four hundred years later during an invasion by Nebuchadnezzar, king of Babylon, so it was not the temple standing in Jesus' day.

ACTS 7:1-29

We read yesterday that when Stephen was about to make his defense before the Sanhedrin, his face took on the appearance of an angel. Not only was it an amazing defense, but the Holy Spirit revealed insights into Old Testament stories that we would not have known otherwise. For example, Moses knew forty years prior to the Exodus that God was going to use him to deliver Israel, but he jumped the gun on God's timing (see v. 25). We also learn that before Moses was forty years old he "was educated in all the learning of the Egyptians, and he was a man of power in words and deeds" (v. 22). That means Moses probably had a high political position in Egypt before he murdered the Egyptian. Moses tried to fulfill his calling in his own power and failed miserably.

PSALM 127:1-5

Are you the kind of person who has so much to do that you go to bed late and get up early? Then you're wasting your time doing more than God ever called you to do. Someday you will see all your labor as futile because God wasn't in it with you. God promises us sleep (see v. 2). That's a promise you may need to claim!

PROVERBS 16:28-30

Oh, the damage that has been done by slanderers! They have separated intimate friends (see v. 28). Gossip falls into the same category. It is best that we never discuss the faults of anyone lest we misrepresent the truth about them to another person. Rarely do we possess all the facts. Besides, we all have preconceived opinions and prejudices. We should always endeavor to believe the best of everyone.

JUNE 10

1 KINGS 7:1-51

Today's reading wasn't too exciting, was it? Essentially we have read of the bronze-work of Hiram of Tyre, who fashioned two huge pillars (each approximately twenty-seven feet high) to stand in front of the temple and a bowl (fifteen feet in diameter) that could have held ten thousand gallons of water; it was supported by twelve bronze oxen all facing outward. Hiram also fashioned smaller bowls on wheeled stands and other small utensils. This was probably exciting reading at one time, because this kind of work was awe-inspiring to people in that day. They viewed Hiram's work as we would a space shuttle or a super computer. Tomorrow we will read of the building dedication ceremony, for which God has a surprise planned!

ACTS 7:30-50

You should be so happy with yourself that you know all about the events of which Stephen spoke during his defense. You can see why it's so important to know the Old Testament in order to understand the New. And isn't it nice that Stephen finished his history lesson with the building of Solomon's temple, which we just read about yesterday?

PSALM 128:1-6

This psalm reveals that the basis for a happy family life is the fear of the Lord. How true. The man who fears the Lord is promised that his wife will be like a fruitful vine, which is a promise to childless couples who want to have children. When the Scriptures say that man will have children like olive plants, it's a reference to how olive trees reproduce. They never die, but new plants spring up from the old roots. The picture is of a man who has children springing up all around him in his home, and also of the blessings of grandchildren (see v. 6). How sad that so many people in our society have bought the lie that the "care-free" single life is the best, or that children are undesirable career-killers. The day will come when those career-seekers will wish they had had children and thus grandchildren to enjoy in their later years. It doesn't get any better than having your own family and watching children grow!

PROVERBS 16:31-33

If verse 31 doesn't make you proud of your gray hair, nothing will.

JUNE 11

1 KINGS 8:1-66

It surprises me when Christians criticize the charismatics because people sometimes fall down in their meetings (we call it being "slain in the Spirit"). When God's glory comes over a people, they may fall down, just as the priests at Solomon's dedication service did when the glory of the Lord filled the temple. We read in verse 11 that "the priests could not stand to minister because of the cloud." I take that to mean that they literally couldn't stand up to minister, which means they fell down.

Did you also notice how Solomon prayed his prayer of dedication? He was on his knees with his hands uplifted to God (see v. 54). It's scriptural to pray that way.

If you have ever been around Orthodox Jews during their times of prayer, you probably noticed that they always face in one direction—toward Jerusalem. This custom originated from Solomon's prayer that if an afflicted Israelite would pray toward the temple, God would hear and answer. So in the United States Orthodox Jews pray toward the east.

Finally, notice that Solomon recognized that God's discipline could come in various forms—defeat in battle, famine, pestilence, attack from enemies, capture by enemies and so on. But also notice that the way out from judgment was always the same: sincere repentance. Under the new covenant God is still a disciplinary God. When we find ourselves in adversity, we need to pray to see if we have opened the door through disobedience. Of course, not all adversity is an indication of sin in our lives. That's why we need to pray. If we have opened the door through sin, we can close the door through repentance. If we have no conviction of sin, we simply need to stand on the promises and see the salvation of the Lord.

ACTS 7:51-8:13

Why did God allow Stephen to be martyred? I don't know, but He did. Of course, it was Satan who inspired the whole thing.

I can't imagine that Stephen's final words, "Lord, do not hold this sin against them!" (7:60) didn't leave a lasting impression on his killers. One of them was Saul of Tarsus, who wound up writing the majority of what we have yet to read in the New Testament. At that time he was in hearty agreement with putting Stephen to death.

On the day of Stephen's stoning a great persecution arose against the whole church in Jerusalem. Some have suggested that God allowed this persecution in order to help spread the gospel to people outside Jerusalem. I agree. Jesus told His disciples to take the gospel to Jerusalem, Judea and Samaria and to the uttermost parts of the earth. Where were the Jerusalem Christians scattered? To Judea and Samaria (see 8:1). Wherever they went they shared the gospel.

Philip, who had had hands laid on him to be a deacon, now entered into his calling as an evangelist. He traveled to Samaria, where Jesus had begun a revival a few years before (see John 4:7-42), and began to preach the gospel. Notice that his ministry was anointed with certain gifts of healings. It seems his specialty was healing paralyzed and lame people, as well as casting out demons. Have you noticed that a person who is used by God in a healing ministry normally has more success with certain kinds of sicknesses or diseases than others? Maybe that is why the Bible refers to them as gifts (plural) of healings (plural), since there appear to be different gifts for different sicknesses.

In effect, Philip was the first missionary, because he was the first Christian who crossed a culture to spread the gospel. Remember that Jews and Samaritans hated each other. But God loves everybody, and the world needed to hear the gospel, even if it took a martyrdom to inspire the Christians to spread it. God so loved the world that He let His own Son be killed, so it shouldn't surprise us if He allowed a Christian to die a martyr's death in order that the unsaved might be reached.

PSALM 129:1-8

PROVERBS 17:1

JUNE 12

1 KINGS 9:1-10:29

You have just finished reading of Israel's golden age under Solomon's rule. We read that "all the earth was seeking the presence of Solomon, to hear his wisdom which God had put in his heart" (10:24). Can you see that God had an ulterior motive in blessing Israel? He wanted to draw the world to Himself. The queen of Sheba was just one example of a mighty ruler of a foreign nation traveling to see Solomon. There is a good possibility that she became a true believer in Israel's God (10:9). Perhaps other world leaders also came to believe in God as a result of Solomon's testimony.

If the queen of Sheba came from modern-day Yemen as many suggest, she traveled more than one thousand miles. Jesus said that she would stand up during the judgment and condemn the Jews of His day because she traveled such a long distance to hear the wisdom of Solomon, yet they were unmoved by the arrival of the very One who gave Solomon his wisdom.

We should realize that when God prospers the righteous, it is partly due to His love for the unrighteous who might see the wisdom of serving and trusting Him. We can also use our properity to be generous and share with those that are in need so that God's love in us might draw others to Him. God *does* desire to prosper us, but even Solomon said that all his wealth was just "vanity" that had no real meaning and brought no real happiness. We need to keep a balanced perspective.

ACTS 8:14-40

It's a good thing Peter and John didn't believe there is only one work of the Holy Spirit, or else the Samaritans would have missed out on a great blessing (see vv. 14-17).

The Scripture plainly says that the Holy Spirit "had not yet fallen upon any" of these thoroughly saved believers. The Holy Spirit was *in* them through the new birth, but He had not come *upon* them. They still needed to be clothed with power. When Peter and John prayed for them, something supernatural happened.

Notice that the Holy Spirit was imparted through the laying on of hands (vv. 17-19). This is another example of how "laying on of hands" is more than a symbolic ritual, but a point of contact to actually release a transfer of power.

The story of the Ethiopian eunuch can teach us a lot, but one message that stands out is this: God knows how receptive every person's heart is, and He will lead us to spiritually hungry people. This eunuch was ripe for salvation, wouldn't you say? We should ask God to guide us to receptive people rather than trying to use the sledgehammer method of witnessing to everyone we meet.

All Philip required of this man was that he believe Jesus Christ is the Son of God. Notice that immediately after he made his confession of faith in Jesus, Philip baptized him (immersed, not sprinkled) in water. People who say they believe in Jesus but are unwilling to obey the simple command to be baptized in water are fooling themselves.

PSALM 130:1-8

Do you get the idea from reading all these psalms that God is a good God? If you do, you're getting the right idea!

PROVERBS 17:2-3

What is the correlation between refining silver and gold and God's testing hearts? When silver and gold are refined, they are heated up until the impurities rise to the top and then are scraped off. In the same way, you'll notice that when we're "heated up" our impurities tend to surface. God can use adversity to cause us to grow, and He does. Those are what we call "testing times," and it becomes abundantly clear what is in our hearts. God is dedicated to our spiritual growth!

JUNE 13

1 KINGS 11:1-12:19

If ever there was a portion of Scripture that proved the doctrine of the free moral agency of humanity, this is it. Solomon, possessor of more God-given wisdom than any person, made the wrong choice and disobeyed God. He had three hundred concubines and seven hundred wives. Not only did he have a lot of wives, but he had a lot of the wrong kind of wives. He became "unequally yoked" to heathen women, and they led him away from God just as God had warned they would. Apparently this happened in Solomon's old age (see 11:4), so we know that he served God for many years. But his story teaches us that no matter how long we have served the Lord, if we allow Satan any foothold in our lives, we're living dangerously.

I can't imagine why Solomon married so many women. No doubt many were politically motivated marriage alliances. But his primary motivation had to have been a desire to be envied, or maybe it was just plain lust. Regardless, he disobeyed the Lord and was leading the people of Israel astray by his bad example so God "raised up adversaries" against him. By the same token, when God's people under the new covenant persist in disobedience, God may permit the devil to afflict them in order to bring them to repentance.

We read that God chose Jeroboam to be king over ten of the tribes of Israel once Solomon died. What's amazing is that when Solomon learned of God's plan, he tried to have Jeroboam killed. He displayed the same evil motivation as Saul had against David. We don't know if Solomon ever repented. But it's obvious that possessing wisdom is not enough. The possessor must choose to act on his wisdom.

How many people today know the right thing to do yet don't do it? For example, we all know that smoking cigarettes is bad for our health. But so many don't act on the wisdom God has given them. That is only one of many examples.

It may seem unfair that God didn't tear the kingdom away from Solomon but promised to tear it from his son. We'll read similar statements in the Bible regarding the sins of fathers for which their sons apparently paid the consequences. Was God punishing a son for his father's sins? No, that would be contrary to God's character. Actually God was showing mercy to the sinful Solomon by not bringing immediate judgment. It's obvious from what we read in chapter 12 that Solomon's son Rehoboam was equally deserving of judgment. I can assure you that if Rehoboam had been a righteous man, God would not have brought judgment upon him. Any time we read of God's promising to send major judgment on a man's son, it is only because God foreknew that the son would be equally or more deserving of judgment than his father. It is also an indication of God's great mercy upon the father by not sending the promised judgment immediately.

Rehoboam acted on his own free will in following the foolish advice of his young counselors. Yes, it was "a turn of events from the Lord" (12:15), but God worked through Rehoboam's free moral agency to bring about His will. The one nation of Israel now became two: Israel (the ten northern tribes) and Judah (the combined southern tribes of Judah and Benjamin).

ACTS 9:1-25

Most Christians have no idea how terrible a person Saul of Tarsus was before he was saved. We know he held the coats of the men who stoned Stephen. We also read two days ago that in Jerusalem he "began ravaging the church, entering house after house; and dragging off men and women, he would put them in prison" (8:3). In his letter to the Galatian Christians Paul said that before his salvation he "persecuted the church of God beyond measure, and tried to destroy it" (Gal. 1:13). In his first letter to Timothy Paul described himself as formerly being a "blasphemer and a persecutor and a violent aggressor" (1 Tim. 1:13). During his testimony to King Agrippa recorded in Acts 26, Paul testified: "I thought to myself that I had to do many things hostile to the name of Jesus of Nazareth. And this is just what I did in Jerusalem; not only did I lock up many of the saints in prisons...but also when they were being put to death I cast my vote against them. And as I punished them often in all the synagogues, I tried to force them to blaspheme; and being furiously enraged at them, I kept pursuing them even to foreign cities" (26:9-11).

From these scriptures I think we can agree that Saul was a former murderer and an extremely evil man! Yet God forgave him. There is no person whom God won't forgive, and it saddens me when I meet Christians or non-Christians who think they have committed too many sins to receive mercy. Paul wrote in 1 Timothy 1:15-16: "It is a trustworthy statement, deserving full acceptance, that Christ Jesus came into the world to save sinners, among whom I am foremost of all. And yet for this reason I found mercy, in order that in me as the foremost, Jesus Christ might demonstrate His perfect patience, as an example for those who would believe in Him for eternal life." So even if you're the world's second-greatest sinner, God has already proved He will forgive you, too!

Notice that when Jesus spoke to Saul

on the road to Damascus, He said, "Saul, Saul, why are you persecuting Me?" (v. 4). Was Saul physically persecuting Jesus? No, because Jesus was in heaven at the right hand of the Father. Saul was persecuting the *church of Jesus*, which is His body. When someone persecutes the church, he persecutes Jesus. Let me take that one step further. How you and I treat the church is how we treat Jesus. Christians who say, "I love Jesus, but I don't go to church," are fooling themselves. Christians who say, "I love Jesus, but I don't support my church financially," are fooling themselves. If we're all members of Christ's body, then how we treat each other individually is how we treat Jesus. Let me bring that fact real close to home: *how you treat your spouse is how you treat Jesus.* Having pastored for a number of years, and having been involved in many counseling sessions between husbands and wives, I believe Jesus is asking many married couples essentially the same question He asked Saul: "Why are you treating Me like this?"

Keep in mind God's divine destiny for Saul—to bear His name before the Gentiles and kings and the sons of Israel. God also said that Saul would suffer greatly (see vv. 15-16). We will read of the unfolding fulfillment of God's calling on Saul throughout the book of Acts.

PSALM 131:1-3

This is a short psalm but one of my favorites. Why are we so troubled so much of the time? Because we overcommit ourselves and involve ourselves in "things too difficult." God wants us to experience His peace in the same way a child rests peacefully against his mother. Now that's a picture of peace! Can you imagine yourself leaning against the breast of Jesus, completely secure in His care?

PROVERBS 17:4-5

JUNE 14

1 KINGS 12:20-13:34

Jeroboam, new king of the ten northern tribes, received a wonderful promise from God in 11:38. Jeroboam knew that God tore the majority of the kingdom from Rehoboam because of Solomon's idolatry, yet he (Jeroboam) led Israel into further idolatry and became a cult leader. What was his motive? Very simply, power had corrupted him, and for fear of ever losing his power he invented a new religion (see 12:26-27).

In chapter 13 we read one of the most amazing prophecies in Scripture. An unnamed prophet predicted that someday a descendant of David named Josiah would burn the bones of Jeroboam's false priests on the very altar on which Jeroboam was offering incense. What makes this prophecy so fantastic is that the future person was called by name. And sure enough the prophecy was fulfilled, but not for three hundred years. We won't read of that incident until the end of 2 Kings.

Today's reading ends with a strange story of this unnamed prophet who delivered God's warning to Jeroboam. He had been given specific instructions by the Lord to eat no bread and drink no water, nor return by the way he had come (see 13:9,16-17). But an old prophet lied to him and said the Lord had changed His mind about His first instructions, and he then enticed the first prophet to come and eat with him. It resulted in a judgment of death upon the first prophet. We can learn at least two lessons from this story. First, what God says, He means. Second, we shouldn't listen to every prophecy. If you hear something that doesn't agree with God's revealed Word, it isn't a true prophecy. God won't contradict Himself.

The question that comes to my mind is this: why did the first prophet die, but the second, who lied to the first, seemingly was not judged? But this passage doesn't answer my question. The rest of the Bible, however, gives us plenty of information about God and His fairness, so we can safely trust that God did the right thing.

Did you wonder how God could have used the lying second prophet to prophesy to the first that judgment was coming because of his disobedience? This is one of the foremost proofs from the Bible that gifts of the Spirit aren't passed out to people based on their holiness. They are gifts of God's grace. That's why, as I mentioned some days ago, preachers can be involved in immorality and yet still be anointed to minister. Eventually judgment comes upon them for their sin if they don't repent, but their anointing remains for the duration. Apparently this second prophet felt some guilt for his actions, because he asked to be buried with the first prophet's bones when he died.

ACTS 9:26-43

For the next four or five days we will be reading of Peter's ministry; from then on until the end of the book of Acts, Paul's (Saul's) ministry is highlighted. We read today that Peter was involved in the beginnings of at least two major revivals, one in Lydda/Sharon and the other in Joppa. Notice that both revivals were precipitated by miracles, not programs.

Notice also the difference in receptivity between the people of Lydda/Sharon and the people of Joppa. As a result of the miracle of Aeneas's healing, "all who lived at Lydda and Sharon...turned to the Lord" (v. 35). In Joppa, as a result of Tabitha's being raised from the dead, "many believed in the Lord" (v. 42). All these cities were near one another, yet the people in Lydda/Sharon were more open to God than the people of Joppa. I've seen the same thing in my hometown of Pittsburgh. I know of various suburbs where the people are more or less receptive than in other suburbs. In fact, being in the right place at the right time is one major key to church growth that rarely seems to be mentioned. However, God may call pastors to areas that are not very receptive, thus they will not have large, thriving churches. Yet God still wants to reach the few receptive ones in those areas. Don't judge pastors by the size of their churches.

PSALM 132:1-18

PROVERBS 17:6

JUNE 15

1 KINGS 14:1-15:24

Was the death of Jeroboam's children a case of kids being punished by God for their parents' sins? We've seen several times already that God doesn't do that. As with David and Bathsheba's child, Jeroboam's child went immediately to paradise, which was a great blessing for the child. The ones who suffered were Jeroboam and his wife. The other sons of Jeroboam would die for their own sins. We'll read tomorrow in 15:26 that Jeroboam's son Nadab, who succeeded Jeroboam to the throne, was just as evil as his father. Notice also that in 14:13 God said He found any good only in Jeroboam's one son (the one whom Ahijah had prophesied would soon die). That means the others were totally corrupt like their father. In 14:10 they are all described as "dung."

Ahijah the prophet accurately foretold that God would judge all of Israel by removing them from the promised land and sending them beyond the Euphrates River, though it didn't happen for about another two hundred years.

We also read today that King Asa had a disease in his feet during his old age (15:23). Since God promised all of Israel that he would be their Healer if they would trust and obey Him (Ex. 15:26, 23:25), either Asa wasn't trusting God or he was living in disobedience. The fact that Asa imprisoned a prophet for telling him the truth makes me wonder if God permitted the disease in order to bring about his repentance. We read that "his disease was severe, yet even in his disease he did not seek the Lord, but the physicians (2 Chron. 16:12-13; italics mine). Asa could have been healed if he had repented. It was God's will for him to be healed, but he missed God's best through disobedience.

ACTS 10:1-23a

Cornelius, a Roman army commander over one hundred men, had been attracted to the Jewish faith and believed in the true God. In fact, he prayed to God continually and gave alms. He was a good candidate to be the first Gentile to hear and believe the gospel. The only problem was that the early church was made up entirely of Jews who believed that only Jews could be saved! So God had to take drastic action to have someone cross a culture to reach different people. Thus, Peter was chosen to be the first "real" missionary. (Philip had crossed a culture in Samaria, but the Samaritans observed the Law of Moses and were considered half-Jews.)

Peter didn't immediately understand his God-given vision, but within time it became abundantly clear to him. Not only has God declared all foods clean under the new covenant (see Mark 7:19), but the "unclean Gentiles" could be made clean by the blood of Christ. It's obvious that the early church still followed the dietary restrictions of the Law of Moses. Furthermore, they had no social intercourse with Gentiles. We'll read in two days that the church in Jerusalem called Peter on the carpet because he went and ate a meal with Gentiles! So you can see why God had to do something supernatural to make the church realize that Gentiles could be saved simply by believing in Jesus. God gave that vision to Peter because He loves all of us Gentiles!

Incidentally, we are only to the tenth chapter of Acts, but already angels have appeared on four occasions and given directions (1:10-11; 5:19-20; 8:26; 10:3-6). We shouldn't be surprised if angels sometimes appear and speak to God's servants today.

PSALM 133:1-3

The oil with which Aaron was anointed represented his anointing to minister. Probably this psalm is saying that where there is unity between brothers, there the anointing of God will be also. If you have ever experienced true unity in a church or fellowship of believers, you understand what I'm talking about. God blesses unity.

PROVERBS 17:7-8

Verse 8 is not an endorsement of bribery. It is simply stating unfortunate realities.

JUNE 16

1 KINGS 15:25-17:24

Throughout the books of 1 and 2 Kings we will jump back and forth from the line of kings of Israel and Judah. Remember that Israel never had a good king. Ahab was the cream of the crop as far as wickedness is concerned, and God allowed a famine to come upon Israel during his evil reign. It was a direct slap in the face from God to Baal, the god who supposedly was in charge of the rain and good crops.

Notice that Elijah didn't have to suffer along with the rest of Israel during the three-and-a-half-year famine. However, Elijah had to obey God's instructions if his needs were to be supplied. Do you know what would have happened to Elijah if he had just sat around and made positive confessions such as, "I'm trusting God to supply all my needs?" He would have starved. There is more to prosperity than just trusting God's promises. We must also listen to and apply the wisdom God gives us. Elijah obeyed God's instructions to go to the brook Cherith, and God provided for him there.

If Elijah had been like a lot of Christians, when the brook dried up he would have said, "God doesn't love me anymore!" But Elijah was more mature than that, knowing that if one source dries up it simply means God has another source waiting. If you have lost your job or source of income, don't doubt God. Trust that He has something better for you. God never promised us that there wouldn't be times when we might lose our jobs or a source of income might dry up. He only promised to supply our needs. I guarantee there will be times when you'll have to trust Him.

God's next source for Elijah was a little widow woman who lived in Zarephath in the land of Sidon. She wasn't an Israelite, but quite possibly she was a believer in Israel's God. One significant aspect of this story that's often overlooked is that this widow knew Elijah was coming even before Elijah knew he was going! God said to Elijah in 17:9, "Go to Zarephath...behold, I have commanded a widow there to provide for you." If God hadn't revealed that knowledge to her before Elijah requested her last meal, she would have chased him out of the country!

She obviously was not prepared, however, for the *way* God was going to use her to provide for Elijah. She was required to give what little she had to Elijah, and only then would God provide for her. It was a supreme test of her faith, but she passed with flying colors. This is a beautiful example of the divine principle "Give and it shall be given unto you." Did you know that all of us have been given a similar test? God commands us to give to His work, and if we will, He promises to supply all our needs. It is such a shame when Christians don't give to God what He says to give because they think they can't afford it. They are stopping miracles from happening! I know it takes faith, but faith in God's Word knows no failure.

Most of the time we talk about the faith of this widow, but I think it took a lot of faith on Elijah's part too. What if God didn't multiply the flour and oil as he predicted? He would have watched that poor woman and her son die, knowing that he had consumed their last meal! Pastors should take courage from Elijah's example. As a pastor, it was sometimes difficult for me to watch people who were hurting financially to put their tithes in the offering. Yet I knew God couldn't lie and would bless them for it. And do you know what? He did!

When this widow's son died, God used the tragedy to confirm His calling upon

Elijah and draw the widow woman closer to Himself. God didn't cause her son's death, nor was his death good, but God caused it to work for good (see Rom. 8:28). This was the first time in history that any person had been raised from the dead. You can imagine how surprised that woman was!

ACTS 10:23b-48

Peter, who walked with Jesus for three years, spoke of Jesus' "healing all who were oppressed by the devil" in his message to Cornelius's household (see 10:38). God is not the author of sickness, as some uninformed Christians unfortunately believe. Satan, who desires to "steal, kill and destroy" (John 10:10), is responsible for much sickness and disease. Jesus came to "destroy the works of the devil (1 John 3:8)!

As soon as Peter mentioned the way to salvation as being faith in Jesus Christ, Cornelius and his household didn't wait for the altar call to pray the sinner's prayer. They immediately put their faith in Jesus and were all saved. Then God sovereignly baptized them in the Holy Spirit. How did Peter and the others know these new Christians had received the Holy Spirit? They heard them speaking in other tongues (see vv. 45-46).

Within a few minutes these new converts were baptized in water as well. This was a historic moment for Christianity, as it marked the first time any of us Gentiles were born again.

PSALM 134:1-3

Have you ever lifted your hands to the Lord? If not, you should, because the Bible says you should (v. 2). Lifting our hands signifies complete surrender to Him.

PROVERBS 17:9-11

JUNE 17

1 KINGS 18:1-46

What a tremendous story about Elijah and the prophets of Baal! Elijah didn't just dream up this test that took place on Mount Carmel: he was simply acting on divine command. He was also obeying God when he put the prophets of Baal to death (see Deut. 13:1-5, which says that false prophets should be executed).

Did Elijah pray seven times for it to rain, as some say? No, the Scripture doesn't say he prayed seven times; it only says he sent his servant to look for a cloud on the horizon seven times. Elijah prayed once for the rain to come and simply persisted in faith. Notice that he said to Ahab *before there was even a cloud in the sky*, "Go up, eat and drink; for there is the sound of the roar of a heavy shower" (v. 41). Faith speaks as though the promise has already come to pass. You can imagine the celebration they had after three and a half years of no rain!

One final miracle of which we read today is how Elijah outran Ahab, who was in a horse-drawn chariot, to Jezreel, about seventeen miles away. The Lord was his strength.

ACTS 11:1-30

In today's reading we get a glimpse of the hottest controversy that confronted the early church: the role of the Law of Moses in a new covenant believer's life. God was slowly helping the early Jewish Christians to realize that the old law had passed away. Peter, who previously was so well-known for his brashness and lack of self-control, diplomatically explained what God had revealed to him through the revival at Cornelius's house. There was no way his questioners could argue with what God had done.

It was in a Gentile church in Antioch where the disciples were first called Christians, which means "like Christ." You can see by that definition that many people who are born again aren't "Christians," because they're not committed disciples and don't act like Christ.

One aspect of the ministry of true New Testament prophets is revealed in the final portion of today's reading. Agabus foretold a coming famine that the Christians in Antioch apparently knew would affect the brethren living in Judea, so they sent them an offering. Are there prophets today in the body of Christ? As long as the saints need perfecting, there will be prophets (see Eph. 4:11-13). Remember that just because God uses a person to prophesy doesn't mean that person is a prophet. I believe that a true prophet will be a minister with a teaching or preaching ministry, not simply a lay person who prophesies at times. A prophet is used consistently in other gifts of the Spirit besides prophecy, most commonly the "word of knowledge," the "word of wisdom" and "discerning of spirits." We'll look further into each of those gifts when we read about them in 1 Corinthians.

PSALM 135:1-21

PROVERBS 17:12-13

JUNE 18

1 KINGS 19:1-21

It's hard to believe that anyone could be as wicked as Queen Jezebel. Even after hearing the first-hand report from her own husband about how the fire of God fell on Mount Carmel, her only thought was to murder Elijah. Consequently, Elijah ran for his life. Elijah's fear proves to me that he was just an ordinary man subject to the same doubts as you and I are.

I sure would like to get my hands on some of that special food the angel prepared for Elijah. One meal nourished him for forty days!

Elijah journeyed two hundred miles to Mount Horeb, where God had appeared to Moses in the burning bush and given him the Ten Commandments. There the Lord asked him, "What are you doing here, Elijah?" (v. 9). (The implication was that he didn't have any good reason for being there if he were trusting God.) After the wind, earthquake and fire, the Lord gently encouraged Elijah by telling him there were still seven thousand people in Israel who had not bowed their knees to Baal. Remember the names of the men God told Elijah to anoint. God raised them up to bring judgment upon Israel for her apostasy (see v. 17), and we'll read about them again.

Elisha knew exactly what it meant when Elijah threw his mantle over him. The mantle represented the anointing that was upon Elijah and would eventually be transferred to Elisha. He was willing to give up everything he possessed to follow Elijah; he slew his oxen and burned them with their yokes. There was no turning back from the call of God on his life now, no "Plan B." He began his ministry being faithful in small things by ministering to Elijah. He operated in this ministry of helps until the time came when he was to carry on Elijah's ministry. In time Elisha would be the one who would fulfill God's command to Elijah to anoint Hazael and Jehu (see 2 Kin. 8-9).

ACTS 12:1-23

To me, this section of the book of Acts reveals that God loves to plan surprises. Isn't it amazing that on the eve of Peter's execution he was sleeping soundly in his jail cell? Either Peter was given the gift of special faith or else he had highly developed his ability to walk in God's peace. It's a good thing he didn't lose any sleep, because God has a tremendous "jail ministry"! He specializes in escapes! Even with two soldiers chained to Peter and more guarding his cell and the entire prison, it was no problem for God to deliver him.

Why did God deliver Peter from death but allow James to be martyred? I don't know. But maybe we should ask that question this way: "Why did God let James go to heaven so soon but keep Peter on this lousy earth?" Death is a great blessing to those in Christ (see Phil. 1:21-23).

During Peter's stay in prison, "prayer for him was being made fervently by the church to God" (v. 5). This part makes me laugh. Peter's first stop after his escape was at a prayer meeting being held on his behalf. They didn't believe their own prayers had been answered! I'm sure the Lord was having a good chuckle at this point!

Notice that everyone in the prayer meeting thought that Rhoda had been talking to Peter's angel (v. 15). Apparently they believed that Peter had a personal angel. Did you know that you have an angel assigned to you too? He's watching you right now as you are reading this!

Herod accepted glory that belonged only to God (see v. 23). His judgment came through worms. What can we learn from this story about giving God the glory that is rightfully His?

PSALM 136:1-26

All the works God has done, from creation even to judgment upon the wicked, have been done because of His great love for us. How could we ever doubt His love? This psalm makes that point like no other.

PROVERBS 17:14-15

Strife is always nonproductive, because a person's pride is usually involved. That's why we're admonished to "abandon the quarrel before it breaks out." Of course, there is a difference between an argument and two mature, open-minded parties having a lively discussion. You can tell that a discussion has turned into strife when voices rise above normal volumes. That's the time to call it quits

JUNE 19

1 KINGS 20:1-21:29

Samaria was the new capital of the ten northern tribes of Israel, while Jerusalem remained the capital of Judah. It was Samaria that Ben-hadad, king of Syria, had surrounded and was fighting. Although Israel had essentially forsaken God, the Lord continued to show the people mercy by supernaturally assisting them in battle against the Syrians on two occasions. It was during the second battle that Ahab made the error of allowing Ben-hadad to live, a man God had intended to destroy.

One story that may need a little explanation is this one of the prophet who requested that another prophet strike him (see 20:35). When he refused, the first prophet pronounced that he would be killed by a lion. (Lions were common in Palestine in those days.) Sure enough, shortly thereafter, the disobedient prophet was killed by a lion. Was God's judgment severe? Yes, but we can be certain it was deserved. This prophet willfully disobeyed God's command to him, and such a man has no right to be a prophet of God.

King Ahab's selfish nature was outdone only by his wife's incredible wickedness, as we read in this story of Ahab's coveting Naboth's vineyard. By refusing to sell or trade his land to Ahab, Naboth was only obeying the tradition that the land should pass from generation to generation in the same family. Of course, nothing escapes God's notice, and because God is not mocked, both Ahab and Jezebel would reap what they had sown. Where the dogs licked up the blood of Naboth, they would lick up the blood of Ahab, and dogs would eat the body of Jezebel in her hometown. *All* of Ahab's descendants would die shamefully.

What amazes me is that God showed remorseful Ahab some mercy and promised to forestall judgment on Ahab's house until after he was dead. Again, this wasn't a case of the sons being punished for the father's sins, but God showing mercy on a wicked father until the time of his equally evil sons. Ahab was still destined to die for his wickedness.

ACTS 12:24-13:15

The church in Antioch included prophets and teachers (see 13:1). *Every* local church doesn't have to have prophets and teachers, but I would certainly hope there would be prophets and teachers in every *city* where the body of Christ exists.

The Holy Spirit spoke in some manner, possibly through prophecy, to "set apart for Me Barnabas and Saul for the work to which I have called them" (13:2). Notice that the Spirit didn't specify what "the work" was, but simply that it was time for Barnabas and Saul to be set apart for it.

Under the new covenant we're not to be led by prophecy, which should serve only as a confirmation of what has already been revealed to us by the indwelling Holy Spirit.

The various prophets and teachers there in Antioch laid their hands on Barnabas and Saul to impart the anointing that would be necessary for their new ministries (see 13:3). Whatever they lacked to be apostles before that prayer meeting, they had it after it was over.

The apostolic anointing that was imparted was first evident on the island of Cyprus. Notice the words, "Paul, filled with the Holy Spirit...." This indicates a sudden anointing which came upon Paul to rebuke the false prophet Bar-Jesus, and which caused him to be struck blind. After witnessing this miracle, Sergius Paulus believed in the Lord.

How was the church started on the island of Cyprus? It started from one miracle, worked through an anointed man (see 13:9).

PSALM 137:1-9

This psalm refers to the time (of which we will soon read) when the Jews were deported from Judah and Jerusalem to Babylon. God used Nebuchadnezzar as a tool of His judgment upon the apostate Jews, and they remained in exile for seventy years before they were permitted to return to their homeland. The Babylonians were cruel captors who destroyed Jerusalem, and this psalmist prayed for a repayment to come upon them, which eventually happened.

PROVERBS 17:16

JUNE 20

1 KINGS 22:1-53

Although Jehoshaphat was a good king of Judah, he made a poor decision to ally himself with evil King Ahab of Israel to fight against Syria. He was "unequally yoked." At least he had the sense to seek God's will in the matter, apparently doubting that Ahab's proposed endeavor was blessed of the Lord.

Commentators differ on whether those four hundred prophets were true prophets of the Lord. I have to think not in light of the fact that they were unanimously wrong about Ahab's battle against Syria. Even Jehoshaphat seemed to know that they were false, because he requested a "prophet of the Lord" after hearing their prophecies (see v. 7).

Did God actually allow one of His angels to put a "deceiving spirit" in the mouths of all of Ahab's prophets in order to bring about Ahab's death? If we believe what we've just read, the answer is yes. God can do anything He wants to do. It certainly wasn't contrary to His character to deceive an evil person to bring about His judgment. We read in 2 Thessalonians that in the last days God will send a "deluding influence" upon people who have rejected the truth so that they might be deceived by the Antichrist (see 2:10-12). Remember that God would only deceive evil people who are beyond repentance. God even revealed to Ahab how He had allowed a deceiving spirit to enter into the mouths of his prophets, yet still Ahab would not take heed. The "randomly shot arrow" that took his life wasn't really so random. In addition, the Lord's word through Elijah was fulfilled that the dogs would lick up the blood of Ahab where they had licked up the blood of Naboth (see 21:19).

Thankfully, God protected Jehoshaphat even though he had no place joining himself in battle with Ahab. Unfortunately, he became no wiser for the incident, and we'll read later that he joined himself in another alliance with Ahab's son, even after receiving rebuke from a prophet for helping "those who hate the Lord" (see 2 Chron. 19:2).

ACTS 13:16-41

It would be helpful for you to look at the maps in your Bible to find the one that depicts the first missionary journey of the apostle Paul. Today's reading takes us to Pisidian Antioch, a city in the region of Galatia that is now located in Turkey, a Muslim country, which has forty million people but fewer than one thousand Christians (1988 figures).

During his sermon at the synagogue in Antioch, Paul quoted a verse from the second Psalm as a reference to Jesus' resurrection (see v. 33). What does it mean that Jesus was "begotten" on the day He was resurrected? It might be a reference to His body's being reborn (or coming back to life). On the other hand, some believe Jesus died spiritually on the cross when He "became sin" (2 Cor. 5:21) and therefore of necessity had to experience a spiritual rebirth. Jesus, of course, never sinned and didn't become a "sinner" on the cross. It's a difficult and controversial subject, so I'm not going to delve any deeper into it. You can still be saved no matter what you believe concerning this topic.

PSALM 138:1-8

David said in verse 7, "Though I walk in the midst of trouble, Thou wilt revive me...Thy right hand will save me." If you're in some kind of difficulty, don't think that by faith you have to deny the problem exists. But you do need to believe and confess that God is working on your behalf according to His promises. Hold fast in faith!

PROVERBS 17:17-18

You probably have discovered that some people don't become your friend because they love you, but because they want something from you. Thank God for a friend or brother who loves you at "all times" and is "born for adversity"! I can guarantee you that Jesus is one of those friends. He loves you even when you make a mistake.

JUNE 21

2 KINGS 1:1-2:25

This story of Ahab's son Ahaziah becoming ill and inquiring of Baalzebub about the outcome of his sickness certainly raises some questions. First of all, it's quite obvious that Ahaziah's sickness had been permitted because of God's judgment. Probably God was trying to bring about Ahaziah's repentance in the sickness, but Ahaziah didn't even think to seek the Lord. God therefore decreed that the result of his illness would be death.

We read that Ahaziah sent three groups of fifty soldiers to bring Elijah to himself, and the first two groups were consumed by fire from heaven. We tend to question why God would wipe out one hundred supposedly innocent men. However, maybe we should be marveling that He spared fifty. Everybody gets what he deserves, but only after God has shown ample mercy. It's my opinion that the first captain of fifty men called Elijah "a man of God" in a mocking tone (see 1:9). That's why Elijah replied, "If I am a man of God, let fire come down from heaven and consume you and your fifty" (1:10). In other words, Elijah was saying, "So you make fun of God and me? Let God teach you a lesson!" The same was probably true concerning the second captain and his fifty men.

Also keep in mind that the first two groups would have been shown the same mercy that the third group was shown if they had approached Elijah *as* the last group did—with humility and respect.

If there is one overriding message in this first chapter it's that when we get into trouble, we should seek God first. Too many times we seek God's help only when every other avenue for assistance has failed.

The story of Elijah's "homegoing" is amazing, and it demonstrates at least one spiritual principle—that the anointing on one person can be transferred to another if it is God's will. The sons of the prophets remarked, "The spirit (or anointing) of Elijah rests upon Elisha" (2:15). It was obvious!

Elijah actually tried to discourage Elisha from following him from Gilgal to Bethel, to Jericho and to the Jordan River. It must have been a test to see if Elisha was willing to pay the price for the ministry and anointing. Elisha's tenacity paid off, as Elisha received a double portion of Elijah's anointing. If you study the Scriptures you'll discover that Elisha did twice as many miracles as Elijah did.

Many have been disturbed while

reading the story of the forty-two young boys who mocked Elisha. Why would God have two bears kill those boys for such a trifling matter? First of all, the Scripture doesn't say that the two bears killed forty-two boys. That would have constituted a major miracle, because if that were the case, either those boys were slow runners or those two bears were superbears! The Bible says the bears "tore up" forty-two lads. I believe a few of them got some good scratches, all of them got a good scare and all of them learned a good lesson: don't make fun of God's men!

ACTS 13:42-14:7

Do you remember when God spoke to Ananias concerning the Apostle Paul's ministry and said "for I will show him how much he must suffer for My name's sake" (Acts 9:16)? Today we read about the beginning of Paul's sufferings.

Notice that his sufferings were the result of persecution from ungodly people, not sickness or disease. Occasionally Christians read in the Bible about the sufferings that we as Christians must face sometimes, and they try to throw sickness and disease into the same category as suffering persecution. They speak of their infirmity when they say "I'm suffering for Jesus." Jesus bore our sicknesses and diseases, but He didn't promise that we would never suffer persecution.

Just as Jesus had taught His disciples to do, Paul and Barnabas shook the dust from their feet in protest to the unreceptive Jews in Pisidian Antioch (see v. 51). But many believers were in that city (especially Gentiles), and a church was established there. For Paul and Barnabas it was on to Iconium, another city of Galatia. Once again they faced opposition, but they continued to rely upon the Lord, who was granting that signs and wonders be done by their hands.

Note how God always built the church through the power of the Holy Spirit. Paul would later write in his letter to the Romans, "For I will not presume to speak of anything except what Christ has accomplished through me, resulting in the obedience of the Gentiles by word and deed, in the power of signs and wonders, in the power of the Spirit; so that from Jerusalem and round about as far as Illyricum I have fully preached the gospel of Christ" (Rom. 15:18-19). Without the power of the Holy Spirit demonstrated through signs and wonders, we can never hope to accomplish the great commission.

PSALM 139:1-24

What a great psalm this is! I take comfort in the fact that God knows me better than I know myself, and there is no place I can go that He will not be with me. Under the new covenant we have it even better than David, the author of this psalm. He only had God *with* him, whereas we have God *in* us.

This psalm also arms us with a scriptural argument against the sin of abortion. David said that God formed him in his mother's womb (see v. 13). What the abortionists call a "fetus," God calls a person.

PROVERBS 17:19-21

JUNE 22

2 KINGS 3:1-4:17

Once again good King Jehoshaphat foolishly allied himself with an evil king of Israel, this time to fight against the Moabites. Jehoshaphat shouldn't have been involved at all, but it was fortunate for Jehoram that he was, or else Jehoram and his army might have perished.

Notice also that Elisha called for a minstrel, and when the minstrel played, "the hand of the Lord came upon him [Elisha]" (v. 15). There is a definite correlation between music and the move of the Spirit. So many churches have no move of the Spirit in their services because they've never learned to create an atmosphere in which the Spirit can move. They sing three hymns and then sit down. Sincere worship brings the presence of God on the scene. Anybody who has ever been involved in a worship service where the people truly concentrate on ministering to the Lord knows what I'm talking about.

Many charismatic churches, unfortunately, know nothing about spiritual worship. They only sing fast songs to bring people to an emotional high. Sometimes I've sensed that the Spirit was grieved by their song service because it was so man-centered.

Elisha's prophecy carried a command to dig trenches in the valley, because God was going to miraculously send water to the thirsty troops. I like that. They had to prepare for the blessing by faith. We, too, need to get ready to receive what God has promised us if we are truly believing Him.

The story in chapter 4 about the widow's oil displays that same principle. I'm sure the widow and her sons felt reluctant to ask all their neighbors for every receptacle they owned. No doubt many of them asked, "What for?," and the widow and her sons had to confess their faith in what God had promised through Elisha. Truly it was done to them "according to their faith." As soon as they ran out of receptacles, the oil stopped flowing.

God may not choose to supply your needs in such a miraculous manner, but this story is one more proof that He will go to great lengths to supply your needs. If you will trust and obey Him, He will "supply all your needs according to His riches in glory" (Phil. 4:19).

Finally, we read about the Shunammite woman who showed Elisha hospitality. When people are good to God's anointed ones, God is good to them in return. This childless woman received the blessing of a son not because of her faith, because she didn't believe Elisha when he promised she would have a son, but because she was kind to the man of God. Don't forget this story, because tomorrow we will discover that what the Lord gives, the devil tries to take away.

ACTS 14:8-28

This story of the crippled man in Lystra beautifully illustrates the power of the "full gospel"—the gospel that includes healing as well as salvation. According to the Scripture, Paul was preaching "the gospel" in Lystra (see v. 7). He was not only proclaiming that in Christ there is forgiveness of sins, but that physical healing is available also. That had to be the case, because this man received faith to be healed from listening to Paul's message (see v. 9). Paul "perceived" that the man had faith, and he did so either through the gift of "the word of knowledge" or by the fact that the man was receiving what he was saying. (People who have faith are easy to spot—they're smiling!)

Notice that even though the man "had faith to be made well" he still was not healed (v. 9). Why? Because he had not yet acted upon his faith. It wasn't until this man stood up at the command of Paul that his healing was manifested. Now don't try to concoct some formula such as, "If I quit taking my medicine, God will have to heal me." That's not faith, that's foolishness. Work on getting faith down in your heart. When you do, the corresponding actions will come naturally, as they did with this man at Lystra.

I'm amazed that Paul got up after being stoned and went back into the city. He was no wimp! We really shouldn't complain about the small amounts of persecution we receive, should we?

PSALM 140:1-13

PROVERBS 17:22

The truth of this proverb has been proved by modern medical science. People who have a bright, optimistic attitude tend to recover faster from surgery and illness. I once read about a man who had a fatal disease but gradually recovered by watching old Laurel and Hardy movies. He said he "laughed himself to health"!

There is no doubt that our emotions affect our health. Depression, anxiety, bitterness as well as many other negative emotions can reduce the body's resistance to certain sicknesses.

Remember that happiness is a choice. The Bible teaches that we should rejoice in every situation (see 1 Thess. 5:16-18). The only way to rejoice always is to have faith in God. And the only way to have faith in God is to know His promises.

JUNE 23

2 KINGS 4:18-5:27

It is somewhat amazing that after her child died this Shunammite woman kept it a secret from her husband (even during his questioning) and made a beeline for Elisha.

We don't fully understand why Elisha's staff didn't work, but my opinion is that the Shunammite woman had no faith in it—she had faith that when *Elisha* arrived on the scene something would happen, as indeed it did. This story teaches that just because great blessings come our way, it shouldn't surprise us if fiery trials come our way as well.

Naaman, like so many of us, thought he had God's ways all figured out, *but God cannot be made to fit into anyone's box!* Naaman had to humble himself to obey God. When he did, his leprosy was cleansed.

Could Elisha heal any leper he desired? No, this was a manifestation of the "gifts of healings" working through him. Jesus Himself said about this story, "There were many lepers in Israel in the time of Elisha the prophet; and none of them was cleansed, but only Naaman the Syrian" (Luke 4:27). Gifts of the Spirit work only as the Spirit wills (see 1 Cor. 12:11).

This story also demonstrates that the gift of "the word of knowledge" cannot be turned on or off by human will. If Elisha had possessed the ability to know anything any time he wanted, Gehazi never would have had the nerve to lie to him. Gehazi's dirty deed was supernaturally revealed to Elisha by the Holy Spirit this one time. Naaman had brought with him a huge amount of silver and gold as payment for his healing (see 5:5), but Elisha knew he was not to receive it lest anyone (including Naaman) should think he could buy God's blessings. Healing comes because of God's grace.

The judgment of leprosy upon Gehazi was pronounced by Elisha as lasting forever, yet I have to think that Gehazi could have repented and sooner or later been healed, just as Miriam, Moses' sister, had been stricken with leprosy in judgment and was healed seven days later (see Num. 12:10-15). But we don't know for sure.

ACTS 15:1-35

Did you notice how the elders and apostles in Jerusalem arrived at their determination that the Gentiles could be saved simply by faith in Jesus, regardless of whether they kept the Law of Moses? First they took into consideration what God had already done and the attitude He had demonstrated toward Gentiles. Peter retold his story of how God used him to be the first one to preach to the Gentiles approximately ten years before and how God sovereignly baptized them in the Holy Spirit. Paul and Barnabas related the various signs and wonders that God did among the Gentiles through their ministry, as well as how God had accepted them without any requirement of keeping the Law. Finally, James quoted several supporting scriptures.

Of course, salvation by grace doesn't mean we can continue in sin once we believe in Jesus, because a truly born-again person will want to serve Jesus.

The leaders in Jerusalem *did* suggest that the Gentile converts follow certain Jewish social customs, probably so they could meet with Jewish Christians without offending them (see vv. 20-21).

Notice that the prophecies of Judas and Silas "encouraged and strengthened the brethren" (v. 32). The Bible teaches that the simple gift of prophecy is for "edification and exhortation and consolation" (1 Cor. 14:3). It doesn't say that prophecy is for condemnation. True prophecy should lift us up!

One verse you may have skimmed over but which is really significant is verse 34: "But it seemed good to Silas to remain there." How does the Holy Spirit lead us? By "seems good" (if you'll pardon my English). I've done many things because they "seemed good" down in my spirit. It's a peace, or a conviction, that what you're about to do is God's will.

PSALM 141:1-10

You've probably figured out by now that we will be through all the Psalms within about one week. Our Bible reading plan has us going through the Psalms twice, so I will list the daily reference for each psalm, but I won't add any comments the second time through. Whether you read through the Psalms again is up to you. I recommend that you do, because we can learn so much about how to pray from them.

PROVERBS 17:23

JUNE 24

2 KINGS 6:1-7:20

Miracles, miracles, miracles! If nothing else, today's reading should encourage us to believe that God is concerned about every small detail of our lives, and that He wants to protect us and supply our needs. Think about it. The God who created the universe takes notice when somebody loses a small borrowed item. His love is so great!

How did the axe head float? I have no idea, but maybe an angel dove in and lifted it to the surface. Maybe God just made it lighter than water. The point is that nothing is too difficult for the Lord.

Don't you love the story of when the Syrians tried to capture Elisha, but instead Elisha captured the entire Syrian army? The part of the story that blesses me the most is when Dothan was completely surrounded by the Syrian army with Elisha and his servant inside, and Elisha said to his servant, "Do not fear, for those who are with us are more than those who are with them" (6:16). I can imagine Elisha's servant looking at him with disbelief and then counting how many they had on their side: "One, two!" But Elisha asked God to open his servant's eyes (or to impart to him the gift of "discerning of spirits"), and God allowed him to see the host of angelic warriors that were on their side. Praise God! Those angels were actually there! God has legions of angels that are ready to assist us. We can always say, "There are more with me than with them!" Not only that, but we can say, "Greater is He [God] who is in [me], than he [Satan] who is in the world" (1 John 4:4).

The king of Israel wanted to kill all the Syrians, but God manifested His merciful character by instructing him to feed the Syrian army a good meal and send them on their way. I'll bet those Syrians were surprised and talked about what happened for the rest of their lives! I wonder if any of them got saved as a result?

Warfare was much different in Bible days from what it is today. There were no long-range weapons other than catapults, so combat was hand to hand. All major cities were surrounded by huge walls with various large gates in them, and when an invading army approached, all the gates were closed to keep the invaders out. Many times the strategy of the invaders would be to simply surround smaller cities and keep anyone from going in or out. Eventually there would be no more food in the city, and the people within would begin to starve. Food prices, according to the law of supply and demand, would go sky high. People would resort to cannibalism, even eating their own children. This is what happened when Syria tried to capture Israel's capital city, Samaria. Apparently Elisha had promised eventual deliverance, so the people of Samaria waited it out. But when a mother reported to the king that she and a friend had eaten her baby, the king decided he had waited long enough for the fulfillment of Elisha's word. He wanted Elisha's head. I have to assume that God allowed the Syrian army to prosper as much as it did as a form of discipline upon Samaria.

The end of the story is self-explanatory, but let me point out one significant aspect. The four lepers who "happened" to discover that the Syrian camp had been abandoned realized that they were doing wrong in not notifying the people of Samaria. They said, "This day is a day of good news, but we are keeping silent" (7:9). They knew that God didn't chase the entire Syrian camp away simply for their benefit. We, too, must never forget that Jesus didn't die only for those of us who have heard the gospel and believed it. He died for the whole world. We must guard our churches from becoming "Rich Leper Clubs" and do all we can to share the good news with every person in the world.

ACTS 15:36-16:15

I'm glad the Bible is honest. I don't know of any other book that so readily discusses people's sins. Today we read of a "sharp disagreement" between good friends Paul and Barnabas over whether Mark should be permitted to travel with them on their second missionary journey (see 15:39). We don't know all the details, so we can't make a judgment on who was right and who was wrong. (However it does appear that Paul's decision was endorsed by the brethren in Antioch.) The point is that each man did what he felt was right; in the end they doubled their effectiveness for God by dividing.

Why did Paul have Timothy circumcised (see 16:3)? Not because he thought it made any difference to God, but because he knew it would make a difference to the Jews whom he would be trying to reach with the gospel. Paul taught that we should "become all things to all men that [we] may by all means save some" (1 Cor. 9:22). We should do all we can to avoid offending non-Christians in nonessential things such as social and cultural practices. How can you reach a businessman in a three-piece suit if you look like a hippie? On the other hand, how can you reach a street person if you look like a senator?

Why didn't the Spirit allow Paul to preach the Word in Asia (the western section of modern Turkey)? I don't know, but I'm sure God had a reason for it. On Paul's very next journey God directed him to preach there. God wants to reach the whole world as quickly as possible, so there's no doubt in my mind that the gospel would be spread over the whole world faster by having Paul first preach in Macedonia (modern Greece).

It was in the Roman city of Philippi that the first European convert was won to Christ, a lady named Lydia.

Notice that sometimes the Holy Spirit will lead us through visions (see 16:9). But notice that Paul and Silas were *on the go, and the Holy Spirit led them as they were going*. We must obey the direction we have if we expect to gain further direction from God.

PSALM 142:1-7

This psalm was probably written by David when he was hiding from Saul in a cave. Was David's prayer answered? Was he delivered? Yes! But notice that final phrase of his prayer: "For Thou wilt deal bountifully with me" (v. 7). David had the victory before he experienced the victory. Our battles are won in believing prayer.

PROVERBS 17:24-25

JUNE 25

2 KINGS 8:1-9:13

We can always trust that God's timing is perfect. He is never too early or too late. Isn't it amazing that just when the Shunammite woman came before the king to request repossession of her former house and land, Gehazi was relating the amazing story of her son's resurrection to the king? Have you ever had something "just happen" at the perfect time? The Lord specializes in those kinds of things!

Remember that when Elijah was fleeing from Jezebel in the wilderness, the Lord commissioned him to anoint Hazael king over Syria (see 1 Kin. 19:15-17). Hazael ascended by murdering Ben-hadad (see 8:15), so God obviously was not exalting Hazael because of his righteousness but simply to serve His purposes.

When Elijah was fleeing from Jezebel, God not only commissioned Elijah to anoint Hazael as king over Syria but also to anoint Jehu as king over Israel. God planned to use Jehu to put an end to the dynasty of Ahab and destroy all of his wicked family. The Scripture doesn't say anything about Elijah anointing Jehu, but we read today of Elisha sending a young prophet to anoint him. Because Elisha had "the spirit of Elijah," we assume that Elisha carried on what Elijah never finished. God's plans cannot be stopped.

It's hard for me to believe that Jezebel was still alive at this point, but she was. If I had been God, I would have had her killed years before! But God is much more merciful than any of us are. (Aren't you glad He had mercy on *you* for as long as He did?) He delayed His judgment upon Jezebel because He was giving her time to repent. He knows the full extent of the terribleness of hell.

ACTS 16:16-40

Divination is a demonic ability to foretell future events or reveal occult knowledge. This slave girl whom Paul delivered was possessed with such a spirit, and her masters were making money from her demon-given abilities. Why the evil spirit followed Paul and Silas around and proclaimed that they were "servants of the Most High God, who are proclaiming to you the way of salvation," I don't know. Regardless, once the girl was delivered through Paul's command of faith she could no longer foretell the future. Whether or not she was saved as a result we don't know, but the chances are good that she was.

Keep in mind that God supernaturally led Paul and Silas to preach in Philippi, yet just a few days after their arrival they found themselves beaten with rods and cast in prison with their feet in stocks! *We can never try to determine God's will by circumstances.*

Did Paul and Silas complain or question God? No, they were praying and singing hymns of praise to God at midnight! They trusted that "all things work together for good," and God marvelously delivered them from their trial. God is no respecter of persons. I believe that if you had been in that prison and displayed the faith of Paul and Silas, you would have been delivered too.

I believe that you can "praise" your way out of a difficulty or trial. Don't try to figure a way out. Praise your way out! Perhaps the reason many Christians remain in difficulties for such a long time is because they keep asking God over and over again for help and deliverance when they should be praising God for the answer!

Paul was not saying in verse 31 that if the jailer believed, it was guaranteed his whole family would be saved. That would contradict what Paul said in 1 Corinthians 7:16 and a host of other scriptures that make it plain that every person is responsible to believe for his or her own salvation. Paul was simply saying that if the jailer and his family believed in Jesus, they would be saved. (Normally, if a man gets saved, his wife and children do follow him.) My point is that we cannot "claim" Acts 16:31 for our families. Unfortunately, many good Christians believe they can and have prayed once, "believing" God for the salvation of family members. What they should be doing is interceding every day for their unsaved loved ones (or as much as they feel led). Notice the Scripture says that all the members of the jailer's household did individually trust in Jesus (see 16:34).

In explanation of verses 35-39, it was not lawful to punish citizens of the Roman empire without a fair trial. The magistrates of Philippi had broken national law and feared that if they were discovered, they would be punished. Paul knew they had broken the law and so requested that they themselves come and release him. (He and Silas must have gone back into their jail cell, now knowing the jailer was one of them. Praise God!) At this point the Philippian church included a woman who sold purple fabrics, a formerly demon-possessed slave girl, a jailer and his household and probably a number of prisoners who were in jail when the earthquake hit! I would like to have been in some of their church services! All of them were testimonies to the grace and goodness of God.

PSALM 143:1-12

Another prayer for help that we know was answered!

PROVERBS 17:26

JUNE 26

2 KINGS 9:14-10:31

All you needed to keep in mind during this reading was that everybody got what he deserved. God was "cleaning house" in Israel and Judah by the hand of Jehu.

Jehu started off as a king who obeyed the Lord, but it probably wasn't his love for God that made him so zealous. It was his eagerness to establish his rulership over Israel by destroying all of the former dynasty's family. But after a glorious start it was downhill from then on for Jehu. He walked in the sins of Jeroboam, the evil first king of divided Israel.

ACTS 17:1-34

Today we continue to read of Paul's second missionary journey, during which he traveled to Thessalonica, Berea and Athens, all located in modern Greece. Today (1990) it is illegal to "proselytize" in Greece—to try to lead people to the Lord—even though the majority of people consider themselves Greek Orthodox Christians.

Notice the principle of "varying receptivity" in today's reading. The people of Berea were "more noble-minded than those in Thessalonica, for they received the word with great eagerness, examining the Scriptures daily, to see whether these things were so" (v. 11). The people in Athens spent "their time in nothing other than telling or hearing something new" (v. 21). Some of them made fun of Paul's message, some were interested in hearing more and some believed (see vv. 32-34). However, churches were established in all three cities. I encourage you to take a look at the map in the back of your Bible titled "Paul's Second Missionary Journey."

While in Athens, Paul's "spirit was being provoked within him as he was beholding the city full of idols" (v. 16). Have you ever sensed your spirit being provoked? I'm sure you have if you've been a Christian for very long, but possibly you didn't realize it. This is a good way to learn the leading of the Spirit through your spirit. Let me give you an example. Do you know the feeling you get inside you when you drive past an adult bookstore? That is your spirit being provoked. Try to follow those holy intuitions that float up out of your spirit.

Notice that, according to Paul, God expects all people to seek Him and find Him (see v. 27). It's amazing to me that some people don't seem to have the slightest interest in God and apparently are not seeking Him at all. Praise God that Jesus said, "Seek, and you shall find" (Matt. 7:7). I believe that if any person anywhere on the face of the earth sincerely seeks to know God, God will see to it that the person finds Him. I recently heard about a Christian woman who was shopping, and while in the grocery store she felt led to speak to a lady she didn't know. She felt as if the Lord was telling her to go up to that lady and say that God knew she was having trouble with her daughter, and that God cared. After debating within herself for a few minutes she finally "threw caution to the wind" and spoke to the woman. Do you know what the lady's response was? She broke down into tears, exclaiming that she had been having great troubles with her daughter and that she had prayed just that morning, "God, if you're real, please send someone who can help me!" She was born again right there in that grocery store aisle.

PSALM 144:1-15

What an encouraging psalm this is! Not only was it David's usual faith-filled request for deliverance, but it was also a request for God to send material prosperity. David believed in the goodness of God.

PROVERBS 17:27-28

Have you ever noticed that too often the people who have the most to say are the people who say the least, and the people who have the least to say, say the most?

JUNE 27

2 KINGS 10:32-12:21

Old Athaliah sure sounds like a nice lady, doesn't she? When her son, King Ahaziah of Judah, was killed by Jehu, she had all her own grandchildren slaughtered so that she could gain and keep the throne of Judah. Thankfully she was prevented from having one of her grandsons, Joash (or Jehoash), murdered.

The moral of this story is clear. But don't fail to realize that we're reading about something more significant than just what concerned Judah several thousand years ago. The story concerns *you*, because God had promised that the Messiah would come through David's lineage, and Athaliah almost destroyed every male descendant of David! It's easy to see that Satan was motivating evil Athaliah. Aren't you glad he lost that round (as well as every round before and after that one)?

Joash was only seven years old when he became king of Judah, but he was under the guidance of Jehoiada the priest, who instructed him in the ways of the Lord. Verse 12:2 says that as long as Joash remained under Jehoiada's guidance, he followed the Lord. We will learn when we read the book of 2 Chronicles that Jehoiada died at the age of 130, and then Joash and the people of Judah began to serve idols. Joash even had Jehoiada's son murdered because he prophesied against him (Joash). That is exactly why we read today that Joash was murdered in a plot by his own servants (see 12:20-21). He, too, reaped what he sowed.

It's sad that a man who started off so well could end up so bad. We need to be ever cautious of giving the devil even the smallest place in our lives because it could lead to further steps away from God. I'm sure that as a young man Joash had no plans to backslide when he grew older. But he did. It greatly concerns me when I witness Christians slowly becoming less devoted to the Lord. I know that if they continue on that same path, eventually they will no longer be serving the Lord at all. I strongly encourage you to guard yourself from allowing anything to come before the Lord in your life.

ACTS 18:1-21

Corinth was the capital of a region called Achaia, which today is part of southern Greece. It was a strategic location for Paul to preach the gospel, as it was a commercial center through which people from many places in the ancient world would pass. It was there that Paul lived for a year and a half teaching the Word of God. The Lord told Paul, "I have many people in this city" (v. 10). God knows the hearts of all people, and He knew there were many receptive people who would open their hearts to Him once they heard the gospel.

What's amazing is that Corinth was one of the most licentious cities in the ancient world. A thousand temple prostitutes worked as an integral part of the Corinthian religious practices at the temple of Aphrodite, "goddess of love." The words "to Corinthianize" were synonymous with taking excessive sexual license. Corinth was a seaman's paradise. But God loved them, and Paul established the church there.

PSALM 145:1-21

This psalm is filled with beautiful descriptions of the Lord's wonderful character. He is gracious and merciful, slow to anger, great in lovingkindness and good to all. He sustains all who fall; He is near to all who call upon Him in truth. He fulfills the desire of those who fear Him, and He hears their cry and saves them. He keeps all who love Him. Remember all that the next time you get discouraged.

PROVERBS 18:1

Beware of lone rangers! They are only concerned with their own interests.

JUNE 28

2 KINGS 13:1-14:29

Why did Elisha die from a sickness? We don't know because the Bible doesn't say. Just because a person has been anointed with a healing ministry doesn't guarantee he will always be healthy. Hopefully by now you have learned to "fill in the blanks" with what you know of God's character from the rest of the Bible. If so, this incident involving Elisha's sickness and death won't faze you. This one scripture doesn't do away with the hundreds of others that show us that God does want to heal us.

Obviously God was using Syria to discipline Israel at this point in history. Yet in this short reading we have seen four different instances of God's giving Israel victory over Syria when Israel and its king sought God (see 13:5, 23-25).

According to 2 Chronicles, Amaziah, after he defeated the Edomites, began worshipping their gods. That's why God allowed him to be defeated before Jehoash, king of Israel, and murdered.

ACTS 18:23-19:12

We read today of what is commonly referred to as Paul's third missionary journey. Paul traveled through some of the same cities in which he had established churches before, strengthening the disciples, but he also traveled to a number of previously unvisited cities.

Apollos is probably an example of the New Testament ministry of a "teacher." The teacher doesn't lay a foundation as an apostle would, but "he [helps] greatly those who [have] believed through grace" (18:27). The apostle establishes the church, whereas the teacher strengthens the church that already exists.

Notice that the baptism in the Holy Spirit was a second experience after salvation for the new believers in Ephesus according to 19:5-6. Also notice that the initial sign of their baptism was that they spoke in other tongues. These twelve men also prophesied, which indicates to me that baptism in the Holy Spirit is the door to the rest of the spiritual gifts. All twelve men spoke in tongues, which is another proof that speaking in tongues is something that is available to all believers, not just a select few.

It was God who anointed Paul at this time so that handkerchiefs and aprons were carried from his body to heal the sick and cast out demons. God can and does do miraculous healings today, but I wouldn't believe every so-called minister who claims to have such an anointing. Most often the ones who advertise that they do are also asking you to send them money, and then they'll send you an "anointed cloth." That's ridiculous. It doesn't say that Paul sold anointed handkerchiefs and aprons.

PSALM 146:1-10

PROVERBS 18:2-3

JUNE 29

2 KINGS 15:1-16:20

In the beginning of chapter 15 we read that King Uzziah was a good king who reigned in Jerusalem for fifty-two years. But we also read that "the Lord struck the king, so that he was a leper to the day of his death" (15:5). Why? In 2 Chronicles we'll read that Uzziah became proud in his old age and assumed a responsibility that only belonged to the priests: he offered incense in the holy place of the temple. When Uzziah was rebuked by the priests, he became enraged at them, and immediately leprosy broke out on his forehead.

Much of what we read today is just the history of the final evil kings of Israel. What God had warned them of had begun to come to pass. An Assyrian king named Tiglath-pileser invaded the land and deported many of the people (see 15:29). The year was about 733 B.C. This was the first of two deportations. Later, when we read some of the minor prophets such as Amos and Hosea, we will gain a clear picture of the spiritual corruption that existed in Israel at that time.

ACTS 19:13-41

The seven sons of Sceva, who apparently practiced exorcism, tried to use the authority of the name of Jesus "whom Paul preached." Their only problem was that they had no right to use the name of Jesus because they didn't belong to Him. God used their failure for His glory, and the news of their humiliation was spread among all the Jews and Greeks in Ephesus.

Notice that Paul "purposed in the spirit to go to Jerusalem after he had passed through Macedonia and Achaia," and then he planned to go to Rome as well (see v. 21). This is important to keep in mind as we read Paul's continuing story, because Paul encountered many difficulties even though he was following the leading of the Holy Spirit. Once again, we must not allow circumstances to dictate to us what God's will is. We must rely upon the Spirit who lives within.

Ephesus obviously had some very religious people who worshipped the goddess Artemis, also known as Diana. They were proud of their temple that was devoted to her; it was considered one of the seven wonders of the world and was four times the size of the Parthenon in Greece. Nevertheless, Paul's ministry in Ephesus was so successful that the Ephesians were burning thousands of dollars worth of magic books, and even the silversmiths who manufactured shrines for Artemis were losing profits as people turned to Jesus!

PSALM 147:1-20

Verse 11 says, "The Lord favors those who fear Him, those who wait for His lovingkindness." The problem with so many of us is that we don't exercise the faith to wait. We want everything immediately. Let's have the faith and patience that it takes to experience all of God's favor.

PROVERBS 18:4-5

JUNE 30

2 KINGS 17:1-18:12

It had now been about two hundred years the nation of Israel was divided into two kingdoms. After enduring nineteen evil kings in the northern kingdom, God had had enough. He permitted Shalmaneser, king of Assyria, to capture Samaria, the capital of Israel, and then the majority of the population was deported to the area where today Syria, Turkey and Iraq meet. About 136 years later Judah would run out of mercy as well. I can't blame God for disciplining them in that way.

Assyria repopulated the land with exiles from other conquered countries, and those people developed a strange religious mixture of worshipping Jehovah and their former gods as well. Their descendants intermarried with Jews and became known as the Samaritans, with whom the Jews in Jesus' day had no dealings.

Hezekiah was one of the best kings of Judah. We learn that he broke into pieces the bronze serpent Moses had made in the wilderness because the people of Judah had been worshipping it. Do you remember the story of how God sent fiery serpents to bite the Israelites, and God instructed Moses to fashion a bronze serpent and place it on a pole? Any bitten person who looked at that bronze serpent would live (see Num. 21:8-9). That happened seven hundred years before the time of Hezekiah.

ACTS 20:1-38

I've stopped feeling bad if people fall asleep when I'm preaching ever since I read that Paul had someone fall asleep during his sermon in Troas! This young man named Eutychus was "bored to death"! Paul embraced the dead man's body (see v. 10) just as we read of Elijah and Elisha doing when they raised people from the dead. I assume all three were led by the Spirit to do so.

In Paul's farewell sermon to the elders of Ephesus he said, "And now, behold, bound in spirit, I am on my way to Jerusalem, not knowing what will happen to me there, except that the Holy Spirit solemnly testifies to me in every city, saying that bonds and afflictions await me" (vv. 22-23). This is significant for several reasons. First, Paul was being led by the indwelling Holy Spirit to go to Jerusalem. We will read that when he arrived, years of trouble started for Paul. Thus, a number of commentators sincerely but wrongly believe that Paul missed God's will by traveling to Jerusalem. But twice we have already read that Paul knew he was being led to Jerusalem by the Holy Spirit.

Second, this short statement from Paul's lips reveals that God doesn't always tell us everything or give us the complete picture. Paul knew he was being led to Jerusalem, but he admitted he didn't know what would happen to him once he arrived. However, he suspected he would face intense persecution, because the Holy Spirit had already told him in every city that bonds and afflictions awaited him there.

Although none of the Gospel writers recorded it, Paul stated that Jesus once said, "It is more blessed to give than to receive" (v. 35). Most of us spend our efforts in trying to receive more for ourselves. But Jesus said we should live to give. True joy is found in serving others. However, keep in mind that Jesus didn't say it is only blessed to give. He said it was more blessed. That means it's blessed to receive as well! It was a blessed day when you received Jesus as your Savior, wasn't it?

PSALM 148:1-14

Praise the Lord!

PROVERBS 18:6-7

JULY 1

2 KINGS 18:13-19:37

Although Hezekiah was a godly king, he still faced difficulties. One of his major challenges came during the invasion of Sennacherib, king of Assyria. Hezekiah's situation looked hopeless, but nothing is impossible with God (see Luke 1:34-37).

Sennacherib had become prideful because of his victories over other nations. He failed to recognize that he was winning his battles only because God was using him as a tool of His judgment against ungodly people (see 19:25-28). Now he had even grown arrogant against the One who had designed his triumphs. He and his army *had* to be judged, so God sent an angel who destroyed 185,000 Assyrian troops in one night.

God brought Hezekiah safely through this dangerous time. We should take courage from today's reading and remember that "if God is for us, who can be against us?" (Rom. 8:31). When the odds are stacked against you, remember: God is bigger than the odds!

ACTS 21:1-16

When Paul arrived in Tyre, the disciples there told him through the Spirit "not to set foot in Jerusalem" (v. 4). This verse confuses many people because it seems to contradict Paul's conviction that the Holy Spirit was sending him to Jerusalem. William's Translation helps us to better understand what was really happening when it says, "Because of the impressions made by the Spirit, they kept on warning Paul...." In other words, they picked up in their spirits that Paul was going to be in danger in Jerusalem and so they *interpreted* it to mean that Paul shouldn't go. But that was not the case. The danger was real, but God was still sending him there.

Because of this passage and the incident with Agabus, some people believe Paul made a mistake in going to Jerusalem. I disagree. Agabus didn't tell Paul to avoid Jerusalem. He simply told him what would happen when he arrived (see v. 11). God could have easily warned Paul not to go, but He didn't. Everyone who heard the prophecy wanted Paul to avoid Jerusalem, but Paul knew God's plan in his own spirit. He apparently convinced them because they finally remarked, "The will of the Lord be done" (v. 14).

PSALM 149:1-9

Did you know that you can praise the Lord with dancing? Have you ever done it? I guarantee that when you do, you'll be blessed.

PROVERBS 18:8

JULY 2

2 KINGS 20:1-22:2

I want you to go out today and treat yourself to a double-decker ice-cream cone, because you have completed reading *more than half the Bible*. Congratulations!

Hezekiah's second great trial was a terminal illness. We don't know all of the circumstances that surrounded the trial but we do know that it wasn't doctors who promised Hezekiah that he was going to die, it was God Himself! Yet through prayer, Hezekiah changed God's decree. I know that sounds wrong, but that is what happened. To me this is a great proof that it is God's desire to heal. Even if *God* says you are going to die, there is still hope that you can be healed. How much more if only the *doctors* say that you are going to die!

Isaiah prophesied to Hezekiah that someday all his treasures would be carried to Babylon (see 20:17). That was an amazing prediction, because at the time, Babylon was a small state located just south of Assyria. But within the next one hundred years, it would overrun Assyria and become a dominant power. Isaiah also prophesied that some of Hezekiah's descendants would become officials in the palace of the king of Babylon (see 20:18). This prophecy was fulfilled when Nebuchadnezzar, king of Babylon, chose Daniel, one of the "royal offspring" of Judah, to serve in his court.

After Hezekiah died, his son Manasseh became king and led the people of Judah to new depths of degradation. According to Jewish tradition, Manasseh had Isaiah sawn in half, and we know from Scripture that he had many innocent people murdered. However, 2 Chronicles 33:11-19 records that, near the end of his life, Manasseh repented and had a complete change of heart.

ACTS 21:17-36

Although many Jews in Jerusalem believed in Jesus, many more lived by the traditions and laws of their Jewish heritage. The church leadership in Jerusalem realized Paul was in danger because of the rumors circulating about him. These rumors said he was teaching *all Jews* to forsake the Law of Moses and was telling them not to circumcise their children (see v. 21). Paul actually taught Jewish *Christians* that circumcision and keeping the Law of Moses were unnecessary for salvation. To stop these rumors, the leaders wanted Paul to be seen obeying the Law.

The plan worked until Paul was recognized by certain Jews "from Asia" (see v. 27), where he had done so much of his missionary work. They stirred up the crowds and would have killed him, except for a providential rescue by Roman soldiers. I'm sure that Paul had perfect peace during this incident because he knew beforehand that the Jews would bind him and hand him over to Gentiles (see 21:11)!

PSALM 150:1-6

And you thought God only liked church organ music!

PROVERBS 18:9-10

Let verse 9 sharpen your conscience. If you are slack in the work for which you are being paid, you are stealing from your employer.

JULY 3

2 KINGS 22:3-23:30

Today, we see how far the people of Judah had strayed from God's law. Nobody even knew what God required until they discovered the books of Moses in the temple. Even though God's Word was lost, God Himself had not changed. Through Huldah, the prophetess, God promised to withhold judgment until King Josiah was dead because he humbled himself and wept when he heard the law. Josiah instituted sweeping reforms, fulfilling a prophecy given more than three hundred years before (see 1 Kings 13:2), and the Passover was celebrated for the first time since the days of Hezekiah.

Why did God promise to judge Judah, even after Josiah's reforms? Probably because the hearts of the people weren't changed. Once Josiah was gone, God knew the people would fall back into idolatry. We won't have the full picture until we read the books of Habakkuk, Zephaniah and Jeremiah, who all prophesied during Judah's final years.

ACTS 21:37-22:16

Do you remember God's original calling of Paul? God said to Ananias about Paul, "He is a chosen instrument of Mine, to bear My name before the gentiles and kings and the sons of Israel" (Acts 9:15). Today, we see Paul begin to testify before kings. This was only possible because he followed the leading of the Spirit to Jerusalem. Paul would eventually present Christ to several kings, including the Roman Emperor Nero, the most powerful man on earth.

PSALM 1:1-6

PROVERBS 18:11-12

JULY 4

2 KINGS 23:31-25:30

There were three different times when people from Judah were deported to Babylon. The first was in 605 B.C., when Nebuchadnezzar came to Jerusalem and bound King Jehoiakim (see 24:1). This was when Daniel and his three friends were taken to Babylon. The second time was in 597 B.C., when Nebuchadnezzar removed King Jehoiachin, his family and ten thousand leading citizens (see 24:10-16). At that time, the prophet Ezekiel was also taken to Babylon. The final deportation was in 586 B.C., when Jerusalem, its walls and the temple were all destroyed by Nebuzaradan, captain of Nebuchadnezzar's guard. Only the very poor were left behind (see 25:8-12). Nebuchadnezzar then installed Gedaliah as king in Judah. He was assassinated, and the conspirators fled to Egypt (see 25:22-26).

It's important to keep these incidents in mind, because they'll help us understand the writings of Jeremiah and Ezekiel. For example, in Jeremiah 42:7-22, the remaining people of Judah are warned not to flee to Egypt after Gedaliah's death. They refused to heed this God-given admonition and suffered the consequences.

ACTS 22:17-23:10

Paul's audience listened to his amazing story until he mentioned his mission to the Gentiles. They thought that Paul was setting the stage to justify the rumors that he was teaching Jews to forsake the Law of Moses. Consequently they cut off his defense by shouting and throwing dust in the air.

Paul was saved from scourging by his Roman citizenship and was brought before the Sanhedrin the next day by the Roman commander. Paul's words to the high priest, "God is going to strike you, you white-washed wall" (23:3), show that even Paul's patience ran short sometimes! (On the other hand, Paul may have been speaking by the inspiration of the Holy Spirit, because Ananias was later assassinated.)

During the meeting, Paul was suddenly (and perhaps mischievously) inspired to create division among the members of the Sanhedrin. He proclaimed his loyalty to the Pharisees and their doctrine of the resurrection, a doctrine denied by the Sadducees. Pandemonium resulted, and in the confusion, Paul was removed to safety by the Romans. Don't you wish you could have been there to see it all happen? I hope there are reruns of all this in heaven!

PSALM 2:1-12

PROVERBS 18:13

Have you ever spoken too soon? We all have. It is always best to know what you are talking about before you speak!

JULY 5

1 CHRONICLES 1:1-2:17

Welcome to the books of 1 and 2 Chronicles. You may have already figured out that we are going to be repeating some information previously covered in other books of the Old Testament. The first nine chapters are genealogies, concentrating mostly on the lineage of Judah, Benjamin, Levi and David. Next, we will read stories that are similar to those in 2 Samuel and Kings, but these stories place a greater emphasis on moral lessons. God probably gave these books for the benefit of the exiles in Babylon, who eventually returned to the promised land. They needed a link to their past and a reminder of the consequences of unfaithfulness toward God.

ACTS 23:11-35

Today's reading shows us again that Paul did not miss God's will by going to Jerusalem. Jesus appeared to Paul while he was in jail and said, "Take courage; for as you have solemnly witnessed to My cause at Jerusalem, so you must witness at Rome also" (v. 11). If Paul had missed God certainly Jesus would have mentioned it at that time. Instead He implied that Paul was just where God wanted him.

You may ask why Paul had so many supernatural confirmations of God's will at this time in his ministry. It seems that most of us are led through the "inward witness" of the Holy Spirit in our spirits. Do you wonder why someone hasn't prophesied to you, or why Jesus hasn't appeared to you in a vision? The reason is that you don't need that type of "spectacular guidance." Paul was about to face years of suffering when he would often be tempted to doubt God and give up. Because God led him in spectacular ways, Paul had the stamina to continue.

Notice that Paul had perfect assurance that he was going to arrive safely in Rome. He was able to stay calm during the most adverse circumstances because he knew the end from the beginning! We too can have peace in adversity if we'll trust God's promises to us. His word cannot fail. We know that everything will turn out fine in the end!

PSALM 3:1-8

PROVERBS 18:14-15

JULY 6

1 CHRONICLES 2:18-4:4

You have just read (or skimmed over) part of the lineage of Judah, David's dynasty of kings, before and after the exile. Like David, Jesus descended from the tribe of Judah.

ACTS 24:1-27

Felix, the Roman governor of Judea from A.D. 52-59, was living in Herod's royal palace at the port of Caesarea. At that time, he was married to his third wife, Drusilla, the daughter of Herod Agrippa, who had murdered the apostle James. In his meeting with Felix, Paul's calling to testify before kings was further fulfilled (see Acts 9:15).

Apparently Paul sparked some interest in Felix, and he requested to hear Paul speak more. However, when Paul began to talk about the judgment at which all men must stand before God, Felix became frightened and used the familiar excuse, "Now is not the time. But I'll think about what you have said, and when I find time, I'd like to hear more." People haven't changed since then, have they?

Paul remained a captive for *two years* in Caesarea, but he never forgot that Jesus had promised he would make it to Rome. Paul would spend at least two *more* years in prison at Rome. During those confinements, he wrote letters that invigorated and revolutionized the church of the first century. Today, many of those letters are part of the New Testament, and they continue to revolutionize our lives. God causes all things to work together for good!

PSALM 4:1-8

PROVERBS 18:16-18

JULY 7

1 CHRONICLES 4:5-5:17

ACTS 25:1-27

The second ruler before whom Paul testified was Felix's successor, Festus. It's amazing that the Sanhedrin in Jerusalem still wanted Paul dead, even though he had been imprisoned in Caesarea for two years. Festus had only been in office for three days when the Sanhedrin requested Paul's transfer to Jerusalem. They wanted to kill Paul on the journey. Instead, Festus required Paul's accusers to come to Caesarea. Paul must have known the Jews planned to ambush him on the way to Jerusalem. It is no wonder that he appealed to

Caesar when Festus asked him if he would be willing to stand trial in Jerusalem. I personally believe that he was led of the Spirit to appeal to Caesar, because we know that it was God's will for Paul to testify in Rome.

King Agrippa was Festus's superior and the ruler over most of Palestine. His acting wife, Bernice, was also his sister. She later left him and would become the mistress of the Roman Emperor Vespasian and his son Titus, who destroyed Jerusalem in A.D. 70. Both Agrippa and Bernice had a great need to hear of the Man who died on the cross for their sins. They would hear it from a man whose knowledge, eloquence and holy passion have seldom been equaled.

PSALM 5:1-12

PROVERBS 18:19

JULY 8

1 CHRONICLES 5:18-6:81

You have just read the genealogies of Reuben, Gad, Manasseh and Levi.

One verse that made an impression upon me today was 5:20, "...And they were helped against them, and the Hagrites and all who were with them were given into their hand; for they cried out to God in battle, and He was entreated for them, *because they trusted in Him*" (italics mine). According to this verse, "crying out to God" is not enough to guarantee an answer to prayer. This verse said that God was entreated "because they trusted in Him."

Why not do a check-up on your life right now? Are you just praying, or are you praying and trusting God? I'm convinced many of us are living way below our privileges because we simply are not trusting God in every area of our lives. Let's agree with what God says, and act as if His Word is true—because it is!

ACTS 26:1-32

As Jesus promised (see Luke 21:13-15), the Holy Spirit gave Paul the words to speak when he stood before Festus, Agrippa and Bernice. His words were so convicting that Agrippa exclaimed, "In a short time you will persuade me to become a Christian" (v. 28), which was the whole purpose of Paul's speech in the first place. But even the apostle Paul wasn't always successful in his witnessing endeavors. He was working with the same limitation as you and I are, which is the fact that every person is a free moral agent. Even with the Holy Spirit's help, there is no guarantee that we will win every person with whom we share the gospel.

In his defense, Paul stated that those who believe in Jesus *have been delivered from darkness and the dominion of Satan into light and the dominion of God* (see v. 18). If you believe in Jesus, that means Satan no longer has any right to rule you, oppress you or afflict you!

PSALM 6:1-10

PROVERBS 18:20-21

If the tongue has the power of death and life, we had better be careful how we use it. Our words of faith can produce life, and our words of doubt can produce death. What are you speaking?

JULY 9

1 CHRONICLES 7:1-8:40

Today we read the genealogy of Jacob's sons Issachar, Benjamin, Naphtali, Manasseh, Ephraim and Asher. Don't worry, tomorrow we'll be out of the genealogies!

ACTS 27:1-20

Find a map (perhaps in the back of your Bible) that traces Paul's journey to Rome. If you spend some time studying it, the next few readings in Acts will be more meaningful.

Today we see a great example of how the Holy Spirit leads us. Paul said, "Men, I *perceive* that the voyage will certainly be attended with damage and great loss, not only of the cargo and the ship, but also of our lives" (v. 10, italics mine). How did Paul know what was going to happen? He "perceived" it. He didn't have a vision or hear a voice. He simply had an impression in his spirit. Also notice that God tried to prevent the loss of the ship and the cargo. He warned them in advance, but they wouldn't listen. No one on that boat had any right to blame God for their calamity.

PSALM 7:1-17

PROVERBS 18:22

JULY 10

1 CHRONICLES 9:1-10:14

Now that we are through the genealogies, you will discover that we will be reading many of the same stories found in 2 Samuel and Kings. However, the writer of Chronicles divulges unknown facts and adds moral commentary to help us better understand previously read stories.

ACTS 27:21-44

Once again we see the ministry of angels. An angel appeared to Paul to assure him there would be no loss of life (see vv. 23-26). Angels also must have helped the 276 people reach shore safely when the ship was destroyed.

Have you ever wondered why God didn't just stop the storm in the first place? And if He could supernaturally rescue the crew members and passengers, why didn't He keep the ship from running aground? I don't have the answers, but I do know that God's overriding motivation is to reach people by revealing Himself to them. God was trying to reach the people on that ship, and after all that they had heard and seen, they had no excuse not to seek to know Paul's God.

In addition, we will learn tomorrow that God was also interested in reaching the people of the island on which Paul and his shipwrecked companions would land. In a situation that appeared to be completely circumstantial, God was still working out His plan of love to reach unreached people!

I love this whole story. Paul was taken aboard that ship as a prisoner, but by the time of the shipwreck, everyone was following his orders (see vv. 30-36). I believe that people who are filled with the Holy Spirit ought to rise to the top in every circumstance!

PSALM 8:1-9

PROVERBS 18:23-24

What a commentary on life! Wealthy people often feel and act self-sufficient, while poor people realize they are at the mercy of others.

The original word for "friend" probably meant "covenant partner." This is a warning for people who tend to become overcommitted. Too many promises will ruin you. We also know that Jesus is a covenant partner who sticks closer than a brother.

JULY 11

1 CHRONICLES 11:1-12:18

ACTS 28:1-31

Paul and the other people on board found themselves on the island of Malta, located in the Mediterranean Sea off the coast of Sicily. A revival began there when Paul was bitten by a poisonous snake, and God turned something bad into good. No doubt he claimed Jesus' promise that true believers would "pick up servants" (Mark 16:18) and not be harmed, because he did not die or suffer any ill-effects as the natives expected. Just like other revivals in the book of Acts, God used a supernatural miracle to get the ball rolling.

Paul finally made it to Rome at the expense of the Roman government and waited for his trial before Nero (Caesar). We don't have a detailed biblical record of what happened to Paul during and after his two years in Rome. We do know that the Lord used him greatly while he was waiting for his trial, and many people became believers as a result. Paul was probably released and continued his ministry for about seven years. He was martyred in about A.D. 67. During his imprisonment at Rome, he probably wrote Ephesians, Colossians, Philippians and Philemon.

PSALM 9:1-12

PROVERBS 19:1-3

JULY 12

1 CHRONICLES 12:19-14:17

ROMANS 1:1-17

Today we begin the most applicable part of the Bible: the letters to the churches. You will find that the letters fit your own life because they were written to people just like you—born-again, Spirit-filled believers in Jesus. Some of the letters are easier to understand than others, and Romans is one of the more difficult. Here we should keep in mind the words of Peter that some of Paul's writings were "hard to understand" (2 Pet. 3:15-16). If Peter had a hard time understanding some of Paul's writings, I don't feel so badly!

This letter was obviously written before Paul ever reached Rome (see v. 10). Someone else brought the gospel to Rome, but Paul was moved to write this letter so the Roman Christians might be grounded in solid doctrine. The church in Rome was comprised of Jews and Gentiles, and within a few years of this letter it would endure severe persecution under Nero, who would blame the Christians for the devastating fire that consumed Rome.

In Paul's salutation, he referred to the believers as "saints" (v. 7). All who have been washed by the blood of Jesus are righteous in God's eyes and therefore have already obtained sainthood. You've been canonized by God Himself!

Paul had prayed many times that he might visit the saints in Rome, but he realized he couldn't go until God's time (see v. 10). Only when we know the will of God can we pray with full assurance that our prayer will be answered. If we don't know God's will, we should pray repeatedly until it becomes clear.

Paul said the gospel is "the power of God for *salvation* to everyone who believes" (v. 16, italics mine). The word translated "salvation" also implies deliverance, safety, healing and soundness. God is offering more than just heaven when we die.

Notice that the gospel will work in the life of anyone "who believes" (v. 16). A dominant theme in the book of Romans is that we are not saved by anything we have done, but by faith in the work Jesus did on the cross. Paul's quotation of Habakkuk 2:4 inspired Martin Luther and contributed to the Reformation: "But the righteous man shall live by faith" (v. 17). This means that our righteousness (right standing with God) stems from our faith, not from our works. The righteousness of God has been *given* to us. Make this positive confession today: "I am righteous now before God because of my faith in Jesus. I cannot become more righteous than I already am!"

PSALM 9:13-20

PROVERBS 19:4-5

JULY 13

1 CHRONICLES 15:1-16:36

ROMANS 1:18-32

The *foundation* of every person's guilt before God is this: God has revealed Himself to everyone through His creation. No one has any excuse not to believe in God and to understand some of the attributes of His character (see vv. 18-20). God's work of creation is amazing in a million ways. The more scientists discover, the more proof there is for the existence of God. Let me give you some examples.

If the thickness of one sheet of paper represented the distance from the earth to the sun (93 million miles), the distance to the next nearest star would be represented by a stack of paper *71 feet high*. The diameter of our Milky Way galaxy would be represented by a stack of paper *310 miles high*. To reach the edge of the known universe would take a stack *31 million miles high*.

Did you know that if the sun were hollow, it could hold more than *1 million* earths? That the star Antares could contain *64 million* suns? That in the constellation Hercules, there is a star that could contain *100 million* Antares? That the largest known star, Epsilon, could easily contain *several million* stars the size of the star in the constellation Hercules? The phrase "God is great" takes on new meaning when you encounter such facts.

Even though unsaved people know *about* God, none honor Him or give Him thanks. Instead they follow their selfish desires. So God has permitted people to have their own way. God "gave them over in the lusts of their hearts to impurity" (v. 24), and the end result is every kind of perversion and wickedness imaginable.

People's insurgency against God is revealed in a thousand sins from which no one can claim innocence. This is the foundation upon which the gospel is built. All of us are sinners who desperately need the Savior if we ever hope to obtain a righteous standing before God.

PSALM 10:1-15

PROVERBS 19:6-7

Today we read a commentary on the character of most people. Generous people normally have many friends. On the other hand, poor people have little to give and so have fewer friends. Examine yourself. Do you cater to the powerful, the wealthy or the influential? If your friends suddenly became less powerful, wealthy or influential, would you still seek their company?

JULY 14

1 CHRONICLES 16:37-18:17

ROMANS 2:1-24

Yesterday we learned two foundational truths. First, no one has an excuse not to believe in God, because we all know something of His character. Second, all of us have rebelled against God, and God has let us have our way. Today's reading adds these facts: God is holy, and everyone will stand before His throne of judgment. God shows no partiality to anyone, not even to Jews.

There were many people in Paul's day who were self-righteous; they had high moral principles and appeared to be outwardly holy. The Jews, to whom Paul referred in our reading today, were the most likely candidates for this category of moralists. They were proud that they were chosen by God and had been given the laws of righteous living. Yet it's not the hearers of the Law who are just before God, but the doers of the Law (see v. 13).

The modern parallel is found in church-going people who hear their sermons on Sunday, gossip on Monday, harbor grudges on Tuesday, steal from their companies on Wednesday, envy their neighbors on Thursday, boast about themselves on Friday, get drunk on Saturday, and proudly visit church again the next Sunday.

God gave the Law to the descendants of Israel, so only they would be judged by its standards. The Gentiles were all given a conscience and will be judged by it (see vv. 12-16). Everyone has violated his conscience time and time again. At the judgment, each person will receive either justice or mercy. The only way he can receive mercy is to have made Jesus Christ his Lord and Savior.

Paul states that glory and honor and peace will be given to every man who does good, and that tribulation and distress will be given to every man who does evil. This does not mean that we are saved by our good deeds. The only people who are truly "good" are those who have been born again through faith in Jesus. Even the so-called "good deeds" of unsaved people are evil because they are done with the wrong motives. Every man *will* be recompensed "according to his deeds" (v. 6). But Jesus, our substitute, has already received the recompense for our sins!

PSALM 10:16-18

PROVERBS 19:8-9

JULY 15

1 CHRONICLES 19:1-21:30

For an explanation of David's census, please see my comments on 2 Samuel 24:1-25. First Chronicles indicates that Satan moved David to number Israel, while 2 Samuel 24:1 indicates it was the "anger of the Lord." Apparently, God *permitted* the devil to tempt David. God was already angry with the children of Israel (see 2 Sam. 24:1) and chose these means to discipline them. This is an incident I don't fully understand.

ROMANS 2:25-3:8

Many Jews of Paul's day considered themselves righteous because they were circumcised as babies, according to the Law. Today, people think they are right before God because they're church members or because they've been baptized. Those are false assumptions. Righteousness begins on the inside, which is why Paul referred to the "circumcision of the heart." Everyone needs a spiritual rebirth.

Though being a Jew didn't guarantee righteousness, it did have some advantages. The Jews had received the revelation of God. No one else could know God as they did because they possessed the written Word of God. Gentiles had only their consciences and the creation through which to learn about the Creator.

Some apparently justified their sin by saying their disobedience allowed God to manifest His goodness by showing mercy to them (see 3:5-8)! Since their sin served a positive end, they reasoned, wasn't God unjust to punish them? These same people were slanderously reporting that Paul was teaching this absurd line of reasoning (see 3:8).

PSALM 11:1-7

PROVERBS 19:10-12

Wise people are slow to anger (see v. 11). They enjoy the privilege of overlooking someone's sin against them. Are you the kind of person who blows your horn at everyone who cuts you off in traffic or makes a mistake that affects you? If you are, *please* meditate on this verse!

JULY 16

1 CHRONICLES 22:1-23:32

ROMANS 3:9-31

Paul quoted seven different Old Testament texts to prove that Jews as well as Gentiles are classified as sinners (see vv. 10-18). The Jews had a tendency to think that because they had so much knowledge of the true God and His laws that they were better than the Gentiles. However, Paul tells us that the Law cannot save anyone, and it is through the Law that man gains knowledge of sin (see v. 20).

If we cannot be justified by the Law, how can we be justified? Through faith in Jesus Christ. All have sinned and fallen short of God's glory, and God is now offering the free gift of salvation to anyone who will believe in His Son (see vv. 22-24). God can offer us a pardon because Jesus has been punished in our place for our sins. He has paid our penalty in full. We have been "justified by faith apart from works of the Law" (v. 28). The word *justified* means much more than "forgiveness." When God justifies, He declares us righteous, and He treats us just as if we had never sinned.

Can you see how tragic it is when so many people are deceived into thinking that their good works will save them? If you ask them if they think they will go to heaven when they die, most will say that they hope so, because they hope that they are good enough. The point that Paul is making is that no one is good enough to make it into heaven because all men have sinned (v. 23). Every man is guilty before God, and if he gets what he deserves, he will be eternally condemned.

Does that mean we can believe in Jesus and then go on sinning (see v. 31)? No, because real faith always leads to obedient action (see Rom. 6). If you believe Jesus is the Son of God, you will want to *obey* Him. When someone tells me that he believes that Jesus Christ is the Son of God, yet he lives his life no differently than someone who doesn't believe in Jesus, I know he is foolish himself. You can't have a casual relationship with Jesus.

When we exercise faith in Jesus Christ, our spirits are reborn and our desires change. We find that something inside us resists sin (see 2 Cor. 5:17).

PSALM 12:1-8

PROVERBS 19:13-14

The most frequent complaint I hear from husbands is that their wives nag them too much. (I'm sure there are plenty of nagging husbands, too.) We will rarely change anyone by criticizing. Real change is created by positive words of praise and encouragement. By the way, did I tell you how proud I am of you for reading through the Bible?

JULY 17

1 CHRONICLES 24:1-26:11

ROMANS 4:1-12

No one has ever been justified before God by keeping the Law, not even under the old covenant. The Law was given to help people understand their sinfulness and their need for a Savior. Paul proved this point by establishing that Abraham (Abram), the father of all Jews, was made righteous because of his faith and not because of his circumcision or his works. Paul quoted Genesis 15:6, which says that Abram "*believed* in the Lord; and He reckoned it to him as righteousness" (italics mine). The Scripture says this about Abraham *before* he was circumcised (see vv. 9-11 and Gen. 17:9-14). Just as Abraham was justified by his faith, so are we. Paul also referred to Psalm 32:1-2, which shows the same pattern of righteousness without works (see Rom. 4:6-8).

If God were to ask you, "Why should I let you into My heaven?", the only correct response would be, "Because Jesus shed His blood on my behalf, and my sins have been atoned for by Him. There is nothing that I have done that could ever merit me a place in heaven." Unfortunately, the average person would probably say, "I've tried to live a pretty decent life, and I've never murdered anybody or stolen any large sums of money."

They would be trying to save themselves by their own good conduct. And that is not good enough.

PSALM 13:1-6

PROVERBS 19:15-16

I've met very few Christians who are lazy. Most are hard-working, industrious people. However, we must be careful to avoid the opposite of laziness: addiction to work. If you're working night and day, all the time, either your priorities are out of order or you've set unrealistic expectations for yourself. If God needed rest on the seventh day, who are we to work seven days a week?

JULY 18

1 CHRONICLES 26:12-27:34

ROMANS 4:13-5:5

Today we learn several keys to Abraham's strong faith that enabled him to father a son in his old age. First, Abraham had a promise from God that became a foundation for his faith. He knew God wanted him to have a son. You or I could never trust God to have a son when we are one hundred years old because we have no promise of such a thing. However, don't be discouraged, because we do have plenty of good promises in the Bible that apply to us. Those we can believe!

Second, Abraham was fully aware of his circumstances (see 4:19-21). When we exercise faith, there are always contradicting circumstances. We don't ignore them but by faith we can learn to disregard their message.

Third, Abraham grew in faith. We feed our faith by meditating on God's promises. We exercise our faith by acting upon them. Use the faith you have now, feed it, and you will find your faith growing.

Fourth, Abraham gave glory to God *before* he saw the promise fulfilled (see v. 20). We read in verse 17 that "God calls things which do not exist as existing." That refers to the time when God called Abraham a "father of many nations" while Abraham was still childless. Abraham was simply imitating God when he acted like he had already seen his son. We, too, must express as much joy over the promise as we would over actually experiencing the answer to our prayer.

What does justification by faith mean for us? We have peace with God, and we don't have to be afraid of His wrath (see 5:1). We can exult in our tribulations, because God uses them to develop perseverance. This creates proven character (see 5:3-4). I like spending time with people who have come through tough times and can tell how God was faithful to them. They're fascinating and inspiring.

One other fabulous fact that is brought to light today is that God's love "has been poured out within our hearts through the Holy Spirit" (5:5). It shouldn't come as a surprise to us that God's own love is in our hearts, because God Himself lives in each of us by the Holy Spirit, and the Bible says that "God is love" (1 John 4:8). If you have God in you, you have His love too! We need to learn to let God's love within dominate us in every situation. When we do, we will find ourselves being more patient, more merciful, and more concerned with others. I've said to myself a number of times, "I can't love that person! It is too hard after what they've done to me!" But something on the inside says to me,

"You can't love them, but God's love in you can." We can learn to use His love in every situation.

PSALM 14:1-7

PROVERBS 19:17

How would you like to make a loan to God? Do you think He would repay you? This promise informs us that when we give to someone in need, God takes it onto His personal account to guarantee the repayment. I can say from experience that God offers tremendous interest rates too!

JULY 19

1 CHRONICLES 28:1-29:30

ROMANS 5:6-21

If you were going to die to save someone's life, would you rather die for a good person or an evil one? Jesus proved His great love for us because He died for us when we were sinful and certainly not worth His sacrifice. *If God loved us that much when we were His enemies, think how much He loves us now as His own children.* Paul actually says that we were reconciled to God while we were still God's enemies (v. 10)! Now think about that. Every person in the world today has already been reconciled to God because the price for their sins has been paid. But that doesn't mean that everyone is automatically saved, because each person must personally receive his reconciliation (vv. 11,17).

Verses 12 through 21 are admittedly difficult to interpret, but I will do my best to share what I understand. Paul said that through one man sin entered the world (v. 12). That obviously is referring to Adam and his original transgression. Through Adam's sin, spiritual death invaded the world—that spiritual force that infects men's spirits. The day Adam sinned he died spiritually. He passed from a state of being spiritually alive to a state of being spiritually dead.

As a result, spiritual death eventually spread to all people, not just because Adam sinned, but because all people sinned as well (v. 12). All of this started because of one man. But don't get unbalanced by placing all the blame on Adam. All of this spread because of everybody's sin. You and I both helped the spread of spiritual death, first by sinning ourselves, and secondly by influencing others to sin. On the other hand, all of this can end because of one Man, Jesus Christ, the "second Adam." You and I can help the spread of "spiritual life" by first receiving it ourselves, and secondly by sharing the gospel with others.

The majority of these verses are making a comparison between what happened as a result of what Adam did and what happened as a result of what Jesus did. Both men hold unique roles in human history. One opened the door for sin, spiritual death and judgment to come to all men, and one opened the door for holiness, spiritual life and justification to all men. Verse 18 says, "So then as through one transgression there resulted condemnation to all men, even so through one act of righteousness there resulted justification of life to all men."

Again this does not mean that everybody is automatically saved just because Jesus died for them, just as it does not mean that everybody was automatically damned just because of Adam's sin. If you had lived a life of sinlessness, spiritual death would never have infected your spirit. But you obviously haven't lived a sinless life, and so you were condemned by your own sin, not the sin of Adam. Adam just got the whole thing started.

I disagree with those who teach that Adam's sin and guilt were imputed to all of us. That is said nowhere in what we read today and would be totally contrary to God's character (see Ezekiel 18). Why would I be held accountable for something someone else did? The Scripture plainly says that death spread to all men "because all sinned," not because Adam sinned. Adam simply opened the door to sin and spiritual death. His sin didn't guarantee our damnation any more than Christ's atonement guaranteed our salvation. We had to sin to be damned, and we had to believe in Jesus to be saved.

PSALM 15:1-5

PROVERBS 19:18-19

Verse 18 tells us that there will come a time when our children are "out of the nest" and we will not be able to discipline them any longer. Therefore, we need to take advantage of the opportunities we have while they're young to discipline them. With the pervasiveness of sin in our day, Christian parents need to work extra hard at raising their children in the "nurture and admonition of the Lord."

JULY 20

2 CHRONICLES 1:1-3:17

ROMANS 6:1-23

This chapter begins with a foundational truth: our identification with Jesus in His death, burial and resurrection. Now that we are "in Him," everything that happened to Jesus affects us. When Jesus died, we died. When Jesus was buried, we were buried. When Jesus was resurrected, so were we. This is what your baptism symbolized. You died and were buried under the water. Then you were raised from the dead as a new person who was washed clean. Praise God! Your reborn spirit is dead to sin because it now has a new nature, the nature of God Himself. We are no longer slaves to sin. We can walk in righteousness if we will allow our spirits, rather than our flesh, to dominate us.

Even though we have been freed from sin, we can still choose to sin (see v. 12). Our spirits have been changed, but our bodies have not. There's a war going on between the spirit and the flesh, and we must determine that the spirit will prevail. When you're tempted to sin, keep in mind that this desire does not come from you, but from your "container." Your reborn spirit resists sin.

Memorize Romans 6:23: "For the wages of sin is death, but the free gift of God is eternal life in Christ Jesus our Lord." Notice the contrasts: "wages" and "free gift"; "death" and "life." All we *earned* from sin was the "reward" of spiritual death, but eternal life is *freely given* to us by God. Eternal life is something you possess *now*. It is the life and nature of God residing in your spirit.

PSALM 16:1-11

PROVERBS 19:20-21

JULY 21

2 CHRONICLES 4:1-6:11

I think we can readily see some of the contributing factors for the glory of God being manifested during the dedication of Solomon's temple. We know that the musicians and singers were all in unison and made "themselves heard with one voice to praise and glorify the Lord" (5:13). Sincere, unified worship brings God's holy presence on the scene. Notice also that all the people were magnifying the Lord by saying, "He is indeed good for His lovingkindness is everlasting" (5:13). It was then that the house of the Lord was filled with the cloud so the priests couldn't stand to minister. I have found that when we are involved in sincere worship with other believers and we are unified, we can sense the presence of the Lord. Sometimes it can get pretty strong!

ROMANS 7:1-13

Paul explained to Jewish Christians that the Law had no authority over them, because their death "in Christ" had removed them from its influence. They didn't have to obey the Law, and neither do any of us who are true believers in Christ. Our guide is not a list of rules and regulations, but the Holy Spirit who lives in us.

Sin is not simply an *act* of disobedience; it's a *spiritual force* that flows from spiritual death. Unsaved people don't just commit sins; they're sinners by nature. Paul described how the sinful nature in him used to take "opportunity through the commandment" to sin against God before he was born again (see v. 8). I'm sure you can remember that feeling. Something inside drove you to disobey God, even when you were fully aware that what you were doing was wrong. That old nature is now gone from your spirit.

PSALM 17:1-15

PROVERBS 19:22-23

JULY 22

2 CHRONICLES 6:12-8:10

ROMANS 7:14-8:8

In Romans 7:14-25, was Paul speaking of his life in Christ or before Christ? As a Christian, I can certainly identify with his feelings. Paul implied that something good *did* dwell in his spirit (see v. 18), and this is only true of those who have been born again. He stated, "For I joyfully concur with the law of God in the inner man" (v. 22). This also points to spiritual transformation. I believe Paul was speaking of his experience as a Christian, of the war between the spirit and the flesh.

We all battle the flesh and struggle to let Christ live through us. Only Jesus, who indwells us, can enable us to live victoriously over sin. He is the One whom we must trust for power to subdue the desires of the flesh.

In chapter 8, we learn that if we're to please the Lord, we must set our minds on the things of the Spirit (or possibly spirit) rather than on the things of the flesh. The mind set on the flesh will actually be hostile toward God (see v. 7). However, the mind set upon the Spirit (or spirit) experiences life and peace (see v. 6). Our minds decide who wins the war between the spirit and the flesh. That is why it's so important to have our minds renewed with the Word of God (see Rom. 12:2). Renewed minds will side with our transformed spirits to win the war.

PSALM 18:1-15

PROVERBS 19:24-25

JULY 23

2 CHRONICLES 8:11-10:19

ROMANS 8:9-21

Those who are born again have the Holy Spirit within. They are not controlled by their flesh, as unsaved people are. Because our flesh is still unregenerate, however, we will have to deal with it. We can choose to follow our flesh or our spirit (see vv. 13-14).

If we're living according to the flesh, we must die (see v. 13). Was Paul talking about spiritual or physical death? Probably he meant physical death, because we know that Christians who persist in sin can be judged by physical death (see 1 Cor. 11:30).

Notice that the Holy Spirit was referred to as a *Person*: "The Spirit *Himself* bears witness with our spirit that we are the children of God" (v. 16, italics mine). The Holy Spirit is also God (see v. 14).

The suffering and redemption of the creation is the theme of verses 18-21. During the millennial reign of Christ, nature itself will be completely changed. Isaiah 11:6-8 says, "And the wolf will dwell with the lamb, and the leopard will lie down with the kid, and the calf and the young lion and the fatling together; and a little boy will lead them. Also the cow and the bear will graze...and the lion will eat straw like the ox. And the nursing child will play by the hole of the cobra, and the weaned child will put his hand on the viper's den." That will be something to see, won't it? Paul said that then "creation...will be set free from its slavery to corruption...." Someday, according to Revelation 21:1, there will be a "new heaven and a new earth."

PSALM 18:16-36

PROVERBS 19:26

JULY 24

2 CHRONICLES 11:1-13:22

I can't resist commenting on one verse which we read today. In chapter 13 verse 18 we read that "the sons of Judah conquered because they trusted in the Lord, the God of their fathers." Although I've said it many times before, may I say once again that it is he who trusts in the Lord whom God blesses. That means that when it looks bad, he holds his confidence and continues to rejoice. Take that verse as a personal word for yourself today. Whatever difficulty you are facing, trust in the Lord and know that you will come out a conqueror!

ROMANS 8:22-39

Are you looking forward to getting your new body? You will receive a new one at the rapture of the church. At that time, we'll begin to realize all the blessings of being adopted into God's family. Paul spoke of that event as "the redemption of our body" (v. 23). There will no longer be any battle between the spirit and the flesh, because our new bodies will have no sinful nature. Paul says that now we groan within ourselves, waiting anxiously for that time to arrive (v. 23).

The Holy Spirit helps us in our prayer lives. He "intercedes for us with groanings too deep for words" (v. 26). We need more intercessors today, especially those who will learn to cooperate with the Holy Spirit. How about you?

Romans 8:28 is often misquoted. It does not say that "God causes all things" or that "all things are good." It reads, "God causes all things to work together for good to those who love God, to those who are called according to His purpose." God can take our mistakes, our most depressing circumstances, and even things that the devil does and turn them around for good.

Verses 29-30 have been a source of great controversy throughout the church's history. But I don't believe Paul meant that God predestines some to be saved and some to be damned (see v. 29). Jesus said that "*whoever* believes in Him should not perish, but have eternal life" (John 3:16, italics mine). God did decide long ago, however, that we who would believe in Jesus would become like Him; would be called to serve Him; would be justified by Him; and would be glorified with Him (see vv. 29-30).

God did have some sort of foreknowledge of us. But these verses don't say that God pre-picked the ones who would be saved. Salvation is offered to every person because Jesus shed His blood for every person.

I'm so glad nothing can separate us from the love of Christ! Aren't you? Even if we're persecuted to death, we are still overwhelming conquerors, because death cannot stop God's love (see vv. 36-37).

PSALM 18:37-50

PROVERBS 19:27-29

JULY 25

2 CHRONICLES 14:1-16:14

I love what God said through the prophet Azariah: "The Lord is with you when you are with Him...be strong and do not lose courage, for there is a reward for your work" (15:2,7). There *is* reward for what we do for the Lord, but we sometimes need encouragement from God's Word, just as King Asa did. Take these heartening words for yourself today, and be encouraged. God knows your situation, He is keeping track of your work for Him, and He will reward you.

ROMANS 9:1-21

Paul explained that God has the right to do anything He wants. He may choose to show mercy or withhold it. No one ever has any right to question God's dealings (see vv. 20-21).

But what about Jacob and Esau? Why did God decree before they were born that Esau, the older, would serve the younger Jacob? God was not speaking about the *individuals* Jacob and Esau but about their descendants (see Gen. 25:23). Esau never served Jacob, and God blessed both of them as individuals.

But why did God say, "Jacob I loved, but Esau I hated" (v. 13)? God didn't say this before the two boys were born, nor is it a reference to those two individuals. It was spoken through the prophet Malachi and refers to the two tribes that descended from Jacob and Esau (see Mal. 1:2-4). The statement was made when God was judging the descendants of Esau (the Edomites) hundreds of years after Jacob and Esau.

Paul said that God can show as much or as little mercy as He desires. Thank God that He always shows a lot of mercy! No one can complain.

PSALM 19:1-14

PROVERBS 20:1

JULY 26

2 CHRONICLES 17:1-18:34

ROMANS 9:22-10:13

Romans 9:22 raises some difficult questions. Has God prepared some "vessels for destruction"? I don't believe so. The Greek word for "prepared" suggests God is not the one responsible for the "preparing." God didn't create people to be damned any more than a potter creates a pot just to destroy it. Again, the point is that God shows incredible mercy to undeserving people.

Most of chapters 9-11 deal with the Jewish question. By the time Paul wrote his letter to the Romans, the majority of the church was made up of Gentiles rather than Jews. Had God rejected His chosen people? By no means. They had rejected God, because they were trying to attain a righteous standing before Him based on their keeping of the Law. On the other hand, Gentiles by the thousands were accepting God's free gift of righteousness (see 9:30-32).

The first portion of chapter 10 contains some of the Bible's strongest statements regarding justification by faith apart from the works of the Law. Our righteousness depends on our faith, and our faith depends on the promises of God.

Notice the relationship between faith and confession: "That if you *confess with your mouth* Jesus as Lord, and *believe in your heart* that God raised Him from the dead, you shall be saved; for *with the heart man believes*, resulting in righteousness, and *with the mouth he confesses*, resulting in salvation" (vv. 9-10, italics mine). If we believe, the words we speak will be words of belief.

PSALM 20:1-9

PROVERBS 20:2-3

JULY 27

2 CHRONICLES 19:1-20:37

Even though Jehoshaphat was a good man, he still faced trials, and his faith brought him through them. When Judah was being invaded by the Ammonites and the Moabites, God promised, "The battle is not yours but God's" (20:15). Our fight is the fight of faith. We should trust God to fight on our behalf.

God told Judah through prophecy to go out and face the enemy. I'm sure it took a great deal of faith for the people to obey. The natural thing would have been to run. Jehoshaphat exhorted the people to trust God. Then he placed the singers and praisers in front, and the people marched into battle. When they began praising and thanking the Lord—

always a good way to display our faith—God routed their enemies.

ROMANS 10:14-11:12

The spread of the gospel begins with those who give money to send preachers (see vv. 14-15). If no one gives, no one can be sent. If no one is sent, no one can hear the gospel. If no one can hear the gospel, no one can believe it. I'm so glad we all can have some part in reaching people throughout the world.

How do we get faith? By hearing the Word of God (see 10:17). But some who hear won't believe. Paul was still speaking of the Jews in this passage. He said they have heard but haven't all believed (see 10:16). Apparently part of God's strategy for reaching the Jews was to make them jealous of the Gentiles whom He blessed with salvation (see 10:19; 11:11).

Chapter 11 addresses the subject of biblical predestination. Paul was proving that God had not cast away the Jewish people because of their rejection of Christ. He referred to the incident where Elijah ran from Jezebel. Elijah claimed he was the only one still serving God, but God told him, "I have kept for Myself seven thousand men who have not bowed the knee to Baal" (11:4). Notice God said He had *chosen* seven thousand men. Those men had also *chosen* God.

Paul then explained, "In the same way then, there has also come to be at the present time a remnant according to *God's gracious choice*" (v. 5, italics mine). God has chosen us because He knew we would believe! That is true biblical predestination. A long time ago, God chose to save all those who would believe in His Son.

PSALM 21:1-13

PROVERBS 20:4-6

Rather than proclaiming our loyalty, let's concentrate on *demonstrating* it (see v. 6).

JULY 28

2 CHRONICLES 21:1-23:21

This passage proves that God will sometimes discipline or judge sinful people through sickness. The story of Jehoram, whom God struck with a disease in his bowels, is one of numerous examples of this process (see 21:15, 18-19). The New Testament teaches that Satan is an author of sickness and that God may *permit* him to attack someone with illness. Of course, just because people get sick doesn't mean they're being judged by God. It could mean they ate the wrong food! When sickness attacks, however, we need to have a spiritual checkup to insure that we haven't opened the door to illness through our own disobedience.

ROMANS 11:13-36

The time is coming when there will be a mass conversion of Jewish people to Jesus, even though most of the Jews are now hardened to Him (see 11:12,15,25-27). That will be a great day. We should never be arrogant toward the Jewish people, because they are the roots of the "Christian tree." True Christians love the Jews. (True Christians love everyone.)

Because you didn't obtain your salvation by good works, you can't lose it by bad works. When you sin as a believer, you're simply a disobedient believer. You have broken your *fellowship* with

God, but not your *relationship* with Him. He is still your Father, and you're still His child. You can have your fellowship immediately restored by confessing your sin (see 1 John 1:9).

Paul said, "Behold then the kindness and severity of God" (v. 22). People always want to overemphasize either God's kindness or His severity, but we need balance. How kind is God? Anyone who would have His own Son die for us must be extremely kind. How severe is God? Anyone who would send someone to an eternal hell must be extremely severe. But remember, God is kind to everyone and only severe to those who rebel against Him.

Romans 11:32 is a beautiful synopsis of this major theme: "For God has shut up all in disobedience that He might show mercy to all." That's hard to fathom. How many courts convict people for the sole purpose of showing them mercy?

PSALM 22:1-18

PROVERBS 20:7

JULY 29

2 CHRONICLES 24:1-25:28

ROMANS 12:1-21

We are transformed by the renewing of our minds (see v. 2). Why? A mind renewed by the Word of God will embrace the reborn spirit rather than yielding to the desires of the flesh. We not only worship by singing and praising God, but also by daily obedience to Him. One of our greatest enemies is the old nature that resides in our flesh. When our spirits dominate our flesh through our renewed minds, we bring glory to God through our lives. That is our "spiritual service of worship" (v. 1).

If we're filled with Christ, we are the body of Christ (see vv. 4-5). As individual members of that body, we all have different functions and gifts that are for God's glory. Most important, we need each other because we are "members one of another" (v. 5). A hand needs the arm, elbow and shoulder in order to function.

One of the greatest tragedies in the body of Christ today is the shortage of people exercising their gifts. Also, many parts refuse to cooperate with each other because of doctrinal differences and personality conflicts.

What's your gift or function? Paul listed several possible functions for your prayerful consideration. Some have a ministry in prophecy; some have gifts to serve in specific ways. Others have an anointing to teach or a call to exhort others. Some can give or lead. Many show mercy to those in need. Paul didn't give us an exhaustive list, but all of us need to pray and discover our particular calling from God.

Romans 12:9-21 is full of practical instruction on how to live in a godly manner. Did you do a check-up on yourself as you read through this section?

Notice the strong verbs Paul used to describe the appropriate attitudes and actions of Spirit-filled believers (see vv. 9-13). God hates half-heartedness!

The real test of our spirituality is how we react when others wrong us (see vv. 14-21). Our kindness, shown in response to their hatred, will shame them. God wants us to overcome evil with good.

PSALM 22:19-31

PROVERBS 20:8-10

JULY 30

2 CHRONICLES 26:1-28:27

Sometimes, God allows a calamity to draw those who are straying from His paths back to Him. This was true of Ahaz. The king should have returned to the Lord as a result of his troubles. He's a prime example of those who become progressively hardened to God no matter what He does or permits. On the other hand, many have turned back to God when they suffered (the prodigal son for example).

ROMANS 13:1-14

Governments exist only because God permits them. However, when any government makes demands that are contrary to God's Word, we must obey God. The Scripture is full of examples of people who disobeyed the government to obey God. Paul himself is a prime case. As long as the law of the government doesn't contradict the law of God, however, Christians should be law-abiding citizens.

When Paul said, "Owe nothing to anyone except to love one another" (v. 8), did he mean that Christians should never borrow money? Not in light of the rest of Scripture. God doesn't want us to be delinquent on loan payments, because that would be a bad testimony. He doesn't want us to be in debt beyond our ability to repay, or to borrow money because of a lack of contentment with what we already have. My personal policy is that I will never borrow money for anything except a house and a car. I admire people who have more stringent convictions.

If we love others, we fulfill the law (see v. 10). If we walk in love, we won't commit adultery or steal from anyone. I like having to keep only one commandment rather than hundreds. Let's judge our every thought, word and deed by the law of love.

We should "make no provision for the flesh in regard to its lusts" (v. 14). All of us, even though we're born again, live in a body that has wrong desires. To live victoriously over the flesh, we must make no provision for it. For example, if you struggle with the temptation to watch inappropriate movies on television, you should take measures to eliminate the source of the temptation. Either get rid of the cable network that brings those movies to your home, or get rid of your television altogether! If you struggle with the temptation to eat more than you should, quit buying ice cream at the grocery store each week! By eliminating temptations, we will eliminate many sins.

PSALM 23:1-6

PROVERBS 20:11

JULY 31

2 CHRONICLES 29:1-36

ROMANS 14:1-23

In Paul's day, several sensitive cultural issues divided Christians. How were those on each side of an issue to treat one another? Paul said they should accept and love one another. We know there are no dietary laws for Christians, for example, but we shouldn't criticize those who think differently. The church in Rome contained both Jews and Gentiles, and some of the Jewish Christians were still following their old dietary laws. Paul said that one group shouldn't despise the other; both were trying to obey God. Who are we to judge someone else's servant (see v. 4)? We should only judge ourselves—so that we're ready to stand before the Lord.

We should also be careful not to put a stumbling block before a fellow believer who is "weak in faith" (v. 1). If a certain brother in the Lord believes it's wrong to eat pork chops, I shouldn't eat pork chops in his presence.

Every year, as Halloween approaches, many pastors begin to have nightmares. They aren't afraid of Halloween, but they hate the strife that occurs between church members whose opinions differ about that day. Some Christians think it's a sin even to mention the word *Halloween.* Some are sure it's a sin to send their children out trick-or-treating. Some want the church to provide an alternate activity for their children. Others think it's all right to send their children out trick-or-treating as long as they aren't dressed like witches or ghosts. What's the proper attitude? We *must* love and respect those with differing opinions.

PSALM 24:1-10

PROVERBS 20:12

AUGUST 1

2 CHRONICLES 30:1-31:21

ROMANS 15:1-22

The divisions in the church of Rome were often between Christian Jews and Gentiles (see vv. 7-12). Paul admonished both groups to accept each other and live in harmony. This is also a good lesson for our churches, because the most segregated hour of the week is still on Sunday morning.

Paul gave all the credit for the success of his ministry to Jesus, working through him in the power of signs and wonders (see vv. 18-19). That impresses me. Here was a man who had planted churches all over modern Syria, Turkey, Greece, Cyprus and Yugoslavia without a mission board or any promise of regular support, without a car, printing press or mailing list, and who had faced incredible hostility almost everywhere he preached. No one could have done what he did without supernatural assistance. *Paul's ministry demonstrates what can be accomplished through a person who is called by God and relies on Him completely.* No matter what God has called *you* to do, He can and will make a way!

PSALM 25:1-15

PROVERBS 20:13-15

Verse 14 is another true-to-life commentary on the nature of the average person. If you are selling something, potential buyers normally try to find its flaws in order to drive the price down. But once they have made the purchase, they boast to their friends about the good deal they got on such a fine item!

AUGUST 2

2 CHRONICLES 32:1-33:13

Second Chronicles 32:1 emphasizes that even when we're following the Lord with all our hearts, difficulties may come our way. King Hezekiah had just instituted sweeping reforms throughout Judah, and yet we read, "After these acts of faithfulness Sennacherib king of Assyria came and invaded Judah and besieged the fortified cities" (32:1). The same difficulties that assailed idolatrous kings came to Hezekiah in his faithfulness. The difference was the outcome. Hezekiah experienced a marvelous deliverance.

Jesus said the storms of life come to everyone, and only the doers of the Word are not washed away in the flood (see Matt. 7:24-27). Don't be surprised when difficulties come your way. View them as times to grow closer to the Lord and as opportunities to see miracles.

Today's account also reveals that Hezekiah "gave no return for the benefit he received, because his heart was proud" (32:25). I wonder how guilty we are of ingratitude for all the Lord has done for us? Truly, above all people on the face of the earth, we should be thankful. Let's never take God's grace for granted.

The reading gives one other detail of Hezekiah's life: "And even in the matter of the envoys of the rulers of Babylon, who sent to him to inquire of the wonder that had happened in the land, God left him alone only to test him, that He might know all that was in his heart" (32:31).

God tests each one of us in the same way. He may permit circumstances in *our* lives that tempt us to take more credit than we should. Will we give glory to God, or will we take the credit ourselves? *If we give God His due credit, He can trust us and use us to a greater degree.*

King Manasseh's life is a testimony to God's mercy and love toward a terribly evil man who had led his nation astray. God permitted calamity to come his way in order to reach him (33:11-13). "And *when he was in distress*, he entreated the Lord his God and humbled himself greatly before the God of his fathers" (italics mine). Notice that Manasseh had a very different reaction to calamity than King Ahaz. Manasseh was softened by it, Ahaz was hardened.

ROMANS 15:23-16:7

Paul hoped to mend the differences between Jews and Gentiles by taking an offering from the Gentiles of Macedonia and Achaia to the poor Christians in Jerusalem (see 15:25-31). He was confident that the legalistic, unsaved Jews in Jerusalem would be moved by such an act. But we know how warmly Paul was received when he came to Jerusalem—the Jews bound him in chains!

Paul obviously had an intimation of what would happen when he arrived in Jerusalem, because he requested prayer that he would be delivered from those "who are disobedient in Judea" (15:31). Incidentally, those prayers were answered. Paul could have easily been killed during the riot that broke out when he arrived in Jerusalem. But he was rescued from death and eventually made it to Rome.

Romans 16 contains a list of salutations to people Paul knew from his travels. First mentioned is Phoebe, a "servant" of the church of Cenchrea. The word *servant* is the same word translated "deacon" elsewhere. There is no doubt that Phoebe was a woman. Can women be deacons? Yes. Women can serve, and that's what a deacon is: a servant.

In verse 7 notice that Paul talks about

Andronicus and Junias, two apostles not previously mentioned. God sent more than just twelve apostles to plant churches in the ancient world. It is my understanding that at least twenty-four people were listed as apostles in the New Testament.

God is still calling, equipping and sending apostles today. The world needs them more than ever!

PSALM 25:16-22

PROVERBS 20:16-18

AUGUST 3

2 CHRONICLES 33:14-34:33

ROMANS 16:8-27

I am blessed by Paul's efforts to send personal greetings to many saints in Rome. He warmly compliments them for their faithfulness and labor for the Lord. Paul would have been a nice person to be around. He was always encouraging others and building them up. He wasn't such a "big-time apostle" that he couldn't take time to mention people by their first names.

A number of times in Paul's letters, he mentioned "the mystery" that had been revealed to him. Today we read, "Now to Him who is able to establish you according to my gospel and the preaching of Jesus Christ, according to the revelation of *the mystery* which has been kept secret for long ages past, but now has been manifested" (v. 25-26a, italics mine). What was this mystery? The revelation contained in the New Testament epistles.

The mystery includes the plan of our redemption through Jesus' death; the entire church age in which we're now living; the revelation of our identification with Christ in His death, burial and resurrection; the knowledge of the indwelling of the Holy Spirit in every believer; and the rapture of the church at the end of the age. The mystery was written down by Paul and the other New Testament authors as it was revealed to them by the Holy Spirit.

Do you remember when Jesus told His disciples that He had many more things to tell them, but they weren't ready to hear them? It was then that He promised to send the Holy Spirit to lead them into all the truth (see John 16:12-13). That was the mystery. Praise God it's not a mystery anymore!

PSALM 26:1-12

PROVERBS 20:19

Simply put, don't associate with a gossip. That means Christian as well as non-Christian gossips I might add!

AUGUST 4

2 CHRONICLES 35:1-36:23

The writer of 2 Chronicles tells us that when the people of Judah were deported to Babylon by King Nebuchadnezzar, "they were servants to him and to his sons until the rule of the kingdom of Persia, to fulfill the word of the Lord by the mouth of Jeremiah, until the land had enjoyed its sabbaths...seventy years" (36:20-21).

What does this mean? Under levitical law, the land was supposed to have a sabbath rest every seven years (see Lev.

25:3-4). But for 490 years, the Jews didn't obey that law. During that time, the land should have enjoyed seventy years of rest, so God was going to make up for the disobedience and give the land its due. Jeremiah, whose book we'll read in a few months, foretold that the Babylonian captivity would last exactly seventy years (see Jer. 25:12; 29:10). After that, Babylon, the world power, was overthrown by the Persians. The first king of Persia, Cyrus, decreed that the captive Jews could return to Jerusalem to rebuild the temple.

1 CORINTHIANS 1:1-17

First Corinthians was written by the apostle Paul around A.D. 55 in response to a letter from the church in Corinth. In this letter, Paul answered questions raised by the church and dealt with other areas needing correction.

Corinth was a commercial crossroads of Greece and was known for its licentiousness. The city boasted of its temple of Aphrodite, goddess of love, at which a thousand temple prostitutes earned their living as a vital part of the Corinthian "religious experience." Corinth was a sin-sick cosmopolitan city that needed to hear the gospel from the church Paul had established several years before. Unfortunately, that church was having some problems of its own.

Notice that Paul spoke of the Corinthian Christians as "saints" in his introduction (see v. 2)—a term that would hardly characterize their lifestyles. But Paul was speaking of the Corinthians as God saw them: washed clean and made righteous by the blood of Christ. If the carnal Corinthian Christians could be classified as saints, anyone who is in Christ can claim that title. Paul even promised the Corinthians that God would confirm them "blameless in the day of our Lord Jesus Christ" (v. 8). There could hardly be more convincing proof of the doctrine of justification by faith alone than that one statement by Paul.

The foremost problem at Corinth was division in the church. The Corinthians were breaking into factions based on their favorite teachers (see vv. 10-12). Disunity is one of the greatest signs of carnality. I wonder what God thinks of the more than three hundred different Protestant denominations in the United States alone.

The situation wouldn't be so bad if the various groups had something to do with each other, but so often they grow exclusive. Each one claims to have more perfect doctrine. By the same token, many nondenominational churches are nothing more than one-church denominations. They don't associate with anyone. We need to draw circles that *include* other Christians rather than *exclude* them.

Let's endeavor to love all Christians no matter what their particular pet doctrines might be. God loves us all!

PSALM 27:1-6

PROVERBS 20:20-21

AUGUST 5

EZRA 1:1-2:70

The book of Ezra picks up where 2 Kings and 2 Chronicles left off. The Jews had been in captivity in Babylon for seventy years, and Persia had just overthrown Babylon. This took place at about 536 B.C. The story begins when God used Cyrus, a heathen king, to release all the Jews so that the temple in Jerusalem could be rebuilt.

Not all the Jews returned to Jerusalem, but Cyrus decreed that any who remained in Babylon were to support the exiles' return with gifts and an offering for the construction of the temple. It's likely that not just the people of Judah returned, but that a few members of the northern tribes who had been deported to Assyria returned as well. (Assyria had been overthrown by the Babylonians, who were in turn deposed by the Persians.) All totaled, there were 42,360 people who returned to Jerusalem with Zerubbabel as their leader. The majority remained, comfortable with their now-familiar home in Babylon.

1 CORINTHIANS 1:18-2:5

The message of the gospel is foolish by human standards. That's why it is normally a waste of time to try to *reason* with people about God and His plan of salvation from philosophical, psychological or even scientific viewpoints. The message of the cross itself is what pierces people's hearts, and it demands a decision from the hearer.

That's why, when Paul first came to Corinth, he determined to "know nothing among [you] except Jesus Christ, and Him crucified" (2:2). Paul said he didn't come "with superiority of speech or of wisdom" (2:1) and claimed that his message and preaching were not "in persuasive words of wisdom" (2:4). We should follow his example in our witnessing opportunities. We simply need to tell people that Jesus died for them and that if they'll place their trust in Him, they will be saved. Some will laugh, but some will believe. Their responsibility begins where ours ends.

You might notice, as Paul observed, that the majority of Christians are not considered wise, rich or famous by the world's standards (1:26). Don't ever be envious of the rich, powerful and famous. Because they have attained everything that the world is seeking, they don't see their need for Christ. God has chosen the foolish things of the world to shame the wise.

Keep your eyes open for any phrases in the New Testament epistles that include the words "in Christ," "in Him" or "through whom." Those words indicate something we now have because of Jesus' work on the cross. In this chapter, we read that we're now "in Christ Jesus, who became to us wisdom from God, and righteousness and sanctification, and redemption" (v. 30). Thus, according to God's eternal Word, you can boldly claim that you are righteous, sanctified and redeemed through Christ!

PSALM 27:7-14

PROVERBS 20:22-23

A Chinese proverb says, "He who pursues revenge should dig two graves." It is never right for us to repay others for the evil that they have done to us.

AUGUST 6

EZRA 3:1-4:24

Zerubbabel and 42,360 exiles traveled nine hundred miles to the ruined city of Jerusalem to rebuild the temple. It took about forty-three years to complete the project because of its size and because of hindrances during construction.

Did you notice that the Jews shouted with a great shout when the temple's foundation was laid (see 3:11)? Praise God for the freedom to shout with joy.

Don't ever think God requires silent worship from us.

1 CORINTHIANS 2:6-3:4

We read in 1 Corinthians 2:9, "Things which eye has not seen and ear has not heard, and which have not entered into the heart of man, all that God has prepared for those who love Him." Often, this verse is applied to what heaven will be like. But in this context, Paul wasn't speaking of heaven. He was speaking of the blessings of our redemption that we experience *now*.

No one could have imagined all the blessings that would blossom from the new covenant. But "to us, God revealed them through the Spirit" (2:10). Notice that "revealed" is in the past tense. The Holy Spirit was able to do this because He knows the thoughts of God, just as the spirit of a person knows the thoughts of the person (see 2:11). Because all of us have been given that same Spirit, we can all know the things that have been "freely given to us by God" (2:12).

Unfortunately, too many members of the body of Christ aren't listening to the Holy Spirit, so they're missing blessings God intended for them to enjoy. They are more apt to listen to the traditions of men and their particular church creed than the Holy Spirit within them. Often they don't even realize the Holy Spirit is in them. However, those who *are* listening to the Spirit can say with Paul that they "have the mind of Christ" (2:16).

In chapter three, Paul spoke of the Corinthian Christians as "men of flesh," as "babes in Christ," and as "fleshly" or "carnal." He was saying they were dominated by their flesh rather than by their recreated spirits.

What gave them away? The jealousy and strife among them. They weren't acting as Jesus would but like unbelievers, "walking like mere men" (v. 3).

Carnal Christians are only able to handle the milk of the Word (see 3:2). They aren't ready to digest deeper revelation. If you've made it this far through the Bible, you're probably beyond the babyhood stage of Christianity. But you will still have a daily battle against the flesh. May your spirit be winning the battle more and more!

PSALM 28:1-9

PROVERBS 20:24-25

AUGUST 7

EZRA 5:1-6:22

We read today that the prophesying of Haggai and Zechariah inspired the Jews to rise up and begin to build the temple again. What did these two prophets say that motivated the Jews to start building again?

In the first chapter of Haggai God asks the people, "Is it time for you yourselves to dwell in paneled houses while this house lies desolate?... You look for much, but behold it comes to little; when you bring it home, I blow it away. Why? Because of My house which lies desolate, while each of you runs to his own house. Therefore because of you the sky has withheld its dew, and the earth has withheld its produce."

The people were not seeking first the kingdom of God (see Matt. 6:33). Consequently, they experienced lack. The same will be true for Christians who put their own desires ahead of obeying the Lord. God will lovingly discipline them to bring them to repentance.

This portion of the story also demonstrates how God can cause "all things to work together for good" (Rom. 8:28). When Governor Tattenai decided to report to Darius about what the Jews were doing, it looked as if they would be stopped once again. However, Darius taxed Tattenai and his subjects to finance the rebuilding of the temple. What could have been a crushing fist turned out to be a hand of support.

God will do the same for you. When people work evil against you, God can make it work for good. Keep working and rejoicing, because God is on your side!

1 CORINTHIANS 3:5-23

Still discussing division in the Corinthian church, Paul tried to impart a correct perspective of his, Peter's and Apollos's ministries. Each was only a servant of Christ to whom the Lord had given opportunity to minister, so it is God who should be credited and revered, not God's people.

We also see more of the difference between the ministry of apostles and the ministry of teachers. Paul said he planted but that Apollos watered (see v. 6). Apostles plant churches, and teachers water them with the Word to help them grow. But God causes the growth.

Did you know that we will be rewarded for what we do in our service to the Lord when we get to heaven? This does not affect our salvation, but is an evaluation of our works.

Paul tells us that all works done in the Lord's service fall into one of six categories: gold, silver, precious stones, wood, hay and straw (v. 12). These categories can be divided again into those which are flammable and those which are not.

One day our works will be presented to God and will go through His purging fire. Those things that were not God's will or which were done with wrong motives will be burned in the fire. For those works, we will receive no reward.

But those works which are classified as gold, silver or precious stones will not be consumed by the fire, and for those we will receive reward (vv. 14-15). The important thing is that we do our best to accomplish what the Lord tells us to do with the right motives.

Paul stated that we are a temple of the Holy Spirit (see v. 16). In this context, he was not referring to each of us as individuals, but saying that all of us together, *corporately*, are the temple of the Holy Spirit. (For context, see verse 9, where Paul said the Corinthians were God's building.) Paul went on to say that if anyone destroyed the temple of God, God would destroy him. This was clearly a reference to the division that existed in Corinth and was a stern warning against engendering strife.

PSALM 29:1-11

PROVERBS 20:26-27

AUGUST 8

EZRA 7:1-8:20

About eighty years after the first group of exiles returned to Jerusalem with Zerubbabel, a second group prepared to return under the leadership of Ezra. This happened at about 458 B.C. Sometime during the preceding eighty years, Esther had saved the Jewish race from annihilation. The temple was rebuilt, but the people still needed instruction about how to carry out all the requirements of the Law. Ezra was assigned to this task. He had the God-granted favor of King Artaxerxes of

Persia, who also commissioned Ezra to set up a complete judicial system and decreed that abundant provision be supplied for adorning the temple and presenting offerings. God was in it!

1 CORINTHIANS 4:1-21

Paul labeled himself and Apollos stewards of God's mysteries and stated that stewards must first be found trustworthy (see vv.1-2). A steward is someone responsible for someone else's possessions. If I were going to be your steward, I doubt you would entrust me with one million dollars my first day on the job. You might start off by testing me with one hundred dollars. Why? Because trust must be earned. If we expect God to entrust us with more, we must prove ourselves faithful by properly using what He has already given us.

Paul went on to say that only the Lord is the Judge, so none of us should be passing judgment on others. We can't see people's hearts as God can, who someday will "disclose the motives of men's hearts; and then each man's praise will come to him from God" (v. 5).

PSALM 30:1-12

PROVERBS 20:28-30

I wonder if ancient justice was more effective and humane than what we administer today. If a man was caught in a crime, he was usually punished by receiving a whipping. It was very painful, but it brought reformation.

Today, we punish a man by putting him in jail where he can be influenced by other criminals, increasing the chances that he will wind up back in prison. Effective punishment should not only deter future offenses, but do a work of reformation in the life of the offender as well.

AUGUST 9

EZRA 8:21-9:15

Today we read of Ezra's journey from Babylon to Jerusalem, a journey of about nine hundred miles. His group was much smaller than Zerubbabel's, but they were carrying about a million dollars' worth of gold and other treasure, causing them to invoke divine protection from the Lord.

Once safely in Jerusalem, they discovered that some of the returned exiles had intermarried with women from the surrounding nations: nations with whom God had forbidden marriage. Some of the Israelites had even divorced their Jewish wives in order to marry foreigners. Ezra was appalled. Such compromise had precipitated Israel's downfall before and had led to the eventual exile to Assyria and Babylon. Ezra's prayer reveals his deep relationship with the Lord and his knowledge of God's Word.

1 CORINTHIANS 5:1-13

With problem number one behind him, Paul next turned his attention to problem number two: immorality in the church. One of the men in the church was living in sin with his stepmother. This was a stain on the church since even the heathen knew such a relationship was wrong (v. 1).

Paul instructed the church to publicly turn the offender over "to Satan for the destruction of his flesh, that his spirit may be saved in the day of the Lord Jesus" (v. 5). The man would be attacked by Satan in his body, contracting some sickness or disease, in hopes that this would bring him to repentance.

Paul said the church had the authority to judge church members (see v. 12), but he wasn't talking about judging someone's motives or jumping to conclusions. You can't turn everyone over to Satan who is guilty of some little offense against you. He was referring to situations where the continued, unrepentant, serious offense of the offender cannot be debated. In those cases, the church has the authority to excommunicate and to turn the offender over to Satan.

Paul's main concern was that the church should be holy. His instruction was clear: we are not to associate with any so-called Christian who is immoral, covetous (a reference to coveting someone else's wife or husband), a swindler, idolater, reviler or drunkard. Those kinds of professing Christians can bring reproach on the church.

PSALM 31:1-8

PROVERBS 21:1-2

AUGUST 10

EZRA 10:1-44

I have to question whether the decision of the people of Judah and Benjamin to divorce their foreign wives was the best one, especially since some of them had children by their foreign wives. However, we have to admire their sincere repentance. And because the Bible doesn't reveal God's viewpoint on their decision, we have to leave that question unanswered. My opinion is that God would have been satisfied with a confession on the part of the offenders and a resolve from the rest that they would not marry foreign wives.

1 CORINTHIANS 6:1-20

The third problem Paul addressed in 1 Corinthians was that Christians were bringing lawsuits against one another. It's a reproach against the life-changing power of the gospel when two believers go to court and stand before an unsaved judge to settle their case. Paul said it would actually be better to be defrauded by a brother than to try to settle the difference in court (see v. 7).

Was this a license for Christians to defraud fellow believers? No. Paul condemned those in the Corinthian church who had defrauded others. He placed them in the same category as fornicators, idolaters, adulterers, homosexuals, thieves and drunkards, all of whom assuredly will not inherit the kingdom of God (see v. 9-10).

This chapter also gives several "in Christ" revelations. First, our bodies are members of Christ (see v. 15). Our bodies are owned by God, and we don't have the right to do with them whatever we want.

Not only are our bodies members of Christ, but we're also one spirit with Him (see v. 17). You now have His nature in your spirit.

We learned in chapter 3 that the church corporately is a temple of the Holy Spirit. Now we take it one step further and learn that each of us *individually* is a temple of the Holy Spirit (see v. 19). Think about it. God lives in you! The more conscious we are of God's ownership and His indwelling presence, the more we'll try to please Him.

PSALM 31:9-18

PROVERBS 21:3

AUGUST 11

NEHEMIAH 1:1-3:14

The story of Nehemiah begins about twelve years after the return of the second group of exiles to Jerusalem. The temple had been rebuilt, but the city wall and its gates were still in disrepair, broken down almost one hundred and fifty years earlier in the days of Nebuchadnezzar. Nehemiah, King Artaxerxes' cup-bearer, received the burden from the Lord to rebuild them. The only problem was that the king had ordered that the rebuilding of Jerusalem's walls should stop because he had been told that the city had a rebellious history (see the parenthetical information found in Ezra 4:7-23). No wonder Nehemiah was afraid to make his request! It could have cost him his life. Artaxerxes' granting Nehemiah's request was miraculous. This is one more illustration that with God, we can do all things.

Just as in the case of the rebuilding of the temple, Nehemiah and his helpers encountered opposition right from the start (see 2:19). Did God remove the adversaries? No, He used them to develop spiritual growth, just as He uses irritating people in your life to cause you to grow. It's easy to love people who are nice, but it is a challenge to love people who are not so nice. It's easy to have faith when everything is going smoothly, but it's much more challenging when it looks as though your world is falling apart.

1 CORINTHIANS 7:1-24

Today we begin the part of Paul's letter where he addressed questions from the Corinthian church. Chapter 7 deals with the sticky subject of marriage, divorce and remarriage.

The first few verses of the chapter are plain. The Corinthians asked if it was good for a man not to touch a woman. (I assume they were asking about unmarried men and women.) Paul said they were correct. However, because of sexual drives and the resulting temptation for sin, marriage is the answer for most people. Sex is designed by God to be enjoyed, but only within the bonds of marriage. Paul wished that everyone could remain unmarried, but he recognized that for most of us, "it is better to marry than to burn" (v. 9). Also, because the normal sexual drives are designed by God, it is wrong to deprive your mate of sexual fulfillment (see vv. 3-5).

What about those who are contemplating a divorce? Paul first addressed the case of two Christians who were married (see vv. 10-11). The wife should not leave her husband, but if she did, she should remain unmarried or be reconciled to her husband. Sometimes when a Christian husband acts like an unsaved person, separation can bring him back to right living. The same rule applies when the roles are reversed.

Next, Paul addressed the Christian who was married to a non-Christian (see vv. 12-17). In general, the Christian should remain married, but if the non-Christian spouse desires a divorce, the Christian is to let the spouse go. Paul said that the unbelieving one is "sanctified" through the believing one (see v. 14). This means that the unbelieving spouse is "set apart" for special mercies from the Lord because he or she is married to one of His children. But there is no guarantee an unbelieving spouse will be saved (see v. 16).

I realize that these scriptures don't offer an answer for every situation. For example, what should a woman do if she is married to an unbelieving husband who comes home drunk every night and beats her and her children? She should not put up with that kind of treatment year after year, as I've seen some Christian women do. But seeking a divorce may not be the best thing for her and her children. I think she should separate from her husband and give him time to repent. Her husband won't normally change as long as she puts up with his behavior. Only when he suffers the consequences, through separation or the threat of divorce, is there any chance that he will repent and be transformed.

What about the woman married to a Christian who acts like a saint in church but a devil at home? The rule that applies to being married to a non-Christian would also apply here. Apparently, Paul allowed some variation for each individual case. He said, "Only, as the Lord has assigned to each one, as God has called each, in this manner let him walk" (v. 17). The guidance from this commentary will never replace your pastor. If you need more help, see him.

Please note: we who have never been divorced have no right to judge those who have. No one hates divorce more than those who have been through it. No one ever got married with plans of eventually being divorced.

And one more thing: you may have been a "divorced person" before your salvation, but you aren't anymore. Sins committed prior to your new birth are forgiven and forgotten. We are new creations in Christ. And if you've been wrongfully divorced as a Christian, God will not hold it against you if you simply ask His forgiveness.

PSALM 31:19-24

PROVERBS 21:4

AUGUST 12

NEHEMIAH 3:15-5:13

Sanballat and Tobiah harassed the Jews who were rebuilding the wall, but God got the last laugh when it was rebuilt with miraculous speed.

Notice that God did not remove Jerusalem's adversaries. In Daniel 9:25 we are told that Jerusalem would be rebuilt "in times of distress." The threats which were made against the builders motivated the Jews to trust God even more, allowing God to use their trials to draw them closer to Himself. Hopefully we allow difficulties in our lives to draw us closer to God.

We read of another crisis in chapter 5. Some of the wealthier Jews were lending money at high interest rates to their fellow Jews. Some were even selling their debtors as slaves to collect on the loss. According to the Law, they were forbidden to charge any interest on loans to other Israelites (see Exod. 22:25). Nehemiah set them straight, not only by preaching the truth, but also by example.

1 CORINTHIANS 7:25-40

Today we read Paul's suggestion that "in view of the present distress," virgins should remain unmarried (v. 26). Notice that Paul was offering his opinion, not necessarily speaking for God. We don't know what the "present distress" was, but a more accurate translation might be "impending distress." Paul was probably referring to outside persecution of the church. Another reason Paul recommended that single people remain unmarried was so they could serve the Lord with undistracted devotion.

Plainly, it's not a sin for divorced

people to be remarried: "Are you *released* from a wife? Do not seek a wife. But if you should marry, *you have not sinned*; and if a virgin should marry, she has not sinned" (vv. 27*b*-28, italics mine).

In Paul's day fathers had the authority to decide whether or not their daughters could marry and who they would marry (vv. 36-38). Most daughters today would have a hard time believing this. But as a general rule the best person to offer advice on her prospective husband is her own father, providing that her father is a mature Christian. He knows his daughter. He knows about men. He knows about marriage. And no one loves his daughter as much as he does!

PSALM 32:1-11

PROVERBS 21:5-7

AUGUST 13

NEHEMIAH 5:14-7:60

I like Nehemiah. He held to a very high standard of integrity and lived above reproach. Although he may have sounded a little self-centered when he prayed that God might remember him for all the good he did (see 5:19), I have to admire his honesty. Don't all of us want God to remember us for the good we do?

Four times Nehemiah's enemies tried to distract him from his work, but Nehemiah stayed with what God had called him to do. Nehemiah's unflinching persistence in the face of ridicule and discouragement reminds me of the story of Colonel George Washington Goethals, who was in charge of building the Panama Canal. Back in the States, he was publicly criticized by many who predicted that he would never complete his task. When asked how he was going to answer his critics, he simply replied, "With the canal!"

Remember that sometimes the devil sends people our way just to waste our time. We are called to bring others to a saving relationship with Christ. As Christ's ambassadors, we don't have time to waste.

1 CORINTHIANS 8:1-13

The second question the Corinthians had asked Paul concerned the eating of things sacrificed to idols. Obviously, those idols didn't eat the food, so it was sold in the marketplace and to restaurants. Was it a sin for a Christian to eat food that had been dedicated to an idol? It wasn't a sin, because an idol is just an object. However, the same principle that Paul discussed in Romans 14 applied to this situation as well.

If a Christian brother was convinced it *was* a sin, the brother who didn't believe it needed to be careful not to offend. If the one who believed it was a sin saw another brother eating at a temple restaurant, he might have thought, *That brother is sinning and yet calls himself a Christian.* It might have weakened his conscience and caused him to sin in some other way. So Paul wrote, "If food causes my brother to stumble, I will never eat meat again, that I might not cause my brother to stumble" (v. 13). We should always do what's best for others, even if it means sacrificing ourselves.

PSALM 33:1-11

PROVERBS 21:8-10

AUGUST 14

NEHEMIAH 7:61-9:21

Remember that it had been almost 150 years since Jerusalem was destroyed and the Jews were deported to Babylon by Nebuchadnezzar. The group that returned with Nehemiah had grown up in a foreign land, and now for the first time in their lives they were in the birthplace of their forefathers. Apparently during those 150 years, a common knowledge of the Law of Moses had diminished greatly. This is easy to understand when we realize that Nehemiah lived during a time when copies of the biblical books had to be transcribed by hand.

Did you notice the tremendous respect for the Law that the people demonstrated as Ezra read from it for about six hours? They stood up, and as Ezra blessed the Lord, they all answered, "Amen, Amen." Then they lifted their hands in surrender to the Lord and "bowed low and worshiped the Lord with their faces to the ground" (8:6). And when the people heard the words Ezra read, they began to weep. Whenever you find people who display such an attitude of respect, you are likely to have a revival. And so they did, and began by celebrating the Feast of Booths!

1 CORINTHIANS 9:1-18

This chapter flows naturally from the previous one where Paul taught the Corinthian Christians that they should set aside their own rights if exercising them hindered others from following God. Here, Paul listed several of his God-given rights and privileges that he relinquished.

Paul had a God-given right to expect financial support from the Corinthians. He proved this principle with many examples (see vv. 6-14). However, Paul had never taken up an offering for himself while with them in order that there would be no potential hindrance to the gospel. In other words Paul had relinquished his right so that he wouldn't offend some of them.

Many times we're guilty of thinking, *There's nothing wrong with what I'm doing, so if people are offended by it, that's their problem.* But God is calling us to a deeper love than that. Our ideal should be "Live to give."

PSALM 33:12-22

PROVERBS 21:11-12

AUGUST 15

NEHEMIAH 9:22-10:39

I'm impressed by the oath the Jews made to keep God's law. However, over the next few days we'll see that it is only a matter of time before they begin to break their covenant with God and a new reformation is needed.

1 CORINTHIANS 9:19-10:13

Paul continued to discuss the principle of relinquishing our rights to better serve others. He knew he was not under the requirements of the Law of Moses, because he was in Christ. The only law he was compelled to obey, as all Christians are, was the law of Christ (to love one another). However, when Paul was ministering to Jews, he followed the Law so he wouldn't offend them and thus hinder *them* from receiving Christ. When he was ministering to Gentiles, he didn't act like a law-keeping Jew, lest he misrepresent the gospel as being a strange list of rules and thus hinder *them* from receiving Christ.

When Paul referred to how he related to the weak, he was speaking of those who had "weak consciences." He was saying the same principle that applied to his treatment of Jews and Gentiles applied to the treatment of Christians with "weak consciences." In their presence, Paul would not eat meat lest he cause one of them to stumble. He became "all things to all men" that he might "by all means save some" (9:22).

We, too, should be willing to lay down our personal rights and preferences when someone's conversion or spiritual growth is at stake. Too often, we expect others to make adjustments for us while refusing to make similar adjustments for them.

Paul also explained why we need to read the Old Testament (see 10:1-11). Those stories were recorded for our benefit, so we wouldn't make the same mistakes the children of Israel did. The people of Israel experienced God's great deliverance, protection, power and provision, yet God wasn't pleased with most of them because they craved evil things, engaged in idolatry, acted immorally, "tried the Lord," and grumbled against Him. He had to discipline them.

Keep in mind that God is no different today. Praise God that He has promised not to allow us to be tempted beyond what we're able to resist. No one can ever say, "I had to sin," or, "The devil made me do it." God obviously allows temptations to come our way, but never more than He knows we can handle. He always provides a way of escape (see 10:13). That promise is essential for all Christians to memorize.

PSALM 34 1-10

PROVERBS 21:13

I don't think "the cry of the poor" is just for money. More than money, the poor need the gospel, and they have just as much right to hear it as anyone else. In James 2:5 we are told that "God has chosen the poor of this world to be rich in faith and heirs of the kingdom which He promised to those who love Him." One-half of the world's population has never heard Jesus' name. Most of them are poor. We shouldn't shut our ears to their cries.

AUGUST 16

NEHEMIAH 11:1-12:26

Tomorrow we will have completed the record of Old Testament Jewish history except for the book of Esther. The story of Nehemiah ended around 433 B.C. The Old Testament prophet Malachi prophesied during Ezra and Nehemiah's time, and his book will be the last one we read in the Old Testament. After his time, God was silent for four hundred years until Jesus' incarnation. So I want to congratulate you; you know more about Jewish history than the large majority of Christians.

1 CORINTHIANS 10:14-11:2

As Paul pointed out in chapter 8, part of the division in the Corinthian church centered on meat that had been sacrificed to idols. Those who ate meat sacrificed to idols were being slandered as unholy Christians by those who didn't (10:30). Those who didn't eat the meat that was sacrificed to idols were judged by those who did as "in bondage." Paul masterfully rebuked and commended both sides, then admonished them to walk in love toward one another. The primary principles are that all we do should be done for God's glory (see v. 31), and that we should endeavor not to offend any other person (see v. 32).

These last three chapters say a great deal about the specifics of walking in love. We should strive to "please all men in all things, not seeking [our] own profit, but the profit of the many, that they may be saved" (10:33).

Notice that Paul said, "Be imitators of me, just as I also am of Christ" (11:1). Could you, in good conscience, tell someone to imitate you?

PSALM 34:11-22

PROVERBS 21:14-16

AUGUST 17

NEHEMIAH 12:27-13:31

Today we read the last recorded acts of Nehemiah's governorship. True to their previous pattern, the Jews fell back into disobedience whenever they had no strong leader to make them toe the line. While Nehemiah was reporting back to the king of Persia, the Jews began to neglect their covenant with God. First, they stopped paying their tithes (see 13:10). Second, they began breaking the Sabbath (see 13:15). Third, they married foreign women (see 13:23). I've noticed that when Christians begin to backslide, similar signs show up.

Also notice that when the Jews began to disregard God's laws, they allowed their enemies to move in. Tobiah, who had caused so much trouble when the Jews were rebuilding the walls of Jerusalem, moved into a furnished apartment adjoining the temple at the invitation of Eliashib the priest! This is a perfect picture of Christians who disregard God's commandments: they open the door for the devil to move right in with them.

1 CORINTHIANS 11:3-16

In the Greek language, there were no words for "husband" or "wife," only for "man" and "woman." So we must ascertain from the context how those Greek words should be translated. In this passage, we're reading about husbands and wives. It's absurd to think that "every man" is the head of "every woman" based on verse 3. Only the husband is the head of his wife, and no other man can claim headship.

Paul was not saying the husband is the spiritual head of his wife. Jesus is the head of the body of Christ and therefore is the spiritual head of every member of the body, including women. If the husband were the spiritual head, then Christian women who have unsaved husbands would have spiritual heads who are under the dominion of Satan.

Paul was simply pointing out the correct family order. The husband is the head of the family. That doesn't mean he is to be a dictator. Instead, the husband should be the family's leader. A woman will gladly submit to an unselfish, Christlike man.

What about this discussion of having heads covered during prayer? Most of Paul's discussion deals with the customs of the day. A covering on a woman's head meant she was under the authority of someone visibly present. For a wife to take off her head covering in worship would have been disrespectful to her husband (see v. 5). An uncovered woman would be equivalent to a woman whose head was shaved, a practice of the Corinthian prostitutes.

On the other hand, men didn't wear head coverings in worship, and if a man did, it would have been considered disrespectful to his head, Christ.

Paul didn't say anything about these rules' being commands from God. The Corinthians were deferring to their culture's custom. Every culture has its customs, and you'd better know what they are or you'll embarrass yourself and offend others. Once again, this is an example of "becoming all things to all men."

Paul never said women are inferior to men. In fact, he supported the mutual dependency of men and women. The first woman originated from man, but every man since then has come from a woman (see v. 12).

PSALM 35:1-16

PROVERBS 21:17-18

AUGUST 18

ESTHER 1:1-3:15

The story of Esther is set in Persia during the reign of King Ahasuerus and took place sometime between the rebuilding of the temple and Ezra's return to Jerusalem. This dramatic story reveals one of Satan's final attempts to prevent the coming of Messiah. This story becomes even more interesting when you realize that the outcome affects your eternal destiny!

The Greek historian Herodotus described King Ahasuerus as a cruel, temperamental and sensual man. This account of him in Esther certainly agrees.

Ahasuerus was drunk when he asked Vashti to appear before his guests (see 1:10). Some commentators suggest the king ordered Vashti to stand naked. They base this upon his requesting that she display her beauty (see 1:11).

You may have wondered if you were reading the story correctly, but it is true that Ahasuerus gathered all the beautiful young virgins from his kingdom. He "tried each one out" for a night to choose Vashti's successor. One would be chosen queen, and the rest would remain in Ahasuerus's harem. As you read, Esther was his choice, yet she never revealed she was a Jew. (The Persian kingdom included many different nationalities, extending from the Middle East into Africa and southwest Asia.)

We parenthetically learn that Esther's uncle saved the king's life, and then we meet self-centered Haman. He was enraged that Mordecai would not bow down to him. (It was against God's laws for Mordecai to bow down to Haman.) The stage was now set for Haman's plot against the Jews and God's great deliverance through Queen Esther.

1 CORINTHIANS 11:17-34

If the cause of all of the Corinthian Christians' problems could be placed under one heading, it would be "selfishness." That's why Paul spent more time discussing the Christian's love-walk in this book than in any other. With an overflow of division, disagreements and self-centeredness in the Corinthian church, selfishness had even surfaced during the Lord's supper.

Apparently, those who arrived first didn't have the courtesy to wait for the others to arrive, and some used the communion elements as their supper. Some even got drunk from the wine. That's why Paul said, "Do you not have houses in which to eat and drink? Or do you despise the church of God and shame those who have nothing?" (v. 22). Many in the body brought wine and bread for everyone to use in partaking of the Lord's supper. But with some arriving first and eating and drinking everything, those who arrived later were left out. And they were arriving to discover that some people were drunk from the communion wine. What a church service!

The result of the Corinthians' selfishness was that they were eating the bread and drinking the cup of the Lord in an unworthy manner. Consequently, God had disciplined a number of the Corinthian Christians by permitting sickness and even death (see v. 30). How can we avoid God's discipline if we've been selfish? Simply by examining ourselves (see v. 28) and, if we find any selfishness, confessing our sin to the Lord (see v. 31).

However, if we find ourselves judged by God, we should remember that it's only because He loves us and wants us to share in His holiness. If God didn't arrest our attention through discipline, we might continue on our downward path of sin. Some Christians have such a serious problem that God must discipline them by allowing Satan to bring death. But again, it is only for their good. They will go to heaven, and God will no longer be dishonored.

The Lord's supper is a holy time, and we should treat it with reverence. If not, we can actually bring judgment upon ourselves when we partake of the elements.

PSALM 35:17-28

PROVERBS 21:19-20

AUGUST 19

ESTHER 4:1-7:10

Although Esther is usually viewed as the heroine of this story, I have to give my first applause to Mordecai. When Esther sent word to him that intruding upon the king's presence could easily mean death for her, he replied that she herself would not be exempt from annihilation and warned her that if she didn't act, God would bring deliverance from another source. That's faith. Mordecai knew that God wasn't limited to one plan.

One other thing I like about Mordecai is that he didn't presume to have God's will all figured out (see 4:14). If we had been in Mordecai's shoes, we might have said, "Esther, God spoke to me and showed me that He knew this would happen one day, and so He exalted you to be queen so you could bring us deliverance." Mordecai certainly recognized that was a possibility, *but he didn't claim to have a revelation when he really didn't have one.*

Although God is never mentioned in this book, we can certainly see Him working providentially as the story unfolds. It must have been God who kept the king from sleeping that one fateful night. I don't know if God pricked his conscience concerning the oversight of rewarding Mordecai's service or if the king thought that the reading of the official book of records would put him to sleep, but God had His hand in it!

1 CORINTHIANS 12:1-26

Apparently the Corinthians had also requested information concerning the operation of spiritual gifts. This chapter literally begins, "Now concerning *spirituals* brethren, I do not want you to be unaware." The word "gifts" is not part of the original text. Paul wanted to pass along information about the ministry of the Holy Spirit through us, not just the spiritual gifts.

In Corinth, the people had encountered the spiritual realm long before their encounter with Christianity, though only through demonic manifestations. This included "channeling"—that is, a *demon spirit* speaking through a human vessel. It's the demonic counterfeit of true prophecy given by the *Holy Spirit.*

Because the Corinthians had already been exposed to both channeling and true prophecy, there was some confusion about the gift of prophecy. Paul stated that no person under the inspiration of the Holy Spirit could ever say, "Jesus is accursed." On the other hand, no person under demonic influence could ever say, "Jesus is Lord" (v. 3). *This is only true during a time of spiritual manifestation.* Anyone can say "Jesus is Lord." But no demon speaking through a person could ever say, "Jesus is Lord." True gifts of the Holy Spirit will always magnify the Lord.

Paul then mentioned three aspects of "spirituals": gifts, ministries and effects or operations (see vv. 4-6). There is great variety in manifestations of the Holy Spirit, but one God gives them all. Each manifestation is for the good of the *entire* body (see vv. 6-7).

This was a principle the Corinthians needed to learn. Once they did, it would end their selfishness in how they related to ministries (such as in their conflict between followers of Paul and Apollos) and how they operated in the gifts of the Spirit. Thus, this twelfth chapter is also a greater lesson on walking in love.

The nine gifts can be divided into three categories: three gifts that *reveal* something (the revelational gifts), three gifts that *say* something (the gifts of utterance), and three gifts that *do* something (the power gifts).

The revelational gifts include the "word of wisdom," the "word of knowledge," and the gift of "discerning of spirits." The word of wisdom is the supernatural imparting of knowledge concerning the future. The word of knowledge is similar but concerns knowledge of the past or present.

Notice that these are *words* of wisdom and knowledge. Words are fragmentary portions of sentences. When God reveals supernatural information, He gives only a small portion. A person with the gift of the word of knowledge can't read people's minds or know everything about a person's past.

The gift of discerning of spirits is a supernatural ability to see into the spiritual realm. All visions fall under this category. A person with this gift might see demons, angels or even Jesus, as did the apostle Paul on several occasions (see Acts 23:11; 27:23-24).

The three gifts of utterance are "the gift of prophecy," "various kinds of tongues" and "the interpretation of tongues." The gift of prophecy is a message from God through an individual, spoken in the language of those present. The gift of various kinds of tongues is the same, except the message is spoken in a language unknown to the speaker. It requires the accompanying gift of the interpretation of tongues in order for those present to understand.

The three power gifts are the "gift of special faith," "gifts of healings" and "working of miracles." The gift of faith is a sudden supernatural impartation of faith to receive a miracle. When Daniel was thrown into the lions' den, it took the gift of special faith to sustain him (see Dan. 6). The gifts of healings are a sudden, supernatural ability to heal some sickness regardless of the faith of the individual who needs the healing. The working of miracles is a sudden, supernatural ability to work a miracle, such as dividing the Red Sea (see Exod. 14:21-31).

All these gifts work only as the Holy Spirit wills; we cannot turn them on or off (see v. 11). God may consistently use a person in a certain gift over a period of time, but no one ever possesses any of the gifts. They are given spontaneously, not continuously.

Once again, Paul broached the subject of walking in love, but this time in the area of gifts, ministries and operations of the Holy Spirit (see vv. 12-26). We are one body in Christ. There is only one Spirit who places us in that body and who imparts the various gifts and ministries as He desires. We all need the entire body. If my gift or ministry differs from yours, it doesn't mean we're in two different bodies. As in the case of the human body, there are many parts. All have different functions and are interdependent. If we were to heed Paul's instruction in these few verses, there would be "no division in the body," and all the members would "have the same care for one another" (v. 25). Thank God for every member of the body of Christ! Thank God they're not all like you or me! Or like your pastor or your church! We need each other, and we need to find our place and do our part.

PSALM 36:1-12

PROVERBS 21:21-22

AUGUST 20

ESTHER 8:1-10:3

Because a decree made by the king and sealed with his signet ring could not be revoked, Ahasuerus couldn't stop the enemies of the Jews from attacking on the designated day. However, he could decree that the Jews could fight back against their enemies. As a result, many people became Jews (see 8:17), and many others became the Jews' supporters. Notwithstanding everyone else's support, it's obvious God was supernaturally assisting the Jews in their battles throughout the kingdom. Even Ahasuerus was astonished when he learned of how many enemies the Jews had in Susa and of the great Jewish victory there. Recognizing the hand of God, he granted Esther's request of another day of battle in Susa and the hanging of Haman's already dead sons from the gallows.

Now you know where the Feast of Purim originated. It's still celebrated by the Jews. At that feast, the book of Esther is read aloud. If God is for you, who can be against you (see Rom. 8:31)?

1 CORINTHIANS 12:27-13:13

Today we have listed some of the ministries that are given to various members of the body of Christ. According to 1 Corinthians 12:29-30, there are those who have ministries of gifts of healings, indicating the gifts of healings operate through them frequently.

There is also a ministry of helps, given to those who are called to work behind the scenes.

The ministry of various kinds of tongues (see 12:28) is given to those who are called to use that gift frequently, although God might use anyone occasionally in one of the utterance gifts.

Paul's main purpose in listing these various gifts and ministries of the Holy Spirit was not to give us an exhaustive catalog, but to impress upon us the diversity that exists in "spirituals." All are not apostles. And all do not have a ministry in the gifts of various kinds of tongues or the interpretation of tongues. However, God wants to use us all in some way through a manifestation of the Holy Spirit. For further possibilities of what your gift or calling might be, see Romans 12:6-8.

When Paul asked, "Do all speak in tongues?" (12:30), he was referring to the public use of the gift of various kinds of tongues. *He was not referring to using the devotional ability to pray in tongues that every Spirit-baptized believer can exercise.*

There are several distinct differences between using the gift of various kinds of tongues and exercising the ability to pray in other tongues. First, the gift of various kinds of tongues can only be operated as the Holy Spirit wills and comes as a sudden inspiration. On the other hand, praying in tongues can be done often (see 14:15). Second, the gift of various kinds of tongues is primarily for use in a public assembly, whereas the ability to pray in tongues is primarily for private use (see 14:18-19). Third, the gift of various kinds of tongues is normally accompanied by the gift of interpretation so that the church can be edified by what's said. When we pray in tongues, however, usually our "minds are unfruitful" (see 14:14), which means we have no interpretation. Finally, through the gift of various kinds of tongues, God speaks to us. But when praying in tongues, we speak to God.

Now we have arrived at chapter 13, the great love chapter of this great love book. Notice that it sits right between the two chapters on "spirituals." Why? Because we can have faith to move mountains, operate in the gift of prophecy, and speak with tongues, but without love, we're nothing. Paul described *agape* love beautifully (vv. 4-8), but all of its attributes can be summed up in the word *unselfishness. Agape* love seeks the good of the receiver and does not give based on merit.

Prophecy and tongues will cease when "the perfect comes" (see 13:8-10). Some say "the perfect" refers to the completed New Testament, but God has not done away with any of the ministries or gifts, and He won't do so *at least* until Jesus sets up His kingdom on this earth. Right now we only "know in part, and we prophesy in part" (v. 9). When "the perfect comes, the partial will be done away" (v. 10). Obviously "the perfect" hasn't arrived yet or we would no longer have partial knowledge.

PSALM 37:1-11

PROVERBS 21:23-24

Our tongues cause most of our troubles. We think we're guarding our mouths if we don't use any curse words, but that's just the beginning. God wants us to clean out all gossip, all doubt, all complaints and anything else that doesn't minister to the hearers (see Eph. 4:29).

AUGUST 21

JOB 1:1-3:26

In our study, we have come across many references to God's testings. Still, some skeptics say that God never tests anyone. Job, who lived during the age of the patriarchs, was *severely* tested, and no one can say otherwise.

Why was Satan permitted to bring such calamity into Job's life? The answer is clear. God and Satan got into an argument about Job. God thought very highly of Job (see 1:8). Because Job was such an upright man, he was a prime target for Satan.

Satan accused Job of serving God only because of his possessions and health. God's permission for Job's testing should teach us that *God does not want us to serve Him just because of what He does for us.* How about you? If God suddenly stopped blessing you, or if He allowed Satan to take the blessings you already have, would you continue to serve Him?

Satan was permitted to kill Job's children, most of his servants, his oxen, donkeys, sheep and camels. What was Job's reaction? He worshipped God. He didn't praise God *for* his calamity. He simply recognized that it was the Lord who had given him all of his blessings and that he had no right to complain if God took them away. How would you have reacted if you had been in Job's place?

Apparently Job had no understanding of the devil's existence and character. He thought everything was God's doing (see 1:21). God *permitted* Job's possessions to be taken, but God didn't take them.

God pointed out to Satan that Job had done admirably in the first test. Satan suggested another test, so God allowed him to steal Job's health. Even with his skin covered with painful boils, Job didn't curse God. As the test continued, however, he did question God. (I can hardly blame him. Can you?)

Some have suggested that Job was responsible for "opening the door to Satan" through his own fear (see 3:25). But an honest examination of the first two chapters shows that Job's trials were a test permitted by the Lord. We cannot base our entire interpretation of this book on one verse in which Job said, "For what I fear comes upon me...." If so, we could just as easily read the verse in which Job says, "When I expected good, then evil came..." (30:26) and say that we can open the door to the devil by expecting good! Fear *can* open the door to Satan, but it is not appropriate to suggest that all Job's troubles were caused by fear.

Let's not make the same mistake that Job's three friends made when they thought they had figured everything out. As we study more about how God tests us, the book of Job will be easier to understand.

1 CORINTHIANS 14:1-17

The Corinthian church wasn't using the utterance gifts properly. The services were characterized by an overabundance of speaking in tongues. Because there was no interpretation, no one but the individual speaking was being edified. Paul instructed that the utterance gifts should teach the *entire* church. He encouraged them to seek the gift of prophecy with this goal in mind.

The ability to pray in tongues is primarily a devotional gift to be used privately. We should pray in tongues often, as we converse with the Lord throughout the day. This will "charge up" our spirits. I could never adequately express the blessing that tongues has been in my life. It helps me to respond to the Holy Spirit, because my spirit is active when praying in tongues (see v. 14). We can also sing in tongues by simply adding a melody to the utterances that escape our lips (see v. 15).

The gift of prophecy (what you would normally hear in church) is for "edification and exhortation and consolation" (v. 3). It sounds a lot like Scripture, but it doesn't contain any new truth except to those ignorant of the Scriptures. However, the gift of prophecy can also work with the word of knowledge or the word of wisdom. If you hear a prophecy that foretells future events, some combination of gifts is in use.

I'm convinced that we charismatics have much more to learn about 1 Corinthians 14. We need the Holy Spirit's help to find all the truth that's here.

PSALM 37:12-29

PROVERBS 21:25-26

AUGUST 22

JOB 4:1-7:21

This long section of Job records one part of the debate between Job and his friends. In their discussions, they tried to answer this question: Why is Job suffering? None of them had the correct answer. They didn't understand the character of God or the reality of Satan.

Job's friends thought they had God all figured out. They were sure that God blesses the righteous and punishes the unrighteous. That's a scriptural principle, but it isn't a complete explanation of suffering. If we follow their logic, anyone who is suffering must be sinful. Sometimes, however, people suffer because of their *obedience* to God.

Job himself had very little idea why he was suffering. Before all these calamities, he may have thought he had God figured out, too. Now he was experiencing great misery, yet he knew he was a holy man who walked according to God's commandments. So he started questioning God's justice, fairness and love. By the end of the book God rebukes Job and his friends for their various faulty assumptions.

None of Job's friends had any concept of a God who sometimes tests, although Job admits the possibility when he says, "What is man that Thou dost magnify him, and that Thou art concerned about him, that Thou dost *examine* him every morning, and *try* him every moment?" (italics mine).

Will God ever test you like He did Job? While I'm certain that you will be tested by God at some time, I don't know of any other case in the Bible that was as severe as that of Job.

When you do go through such a time, try to be balanced in your response. Acknowledge the possibility that God indeed can be testing you, but don't magnify every trial you experience as if it is a result of an argument between God and Satan. Don't allow yourself to be discouraged, but follow God's command to rejoice always. Trust in the Lord, and know that the trial is only temporary—it will pass. Job only suffered for several months (7:3) and came out with twice as much in the end! In the same way, your trials will mean certain victory if you hold fast your faith.

1 CORINTHIANS 14:18-40

One commentator said, "Paul took a very dim view of speaking in tongues because he said that he would rather speak five words in an intelligible language than ten thousand words in an unknown tongue" (14:19). However, that commentator failed to read the first part of the sentence in verse 18 which says, "I thank God I speak in tongues more than you all; however, in the church...."

Paul was not diminishing tongues. He was correcting the Corinthians' abuse of them in church services. Individuals were speaking in tongues publicly, without interpretation, and no one was learning anything. Verses 21 and 22 seem to contradict the next two verses. In verses 21 and 22, Paul might have been quoting from a letter sent to him by the Corinthians. Then he might have been giving his responses in verses 23 and 24. He responded to written questions in other parts of this epistle (see 7:1; 16:1). I don't claim to have any final answer for this problem, however.

No matter what spiritual gifts or

manifestations were received in the assembly, they were all to be used for the common good. Obviously, the Corinthians' services were characterized by more Spirit-given manifestations than most churches allow today (see v. 26). Paul wasn't limiting the number of "messages in tongues" that could be spoken in a church service, but the number of *people* who could speak them (see v. 27). He stated that only one person should interpret each message in tongues. That eliminates "competitive interpretations." Otherwise any number of people who are used frequently in the gift of interpretation of tongues might try to give a "better" interpretation of what was said.

Keep in mind that we are talking about *interpretation* of tongues and not *translation* of tongues. This explains why a long message in tongues may be followed by a short interpretation, or vice versa.

Apparently, there were several prophets in the Corinthian church (see v. 29). New Testament prophets are ministers who preach or teach, not just laypeople who prophesy occasionally. They will have other revelation gifts and will use them frequently. If prophets receive a revelation, they must wait their turn to speak rather than speaking all at once (see v. 31). Paul said the "spirits of the prophets are subject to the prophets" (v. 32), simply meaning that prophets can control their utterances.

When Paul said, "You can all prophesy one by one," he meant all the prophets who were present (see vv. 29,32). He didn't mean every person in the assembly had the ability to prophesy.

The main problem was one of order. There was great confusion during the Corinthian services, because they were all doing what they wanted without concern for anyone else. People were speaking in tongues and prophesying at the same time. Also, some of the wives were asking their husbands questions during the teaching times (see v. 34). Some scholars have suggested that because husbands and wives sat in different sections of the church, the wives were shouting their questions to their husbands. Paul did not mean that all women should never say a word in church; he had already allowed them to pray and prophesy (see 11:5.)

Paul concluded this entire section on "spirituals" by saying, "Let all things be done properly and in an orderly manner."

PSALM 37:30-40

PROVERBS 21:27

AUGUST 23

JOB 8:1-11:20

Poor Job! His three friends believed he had committed some great evil, his wife had encouraged him to curse God, and his children, servants and livestock were dead. No doubt his entire community of friends considered him a sinner whom God was judging. He was living in misery with a disease that caused his entire body to be broken out in boils, and he wished he were dead. I'm glad this story has a happy ending!

1 CORINTHIANS 15:1-28

Chapter 15 is written to correct a serious doctrinal error that had crept into the Corinthian church. Some were teaching that there was no resurrection. The word *resurrection* refers to the physical body's coming back to life. The Bible teaches this will happen one day to everyone who has ever lived, righteous and unrighteous. For Christians, their bodies will be resurrected at the rapture of the church when Jesus returns. The spirits of those who have died in Christ go immediately to be with Him in heaven. When Jesus comes back, the bodies of those dead saints will be resurrected and rejoined with their spirits as they return with Jesus. Their bodies will be radically changed to what we call "resurrection bodies," which will be incorruptible. Those Christians who are alive at the time will also receive resurrection bodies (see vv. 51-57; 1 Thess. 4:13-17).

Denial of the resurrection is a major error because it makes the resurrection of Jesus impossible. If Jesus was not raised from the dead, there is no sense believing in Him (see vv. 16-19). That's why Paul emphatically asserted that Jesus was raised from the dead and that more than five hundred people saw the resurrected Christ during one of at least six different appearances (see vv. 4-8).

Jesus was the first to be resurrected and given an incorruptible body. Next will be those who are Christ's at His coming (see v. 23). Soon after will come the time when Jesus rules and reigns, abolishing "all rule and all authority and power" and putting "all His enemies under His feet" (vv. 24-25). This is a reference to the end of Satan's rule over the world and the end of death, both physical and spiritual (see v. 26). Finally, Jesus will deliver the kingdom to God the Father, who is the only One who will not be under Christ's authority during His thousand-year reign on earth (see v. 27). From then on, God the Father will rule over all.

PSALM 38:1-22

PROVERBS 21:28-29

AUGUST 24

JOB 12:1-15:35

Job never doubted God's existence or His power; he only doubted God's fairness to him. Job knew that as long as he was alive there was hope that God would answer him. He expressed his conviction that he would eventually be vindicated (see 13:15,18). However, he still thought God viewed him as His enemy.

The most difficult part of Job's suffering was God's silence. If Job had only understood the "why" of his difficulties, it wouldn't have been nearly as hard. Job thought God hated him, when in reality there was no one on the face of the earth of whom God was more proud.

1 CORINTHIANS 15:29-58

Verse 29 is difficult to interpret, but we can be certain Paul was not teaching that we can be baptized for dead people, thus insuring their salvation. Perhaps Paul was saying that some Corinthians had received salvation and baptism in order to be reunited eventually with Christian friends and relatives who had died in Christ. Or he may have been referring to Christians who were baptized in the place of other believers who had died unbaptized. I don't know, but this is the only verse in the Bible that mentions the subject.

Apparently some questioned the idea of a resurrection because of its practical difficulties (see v. 35). They wondered how a dead, decayed body could ever come back to life. Paul compared the process to the planting of a seed. The seed is dead when planted in the ground, but it comes to life and produces a more "glorious" creation. It's the same with our bodies. They are buried perishable but will be raised imperishable. Our new bodies will differ from the old bodies just as a new plant differs from the dead seed from which it grew.

But what about those who have been dead for centuries and whose bodies have completely decayed? What about those who were buried at sea, or those whose bodies have been cremated? It's very simple. It is impossible to destroy matter. You can alter its state, but you can't destroy it. For example, you can boil water and change it into steam, but you haven't destroyed any hydrogen or oxygen molecules. They're still out there somewhere. It's the same with the molecules that made up each now-dead human body. They're out there somewhere. At the rapture, God will reconstruct all those molecules from each individual body and form them into new bodies.

Part of the mystery which had been revealed to Paul was the details of the resurrection and information about the rapture of the church. Not all of us will die, but all of us will receive resurrection bodies. It will all happen in a split second at the last trumpet (see v. 52). At that time, physical death will no longer have any hold on us. The thought of dying will never be a concern again (see vv. 54-55).

PSALM 39:1-13

PROVERBS 21:30-31

"The horse is prepared for the day of battle, but victory belongs to the Lord" (v. 31). We can plan our works and work our plans, but without God, we won't succeed. Do we give Him the glory for all He has allowed us to accomplish? Apart from Him, we can do nothing (see John 15:5).

AUGUST 25

JOB 16:1-19:29

I'm sure you're beginning to notice the redundancy in this argument between Job and his friends. No one budged from his position, and the conversation grew hotter and hotter. Sarcastic remarks turned to insults as tempers flared. Eventually, they reached an impasse. Then God spoke, but we'll have to wait another week to read His words.

Job expressed a new level of trust when he exclaimed that he knew his Redeemer lived and that he would be vindicated before his accusers. He warned them that by passing judgment, they were in danger of being judged themselves (see 19:25-29). One thing we can learn from this story is never to pass judgment on another person; we never have the full picture God possesses.

1 CORINTHIANS 16:1-24

Paul's closing remarks in this section are self-explanatory. The whole letter is summed up in these words: "Let all that you do be done in love" (v. 14). If the Corinthians followed that one charge, all their church problems would be solved. If you and I followed that one charge, how many of our problems would be resolved?

Paul also gave instructions for the taking up of collections for the poor saints who lived in Jerusalem (see 16:1-4). It blesses me that an anointed man of God like Paul would consider gathering money for the poor as part of his ministry.

PSALM 40:1-10

PROVERBS 22:1

AUGUST 26

JOB 20:1-22:30

Job asked why experience didn't always line up with his friends' theology. Here he was, a righteous man, suffering terribly. What about all the evil people who lived securely and happily and who died peacefully? Just as Job's friends had somewhat overstated the *plights* of the wicked, Job somewhat exaggerated the *prosperity* of the wicked.

Job anticipated that the response to his question would be the standard theological line of that day: God will repay the evil man's sons after he is gone. Job asked how that was fair. "Let God repay him so that he may know it" (21:19b). More than his friends, Job recognized that God is merciful toward sinners while remaining just. We know that if an evil person is not repaid in this life, he will be in the next. But Job and his friends apparently had little understanding of the afterlife.

2 CORINTHIANS 1:1-11

Actually, 2 Corinthians could be named 4 Corinthians, because it was Paul's fourth letter to that church. In 1 Corinthians 5:9, Paul mentioned an earlier letter, making 1 Corinthians the second letter he sent them. Between 1 and 2 Corinthians, Paul had written another brief and to-the-point letter that caused him much anguish (see 2 Cor. 2:3-4). He eventually discovered that his third letter had put the Corinthian church back on course. This fourth letter expressed his relief and focused on a few matters that still needed straightening out.

Today's passage is only Paul's introduction, but in it we learn that Paul had suffered a great deal of persecution and had almost lost his life. He had also experienced the comfort of the Holy Spirit, however, thus enabling him to be a greater comfort to others (see 1:4-5). I'm sure you, too, have the greatest amount of empathy for people who are going through a difficulty you've already experienced. You know what it's like.

PSALM 40:11-17

PROVERBS 22:2-4

AUGUST 27

JOB 23:1-27:23

For the second time, we learn that Job suspected the "silent" God was testing him: "When He has *tried* me, I shall come forth as gold" (23:10*b*, italics mine).

Again, Job questioned why God seemed to ignore the evil deeds of the wicked. In 24:18-25, it appears that Job was quoting his friends' arguments and not expressing his own opinion since these verses contradict what he had been saying. Perhaps Job still believed in the reward of the righteous and punishment of the wicked, but he had his eyes opened to God's mercy.

Bildad's third and final speech was short and lacking any significant new revelation. All he could say was that no person can claim to be just before God, because all are sinners. That's true, but it didn't help Job.

Some see Job 27:7-23 as Zophar's

missing third speech because it matches the opinions of Job's three friends rather than those of Job himself. (Eliphaz and Bildad both spoke three times.) I think Job kept his faith in the justice of God but became less idealistic concerning the sure punishment of the wicked and blessing of the righteous. Once he experienced misery, he began to see how things really are. Justice would be meted out, but not always as surely and swiftly as Job's friends claimed.

Job was having severe doubts by this time, because his suffering didn't fit into any theological mold. His confusion was compounded by the fact that he was suffering and he knew he wasn't guilty.

2 CORINTHIANS 1:12-2:11

The opposition group in the Corinthian church had apparently accused Paul of being a vacillator. Hadn't he said he was going to stop at Corinth on his way from Macedonia (see 1 Cor. 16:5)? Apparently he had stopped at Corinth before traveling to Macedonia, but he hadn't returned yet as promised. He explained that he didn't want to come at such a delicate time (see 1:15-2:1). He knew his relationship with the Corinthians was hanging in the balance while they considered his words of correction. Rather than visit, Paul wrote an emotion-packed letter, which apparently moved the church to expel the leader of the opposition. Scholars assume Paul was speaking of this man in 2 Corinthians 2:5-11. (Some think it was the incestuous man of 1 Cor. 5:1.) He now urged the man's restoration, certain of the church's obedient allegiance.

This is Paul's most personal letter, and in it we get a glimpse of the heart of this great man of God: "For out of much affliction and anguish of heart I wrote to you with many tears; not that you should be made sorrowful, but that you might know the love which I have especially for you" (2:4). As their spiritual father, Paul was committed to their well-being. It was for their own good that he had written such an intense letter. Thankfully, it had turned them around!

PSALM 41:1-13

PROVERBS 22:5-6

We shouldn't just suggest to our children the way they should go. The Bible says to *train* them. You train children by giving them no option but to obey! By repetitive training in the early years, we can establish habits that will last a lifetime. Pity the child whose Christian parents allow him to decide for himself if he wants to go to church lest he be turned off because they "forced religion on him."

AUGUST 28

JOB 28:1-30:31

Have you noticed the beautiful poetic form of this book? Job is considered by many to be one of the great literary works of all time. Job's narrative on the value of hidden wisdom in chapter 28 is one of the most beautiful passages in the entire book.

In chapter 29, we're allowed a look into Job's former life, and we gain further proof that he was a righteous man. God Himself praised Job as being upright, turning away from evil. Job had assisted distressed widows and orphans, had given to the poor and had personally brought law-breakers to justice (see 29:12-17). He had "wept for the one whose life is hard" and had "grieved for the needy" (30:25). As a result, he was respected by everyone.

Then he lost that respect. Not only had Job's three friends passed judgment on him, but so had everyone in his community. Job said they even spat in his face (see 30:10)! Job's test was also a test for all who knew him. Would they pass judgment or not? Apparently they all failed their test.

Still Job had no concrete idea of why he was suffering. He began to question God more and more. He even stated that God had become cruel to him (see 30:21).

2 CORINTHIANS 2:12-17

This short reading offers us further insight into events that had occurred since Paul sent his third letter to the Corinthians. Paul was so concerned about their reaction that he left Troas, where the Lord had opened a door for him to preach the gospel. He then crossed the Aegean Sea to Macedonia, hoping to hear about Corinth from Titus. Apparently he met Titus somewhere in Macedonia and heard the good news that the church had repented as a result of Paul's strong letter. Paul rejoiced over the Corinthians' change of heart (see v. 14).

In ancient Rome, when a general returned from winning a battle, he would lead a procession through the streets. After the incense-bearers came the enemy captives bound in chains. To the conquerors, the incense was the smell of victory. To the captives, the incense signified death. Paul's analogy (see vv. 15-16) means that Jesus is our conquering general who is leading us in His triumphant procession. We who follow Him are like incense-bearers. We give off the fragrance of eternal life. But to those who reject the gospel, we are giving off an aroma of death. When they reject our message, they seal their doom.

PSALM 42:1-11

PROVERBS 22:7

This proverb is probably referring to borrowers who couldn't pay their debts and were forced to sell themselves as slaves to their creditors. That is not a normal occurrence in our modern culture. However, you may have felt somewhat like a slave to anyone or any bank to whom you are paying off loans. This thought should keep you from needless borrowing that could ultimately enslave you!

AUGUST 29

JOB 31:1-33:33

Chapter 31 records Job's final defense—his oaths of innocence. We learn that he followed a strict moral code. He had determined not to lust after women (see v. 1). He walked in truthfulness and sincerity. He treated his servants with fairness and equality. He shared his wealth with the less fortunate. He had not placed money before God or served any false gods in his heart. He had not rejoiced at the calamity of his enemies. He had taken care of travelers. He had not hidden his sins from others as a hypocrite would.

Job had finally silenced his critics except for one angry young man. Elihu couldn't remain silent because Job had "justified himself before God" and had resisted his friends' arguments (see 32:2). Elihu's tirade isn't much more than a repeat of what had already been said: Job must be a terrible sinner.

2 CORINTHIANS 3:1-18

The church in Corinth was born out of Paul's ministry and was therefore his "living letter of recommendation" (v. 2). He possessed a supreme awareness of his great responsibility as their apostle. His ability in ministry came from the Lord (see vv. 5-6).

Paul compared his ministry with that of Moses, who was responsible to deliver the revelation of the old covenant to the people of Israel. That was a momentous time in history. Moses' face actually glowed when he spoke to the Lord and received the oracles to pass on to the people. Paul said the new covenant revelation carries *even more* glory. The old covenant law brought death when it was broken by Israel. But the new covenant revelation brings life to all who will believe (see vv. 7-8). The fading glory on Moses' face was like the eventual fading away of the old covenant. In contrast, the new covenant will be in effect forever (see vv. 10-11).

The veil on Moses' face was also symbolic of Israel's blindness to the full glory of the old covenant. In Christ, that veil has been torn away, and our hearts have been exposed to the full glory of the new covenant. Spiritually speaking, we can look in the mirror with an unveiled face and actually see Christ. He lives in us by His Spirit, and we are being transformed to be like Him!

PSALM 43:1-5

PROVERBS 22:8-9

AUGUST 30

JOB 34:1-36:33

Elihu continued his harangue with a scathing condemnation of Job (see 34:8,37). He tried to defend God's honor against Job's questioning.

More than any of Job's other "comforters," Elihu attacked Job for his wrong attitudes. Job's other friends concentrated on his supposed past sins. Elihu also stated that God used suffering to get the attention of those who were going astray. Job needed to be careful not to harden his heart toward God, lest he perish (see 36:7-15).

Before we read God's reply tomorrow, why not evaluate yourself? If you had been in Job's place, knowing only what he knew, how would you have reacted? Would you have abandoned your faith? Would you have stopped serving God, concluding there was no profit in obeying Him? What could happen that would cause you to doubt God's love and justice? *Unfortunately, many Christians have discarded their faith while suffering much less than Job.*

2 CORINTHIANS 4:1-12

Paul stated that the gospel is veiled to those who are perishing, "in whose case the god of this world [Satan] has blinded the minds of the unbelieving, that they might not see the light of the gospel of the glory of Christ, who is the image of God" (v. 4). When we pray for the lost, we make it easier for them to make the right choice.

The gospel is not veiled to Christians. Our living knowledge of Jesus is a treasure we keep in "earthen vessels" (our bodies). These vessels are fragile and aging, but God, who lives in us by the Holy Spirit, remains strong.

The strength of Christ in us does not exempt us from persecution. Paul, who was often persecuted, looked on this suffering as part of his identification with Christ (see Phil. 3:10). When we're persecuted, our bodies suffer, but the Spirit of Christ within us remains unconquered. Paul's body was afflicted, but his spirit was never crushed. His mind was perplexed, but his spirit never despaired. His body was persecuted, but Jesus in him never gave up. His body was struck down, but his spirit was never destroyed (see vv. 8-9). Jesus sustains us with His eternal life (see vv. 10-11).

As the eternal life of Jesus surges through us in response to persecution, it affects the lives of many around us. Revival and renewal can grow out of such times. That's why Paul could say, "So death works in us, but life in you" (v. 12).

PSALM 44:1-8

PROVERBS 22:10-12

Verse 10 is important for pastors. When there is strife in the church, we try to treat everyone gently to reduce tensions. But sometimes, when there are obvious troublemakers, the pastor should boldly drive them out.

AUGUST 31

JOB 37:1-39:30

You now have another reason to celebrate: you're officially two-thirds of the way through the entire Bible. Congratulations!

In today's reading, we hear God's view of things. You might have expected Him to say, "Now, Job, let me explain why all this happened. You see, the devil and I had a disagreement about you." If you did, you've been surprised.

God first asked a rhetorical question: "Who is this that darkens counsel by words without knowledge?" (38:2). Job was caught with his foot firmly in his mouth. God then asked a series of wonderful but unanswerable questions. They helped Job understand the severe limitations of his knowledge. If the whole world would consider those same questions, more people might seek and serve the living God. So often, we take the wonders of life on earth for granted and never stop to worship the Creator.

Later in this discourse, the Lord refuted Job's accusation concerning His "unjust" treatment of the righteous and the wicked (see 38:12-15). God upholds his righteousness and justice. He doesn't treat sinner and saint alike, as Job had suggested.

We also learn that God is the source of all wisdom: "Who has put wisdom in the innermost being, or has given understanding to the mind?" (38:36). The answer, of course, is God. When we begin to feel independent and proud, we should stop and remember that human beings can do only what God enables them to do.

2 CORINTHIANS 4:13-5:10

In 2 Corinthians 4:16, we have a beautiful description of the difference between the spirit and the body. Paul called the body our "outer man" and said it is decaying or growing older. The spirit is called the "inner man," and it is "being renewed day by day." Only Christians can truly say, "We're not getting older; we're getting better."

The persecution we endure as Christians is nothing in comparison to the reward we'll receive in heaven. Our suffering is producing an "eternal weight of glory" (4:17).

If our physical body is killed, we all have the guarantee of a resurrection body, our "dwelling from heaven" (5:1-2). When Paul said we're absent from the Lord while living in our present bodies (see 5:6), he was talking about seeing Jesus face to face.

Some day, we will stand before the Lord and give an account of our lives. Then we'll be repaid for what we've done, "whether good or bad" (5:10). God is not going to send us to hell for the "bad" things, but He will make us aware of them. Of course, sins we've confessed on earth will not be mentioned, because they were forgiven and forgotten (see 1 John 1:9). It's sobering to think we will one day stand before Jesus and review our lives. What will you say when He asks you, "Did you follow My plans for your life, or your own?"

PSALM 44:9-26

PROVERBS 22:13

SEPTEMBER 1

JOB 40:1-42:17

It's obvious the Lord was not happy with Job's finding fault in Him (see 40:2). According to the Lord, Job had reproved Him, annulled His judgment, and condemned Him in justifying himself (see 40:2,8). Lest we become too critical of Job, we should realize we're guilty of the identical sins when we doubt God's Word or question His justice.

Job was finally speechless, realizing he had spoken presumptuously. God helped Job understand how great He is by describing two of His created creatures—the hippopotamus and crocodile (see 40:15-41:34). It's not wise to tangle with either; we certainly don't want to tangle with the One who invented them!

Finally, Job saw his circumstances from a new perspective. He was wrong to doubt, question or accuse God. Job could simply trust that the Lord is great and knows what He's doing. God is always consistent. We, too, can always trust the Lord, even when we don't fully understand.

Did Job pass his test? Yes, because he never cursed God as Satan claimed he would. Job's fault was that he doubted God.

After God dealt with Job, He turned His attention to Job's three friends. It's interesting that the Lord said, "You have not spoken of Me what is right as My servant Job has" (42:7). Even though Job had said some things that were wrong, he must have said something right that contradicted his friends. I assume it was that Job's friends believed that all suffering was a result of sin. After all his suffering, Job knew there had to be more to it.

It's interesting that very little is said throughout the entire book about God's longsuffering and mercy toward those who deserve judgment, which is one reason Job's three friends' viewpoints were wrong. Their theology left no room for anyone to receive mercy from God. It's also interesting that Job's three friends almost experienced the wrath of God themselves, which they so heartily agreed came upon all the unrighteous (see 42:7-8). But the wrathful God showed mercy.

God does show mercy to those deserving His wrath. Notice also that God showed them mercy through an atoning sacrifice, pointing to Christ (see 42:8).

God restored Job's fortunes when he prayed for his friends (see 42:10). It took a double dose of forgiveness from Job for him to be able to pray for the ones who passed judgment on him. But when Job walked in love, the blessing began to flow once again. Unforgiveness can hinder God's blessings from coming into our lives.

Finally, Job was completely vindicated before his family and friends and before everyone who has ever read this book. Job received twice as much as he had prior to his test and lived 140 years after it was over. As Moses said in Deuteronomy 8:16, the only reason God tests believers is to do good to them in the end.

2 CORINTHIANS 5:11-21

We should ask ourselves if God's love is controlling us as it was Paul (see 5:14). Christ's love drove Him to die for us, and if we're controlled by His love, we too will lay our lives down for others. Essentially, there are only two options from which to choose—we either live for ourselves or live for Christ (see 5:15).

When we first believe in Christ, we die. That is, the person with the unregenerate spirit is replaced with a new nature. We become new creations in Christ (see 5:17). We should recognize ourselves and other members of the body of Christ as new persons.

Now that Christ lives in us, He wants to use us in His work of reconciling the world to Himself, just as He did when He was here in the flesh (see 5:18-19). We are Christ's ambassadors, representing heaven and the message of the cross (see 5:20). That message proclaims that Jesus became sin on the cross and that because of it, we who believe in Him are made righteous before God (see 5:21). Hallelujah!

PSALM 45:1-17

PROVERBS 22:14

SEPTEMBER 2

ECCLESIASTES 1:1-3:22

Ecclesiastes is not the easiest book in the Bible to understand. The overriding message, however, comes through loud and clear: without God at the helm, life is empty. The author is Solomon, who the Bible tells us lapsed from holy living to idolatry because his foreign wives turned his heart from God. Perhaps this book was written in his old age—after his life had gone full circle—and now he imparted to us what he learned through it all.

Before we seek to understand Solomon's observations of life, let's see what he concluded: "The conclusion, when all has been heard is: *fear God and keep his commandments,* because this applies to every person. Because God will bring every act to judgment, everything which is hidden, whether it is good or evil" (12:13-14, italics mine). Knowing that positive final note, it is safer to wade into Solomon's critique of life.

Solomon sounds like a person who has come through a mid-life crisis. He tried to find fulfillment in the acquiring of earthly wisdom and knowledge (see 1:13-18), through pleasure (see 2:1-3), through the acquiring of many possessions (see 2:4-8), and through sex (see 2:8). But nothing quenched his inward thirst. He found that everything is temporal. When death arrives, all life's accumulations are left behind (see 2:18-23).

That doesn't mean we shouldn't acquire wisdom and possessions or do anything that brings pleasure. Solomon's point was that true fulfillment can't be found in any of those things when they're an end in themselves. Life should be enjoyed, but as Solomon said, "For who can eat and who can have enjoyment without God?" (2:25). Therefore, we should rejoice and do good during our lives and see good in our labor (see 2:24, 3:12-13).

I haven't quit mowing my lawn because I know I'll just have to mow it again and someday I'm going to die. I confess that after I finish mowing my lawn, I usually sit down and admire the results. That isn't wrong. Not only can I take pleasure in my accomplishment, but I can also marvel at how my body works as I push the lawnmower. I enjoy part of God's creation as I breathe the air He created and feel the warmth of His sun!

2 CORINTHIANS 6:1-13

This short section was written by Paul to win back any lost affection from the Corinthians. He had proved that he truly was a sincere servant of Christ through all the hardships he endured, through his demonstration of Christlike character, through his knowledge of God's Word, by his demonstration of gifts of the Holy Spirit, and so on. His apostleship was authenticated by the contradictory ways people reacted to his ministry, for example, by glory and dishonor, by evil report and good report (see 6:8).

It was only to be expected that people would malign such a servant of Christ, but it was wrong for the Corinthians to believe the slanderous reports. It amazes me that we Christians will listen to reports from the news media concerning well-known ministers and believe what we hear. Those who are being used greatly by God are Satan's prime targets!

When we witness to our neighbors, we may be slandered in our neighborhoods. When a church is planted in a community, the pastor may be slandered in that community. When the gospel is proclaimed via television, the preacher may be slandered on television! Why? Because Satan wants to stop the spread of the gospel.

PSALM 46:1-11

PROVERBS 22:15

The word *foolishness* here could also be translated "stubbornness." Parents know their children will go to great lengths to get their own way. If it means crying for an hour or having a temper tantrum, many children persist so that their selfish desires are satisfied. The cure for self-willed stubbornness is the rod of discipline, better known as the board of education applied to the seat of learning.

SEPTEMBER 3

ECCLESIASTES 4:1-6:12

Solomon observed how rivalry motivates so much of humanity's doings. But what does it accomplish? In the end, one person can say he's better than the other. That's it. It's vain to have competitiveness as your motivation, but sad to say, that's the chief motivation of many people. Their desire to be first drives them to work long hours at the expense of priorities that should be more important. The workaholic is described in detail in 4:8.

Today we read that money can never satisfy. Solomon had seen people hoard money and knew the vanity in it (see 5:13). If a person lived a long, prosperous life but never was able to enjoy it, he would have been better to have never been born (see 6:1-6). For the third time, Solomon emphasized that people should eat and drink and enjoy themselves in their labor (see 5:18). That's simple to understand, but how many of us are really enjoying the thrill of daily living? We work harder to improve our lot, and when it's improved, we discover we've missed enjoying those blessings God gives freely to us all, like watching our children grow or watching the clouds roll by.

2 CORINTHIANS 6:14-7:7

This passage is a continuation of Paul's efforts to regain the full affections of the Corinthians. It seems to be implied that the person or persons leading the opposition party against Paul were not even saved. Thus, Paul's admonition was to avoid close association with unbelievers.

It is perfectly acceptable for Christians to have non-Christian acquaintances, but it's a mistake to be bound together with unbelievers. That would include not only marriage covenants, but also business partnerships. To do so would be like trying to join light with darkness or Christ with the devil (see 6:14-15).

Notice Paul used the words *righteous, light, Christ* and *the temple of God* in reference to believers. Those words illuminate who we are! We have been made righteous by Jesus' blood. We're the light of the world, according to Jesus (see Matt. 5:14). We're members of Christ's body, and God lives inside us by the Holy Spirit. It's hard to think badly of ourselves when we know how wonderful we are (in Christ, of course)!

Because God lives in us, we ought to be acting like it, and "cleanse ourselves from all defilement of flesh and spirit, perfecting holiness in the fear of God" (7:1). The one thing that has motivated me more than anything else to live holy before the Lord is the consciousness that He lives within me.

PSALM 47:1-9

PROVERBS 22:16

Is it wrong to give gifts to wealthy people? No, except when it's done in an attempt to buy their favor. Both he who oppresses the poor to make money and the one who tries to buy rich people's favor are motivated by greed.

SEPTEMBER 4

ECCLESIASTES 7:1-9:18

It almost seems as if Solomon contradicted himself and various sound biblical doctrines throughout today's discourse. For that reason, some commentators think Solomon wrote this book during a backslidden state. I will admit again that this book is difficult, so I simply follow the policy that we ought to thank God for what we do understand and not worry about what we don't. Remember that the main theme of this book is the vanity of human works.

With that in mind, it's easier to understand verses like 7:2. Let's face it, most people don't live as if they'll ever die. If more people would face up to the reality of their eventual death, more would accept the gift of eternal life through Jesus Christ.

Solomon sounded like Job when he stated that he had seen righteous men perish in their righteousness and wicked men prolong their lives in their wickedness (see 7:15). Beyond that, Solomon advised us not to be excessively righteous or excessively wicked (see 7:16-17).

How could he say such things? One possibility is that Solomon *did* author this book in somewhat of a backslidden state, but that negates the possibility that anything he said was inspired by the Holy Spirit. I think Solomon was simply remarking on what has always perplexed many of those who serve God: the suffering of the righteous and the seeming prosperity of the wicked. When Solomon advised against being overly righteous, he was probably referring to those who had become *self*-righteous.

Notice also that Solomon affirmed what we all hold to be fundamentally true: "Although a sinner does evil a hundred times and may lengthen his life, still I know that it will be well with those who fear God...but it will not be well for the evil man and he will not lengthen his days like a shadow, because he does not fear God" (8:12-13). Solomon also noted that God's judgment didn't always fall immediately upon wrongdoing, and therefore wrongdoers had the tendency to think they were getting away with their sins (see 8:11).

Solomon affirms that there is not a man on the earth who can claim to be perfectly righteous. When we are hurt by the sins of others, we should realize that we ourselves have been guilty of the same.

Solomon questioned the perplexities and enigmas of life throughout his discourse, but he concluded that although we can't understand everything, we can trust God. Regardless of what life brings, we know that God is for us and loves us. Eternity will reveal the whole picture, but until then, the wise person will trust and obey the Lord.

Notice that the man who had seven hundred wives and three hundred concubines now recognized that one wife is God's ideal (see 9:9)!

2 CORINTHIANS 7:8-16

Paul wrote of two kinds of sorrows—the world's sorrow and sorrow that is according to the will of God (see 7:10). The latter is a sorrow for unconfessed sin and leads to repentance and life. The world's sorrow is everything but that. For the Christian, there is only one thing to be sorrowful about—personal sin. Other than that, God wants us to rejoice in everything.

Let's take stock of our lives right now. If you're sorrowful about anything other than an unconfessed sin, you need to purge that sorrow out of your life, because it is not according to the will of God.

PSALM 48:1-14

PROVERBS 22:17-19

SEPTEMBER 5

ECCLESIASTES 10:1-12:14

In biblical times, right and left had somewhat different connotations from what they do in our society. The right represented that which is good and pure, whereas the left represented that which is cunning and impure. Jesus said, "Don't let your left hand know what your right hand is doing" (Matt. 6:3). At the great judgment of which Jesus spoke in Matthew 25, the blessed sheep are on the right and the cursed goats are on the left. Now you can understand why Solomon said that a wise man's heart directs him to the right, and a foolish man's heart directs him to the left (see 10:2).

What did Solomon mean when he said "money is the answer to everything" (10:19)? His comments must be taken in context with the surrounding verses. He lamented for the country that has a lad as a king and whose princes eat for the purpose of drunken revelry rather than for strength. Their work is neglected (see 10:18). In the minds of those kinds of leaders, wine makes their lives merry, and money is the answer to everything. Sounds like some of our modern leaders, doesn't it?

People have a tendency to think more about God in their old age, because they know their time of death is closer. But in today's reading, Solomon admonished young men to align their lives with God's Word, because God will bring every act to judgment (see 11:9, 12:14). Even youth were admonished to remember the Creator (see 12:1).

In 12:2-6, we have an interesting allegorical description of old age. The "watchmen of the house tremble" are probably the arms; the "mighty men who stoop" are the legs; the "grinding ones who stand idle because they are few" refer to the teeth; "those who look through the windows" who grow dim must be the eyes. For the elderly, the "doors of the street are shut as the sound of the grinding mill is low," probably referring to the impairment of hearing, yet they "arise at the sound of a bird, and all the daughters of song will sing softly." Perhaps Solomon was speaking of insomnia. In verse 5, "the almond tree blossoms," referring to the graying of the hair.

Regardless of what we didn't understand about this book, no one can miss the clearness of the conclusion. Every person should fear God and keep His commandments, because "the fear of the Lord is the beginning of wisdom" (Prov. 9:10). Furthermore, we must all someday stand judgment before God. As has been said, "You aren't ready to live until you are ready to die."

2 CORINTHIANS 8:1-15

This chapter and the next deal with the subject of receiving an offering for the poor Christians in Jerusalem. Why there were so many poor Christians in Jerusalem we don't know, but we assume that because Jerusalem was the Jewish stronghold, persecution against the Christians was very intense. Many Christians could no longer obtain jobs or purchase certain goods.

Apparently the persecuted churches of Macedonia had already sacrificially given a large contribution to the fund (see 8:1-4), and Paul expected the Corinthians would do the same. The Macedonian Christians didn't have to be begged to give, but actually begged Paul for the "favor of participation in the support of the saints" (v. 4). Talk about cheerful givers!

PSALM 49:1-20

PROVERBS 22:20-21

SEPTEMBER 6

SONG OF SOLOMON 1:1-4:16

Song of Solomon, obviously written by Solomon, is a love poem that has been interpreted in a number of ways. At the very least, it expresses the virtues of true love between a man and a woman.

At most, it is an allegory of the love Christ has for His church.

The major difficulty in interpreting the poem is that there are several speakers interjecting their thoughts throughout, and we don't always know who speaks when. Beyond that, the story the poem tells isn't always clear. We do know that the primary players in the narrative are Solomon, a young Shulammite maiden, and her betrothed shepherd-lover.

One common interpretation is that Solomon, attracted by the beauty of the Shulammite, abducts her and tries to win her affection. He is unable to do so because of her devotion to her intended. In the end, King Solomon allows her to return to her betrothed after exhausting all attempts to gain her love. If this poem is based on an actual occurrence, perhaps it was the Shulammite's devotion to her fiancé that opened Solomon's eyes (the one who was married to seven hundred) to the superiority of love that is faithful to one.

If we take the above interpretation, the book opens with the Shulammite speaking of her love for her fiancé, although she is now in the *king's chambers* (see 1:2-4). In 1:8-3:4, we find Solomon extolling her beauty, as she in return extols her fiancé's virtues and reminisces of their past days together. Longing to be reunited, she dreams of seeing him again.

Chapter 3:6-11 may be recounting the story of how Solomon met the Shulammite girl, and chapter 4 is most likely the bridegroom's description of her beauty. This is all subject to individual interpretation, but no one can argue that this is a beautiful poem, and it certainly dissolves the Victorian myth that God is prudish! He invented sex, which was obviously intended for more than procreation, but only to be enjoyed within the bonds of marriage.

2 CORINTHIANS 8:16-24

To collect the monetary gifts of the Corinthians, Paul sent Titus and several others to Corinth so that he could not be accused of misappropriation of funds. Paul realized he was accountable not only to do things properly in the sight of God, but also in the sight of men. We should be careful that money we give for charitable purposes is administered with accountability.

PSALM 50:1-23

PROVERBS 22:22-23

SEPTEMBER 7

SONG OF SOLOMON 5:1-8:14

Chapter 5:5-7 is usually viewed as referring to a dream of the Shulammite in which she imagined being reunited to her beloved—but the dream turns into a nightmare. Waking, she adjures the daughters of Jerusalem (probably the king's court or harem) that if they find her fiancé, they should tell him she is lovesick. They ask what makes her beloved so special, and she replies with the description of him in 5:10-16.

In chapter 6, Solomon once again flatters her, comparing her to his other queens and concubines. At this time he only had sixty of the former and eighty of the latter! He is enraptured by her beauty and graphically describes his carnal desires for her in 7:1-9. But Solomon is an intruder upon a heart already possessed by another. The Shulammite exclaims: "I am my beloved's, and his desire is for me" (7:10).

Verses 7:11-8:7 are viewed as the time

when the bride and her bridegroom are reunited and journey together to their home village in the countryside. The poor country girl resisted the rich king's advances because of her devotion to her betrothed shepherd. Her love for him cannot be swayed or diminished (see 8:7). This may be a reference to Solomon's promises to her—providing she would consent to join his *marriage club*. Apparently, he had promised her a huge vineyard worth thousands of shekels of silver, but she was contented with her small vineyard (see 8:11-12). Wasn't that a wonderful story?

2 CORINTHIANS 9:1-15

The Corinthians had previously promised a bountiful gift, and Paul wanted to make certain they were prepared for his arrival, because some Macedonian Christians to whom he had boasted of the Corinthians' generosity would be arriving with him. He sent Titus and others to arrive before he did to make sure he and they were not embarrassed (see 9:2-5).

Paul affirmed that those who give will be blessed by God in proportion to their giving (see 9:6). However, he didn't want them to give grudgingly, because God "loves a cheerful giver" (9:7). The reason God loves cheerful givers is that they're motivated by love and faith. Too many times, giving is motivated by compulsion and fear. The cheerful giver says: "I love to give money, because I love to help people, and I know God will bless me in return." The non-cheerful giver says, "I'll give, because if I don't, people will think I'm stingy. But I'd rather not, because when I do I have less for myself."

Paul not only affirmed that God will repay those who give, but also that God is more than able to supply all their needs abundantly so that they can continue to give liberally (see 9:10-11). What impresses me most is Paul's statement that their ministry of raising money for the poor saints in Jerusalem was "fully supplying" their needs (v. 12).

PSALM 51:1-19

PROVERBS 22:24-25

Have you ever noticed how easy it is to acquire the same bad habits as those with whom you associate frequently? All bad behavior, not just anger, is contagious, which is why it's wise to choose friends carefully. As Christian parents, we also need to be careful with whom our children associate.

SEPTEMBER 8

ISAIAH 1:1-2:22

To understand the prophetic books, it's vital to know the time setting of each prophecy and to whom the prophecies were directed. It bothers me when I hear contemporary preachers quoting the prophets, trying to apply their words to the church. Most of the prophets were forewarning rebellious people of impending judgment, so their prophecies would apply only to the modern reader who rebels against God.

We'll see plenty of gloom and doom as we finish reading the Old Testament, but we'll also gain a greater revelation of God's love and mercy, marvel at God's faithfulness to His Word, have our faith in Jesus' divinity strengthened, and learn of many events that will be happening in our future.

All the prophets we'll be reading prophesied during a period of 300 years, mainly during crises when Israel was declining, and the people were being exiled, or returning to their homeland. Isaiah was one of the five earliest prophets who lived in Judah during the reigns of Uzziah, Jotham, Ahaz and Hezekiah (see 1:1). Therefore, Isaiah's book parallels part of the books of 2 Kings and 2 Chronicles. Although Isaiah lived about 750 years before Jesus was born, he spoke accurately of His birth, His atoning death, and His millennial reign.

The first twelve chapters contain prophecies against Judah and its capital, Jerusalem. God had numerous points of contention with His people, and His judgment had already come in the form of an enemy invasion (see 1:5-7). Only Jerusalem stood, but like a "watchman's hut in a cucumber field" (1:8). Yet even in judgment, God had shown mercy (1:9).

How degraded had the people of Judah become? God compared them with the inhabitants of Sodom and Gomorrah. Their sacrifices had deteriorated into meaningless ritualistic obligations as they neglected the ethical and moral commandments of the Law. Jerusalem was full of murderers, ruled by "rebels and companions of thieves" (1:23). Bribes were the normal way of business, and orphans and widows were exploited. God was tired of their hypocrisy, yet there was still time to repent and receive His mercy. He offered them complete forgiveness if they would consent and obey, but He promised they would fall by the sword if they didn't mend their ways. We know, of course, that they didn't heed the prophet's warning and eventually endured a holocaust at the hands of Nebuchadnezzar.

God promised that after His judgment, He would restore Jerusalem, and it would be known as a city of righteousness (see 1:26). He did this, as we've already read in the books of Ezra and Nehemiah. However, God's promise to Jerusalem has its ultimate fulfillment during the millennial reign of Christ, which is described somewhat in Isaiah 2:1-4 (note the phrase in 2:2, "In the last days..."). During that time, Mount Zion will be raised up as "chief of the mountains" (2:2), because from there Jesus will rule all the nations. People will travel from near and far to learn the ways of God, and Jesus will "render decisions for many peoples" (2:4). There will be no wars anywhere on the earth during His reign (see 2:4)!

The prophets frequently seem to speak as if there were no such thing as time. That's probably because with God there *is* no time; He always has been and always will be. For example, from the restoration of Jerusalem, Isaiah jumped to the millennium. From a warning to the inhabitants of Jerusalem of impending judgment, Isaiah jumped to a warning of God's day of judgment upon the entire world (see 2:12-22). What was about to happen in Jerusalem was just a foreshadowing of what will happen to the whole earth. Just as Jerusalem was restored, so will the earth be after God's day of reckoning.

2 CORINTHIANS 10:1-18

From here to the end of the book, Paul faced his critics in Corinth and answered every challenge. Some had apparently declared that Paul was bold in his letters but weak when actually present (see 10:1). Paul's reply was that if they thought that was the case, they should wait until he arrived. Then he would change their opinion (see v. 11).

However, he hoped there would be no need to come wielding the rod of authority God had given him (see 10: 2,8). Paul warned the opposition that God had armed him with spiritual weapons, which included gifts of the Spirit, an apostolic anointing, and revelation of God's Word. The weapons of his warfare were divinely powerful (see v. 4).

Apparently some of the opposition group claimed authority by listing their qualifications and by comparing themselves with others. But Paul reminded them that his being the first to come and preach the gospel in Corinth gave him the greatest authority there (see 10:12-14). Paul also expresses his desire to take the gospel to regions even beyond Corinth, backed by their financial support (see v. 15). He recognized that God had given him a sphere of apostolic influence and that it wouldn't be ethical for him to take credit for what had been done by another person's labors, as some were doing to Paul's discredit. Truly, Paul's boastings were "boastings in the Lord" (10: 17).

PSALM 52:1-9

PROVERBS 22:26-27

Do you remember what it means to be one who "becomes sureties for debts"? It would be equivalent to the modern practice of cosigning a loan. Be careful!

SEPTEMBER 9

ISAIAH 3:1-5:30

Today we continue Isaiah's prophecies against Judah and Jerusalem. Isaiah 3 speaks of famine and deportation (see 3:1-3) that were yet to come if there was no repentance. Those who survived and were left behind would themselves be in a pitiful state of oppression and lawlessness (see 3:4-7). Children would rule over them (see 3:4), which actually came to pass when wicked King Manasseh came to the throne at age twelve (see 2 Kin. 21:1). God specifically condemned the injustice of Judah's leaders and the pride and immorality of Judah's women in 3:13-16. Their judgment would be severe (see 3:17-24).

Then in Isaiah 4:2, we jump to the future, when Jerusalem has been permanently purged of her sinfulness, and Christ, the "Branch," rules. The reference to the Messiah as the Branch points to Jesus, who is of the branch, or lineage, of David (see 11:1). And during that time, a cloud, like the one that led Israel through the wilderness, will cover Jerusalem like a canopy.

The parable of the vineyard in chapter 5 is easy to understand. Jesus used the same analogy during His earthly ministry (see Matt. 21:33). Once again, through Isaiah, God condemned various sins of His people and foretold the coming judgment.

Have you noticed the poetic quality of God's words in this book so far? God is a master communicator. The imagery He created is unsurpassed.

2 CORINTHIANS 11:1-15

This chapter authenticated Paul's God-given apostleship before his accusers in Corinth who were trying to rob him of his authority over the church. He didn't want to boast of his credentials, but he saw no other way to prove his point. His jealousy for the church was a godly, unselfish jealousy (see v. 2). Apparently Paul's critics were claiming to be apostles themselves, but Paul called them "false apostles, deceitful workers," and "servants of Satan" (11:13-15). It also seems that some had said Paul was inferior as an apostle since he wasn't on the Corinthian payroll. Paul justified himself by saying he didn't want to be a burden to the Corinthians but took his wages from other churches instead (see 11:7-9). This not only further proved his deep love for them, but it probably exposed the true motives of his opposition as well.

Paul had no problems with false humility but knew full well that God had made him someone special. He said explicitly in 11:5, "For I consider myself not in the least inferior to the most eminent apostles." He realized that by making such statements, his critics would accuse him of being prideful. We'll read tomorrow how he qualified his boast.

PSALM 53:1-6

PROVERBS 22:28-29

Rather than trying to be a *jack of all trades and master of none,* why not develop some skills that few possess? That's what sets some apart from the rest. They work on doing one thing well instead of doing several things in a mediocre fashion.

SEPTEMBER 10

ISAIAH 6:1-7:25

Isaiah's book was not recorded in chronological order but is rather a compilation of the visions and prophecies of his forty-year ministry. Chapter 6 tells us the story of his initial vision, when he was called to be a prophet. But don't skim over this passage, because the day is coming when we'll see God ourselves! Notice that Isaiah's first reaction to seeing the Lord was a realization of his sinfulness in comparison to God's holiness. Even the seraphim (angels) who stood above the Lord cried, "Holy, Holy, Holy, is the Lord of Hosts..." (6:3).

Isaiah's commission was simply to preach to unreceptive people (see 6:9-10). How would you like to have such a calling? God said the people would be insensitive until a complete devastation had taken place and the majority of people had been exiled (see 6:11-12). Isaiah never lived to see the Babylonian invasion and captivity he predicted more than 120 years in advance, but God knew the nation was past the point of no return. However, even after judgment, God promised a holy remnant of the Jewish race would survive. Yet even that remnant would face further devastation (see 6:13).

Did you notice that God said, "Who will go for *us?*" (6:8, italics mine). Once again, we have clear Old Testament evidence of the trinity.

Chapter 7 has its historical setting around 734 B.C. We have already read this incident—the attack on Jerusalem by the Israeli-Syrian alliance during the reign of evil King Ahaz in 2 Kings 16. God sent Isaiah to tell Ahaz not to be concerned about the plans of Rezin, king of Syria, and Pekah, king of Israel. Within sixty-five years, Ephraim (speaking of the ten northern tribes of Israel) "will be shattered, so that it is no longer a people" (referring to their destruction by Assyria, which came much sooner than sixty-five years). However, he also warned Ahaz that if he wouldn't believe, he wouldn't be established (see 7:9). But rather than relying on the Lord, Ahaz hired Assyria to attack Damascus, capital of Syria.

The Lord also said that Ahaz could request a sign from Him to authenticate Isaiah's message, but evil Ahaz piously waived his opportunity. So God gave a sign of His own choosing—a virgin would conceive a child named Immanuel, meaning "God with us"! What a sign! It was, of course, a reference to Jesus.

God also promised that before the child knew the difference between right and wrong, both Syria and Israel would be "forsaken" (7:16). God wasn't actually referring to the time when the child Jesus would be old enough to know right from wrong, because that wouldn't be for another 736 years! He was more likely saying something such as, "Within about two years time (the time it takes for a baby to grow to where it knows right from wrong), Israel and Syria will no longer present any threat." As God promised, the plans of Syria and Israel to defeat Judah and set up their puppet king in Jerusalem never came to pass. Within two years, Syria was crushed by Assyria, and Israel fell to Assyria over a period of twelve years, from 734 to 722 B.C.

2 CORINTHIANS 11:16-33

Paul obviously didn't enjoy having to list his qualifications for apostleship, but he felt he had no choice because of the "false apostles" who were undermining his authority. They had enumerated their qualifications. So did Paul, and even by natural comparison, apart from divine calling, he proved to be far more worthy of the Corinthians' allegiance.

PSALM 53:1-6

PROVERBS 23:1-3

In the world, they wine you and dine you for selfish motives, to get something in return. Beware!

SEPTEMBER 11

ISAIAH 8:1-9:21

Chapter 8 flows naturally from chapter 7, which contains a prophecy of the downfall of Syria and Israel. In today's reading, Isaiah and his wife "the prophetess" had a child whom they named "Maher-shalal-hash-baz." The name literally means "Swift is the booty, speedy is the prey" and was a prophecy in itself. Damascus and Samaria, the respective capitals of Syria and Israel, would be attacked by Assyria, and their spoil would be carried away before Isaiah's son knew how to say "Mommy" or "Daddy" (8:4). This helps us to better understand the prophecy we read yesterday in Isaiah 7:16, referring to the destruction of Syria and Israel before a child knew the difference between right and wrong.

We also read that during the Assyrian invasion of Syria and Israel, Judah would suffer as well, as the armies of Assyria were figuratively compared to the flooding Euphrates River in 8:6-8. We read the historical account of the Assyrian invasion of Judah in chapters 36-37.

The saddest part of this story is that Judah and Israel were not seeing God's hand in the Assyrian threat. As natural man does, they looked only at their circumstances. They were afraid of Assyria, but they should have been afraid of God (see 8:1213)!

If they had feared God, He would have become their sanctuary. But because they didn't fear Him, He became a striking stone and a stumbling rock as He said in Isaiah 8:14. In desperation, they consulted the mediums and spiritists to know what the future held (see 8:19), but God proclaimed that their destiny was dark.

Isaiah 9:1-7 is clearly a messianic prophecy, part of which is quoted in

Matthew 4:15-16. Jesus spent a great deal of time in the regions of the tribes of Zebulun and Naphtali, better known in His day as the Galilee. In 9:1, God was saying that even though the people of Zebulun and Naphtali were about to be invaded and deported by Assyria (they were part of the ten northern tribes of Israel), there were yet good things in store for them. This is one of the things I love about God. He is always encouraging, even in the midst of predicting judgment. Because of His great love, there is always hope! Jesus would walk in the midst of their land; He would be the light that shines in the darkness.

Notice in 9:6 that the Word of the Lord said, "For a child shall be born to us, a son shall be given to us." Jesus was 100 percent God and 100 percent man. He was God clothed in flesh. He wasn't born when Mary gave birth to that baby in Bethlehem, because He always existed. It was only His human body that was born that day. Therefore, Isaiah accurately described the incarnation when he said that the child was born, but the Son was given.

Part of Isaiah's prophecy will be fulfilled during Christ's millennial reign. Then the earth's government "will rest upon His shoulders," and the whole world will know Him as "Wonderful Counselor, Mighty God, Eternal Father" and "Prince of Peace." Aren't you glad He's all those and more to you *now?* Verse 7 sends a thrill through my spirit: "There will be no end to the increase of His government or of peace...from then on and forevermore."

In 9:8, we return from the glorious future to the fateful present.

2 CORINTHIANS 12:1-10

Still trying to win the complete allegiance of the Corinthians and authenticate his calling and ministry, Paul described a vision he had. Although Paul didn't specifically say that he was "the man in Christ" who had been caught up to heaven, it seems it must have been him in light of the context of this passage. While in heaven, Paul heard *inexpressible words* which he was not permitted to repeat (12:4). Beyond this one experience, Paul had many other revelations and visions, but apparently this one was the most spectacular.

Because of the "surpassing greatness of the revelations," Paul was given a "thorn in the flesh" that he said was a "messenger of Satan" (v. 7). The word *messenger* is the Greek word *angelos,* which is found 184 times in the New Testament. And 177 of those 184 times, it is translated "angel." So Paul's thorn in the flesh was most likely an angel of Satan. I make that point because many modern theologians suggest that Paul's thorn was some kind of disease, perhaps a disease of his eyes, malaria or epilepsy.

Wherever Paul traveled there was trouble. Now we have a better idea as to why. That satanic angel was following Paul wherever he went to stir up trouble and attempt to hinder the gospel.

Why was Paul given this thorn in the flesh? Paul said, "to keep me from exalting myself" (12:7). Perhaps God allowed a satanic angel to harass Paul to keep him humble, lest he be lifted up in pride because of his visions and revelations. So what did Paul do about his situation? He did what you and I would have done: he prayed about it three times.

God did not remove the satanic angel, but He reassured Paul that he had been given the grace to endure. He also revealed to Paul that when he was at his weakest, God could be at His strongest. We, like Paul, won't be exempt from Satan's attacks until we die. The more we're used by God, the more of a threat we are to the devil, and the more he'll try to defeat us. When Christians say to me, "I don't ever have any trouble with the devil," that tells me they aren't any threat to the devil, either! When trials come, on the other hand, we ought to rejoice at another opportunity to see God manifest His glory on our behalf!

PSALM 55:1-23

PROVERBS 23:4-5

This proverb doesn't say we shouldn't work hard to better our position in life, but it warns us of the vanity of making the accumulation of wealth our highest priority. Once you weary yourself amassing money, you'll have to weary yourself with how you can retain it, because as we just read, without warning fortunes can fly away.

SEPTEMBER 12

ISAIAH 10:1-11:16

Today we start off with more gloom and doom, but it's not just directed at Israel and Judah. Beginning with 10:5, God warned Assyria that her day of judgment was coming as well for two specific reasons. First, God intended to use the Assyrian armies to overthrow Israel and Syria, as well as other nations, but the Assyrians had overstepped their commission and planned to *destroy* many nations, including all of Judah and Jerusalem (see 10:6-11). Second, the Assyrians had become proud, taking credit for their victories that rightfully belonged to God.

Darkness comes before the dawn, and after the gloom of chapter 10 we're presented with the glorious promises of chapter 11. "A shoot will spring from the stem of Jesse....And the Spirit of the Lord will rest upon Him" (vv. 1, 2). Jesse was the father of David, so we have a promise of the Messiah's coming through Jesse's family.

Parts of this messianic prophecy have their fulfillment in the millennium. For example, there will be a complete change in the nature of animals, because "the wolf will dwell with the lamb, and the leopard will lie down with the kid" (11:6-9). Jesus will then be known as the "Prince of Peace." Believe it or not, there won't even be any fighting among Christians! That will be a bigger miracle than the one involving the wolf and the lamb. (Whenever I hear some misguided preacher say we're in the millennium right now, I'm tempted to ask how many bears he's got grazing with his cows!)

At that time, God will once again gather His scattered people from around the world to Palestine. Many see the present regathering of Jews to the independent nation of Israel as a foreshadowing of this promise.

2 CORINTHIANS 12:11-21

Winding up his defense, Paul made one final claim to his true apostleship—signs, wonders and miracles that were wrought through him (see 12:12). He promises again that when he returned, he would take no money from them in payment for his service (see 12:14-18). He longed to return this third time to Corinth and find a church that was truly walking in holiness and fully loyal to Jesus Christ rather than to some "false apostles."

PSALM 56:1-13

PROVERBS 23:6-8

This proverb is similar to the one we read in the first three verses of the same chapter.

The kind deeds of selfish people are designed only to gain a personal advantage. Many people appear outwardly kind but are inwardly evil (see v. 7). Beware!

SEPTEMBER 13

ISAIAH 12:1-14:32

Chapter 12 speaks of a song of praise that will be sung by the believing remnant who are restored to the promised land in the millennium. Some differ with that understanding of the timing, but I believe it's the best interpretation within the context. Notice that Isaiah 12:6 states, "Cry aloud and shout for joy, O inhabitant of Zion, for great in your midst is the Holy One of Israel." That's directed toward people living in Jerusalem when Jesus is living and ruling there.

Chapters 13-14 are not quite as easy to interpret, but in my opinion they're much more interesting. We learn in 13:1 that we'll be reading something that concerns Babylon, but the next thirteen verses clearly foretell God's great judgment on the whole earth. This is in keeping with the *style* of Isaiah's book—themes remain constant, while time periods fluctuate over thousands of years. In those two chapters, we jump from events that happened before the creation of Adam and Eve, to events that would happen within about 150 years of Isaiah's writing, to events that wouldn't happen for at least 2,700 years. The theme is consistent throughout: God judges sinful pride.

It's difficult to separate which verses are speaking of which judgment, so I take the position that verses applicable to both, I apply to both. Verses that apply to only one, I apply to only one.

For example, 13:10-11 clearly can be applied only to the great day of God's wrath upon the earth. On the other hand, verses such as 13:17, 19 can be applied to God's judgment upon Babylon.

The primary subject of chapter 14 jumps from God's judgment upon the king of Babylon to the judgment of Satan himself, beginning with verse 12. The Hebrew word for Satan, "the star of the morning," is Helel, which means "shining one." The King James Version translates it "Lucifer." The verses that follow could also apply to one of the kings of Babylon, who proudly proclaimed their divinity. They, like Satan, exalted themselves, and they, like Satan, would be humbled. We also realize that Satan is the energizer behind the Antichrist and all evil earthly rulers.

Finally, we have prophecies against Assyria and Philistia in Isaiah 14:24-32. This entire section of Isaiah, from chapters 12 through 23, contains numerous prophecies against Israel's neighboring nations. Those chapters will have little direct application to our lives, but they'll help us to better understand God's full character. He's a God of love, but He's also a *consuming fire.*

2 CORINTHIANS 13:1-14

With a threatening tone, Paul admonished the Corinthians to put their lives in order before he arrived for the third time. He told them to test themselves to see if they were "in the faith," because if they were, Christ lived in them (see v. 5). And if Christ lived in them, they should be acting like it!

This is a revelation that can transform any carnal Christian: Christ lives in us!

If we practiced His presence in our lives, what would we do differently?

PSALM 57:1-11

PROVERBS 23:9-11

SEPTEMBER 14

ISAIAH 15:1-18:7

Most of chapters 13-23 contain various prophecies against Israel's neighboring nations. Those words are not directed at the church, so beware of anyone who tries to make you believe they are. The only way those denunciations could be applied to a Christian is if that Christian were grossly backslidden and in danger of severe judgment.

One bright spot in the dark prediction against Moab is found in 16:5, another messianic promise: "A throne will be established in lovingkindness, and a judge will sit on it in faithfulness in the tent of David; moreover, he will seek justice and be prompt in righteousness." Sounds like Jesus to me!

If you're having difficulty understanding these particular prophecies, it's probably because there are so many names of cities or other geographical locations that Isaiah's contemporaries would have recognized. And some of the prophecies of judgment are repeated from earlier in the book because Isaiah didn't just sit down one day and write his entire book. Rather, it was compiled over a period of years as he would receive words from the Lord. When God repeated His warnings, it was only because of His great mercy; He wanted His hearers to repent.

GALATIANS 1:1-24

Looking at a map of Paul's journeys, you will discover that Galatia was not one city, but a region containing numerous cities in what is now central Turkey. We've already read of Paul's visits to some of those cities—Antioch, Lycaonia, Lystra, Derbe, and Iconium—in the book of Acts (see Acts 13:14-14:23; 16:1-6; 18:23). In all the cities of Galatia, Paul ran into severe opposition and persecution. In the Galatian city of Lystra, for example, Jews from Antioch and Iconium actually stoned Paul and left him for dead (see Acts 14:19).

We know that Paul made at least three visits to Galatia, and this letter was written in about 49 A.D, after his first journey, in response to some problems that had developed in the church. After Paul's departure, some Jewish legalists arrived and began teaching the Galatian Christians that if they wanted to be saved, they had to be circumcised and keep the other requirements of the Law of Moses.

Such a view is totally false, because it would mean that we can earn our salvation through works rather than receive it by grace through faith. Therefore, we have contained in this letter the best single theological argument against *salvation by works*. We assume this letter was written before the council of Jerusalem, which convened for the very purpose of resolving the same problem (see Acts 15).

Notice that from the start, Paul built a case for *his* gospel (the gospel of grace) by claiming that his apostleship came from the Lord. Without a long introduction and without mincing words, Paul fired right at the heart of the problem. The Galatians were abandoning the gospel of grace for a distorted gospel of works (see Gal. 1:6-7). Anyone who preached a gospel contrary to the one Paul delivered should be cursed.

No one told Paul what to preach except

Jesus Himself, by revelation (see 1:11-12). Paul didn't even confer with any of the apostles in Jerusalem for at least the first seventeen years of his Christian life (except for a two-week visit with Peter and James a little more than three years after his conversion; see 2:1). Again, Paul was simply authenticating the divine nature of his message, as opposed to the human nature of the contradictory gospel the Galatians were now hearing. Thank God we have Paul's words recorded in the pages of his letters to the churches!

PSALM 58:1-11

PROVERBS 23:12

SEPTEMBER 15

ISAIAH 19:1-21:17

Starting with a prediction of civil war in Egypt, God also foretold near-term events in Ethiopia and Assyria. Around 19:17 or 18, Isaiah began to speak of the final judgment upon Egypt and its subsequent turning to the Lord. At that time, Egypt will be deathly afraid of Judah and will swear allegiance to the Lord. That will be quite amazing, since Egypt is now a Muslim nation, and most Egyptians are anti-Israel. They will come to believe in Jesus as Lord and Savior, who is the champion and deliverer of 19:20. Not only that, but the Assyrians will one day serve the Lord as well (see 19:23-25). Ancient Assyria was located in the modern region of Iraq, also presently a zealous Muslim country.

In 20:2, God instructed Isaiah to go naked and barefoot for three years as a sign to Egypt and Ethiopia that their captives would go naked and barefoot as exiles. Isaiah probably wasn't a nudist for three years, however, but removed only his outer garment of sackcloth, and continued to wear his undergarments.

In Chapter 21, Isaiah predicted an alliance between Elam (Persia) and Media, who together would conquer Babylon. History records that occurred in 539 B.C.

Those prophecies aren't so startling to us, but can you imagine the effect they had on people in Isaiah's day who believed them? It would be equivalent to God's revealing what's going to happen to America, the Soviet Union, and China over the next two hundred years!

GALATIANS 2:1-16

Continuing to validate his gospel, Paul related his experience of traveling to Jerusalem for the first time to discuss his revelation with the apostles there. For at least seventeen years, Paul had been preaching that salvation comes by grace through faith, and that circumcision and keeping the law are not requirements for right standing before God. After consultation with James, Peter and John, Paul had no doubt that his message was identical to what God had given them. To prove he had received the sanction of the Jerusalem church at that time, Paul remarked that Gentile Titus, who was with him then, was not compelled to be circumcised as a result of the meeting (see v. 3).

However, Paul was apparently forced to rebuke Peter at a later date in Antioch when Peter temporarily yielded to the pressure of the Jewish legalists. Antioch was the first true Gentile church, and Paul and Barnabas ministered there for at least a year (see Acts 11:20-26).

PSALM 59:1-17

PROVERBS 23:13-14

Nobody enjoys spanking children, and even though kids wiggle like worms, they won't die when disciplined! The seriousness of the matter is summed up in verse 14—spankings can ultimately mean deliverance from hell, because the discipline sets a child on the right course.

SEPTEMBER 16

ISAIAH 22:1-24:23

Isaiah saw about a century into the future, to the time of Jerusalem's terrible fall before Babylon in 22:1-14. We've already read about it in 2 Kings 25 and 2 Chronicles 36. He lamented the fact that the people thought they were fighting against a foreign army, when in actuality they were fighting God and His decree (see 22:11).

Verses 15-25 of the same chapter deal with a more current event of Isaiah's time: the fate of two king's treasurers named Shebna and Eliakim. And in chapter 23, Isaiah foretold the fall of the Mediterranean port city Tyre. However, God promised a place in His millennial kingdom for Tyre, saying that one day her goods "will be set apart to the Lord" and "will become sufficient food and choice attire for those who dwell in the presence of the Lord" (23:18).

Thus ends the section of Isaiah referred to as the "prophecies to the nations." With chapter 24, we begin a new section that deals not with God's judgment on individual nations but with God's great day of judgment on the entire earth, and then His millennial kingdom. Those prophecies are obviously yet to be fulfilled.

If chapter 24 doesn't put the fear of God into you, nothing will! The whole earth will one day experience the cataclysmic wrath of God, including Satan and his demons (see 24:21). All the unsaved people who are alive at that time will be bound in hell. Then after a thousand years ("after many days"—24:22; compare with Rev. 20:5, 13-15), they will be judged and thrown into the lake that burns with fire and brimstone.

When will this great tribulation occur? Right before the beginning of the millennial reign of Christ (see 24:23).

GALATIANS 2:17-3:9

Paul couldn't have made his point more clear in 2:16: "Knowing that a man is not justified by the works of the Law but through faith in Christ Jesus, even we [speaking of the Jews] have believed in Christ Jesus, that we may be justified by faith in Christ, and not by the works of the Law; since by the works of the Law shall no flesh be justified."

We always need to be on guard against legalism creeping into our spiritual lives. Legalism doesn't mean holy living. It means trusting in one's own works to merit salvation. Legalism is adding anything to the requirements of John 3:16 for salvation. How many churches are guilty of that? Some say, "You must believe in Jesus and join our church to be saved." Others say, "You must believe in Jesus and be baptized according to our formula."

Legalism can also creep into our lives in more subtle ways—for example, when we doubt our salvation because of some sin we've committed. Those are all Satan's tactics to fool us into trusting that salvation depends on something we do or don't do.

We stand in Christ by God's grace alone. Our salvation was God's work from start to finish! What if we sin as

Christians (see 2:17)? It doesn't mean we lose our salvation. If it did, salvation is earned by our conduct. Sin breaks our fellowship with God, but not our relationship. As far as God is concerned, when Jesus died, we died. The Law has no authority over our lives because we're dead. Now Christ lives in us and through us. However, if we try to earn our salvation or think our conduct is what saves us, we have nullified the grace of God, and Christ's death was needless (see 2:21).

In chapter 3, Paul strongly rebuked the Galatians for being *bewitched* by false, legalistic teachers. They should have known better.

Just as salvation comes by faith, so, too, the miracles that occurred in the Galatian church didn't happen because of the Galatians' keeping the Law but because of their faith (see 3:5).

Finally, Paul pointed to the example of Abraham, who was justified by faith before he was circumcised and without the Law.

PSALM 60:1-12

PROVERBS 23:15-16

SEPTEMBER 17

ISAIAH 25:1-28:13

This is a beautiful portion of Isaiah's book. The psalm of 25:1-5 will be sung by those who are looking back at the tribulation and praising God for His deliverance. It gives us a glimpse of a great banquet that God Himself will prepare on Mount Zion. Some see this as the "marriage supper of the Lamb" referred to in Revelation 19:7-9.

The next two chapters are also set during the future millennium. They give a promise of a resurrection (see 26:19). This, too, agrees with the timing found in Revelation. We also find a prophecy foretelling Satan's doom (see 27:1).

Chapter 28 begins a new section of Isaiah in which God pronounced more woes upon disobedient Israel. Keep in mind that "Ephraim" was the dominant tribe of the northern kingdom of Israel. Remember, too, that all these prophecies were given to Isaiah over a period of years, and we're reading them within a few weeks. Apparently those drunken, sinful people complained that they were tired of God's messages, so He promised to teach them through another language—the Assyrians (see 28:11).

GALATIANS 3:10-22

Anyone trying to obtain salvation by keeping the Law will only be disappointed, because the Law promises a *curse* to those who don't obey it fully. Since no one but Jesus has ever kept all the requirements of the Law, every person who tries to be justified by it is guaranteed condemnation (see 3:10). As our substitute, Jesus redeemed us from the Law's curse and paved the way for us to receive the blessing God promised Abraham—that all the nations would be blessed through his seed, the Messiah. That promise to Abraham is received by us through faith (see 3:14). Through Christ, we, too, become Abraham's spiritual children, or seed (see 3:29).

The Law wasn't even given until 430 years after Abraham received his promise, which indicates the promise given to him had no relationship whatsoever with the Law! So why was the Law given if it had no bearing on anyone's salvation? It was given to reveal sinfulness, and thus to help its hearers recognize their need for a Savior (see v. 22).

PSALM 61:1-8

PROVERBS 23:17-18

SEPTEMBER 18

ISAIAH 28:14-30:11

What blesses me most about today's reading is that in the midst of forewarning Judah and Jerusalem of the coming holocaust, the Lord added encouragement—after judgment, the future was glorious. The promises of 29:17-21 foretell the millennial blessings.

In Chapter 28, God warned that there was no way Jerusalem's rulers could stop the coming destruction, even though they had made a "covenant with death" (28:15). That could be a reference to their attempt to find protection from Assyrian invasion by an alliance with Egypt. Remember that in chapters 19-20, we read of Egypt's impending fate at the hands of the Assyrians.

In chapter 30, God again warned Judah that the Egyptian alliance was not His plan. The only way Judah could be spared was through repentance. As we read in 2 Kings and 2 Chronicles, God did spare Jerusalem from Assyrian destruction because of the reforms under good King Hezekiah. However, the hearts of the people experienced no permanent reformation, and eventually full judgment arrived from Babylon.

The description of the people of Judah in 29:13 sounds like some religious folk in our day. Jesus ascribed the message of that verse to the Pharisees of His day (see Mark 7:6). "Ariel" in 29:1 is a term speaking of Jerusalem. The "Negev" (30:6) is the southern portion of Israel, including the Sinai Peninsula, which connects Israel with Egypt. God was saying that those who fled through the Negev into Egypt were wasting their time. You can't hide from God!

We find a reference to Christ in 28:16. Both Peter and Paul plainly declared that Jesus is that "cornerstone" who became a stumbling block to those who do not believe in Him (see Rom. 9:32-33; 1 Pet. 2:6).

GALATIANS 3:23-4:31

Under the old covenant, God's people were only His servants. They related to Him as any servant relates to a master. Under the new covenant, we are God's children, which means we relate to Him as a father. Obviously, the father-child relationship is far superior to the servant-master relationship.

Paul wasn't saying we're no longer servants of God, however, because we are. Children should obey their fathers. But, our relationship to God is not based solely on keeping His commandments. We're born of His Spirit! He is our Father! We're His children!

Our relationship with one another has also been changed. The old distinctions of race, nationality, social status and sex have all been erased, because we all fall into the one category of being children of God (see 3:28). Furthermore, we have now been "baptized into Christ" (3:27) and therefore qualify as "Abraham's offspring," which makes us "heirs according to promise."

We see again in 3:24 that the Law's purpose was not to save us but to point us to the Savior.

In Paul's day, slavery was common. And we used to be slaves under the domination of a harsh taskmaster, the Law. But when the right time came, God sent His Son Jesus, to buy us (redeem us) at the slave market (see 4:4-5). The price He paid was His life. Then He set us free and made us children of God!

Once you are a set-free child, why would you ever want to go back to being a slave? Yet that's what the Galatian Christians were doing. They were getting back under the Law, observing the various feast days, and so on. That's what *we* do if we try to earn or deserve our salvation or think we lose our salvation when we sin. We once again become slaves to a taskmaster that cannot be satisfied and cannot save us. *We stand in Christ by our faith, through God's grace.*

Paul's second analogy in this passage is a little more difficult to understand. In Genesis we read that Abraham had two sons, Isaac and Ishmael. Ishmael was born because of Abraham's works. On the other hand, Isaac was born supernaturally because of Abraham's faith. Ishmael's mother was a slave, whereas Isaac's mother was free. Paul allegorically compared Ishmael's mother to the covenant God made at Mount Sinai, that is, the giving of the Law of Moses. She and the Law only bore slaves. Isaac's mother, although not specifically stated, was compared to the new covenant. Both she and the new covenant produce offspring who are not slaves but full-statured children and heirs (see 4:21-31).

Finally, Paul stated that it "was because of a bodily illness" that he preached to the Galatians the first time (4:13). Was Paul sick? I don't believe so. The Greek word translated "bodily illness" is the word *asthenia.* It literally means "weakness," and doesn't always refer to sickness. For example, Jesus said in Matthew 26:41, "The spirit is willing, but the flesh is weak." The word "weak" there is this same word: *asthenia.* Could it have been translated "bodily illness" or "sickness"? Of course not. (See also 1 Cor. 1:25 and 1 Pet. 3:7, where *asthenia* is also translated "weakness" and couldn't possibly be translated "sickness.") It's evident something was wrong with Paul's body other than just being weak, though, because in 4:14 he said that his bodily condition was a trial to the Galatians that they could very well have loathed.

So what was wrong with Paul's body in Galatia? A likely answer is found in Acts 14:6-21, where we read how Paul was stoned and left for dead in the Galatian city of Lystra. How do you think a person looks and feels after he's been stoned and left for dead? I would imagine he would be weakened for a while and would be an awful sight to see.

PSALM 62:1-12

PROVERBS 23:19-21

SEPTEMBER 19

ISAIAH 30:12-33:12

While many in Judah were plotting to escape the Assyrian threat by fleeing to Egypt, God prescribed that "in repentance and rest you shall be saved, in quietness and trust is your strength" (30:15). Their deliverance would come only through repentance and then resting, or trusting, in the Lord. That's how our salvation and deliverance come as well. We repent, and then we trust in Jesus.

Note how the Lord used the words "rest," "quietness" and "trust." They're almost synonymous terms in this context and are always elements of faith. If we are truly trusting in the Lord, we, too, will have a "quiet rest" in Him. People who are always scheming and making a lot of worrisome noise in the process are doubters. But people who have faith possess "peace that surpasses all understanding." Their strength is displayed through their rest from worry and their quietness in the midst of trial.

God's heart of love is so wonderfully revealed in His words of 30:18, which were addressed to very sinful people: "Therefore the Lord longs to be gracious to you, and therefore He waits on high to have compassion on you. For the Lord is a God of justice: how blessed are all those who long for Him." Why did God permit calamity to come to Judah? Because He is just and holy. Why did He wait so long before allowing it? Because He is so compassionate. If Judah would only repent and obey, He would bless them abundantly with prosperity (see 30:23-25). We know Judah never did obtain the blessings of obedience that the Lord wanted her to enjoy, but God's promise is still good.

Those promises of prosperity were followed by what is obviously a millennial prophecy, when "the light of the moon will be as the light of the sun, and the light of the sun will be seven times brighter...on the day the Lord binds up the fracture of His people and heals the bruise He has afflicted" (30:26). Because of intertwined passages like these, many interpreters apply "the law of double reference" throughout Isaiah's entire book. We know that Israel will be invaded at least once more during the time of the Antichrist according to biblical prophecy (see, e.g. Zech. 14), and conditions will be similar then to those in Isaiah's day. Just as Jerusalem was suddenly delivered when surrounded by Assyrian armies, so, too, Jerusalem will be surrounded one day once again by her enemies and be miraculously saved. The "Assyrian" spoken of in 31:8 could very well be the Antichrist.

Although it is debated among Bible scholars, I assume that chapter 33 is a prophecy directed toward Sennacherib, the invading king of Assyria, and the Antichrist of the end times. We know from other scriptures that the Antichrist enters into a covenant with the nation of Israel and then breaks it after three and a half years. Here Isaiah spoke of "the destroyer" who "has broken the covenant" (33:8).

In summary, today we have a combination of a call to repentance with predictions of future judgment and blessing, all which may have been referring to more than one time in the future. We've also read a prediction of the reign of our Savior and soon-coming king in 32:1-8, 15-20. He is the "King who will reign righteously" (32:1). It will be during His reign that Joel's prophecy (Joel 2:28-32) of the outpouring of God's Spirit upon "all flesh" will be completely fulfilled. Isaiah saw that day as well in 32:15. God's Spirit has been poured out on the church, but not yet on "all flesh," mainly because not all people are born again and able to receive the Holy Spirit. At least at the start of the millennium, everyone will have experienced a baptism in God's Holy Spirit.

Passages like these cement our faith that the Bible is a special, timeless book. We will be reading it at least until the end of the millennium, because we'll always want to know what's going to happen next. And as time progresses, prophecies like the ones we've been reading today will become clearer.

GALATIANS 5:1-12

Is it possible to "fall from grace"? According to Paul, it is if a person who was once trusting in Christ for salvation starts trusting in works (see v. 4). Those people have "severed themselves from Christ." Paul said the person who receives the rite of circumcision is obligated to keep the whole law, and Christ is of no benefit to the person trying to merit salvation through works (see v. 3).

Those are strong statements, but can you see how applicable this book is to the modern church? Many church members will tell you that they hope God will let them into heaven because of their good works. Those church-going folks have missed the entire message of the gospel of Jesus Christ.

Paul fully expected God would deal with the person or persons who had been leading the Galatian Christians astray. He was personally so aggravated with those deceivers that he said in verse 12, "Would that those who are troubling you would even mutilate themselves." The word *mutilate* in the Greek means to "cut themselves off."

In other words, Paul was saying that he wished the circumcision-pushers of Galatia would castrate themselves! If a little cutting off of the foreskin is so beneficial, why not cut it all off? Then they could be really righteous before God!

PSALM 63:1-11

PROVERBS 23:22

SEPTEMBER 20

ISAIAH 33:12-36:22

There is no doubt that chapter 33 speaks of the future coming of Christ and the establishment of His kingdom, although not everything is clear. Jesus is the king whom we will see "in His beauty" (33:17). Isaiah also foretold that Jerusalem will have rivers and wide canals at some point in the future, "on which no boat with oars shall go, and on which no mighty ship shall pass" (33:22). There is nothing like that now in Jerusalem. Exactly what Isaiah was talking about is open to debate, but we do know that the New Jerusalem, which will come down from heaven after the millennium, was described by John as having a river "of the water of life, clear as crystal, coming from the throne of God" (Rev. 22:1). If that's one of the rivers Isaiah was talking about, we have the explanation of why there will be no boats on that river. Isaiah also told us that no one who lives there will be sick (see 33:24).

Chapter 34 is another prophecy against the end time nations and the final judgment before Christ's return. This is the "battle of Armageddon." The prophecy is particularly directed toward the land of Edom (Esau), which would be a portion of modern day Jordan. Chapter 35 explodes with joyous predictions of what wondrous works God is yet to perform in Israel. Much of the landscape in Israel is barren desert, yet God said here in Isaiah that someday the desert will blossom profusely. Some try to convince us that this prophecy is currently being fulfilled with the wonderful strides made in drip irrigation, but there's still a lot of desert! This prophecy speaks of the time when "waters will break forth in the wilderness and streams in the desert and the scorched land will become a pool, and the thirsty ground springs of water" (35:6-7). That sounds like a little more than the drips of irrigation pipes that presently empty the Jordan River.

Beyond that, it will be a time of miraculous healing, when "the eyes of the blind will be opened, and the ears of deaf will be unstopped....Then the lame will leap like a deer, and the tongue of the dumb will shout for joy" (vv. 5-6). Perhaps that will be when Jesus' promise will be completely fulfilled—that every believer will do the works that He did and even greater works (see John 14:12). If God doesn't just automatically heal everyone at that time, I assume He'll use us.

Those worthy, by Christ's blood, to enter that great city will have "everlasting joy" on their heads, and "sorrow and sighing will flee away" (35:10).

Chapter 36 should have been recognizable, as we have already read it twice, in 2 Kings and 2 Chronicles. This time, we have a better perspective, because we know what Isaiah has been prophesying over the previous years. This is the invasion of Sennacherib the Assyrian king, of which Isaiah had been warning Judah. God was using Sennacherib to judge the nations, but it was His intent only to discipline the people of Judah and bring them to a place of complete repentance. Sennacherib had become proud, thinking it was his own power that brought him repeated victories. He even went so far as to say the Lord couldn't stop him from destroying Jerusalem (see 36:18-20). As you might have expected, the Lord heard what he said and was about to rise to meet the challenge!

GALATIANS 5:13-26

Just because we've been liberated from the Law doesn't mean we have a license to sin. We're now under the law of the indwelling Christ—the law of love. Essentially, the entire moral message of Moses' Law can be summed up in that one command (see 5:14). Now that we have Jesus living in us, we have an inner drive to do what's right. Our spirits have undergone a radical transformation. We have a new nature!

All Christians discover they are two-natured, and those two natures are the flesh and the reborn spirit. They are constantly at war with one another. The reborn spirit will prevail in those who are sold out to Jesus and whose minds are renewed by the Word of God. Wrong desires do not emanate from the spirit but from the flesh. The spirit resists when the flesh engages in following its desires. If it does not, true regeneration has not occurred. Our re-created spirits make us feel guilty when we sin. That's the signal to confess the sin to the Lord.

If Christians follow the desires of their flesh, they will engage in acts of immorality and sensuality. They will be guilty of idolatry or putting other things before serving God. They might take drugs, be argumentative and hateful, throw temper tantrums, cause divisions, be envious of others, get drunk, go to wild parties, and so on (see 5:19-21).

Paul warned that those who practice such behavior will not inherit the kingdom of God. Note the word *practice.* Those who constantly, habitually do such things cannot be truly saved. Christians may temporarily fall into one of those sins, but when they do they will be absolutely miserable until they confess it and receive forgiveness.

On the other hand, Christians dominated by God's Spirit living within will display unselfish "love, joy, peace, patience, kindness, goodness, faithfulness, gentleness, and self-control" (5:22-23). All of us need improvement; fruit can grow. It is our duty to "crucify" our flesh (see v. 24). That hurts, but it's essential. Those who are led by the Spirit in their spirits have no need of any outward laws, because they're restrained by an inward law (see v. 18).

PSALM 64:1-10

PROVERBS 23:23

SEPTEMBER 21

ISAIAH 37:1-38:22

Having already read these stories twice of the life of King Hezekiah, there's not much more I can say. The outcome of the two incidents recorded here, the Assyrian invasion and Hezekiah's terminal illness, demonstrate the tremendous power of prayer. In response to Hezekiah's prayer concerning Assyria, God said, "Because you have prayed to Me about Sennacherib..." (37:21). I wonder what would have happened if Hezekiah had not prayed? And in the incident of Hezekiah's mortal illness, it's obvious the situation completely turned around because Hezekiah prayed.

God granted Hezekiah a sign: the sun's shadow went back ten steps on "Ahaz's staircase" to confirm to him that he would be healed and that God would deliver Jerusalem from Assyria (see 38:7-8).

While studying Joshua, I wrote there is scientific proof that the sun did stand still for a day at Joshua's command (see my comments on Josh. 9:3-10:43). I didn't tell the whole story at that point, however. The scientists who were figuring the future position of the planets had come up with a full missing day in elapsed time. One of the "religious fellows" suggested Joshua's incident as an explanation. Sure enough, when they ran their computers back to Joshua's time, they found a day missing since then—but not quite. Actually, there were twenty-three hours and twenty minutes missing from time. So they were still missing forty minutes from Joshua's time to the present. Then that same "religious fellow" told them this story about Hezekiah. Voila! The missing forty minutes could be biblically accounted for—when God made the sun's shadow go back ten steps on Ahaz's stairway.

GALATIANS 6:1-18

The church has been described as the "only army that kills its wounded," and unfortunately that's often the case. When people in the body of Christ make a mistake or fall to temptation and are discovered, too many times they're criticized and abandoned rather than loved and restored. You can always tell who the spiritual ones are by how they treat fallen saints. Truly spiritual Christians work toward the restoration of a fallen brother or sister, realizing they themselves might sometime need restoration (see v. 1).

Verses 6-9 speak of giving money to those who teach the Word of God. We have an obligation to feed those who spiritually feed us. When we give to a minister or ministry, we're "sowing to the Spirit." That is, we are contributing to the ministry of the Holy Spirit. But when we withhold what's due to the Spirit and spend the money on something for ourselves, we're "sowing to the flesh" (v. 8).

Sowing to the Spirit results in eternal life, or simply "life." Sowing to the flesh only results in "corruption": carnal, natural, selfish and temporary "benefits." Spending God's money on carnal pleasures is sin.

Some take Paul's words in verse 11, "See with what large letters I am writing to you with my own hand," as another proof that Paul had an eye disease. But I believe the large letters may simply have been his own style of writing. Perhaps to thwart others who may have tried to write in his name, Paul was calling attention to his way of writing. For example, Paul wrote at the end of his second letter to the Thessalonians, "I, Paul, write this greeting with my own hand, and this is a distinguishing mark in every letter; this is the way I write" (2 Thess. 3:17). There is no doubt that the Thessalonians had received false letters in Paul's name (see 2 Thess. 2:2).

This Galatian letter ends with a positive summary of the entire letter's message: circumcision is unimportant—what matters is whether a person is a new creation. "New creations" only boast in the cross of Christ, not in their works.

They are the "Israel of God," as opposed to those who were simply descended from Jacob.

PSALM 65:1-13

PROVERBS 23:24

SEPTEMBER 22

ISAIAH 39:1-41:16

This portion of Isaiah begins a new section that turns its attention away from the present threat of Assyria to the future threat of Babylon. Hezekiah pridefully and foolishly showed all his treasures to the envoys from Babylon; Isaiah predicted that the day would come when all those treasures were removed to Babylon. Hezekiah was thankful it wouldn't happen until after he was dead. Isaiah also promised him that some of his descendants would become officials in the palace of the king of Babylon (see 39:7). That promise was fulfilled in the stories of Daniel and his three friends.

Chapter 40 begins with words of comfort to Jerusalem that the time will come when she will no longer be in danger from war (see 40:1-2). This may have been fulfilled to a small degree when Cyrus, king of Persia, allowed the Jews to return to Jerusalem after seventy years of exile; however, that prophecy is obviously yet to be completely fulfilled.

According to Matthew, Mark, Luke and John, Isaiah 40:3-5 prophetically speaks of the ministry of John the Baptist, who was "the voice crying in the wilderness" (Matt. 3:3). The verses following tell of the coming of the Lord, but not just as a good shepherd, as Jesus did when He came 2,000 years ago (see John 10:11), but as a mighty, ruling king. He is a great God, as described in Isaiah 40:12-26. God's main point in describing Himself was to compare His overwhelming awesomeness to the mundane earthliness of idols (see 40:18-20).

Isaiah 40:31 should be memorized: "Those who wait for the Lord will gain new strength; they will mount up with wings like eagles, they will run and not get tired, they will walk and not become weary." God not only wants to provide spiritual strength, but He wants to provide physical strength as well.

Chapter 41 starts with a warning to the "coastlands," which may have referred to the coastal nations of the eastern Mediterranean. Their destruction was coming "from the east" (41:2)—from Cyrus, king of Persia, the great Jewish liberator. In the midst of warning the nations, the Lord once again comforted His people and promised them a time when they would be victorious over their enemies because of His help. We assume that this promise has end-time application, although it was somewhat fulfilled after the Babylonian captivity. God promised that "those who are angry at you...will be as nothing and will perish" (41:11). Indeed, Babylon and Assyria don't exist anymore.

EPHESIANS 1:1-23

Ephesus was a coastal city near the Aegean Sea in what today is the nation of Turkey. Paul established a church there during his third missionary journey. The church started with twelve disciples' being filled with the Holy Spirit and speaking with other tongues. He stayed in Ephesus about three years, during which time "all who lived in Asia heard the word of the Lord, both Jews and Greeks" (Acts 19:10). We know the church there was made up of Jewish and Gentile converts who had a difficult time accepting one another, which is one of the reasons Paul wrote this letter.

In Ephesus God performed "extraordinary miracles by the hands of Paul, so that handkerchiefs or aprons were even carried from his body to the sick, and the diseases left them and the evil spirits went out" (Acts 19:11-12). The seven sons of Sceva unsuccessfully tried to cast out a demon "by Jesus whom Paul preaches" (Acts 19:13-17). A great many people repented of their practice of magic and publicly burned their books worth "fifty thousand pieces of silver" (Acts 19:19). A riot started because the "idol business" suffered a great loss in profits after so many people came to Christ! There is no doubt that Ephesus and the surrounding regions of Asia Minor experienced a great move of God through Paul's ministry. Now he wrote a letter from a Roman jail to strengthen and admonish the thousands of new Christians.

In the first chapter, Paul listed numerous "in Christ" realities that can be applied to every member of the body of Christ. Stated simply, we are now joined together with Christ, and in God's eyes, everything that happened to Jesus happened to us. Notice how many times the phrases "in Christ" and "in Him" are found in the first thirteen verses, as well as the phrases "through Jesus Christ" and "in the Beloved." They all mean the same thing.

To start with, we have been blessed with "every spiritual blessing in the heavenly places" (1:3). We have been chosen "in Him before the foundation of the world" (v. 4). In my opinion this doesn't mean that some have been predestined to be saved while the rest are predestined to be damned. Keep in mind that these are "in Christ" realities. It is only because we have believed in Jesus and been baptized into Him that God sees us as chosen before the foundation of the world. If you take away the "in Christ" portions of these spiritual facts, you must not be saved, because you're not physically seated with Christ in the heavenlies right now (see 2:6)—you're on the earth reading this commentary! But in Christ you are seated in heavenly places, because that's where Christ is. Since Christ was chosen before the foundation of the world and we have chosen to believe in Him and therefore are "in Him," we, too, have been chosen from the foundation of the world.

God predestined us to adoption as children of God "through Jesus Christ" and has freely bestowed His grace on us "in the Beloved" (1:5-6). We now have redemption through Christ's blood and forgiveness of all our sins. We have obtained an inheritance (which is all yet to be realized) and have been sealed "in Him" with the Holy Spirit, who is given as a pledge of our future glorious inheritance in God's kingdom (see 1:7,11,13,14). Possessing all those things in Christ, all we need is the understanding of how to walk in what God has done for us and who we are in Christ. Consequently, Paul prayed that God might give the Ephesian Christians understanding of what the future holds, what they have in Christ, and how God will work on their behalf (see vv. 17-19).

The greatest show of God's power on behalf of we who believe is that He raised Jesus from the dead and seated Him at His right hand in heaven, "far above all rule and authority and power and dominion" (the various categories of demon rankings who inhabit the atmosphere) "and every name that is named, not only in this age but also in the one to come" (1:21). I think it's safe to assume that every demon power that existed tried to stop the resurrection and Jesus' journey through the atmosphere to heaven. But God was big enough to "pull it off." Now everything is under Jesus' feet. And because we're in Him, so, too, are all the demons under *our* feet. Jesus is the head of the church, which is His body, "the fullness of Him who fills all in all." That means that the church, corporately, contains Christ's fullness, and He lives in every one of us who are members of His body. Hallelujah!

PSALM 66:1-20

PROVERBS 23:25-28

SEPTEMBER 23

ISAIAH 41:17-43:13

In the beginning of today's reading, we have further promises from the Lord that He will one day change the desert of Israel into a land of lush vegetation (see 41:17-20). This must be referring to the millennium. The remaining verses of chapter 41 are a challenge from the God of the universe to the gods of men. They couldn't predict the future or even tell of the events of the past (see 41:22-24). Yet God foretold of one who would come from the north, whom He would later name as Cyrus, approximately one hundred years before the man was even born!

"The Servant" of whom God spoke in chapter 42 is Jesus. Isaiah 42:1-4 is quoted in Matthew's Gospel as a reference to Jesus (see Matt. 12:18-21). Those verses strongly state that Jesus would not come as a worldly conqueror, but as a humble, merciful servant. His ministry would extend beyond Jewish persons to all the Gentiles of the earth. He would be a covenant to the people and "a light to the nations" (42:6). He would open blind eyes and set prisoners free.

This passage also speaks of Christ's going forth like a warrior against His enemies (see 42:13). When that role of Jesus' ministry is fulfilled, there will be widespread devastation, as we read in 42:15 and in the book of Revelation.

The blind and deaf of Isaiah 42:18-25 are the unbelieving of Israel, also referred to as God's servant. God declared that He is the one who gave His people up as spoil to their enemies, but they didn't recognize the hand of God in their calamity (see 42:24-25).

Yet amazingly in chapter 43, God assures His people that their redemption will be accomplished. Notice how God speaks as if it has already happened, as He typically did. Even in judgment He was still with them, and eventually they would return from the lands of their exile (see 43:5-6). Then Israel would fulfill her calling to witness to the pagan nations that the Lord is the only true God (see 43:10-13).

EPHESIANS 2:1-22

Before salvation, we were all spiritually dead because of our trespasses and sins, just like the rest of humanity who are under the control of "the prince of the powers of the air"—Satan. All unsaved people have Satan's nature residing in their spirits (see 2:1-2). Their nature is all wrong, and they need a new one. Until they are born again, they can rightfully be called "children of wrath" (v. 3). Their lives are characterized by complete domination of the desires of the flesh. But because of God's great love for us, He has caused our spirits to be regenerated, and now we are spiritually alive (see 2:4-5). Beyond that, God has raised us with Christ and seated us with Him in the heavenly places (far above all evil spirits) "in order that in the ages to come He might show the surpassing riches of His grace in kindness toward us in Christ Jesus" (v. 7).

Our salvation is a result of God's grace and our faith. It's a gift, which means it can't be earned (see 2:8-9). God Himself is the one who has re-created us, and He has a divine destiny for us to fulfill, a ministry prepared for us (see v. 10). That one verse should be memorized and pondered by every Christian. Too many of us think that God's plan for us is simply to go to heaven when we die, and that we can pretty much follow our own course until we get there as long as we live reasonably holy lives. But that's not so. God has a divine plan for our lives that we need to discover and follow. There are certain good works he has specifically prepared for each one of us.

Verses 11-22 served to teach the Ephesian Christians and us that we should get along with each other in spite of our spiritual backgrounds. Jesus has placed us all into one body. In the early church, problems typically developed between antagonistic Jewish and Gentile Christians, who admittedly came from radically different backgrounds. However, the same principle applies to Christians of all ages, and it would be well worth the effort for us to learn this divine truth, since we are probably the world's most divided group! Paul admonished the Gentiles to realize that Christianity grew from Jewish roots, and he reminded both Jewish and Gentile Christians that Gentiles now have just as much of a claim on God as Jews do—through Jesus Christ.

PSALM 67:1-7

PROVERBS 23:29-35

SEPTEMBER 24

ISAIAH 43:14-45:10

At least seventy-five years before any Jews were taken into Babylonian captivity, God promised they would be released (see 43:14). About one hundred years before Jerusalem was destroyed, God promised that the city and temple would be rebuilt (see 44:26,28). Isn't God's love and mercy amazing?

Isaiah 44:28 and 45:1 contain an astounding prophecy that names the man whom God would use to liberate His people from captivity—Cyrus. Isaiah spoke this prediction about 140 years before it happened! It's possible that Cyrus himself came to have knowledge of Isaiah's prophecy, because we read in Ezra 1:2 that Cyrus claimed it was his divine commission from the Lord to release the Jews so that they might return and rebuild the temple in Jerusalem.

God also foretold Cyrus's conquests of the nations (see 45:1-3). His army easily defeated Babylon by diverting the course of the Euphrates River, which ran under the walls of Babylon, and then entered the city through the dry riverbed. Babylon fell to Persia in 539 B.C., during the days of Daniel.

Incidentally, when we read of the "Chaldeans," we're reading about the people of the Babylon. Chaldea was a part of southern Babylonia, and its kings came to power in Babylon. So the names "Babylonians" and "Chaldeans" are essentially synonymous.

God satirically exposed the foolishness of idolatry in Isaiah 44:9-20. No one could have used better logic than God: a man cuts down a tree and uses half its wood to bake bread, and the other half he carves into something to which he can pray!

Some versions translate God as saying

in Isaiah 45:6-7, "I...create evil." This is translated more accurately, "I bring calamity," speaking of His judgment on wicked nations. God doesn't create any moral evil and is not the author of sin.

EPHESIANS 3:1-21

I wrote of "the mystery" in Paul's letter to the Romans (see my comments on Romans 16:8-17). The mystery was essentially the revelation that was given to Paul by Jesus that we don't find anywhere in the Old Testament or Gospels. Paul said in today's reading that the "mystery which in other generations was not made known to the sons of men as it has now been revealed to His holy apostles and prophets in the Spirit" (v. 5).

Part of that mystery was the truth that Gentiles would have equal access to all the blessings of salvation (see v. 6). Paul's calling was specifically to the Gentiles, so it's no wonder that the Holy Spirit gave him that revelation. We do find hints in the Old Testament that God would bless the Gentiles through the coming of the Messiah, but Paul was given the fullness of the revelation. Paul said he was to preach the unfathomable riches of Christ to the Gentiles, and that he was to "bring to light...the mystery... in order that the manifold wisdom of God might now be made known through the church to the rulers and the authorities in heavenly places" (Eph. 3:9-10). That means the church is supposed to demonstrate to all the evil spirits God's age-old plan for their defeat and our victory.

Verse 15 speaks of our heavenly Father, "from whom every family in heaven and on earth derives its name." I like the King James Version which says, "of whom the whole family in heaven and earth is named." That means our Father has a large family—some who are in heaven, and some who are on the earth. Spiritually speaking, there are only two families in the universe—God's family and Satan's. It doesn't matter which church you belong to; what matters is which family you're in.

Paul's second prayer for the Ephesians is every bit as good as the first one, found in 1:17-19. Both were inspired by the Holy Spirit and are worthwhile for us to pray for fellow Christians. In this second prayer, Paul prayed that they might be strengthened with power through God's Spirit in the inner man. Paul also prayed that the Ephesian Christians would be able to comprehend the "breadth and length and height and depth, and to know the love of Christ which surpasses knowledge," that they might be filled up to all the fullness of God (3:18-19). There's no doubt that if we're going to be all that God intended for us to be, we need a revelation of His great love. The greater revelation of God's love we possess, the more faith in Him we will also possess. We naturally have faith in those whom we know love us!

Finally, in verse 20, we get a glimpse of how much power is actually within us through the Holy Spirit. With that power, God is able to do "exceeding abundantly beyond all that we ask or think."

PSALM 68:1-18

PROVERBS 24:1-2

SEPTEMBER 25

ISAIAH 45:11-48:11

Keep in mind that throughout the book of Isaiah, there are prophecies that were partially fulfilled within a few hundred years but will not be completely fulfilled until Jesus is physically reigning from Jerusalem. Key words to look for in this kind of prophecy are "everlasting" and "eternity," as we find in 45:17. It would be easy for those reading in Isaiah's day to think that when Cyrus permitted Judah to return to her homeland, it would usher in a time of blessing for Israel that would never end. But looking back, we know that wasn't the case. We can be certain that all God's promises will one day come to pass. For example, we know that in the future, Egypt, Ethiopia and the Arabs (Sabeans) will acknowledge the true God of Israel (see 45:14).

Some (like myself) take God's statement in 45:18 to further prove their belief that before Adam there was some kind of a creation that suffered God's judgment. We read in Genesis 1:1 that God created the heavens and the earth, but in the next verse we read that the "earth was formless and void." In Hebrew the word for "formless" is *tohuw.* It is the same word God used here in Isaiah 45:18 when he said concerning Himself, "He is the God who formed the earth and made it, He established it and did not create it a *waste place*" (italics mine). The words "waste place" are one word in the Hebrew—*tohuw.* So why was God saying here that He didn't create the world *tohuw* when Genesis 1:2 states the world became *tohuw* after God created it? The answer could be that He didn't originally create it "formless and void," but that it became that way after He judged the original creation. Therefore, there may possibly be a gap of millions of years between Genesis 1:1 and 1:2. God created the world to be inhabited, but it became a waste place after He judged the previous creation.

The same themes of the coming deportation to Babylon, the release of the exiles, judgment on Babylon, future glories for Israel, and the folly of idolatry fill the pages of today's reading. In chapter 46, God once again compared Himself to the idols of Babylon, who will become burdens on the backs of the captives of Babylon. In contrast to the idols that are carried by their worshippers, God carries His people from birth to old age (see 46:1-4).

All of chapter 47 speaks of the coming fall of Babylon, which again has a "double reference" in light of the future fall of Babylon that we will read about in the book of Revelation. We once again see God's purposes revealed in 47:6: "I was angry with My people, I profaned My heritage, and gave them into your hand. You did not show mercy to them, on the aged you made your yoke very heavy." Keep in mind that Isaiah was saying these things almost a century before Judah was deported to Babylon! God could see that Babylon would become proud of her own power, not acknowledging the power of God in her conquests, and that she would reap disastrous consequences for her cruelty, idolatry and sorcery.

Chapter 48 is addressed to God's own obstinate people for whom—for the sake of His name and His praise—He had delayed and restrained His wrath (see 48:9). They had been refined and tested in the "furnace of affliction." Now it was time for judgment to fall. God is truly a God of judgment, and He will not put up with the wickedness of the earth forever. The day of God's wrath is coming, but people take advantage of His patience, not realizing they're only storing up additional wrath for themselves.

EPHESIANS 4:1-16

The first three chapters of Ephesians provide a great deal of revelation concerning who we are in Christ, and the last three chapters offer us practical help that we might walk in the light of that revelation. There are four traits found in verse 2 that we should all possess:

"humility," "gentleness," "patience" and "forbearance."

Verses 3-6 admonish us to preserve the "unity of the Spirit," and Paul listed a number of reasons why we should. No part of God's plan of redemption makes provision for division. There is only one body of Christ, one Holy Spirit, one place where we are going to live when we die, one Savior, one faith, one baptism (into the body of Christ), one God, and one Father who is over us all and in us all!

There is no doubt that Jesus' spirit descended into the heart of the earth, according to verse 9. He spent three days there, and it wasn't until after His resurrection that He ascended into heaven. Many commentators assume that "the captives" spoken of in verse 8, whom Christ "led captive," are the Old Testament saints who were kept in "Abraham's bosom," but whom Jesus took to heaven at His ascension.

After His ascension, Jesus now (from heaven) gives various gifts to us who are on the earth (see v. 8). What kinds of gifts does He give? Because God's main concern is for our spiritual growth and service to Him, He naturally gives gifts that will help us in those areas. God's greatest gift to the church is His Holy Spirit. But after the Holy Spirit, God's best gifts to us are the apostles, prophets, evangelists, pastors and teachers (see v. 11). Paul was not speaking of the actual people who stand in those offices, but of the anointings that rest upon people that equip them.

What purpose do the five offices fulfill? God gives them to the body to equip us to serve, with the result that the body of Christ will grow and mature. The final result is that the church grows as much as possible numerically, because every member is properly functioning (see 4:12-16). Many churches and ministries have lost sight of this simple truth. The pastor's role is to equip the believer to serve and to mature spiritually. Too many Christians see their pastor as a hired hand who waits for a beckoning call to be a doctor, psychologist, mechanic, baby-sitter, and so on.

How does one know whether he or she is a mature Christian?

Very simply. Spiritual adults have found their place of ministry in the body of Christ (see v. 16). Children are not dependable and are easily distracted and carried away every time some new doctrine blows through the church (see v. 14). They're easily influenced by people whose motives are all wrong, because they, like children, are not able to discern the good people from evil ones (see v. 14). Those children are the first ones to leave a church whenever there is any strife or internal problem, because they'll listen to anyone who carries a rumor about their pastor or the church leadership.

PSALM 68:19-35

PROVERBS 24:3-4

SEPTEMBER 26

ISAIAH 48:12-50:11

Continuing on in chapter 48, we find more predictions of the destruction of Babylon by Cyrus (see 48:14-15) and the release of the captives of Judah shortly thereafter. God also lamented that there ever had to be a Babylonian captivity suffered by His people. Things would have been so much better for them if they had only obeyed in the first place (see 48:17-19).

In chapter 49, the theme of God's Servant surfaces once again, and it climaxes in chapter 53—the most well-known chapter of Isaiah. Only the context of each passage can determine who the "Servant" is, but God is usually speaking of either his people Israel or the future Messiah. In chapter 49, the description of the "Servant" seems to best fit Jesus. He is the one whose mission was first to the Jews (see 49:5). He is also "a light to the nations" (49:6)—a reference to His ministry to the Gentiles. Further, He is the one who was "despised" and "abhorred by the nation" (49:7). He became "a covenant of the people" (49:8). He is the one through whom all blessings will ultimately come to Israel—whom He has not forgotten (see 49:15).

Isaiah 50:4-9 is speaking of Jesus. He said, "I gave My back to those who strike Me, and My cheeks to those who pluck out the beard; I did not cover My face from humiliation and spitting" (v. 6). We have already read the fulfillment of those predictions in the Gospels. Isn't it amazing that Isaiah wrote his book seven hundred years before Jesus was born?

God also foretold the redemption of His people and the accompanying blessings (see 49:14-26), which could be applied to Judah's release from Babylon or to the final redemption of believing Israel from the nations to which they're now scattered. The latter seems to be a better possibility since God promised the result of His deliverance will be that "all flesh" will know He is the Savior (see 49:26).

EPHESIANS 4:17-32

One of the best descriptions in the Bible of unregenerate people is found in verses 17-19. First, their perception of reality is darkened, and their understanding is clouded. They're ignorant of what it means to walk in a relationship with God. Why are they so blind? Because their hearts are hardened. They have become callous toward God, and the result is that they give themselves to sensuality—that is, their motivation for living is to satisfy their senses. Because their conscience has no bearing on their life-style, their sensual search is never satisfied, and it ultimately leads them to perversion and greed.

As Christians, we are to lay aside our old life-style (maybe it would be better called a "death-style") and "be renewed in the spirit of our mind" (v. 23). That means we should have a completely different attitude toward how we live. We should be motivated to please our conscience rather than our flesh. We haven't turned over a new leaf but have been given a brand-new life.

Paul also admonished us to give the devil no opportunity. It's not God's responsibility—it's ours. How can we give the devil an opportunity? By lying, by staying angry longer than after the sun goes down, by stealing, by speaking unwholesome words, by allowing bitterness to hold us captive or by slandering others (see 4:25-31). Through any sin, we allow Satan the opportunity to work in our lives and circumstances, because we're obeying him when we disobey God.

Verse 29 needs to be memorized and then practiced: "Let no unwholesome word proceed from your mouth, but only such a word as is good for edification according to the need of the moment, that it might give grace to those who hear." How much of what comes out of our mouths is within the confines of that command? Everything we say should be helpful, uplifting or encouraging. If it's not edifying, God considers it "unwholesome."

Finally, we are commanded to forgive others "just as God in Christ has forgiven you" (v. 32). We have no right to harbor grudges against others when we have been freely forgiven of so much ourselves. How can you tell if you have truly forgiven a person? If you find yourself consistently dwelling on what someone did to you, you haven't forgiven. Of course the devil will try to draw you into unforgiveness by bringing to your mind wrongs that have been done against you. That doesn't mean you have unforgiveness. As Martin Luther said, you can't keep the birds from flying over your head, but you can keep them from making a nest in your hair!

PSALM 69:1-18

PROVERBS 24:5-6

SEPTEMBER 27

ISAIAH 51:1-53:12

We begin today with several references to the blessings that will be experienced by the redeemed during the millennium (see 51:1-11). Verse 3 promised that the wilderness of Zion will become like Eden, and her desert like a garden. In her (Jerusalem) will be found joy, gladness, "thanksgiving, and the sound of a melody" (v. 3). The law of God will go forth to the world, and His justice will be a light for the people (v. 4).

We know, according to 51:6, that the time will come when "the sky will vanish like smoke, and the earth will wear out like a garment, and its inhabitants will die in like manner." However, God's salvation will last forever! That's a reference to the time after the millennium when God creates a new heaven and a new earth. We'll read about it at the end of the book of Revelation. Jesus Himself said that heaven and earth would one day pass away. You will see it, but it won't be for at least another thousand years. Unfortunately, we aren't given a large amount of information about the time after the millennium in the Bible. Theologians refer to that time period as the "eternal state."

Once again, we find the Lord promising blessing after judgment (see 51:12-52:12). Those verses must ultimately be fulfilled in the millennium, because we read God's promise that Israel will never again drink the "chalice of His anger." Israel experienced God's judgment at least once more after the Babylonian captivity when, as Jesus predicted, Jerusalem was destroyed by the Romans in A.D. 70. Furthermore, in Isaiah 52:1, God promised that the uncircumcised and the unclean will "no more come into" Jerusalem. That will not be fulfilled until after the millennium, in the new Jerusalem, according to Revelation 21:27: "And nothing unclean and no one who practices abomination and lying shall ever come into it, but only those whose names are written in the Lamb's book of life."

Isaiah 52:7-10 will only be truly fulfilled in the millennium as well, when it is proclaimed to Zion, "Your God reigns!" Jesus is now reigning only in the lives of the believers, but then He will rule the earth. Then "all the ends of the earth may see the salvation of our God" (52:10).

Starting with Isaiah 52:13, we once again are reading about God's Servant—Jesus Himself. In the millennium, He will prosper and "be high and lifted up, and greatly exalted" (52:13). Isaiah said that Jesus' appearance was "marred more than any man, and His form more than the sons of men." (52:14). That is no doubt a reference to how Jesus' body was mutilated under the abuse and scourge of the Roman soldiers. But it was allowed in order that His blood would "sprinkle many nations" (52:15).

Reading chapter 53 is like reading a part of the New Testament, and if I didn't know it was inspired by the Holy Spirit, I would have thought it had been written 750 years later. This Old Testament chapter contains more specific details concerning Jesus than any other I know of. Jesus was the tender shoot that grew out of parched ground (see 53:2). Although He was destined to be king of the world, when He walked this earth 2,000 years ago, He had "no stately form or majesty that we should look upon Him" (53:2). Throughout His ministry, and especially while hanging on the cross, He was "despised and forsaken of men" (53:3).

Verse 4 states that Jesus has surely borne our griefs and carried our sorrows. The words *griefs* and *sorrows* would be better translated "sickness" and "pains" as proved by comparison with the Hebrew translation of those same words in Deuteronomy 7:15 and 28:61, as well as Job 14:22 and 33:19. Matthew, in quoting this same verse, translated it: "He Himself took our infirmities and carried away our diseases" (8:17). Matthew quoted Isaiah's promise as being fulfilled by Jesus when He physically healed Peter's mother-in-law as well as numerous other physically sick people (see Matt. 8:14-17).

Jesus was "pierced through for our transgressions, He was crushed for our iniquities; the chastening for our well-being fell upon Him, and by His scourging we are healed" (53:5). Isaiah predicted, "Like a lamb that is led to slaughter and like a sheep that is silent before its shearers, so He did not open His mouth" (53:7). Remember how Pilate was shocked when Jesus wouldn't defend Himself (see Matt. 27:13-14).

Truly Jesus was taken away by oppression and judgment (see 53:8). His trial was a travesty of justice. Jesus' grave was "assigned to be with wicked men," and "with a rich man in death" (53:9). Jesus was crucified between two criminals, and Joseph of Arimathea, a rich man, buried Jesus' body in his own specially cut tomb (see Matt. 27:57-60).

This section of Scripture even predicted Christ's resurrection! "He will see His offspring, He will prolong His days" (53:10). The only way this prediction could come to pass (along with Isaiah's prediction that the Messiah would die an untimely death) would be for the Messiah to be killed and resurrected!

The gospel message is clearly evident in this one chapter. In verse 11, God stated, "My Servant will justify the many, as He will bear their iniquities" (53:11). Jesus was "numbered with the transgressors,"—that is, crucified between thieves—and "interceded for the transgressors" (53:12). Some see this as His intercession for the one criminal who asked for forgiveness, but it really applies to all of us. Jesus is our intercessor who gave us the right to approach a holy God.

EPHESIANS 5:1-33

Paul admonished us to imitate God (see 5:1). We should ask ourselves in every situation: "What would Jesus do?" The outstanding character trait that will mark us then will be unselfish love (see 5:2).

Our lives should be radically different from those in the world. There should be no impurity, immorality or any greed even named among us (see 5:3). Those who are guilty of such things are considered idolaters by God, and they're bound for hell (see 5:5-6).

Paul stated that those who are filled with the Spirit will "speak to one another in psalms and hymns and spiritual songs, singing and making melody in your heart to the Lord; always giving thanks for all things..." (5:18-20). That means that those filled with the Spirit are fellowshipping with the Lord all day long, and in so doing, they speak forth by sudden inspiration "psalms" and "spiritual songs," as well as songs that are memorized. Spiritual songs are songs that are given by the Holy Spirit, and psalms would be the same without a melody.

Should we really "give thanks for all things" (5:20), even for wars and disease and tragedy? This is a difficult verse, since it doesn't seem to make sense to thank God for bad things caused by sin, Satan or the fallen state of our world. However, we can always give thanks to God *in* spite of adverse circumstances, because we know, by faith, that He is our deliverer and that He will "cause all things to work together for good" (Rom. 8:28).

The final portion of chapter 5 deals with husband and wife relationships. It really begins in verse 21, yet too many preachers take the text of their sermons on marriage beginning with verse 22. Verse 21 says, "And be subject to one another in the fear of Christ." That means all of us ought to be agreeable with one another, giving preference to each other, as true Christians. Verse 22 literally says: "Wives, to your own husbands, as to the Lord." The words "be subject" aren't in the original Greek but were added by the translators, which is why they're italicized in the Bible. Paul was simply saying that wives should get along with and be agreeable with their husbands.

I might add that this verse is not written to husbands, but to wives, so it's not granting permission for husbands to dominate their wives. Paul admonished "husbands to love your wives just as Christ loves the church" (v. 25). Jesus loves the church so much that He died for her!

Paul was not a woman-hater as some suppose, but was outlining God's plan for families. Anything but God's plan is a perversion. The husband is to be the head of the family, but not a dictator. No Christian wife wants a spineless, Milquetoast man as a husband. She wants a godly man whom she can trust, respect and honor.

Don't forget, husbands, that it's not your job to make your wife submit to you! Your job is to love her as Christ loves the church. When you do, you'll usually find her much more submissive. And wives, it's not your job to make your husband love you as Christ loves the church! Your job is to submit to him as the church submits to Christ. If you do, he'll start to treat you better too. Some wives live as if they have no husband, and it's no wonder their marriages are such a mess. They have allowed the worldly independent-woman spirit to motivate them, and their husbands resent their attitude. Husbands need to feel needed by their wives, and wives need to feel needed by their husbands.

PSALM 69:19-36

PROVERBS 24:7

SEPTEMBER 28

ISAIAH 54:1-57:13

Isaiah wrote almost three thousand years ago! The reason those words have survived so long is that they're God's own words, and through the centuries, spiritual people have recognized their pricelessness. I doubt that anyone in Isaiah's day ever dreamed that it would be at least thirty-seven hundred years before some of his predictions were fulfilled.

One of those predictions is found in

chapter 54. The entire chapter is once again speaking of the time that is yet to come—the millennium and beyond. It anticipates a time of great population growth in Jerusalem, when Israel's descendants will "possess nations" and will "resettle the desolate cities" (54:1-3). Don't ever feel left out when you read about the future blessings for the children of Israel, because as we read in Galatians, we Gentiles who are "in Christ" are now "the seed of Abraham." Therefore, I believe that any promise that applies to the future children of Israel applies to us as well. And none of the promises to future Israel apply to them apart from Christ.

I love the words of 54:7-8: "For a brief moment I forsook you, but with great compassion I will gather you. In an outburst of anger I hid My face from you for a moment; but with everlasting lovingkindness I will have compassion on you." From the context of this promise, we know it has greater application than just to the Jews' return from Babylonian exile; in the next verses, God promises He will never again be angry with His people (see 54:9-10).

There is no doubt that 54:11-17 speaks of the day of the New Jerusalem, because God promised, "I will set your stones in antimony, and your foundations I will lay in sapphires. Moreover, I will make your battlements of rubies, and your gates of crystal, and your entire wall of precious stones" (54:11-12). Are those words only to be applied figuratively? No! When John described the New Jerusalem in the book of Revelation, he said: "And the material in the wall was jasper; and the city was pure gold, like clear glass. The foundation stones of the city wall were adorned with every kind of precious stone. The first foundation stone was jasper; the second, sapphire; the third, chalcedony; the fourth, emerald....And the twelve gates were twelve pearls; each one of the gates was a single pearl. And the street of the city was pure gold, like transparent glass" (Rev. 21:18-21).

Isaiah 55:1-56:8 contains God's free extension of mercy to all who will accept His pardon. And throughout the chapter, God promised more wonderful millennial blessings to those who will come to Him. During the millennium, Israel will be chief among the nations, because her ruler will be Jesus. He is the One who will then sit on the throne of David and inherit the promises of Isaiah 55:4-5.

At that time, as we've already learned, nature itself will undergo a radical transformation. Not only the animal kingdom will be changed, but apparently the plant kingdom as well—we read of mountains shouting and trees clapping their hands in 55:12! God promised that "instead of the thorn bush the cypress will come up; and instead of the nettle the myrtle will come up" (55:13). (Maybe God will do away with flies and mosquitoes, too.)

When Christ rules the earth, it will mean blessings for all races, tongues and tribes, not just Jews. God specifically spoke to "the foreigners and eunuchs" and promised them a place in His kingdom (see 56:3-8). Then on Mount Zion in Jerusalem, God's temple will be "a house of prayer for all the peoples" (56:7). To be an "imitator of God," as Paul admonished us yesterday, we should all be playing some part in reaching people of other nations. Incidentally, Jesus Himself quoted Isaiah 56:7 when He cleansed the temple in Jerusalem (see Mark 11:17).

In Isaiah 56:9-57:13, we travel from the glorious future to the glum reality of the present. The sins of the people were hideous. They were mixing idolatry with perverted sexual rites and were even sacrificing their own children to heathen deities. Still, we end our reading with a positive note of future blessing upon those who repent: "But he who takes refuge in Me shall inherit the land and shall possess My holy mountain" (57:13).

EPHESIANS 6:1-24

Paul addressed children, fathers and slaves in this final chapter of Ephesians. Children are promised long, healthy lives if they're obedient to their parents—a good verse to teach to the next generation.

Fathers are instructed: "do not provoke your children to anger" (6:4). Possibly a better way of saying it would be, "Don't exasperate your children." Kids are kids and won't act like adults. But some fathers (and mothers) have a tendency to be too harsh with their children and expect from them behavior beyond their abilities. Consequently their children become exasperated and develop poor self-images knowing they will never measure up to their parents' expectations. Then they rebel and find someone else who will accept them as they are, such as their exasperated friends. All children need large doses of love and acceptance from their parents.

This doesn't mean that parents shouldn't expect their children's behavior to demonstrate a conformity to realistic expectations however. We read that fathers are also given the two-fold responsibility of raising their children in the "discipline and instruction of the Lord" (v. 4). That means their duty is to instruct their children in the ways of God and enforce their conformity to those ways.

It's interesting that nothing is said about the mother's responsibility in raising the children. The reason is that the father is to be the head of the family. Unfortunately, too many modern fathers have abdicated their God-given responsibilities.

Neither is anything said about the Sunday school teacher's responsibility to instruct the children. Not one word in the entire Bible speaks of Sunday school, and those who have relegated the responsibilities of teaching children about the Lord to Sunday school teachers are making a grave mistake.

We may not have slaves in our society today, but those who work for an employer can surely relate. The instructions Paul gave to slaves apply to anyone who works for someone else. We should be good employees, not just when the boss is present, but even when he's gone. Why? Because we're slaves of Jesus Christ, and He's always with us. We should do our work as unto the Lord, and He will reward us (see v. 8). Christian employers shouldn't try to motivate their employees by threatening them, but rather through positive incentives (see v. 9).

In verses 10-17, we find Paul's beautiful analogy of the Roman soldier's armor and the Christian's defense against the devil and demons. We are first admonished to "be strong in the Lord, and in the strength of His might" (v. 10). Notice he said nothing about being strong in our own strength. How can you be strong in God's strength? Very simply: know, believe and act upon His Word.

Notice that all the various parts of the spiritual armor have some connection with the Word of God. We are to gird our loins with the truth, which is God's Word. It holds the rest of the armor in place. Second, we are to put on the breastplate of righteousness. When we know we've been made the righteousness of God in Christ, we won't be deceived by the devil into thinking we have no right to approach God, God won't answer our prayers, or God may not be for us. Our feet are to be shod with the preparation of the gospel of peace. That means our feet should be taking us to people who need to hear the gospel. In sharing God's love with others, we're taking ground from the kingdom of darkness.

Also, we are to take up the shield of faith, by which we can stop all the flaming missiles of the evil one (see v. 16). When Satan shoots with "God won't answer your prayer!" or any other doubtful suggestion, we can hold up the shield of faith of God's Word and reply, "Thus saith the Lord...!"

Our sword is God's Word, and it can cut! Also, the helmet of salvation guards our minds from assailing doubts, fears and anxieties (see v. 17). Furthermore, because our battle is spiritual, one of our main weapons is prayer (see v. 18), and especially prayer that is "in the Spirit," because we don't always know how to pray in certain situations (see Rom. 8:26). The idea is that we should be victorious, not defeated, because God has given us everything we need to live as overcomers.

PSALM 70:1-5

PROVERBS 24:8

SEPTEMBER 29

ISAIAH 57:14-59:21

The rest of Isaiah's book is a mixture of condemnation for present sins and promises of future glories. Chapter 58 is a rebuke of the hypocrisy of Israel's religious rituals. Apparently the people had been going through all the outward motions of service to God, even to the extent of fastings, yet they questioned why God did not respond. His reply was that they broke other moral and ethical laws during their fasts and fasted for the wrong motives. Their reasons were selfish, but God desired that they fast and pray for the benefit of others who needed help from Him (see 58:6). He also wanted them to share some of their food, which they would have otherwise eaten, with the poor (see 58:7). If they would only line up with God's Word, instead of hypocritically and reluctantly observing its outward obligations and rituals, they would be blessed abundantly (see 58:8-14). God even promised them healing (see 58:8).

Chapter 59 contains the classic statement: "Your iniquities have made a separation between you and your God, and your sins have hidden His face from you, so that He does not hear" (59:2). That's the problem of unregenerate people today—they can't approach a holy God, because their sins have separated them. Their only answer is Jesus Christ, who has paved the way for the unrighteous to receive mercy and salvation. The remainder of chapter 59 is an enumeration of God's indictments against His people and a description of their present circumstances that stemmed from disobedience. They had reached a place where judgment was inevitable, and God no longer had an excuse to withhold His wrath, because not even a single person was interceding on their behalf (see 59:16). However, at the end of His wrath, God promised an eternal redemption through a Redeemer in Zion—Jesus (see 59:20).

Have you noticed that Paul was very familiar with Isaiah's book and alluded to its themes frequently in his epistles? One such example that correlates with what we just read yesterday in Ephesians is Isaiah 59:17: "And He put on righteousness like a breastplate, and a helmet of salvation on His head."

PHILIPPIANS 1:1-26

In my opinion, Philippians is the most uplifting and encouraging letter Paul wrote. Take your time as we read through it together.

You will recall that Paul and Silas were supernaturally led to Philippi by means of a vision to preach the gospel during the second missionary journey. There in the Roman colony of Philippi, located in modern Greece, a woman named Lydia became the first European convert to Christianity. It was also in Philippi that Paul cast out the spirit of divination from a slave girl. The result was that he and Silas were beaten and thrown in jail, because the slave girl's masters saw that "their hope of profit was gone" (Acts 16:19).

And it was in the Philippian jail that God sent an earthquake as Paul and Silas worshipped Him in the midst of their trial, resulting in everyone's chains falling off! Now in prison once again, probably in Rome, Paul wrote a letter to this church he loved so much and which had helped him financially in furthering his ministry. Keep in mind that Paul was writing to Lydia, to the formerly demon-possessed slave girl, and to the Philippian jailer and his family.

Paul began his letter by thanking the Philippian Christians for their "participation in the gospel from the first day until now" (1:5). That was an implication of their financial support, for which he will outrightly thank them at the end of the letter. When we support our church and missionaries with our money, we, too, are participating in the gospel. It should be viewed as our privilege!

Because Paul knew he was following God's plan for his life, he could always see God at work in his circumstances. Of course, it wasn't God who put Paul in prison, but it was God who led Paul to go to Rome and who allowed him to be cast into prison. Paul realized that his imprisonment had wrought "further progress for the gospel," because he was able to share his faith inside the prison with his guards, and also because the preachers outside prison were motivated all the more to preach the gospel, knowing Paul was prevented from doing so. No doubt when they saw his willingness to be persecuted for the sake of the gospel, they were ashamed of their own lack of consecration and repented.

Paul also mentioned that there were some who were preaching Christ from selfish motives, thinking they were causing him distress in his imprisonment. So we know that just as in our day, there existed a carnal attitude of competition among some ministers. Those selfishly ambitious ministers of Paul's day were using Paul's imprisonment as an opportunity to advance their own ministries as they competed for the top slot. However, Paul was not disturbed by it all. He was just happy that the gospel was being proclaimed, even if in some cases it was being proclaimed by preachers with wrong motives. Paul's only desire was to see the gospel progress, even if it meant his death (see v. 20).

For me "to live is Christ" (v. 21). What an amazing statement! Can you say that in your own life, to live is Christ? That means every word you speak, every plan you plan, every deed you do, every thought you think is first judged by the question, "Is this what Jesus would say, plan, do, or think?"

Paul also said that "to die is gain." Any Christian can say that! In fact, Paul said that to depart and be with Christ is very much better (see v. 23). Don't ever feel sorry for Christians who have died. They would never come back if they had the choice! They go immediately to be with Christ in heaven. It almost seems as if Paul himself was making the decision of whether to live or die. I'm glad he decided to live for a while longer, and I'm sure the Philippians were glad as well, because Paul promised to come and see them again (see v. 26). Notice how Paul expressed his faith—even though he was in jail he boldly stated, "For I know that this shall turn out for my deliverance through your prayers and the provision of the Spirit of Jesus Christ." (v. 19). What are you saying about your circumstances—what God says, or what the devil is trying to make you believe?

PSALM 71:1-24

PROVERBS 24:9-10

SEPTEMBER 30

ISAIAH 60:1-62:5

The promises of the blessings of the millennium and beyond apply to all of us who are in Christ. We read today an expansion of the theme of Israel's being exalted to chief among the nations under the kingship of Jesus. As previously discussed, before that time there will be a great awakening among many of the world's Jews, who will recognize Jesus as the Messiah. They will be gathered from all over the world to return to their homeland (see 60:4). The land will experience abundant prosperity as the wealth of the world's nations is poured into it (see 60:5-12), and the kings of the world will lead their processionals into Jerusalem to honor the King of kings. Israel will no longer fear any enemies, because they will all be subdued under Jesus' feet. And God will change the desert into an Eden, even as Jesus promised, "I shall make the place of My feet glorious" (60:13).

As we come to Isaiah 60:11, 19, it almost seems as if we're reading about the time beyond the millennium, because we have a reference to the gates of Jerusalem being open continually so that "men may bring to you the wealth of the nations" (60:11). Also in Isaiah 60:19, God said, "No longer will you have the sun for light by day, nor for brightness will the moon give you light; but you will have the Lord for an everlasting light."

We read similar promises in Revelation 21:23-26, the events of which take place after the millennium: "And the city has no need of the sun or of the moon to shine upon it, for the glory of God has illumined it....And the nations shall walk by its light, and the kings of the earth shall bring their glory into it. And in the daytime (for there shall be no night there) its gates shall never be closed; and they shall bring the glory and the honor of the nations into it."

It's also clear that people living at that time will continue to procreate, because God promised that "the smallest one will become a clan, and the least one a mighty nation" (60:22). Where will God put all those people? I don't know. Maybe He'll create some more worlds! Is anything too difficult for Him?

There is no doubt that 61:1-3 spoke of Jesus. Jesus quoted verse 1 and part of verse 2 as a reference to His own earthly ministry in Luke 4:18-19. Why didn't He quote the rest of verse 2 and verse 3? Simply because those verses weren't fulfilled during His earthly ministry, but they will be during the tribulation and millennium.

The remainder of chapter 61 to the end of today's reading once again predicts the future glories for Zion and its inhabitants. At that time, God will give Jerusalem a new name, and He will rejoice over her as a bridegroom rejoices over his bride (see 62:5). The parallel symbolism with the book of Revelation is very apparent, as the New Jerusalem is spoken of as "the bride, the wife of the Lamb" in Revelation 21:9. Get ready!

PHILIPPIANS 1:27-2:18

We gather from this section of Paul's letter that there existed some division in the Philippian church. We also learn that they were being persecuted to some degree, which Paul viewed as a sure sign of destruction for the church's opponents and a sure sign of salvation for the church (see 1:28). In other words, depending on which side of the persecution you stood, it either marked you as saved or unsaved.

Notice that Paul recognized the permissive hand of God in the Philippians' sufferings of persecution. Paul stated, "For to you it has been granted for Christ's sake [cause], not only to believe in Him, but also to suffer for His sake [cause]" (1:29). The early believers looked upon persecution as an opportunity to prove their faith and devotion to Christ. Persecution, although originating from the devil, can be used as a test by God.

In Philippians 2:1, Paul mentioned the phrase "fellowship of the Spirit." What many Christians call fellowship may be fellowship, but it is not fellowship of the Spirit. It is carnal fellowship, because conversation focuses on worldly things, and no one is really edified. Fellowshipping in the Spirit feeds the spirit that dwells within us.

If you're tired of hearing the phrase "walk in love," Paul offered us a different way to express that command: "Do nothing from selfishness or empty conceit, but with humility of mind let each of you regard one another as more important than himself; do not merely look out for your own personal interests, but also for the interests of others" (2:3-4). If we regard others as more important than ourselves, we will always act unselfishly. That's the same attitude Jesus displayed throughout His life and ministry (see 2:5-8). As a result of His humility, God exalted Him, just as He will you and me if we will humbly serve others.

The name of Jesus is now the highest name in the universe (see 2:9), and every knee should bow at that name—every knee on the earth, under the earth and in heaven. (There's no doubt from Scripture that there are three worlds.) Yet the world uses the highest name in the universe as a curse word. Why is it that you never hear anyone use Buddha's or Mohammed's name as a curse word? Because the devil is motivating all unsaved people, and Buddha and Mohammed are *on his team.*

When Paul admonished the Philippians to "work out their own salvation with fear and trembling," he was certainly not saying that our works earn our salvation. "Salvation" here refers to the practical working-out of our relationship to God and our obedience to Him. We need to "be saved" in every area of our lives. Some people who are saved from hell still need to have their tongues saved, their eyes saved, their feet saved and their minds saved. The practical working-out of our salvation should be our highest priority in life, to the point that we apply ourselves to it with "fear and trembling" (2:12). God is dedicated to our spiritual growth, for God "is at work in you" (2:13).

This letter is appropriately referred to as the epistle of joy. What a positive letter it is! According to 2:14, we should do all things "without grumbling or disputing." It's time for another check up. Are you a complainer? When we complain, our grumblings are not of faith and therefore are ultimately directed toward God.

PSALM 72:1-20

PROVERBS 24:11-12

OCTOBER 1

ISAIAH 62:6-65:25

Congratulations! You've just finished three-fourths of the entire Bible!

Today we again have a mixture of promised future blessings and warnings of imminent judgments. Isaiah 62:6-12 speaks of a time in Jerusalem that is yet to come, when there will no longer be any foreign invasions. Jesus is depicted as the one who has "trodden the wine trough alone," except that the grapes in His wine press are people (see 63:1-6). Just as their garments become splattered with grape juice, so Jesus' garments are red from the blood of the wicked. This is hardly a description of the Jesus most of us know.

God is love, but He is also a God of great wrath. On the final day of His vengeance at the end of the tribulation, He comes to wage war, and none of His enemies are spared. There will be a great slaughter at the battle of Armageddon. The book of Revelation uses the same imagery as Isaiah. Revelation 19:15 says of Jesus' second advent, "And from His mouth comes a sharp sword, so that with it He may smite the nations; and He will rule them with a rod of iron; and He treads the wine press of the fierce wrath of God, the Almighty" (see also Rev. 14:19-20).

Isaiah 63:7-14 recounts God's former gracious deliverance of His people, and then through 64:12 we have recorded a prayer of forgiveness that Judah will be praying after the people have seen their city destroyed by Babylon.

God's reply is found in chapters 65 and 66. There He speaks of His choice of the Gentiles (see 65:1), promises repayment for Israel's sins, salvation for the holy remnant (see 65:1-16), and ultimately eternal blessings for all who will call on His name.

Isaiah 65:17-25 foretells the new heavens and earth, God's inhabiting Jerusalem, the blessings of those who dwell there, and the coming change in the nature of the animal kingdom.

It isn't always easy to determine if we're reading of the millennium or after it, but we do know people will live during that future time of Isaiah 65:17-25, just as they do today. People will be building houses and planting vineyards (see 65:21). They will still die physically, although the long life experienced by the patriarchs will be the normal experience. A person who dies at the age of one hundred will be considered to have died in his youth (see 65:20)!

PHILIPPIANS 2:19-3:4a

A man named Epaphroditus evidently carried an offering from the Philippians to Paul in Rome. If Epaphroditus took the most direct route, it would have been a journey of at least six hundred miles. He risked his health to make the trip and arrived in Rome deathly ill (see 2:27).

In chapter 3, Paul once again admonished the Philippian Christians to rejoice. He warned them to beware of false brethren and the Jewish legalists. They were the false circumcision. Those of us who belong to Jesus by grace through faith are the true circumcision.

Paul said we "worship in the Spirit of God" (3:3). We should experience the presence of the Holy Spirit whenever we worship, and if we don't, something is wrong—our worship is either insincere or unspiritual.

PSALM 73:1-28

PROVERBS 24:13-14

OCTOBER 2

ISAIAH 66:1-24

This final chapter of Isaiah is a good summary of the major themes of the entire book: Jewish hypocrisy in Isaiah's day (see vv. 3-4); promises for the believing remnant (see v. 5); impending judgment on Jerusalem (see v. 6); future blessings for Jerusalem (see 7-14); future judgment upon the whole earth (see vv. 15-18); the gathering of believing Jews from around the world during the millennium, and the inclusion of Gentiles in that kingdom (see vv. 19-21); promise of a new heavens and new earth after the millennium (see v. 22); and finally, eternal punishment for the wicked (see v. 24).

Some people view verse 8 as a prediction of the birth of the nation of Israel as fulfilled in 1948, when for the first time in almost two thousand years, Israel possessed her homeland. There is little doubt that event was nothing short of miraculous. However, these verses probably refer to the conversion of Israel during the tribulation.

Although there will be some rebellion on the earth during the final days of the millennium, thereafter on the new earth, there will be only righteous people living (see v. 23). How will God be certain that the free moral agents of that age will never choose to rebel? By two means: first, they will have been tested already to the point that God knows He can trust them. Second, He will apparently permit the obedient inhabitants of the new earth a permanent opportunity to view the awful fate of the wicked (see v. 24). There's no doubt that Isaiah was referring to the "lake that burns with fire and brimstone" in verse 24. Jesus quoted this verse when He spoke of hell, "where their worm shall not die, and their fire shall not be quenched?" (see Mark 9:43-48). Isaiah adds that "they shall be an abhorrence to all mankind."

PHILIPPIANS 3:4b-21

After reading Paul's list of personal qualifications in verses 4-6, we can see that if anyone was going to be saved apart from faith in Jesus Christ, it would have been Paul! Yet he counted all his qualifications as "rubbish" in comparison to his qualification of being "in Christ." Anything we thought was meritorious in God's eyes before our salvation should be viewed in the same manner. Our church attendance, our good deeds, our gifts to charity—all add up to nothing before the Lord.

Our righteousness comes not from keeping the Law but through our faith in Christ. Having received the free gift of righteousness, we now have the wonderful opportunity to get to know Christ and "the power of His resurrection and the fellowship of His sufferings" (v. 10). How? Through the opportunities we have to prove our love for Jesus as we suffer the same things He did: persecution, rejection and humiliation.

What nationality are you? I'll tell you—you're a "heaven-anian"! Our citizenship is in heaven (see v. 20), which means we are from another planet! We're only visiting here as we wait for the return of our Lord.

PSALM 74:1-23

PROVERBS 24:15-16

No matter how many times a righteous man falls, God will always lift him up again! Maybe you have fallen and been bruised. Maybe you've been taken advantage of and lost some years. Trust

God to lift you back up, because He will if you'll depend on Him.

OCTOBER 3

JEREMIAH 1:1-2:30

Merril Unger, author of *Unger's Bible Handbook*, aptly refers to the time of Jeremiah's book as the "death throes of a decadent nation." Jeremiah ministered approximately one hundred years after the time of Isaiah, during the reign of Judah's last five kings—a period of about forty years. The fall of Judah and Jerusalem was imminent; Jeremiah witnessed the destruction of his city and the three deportations of his people to Babylon.

We will be reading many of the same themes we read in Isaiah. However, the people had sunk into even deeper depths of degradation, and they eventually reached a place where God instructed Jeremiah not to pray for them! Judgment was inevitable, and because of his predictions, Jeremiah became a very unpopular man with his contemporaries.

Just like Isaiah, Jeremiah was supernaturally called to his task of being "a prophet to the nations" (see 1:5). God stated that He had called and appointed Jeremiah before he was even conceived in his mother's womb! In other words, it's hardly likely that Jeremiah would be able to wiggle out of his calling or change God's mind about His selection! His only excuse was that he was too young for the task (he was in his twenties), and he realized his divinely given message was not going to make him popular. However, God reassured him that his youth was of no consequence and that he would be protected from his persecutors. We'll read later how God kept His promises to Jeremiah again and again.

What was the significance of the "almond rod" of 1:11? Probably because the almond tree was the first tree to bud and thus mark the beginning of spring, it was watched closely by the inhabitants of Palestine. So, too, God watches His own Word constantly to insure His promises.

In Jeremiah 1:13-15, we find a prediction of a Babylonian invasion from the north, which would be fulfilled in just a few years. Chapter 2 is essentially self-explanatory. God had had enough of the sins of His people. He chided them to call on their idols to save them now (see 2:28). He had tried to "chasten" them through less severe measures, but to no avail (see 2:30). Those less severe measures could have been slavery to Assyria and then to Egypt (see 2:16-18).

Notice that in Jeremiah 2:13, God referred to Himself as "the fountain of living waters"—the same expression Jesus used in reference to the experience of the new birth when talking to the woman at the well of Samaria (see John 4:13-14).

PHILIPPIANS 4:1-23

Paul listed eight qualifications for things upon which our minds should dwell. This is an area in which so many of us are guilty, because nobody knows our thoughts, and we have a tendency to clean up only our outward sins. Let's make a better effort to keep track of our thoughts. Do they always line up with Philippians 4:8? We shouldn't dwell on thoughts that are impure, hateful, tempting or negative.

The "peace of God that surpasses all comprehension" (v. 7) is supernatural peace that can't be explained. You can experience it even when your world is falling apart and everything is against you, because you're trusting God in the midst of trial. That peace is available, but only to those who place their faith in God, refuse to have anxiety and have control of their thought life.

In verses 10-19, Paul thanked the Philippians for the offering he had just received from them, delivered by Epaphroditus. This is a great section of Scripture. Paul said he had learned the secret of overcoming in any and every circumstance (see v. 12). He stated it in verse 13, which should be memorized: "I can do all things through Him who strengthens me." Paul's secret of successful living was simply that he always relied on the God who was his source for everything. To Paul, to live was Christ (see 1:21).

Paul said he had experienced getting along with humble means, going hungry and suffering need (see v. 12). However, in that same verse, he stated he had also experienced living in prosperity, being filled and having an abundance. Don't forget that Paul was an apostle called to travel to many foreign and hostile places. Naturally, because of his ministry, he suffered lack at times. As he wrote those words to the Philippians, he was in jail and had been experiencing lack—that is, until Epaphroditus arrived! Finally, Paul promised that God would supply all the Philippians' needs as well.

PSALM 75:1-10

PROVERBS 24:17-20

Proverbs 24:17-18 presents a practical way we can love our enemies. When they suffer, we shouldn't rejoice. If we do, Christ's attitude is not our attitude, and God may withdraw his anger from them in order to teach us!

OCTOBER 4

JEREMIAH 2:31-4:18

God metaphorically compared His relationship with Israel to that of a husband and wife. Israel has played the "harlot with many lovers"—their idols of wood and stone (see 3:1). As Christians, we can be guilty of idolatry whenever we allow anything but God to take first place in our lives. In the same way God allowed drought in Israel because of the people's idolatry, so can "showers of blessing" be withheld in our lives when we allow anything to distract us from serving Him (see 3:3).

It was during Josiah's reign when Jeremiah was called to his ministry (see 1:2). King Josiah instituted many reforms during his godly reign. It was during the time when repairs were being made to the temple that the "lost book of the Law of Moses" was discovered, resulting in a national revival. After Josiah's death, however, the people immediately returned to their old ways. There had been no real change in their hearts, as we read in 3:10, "Judah did not return to Me with all her heart, but rather in deception."

In the same passage, God refers to the deportation of the northern tribes of Israel to Assyria, which had occurred about one hundred years prior. In 3:11-13, God invited exiled Israel to repentance and then promised her a wonderful restoration if she accepted. She never did, but the promises of restoration are still good for the time when a remnant of Israel will turn to the Lord through Jesus Christ. Therefore, we have in the verses that follow (3:14-18) some millennial promises: national regathering and restoration of both Israel and Judah; a time when there will no longer be an ark of the covenant, but rather the

Lord's throne will be in their midst; and a time when the nations of the world will gather to the world capital, Jerusalem.

The remainder of our reading today is a warning to Judah of an invasion from the north and a call to repentance. So it's obvious that during Josiah's reign, there was still time for Judah to escape the impending wrath of God.

COLOSSIANS 1:1-20

This is another of Paul's prison letters and was probably written about the same time as his letter to Philippi. Although Paul had not founded the church in Colossae, apparently one of his converts named Epaphras was the first to preach the gospel there. Paul's purpose in writing them was to ground them in truths of the new covenant lest they be carried away by mixing other, mystical, man-made ideas with the Word of God, which they were apparently already doing.

Paul's greatest desire was that the Colossian Christians be rooted and grounded in God's Word, which is why he prayed continually that they would be filled with the knowledge of God's will "in all spiritual wisdom and understanding" (v. 9). The result of knowing God's will is strength, steadfastness, patience and thankfulness (see vv. 11-12).

Paul enumerated several truths in which all Christians should be grounded. First, we have been qualified. We didn't qualify ourselves; God qualified us. Second, we are saints through Christ's blood. Third, we have an inheritance in which to share. However, that inheritance is not just for the saints, but for the "saints in light"—that is, the saints who know God's Word, who have been enlightened with spiritual wisdom (see v. 12).

Fourth, we have been delivered from the "domain of darkness." That means we're no longer under Satan's dominion (see v. 13). We have been transferred into God's kingdom. Fifth, we have been redeemed. That means we've been bought back and are God's property. He owns us.

Sixth, we have been forgiven of all our sins through Christ (see v. 14). Seventh, Jesus Christ was and is God (see v. 15). He created everything, even the demons. He existed from eternity (see v. 16). He is the head of the body of Christ, the church. He started the church. He was the first person to be resurrected and receive a new body (v. 18). God's plan of redemption revolves around Jesus Christ and His work on the cross. Through the shedding of His blood on the cross, we have peace with God (see vv. 19-20).

PSALM 76:1-12

PROVERBS 24:21-22

OCTOBER 5

JEREMIAH 4:19-6:14

In Jeremiah 4:23-26, we have a picture of not only the judgment of Jerusalem, but also the judgment of the whole earth. This is either a picture of the earth after Armageddon, at the end of the tribulation, or a picture of the earth of Genesis 1:2, after God's judgment on the pre-Adamic creation.

Notice that the same words are used in verse 23 as in Genesis 1:2: "the earth...was formless and void." At this time also, the heavens had no light (see 4:23), the mountains were quaking (see 4:24), and there were no men on the planet (see 4:25). Yet there will be survivors on the earth at the end of the tribulation. Therefore, my opinion is that this passage gives us a better idea of the earth after the "creation judgment."

By comparison to that judgment, God spoke to Judah and promised that their land would be devastated as well, but that He would not execute a complete destruction as He did before Adam's time (see 4:27). Chapter 5 enumerates the sins of Jerusalem. God couldn't find a single just person. They were adulterous and lustful, rebellious, stubborn, deceitful, uncompassionate, liars, idolatrous, self-willed, greedy and violent. Again Jeremiah predicted a Babylonian invasion and deportation (see 5:15-18 and chap. 6).

COLOSSIANS 1:21-2:7

Although still in prison, Paul continued to rejoice in the midst of suffering (see 1:24). He said he was filling up that which was lacking in Christ's afflictions (see 1:24), meaning that the church, just like Christ, will always suffer persecution. It just so happened that Paul was one of the parts of the body of Christ that was then experiencing persecution. He didn't mean there was a certain quota of persecution that had to be met! And he didn't mean Jesus didn't suffer enough to purchase our salvation, therefore requiring the church to make up for Jesus' lack by its own sufferings.

Paul admonished the Colossian Christians that they need not search for wisdom from any other source than Christ Himself (see 2:2-3). Apparently those new believers were being tempted to accept some of the contemporary speculative philosophies of their day, which combined Greek "wisdom," Jewish legalism, Oriental mysticism and some form of asceticism.

PSALM 77:1-20

PROVERBS 24:23-25

OCTOBER 6

JEREMIAH 6:15-8:7

After reading passages like this one, how could anyone point his finger at God and accuse Him of being unmerciful? If you or I had been the Lord, we would have destroyed the wicked nation of Judah hundreds of years before God finally did. Those "people of God" were actually taking their babies and offering them as burnt offerings to the foreign god Molech (see 7:31). They were thieves, murderers, adulterers, liars, idolaters, hypocrites and talebearers (see 6:28; 7:9-10).

Did you notice the one verse of our reading today that Jesus Himself quoted? "Has this house, which is called by My name, become a den of robbers...?" (7:11). Jesus used those same words when He cast the money changers from the temple in His day. Knowing that Jesus read this same book that you and I are reading should make our reading even more interesting!

Once more we read a prediction of an invasion from Babylon and the destruction of Jerusalem (see 6:19, 22-26). God had disciplined the Israelites in vain—they would not change (see 6:29). God warned that He would do to His present "dwelling place" what He did to His former dwelling place, Shiloh (see 7:12-14). The tabernacle had first been set in the territory of the dominant northern tribe of Ephraim (sometimes synonymous with "Israel") when Israel came into the promised land. Shiloh had been destroyed by the Philistines several hundred years prior (see 1 Sam. 4). God's point was that He didn't spare a city just because it was formerly a "holy place," and neither would He spare Jerusalem just because it was the "holy city." The people assumed God would never allow Jerusalem to be destroyed, because His temple was there (see 7:4). Their stubborn sinfulness had reached the place, however, where God actually commanded Jeremiah not to pray for them (see 7:16). God informed Jeremiah that even though the people would never listen to him, he should continue warning them anyway (see 7:27).

COLOSSIANS 2:8-23

We gain some idea of the heresies that were being introduced in Colossae from Paul's words today, but not everything is crystal clear. Apparently some were following the rituals of the Law of Moses (see vv. 11, 16-17). However, Paul said that the various festivals of the Law were merely a shadow of things to come and that they all pointed to the finished work of Christ (see v. 17). Some were being led astray into the teachings of asceticism—treating their bodies harshly by means of fastings, and so on—in an attempt to get close to God. However, as Christians, we have power over the evil desires of the flesh through the new life of the inward person. Sin's power has been broken over us, and self-abasement has no value in our walk with God (see vv. 18, 23).

Some were being seduced by those who claimed to have had visions and who espoused the idea of worshipping angels (see v. 18). All these things possessed an appearance of wisdom but were no more than fleshly ideas and self-made religion. They had no foundation in the Word of God and no rightful place in a Christian's walk. This is why it's so important that we be grounded in God's Word—so we can instantly distinguish truth from error.

We also have in this section of Colossians a few more foundational truths in which all Christians should be grounded. Jesus was and is fully God (see v. 9). In Him we have been made complete. We can add nothing to the finished work of Christ in our salvation (see v. 10). Jesus is Lord of all, is above all Satan's demons, and has "disarmed" them as far as believers are concerned (see vv. 10, 15). We have been completely identified with Christ in His death, burial and resurrection, which means our old nature is gone and its power has been broken (see vv. 11-12). We are now spiritually alive and have had all our sins forgiven (see vv. 13-14). Jesus is the head of the body of Christ, and we are members of that body (see v. 20).

Aren't you glad that you know all those things? You are doing better than the Colossians! But are we walking in the light of what we know? Are we still trying to add to Christ's work? Are we victorious over Satan, demons and the flesh? Are we acting as though all our sins have been forgiven? Are we functioning properly in the body of Christ?

PSALM 78:1-31

PROVERBS 24:26

OCTOBER 7

JEREMIAH 8:8-9:26

Have you noticed that some of the words the translators attributed to Jeremiah could just as easily be attributed to the Lord Himself? "My sorrow is beyond healing, my heart is faint within me!" The translators attributed that verse and the first half of the next to Jeremiah, yet they attributed the second half of that same verse to God. I wonder if the entire section (8:18-9:6) and others like it shouldn't be attributed to God (e.g., 4:19-22).

For example, 8:21-9:1 says, "For the brokenness of the daughter of my people I am broken; I mourn, dismay has taken hold of me....O that my head were waters, and my tears a fountain of tears, that I might weep day and night for the slain of the daughter of my people! O that I had in the desert a wayfarer's lodging place: that I might leave my people, and go from them!" Why couldn't it be God who was saying those things? Jesus, God in the flesh, wept. Is He not the personification of unselfish love?

COLOSSIANS 3:1-17

The more revelation we gain of the "in Christ" realities, the more we will act as if they're true in our lives. One of those realities is that we're seated with Christ in the heavenly places. If we act as if that's so, we'll naturally be more mindful of heavenly things than of earthly things. Paul admonished us to "seek the things which are above" and not to set our minds on things "that are on earth" (vv. 1-2). Our old nature is dead and gone, so we should consider the "members of our earthly bodies" as dead to immorality, impurity, passion, evil desire and greed. Those things amount to idolatry (see v. 5).

Paul's other writings, and our own experience, make it clear that we must deal with our fleshly nature. God has done His part; He has given us a new nature in our spirits and broken the power of sin over us. But He hasn't given us a new fleshly nature! It is our job to "put the flesh under," which will be easier to do if we see ourselves "in Christ."

What is the "perfect bond of unity" (3:14)? It's not perfect doctrine! I don't think the body of Christ, or any church for that matter, will ever experience perfect doctrinal harmony. The perfect bond of unity is unselfish love (see v. 14). Love is God's glue!

Paul urged us to "let the word of Christ richly dwell within you" (3:16). That implies more than just reading God's Word; it means *feeding* on God's Word—meditating on it. Just as Paul said in his letter to the Ephesians, we can actually teach and admonish one another with psalms, hymns and spiritual songs, but only if we're allowing the Word of Christ to richly dwell within us.

I encourage you to practice this in your private prayer times. Step out in faith and begin to sing a song that comes from your spirit, not a song you have memorized with your mind. If your spirit is filled with God's Word, you will have no trouble; you will find that you are singing a song that is full of Scripture. Not only will you enjoy this kind of singing, but you will certainly add to the richness of your worship and communion with the Father.

PSALM 78:32-55

PROVERBS 24:27

This is another way of saying, "First things first." Too many of us are trying to build our houses when we ought to be planting our fields.

OCTOBER 8

JEREMIAH 10:1-11:23

Only one new theme is uncovered in today's reading, the persecution of Jeremiah by the men of Anathoth, Jeremiah's hometown (see 11:18-23). When people reject God, they reject His messengers. From the beginning of his ministry, God promised to protect Jeremiah (see 1:8), and His promise was still good. As a result of God's judgment, all the men of Anathoth would die, and unlike other parts of the nation, they would have no surviving remnant. Whether this occurred immediately or not until the Babylonian invasion, we don't know, but it did happen.

COLOSSIANS 3:18-4:18

The first nine verses we read today are similar to the ones Paul wrote near the end of his letter to the Ephesians. (He may have written both from the same prison cell.) They are the same instructions to wives, husbands, children, slaves and masters. I suggest you re-read my comments on Ephesians 5:22-6:9.

Twice in the fourth and final chapters, Paul discussed prayer. First he instructed us to be devoted to it, to stay alert in it, and to maintain thanksgiving in it. Do you have a prayer life? Thank God that we can talk to the Lord at any time and in any place. We need to stay in fellowship with Him throughout each day. And prayer that is full of faith is full of thanksgiving.

Paul also requested that the Colossians pray that the Lord would open up a door for the Word. Isn't it interesting that Paul didn't request that they pray for God to release him from prison? (He did end the letter with, "Remember my imprisonment.") Paul was primarily concerned about getting the Word of God to others. Even in jail, he was continuing to spread the gospel.

In verse 12, Paul once again mentioned Epaphras, a man of prayer, who apparently founded the church in Colossae. It seems that he was an apostle himself, and that possibly he had founded churches in Laodicea and Hierapolis (see v. 13). Remember the church of Laodicea, because it was one of the churches to which John wrote in the book of Revelation.

This chapter also contains some practical wisdom for witnessing (see vv. 5-6). What did Paul mean when he said that our speech should always be with grace, "seasoned with salt"? Simply this: if our conversation is seasoned, people will take notice, and it will open up an opportunity to present the gospel.

Notice that Paul had a word from the Lord for a man named Archippus, which he included at the close of his letter (see v. 17). It was a simple, one-sentence admonition: "Take heed to the ministry which you have received in the Lord, that you may fulfill it." That's a good word for all of us to heed, because we all have a function in the body of Christ. I want to stand before Jesus some day and hear Him say, "Well done, good and faithful servant!"

PSALM 78:56-72

PROVERBS 24:28-29

Revenge is God's, not ours.

OCTOBER 9

JEREMIAH 12:1-14:12

I'm so glad to know that Jeremiah was an ordinary human being. He, too, questioned God about why the wicked prosper (see 12:1), and God's clear answer was that their prosperity is only temporary (see 12:7-13). Judgment was inevitable for Judah and her neighboring countries, yet notice that God was already promising eventual restoration (see 12:15). Jeremiah was now completely disgusted with the sins of his countrymen (they wanted to kill him!), and he prayed for the hastening of their judgment (see 12:3).

Commentators differ regarding who was doing the speaking in 12:5-6, Jeremiah or God. If it was God, the words were an encouragement and a warning from Him to Jeremiah. In verse 5, God in effect was saying, "Hey Jeremiah, if you can't take the heat now, you aren't going to make it, because things are going to get worse!"

In chapter 13, we read about God's symbolic sign of the ruined waistband to the nation of Judah. It seems as if Jeremiah was given simple directions to follow—he only had to bury a waistband near the Euphrates River and then recover it—until you realize that the Euphrates was almost four hundred miles from Jerusalem! Why did God have Jeremiah travel such a long distance, twice? Because the Euphrates was in the land of Judah's forthcoming exile. There was time for Judah to repent, but the chances of that happening were about the same as an Ethiopian's changing his skin and a leopard's changing his spots (see 13:23).

Apparently the false prophets of Jeremiah's time were predicting prosperity ("Every jug is to be filled with wine" [13:12]). God "amened" their prediction, except that He had a little different wine in mind—the wine of His wrath. The people of Judah would be drunk with His judgment and would be shown no mercy. They would be as helpless as drunkards.

As a result of their apostasy, and as a forewarning of further judgment, God allowed a drought to come upon Judah. Most of us have never experienced a severe drought. Can you imagine turning on your faucet and having nothing come out? The Lord graphically described the famine's effects (see 14:2-6). The drought apparently drove Judah to prayer, but not to repentance (see 14:8-10).

1 THESSALONIANS 1:1-2:9

I like Paul's two letters to the Christians of Thessalonica because they're easy to understand, they're very encouraging, and they reveal information about the future. Paul founded the church in Thessalonica during his second missionary journey, and it's assumed this letter was penned by him from Corinth during that same journey around A.D. 51. Therefore, we know that Paul was writing to a young church full of baby Christians (which is probably why this epistle was so easy to understand!).

In Thessalonica, Paul met with severe persecution by the local Jews and was run out of town (see Acts 17:1-10). Despite the harassment, the church there learned to release the "joy of the Holy Spirit" (1:6), which is not dependent on favorable circumstances. Anyone who has the Holy Spirit within can call on the Holy Spirit's joy in times of crisis.

Paul stated that he, Timothy and Silvanus had been "approved by God to be entrusted with the gospel" and that God had "examined" their hearts (2:4). In the original Greek language, the words *approved* and *examined* are the same words and could be better translated "tested." In other words, Paul was saying that God had tested their motives to be certain they weren't in it for money, glory or to take advantage of others in any way, shape or form.

Paul supported his ministry by his own labor while in Thessalonica (see 2:9). He received no offerings, knowing they could hinder the gospel. How does God test preachers to make certain they aren't in it for the money? It's very easy—He calls them to preach for a while with little or no pay. How does He test preachers to make certain they aren't in it for the glory? He calls them to preach to small, ungrateful and many times complaining congregations!

PSALM 79:1-13

PROVERBS 24:30-34

OCTOBER 10

JEREMIAH 14:11-16:15

For the third time, God told Jeremiah not to pray for the people (see 14:11). Mercy had ended, and judgment had begun. God wouldn't be answering anyone's prayers for a while (see 14:12). Even a prayer for mercy that was offered up by the people of Judah and recorded in Jeremiah 14:19-22 went unanswered. The Lord said, "I am tired of relenting" (15:6). In other words, He had shown mercy in response to their cries before, but each time He did, the people returned to their idols. This time, that wouldn't be the case.

The persecution against Jeremiah had increased, and he exclaimed, "Everyone curses me" (15:10). It seems that for a short time he considered backing down from his stand, so God allowed him to be afflicted in some manner (see 15:18). However, the Lord called for his return, and if he *would* return, divine protection from his persecutors would be granted (see 15:19-21). Jeremiah not only had the difficult task of standing up against the entire population of Judah, but he also had to do it practically alone. He wasn't even permitted to take a wife and have children (see 16:2)!

True to God's character, we end with a promise of coming restoration and a return from exile. Even in the midst of His wrath, He was promising future blessings!

1 THESSALONIANS 2:10-3:13

God's Word "performs its work in you who believe" (2:13). Just as a seed must be planted and watered before it can produce fruit, so, too, the Word of God must be planted in our spirits and watered with faith before it will produce fruit in our lives.

The source of the persecution against the Thessalonian church was clearly the Jews, just as it was in Judea and Jerusalem (see 2:14). Isn't it sad that the people who fought God the most were those who had the most revelation about Him?

Paul stated that wrath has come upon those Jews "to the utmost" (2:16) who were persecuting the church in Judea. We don't know in what form that wrath occurred, but we know for certain that within about eighteen years, Jerusalem would be destroyed by the Romans, and at least one million Jews would lose their lives.

Paul said that he had attempted to get back to Thessalonica more than once, but Satan thwarted him (see 2:18). *Thwarted* means "temporarily hindered." It doesn't mean "defeated"! For those who trust in

God, the most Satan can do is thwart them, but he cannot conquer them.

Eventually, Timothy made his way back to Thessalonica and found the Christians standing fast in the midst of their trials (see 3:1-2). The news came as a great relief to Paul, who was only able to spend about four weeks there to establish the church (see Acts 17:1-10). We know Paul did get back to Thessalonica during his third missionary journey, so his prayer of 3:9-11 was answered.

PSALM 80:1-19

PROVERBS 25:1-5

Wouldn't it be wonderful if one person could rule our nation with the authority and power to "remove the wicked from before him" (25:5)? Unfortunately, that won't happen until Jesus reigns, but thank God it will happen!

OCTOBER 11

JEREMIAH 16:16-18:23

It's a good thing the Bible was inspired by God, or both Jeremiah and Paul could be suspected of plagiarism. Jeremiah borrowed the analogy of the "tree planted by the water" (17:7-8) from the first psalm. His analogy of the potter and the clay (see 18:1-6) was borrowed by Paul in Romans 9:20-21. Isaiah also used the analogy of potter and clay several times (see Is. 29:16; 45:9; 64:8).

We find several wonderful passages in today's reading. Jeremiah 17:7-8 says, "Blessed is the man who trusts in the Lord and whose trust is the Lord. For he will be like a tree planted by the water, that extends its roots by a stream and will not fear when the heat comes; but its leaves will be green, and it will not be anxious in a year of drought nor cease to yield fruit." God doesn't promise there won't be an occasional "year of drought." But when the drought does come, those who trust in the Lord won't have any worries over it.

I love God's words to Jeremiah in 18:6-10 that so wonderfully reveal God's sovereign rule over the nations. Paul taught that all governing authorities exist only because of God's ordination or permission (see Rom. 13:1-2). Here in Jeremiah, God's decisions concerning the planting and uprooting of nations are clearly influenced by the obedience of those nations. Few people are able to see God's hand at work in the politics of the world and realize that God is sovereignly working so that His purposes might come to pass. Do you realize that the places of greatest political oppression or instability are many times the places where the greatest revivals are taking place? God's point to Jeremiah was that He deals with entire nations based on their obedience to Him.

Once again we learn of a plot against Jeremiah's life (see 18:18). At one time, Jeremiah prayed for God's mercy on the people of Judah (see 18:20), but now he prayed that God would *stop* showing them mercy (see 18:21-23).

1 THESSALONIANS 4:1-5:3

Writing to a church located in an immoral city, Paul warned the Thessalonians that they should not be imitating the life-styles of the heathen any longer. He specifically targeted sexual immorality and warned that the Lord is the avenger against any brother who "transgresses and defrauds his brother in the matter" (4:6). He was plainly speaking of the sin of adultery. Christians who fall into this sin can expect God's sure judgment if they're unrepentant.

A little knowledge of the Greek in 4:9 would help us greatly to understand what Paul was saying. He used the word *love* two times in this verse, but in the Greek it actually *is* two different words. The first is *phileo* and the second is *agapeo. Phileo* means "to love as a friend." It's natural human love. *Agapeo* means to love as God loves—without regard to the merit of the receiver or the cost to the giver. Paul said in this verse, "Now as to the *phileo* of the brethren, you have no need for anyone to write to you, for you yourselves are taught by God to *agapeo* one another."

Some commentators think that a number of the Thessalonian believers were so taken by the doctrine of the imminent rapture of the church that they had quit their jobs. Why work when Jesus is going to return in the next few days? However, Jesus hadn't come back yet, and now they had gone to sponging from others to survive. Paul commanded them to work so that they didn't bring any reproach to the gospel (see 4:11-12).

The last six verses of chapter 4 explain exactly what happens when a Christian dies, and also what's going to happen at the rapture. At death, the spirit of the Christian goes immediately to be with Jesus in heaven. If that were not the case, how could Jesus bring back with Him those who have "fallen asleep in Jesus" when He returns (4:14)? When Jesus comes back for His church, the dead bodies of the departed saints will be resurrected and glorified, and those bodies will rise in the air to meet the spirits that used to inhabit them! Then, a split second later, we who are alive will be caught up with them, and at that time we, too, will receive glorified bodies. This will all take place at the "sound of a trumpet and the voice of an archangel," and at that time Jesus "will descend from heaven with a shout" (4:16). Now won't that be something? We'll all be "flying high" that day!

PSALM 81:1-16

PROVERBS 25:6-7

Jesus taught this same principle, didn't He (see Luke 14:7-11)?

OCTOBER 12

JEREMIAH 19:1-21:14

Can you imagine the courage it took for Jeremiah to gather the elders of Jerusalem and the senior priests and declare the coming destruction of Jerusalem (see 19:1-13)? He even predicted to their faces that they would eat the flesh of their own children and one another's flesh in the distress of the siege (see 19:9). Exactly as Jeremiah predicted, it all came to pass. Because of the famine within the walls of Jerusalem during its siege, people had to resort to eating the flesh of their dead children and friends to stay alive.

The result of this particular prophecy is that Pashhur the priest had Jeremiah beaten and placed in stocks for a night. But Jeremiah was not intimidated, and upon his release he reiterated his message of doom to Pashhur's face! We can't help but feel sorry for Jeremiah, who then complained that he had become a laughingstock to everyone. He had tried to keep quiet, but like fire in his bones, his divine message had to be proclaimed (see 20:9). All his friends had turned against him and were waiting for an opportunity to kill him. Jeremiah's tenacity ought to encourage us to hold fast in our faith no matter what evil or temptation we face. Observe the faith that is evident in his prayer, "But the Lord *is with me* like a dread champion; therefore my persecutors *will stumble and not prevail....* Sing to the Lord, praise the Lord! For He has delivered the soul of the needy one from the hand of evildoers" (20:11,13; italics mine).

Although he had great faith that the Lord would deliver him, Jeremiah was certainly not enjoying his present circumstances! He wished he had never been born because of his persecution and because he knew he would witness the destruction of his city and the exile of his people (see 20:14-18).

The "Zedekiah" referred to in chapter 21 was the final ruler of Judah, whom Nebuchadnezzar had installed as a puppet king in place of Jehoiachin (see 2 Kings 24:17-20). This took place after the second deportation to Babylon. At that time, Zedekiah rebelled against Nebuchadnezzar, who came once more to Jerusalem to set up his siege works against it. The siege lasted for more than a year. In the end, when Zedekiah was finally captured, the Babylonians killed his sons before his eyes and then blinded him. The setting of this chapter of Jeremiah is during the final siege of Jerusalem. Even then there was still room for mercy if the people would surrender to Nebuchadnezzar. Those who surrendered would live, but the rest would die (see 21:9-10).

1 THESSALONIANS 5:4-28

"God has not destined us for wrath, but for obtaining salvation through our Lord Jesus Christ" (v. 9). Those who teach that the church will be purged, refined and perfected by going through the tribulation have yet to realize the truth of that verse! I'm not going to be made worthy by going through the tribulation; I am already worthy for heaven by Christ's tribulation on the cross!

We are admonished to "rejoice always," to "pray without ceasing" and "in everything give thanks" (vv. 16-18). Paul didn't say to give thanks *for* everything but *in* everything. He didn't mean we should pray twenty-four hours a day, but that we should always be in an attitude of prayer, fellowshipping with the Lord all day long. We shouldn't spend all our time rejoicing, but we should rejoice no matter what kind of circumstances we're facing.

We're told not to "quench the Spirit" (v. 19). Paul was speaking here in the context of the operation of spiritual gifts, as we read his instruction concerning the gift of prophecy in the next verse. We can quench the Spirit if we aren't sensitive to Him and open to His guidance.

It's easy to develop an attitude of "despising prophetic utterances" (v. 20) if we witness enough abuses of the gift. However, we must not discount the real because of so much false. We need to simply "examine everything" and then "hold fast to that which is good" (v. 21). That means to simply disregard what isn't good or what isn't actually of the Holy Spirit.

In verse 23, we have the scriptural basis for understanding that humanity is tripartite in nature: spirit, soul and body. Some teach that the soul and the spirit are the same thing, but if they were the same, why would Paul list them separately?

PSALM 82:1-8

PROVERBS 25:8-10

It's always good to have the facts before you try to present your case. It's not wise to share the secrets of others. Ultimately they may find out you betrayed their confidence and will never trust you again.

OCTOBER 13

JEREMIAH 22:1-23:20

Some historical review of the final years before the fall of Judah would help us in understanding chapter 22. Josiah was the last godly king in Judah. He instituted sweeping reforms after the discovery of the book of the Law while repairs were being made on the temple. Josiah met an untimely death at age thirty-nine, and his son Jehoahaz succeeded him. His was an evil reign of only three months before he was deported to Egypt by Pharaoh Neco, who then made another of Josiah's sons, Jehoiakim, king in place of Jehoahaz.

Jehoiakim's evil reign lasted eleven years, during which time Nebuchadnezzar gained control of Judah. When Jehoiakim rebelled, Nebuchadnezzar came against Jerusalem and deported him to Babylon. This was the first of three deportations of Jews to Babylon. We believe Daniel was taken at this time as well.

After that, Jehoiakim's son Jehoiachin became king, and his evil reign lasted three months. Again Jerusalem was besieged by Nebuchadnezzar, and Jehoiachin was taken captive to Babylon, along with the majority of Jerusalem's inhabitants (including Ezekiel). Jehoiachin's Uncle Zedekiah (another of Josiah's sons) was then installed as king. He, too, rebelled against Babylon, and after his evil reign of eleven years, Nebuchadnezzar sent his army once again. This time he burned the temple and the city and deported almost everyone who was left in it. Zedekiah's sons were slain before his eyes, and he was then blinded and taken captive to Babylon.

So there you have the progression of kings: Josiah, Jehoahaz, Jehoiakim, Jehoiachin and Zedekiah. Jehoahaz, Jehoiakim, and Zedekiah were all sons of Josiah, and Jehoiachin was Josiah's grandson. All, of course, were descendants of David, and Josiah, Jehoiakim, and Jehoiachin are in the lineage of Christ (see Matt. 1:11). Jeremiah ministered during the reigns of all five kings.

In chapter 22, Jeremiah mentioned "Shallum the son of Josiah" (22:11), who must have been Jehoahaz. Jeremiah predicted that he would be led captive to another land and die there. We have already read in 2 Chronicles that he was deported by Pharaoh Neco to Egypt, where he died (see 2 Chron. 36:4).

Jeremiah also mentioned Jehoiakim in 22:13-23 and predicted he would soon die and "be buried with a donkey's burial...thrown out beyond the gates of Jerusalem" (22:19). Finally, Jeremiah predicted that Jehoiachin would be deported to Babylon and never return to Jerusalem (see 22:24-26). God said that "no man of his descendants will prosper sitting on the throne of David or ruling again in Judah" (22:30). This was true, because none of his sons ever ascended to the throne. His Uncle Zedekiah was the last Davidic ruler in Judah.

Chapter 23 contains a wonderful prediction of the future gathering of Israel and the reign of Jesus the Messiah. This is another prophecy that exemplifies the "law of double reference," as it had limited application to the return of the Jews from Persia but will be ultimately fulfilled at the beginning of the millennium.

Jesus is the "righteous Branch" of David referred to in Jeremiah 23:5. Literally, the word *Branch* means "sprout" or "shoot." At the time of the demise of Zedekiah, the "family tree" of David was cut down. There were no more kings of Davidic descent reigning in Israel. But praise God that there was a little "sprout" that sprang out from those dead roots! Jeremiah said that His name would be "the Lord our righteousness" (23:6).

2 THESSALONIANS 1:1-12

This second letter to the Thessalonians was written by Paul a few months after his first letter. His purpose was possibly to clear up some misunderstandings concerning his first letter, particularly on the subject of the return of Jesus. Both of Paul's letters to the Thessalonians may have been his earliest letters, with the possible exception of Galatians. Those letters were penned within twenty years of Christ's crucifixion.

Verses 4-10 have raised some questions that we need to address. Paul referred to the "persecutions and afflictions" (v. 4) the Thessalonian Christians had been enduring. He went on to say that those afflictions were a "plain indication of God's righteous judgment so that you may be considered worthy of the kingdom of God" (v. 5). We know the sure judgment of God's wrath is coming upon this world, and the fact that ungodly people are persecuting the godly is a clear sign that the world deserves God's judgment. Our standing with God is indicated by which side of the persecution we're on. Enduring the persecution doesn't make us worthy in terms of deserving heaven, but it does prove our faith in Jesus—for whom we endure.

God will no doubt repay all the persecutors of the church down through the ages, and those who are alive at His coming won't have to wait until hell to begin to receive what's due them (see v. 6-10). Paul was speaking in this passage of the return of Christ at the end of the tribulation, and not of the rapture. But scriptures like these lead many to believe the rapture does not occur until the end of the tribulation. Again may I say that if the subject were clearer in the Bible, we wouldn't have so many differing viewpoints.

PSALM 83:1-18

PROVERBS 25:11-14

All four of these proverbs deal with words we speak. Solomon lauded the virtues of a word spoken in right circumstances, a word of reproof spoken to a receptive ear, and the refreshing word of a faithful messenger. On the other hand, he disdained the words of a man who "boasts of his gifts falsely." He is compared to clouds and wind that bring no rain.

OCTOBER 14

JEREMIAH 23:21-25:38

Jeremiah had a lot of competition in his day from other "prophets" who were predicting the exact opposite of what he was predicting (see 23:21-40). Today, we must also compete with the false prophets of the world for the hearts of men. Like Jeremiah, we can rely on the authority of God's eternal Word!

Jeremiah 24 is set after the time of Jehoiachin's surrender to Nebuchadnezzar and the second deportation to Babylon. Jeremiah saw a vision of ripe figs and rotten figs, which were comparable to the two groups of Jews. Those exiles then living in Babylon were the good figs, because they would learn their lesson in captivity, and then God would restore them to their land (see 24:5-7).

The bad figs were those who had remained in Jerusalem under the corrupt leadership of Zedekiah and those Jews who had fled to Egypt to escape the Babylonian invasion—the means of God's discipline (see 24:8-10). All of them would be pursued by "the sword, the famine, and the pestilence" (24:10) until they were destroyed.

Chapter 25 comes chronologically *before* chapter 24, during the reign of Jehoiakim (third of the five kings previously mentioned). Jeremiah had been prophesying for twenty-three years, and no one had listened! In this particular prophecy, Jeremiah predicted in great detail what was about to happen over approximately the next eighty years. Babylon would invade and destroy Judah and her surrounding nations, including Egypt, the land of the Philistines, Edom, Moab, Ammon, Tyre and Sidon, and so on. In fact, Babylon would soon rule a good portion of the entire known world (see 25:18-26). Yet after seventy years, God would judge Babylon for its evil, and the exiles would all go free (see 25:11-12). This particular prediction is also mentioned in the book of Daniel, because it is the prophecy that stirred Daniel to begin praying for his nation!

From the promise of imminent judgment upon the known world of Jeremiah's day, we suddenly find ourselves reading about the coming judgment upon the entire world of *our* day (see 25:30-38). At that time, it won't be Nebuchadnezzar whom God uses to judge the nations, but Jesus Himself, as He returns in fury! On that day, "those slain by the Lord...shall be from one end of the earth to the other" (25:33). This couldn't possibly be speaking of God's judgment through Nebuchadnezzar. We can also see the similarity in the way the Spirit of God used Isaiah and Jeremiah—imminent events merged with future events of the same nature. The judgment of the known world through Nebuchadnezzar was just a foreshadowing of the final judgment of the world. Think about it—God has been warning the world of the coming final judgment for over twenty-five hundred years!

2 THESSALONIANS 2:1-17

In this chapter, we see plainly that the beginning of the "day of the Lord" and the rapture of the church are simultaneous events (see vv. 1-2). The "day of the Lord" is not one twenty-four-hour period, but the entire tribulation.

Paul stated that the day of the Lord cannot come unless the "apostasy" comes first. This indicates some great falling away or rebellion against God. Some think the apostasy is a reference to the rapture. Some think it referred to the falling away of the church during the Middle Ages. And others think the falling away is yet to occur.

The day of the Lord cannot come until the "man of lawlessness is revealed"—the Antichrist (v. 3). He will exalt himself as God and will actually seat himself in the temple of God in Jerusalem. When Paul wrote those words, the temple in Jerusalem was still standing, but it would be destroyed within nineteen years by Titus and the Roman legions. So what's going to happen? There is no doubt that the temple must be rebuilt in Jerusalem.

Paul stated that something was restraining the Antichrist from being revealed. He (the Antichrist) would be revealed when "he who now restrains him is taken out of the way" (vv. 6-7). I think the church is "he who now restrains" the Antichrist. When the church is raptured, the Antichrist will have full reign. Only then will he be revealed (see v. 8). Empowered by Satan, the "man of sin" will have the ability to work signs and wonders in order to deceive people into following him (see v. 9).

God will allow all this to happen in

order to further His purposes and will actually send "a deluding influence so that they might believe what is false" (v. 11). God will only send a "deluding influence" upon people who have already rejected the truth and taken pleasure in wickedness (see vv. 10, 12). The hardening of Pharaoh's heart during Moses' time is a foreshadowing of what God will do to the hearts of the wicked during the tribulation. After that, Jesus will slay the Antichrist with the breath of His mouth (see v. 8) when He comes to establish His kingdom.

PSALM 84:1-12

PROVERBS 25:15

"Soft words" are always more persuasive than harsh words.

OCTOBER 15

JEREMIAH 26:1-27:22

During the debate of the elders who were deciding Jeremiah's fate, one of them referred to a prophet name Micah, who in the days of Hezekiah (one hundred years earlier) predicted the destruction of Jerusalem. In Micah 3:12, the prophet predicted that Jerusalem would become ruins, but apparently that destruction was forestalled by the reforms instituted by good King Hezekiah. Regardless, the only effect Micah's predictions had on the present inhabitants of Jerusalem was that they motivated them to spare Jeremiah's life. No one changed his conduct. We also learn that a prophet named Uriah was not as fortunate as Jeremiah (see 26:20-23).

Chapter 27 is set during the time of Zedekiah, the final Davidic king of Judah. Already there had been two deportations to Babylon, and only the poor remnant of Jews remained in Jerusalem. During the second deportation, most of the treasures and vessels of the temple had been taken by Nebuchadnezzar (see 2 Kings 24:13), yet the false prophets were predicting that those vessels would shortly be brought back to Jerusalem (see 27:16).

Jeremiah predicted that the temple vessels would *not* be returned immediately, and furthermore, Nebuchadnezzar would be back to get what temple pieces he had left behind! You can see why Jeremiah wasn't the most popular man in Jerusalem!

Even on the brink of destruction, God was still showing some degree of mercy. He promised the remnant of the people that if they would simply submit to Nebuchadnezzar, they would escape with their lives and remain in their land. Their city would not be ruined. But if they refused to submit, they would be destroyed through war, famine and pestilence (see 27:8). Zedekiah and the people of Jerusalem did not heed Jeremiah's words and suffered the fate God promised.

2 THESSALONIANS 3:1-18

Reiterating the same theme as in his first letter, Paul admonished the Thessalonians to earn their own livings and not be a burden on anyone else. "If anyone will not work, neither let him eat" (v. 10). It was quite possible that some of the Thessalonians saw no reason to work because they thought Jesus was about to return for them momentarily. However, we are to occupy until He comes.

PSALM 85:1-13

PROVERBS 25:16

Good can become bad when moderation is neglected.

OCTOBER 16

JEREMIAH 28:1-29:32

Hananiah the prophet may have been sincere, but he was sincerely wrong; in fact, he was dead wrong. Jeremiah accused him of counseling "rebellion against the Lord" (28:16) simply because his prophecy was partly wrong. Yes, God would eventually "break...the yoke of Nebuchadnezzar...from the neck of all the nations" (28:11), but it wouldn't take place for almost seventy years, not two years as Hananiah predicted. The people of Judah naturally believed Hananiah's good news rather than Jeremiah's bad news, even though Jeremiah's former predictions had all come to pass. As a result, Hananiah suffered God's judgment.

Three other false prophets mentioned in chapter 29 are Ahab, Zedekiah (not to be confused with King Zedekiah) and Shemaiah. All were predicting the imminent release of the exiles and their return to Jerusalem. All would soon die, and apparently Ahab and Zedekiah would be roasted in fire by Nebuchadnezzar (see 29:22). Not only had they prophesied falsely in the Lord's name, but they were also adulterers (see 29:23). False prophets can be known not just by their false prophecies, but also by their "fruits," as Jesus taught (see Matt. 7:15-20). Although Jeremiah's predictions weren't as popular as the others', his were from the Lord.

God instructed the exiles to build houses and plant gardens, because it would be seventy years before He would release them. Only the young would ever return to see their homeland. Notice that God also told the exiles to "seek the welfare of the city" where they were now living and to "pray to the Lord in its behalf" (29:7). Why? Because "in its welfare you will have welfare" (29:27). That promise ties in perfectly with what we are about to read tomorrow in the book of 1 Timothy. We can and should pray for the welfare of our nation, even if it's run by ungodly leaders (as in Jeremiah's and in Timothy's days) because our prayers will make a difference.

1 TIMOTHY 1:1-20

Timothy, a young man from Galatia, was probably converted during Paul's first missionary journey there. He later became Paul's right-hand man and envoy to the churches—a man whom Paul loved and trusted. This letter was likely written to Timothy in the year A.D. 63 or 64, when he was overseeing the young churches in Ephesus. For that reason, Paul's two letters to Timothy and his one letter to Titus are collectively called the "Pastoral Epistles," because in a sense, they're written to pastors.

The same problem that had surfaced in many of the other early churches had apparently surfaced in Ephesus as well—false teaching was drawing away disciples. The kingdom of God is not furthered by human speculations but by faith founded on the solid rock of God's Word (see v. 4). We learn that some Jewish legalists were trying to bind up the Ephesians in the cords of law, but Paul reminded them that laws are for unrighteous people (see v. 9). We who have new natures and who are serving God from the heart have no need for external commandments. All these heresies that were being introduced to the Ephesians were just a ploy of Satan to trap them with the age-old deception of "salvation by works." For that reason, Paul again reiterated that his salvation was wrought purely from God's mercy, poured out upon an unrighteous, undeserving sinner (see vv. 12-16).

Paul states that God placed him into service because He considered him faithful (see v. 12). God entrusts us with more responsibility as we are faithful in our present responsibilities. God has given you a ministry to perform, a task to complete, a divine destiny to fulfill—are you being faithful?

Timothy had received prophecies containing personal promises to him. When God speaks to us by spectacular means such as this, it could mean some rough roads ahead. God normally speaks to us through impressions in our spirits, which is supernatural but not as spectacular as hearing His audible voice or receiving a personal prophecy. We need to be cautious concerning personal prophecies. They are not the everyday, common occurrence that some people make them out to be.

Finally a warning from Paul: those who reject a good conscience jeopardize their very salvation. Paul stated that some had done so and suffered spiritual shipwreck (see v. 19). Two such men are named as Alexander and Hymenaeus, whom Paul delivered over to Satan that they might be taught not to blaspheme.

PSALM 86:1-7

PROVERBS 25:17

Have you ever had a neighbor who stops by for a chat every day? If you have, you can relate to this proverb!

OCTOBER 17

JEREMIAH 30:1-31:26

The prophecy we've just read apparently came to Jeremiah while he was sleeping (see 31:26). God was speaking of more than just Judah's return from captivity in Babylon. He was also referring to future blessings that will come during the millennium (see 30:24; 31:12).

God promised a regathering of both Judah and Israel (see 30:3). As far as we know, there has never been a national regathering of the ten northern tribes of Israel, only of Judah. We assume there were a few exiled Israelis who did return with the remnant of Judah.

The first part of this prophecy speaks of the time of the tribulation, which is referred to as the time of "Jacob's distress" (30:7). (Remember that Jacob's name was changed to Israel.) Speaking of that time, God said, "For that day is great and there is none like it" (30:7). It will be a time of Israel's salvation and great deliverance, and shortly thereafter, "they shall serve the Lord their God and David their king, whom I will raise up for them" (30:9). I presume that the reference to David means that there will be a descendant of David on his throne, and we know that person is Jesus Christ (see Luke 1:32-33). God will regather the believing remnant of Israel and Judah from around the world to the land of their forefathers (see 31:7-8).

Remember that when God talked about "Ephraim," He was referring to the ten northern tribes of Israel that were deported to Assyria. Ephraim was the dominant tribe and therefore served as a representative of all ten (see 31:18-20).

The reference to Rachel's weeping for her children in Ramah (see 31:15) also had a double application in prophecy. In the near future, it referred to Rachel's weeping for the exiled descendants of her sons Joseph (and thus Ephraim) and Benjamin. And Matthew applied this prophecy to Herod's slaughter of the babies of Bethlehem after the birth of Christ there (see Matt. 2:18).

1 TIMOTHY 2:1-15

If our prayers for our government couldn't make any difference, Paul wouldn't have told us to pray for our leaders (see vv. 1-2). But he did, so we can be sure our prayers will make a difference. We sometimes think our battles are all political struggles against the humanists, but in reality we fight evil spirits. Through prayer, we can even change the outcomes of elections.

God's best is that we live in times of tranquility and quietness (see v. 2), because we can more easily spread the gospel around the world with a strong economy and stable government (see v. 4). However, many times political instability and economic hard times open people's hearts to seek the Lord. As Paul wrote these words to Timothy, the church was about to undergo intense persecution under the Roman emperor Nero.

There is only one mediator between God and man, and He is Jesus (see v. 5). You don't need some dead saint or living priest to mediate for you. Jesus is our high priest, and we all have access to God through Him and Him alone!

In verses 9-10, Paul was not saying that women can't get dressed up or wear jewelry, but that they shouldn't spend all their time and energies on their appearance. In Paul's day, women would spend hours braiding their hair and intertwining it with gold thread. Also, women should dress modestly, lest they cause others to stumble.

In verses 12-14 it seems as if Paul was saying that no women can teach in the church. This is a controversial subject. However, from a close examination of the context, I believe Paul was talking about husbands and wives, not all women and men in general. There was no word in the ancient Greek language for "wife" or "husband," only "man" and "woman." The correct translation must be determined by the context. It's obvious that Paul was referring to husbands and wives because of his reference to Adam and Eve. Paul was saying he didn't allow wives to exercise authority over or teach their husbands, as it was a clear perversion of God's intended order of authority in the family (see 2:13). Part of the reason Eve was deceived was that she wasn't properly submitted to her husband. It's clear from Scripture that Adam passed on to Eve God's command not to eat the fruit (see Gen. 2:16-17; 3:1-3). What would have happened if Eve had listened to her husband rather than the serpent? Paul was not teaching that women are inferior, either.

Verse 15 raises some questions that I think are answered by alternate translations. Weymouth's translation says, "Yet a woman will be brought safely through childbirth if she and her husband continue to live in faith and love and growing holiness."

PSALM 87:1-7

PROVERBS 25:18-19

OCTOBER 18

JEREMIAH 31:27-32:44

Today we read of the "new covenant" God promises to inaugurate someday with Israel and Judah. Keep in mind that almost everything we read today has a dual application—first to the return of Judah from Babylon, and then to the restoration of the believing Jews to their homeland during the millennium.

It should be obvious what verses aren't applicable to the return from Babylon. For example, we know that the new covenant wasn't inaugurated when the Jews returned from Babylon, but after Christ's atoning sacrifice. Another example is found in Jeremiah 31:40, where God promised that Jerusalem will never be overthrown again. That is obviously yet to be fulfilled. Jerusalem was destroyed again about six hundred years after the Jews returned from Babylon (in A.D. 70, by the Romans) and has been overthrown many times since.

God promised that the Jewish race would never be completely annihilated, to the degree that the sun and the moon would stop shining first (see vv. 35-36). God has kept His promise now for twenty-five hundred years! It's amazing there are any Jews left in the world today in light of all the persecution they've suffered down through the ages.

Chapter 32 has its setting during the last days of the final Davidic king—Zedekiah. Remember that he was installed as king in place of his nephew by Nebuchadnezzar himself, but he rebelled after about nine years. Now Nebuchadnezzar had returned and was in the process of taking the city by building siege walls around it. Jeremiah was in prison because Zedekiah didn't like his prediction that this was the end for Jerusalem (see 32:2-5).

Somehow Jeremiah purchased land in Anathoth while in prison. It's understandable that he was confused about why God would have him purchase land during an enemy invasion, especially when he knew Babylon would triumph. Property values tend to fall during enemy invasions! Jeremiah's cousin Hanamel, who offered to sell the land to Jeremiah, must have considered himself a real salesman! He received seventeen shekels of silver for a worthless piece of property. However, God explained to Jeremiah that he would one day restore the fortunes of Judah, and Jeremiah's investment would pay off. Jeremiah's purchase was a sign to Judah that he believed what he preached—Judah would return one day. He put his money where his mouth was!

1 TIMOTHY 3:1-16

In the New Testament, when speaking of church government, the words *bishop*, *elder*, and *pastor* are synonymous terms. They all describe the identical office. For example, the word translated "overseer" in verse 1 is the Greek word *episkopos*. The word translated "pastor" in Ephesians 4:11 is the Greek word *poimen*, meaning "shepherd." The word for "elder" in 1 Timothy 5:17 and Acts 20:17 is the word *presbuteros*. So we have *episkopos*, *poimen*, and *presbuteros*—overseers, pastors and elders. In Acts 20:28, Paul tells the elders (*presbuteros*) that the Holy Spirit has made them overseers (*episkopos*). And he tells those elders-overseers to shepherd (*poimaino*—the verb form of *poimen*) the church of God.

Paul was not writing to "Pastor Timothy" to help him choose a board of elders for his church, as some teach. Rather, Paul was giving to fellow-apostle Timothy advice in choosing qualified pastors for the various churches in and around Ephesus. (The church had been founded there probably ten years previously, and the churches desperately needed visible leadership.) These pastors-overseers-elders were paid, full-time, preaching and teaching men who would rule the church (see 5:17-18).

In verses 2-7, we have the qualifications for pastors. A pastor must be above reproach. He can have only one wife. (This doesn't disqualify previously divorced men—Paul was disqualifying men who have two wives.) He can't be addicted to wine. He can't be a lover of money. He must rule his own household well, because he will be ruling the church. He can't be a new convert, or else he may become conceited and fall under the same condemnation that Satan did (i.e., his pride could cause him to fall).

The other church office is that of a "deacon." The Greek word for "deacon" is *diakonos* and simply means "servant." That's what a deacon does: he serves. Sunday school teachers, church janitors, secretaries, sound-equipment operators, and so on, all fall into this category. They, too, must meet certain qualifications, and Paul stated that both deacons and elders should first be tested before being officially commissioned (see v. 10).

PSALM 88:1-18

PROVERBS 25:20-22

If Jesus is God and the Holy Spirit is God, we shouldn't be surprised that the Holy Spirit anointed Solomon to say the same things Jesus said. Here is a classic example in verses 21-22. We should be kind to our enemies. Love is always the best way.

OCTOBER 19

JEREMIAH 33:1-34:22

When God restores Israel's fortunes, the entire earth will fear and tremble at the report (see 33:9). The "righteous branch of David" (33:15) is Jesus Christ. He will "execute justice and righteousness on the earth" (33:15).

We can also see that the descendants of Levi will be restored to their official capacity (see 33:18). They will still administrate the sacrifices, which will be a constant reminder of the sacrifice of the Lamb of God. In Israel today, in anticipation of the rebuilding of the temple, young men who can trace their lineage to Levi are being trained for the priesthood. We must be getting close to the end!

In chapter 34, we learn that during the final days of Jerusalem's siege by Nebuchadnezzar, there was a revival of sorts. The people decided to obey a small part of the Law that required them to set free their Hebrew slaves at the end of seven years of service. They even went so far as to make a formal covenant with God over the matter, and they performed a calf-cutting ceremony (see 34:18). However, their devotion was short-lived, and in a matter of a few weeks they took back their released slaves. This was the last straw before the Lord.

In 34:21, the Babylonian armies had left Jerusalem. This was only a situation, as the troops were needed to battle Pharaoh's advancing army. It was probably during this temporary reprieve that the people of Jerusalem took back their Hebrew slaves.

1 TIMOTHY 4:1-16

Since we're living in the latter times right now, we should heed Paul's warning in verses 1-3. Some will fall away from the faith because they're deceived by demons, but it doesn't have to be you or me! The hypocritical deceivers whom Satan will use will forbid marriage and advocate abstaining from foods. However, we know that "everything created by God is good, and nothing is to be rejected if it is received with gratitude; for it is sanctified by the means of the Word of God and prayer" (vv. 4-5).

Paul exhorted Timothy to discipline himself for the purpose of godliness (see v. 7). It takes discipline to become a godly person. Paul said it would pay off in this life and the next (see v. 8).

We don't know what the "spiritual gift" was within Timothy, which he received by prophetic utterance when hands were laid on him by the presbytery (see v. 14). Possibly the Lord had anointed Timothy to be used frequently in the gift of the word of knowledge or word of wisdom. God equips whom He calls. Regardless of what the gift was, it could be neglected, as can be any gift from God.

The Greek word for "presbytery" is *presbuterion*, and is a presumed derivative of *presbuteros*, which means "elder." So the presbytery must have been a meeting of pastors or ministers in general. If nothing else, this scripture should teach ministers that they need to be in fellowship with other ministers. Beware of "lone ranger pastors" who have no fellowship with any other pastors.

PSALM 89:1-13

PROVERBS 25:23-24

OCTOBER 20

JEREMIAH 35:1-36:32

Both chapters 35 and 36 have their setting during the evil reign of Jehoiakim, the third king in the succession of Judah's five last Davidic rulers.

Chapter 35 is easy to understand—the sons of Jonadab had obeyed the strict commands of their Bedouin father for two centuries, and they were compared to the people of Judah, who had not listened to their God. Notice that God promised to bless the posterity of the sons of Jonadab for their obedience to their father (see 35:18-19).

We get a glimpse of the evil character of King Jehoiakim in chapter 36. God instructed Jeremiah to write down all his prophecies of the last twenty years of his ministry. This task would have taken some amount of time and effort! Baruch, Jeremiah's scribe, read the words of the scroll to the people at the temple and to the princes, and finally it was read before King Jehoiakim, who burned it in his fireplace. All that work up in smoke! Too bad Jeremiah didn't have a copy machine, because God then instructed him to write out the whole thing again (see 36:28)! In response to Jehoiakim's belligerence, God promised that he would have no permanent successor on the throne. This came to pass; his son reigned three months before being exiled. Jehoiakim's brother Zedekiah became the final Davidic king to reign in Jerusalem.

1 TIMOTHY 5:1-25

According to this chapter, there were two classes of people on the church payroll—qualifying widows and pastors-elders-overseers. Paul first discussed what qualifies widows to receive financial assistance from church funds. A widow could not be supported by the church if she had children or grandchildren who were capable of supporting her (see v. 4).

Professing Christians who don't take care of their own are "worse than unbelievers" (v. 8). The church was only to support widows who were devoted to a ministry of prayer, not those who watched soap operas all day long (see v. 6; my own translation). They must be at least sixty years old and have spent their Christian lives in service to God (see v. 10). Apparently these church-supported widows made a pledge never to remarry so that they might devote themselves to the service of the church (see v. 12). God's plan of church-supported widows was not a welfare plan!

Elders-pastors-overseers are to be paid well if they work hard at preaching and teaching (see vv. 17-18). This one verse proves that eldership is a paid, preaching, teaching, ruling position in the church. Notice that Paul used the same expression ("worthy of double honor") as he used in verse 3 when speaking of supporting widows, so there's no doubt that he was referring here to the paying of elders.

In the context of verses 17-22, it seems that when Paul told Timothy to "rebuke in the presence of all those who continue in sin," he was referring to elders who continue in sin. They should be disciplined in the presence of the other elders. Furthermore, Paul instructed Timothy not to lay hands upon anyone too hastily, that is, to confirm an elder publicly. If he did lay his hands on too hastily, he might share responsibility in that elder's sins, having placed him in a position for which he wasn't ready.

Why did Paul instruct Timothy not to drink water, but to take a little wine for the sake of his "frequent ailments" (v. 23)? The wine of which Paul spoke was practically nonalcoholic by modern standards. This scripture does not make drinking alcohol justifiable to you and me. The word for "ailments" here is the Greek word *asthenia*, which is literally translated "weakness." It can mean sickness, but it doesn't have to, as we find in Matthew 26:41, 1 Corinthians 1:25 and 1 Peter 3:7. So it's possible Timothy was weak for some reason other than sickness, or he may well have been sick. Whatever it was, the solution was not to drink the water in Ephesus any longer. Why? I know from traveling in many third-world countries that I should never drink the water, because they rarely have good sanitation or sewers, and my system isn't immune to the germs of each locale. Even though I believe in divine healing, I realize that to drink the water would be a form of testing God (unless I have no other option). Timothy, originally from the Galatian city of Lystra, was about three hundred miles from home in Ephesus, and so his system possibly was not immune to the local germs. The solution was simple—drink fermented grape juice instead of water (alcohol kills germs).

Verses 24-25 simply mean that we don't know about some people's sins until after they've been judged by God. They kept them hidden until then. Just as Solomon wrote in Proverbs 10:9, Paul now stated that all sins will eventually be found out.

PSALM 89:14-37

PROVERBS 25:25-27

Don't give way before the wicked! Stand your ground lest you become a "trampled spring or polluted well."

OCTOBER 21

JEREMIAH 37:1-38:28

These chapters are set during the final days of the last siege of Jerusalem, under the kingship of Zedekiah. God clearly revealed to the king and to those shut up in Jerusalem that if they would surrender themselves to the Chaldeans, their lives and their city would be spared. But the majority refused to listen. Apparently there were only a few who surrendered.

The harassment of Jeremiah grew more severe as the end drew near. He was falsely accused of defecting to the Chaldeans, and then he was beaten, imprisoned and almost executed by means of suffocation or starvation in a cistern. However, God kept his forty-year-old promise to Jeremiah to deliver him (see 1:8)! Why did God allow Jeremiah to undergo such persecution? Only because He loved Jeremiah's persecutors and was still showing them mercy, giving them time to repent.

1 TIMOTHY 6:1-21

This final chapter contains a beautiful balance on the subject of biblical prosperity. First of all, God wants us to be content with what we have (see vv. 6, 8) even if it's only food and covering. We can't take any of our material possessions to heaven with us, so there's no reason to become attached to them.

That doesn't mean it's a sin to have more than food and covering, as is revealed in 1 Timothy 6:17 and many other scriptures. The point is that God doesn't want us to be consumed with acquiring more and more things. Paul said that some have pursued money and wandered away from the faith. Money isn't the root of all sorts of evil, but the "love of money" (v. 10). You can commit that sin and not have a dime! It isn't *how much* money we have that should concern us, but our attitude toward money. It's impossible to serve both God and money, but it is possible to serve God and have money. Paul plainly states that God is the one "who richly supplies us with all things to enjoy" (v. 17), and that "godliness is a means of great gain, when accompanied by contentment" (v. 6). Let's learn to be content and guard ourselves from greed.

Paul spoke of those who are rich "in this present world," which implies they may not be rich in the world to come. However, if they practice generosity and share their abundance, they will insure for themselves "a good foundation for the future" (v. 19).

I like the phrase Paul used in verse 12: "Fight the good fight of faith." Faith is definitely a fight. We must battle doubts and unbelief, and we must fight the testimony of our senses. What is a "good fight"? It's a fight you win!

PSALM 89:38-52

PROVERBS 25:28

A person who has no self-control is very vulnerable.

OCTOBER 22

JEREMIAH 39:1-41:18

Twice before, in 2 Kings and 2 Chronicles, we have read the account of the eighteen-month siege and fall of Jerusalem. However, Jeremiah offered some details that weren't mentioned in those reports. First, notice that even when God's wrath was being poured out on Jerusalem in the form of a Babylonian invasion, He still singled out two righteous men for special treatment: Jeremiah and Ebed-melech (see 39:15-16), the man who rescued Jeremiah from the cistern.

Jeremiah decided to remain in Judah under the appointed governorship of Gedaliah. We will see that he continued to minister to the remaining Jews—the "poorest of the land," whom Nebuchadnezzar left behind, the fighting men of Judah who were "in the field" at the time of the siege, and those who had fled previously to surrounding countries and who returned after the siege. Gedaliah was soon murdered by a wicked man named Ishmael, of the family of David, and the result was that everyone prepared to flee to Egypt, expecting the vengeance of Nebuchadnezzar for Gedaliah's murder. Their preparation for departure was the backdrop for Jeremiah's next prophetic warning to them.

2 TIMOTHY 1:1-18

This letter was Paul's last one and could appropriately be called his dying words. He wrote it from a jail cell during his second imprisonment in Rome, and he knew his death was imminent. The date was around A.D. 67, a time of terrible persecution under the demon-crazed Emperor Nero, who blamed the Christians for the burning of Rome. He instituted a persecution against the church of holocaust proportions, to the degree of covering Christians in tar, setting them on fire, and using them as porch lights. Historians believe that Paul was martyred under the Neronian persecutions, and this epistle may have been written only days before his death. Incidentally, Nero committed suicide in A.D. 68.

One of the purposes of this letter was to encourage a weakening Timothy, who was no doubt suffering himself as a result of the imperial persecution. Paul exhorted him to "kindle afresh" the gift of God that was in him through the laying on of Paul's hands (see v. 6). I assume that he is referring to the Holy Spirit or else Timothy's anointing to preach and teach. The Holy Spirit can be in us, but He will remain dormant if we don't exercise our faith in His ability.

Paul reiterated the fundamental tenets of Christianity—even the doctrine of justification by faith apart from works. Surely Timothy was doctrinally mature and hardly needed reminding that his salvation was by faith. Paul must have known his letter would have a wider audience than just his friend Timothy. I wonder if the Lord revealed to him that his letters would be read for centuries to come, as a means of encouraging Paul as he evaluated his life's work.

Paul may have needed that encouragement, because he mentioned that "all who are in Asia" turned away from him (see v. 15). That means the churches of Ephesus and Colossae no longer listened to Paul. What a disappointment that must have been to this great apostle! However, we have no indication of a pity party in this letter; Paul was full of thanksgiving to the end for His Savior and his few loyal friends.

Every Christian should memorize verse 7: "For God has not given us a spirit of timidity [fear], but of power and love and discipline."

PSALMS 90:1-91:16

PROVERBS 26:1-2

I'm amazed at the number of Christians who talk about some "curse" that has been placed on them or their families. Just talking about such a thing glorifies the devil. We are delivered from the kingdom of darkness and transferred into the kingdom of light! Greater is He who is in us than he who is in the world (see 1 John 4:4). Beyond all that, we have this promise in Proverbs: "A curse without cause does not alight."

OCTOBER 23

JEREMIAH 42:1-44:23

You would have thought that the people who remained in Judah would have realized by now that Jeremiah's word was as good as gold. All his predictions of the past forty years had come to pass without exception! Yet the people persisted in their stubbornness, refused to believe Jeremiah was now speaking on behalf of the Lord, and journeyed to Egypt (taking him along), hoping to escape the wrath of Nebuchadnezzar. There God vowed that the king of Babylon would come and destroy them as His judgment fell on Egypt as well (see 43:8-13). We can hardly blame God, especially when we read the people's response to Jeremiah's final entreaty, which concerns their libations to the queen of heaven (see 44:15-19). Incidentally, Jeremiah's prediction of the Babylonian invasion of Egypt came to pass in 568 B.C.

2 TIMOTHY 2:1-21

Verse 2 relates a principle we need to heed. Paul wrote: "the things which you have heard from me...these entrust to faithful men, who will be able to teach others also." Unfortunately, we've been guilty too much of the time of entrusting what we've learned to unfaithful people. I say "unfaithful" because those whom we have taught have kept the teaching for themselves and haven't shared it. God isn't calling all of us to a full-time teaching ministry, but He is calling all of us to make disciples. And to make a disciple, we'll have to teach what we ourselves have learned.

Those who are involved in ministry find that "the affairs of everyday life" can be their greatest hindrance (see v. 4). No one can avoid those affairs, but we must guard ourselves that we don't become "entangled" by them.

Paul compared God's workers to soldiers, athletes and farmers (see vv. 3-6). As soldiers, we're under the strict command of our commander-in-chief, Jesus. We have an enemy we're fighting—Satan and his hordes of demons. The ground we're taking is the hearts of people. Our emphasis is not on acquiring material possessions, but on winning the war. We travel light, ready to move. We live one day at a time, knowing we might not be here tomorrow (if Jesus should return). We serve proudly for our cause and commander!

As spiritual athletes, we are disciplining ourselves for the purpose of godliness. We have our eyes on a goal of winning the race. We know we must compete according to the rules, because the Judge is watching us closely!

As farmers, we are involved in tilling, sowing, fertilizing and watering with one ultimate purpose—to prepare a harvest that we can present to the Lord at His coming!

In verses 20-21 we're compared to "vessels" in a large house. Some vessels are of silver and gold, and some are wooden and earthenware. In our day, we would say that we have crystal glasses and paper cups. Paul's point was that in God's household, there are some people who bring honor to God, and unfortunately, there are some who bring dishonor (see v. 20). However, whether one is a vessel for honor or a vessel for dishonor is not determined by God, but by each individual. If each one will "cleanse himself," each one will be an honorable vessel (see vv. 20-21). Are you one of God's "crystal glasses" or one of His "paper cups"?

PSALM 92:1-93:5

PROVERBS 26:3-5

OCTOBER 24

JEREMIAH 44:24-47:7

No one knows what became of Jeremiah after the time of his final prophecies in Egypt. Tradition says he was stoned to death shortly thereafter. As we are reading Paul's last words in the New Testament, we are now also reading Jeremiah's last words in the Old.

We read in chapter 44 of God's final promise of calamity that would come upon the Jews in Egypt through the Babylonian invasion. God gave them plenty of warning and plenty of time to repent.

Chapter 46 begins the final major section of Jeremiah's book, which contains various prophecies against some of the nations of the ancient world. We begin this section with the foretelling of two different Babylonian wars against Egypt, the second of which would bring her demise. However, God promised restoration rather than complete and final devastation (see 46:26), proved to be true by the fact that Egypt is still a nation today. Notice also in 46:27-28 that God once again spoke an encouraging word of restoration to His people Israel. Chapter 47 foretold the Babylonian destruction of one of Israel's chief enemies—Philistia. That was fulfilled by 587 B.C.

What impresses me about today's reading is that in the midst of foretelling the destiny of entire nations, God also singled out one man, Jeremiah's scribe Baruch, to encourage him in his faithfulness. Apparently Baruch was distressed over the coming destruction of Jerusalem (this prophecy was spoken in the days of Jehoiakim), so God reassured him that he would survive.

2 TIMOTHY 2:22-3:17

Too often we try to win arguments when we should be trying to win people to the Lord. We're never going to win anyone to Christ by arguing with him (see 2:24). The only way to win someone is to be kind, gentle and patient when wronged. We need to remember that unsaved people are under the control of Satan, and that he has blinded them to the truth of the gospel (see 2:26).

"In the last days difficult times will come" (3:1). What are the "last days" of which Paul was speaking? That's up for debate, but there is little doubt that what he said of the last days has application to our present day. If Jesus doesn't return in my lifetime, I will be very surprised. Note that the characteristics of the last days are an exact description of what we see in the world right now (see 3:2-7). We should be prepared for "difficult times" before Jesus returns. The persecution we now experience will grow more intense, because "evil men and impostors will proceed from bad to worse" (3:13). The world is not going to get any better! And "all who desire to live godly in Christ Jesus will be persecuted" (3:12).

Paul mentioned the sufferings he endured at Antioch, Iconium and Lystra, out of which God delivered him every time (see 3:11). In Antioch, Paul was run out of town. In Iconium, he barely escaped being stoned. At Lystra, Jews from Antioch and Iconium came and succeeded in stoning him, leaving him for dead. But the disciples gathered around him and prayed, and the Lord raised him up! The Lord didn't stop the persecutions, but Paul survived them all.

Why didn't God deliver Paul this final time in Rome? No one can say with certainty, but we do know that Paul had fulfilled his ministry (see 4:7, 17). His time of departure had arrived (see 4:6), and Paul viewed his death as a "drink offering" to the Lord. That is, he saw a divine purpose even in his death that would glorify God.

Thank God that "all Scripture is inspired by God" (3:16)! The words "inspired by God" literally mean "God-breathed." There was an allowance for the individual style of each of the Bible authors, but their words were God's. The Scriptures carry at least a five-fold purpose in the life of the believer: they teach, reprove, correct, train and equip us (see 3:16-17).

PSALM 94:1-23

PROVERBS 26:6-8

OCTOBER 25

JEREMIAH 48:1-49:22

Today we read prophecies directed at the nations of Moab, Ammon and Edom. Remember when God destroyed Sodom and Gomorrah and Lot's two daughters committed incest with him? Their resulting offspring were Moab and Ammon (see Gen. 19:37-38), from whom these two nations arose. Edom is just another name for Esau (see 49:8). This nation came from Jacob's (Israel's) brother, Esau.

All three of these nations were located east of the Jordan River and the Dead Sea, within the modern nation of Jordan. God promised to restore the fortunes of Moab "in the latter days" (see 48:47) and He also promised to restore the fortunes of Ammon sometime in the future—we assume in the "latter days" as well (see 49:6). No such promise was made in regard to Edom, which will suffer permanent devastation.

2 TIMOTHY 4:1-22

We read yesterday that the Word of God is profitable for reproof and correction. Today we read Paul's instructions to Timothy to "reprove, rebuke, exhort," because the time will come when people will listen only to teachers who teach what they want to hear (see vv. 2-3). Those who are preachers of the Word must at times proclaim what is not popular.

Our example of balanced preaching should be Jesus Himself, who didn't always preach on positive subjects. We need a balance. We should find ourselves reproving, rebuking and exhorting. We should be informing people of their responsibilities, not just their blessings.

For those of us who are listening to preaching, let's make sure that what we're hearing is based on the Word of God and not some distortion of His Word. Let's make certain we're receiving a balanced diet of what God has said in His Word, not just one subject all the time.

Paul exhorted Timothy to fulfill his ministry in verse 5. All of us have divine destinies. It would be terrible to stand before Jesus and hear Him say, "You never fulfilled what I called you to do.

You were too busy following your own plans.'' Paul knew that he was near the end of his life and had fulfilled his life's calling. He had finished his course, and it had been a fight (see v. 7). Notice Paul didn't say that it was time for him to die but that the ''time of his departure'' had arrived. He knew it in his spirit; our home-going doesn't have to come as a surprise.

Paul also said he had ''kept the faith'' (v. 7). No matter what, we should never let our faith in Jesus falter. If we endure to the end, we're promised a ''crown of righteousness'' in heaven (v. 8).

Before Paul's second missionary journey, he and Barnabas got into an argument over whether to take Mark along with them. Mark had deserted them during the first missionary journey (see Acts 13:13), and Paul didn't want to trust him again (see Acts 15:37-40). Now Paul wrote to Timothy, ''Pick up Mark and bring him with you, for he is useful to me for service.'' Thank God the story of Paul and Mark's relationship had a happy ending!

The persecution under Nero was obviously intensifying to the point that most of Paul's companions had deserted him in Rome. At his preliminary trial before the emperor, no one had even stood up for him. Paul had no bitterness toward his friends but rather prayed that the Lord would not hold it against them (see v. 16). *That's love.*

However, the Lord, who promised ''I will never leave you or forsake you,'' stood by Paul and strengthened him as he testified of God's grace at his trial (see v. 17). Paul was ''delivered out of the lion's mouth.'' We don't know if Paul was referring literally to being cast to the lions, or if he was speaking figuratively of Nero or Satan. The point is that God supernaturally helped Paul at his preliminary trial, and it saved him in some manner. Nobody knows for certain exactly how Paul died, but there is no doubt that he died shortly after he penned this letter, and we assume he was martyred by Nero.

PSALMS 95:1-96:13

PROVERBS 26:9-12

All these proverbs are about the folly of the fool, yet there is something even worse—being wise in your own eyes (see v. 12)!

OCTOBER 26

JEREMIAH 49:23-50:46

Today we read more prophecies against Israel's neighboring nations of Syria (Damascus, the capital), Kedar and Hazor (located in the Arabian Desert), and Elam (in modern Iran). Elam was promised a future restoration (see 49:39).

Chapter 50 contains the first part of a prophecy against Babylon, located in modern Iraq. It would fall to Medo-Persia in 539 B.C. Babylon had been used as a tool of God's judgment upon the nations, but its time of judgment would soon arrive as well. When that happened, the Jews would be set free to return to their homeland (see 50:4-8, 17-20). We know that when Cyrus the Persian conquered Babylon, he did so without destroying the city or its walls. Eventually, as Jeremiah predicted, the city was ruined and had no inhabitants (see 50:13). To this day, it's a heap of ruins. This prophecy against Babylon also has application beyond the fall of ancient Babylon and the return of the Jews from exile. Its scope includes the fall of the future Babylon of the book of

Revelation and the regathering of believing Israel to Palestine.

TITUS 1:1-16

Crete is a large island in the Mediterranean Sea, and it belongs to Greece. Paul had established the church there, and now he wrote to Titus to instruct him to "set in order what remains" and appoint elders (*presbuteros*) in every city (see v. 5). In other words, Titus was to set pastors over the various groups of new Christians that were meeting in Crete.

The book of Titus is similar to Paul's first letter to Timothy. (It was probably written around the same time.) Paul once again listed qualifications for the pastors. Notice that he also once again interchangeably used the words "elder" and "overseer" (*presbuteros* and *episkopos*) in verses 5 and 7. These pastors would have to be able to stand against false teachings, and therefore they had to be well-grounded in the truths of the gospel.

Especially antagonizing were the Jewish legalists (see vv. 10, 14). Furthermore, they had the challenge of working in a culture that Paul characterized as being full of liars, evil beasts and gluttons (see v. 12). Sounds like fun!

Do you know that there is one thing God can't do? He can't lie. Isn't that what Paul says in verse 2? Although Cretans may be liars, God is not. It is impossible for Him to lie!

PSALMS 97:1-98:9

PROVERBS 26:13-16

God isn't lazy, and He doesn't bless laziness. However, keep in mind that even God took a day of rest.

OCTOBER 27

JEREMIAH 51:1-53

This chapter needs little explanation, as it's a repetition of the now-familiar theme of the fall of Babylon to Medo-Persia. We'll read about it again in Daniel's book. God's people were warned in advance of what was coming so they might escape the future calamity (see vv. 6, 45). Furthermore, we have more promises of the future restoration of the Jews to the land of Judah. Again may I say that this prophecy seems to have further application to the fall of the future Babylon of Revelation.

TITUS 2:1-15

Notice what Paul emphasized the most when he exhorted Titus to "speak the things which are fitting for sound doctrine" (v. 1). The majority of his remaining words centered on the subject of holy living. When we think of "sound doctrine," we usually think of the great subjects of the trinity, the divinity of Christ, the work of His atoning sacrifice and the like. But the result of "sound doctrine" should be a change in the way we live. Knowledge for knowledge's sake is worthless. Our inward beliefs ought to affect our outward actions, lest we be like those whom Paul described yesterday: "They profess to know God, but by their deeds they deny Him" (1:16).

Paul offered specific words to older and younger men and women. Notice that one of the reasons young women should be subject to their husbands is so that "the word of God may not be dishonored" (v. 5). We know the gospel is the greatest women's liberator there ever was, and there's no question that women are treated best in societies that have received Christianity. However, Christian women (especially in the male-dominated society of Paul's day) had to be careful not to take their new-found liberty to the extreme. If they did, it could hinder the gospel.

The same principle applied to the issue of slavery. Paul never endorsed slavery, but he realized that if he encouraged a slave revolt, the true message of the gospel would be obscured. His answer to slavery was to change men's hearts through the gospel. For example, a Christian slave-owner who was allowing Christ to live through him would not treat his slaves harshly, but with compassion and fairness. Chances are that he would eventually release his slaves. The gospel is the most powerful tool we have for instituting social change. Only the gospel of the grace of God causes people to "deny ungodliness and worldly desires and to live sensibly, righteously and godly in the present age" (v. 12).

PSALM 99:1-9

PROVERBS 26:17

Isn't this a good piece of advice? Don't meddle with others' strife!

OCTOBER 28

JEREMIAH 51:54-52:34

This final chapter basically repeats what we read at the end of 2 Kings. It was probably added as proof of the fulfilling of Jeremiah's prophecies. The moral of the story: "Obey God and be blessed. Disobey God and suffer the consequences."

The next three Old Testament books (Lamentations, Ezekiel and Daniel) were written during approximately the same time in Jewish history. The very next book, Lamentations, was written by Jeremiah after the destruction of Jerusalem. Ezekiel and Daniel both were contemporaries of Jeremiah, but they were deported to Babylon and prophesied during the captivity there. Daniel even studied the book of Jeremiah, and he lived to see Jeremiah's prediction fulfilled in the fall of Babylon to Medo-Persia. Isaiah, Jeremiah, Ezekiel and Daniel make up what are known as the "major prophets," whereas all the rest are considered "minor prophets." Of the four "major prophets," I'll have to admit that Daniel is my favorite.

TITUS 3:1-15

Verses 4-7 present several fundamental facts: (1) God is kind and loves all mankind; (2) Jesus (the Savior) is God; (3) He saved us because of His mercy, not because of our works; (4) we have been washed clean and reborn by the Holy Spirit; (5) the Holy Spirit has been poured out upon us; (6) Jesus was and is the one who baptized us in the Holy Spirit; (7) we have been justified by His grace; and (8) we are heirs of God!

PSALM 100:1-5

PROVERBS 26:18-19

OCTOBER 29

LAMENTATIONS 1:1-2:19

You would never know it from reading this book in its English translation, but in the original Hebrew, the first four poems are alphabetic acrostics. That is, each verse begins with a consecutive letter of the Hebrew alphabet. There are twenty-two letters in the Hebrew alphabet, and notice that chapters 1, 2 and 4 each have twenty-two verses, while chapter 3 has sixty-six, or three times twenty-two.

The first four poems were written in the rhythm of a dirge, and truly, this book is like a funeral march for Jerusalem. It was tearfully penned by Jeremiah as he viewed "God's city" after its destruction by Babylon in 587 B.C. It needs little explanation, because its title says it all—this is a lamentation for the consequences of disobedience.

PHILEMON 1-25

This short letter was written by Paul, while imprisoned in Rome, to a Christian friend in Colossae named Philemon—probably one of Paul's own converts. While in jail, Paul had won to the Lord a fellow prisoner named Onesimus, a runaway slave owned by Philemon. Apparently Onesimus was about to be released, so Paul sent this letter encouraging Philemon to forgive and reinstate his runaway slave. As Philemon's legal property, Onesimus could be severely punished for running away (even crucified under Roman law), but Paul assured Philemon that Onesimus was now a changed man.

Paul stated in verse 8 that as an apostle, he had the authority to order Philemon to do what was proper. He had enough confidence in Philemon's love, however, that he needed only to make an appeal on behalf of Onesimus. He even promised to pay back whatever was owed by Onesimus (see v. 18). However, Philemon was in debt to Paul himself, as Paul reminded him (see v. 19)—possibly a reference to the fact that Philemon became a believer through Paul's ministry. Paul expressed his confidence that Philemon would do even more than what he asked of him (see v. 21), which could be an implication that Paul expected Philemon to release his returned slave permanently.

Praise God that through Jesus Christ, men can be forgiven and made new creations! Just as Martin Luther once said, "We are all the Lord's Onesimi." Truly, Jesus is the answer to every social problem, and He can heal any broken relationship. He is the answer!

PSALM 101:1-8

PROVERBS 26:20

Beware of people who always speak in hushed tones. They fan the fires of contention.

OCTOBER 30

LAMENTATIONS 2:20-3:66

This third lament recorded in chapter 3 is somewhat difficult to interpret, because it causes us to question who was doing the speaking. Was it Jeremiah or some other, unnamed Jew? At first it appears that it couldn't have been Jeremiah, because the speaker, in verses 1-18, had obviously suffered the judgment of God for his sins—along with the rest of the population. We know that Jeremiah was one of the few righteous persons in Jerusalem at the time of its destruction, and his sufferings were mainly persecutions by his fellow Jews. He was not exiled to Babylon as a slave.

The only answer I can offer is that possibly Jeremiah was speaking simply as a representative of the Jews of Judah, but not referring to his own experience. Or possibly Jeremiah spoke those words at a low point of despair during his persecutions. The words of verses 1-18 are similar to Job's laments.

Even in the midst of God's dismaying judgment, there was still a ray of hope because of God's never-ceasing compassion (see 3:22). If the Lord brought judgment, He would also bring pardon (see 3:31-32). Therefore, repentance was still in order (see 3:40-42). And the wicked nation God used to judge His people would one day be recompensed in full (see 3:60-66).

HEBREWS 1:1-14

The book of Hebrews was written to Jewish Christians who were being tempted to turn back to Judaism because of intense persecution from fellow Jews and Romans. It was probably written sometime between A.D. 64 and 70, during the Neronian persecutions. Although we don't know the author for sure, I have always thought that it must have been Paul, and I comment on this book with that assumption, even though many would disagree with me.

The theme was "Christ is superior," and the author attempted to dissuade the Hebrew Christians from reverting back to their Jewish tradition. It's a good thing we have already read the majority of the Old Testament, or this book would be impossible to comprehend, as it contains so many references to Jewish practices under the Law of Moses. Everything in the Old Covenant pointed to that which Christ fully accomplished in His redemption. You'll see the Old Testament in a new light—the light of the Holy Spirit's revelation of God's ageless plan for mankind through Jesus.

This first chapter deals with the superiority of Christ over angels. Under the old covenant, the heavenly mediators and messengers between God and humanity were angels; they delivered the words of the covenant to Moses (see Gal. 3:19; Acts 7:38, 53; Heb. 2:2). But Christ is a far superior mediator and messenger! He, unlike any angel, is God's Son (see v. 5). He created the world (see vv. 2, 10). He is one with God the Father (see v. 3). He is the one who "made purification of sins" (see v. 3). He is presently heir of all things and will one day rule the earth from His throne (see vv. 2, 8). Angels are commanded to worship Him (see v. 6). He is sitting at the right hand of God the Father (see vv. 3, 13), a position which no angel can claim. And He has inherited the highest name in the universe (see v. 4).

Angels are "ministering spirits" who work on our behalf (see v. 14). Their ministry to us is invaluable, but they're still no comparison to Jesus our Savior! He created them, and they do His bidding.

The author quoted several Old Testament scriptures which refer to Jesus. One is found in Psalm 2, "Thou art My Son, today I have begotten Thee" (v. 7). Psalm 2 is a messianic psalm which is set during the final days of the millennium. In that light, we see that Jesus truly is "the heir of all things," because God has given Him the nations as His inheritance (see Ps. 2:8)!

The author also quoted from 2 Samuel 7:14, where God, referring to one of David's descendants, promised, "I will be a Father to Him, and He shall be a Son to Me." It beautifully illustrates the law of double reference. God's promise to David was fulfilled in his son Solomon, but it ultimately referred to a fulfillment in Christ.

PSALM 102:1-28

PROVERBS 26:21-22

OCTOBER 31

LAMENTATIONS 4:1-5:22

This sad book ends with a note of despair, but we know that God had not "utterly rejected" (5:22) His people, as it may have seemed to them at the time. They had paid a bitter price for their sin and suffered atrocities, but God would eventually restore a remnant to begin anew in Judah.

HEBREWS 2:1-18

We read today that Christ's message was far superior to the former messages. The author's motive was to prevent his readers, the Hebrew Christians, from drifting away to inferior messengers and messages. The word that came via angels was "unalterable" (v. 2), so how much more "unalterable" is the message God sent us through His own Son! God confirmed His latest message through His apostles with signs, wonders, miracles and various gifts of the Holy Spirit (see v. 4). (Those gifts of the Spirit were manifested as He willed, not as the apostles willed [v. 4].)

How could Christ be superior to angels if He was a mortal human being? He had to become a man, live as a man, and suffer and die as a man in order for God's eternal purposes to be fulfilled. But Jesus was also fully God, and God the Father has subjected the future world to Him, not to angels. The author then quoted Psalm 8:4-6 as a reference to the future worldwide reign of Christ. He is the "Son of Man" spoken of in verse 6—a term Jesus used Himself many times. For a little while (thirty-three years), Jesus held a position lower than the angels, but after His resurrection, He was crowned with glory and honor (see vv. 7, 9). God the Father then put everything under subjection to Him. Verse 8 clearly reveals, however, that the fullness of the Father's promise to Him has not yet come to complete fruition, and it won't until Christ's millennial reign.

Because of what Jesus did, we now have had spiritual death eradicated from our spirits. Physical death has no ultimate hold on us, either, because we have the promise of a bodily resurrection. From a legal standpoint, Satan no longer has the "power of death," because Jesus, by "tasting death for everyone," stripped Satan of his authority—but only over those who receive eternal life into their spirits.

When we read that Jesus was "perfected through sufferings" (v. 10), it can't mean that Jesus was morally imperfect and became more holy because He suffered. It must mean that through His sufferings on the cross, He became the perfect substitute for us. Apart from that suffering, He couldn't have qualified as our redeemer.

Finally, the author stated that Jesus became our "merciful and faithful high priest" (v. 17). The Hebrew Christians could relate to that analogy, because it was only through the mediation of the high priest and the blood sacrifice that their sins could be covered. Jesus is the superior high priest of the new covenant, and it was through the sacrifice of Himself that He made "propitiation for the sins of the people" (v. 17). He is a compassionate high priest, because He knows what it's like to be tempted, and "He is able to come to the aid of those who are tempted" (v. 18). To the suffering Hebrew Christians being tempted to drift away from faith in Christ, this was especially encouraging news.

PSALM 103:1-22

PROVERBS 26:23

NOVEMBER 1

EZEKIEL 1:1-3:15

As Jeremiah was prophesying in Jerusalem, Ezekiel, deported to Babylon in 597 B.C. with King Jehoiachin, was prophesying to Jewish exiles. His ministry warned of the impending destruction of Jerusalem eleven years after his own exile and, after its fall, of the coming restoration that would be fully realized during the reign of Christ. His book is meticulously organized and dated and is strikingly similar to the book of Revelation, which uses many of the same images. As in Revelation, some of the visions in Ezekiel are difficult to interpret. Be assured that God could have made everything plain and simple—if He had wanted to. Every symbol in Scripture will become abundantly clear when God intends it.

In Ezekiel 1 the prophet described God's "chariot-throne." God, who had "the appearance of a man" (vol. 26), sat on His glorious throne and called Ezekiel to speak on the Lord's behalf. God already knew the people wouldn't listen to Ezekiel, but He called him anyway (3:7).

From 3:12-15, it seems that Ezekiel got a ride on God's "mobile throne" and was dropped off at Tel-abib, where he sat for seven days, "causing consternation among" the exiles living there (3:15).

Ezekiel noticed the rainbow around God's throne, as did John (see Rev. 4:3). Both Ezekiel and John saw "four living creatures" (see Rev. 4:6). And both Ezekiel and John ate a book that "tasted like honey" (see Rev. 10:10). Don't be frustrated over these hard-to-understand descriptions of heaven; just enjoy them. We'll spend the first hour in heaven saying, "Oh! Now I understand what Ezekiel was trying to describe."

HEBREWS 3:1-19

This chapter shows that Christ is superior to Moses, who failed to bring God's people into their promised rest. Just as Moses was faithful over the children of Israel, so, too, Jesus is faithful over the church (vv. 5-6). However, we must "hold fast our confidence and the boast of our hope firm until the end" (v. 6).

Paul admonished these Christians to encourage one another to continue in their confidence (see v. 12). The people were facing intense persecution. For some, trusting Jesus meant facing death, yet they were holding on in faith. God will sometimes allow our faith to be tested, and if we can't pass the small tests, how can we expect to pass the major ones?

PSALM 104:1-23

PROVERBS 26:24-26

Hatred is usually hidden, but always eventually manifested. Beware!

NOVEMBER 2

EZEKIEL 3:16-6:14

Consider the demands on Ezekiel: first, he was accountable for delivering a divine message of judgment upon those whom God designated (see 3:17-20). Second, God would silence Ezekiel unless He had a message for him to deliver (see 3:26-27). Third, Ezekiel had to build a model of Jerusalem and act out a pretend siege against it (see 4:1-3). Ezekiel had to lie on his left side for 390 days, and then on his right side for 40 days (see 4:4-6). For 390 days he had to eat a starvation diet of bread and limited rations of water (see 4:9-17).

This is the probable significance of the 390 days and the 40 days: from the division of the kingdom into Israel and Judah to the release of the exiles was almost 390 years. So Ezekiel bore the iniquity of Israel for the corresponding number of days. From the fall of Jerusalem until the release of the exiles was about 49 years, so the 40 years may be a round figure for Ezekiel to bear the iniquity of Judah. Other opinions are offered: the Greek version of Ezekiel lists 190 rather than 390 days. This approximates the number of years between the fall of Israel to Assyria and the return of the exiles.

Ezekiel was possibly supernaturally restrained by God to lie down for 390 days (see 4:8). It would be miraculous for a person to lie continuously on one side for that long.

The sign of Ezekiel's hair is just as graphic (see 5:1-4). He burned a third of it on his model of Jerusalem, signifying that one-third of the people there would die in the plague and famine of the siege. One-third was to be cut with the sword, signifying that one-third of the people would fall by the sword when the city was broken into. Finally, one-third of his hair was scattered to the wind, signifying that one-third of the people in Jerusalem would be scattered to the nations where they would perish, and a small portion of those would be taken as exiles (see 5:3). The only good news we read is that some of those scattered to the nations would eventually come to repentance (see 6:8-10).

How can a compassionate God ask so much of one man? He was simply trying to get the attention of some people He loved very much; He was endeavoring to bring them to repentance. Though the exiles were hoping for a speedy return to their beloved city, God was telling them that it would be destroyed.

HEBREWS 4:1-16

The comparison here is between the readers and the Israelites who failed to enter the promised land because of their unbelief, even though God had delivered them from Egypt and it was clearly His will for them to conquer Canaan. In Psalm 95, God said that because of Israel's unbelief and disobedience, the people would not enter His rest. Paul drew a parallel between God's rest during the seventh day of creation and the rest God referred to in Psalm 95, which prophetically pointed to the believer's rest. When we have faith in Jesus, we, too, enter into God's rest and rest from our works (see v. 10).

Verse 14 begins a new section of the book, detailing the present high-priestly ministry of Jesus. He is a sympathetic high priest because He has faced and endured temptation. Therefore, we can come to Him with confidence to receive mercy and help in time of need (see v. 16).

PSALM 104:24-35

PROVERBS 26:27

Those who plot evil against others will become their own victims.

NOVEMBER 3

EZEKIEL 7:1-9:11

In chapter 8, God supernaturally transported Ezekiel from Babylon to Jerusalem, where He showed him the idolatrous abominations being committed by its remaining inhabitants. This vision occurred at least five years before Jerusalem was finally destroyed. If I had been God, I wouldn't have waited another five minutes, much less five years, before allowing Jerusalem to be devastated. I say that because I want you to see not the obvious—the terrible, consuming wrath of God—but His great, undeserved mercy.

Also notice that in chapter 9, God specially marked the few people in Jerusalem who "sighed and groaned over all the abominations" (9:4), lest they be consumed in His wrath. God may hold nations guilty, but He knows all the innocent individuals and treats them justly. The book of Revelation describes an angel of God who will proclaim during the tribulation, "Do not harm the earth... until we have sealed the bond-servants of our God on their foreheads" (7:3).

HEBREWS 5:1-14

Continuing with the theme of Christ's superiority, this chapter addresses Jesus' preeminence over priests Aaron and Melchizedek. The Hebrew Christians who were being tempted to revert to Judaism would be foolish to go back to a priestly system that was designed to point them to Christ.

Jesus has all the qualifications to be our high priest. First, He didn't appoint Himself; He was chosen by God (see Ps. 2:7; 110:4).

Second, Jesus, being human, knew what it was like to face temptation. But, unlike any other priest, He was sinless. Verse 8 doesn't mean being God, Jesus learned to become obedient by suffering the consequences of disobedience. He learned the cost that is paid by those obedient to God. It meant His life. His sufferings resulted in His complete perfection.

Verses 11-14 are a short exhortation. By this time, the recipients of this letter should have been teachers, but they still needed someone to teach them. Not all are called to the ministry of teaching, but we're all called to make disciples, teaching younger Christians what we know. If you've gone this far with me through the Bible, you have knowledge to share.

PSALM 105:1-15

PROVERBS 26:28

NOVEMBER 4

EZEKIEL 10:1-11:25

Here, Ezekiel described the same four cherubim he saw by the River Chebar at the onset of his ministry. They and their wheels are no easier to imagine this time. But we *can* understand the glory of God departing from the temple; God had departed from His people. Notice that the glory of God departed gradually, almost reluctantly, from the temple's inner sanctuary, to the threshold, to above the cherubim, to the east gate of the temple and finally to the Mount of Olives.

In chapter 11, God denounced some of the evil rulers in Jerusalem. These twenty-five men may have been counseling rebellion against Babylon or falsely reassuring the people, clearly against God's revealed will. Ezekiel was overcome with emotion, witnessing God's swift judgment upon Pelatiah, and cried out to the Lord, asking if all the remnant of Judah would be annihilated. God's promise, that a surviving remnant would be scattered to the nations and one day restored, has its complete fulfillment in the coming millennium.

HEBREWS 6:1-20

Verses 1-2 give six foundational truths in which every believer should be well-grounded. "Repentance from dead works" means no longer trying to earn your salvation by good deeds or by keeping the Law of Moses. "Faith toward God" refers to the doctrine of justification by faith. "Instruction about washings" could be translated "instruction about baptisms": baptism into the body of Christ, baptism in water and baptism in the Holy Spirit.

"Laying on of hands" is the fundamental doctrine of the *transference by physical contact* of healing power, an anointing or the Holy Spirit. "The resurrection of the dead" means that every person's body will be resurrected. Finally, "eternal judgment" is the doctrine that all persons will stand before God, and the results of each person's judgment will be eternal.

Verses 4-8 have caused much controversy. The formerly saved individual described here has turned his back on God after meeting a fivefold qualification. First, this person has been "enlightened" (v. 4), recognizing his sinful condition and need for a Savior. Second, he has "tasted of the heavenly gift" (v. 4), receiving the free gift of eternal life. Third, he has been baptized in the Holy Spirit. Fourth, he has grown in the Word of God. Fifth, he has tasted "the powers of the age to come" (v. 5). If a person has reached that place and then turns away, it is impossible to restore him to repentance. This is not referring to someone committing a sin, but to willfully, knowingly turning his back on Jesus.

Again, Paul wanted to prevent the Hebrew Christians from reverting to Judaism. Verses 9-20 encouraged them to continue on steadfastly; there would be a reward for their perseverance of faith. Abraham's faith was tested, but his patient faith paid off.

God made four promises to Abraham in Genesis 22:16-18: (1) "I will greatly bless you." (2) "I will greatly multiply your seed as the stars of the heavens." (3) "Your seed shall possess the gate of their enemies." (4) "In your seed all the nations of the earth shall be blessed." Christ was the seed of Abraham, and those promises apply specifically to Him. But we also must not forget that we now belong to Christ, and we, too, are considered Abraham's seed (see Gal. 3:29). One promise that particularly comforted the Hebrew Christians was that Abraham's seed would "possess the gates of their enemies." They would one day no longer be victims but victors over their persecutors.

When God ends a promise with an oath, nothing could be more certain (see vv. 13, 16-18). There is no reason to turn away from Jesus. Our full salvation will be realized at His return, when we will enter "within the veil" (v. 19)—in the heavenly holy of holies.

PSALM 105:16-36

PROVERBS 27:1-2

Boasting about ourselves or our own accomplishments reveals our self-centeredness and insecurity. Let others praise you, and let your accomplishments speak for themselves.

NOVEMBER 5

EZEKIEL 12:1-14:11

Ezekiel was told to act out another object lesson for the unbelieving Jews in Babylon by pretending to be a certain exile—Zedekiah, the current king of Judah—departing from Jerusalem. Notice God foretelling that Zedekiah would be brought to Babylon but that "he will not see it" (12:13). You will recall that after Jerusalem was broken into and Zedekiah was captured, his eyes were blinded by Nebuchadnezzar (see Jer. 52:11). God also promised, contrary to popular belief, that Ezekiel's predictions would come to pass shortly, as they did (see 12:22-28).

It's no wonder that this book is so full of gloom and doom. These people were *evil.* Like Jeremiah, Ezekiel had to deal with the undermining work of false prophets, who like plaster over a crumbling wall only served as a facade (see 13:10-12). Ezekiel also had to deal with prophetesses who practiced occult magic (see 13:17-23) and elders who "had set up idols in their hearts" (14:3).

HEBREWS 7:1-17

We have already learned that God appointed Jesus as a priest forever according to the order of Melchizedek (see Ps. 110:4). Who was this man? How is Christ like him? He was the king of Salem (an ancient name for Jerusalem), and his title is translated "king of peace" (v. 2). Melchizedek's name is translated "king of righteousness." Jesus is also a king and a priest. Melchizedek met Abraham after the slaughter of the kings; Abraham gave him a tithe of the spoils. Called "priest of God Most High" in Genesis 14:18, he is a mysterious person. We don't know where he came from, when he was born, when he died or who his parents were (see v. 3). Because those facts are unknown, he is a type of Christ, who had no beginning and has no end.

In this chapter, the writer shows that Jesus is far better than any former levitical priest. Melchizedek was greater than Abraham, because Abraham paid tithes to him, and Melchizedek blessed Abraham, not vice versa (see v. 7). In a sense, the Levites paid tithes to Melchizedek, because they were "in the loins" of Abraham when he paid his tithes to Melchizedek (see vv. 9-10). The point is that the priestly order of Melchizedek was higher than the priestly order of Aaron.

God had promised in Psalm 110 that another priest would arise according to the order of Melchizedek. And God promised that this priest would be eternal. If perfection could be reached under the levitical system of priests, why would God have foretold of another priest who would arise (see v. 11)? Once again, we have to acknowledge that Christ, as high priest, completely overshadows the priests of the old covenant.

PSALM 105:37-45

PROVERBS 27:3

NOVEMBER 6

EZEKIEL 14:12-16:42

In chapter 14, we learn that God can bring judgment to a nation in at least four ways: by famine, wild beasts, war or plague. I don't think anyone can say that *every* war or famine is a direct result of God's judgment. But I don't think we can take the other extreme and say that all famines and wars arise only because of the devil's hatred for mankind (apart from God's sovereignty). I hope you have seen clearly that God's love and mercy were abundantly displayed by years of patience with His people before judgment came.

God mentioned three righteous men—Noah, Daniel and Job—who could not deliver by their own righteousness a country condemned (see 14:14, 16, 20). But God clearly said that they could be individually delivered even when God judged an entire nation. Scriptures like these are great support for a pretribulation rapture.

In Ezekiel 15-16, God spoke most disparagingly of His people. First He compared them to a piece of fire-charred vine, crooked and practically useless (see 15:3). How much more useless was it once it was burned? So, too, Judah was useless to God and fit only for burning.

In chapter 16, the Lord called the nation a harlot (see 16:35). He had found her an abandoned waif and had protected and cared for her since babyhood. He had elevated and blessed her, but she had taken His blessings and used them to serve other gods (see 16:17). She had committed spiritual adultery; unlike a common harlot, she had paid her men (see 16:33-34). Just as a harlot would be judged when discovered, so Judah would be judged. God would use the very nations with which she had played the harlot to bring His judgment on her.

Know that this is not the end of the story. Stay tuned for more developments.

HEBREWS 7:18-28

Here are more reasons why Christ's priesthood is superior to any other. First, the eternal priesthood of Jesus came by an oath from God the Father Himself, which was not true of any other priest before Him (see vv. 20-22). God never promised that the old covenant priesthood would go on forever.

Second, under the old covenant, there were many high priests who followed one another in succession. But Jesus is the only high priest of the new covenant, as He is alive forever. He can offer us eternal salvation, because He will always be around to ensure our covenant with God (see v. 25). He is our intercessor before God the Father.

Third, the old covenant priests had to make daily sacrifices for their own sins and the sins of the people. But sinless Jesus, as the perfect sacrifice, needed to offer Himself only once for our sins. Are you seeing how the rituals of the old covenant were designed to foreshadow the work of Christ in the new covenant?

And fourth, Jesus was a superior priest because He was not mere mortal but also the Son of God (see v. 28).

PSALM 106:1-12

PROVERBS 27:4-6

Thank God for true friends—those who love us enough to tactfully, lovingly tell us the truth, even when it hurts.

NOVEMBER 7

EZEKIEL 16:43-17:24

Here we once again glimpse God's great mercy upon Judah, as God compared Judah to her sisters, Samaria and Sodom. Samaria, the wicked capital of the northern kingdom of Israel, had fallen to Assyria about 125 years before this prophecy. Evil Sodom had been destroyed by God with fire and brimstone in Genesis 19. God said through Ezekiel that *Jerusalem had moved beyond the depravity of those two cities* (see 16:47, 51). Yet God had patiently endured her sin.

We also read two promises of a bright future for Judah: in chapter 16, God promised a future everlasting covenant with Israel (see 16:60). In chapter 17, we have an allegory of two eagles and a vine. The first eagle is Nebuchadnezzar, who took away the top of a cedar tree, representing the Davidic kingly dynasty, specifically King Jehoiachin. Nebuchadnezzar planted him in Babylon and then planted "some of the seed of the land" (King Zedekiah) to rule in Jerusalem (17:5). That seed grew into a vine that was at first subject by oath to Nebuchadnezzar. But Zedekiah broke his oath and began to rebel against Babylon, looking to the second eagle, the Pharaoh of Egypt. Though Zedekiah attempted to join with Pharaoh to break the yoke of Nebuchadnezzar's rule, God said his plans would not succeed. The vine would be rooted up. Zedekiah would be deported to Babylon and die there (see 17:16). This was fulfilled within three or four years. The good news is that God promised that He, like Nebuchadnezzar, shall also "take a sprig from the lofty top of the cedar and...plant it on a high and lofty mountain" (17:22). That sprig is Jesus, descendant of David, who will be planted on Mount Zion. Under His branches, "birds of every kind will nest" (17:23). That refers to people of every tribe, race and tongue.

HEBREWS 8:1-13

Not only is Jesus a superior high priest, but He also has a superior ministry to that of the former priests. The high priests of the old covenant performed their ministry in the earthly tabernacle, a copy of the tabernacle in heaven (see vv. 2, 5). Jesus performed His ministry in the heavenly holy of holies (see v. 2). The high priests of the old covenant stood before a symbol of God's throne; Jesus sits on God's throne. Jesus is the superior mediator of the new covenant, superior to the old covenant because it has been enacted upon better promises (see v. 6). Paul quoted a passage from Jeremiah that listed some of the promises of the future, better covenant. If God had instituted a new covenant, the old covenant had fault and needed to be replaced (see vv. 7-8, 13).

A benefit of the new covenant is that we don't have pages of laws to remember and obey. God has written His law of love in our hearts. Because we have God living inside us by the Holy Spirit, we have an inward, godly nature. "The love of Christ controls us," as Paul said in 2 Corinthians 5:14. Under the new covenant, we can have a personal relationship with Him (see v. 11). Finally, our sins are forgiven and forgotten once and for all (see v. 12).

PSALM 106:13-31

PROVERBS 27:7-9

NOVEMBER 8

EZEKIEL 18:1-19:14

Somehow expressed through the common proverb of Ezekiel 18:2, Ezekiel's contemporaries were blaming their parents' sins for their sufferings. But God said He does *not* punish children for sins committed by their parents. God deals with everyone individually.

Furthermore, God deals with individuals based on their *present* conduct, not their past conduct (see 18:24-28).

God's loving character is revealed in His words: "For I have no pleasure in the death of anyone who dies. Therefore, repent and live" (18:32). God is good and doesn't want anyone to go to hell; He sent His Son to pay the penalty for anyone's sins. But as the moral judge of the universe, He must enforce His laws with their accompanying consequence of punishment upon transgressors. God doesn't enjoy that part of His job.

The "princes" of chapter 19 were among the final kings of Judah: Jehoahaz, who was deported to Egypt (see 19:4; 2 Kin. 23:31-34), and Jehoiachin, who was deported to Babylon (see 19:9; 2 Chron. 36:1-10). The "lioness" (19:2) was the tribe of Judah, also compared to a fruitful vine with many strong branches (see 19:10). The "strong branch" (19:12) was Zedekiah, the final Davidic king of Judah, here viewed as "torn off" the vine. Because of his wickedness, the vine now without a Davidic king ruling her (see 19:13-14) was transplanted to the wilderness of Babylon.

HEBREWS 9:1-10

Only the high priest could enter into the holy of holies, and he only once a year to offer blood on the mercy seat for his and the people's sins. Why couldn't anyone go into the holy of holies after the high priest had offered the blood? That imperfect ritual covered only the sins of the people; it foreshadowed the greater work that would be done by Christ. Through Christ's blood presented in the heavenly holy of holies, we had our sins remitted, not just covered, and our spirits have been cleansed of spiritual death. Our consciences are clean. Now, if we could somehow be translated back to the time of Moses, we could walk into the holy of holies anytime we wanted to.

When Jesus died, the veil in the temple was ripped in half (see Matt. 27:51). We now have confidence to enter the holy place by the blood of Jesus (see 10:19). More about that tomorrow.

PSALM 106:32-48

PROVERBS 27:10

"Do not go to your brother's house in the day of your calamity" must be read in context. If we have good relationships with our neighbors (see v. 10*a*), we won't have to travel a long way to receive help that would have otherwise come from a distant brother (v. 10*c*).

NOVEMBER 9

EZEKIEL 20:1-49

Let me remind you that we have been reading the words of God Himself, spoken through Ezekiel in August 591 B.C., four or five years before the destruction of Jerusalem.

Did you think of God's great mercy as you read His "history lesson" of the children of Israel? Time and again He restrained His wrath and didn't annihilate His people. We learn that Israel had been worshipping other gods even while in Egypt, continuing in idolatry for eight hundred years. It was time for great judgment.

Verses 33-44 point to a day when the Lord will deal with Israel at the end of the tribulation. He will first restore them from the nations to which they have been scattered and then judge them in "the wilderness" (v. 35). He will purge out the rebels, and those remaining He will bring back to the promised land. From then on, all of Israel will serve the Lord, who will dwell on Mount Zion (see v. 40).

HEBREWS 9:11-28

As foreshadowed by the priests of the old covenant, Jesus presented His own blood in the heavenly holy of holies and obtained an *eternal* redemption for us once and for all. He was the sacrifice (see vv. 12, 26). He was the high priest. Because of what He has done, we are cleansed and made righteous before God (see v. 14). The old covenant ritual only cleansed ceremonially and outwardly, but we have been cleansed inwardly and have had our spirits regenerated.

Jesus had to die because a covenant cannot be inaugurated without the shedding of blood, as "without shedding of blood there is no forgiveness" (v. 22). When Jesus appears again, He won't be coming to make another sacrifice for sin. His first and only sacrifice of Himself was sufficient. When He appears the next time, He will be coming for those who have been cleansed (v. 28).

PSALM 107:1-43

PROVERBS 27:11

NOVEMBER 10

EZEKIEL 21:1-22:31

In 21:18-22, God instructed Ezekiel to make a signpost to point the way for Nebuchadnezzar to find Jerusalem and Rabbah (the capital of Ammon, today known as Amman, capital of Jordan). God was promising to bring judgment to both cities. In fact, Nebuchadnezzar attacked Ammon five years after Jerusalem fell. Apparently Nebuchadnezzar used divination to determine what cities he should attack next, by tossing arrows inscribed with cities' names and by examining the livers of dissected animals.

God again foretold Zedekiah's demise in 21:25-27. But notice the messianic promise in verse 27: "This also will be no more (probably referring to the Davidic kingly dynasty) until He comes whose right it is; and I shall give it to Him." As sure as Zedekiah was abased, Jesus will be exalted (see 21:26).

The most amazing verses in this passage are 22:30-31. Even after enumerating the horrific sins of Judah, God said, "And I searched for a man among them who should build up the wall and stand in the gap before Me for the land, that I should not destroy it; but I found no one. Thus I have poured out My indignation on them." God was looking for one person who would intercede to stall His judgment, but since no one was praying in that regard, God poured out His wrath. One person's prayers could have forestalled God's judgment. Many say that judgment is coming to America, but through prayer we may be able to forestall judgment, giving more people time to repent.

HEBREWS 10:1-17

Paul said the Law was "only a shadow of the good things to come" (v. 1).

He also said the sacrifices were proved to be imperfect, not actually "taking away sins" (vv. 4,11). The blood of an animal served only as collateral until the time of the final sacrifice of God's sinless Son. There is now no need for any more animal sacrifices. To continue offering sacrifices would be like going to church every night to rehearse your wedding ceremony, even though you were married ten years ago.

Paul then quoted Psalm 40:6-8, attributing the words to Jesus. From what Jesus said, God took no pleasure in "whole burnt offerings and sacrifices" (v. 6). Through the redemptive work of Jesus, God "took away the first [the sacrificial system of the Law] in order to establish the second [Christ's atoning sacrifice]" (v. 9). Jesus is now seated at the right hand of God (see v. 12), which symbolizes that His work of the redemption of humankind is finished. The promises of the new covenant are now in effect (see vv. 16-17).

PSALM 108:1-13

PROVERBS 27:12

Have you ever found yourself innocently involved in a bad situation you wish you could have foreseen? God can help you avoid that through the wisdom He offers.

NOVEMBER 11

EZEKIEL 23:1-49

Because God's people were guilty of "spiritual adultery," having forsaken Him to join themselves to the gods of Egypt, Assyria and Babylon, God gave them up to their lovers. Assyria destroyed Samaria, and Babylon was about to destroy Jerusalem. As I've mentioned before, the New Testament makes it clear that Christians can be guilty of idolatry—spiritual adultery—if they allow something to have a tighter grip on their hearts than God.

Think about it: these people whose heritage sprang from the true God were tossing their babies into fires in their devotion to idols (see v. 37). And on the same day they would go to God's temple to pay Him respects (see v. 39). Can you blame God for sending judgment?

HEBREWS 10:18-39

Praise God that through our high priest, we have full assurance to draw near to God; we don't have to cringe in condemnation when we come to Him! Many Christians are still coming to God and confessing that they are poor, unworthy, undeserving sinners, never expecting God to answer their prayers. But when we confess our (supposed) unworthiness as Christians, we do an injustice to the cleansing, redeeming work of Christ.

Even in the first century some believers habitually did not attend church (see v. 25). We should be gathering together all the more as we "see the day [of Jesus' return] drawing near."

Under the Law of Moses, those who willfully rebelled against God had no provision of mercy. They were executed.

So, too, under the new covenant, anyone who knows the Lord and willfully, defiantly rebels against Him has no provision of mercy (see vv. 26, 29). If you're reading this commentary, I guarantee you have not committed this sin. Don't allow the devil to deceive you into thinking you have committed the unpardonable sin. *If you're even concerned that you've committed the unpardonable sin, you haven't.* A Christian who has turned his back on God from his heart doesn't care. He doesn't want to and never intends to return to God.

Verses 32-34 give us a glimpse of some of the sufferings those Hebrew Christians were enduring. They had been reproached and persecuted; some had been imprisoned; and apparently many had had their possessions confiscated.

Paul admonished his readers to hold fast to their faith because it would be rewarded (see v. 35). We are now prepared for the greatest chapter of this book. So many times chapter 11 is read by itself, out of context. Not this time. We'll see that persevering faith was rewarded in the lives of numerous Old Testament characters.

PSALM 109:1-31

PROVERBS 27:13

This is actually a continuation of the proverb read yesterday concerning the man with no foresight. He becomes surety for strangers and commits adultery, both indications of foolishness.

NOVEMBER 12

EZEKIEL 24:1-26:21

According to 24:1-2, Ezekiel, although hundreds of miles away in Babylon, knew exactly when the siege of Jerusalem began. Through Ezekiel, God compared besieged Jerusalem to a rusting pot, full of meat boiling on a fire. The wood under the pot represented the besieging armies of Babylon, and the rust represented the bloody sin of the city.

We might question why Ezekiel's wife had to die as a sign to the people of Jerusalem (see 24:16-18), but we can trust that God knew what He was doing. Just as Ezekiel lost the "desire of his eyes," so the people of Judah would see the destruction of their city and temple. As another sign to the people, God would loosen Ezekiel's tongue to speak freely when the siege was completed (see 24:27). He had been under divine constraint for about five years (see 3:26; 33:21-22).

Chapters 25-32 contain Ezekiel's pronouncements of judgments upon Judah's neighbor nations. Chapter 25 denounces four of Judah's oldest enemies—Ammon, Moab, Edom and Philistia—who rejoiced in the destruction of Jerusalem. Chapter 26 centers on the Phoenician coastal and island city of Tyre, located in modern Lebanon. Only a few months after the fall of Jerusalem, Nebuchadnezzar began a thirteen-year siege of Tyre. The prophecy of chapter 25 wasn't completely fulfilled until 250 years later, when Alexander the Great destroyed the island-city by building a causeway out of the debris of the mainland city, unknowingly fulfilling 26:4, 12: "And I will scrape her debris from her and make her a bare rock....and throw your stones and your timbers and your debris into the water."

HEBREWS 11:1-16

There's a difference between hope and faith. Many Christians are substituting hope for faith and wondering why their prayers aren't working. Hope always leaves room for the possibility that you may not get what you want. Hope always says "maybe." Faith is *confidently sure of the outcome of a situation—as if the outcome were already manifested.* Faith is a conviction of a truth, even though that truth cannot be perceived with the five physical senses. For example, I have faith that there is an angel near me—because God's Word promises me so (see Ps. 34:7; 91:11).

The manifestation of what we believe for doesn't always come immediately. We must persevere in faith, even when it looks as if our faith is not working. You see, there's no faith without a test. And through our faith, we gain approval from God. Actually, "Without faith, it is *impossible* to please God" (v. 6, italics mine).

Because of Abel's faith, God accepted his animal sacrifice (see v. 4). Abel had something to base his faith upon—the example of God's clothing Adam and Eve in animal skins. Abel understood the need for an atoning substitute for salvation. Cain, on the other hand, was coming to God by his own works.

Somehow Enoch had faith to be taken up to heaven before his death (see v. 5), and he became a type of the church at the rapture. God must have given Enoch a promise of such, or he, too, would have had no basis for his faith.

Noah acted in faith, trusting that God would keep His promise to flood the earth, and he was saved from God's wrath (see v. 7).

Abraham trusted God enough to obey and leave his homeland. Notice that God didn't immediately tell him where he was to go (see v. 8). We, too, must walk by faith, taking one step at a time. Once Abraham arrived in the promised land, he trusted that God would keep His promise to give his descendants the land, even though he was old and childless. By faith barren Sarah, after her initial unbelief, received ability to conceive a child (see v. 11).

Paul stated that these men and women "died in faith, without receiving the promises, but having seen them and having welcomed them from a distance" (v. 13). Apparently those saints had more knowledge of the future plan of God than we can realize from reading the Old Testament. All those patriarchs had knowledge of and were looking forward to the heavenly country and the city God prepared for them (see v. 16). For that reason, they persevered in faith even when facing many adversaries and obstacles, and they died in faith, still trusting that one day they would behold God's heavenly city. Can you see how this applies to the Hebrew Christians? To us today?

PSALM 110:1-7

PROVERBS 27:14

I think this proverb is speaking of the person who rouses a friend from bed. A sleeping comrade won't feel blessed to be awakened so early. We not only must be careful about what we say, but we should also be careful about when we say it. Bless your friends after they're awake.

NOVEMBER 13

EZEKIEL 27:1-28:26

In chapter 27, the island and coastal city of Tyre is compared to a great trading vessel about to go down in the sea. The main part of the city being on an island, its borders literally "were in the heart of the seas" (27:4).

Tyre traded with many nations, enumerated in 27:12-25, and much of the commerce of the ancient world made its way through this proud and wealthy port (see 27:3). When God judged the city through Nebuchadnezzar's thirteen-year siege (the "east wind" of 27:26), practically every Mediterranean nation lamented its downfall.

In chapter 28, God spoke directly to the prince of Tyre, Ithobaal II, who characterized the arrogance of the city by claiming himself divine. Because of his pride, he would soon die "by the hands of strangers" (28:10).

In 28:11-19, God spoke to "the king of Tyre," or Satan. We gain a glimpse of the double-kingdom principle revealed in Daniel and the New Testament: a spiritual power always rules over an earthly power. In this case, Satan, king of Tyre, ruled over Ithobaal II, prince of Tyre.

Next we read a prophecy against Sidon, a coastal city about twenty miles north of Tyre, which was taken by Nebuchadnezzar about the same time as Tyre. Jesus mentioned the judgment of Tyre and Sidon in Matthew 11:21-22.

At the end of this passage, God promised to restore His scattered people Israel after judging their enemies. This prophecy will be ultimately fulfilled during the millennium.

HEBREWS 11:17-31

Abraham had his love and faith tested when he was commanded to offer up his son Isaac, because God had promised him descendants through Isaac. Abraham trusted that once he killed Isaac, God would raise him from the dead (see v. 19). Though he wasn't killed by Abraham's hand, Isaac became a type of Christ, raised from the dead (see v. 19).

Do you remember aged Isaac's blessing Jacob and Esau, and aged Jacob's blessing the sons of Joseph? Paul revealed that these were acts of faith (see vv. 20-21).

Joseph, too, expressed his faith on his deathbed by predicting the Exodus from Egypt and by requesting that his bones go with the exiles (see v. 22). He believed that God would keep His promise to Abraham, Isaac and Jacob to give their descendants the land of Canaan.

Moses' parents also were people of faith, as revealed when they hid baby Moses (see v. 23). They trusted that God, having a special plan for Moses' life, would save him from death. If they weren't afraid of the king's edict, why did they hide Moses? Though they respected the king's edict, they didn't believe it would be true for their special son. Remember that the Hebrew Christians were being threatened by Nero's edicts. If they became afraid, they might decide to turn their backs on Jesus. The entire life of Moses, as so aptly detailed in verses 24-29, was exemplary to Paul's hearers.

It took faith to circle Jericho silently for seven days within earshot of the mocking Jerichoites, but those walls came tumblin' down (see v. 30). Any doubters would have stopped marching by the second day. And Rahab the harlot found that salvation comes by faith, as she and her family were the only inhabitants of Jericho to survive. She trusted the spies and tied a scarlet thread in her window, possibly a type of Jesus' blood flowing (see v. 31).

PSALM 111:1-10

PROVERBS 27:15-16

Wives, stop nagging your husbands (and vice versa)! We can never hope to change people by nagging them—only by loving and complimenting them.

NOVEMBER 14

EZEKIEL 29:1-30:26

Chapters 29-31 contain several prophecies concerning Egypt, a superpower of the era. God would use Nebuchadnezzar to scatter Egypt as judgment upon its sin and false gods. After forty years He would gather them back (see 29:11-13), though Egypt would never again rise to be the world power she once had been (see 29:15).

Nebuchadnezzar's conquests in Egypt, described in chapter 30, prefigure the judgments of the tribulation ("the day of the Lord" [30:3]). God would bring devastation from Migdol (a northern city on the Nile delta) to Syene (a southern city on the Nile [see 30:6]). In Ezekiel's day, Egypt was not the square land-mass of today, but a thin strip along the Nile.

HEBREWS 11:32-12:13

Here we have a condensed summary of the final "heroes of faith." Maybe I can fill in some details.

First, Paul listed four judges: Gideon, Barak, Samson and Jephthah. Each had his weak points. Gideon, a great doubter, finally displayed great faith by going to battle with an army of three hundred against multitudes (see Judg. 7-8). Barak was the man Deborah the prophetess instructed to go and face Sisera; he agreed to go only if Deborah would accompany him (see Judg. 4). Through his faith, Barak defeated Sisera's army, but Sisera himself was killed by a woman.

Samson paid a bitter price for his weakness for women, but God still used him on numerous occasions because he was a man of faith. He killed more Philistines in his death than in his life (see Judg. 16:30). Jephthah promised that if God would give him victory, he would sacrifice whatever met him first when he returned to his home. It was his daughter (see Judg. 11 and my comments). Despite these men's faults, God used them because of their faith.

The next man mentioned, David, once committed murder and adultery. Nevertheless, he trusted God in battle. Samuel didn't raise his sons to fear the Lord (see 1 Sam. 8:1-3). Yet he, too, demonstrated great faith in God.

It was Daniel who "shut the mouths of lions" by his faith (11:33). His three friends "quenched the power of fire" (11:34). The widow of Zarephath (see 1 Kings 17:17-24) and the Shunammite woman of 2 Kings 4:17-35 "received back their dead by resurrection" (11:35).

We don't know specifically who was tortured and didn't accept release that "they might obtain a better resurrection" (11:35). When people are willing to die for God, they have faith!

Tradition says that Isaiah was sawn in half for his faith (see 11:37). Jeremiah was imprisoned, and Zechariah was stoned. Faith is not only manifested in performing great acts, but also through enduring great persecution. All the above-mentioned people died without receiving the promises of the new covenant (see 11:39). Together with them, we will all one day realize the full reward for our persevering faith.

The greatest example of persevering faith in the midst of suffering is Jesus. He endured the cross because of His faith in the good that it would accomplish—the "joy set before Him" (12:2). We are exhorted to endure the race and lay aside anything that slows down our progress in spiritual growth (see 12:1).

In 12:5-13, we gain at least a partial understanding of why these Hebrew Christians were suffering persecution: God was disciplining them. God chastens only those who are disobedient, and He will, if necessary, use persecution to bring about the obedience of His children. This doesn't mean that if we're persecuted we've been disobedient. Quite the opposite is usually true; when we're most obedient, we're most persecuted. But when there is widespread persecution against a large body of believers, the group should pray to see if their corporate persecution has been permitted by God because of their corporate disobedience.

Discipline is designed to bring us to repentance. Though it isn't a joyful time when we're experiencing it, when it's over, it "yields the peaceful fruit of righteousness" (12:11).

PSALM 112:1-10

PROVERBS 27:17

NOVEMBER 15

EZEKIEL 31:1-32:32

These two chapters and the two read yesterday contain at least *six* different prophecies, given over a period of fourteen years, concerning the fall of Egypt. In today's reading, Egypt was compared to a great cedar tree about to be felled by Babylon and descend into Sheol with the other nations God had already judged.

HEBREWS 12:14-29

The example of Esau (see v. 16) fits perfectly in context with the message of this entire book. He sacrificed spiritual blessings for the sake of fleshly gratification. So, too, these Hebrew Christians, if they were to turn their backs on Jesus for the sake of temporary relief, would be selling their "birthright" cheaply—a birthright obtained with Christ's sacrifice. Later, when Esau tried to inherit the blessing of the birthright that was formerly his, he "found no place for repentance" (v. 17).

The Lord's coming down upon Mount Sinai was a fearful sight (see vv. 18-21). The earth shook at the inauguration of the old covenant. God wanted His people to take it seriously. How much more seriously should we regard the superior covenant under which we live! They were warned from the earth; we are warned from heaven (see v. 25). Their experience at Mount Sinai was incidental compared to the inauguration of the new covenant when Jesus presented His blood in the heavenly holy of holies. And someday we will stand with angels along with the redeemed of all ages before the New Jerusalem. We'll see God face to face! In the meantime, let's trust God regardless of what test or trial comes our way. God is faithful, and we will be glad we endured. Nothing in this world should sway us, because nothing in this world will last—except God's kingdom of which we are now a part (see vv. 26-28).

PSALMS 113:1-114:8

PROVERBS 27:18-20

NOVEMBER 16

EZEKIEL 33:1-34:31

The first portion of this passage is a repeat of information we've read in chapters 3 and 18. Ezekiel's call is likened to a watchman's warning of coming danger (see 33:1-9). And God deals with every individual justly, based on that person's present conduct. He takes no pleasure in the death of the wicked (see 33:10-20).

Jerusalem fell to Nebuchadnezzar in 586 B.C., and the news reached the exiles in Babylon more than a year later (see 33:21). On the day Ezekiel heard the news, his tongue was loosed from the long divine constraint (see 33:22). But did the people repent at the word that their capital city and temple had been destroyed? No, those who survived in the land of Judah were annexing the land suddenly available (see 33:24-26), and those in Babylon came to hear Ezekiel for entertainment (see 33:30-33).

The shepherds addressed in chapter 34 were leaders in Israel, including prophets, priests and king. They had used their God-given ministries for personal advantage. As a result, God's flock had been scattered. The Lord promised to one day regather His flock, judge among the sheep and the goats, and place the sheep under the care of His servant David (see 34:23). This will have its fulfillment in the millennium when Jesus, descendant of David, will reign.

HEBREWS 13:1-25

At the conclusion of this book, we read a few more old covenant analogies. (1) Just as the bodies of the animals whose blood was brought into the holy place were burned outside the camp, so Jesus was crucified outside the walls of Jerusalem (see vv. 11-12). Paul's readers had to depart from the Jewish camp and suffer the reproach of Christ if they wanted to follow Him. Besides, the cities they lived in were only temporal; God had promised them—and us—a place in the New Jerusalem (see vv. 13-14).

And (2) we have no need to continually offer up sacrifices for our sins, because the all-inclusive final sacrifice has been made. Now we're to offer up continual sacrifices of praise to God and continually sacrifice ourselves for others (see vv. 15-16).

If we are true believers in Christ, our faith will manifest itself by our love for fellow Christians, by our kindess to strangers and fellow-believers in jail, and by our love for our spouses (see vv. 1-4). It will be manifested by our attitude toward money, our worship of God, and our submissiveness to God-ordained leaders (see vv. 5, 15, 17).

Please memorize verse 8. Whatever Jesus did for people when He was here in the flesh, He will do for people today from heaven.

Notice that Paul quoted the Lord's promise never to forsake us, and then stated that we can therefore "confidently say, 'The Lord is my helper, I will not be afraid. What shall man do to me?' " (vv. 5-6). Why not make that your positive confession today? If God is your helper, nothing is impossible for you, and there is no reason to be afraid of anything or anybody.

PSALM 115:1-18

PROVERBS 27:21-22

When some people are praised, they're lifted up in pride, and their inward motivations become obvious to all. When others are praised, they become aware of how unworthy they are to receive any adulation; they give the glory to God.

NOVEMBER 17

EZEKIEL 35:1-36:38

When Judah was invaded, destroyed and deported to Babylon, her neighboring enemy Edom (Mount Seir) rejoiced in her calamity and helped to cut off any survivors, greedily taking possession of the vacated land. God was displeased and promised Edom that her day of judgment was coming. The ruins of Edom's main city, Petra, in Jordan, prove that God's word came to pass.

From chapter 36 to the end of the book, Ezekiel spoke of events that are *yet to take place.* Here in chapter 36, God spoke to the mountains of Israel, promising to restore His people Israel to their land.

God promised to bring His people back from all the nations where they've been scattered, not because of their holiness, but for the sake of His own name (see 36:18-24). So God is not going to bring back just those Jews who come to believe in Jesus, but all descendants of Israel around the world. From Ezekiel 20:33-44, we know that God will purge out the rebels. After the physical restoration, there will be a spiritual regeneration among them (see 36:25-27).

From then on, there will never be another famine in Israel (see 36:30). Furthermore, the desolate places will become like the garden of Eden (see 36:35). Israel today is a nice place to visit, but I would hardly call it a Garden of Eden!

JAMES 1:1-18

James, a leader in the church in Jerusalem, was a half-brother of Jesus. This letter, written to Jewish Christians, might be the earliest New Testament epistle, written before A.D. 49. Addressed to the believers driven from Jerusalem after the martyrdom of Stephen, this book draws heavily from the Old Testament and Jesus' Sermon on the Mount, and its doctrinal content is elementary and easy to understand.

This first chapter is not a collection of unrelated thoughts, though it might appear as such. James wrote to encourage Christians who have had to flee for their lives, experiencing persecution and financial hardship—and needing wisdom. James offered us a wonderful promise of wisdom (see vv. 5-8), and we must ask for it in faith without doubting. Faith is the key to answered prayer. In fact, if we doubt, we will not only fail to receive wisdom, but we will fail to receive anything from the Lord (see v. 7).

If Christians are facing financial hardship but have faith, they will "consider it all joy" (v. 2). They will "glory in [their] high position" (v.9).

The rich man addressed in verse 10 is an unrighteous rich man, as we'll learn later in this epistle. In verses 9-10, James referred first to the poor brother, then to the rich man. This unrighteous man will later be exposed as one who has taken advantage of his laborers and exploited others to get gain for himself (see 5:1-6).

The man who perseveres under trial is blessed; he will receive "the crown of life'' (v. 12). Our perseverance under trial proves our faith in Jesus, and one day our faith will be rewarded.

Lest anyone think his trials are from God, James refuted such an idea (see vv. 13-17). Other passages say that God does *test* us, and He may even test us during times of Satan's temptations, but God is not tempting or enticing anyone to do wrong. I am constantly testing my children to see if they're ready to be entrusted with greater responsibilities, but I would never entice them to do wrong. God sends that which is good, and He doesn't have a split personality that changes day to day (see v. 17).

Much of what we blame on the devil we should blame on ourselves. We're tempted when we're enticed by our own lusts (see v. 14). When we yield to sinful desires, we sin, and it ''brings forth death'' (v. 15). That doesn't mean we die spiritually and need to be born again a second time. It means we're in a dangerous place—vulnerable to Satan. If we confess our sins, we shut the door on Satan and spiritual death.

PSALM 116:1-19

PROVERBS 27:23-27

The wise person runs his business prudently, ready for any changes in market conditions.

NOVEMBER 18

EZEKIEL 37:1-38:23

The meaning of the vision of the dry bones is twofold: first, God is going to physically restore the sons of Israel to their homeland. In Ezekiel's day, most of Israel's descendants had given up hope for anything of this sort; the northern tribes were scattered by Assyria, and the southern tribes had been deported to Babylon. But God promised to restore *Israel and Judah* and make them one nation again (see 37:15-22). This has not happened yet.

The second part of Ezekiel's vision speaks of a spiritual regeneration of those returning expatriates, when God puts His Spirit within them. Before God sent His breath upon them, they were just flesh-covered skeletons—walking dead men (see 37:8-10).

After their restoration, rebirth and reunification, God will place one king over them, the One descended from David. Israel will live on the land promised to Abraham, Isaac and Jacob forever, and Jesus will be their prince. His sanctuary will also be in their midst forever (see 37:24-28).

Chapters 38-39 foretell a yet-future battle. This is clear because the enemy from the north comes against a land of ''unwalled villages'' (38:11). Building villages without walls is a relatively new idea (a few hundred years). Also, when Gog invades Israel, the whole earth will shake with a great earthquake (see 38:19-20). That hasn't happened yet.

Who is ''Gog of the land of Magog, the prince of Rosh, Meshech, and Tubal'' (38:2)? Magog, Meshech and Tubal were sons of Noah's son Japheth (see Gen. 10:2). These men reputedly populated the region around the Black Sea and the Caucasus Mountains in modern Turkey and southern Russia. We should be careful about identifying the entire Soviet Union with the descendants of these three or four tribes. The Soviet Union is composed of some 155 ethnic groups who speak 138 different languages. Technically, Ezekiel was referring to a section of northeast Turkey and the Soviet republics of Georgia, Armenia and Azerbaijan. Ezekiel indicated that the invading army will come from the "remote parts of the north" (38:6, 15).

Gog will invade with the help of allies (see 38:5-6). Persia is no doubt Iran. The word translated "Ethiopia" is literally *Cush*, one of the sons of Ham (Noah's son), reputedly the father of the black nations of southern Africa. "Put" was another son of Ham, supposedly the progenitor of the tribes of northern Africa. Gomer was the oldest son of Japheth, supposedly identified with some of the peoples of eastern Europe. Togarmah is reputedly the father of the Armenians. Together they will invade Israel in the "last days" (see 38:16).

Many Bible scholars believe that this battle will take place during the tribulation, but I hold that these chapters describe the final battle *at the end of the millennium.*

Here's just one of several reasons: God says the invaders will come against His people restored from many nations, who are "at rest, that live securely" (38:11). The Jews living in Jerusalem are certainly not living "at rest" and "securely" now and won't be during the tribulation. But during the millennium, Jesus will be living right there in Jerusalem, ruling the world.

JAMES 1:19-2:17

Because our anger is usually selfish, it doesn't "achieve the righteousness of God" (1:20). Therefore, we should be "slow to anger," "slow to speak" and "quick to hear" (1:19).

We are to "receive the word implanted" (1:21). Paul said the same thing in Romans 12:2: "Be transformed by the renewing of your mind."

What did James mean by "receiving the word"? He was referring to receiving and obeying the law of Christ, the law of love. *Agapeo* was a word describing God's love that we find in no classical Greek writings until after the time of Christ. A new word was needed to describe a concept that had been practically foreign to the world before Jesus came: unselfish, sacrificial love. We are to be "doers" of that word, not just hearers who delude themselves (see 1:22). We shouldn't just glance at the great commandment to love one another and forget about it. We should "gaze intently" at it and "abide by it" (1:25). That perfect law is a "law of liberty" (1:25), because we no longer have to follow a list of do's and don'ts; we simply apply the law of love to every situation.

Those who walk in love walk in God's blessings (see 1:25). And those who walk in love will bridle their tongues (see 1:26) and do things to relieve the sufferings of the less fortunate, such as visiting widows and orphans (see 1:27). Those who walk in love will be careful not to show partiality to the rich, dishonoring the poor in the church (see 2:1-8).

Notice how James condemned the rich (see 2:6-7), saying that they oppress Christians and blaspheme God's name. This is in keeping with James's developing theme of the condemnation of the unrighteous rich. Remember that wealthy Job was found blameless by God.

A living faith in Jesus will result in a changed life, affecting the tongue, lifestyle, treatment of others and compassion.

If someone claims to have faith but has no works, can he be saved (see 2:14)? Our faith is to be judged by our obedience to the law of liberty (see 2:12). Therefore, we should sow mercy in order that we might reap mercy (see 2:13).

James was not saying that we're saved by our works. Rather, our works prove that we have saving faith.

PSALM 117:1-2

PROVERBS 28:1

Here's a good positive confession for you to make: "Because I am righteous through Christ, I'm as bold as a lion!"

NOVEMBER 19

EZEKIEL 39:1-40:27

Many commentators believe that the confrontation prophesied here is not the final battle of Revelation 20:7-9, but they will admit it's also not the Battle of Armageddon, the last battle of the tribulation when Jesus destroys the Antichrist. They place this battle sometime during the first half of the tribulation. If that is so, I have two questions. After such a massive divine slaughter of the armies advancing against Israel, would the Antichrist have the nerve to set himself up as being God? God says that *all the nations will recognize the victory as from the hand of the Lord* (see 38:16, 23; 39:7, 21, 23). Second, God says that after this event, He will not allow His holy name to be profaned any more (see 39:7). If this battle occurs during the tribulation, there is no doubt that God's name will be profaned afterward.

Chapter 40 begins Ezekiel's description of the future millennial temple, the order of worship there, and the tribal boundaries.

I'm not going to try to give you a detailed description of the temple, because you'll see it for yourself someday! In this section of chapter 40, Ezekiel and his guide view the outer wall and enter the outer court through the east gate. Ezekiel's measuring stick was about ten feet long.

JAMES 2:18-3:18

James did not contradict what Paul taught about salvation by faith. A Christian doesn't have to go around saying, "I have faith in Jesus!" His faith is obvious because it manifests itself in words and deeds (see 2:18). Even demons have faith that "God is one." They believe and shudder (see 2:19).

Abraham was justified by faith, but *his works were the proof of his saving faith.* The same was true of Rahab the harlot, who sheltered the spies in Jericho. What if Rahab had gone around saying, "I have faith that Jericho is going to be destroyed by Israel," but had never acted on what she supposedly believed? She would have perished with her neighbors. "Faith without works is dead" (2:26).

The message of James in 3:1-12 is enough to make you bite your tongue! If it is under complete control, you're mature (3:2). If you're like the rest of us, you still need improvement in that area.

The tongue is the hardest and most important bodily member to control. As Paul taught, only edifying words should proceed from our mouths. When we use our mouths to bless God, we shouldn't also be using them to curse other people, made in His image (see 3:9-12).

There are two sources of wisdom available to us: God's and the world's, which is really from the devil (see 3:13-18). God's wisdom will always lead us to do things that are pure, peaceable, merciful and so on (see 3:17). Worldly wisdom will drive us to be selfishly competitive, characterized by jealousy, strife and general disorder. We need to evaluate our pursuits to see which wisdom is motivating us.

PSALM 118:1-18

PROVERBS 28:2

We already know that God can judge a land by allowing its government to topple or be overthrown.

NOVEMBER 20

EZEKIEL 40:28-41:26

This detailed description of a future temple no doubt filled the Jewish exiles of Ezekiel's day with great hope. Remember that their former temple had been completely razed. Today, Ezekiel gets a tour of the elevated inner court and the temple itself, including the "most holy place" (41:46).

Why will there be tables for animal sacrifices in the millennial temple (see 40:39-43)? Scripture doesn't say, but I can assure you that they will have no greater significance than the animal sacrifices under the old covenant. They will serve only to commemorate Christ's accomplished redemption.

JAMES 4:1-17

This chapter of James is aimed at backslidden or carnal Christians who are guilty of "spiritual adultery" because of their friendship with the world (see v. 4). They were fighting and quarreling, full of envy and hatred (see v. 2). There is never a valid reason for a Christian to be envious of a fellow-believer; God will give to all His children what He will give to one (see v. 2). However, we can hinder our prayers when we ask with wrong motives (see v. 3) for things God knows will draw us away from Him and closer to the world (see v. 4).

Notice that the promise we often quote, "Resist the devil and he will flee from you," is preceded by the command, "Submit therefore to God" (v. 7). Both go hand-in-hand. Also notice the formula James offers for a closer walk with God (see v. 8). *We are as close to God as we want to be.*

When we speak against a fellow-believer, we're guilty of passing judgment (see vv. 11-12). Rather, we should keep quiet and leave judgment in the hands of God. When we publicly call attention to another believer's faults, we're violating the law of love. Of course, this passage must be balanced with others such as 3 John 9-10 and Galatians 2:11-14, which teach that sometimes it is in order to publicly expose a fellow-believer's sins.

In the context of the entire chapter, verses 13-17 do not say that it's wrong to make business plans. What's wrong is to live in the pursuit of business profits with no regard to *God's* plans. Remember that James was addressing worldly Christians guilty of spiritual adultery and serving money more than God.

PSALM 118:19-29

PROVERBS 28:3-5

NOVEMBER 21

EZEKIEL 42:1-43:27

In Ezekiel's vision of chapter 10, he witnessed the glory of God departing from the temple. Praise God that in the millennial temple, the glory of God will return (see 43:2-5)! There the Lord will sit upon His throne; there He will dwell forever (see 43:7). Notice that God gave Ezekiel this vision in hopes of effecting a repentance among the Jewish exiles (see 43:10-11).

JAMES 5:1-20

James concluded his condemnation of the unrighteous rich in verse 6. Why has it taken so long for Jesus to return? Just as the farmer patiently waits for his harvest, so the Lord is waiting for the final harvest of people from the earth (see vv. 7-8). James exhorted his readers to follow the example of the Old Testament prophets and Job (see vv. 10-11), who endured great sufferings but reaped great reward. These suffering Christians were also to *pray* (see v. 13). Rather than complaining and doubting when we experience trials, we should draw close to the Lord, looking to Him for wisdom, strength and comfort.

Notice that James gave instructions for how the sick can be healed (see v. 14). It isn't the elders or the oil that effects the healing but the *prayer of faith* (see v. 15).

Sometimes, before we can be healed, we must confess a sin to somone we have offended (see v. 16). If our relationships aren't right, our relationship with God isn't right (see Matt. 5:23-24). Verse 15 does not say we ought to confess all our sins to other believers. Don't forget that James was writing to Christians who had been fighting one another (see 4:1).

Praise God that the "effective prayer of a righteous man can accomplish much" (v. 16)! And thank God that we are righteous through Jesus.

PSALM 119:1-16

PROVERBS 28:6-7

The poor man of integrity is better off than the rich man who is crooked, because God sees the long-range outcome. The rich, crooked man has only a temporary advantage.

NOVEMBER 22

EZEKIEL 44:1-45:12

We have learned previously that natural people will be living on the earth during the millennium. They will eat, work, marry and die, just as people do now. But we will have glorified bodies from the time of the rapture onward, and thus much of what we read today is not directly applicable to us.

The faithful sons of Zadok, descended from Levi, will minister in the millennial temple *before the Lord*, and the regulations they follow will be similar to those of the old covenant priests (see 44:14-31). They will be the natural descendants of Levi who lived through the tribulation or were born during the millennium.

Who is "the prince" of 44:3 and 45:7-8? It can't be Jesus, because the priest offers a sin offering (see 45:22). He must be some human leader who ministers in the temple.

Chapter 45 describes the division of the land during that age. A holy area of about eight square miles is designated for the temple. Ezekiel's description of the millennial temple does not mention a veil hiding the holy of holies, an ark of the covenant, a table of showbread or golden lampstands. There will be no need for a veil, because Jesus has opened the way for our access to God's glory. There will be no ark, because God Himself will be present, and the covenant will be fulfilled. There will be no table of showbread, because the living bread from heaven (see John 6:51) will be personally present. There will be no need for lampstands, because the light of the world (see

John 8:12) will illumine the temple area (see Rev. 21:23).

1 PETER 1:1-12

Peter probably wrote this letter from Rome to the persecuted Christians of Asia Minor (now Turkey) just before the great persecution under the sadistic Roman emperor Nero. The theme of this letter is "what to do when suffering." In that respect it is somewhat similar to Hebrews and James. Peter would soon die as a martyr; tradition says he was crucified upside-down.

I don't believe verse 2 means that some are chosen to be saved and some are chosen to be damned. God has chosen to save and sanctify all *who would choose to believe in Jesus.* He apparently has foreknowledge of who will make this choice.

Right from the start, Peter was praising God that through His great mercy we have been born again (see v. 3). We have a lot to look forward to (see v. 4), and we can trust God that everything will turn out for our good (see v. 5). Persecution serves at least one good purpose: it grants an opportunity to prove our faith in Jesus, making our faith "more precious than gold" (v. 7). When your faith is put to the test, just keep on thanking God and rejoicing (see v. 8). Those trials are only temporary!

How wonderful is our salvation, purchased with Christ's own blood? The Old Testament prophets would have loved to live during this age, and even angels are jealous of us (see vv. 10-12).

PSALM 119:17-32

PROVERBS 28:8-10

Usury" is the practice of charging exorbitantly high interest rates on loans, usually to desperate people.

NOVEMBER 23

EZEKIEL 45:13-46:24

Again, the millennial animal sacrifices serve only to represent what Jesus has already accomplished, just as the Old Testament sacrifices served only to represent what Jesus *would* accomplish. The Passover feast, which is rich in relevant Old and New Testament symbolism, will still be practiced (see 45:21).

Why will there continue to be sin offerings? Will people sin during the millennium? Absolutely. That's why Jesus will rule "with a rod of iron" (Rev. 19:15).

1 PETER 1:13-2:10

This is all fairly easy to understand. However, I do want to emphasize the message found in 1:17. I wonder how many Christians are constantly mindful that one day their work will be judged by God Himself?

Today we discover a few more truths we can "positively confess" about ourselves: we are "a chosen race, a royal priesthood, a holy nation, and a people for God's own possession" (2:9). And we have a purpose: to spread the knowledge of the gospel (2:9). The world may think you're a truck driver, banker, homemaker or secretary, but you really are a missionary from heaven.

PSALM 119:33-48

PROVERBS 28:11

NOVEMBER 24

EZEKIEL 47:1-48:35

This river flowing from the millennial temple sounds like the "river of the water of life" described in the book of Revelation. John saw a river "clear as crystal, coming from the throne of God" (22:1). John observed on either side of the river "the tree of life, bearing twelve kinds of fruit, yielding fruit every month; and the leaves of the tree were for the healing of the nations" (Rev. 22:2; compare with Ezek. 47:12). The river Ezekiel saw flowed into the Dead Sea (see 47:8), making its saline waters fresh. I suppose they'll have to change the name of the Dead Sea to the Live Sea!

The remainder of Ezekiel's book outlines the boundaries of the promised land. It is a great testimony to God's faithfulness, as He gave Abraham "all the land of Canaan, for an *everlasting possession*" (Gen. 17:8, italics mine). The boundaries described here are roughly the same boundaries originally apportioned to Israel (see Gen. 15:18-21; Josh. 13:1-19:51). In the millennium, the land will be divided among the twelve tribes. Ezekiel also saw the millennial city of Jerusalem, but it's not the "new Jerusalem" John described in Revelation. The "new Jerusalem" is now in heaven and will come down to earth at the end of the millennium (see Rev. 21:2). That Jerusalem is appropriately renamed "YHWH-shammah," meaning "the Lord is there" (48:35).

1 PETER 2:11-3:7

The majority of our reading today deals with the subject of submission. Christianity isn't for weaklings. If often takes a stronger person to submit to others than to dominate others.

Peter instructed his readers to submit to and honor the king (see 2:13), even when the king was Nero. We shouldn't think God wants us to obey governmental authority only when the leaders are Christians. On the other hand, if the government makes laws contrary to God's, civil disobedience is in order. But as long as the government is "punishing evildoers and praising those who do right," Christians should show themselves to be the finest citizens.

The same thought is emphasized in Peter's instructions to slaves (see 2:18). Do you have an "unreasonable" boss? Then this word applies to you. Claim the promise of 2:20. Have you ever suffered unjustly? Follow the perfect example of Jesus, who did not seek revenge, utter threats at His persecutors or cast insults back at His insulters. He entrusted Himself to the great Judge (see 2:23). Put your case in God's hands.

Peter instructed wives to submit to their husbands, and he was not talking only to wives of Christian husbands (see 3:1). The same rule of "allowable unsubmissiveness" applies here. If a husband forbids his wife to attend church, she has no obligation to submit to him on that issue. The best way a wife can win her husband is not by preaching at him but by her behavior. Many times the only difference a man sees in his wife after she becomes a Christian is her absence; she's always away at Bible studies and prayer meetings.

In 3:3-4, Peter was not saying it's wrong for Christian women to wear jewelry and look their best. They are simply to be more concerned about their inward beauty than their outward appearance. And think about it: inward beauty tends to make a person outwardly beautiful as well.

When Peter called the woman "the weaker vessel" (3:7), he wasn't saying women are inferior or weaker emotionally or spiritually, only that most are physically weaker than men.

Husbands are instructed to grant their wives honor, because their wives hold no subordinate position in God's kingdom. And the husband who does not treat his wife as an honorable equal heir is warned that his prayers will be hindered (see 3:7).

PSALM 119:49-64

PROVERBS 28:12-13

NOVEMBER 25

DANIEL 1:1-2:23

Welcome to my favorite prophetic book! It opens up the events of the end times and prepares us to better understand the book of Revelation.

Daniel was taken as a boy to Babylon with the first group of exiles. He was of noble descent, possibly from the royal line of David (see Is. 39:7, which predicts Daniel's ministry). In Babylon, he and three of his friends were chosen to be educated by the Babylonians and placed in the personal service of Nebuchadnezzar. Daniel and his friends resolved to obey God from early on, requesting not to eat the king's ration of "unclean" food. With divinely granted favor, they subsisted and prospered on a vegetarian diet (see 1:16).

Notice that God gave Daniel and his friends knowledge, intelligence and wisdom (see 1:17). Daniel, Hananiah, Mishael and Azariah were *ten times* wiser than Nebuchadnezzar's "magicians and conjurers" (1:20).

Daniel worked for the Babylonian kings seventy years, until Cyrus the Persian overthrew Babylon (see 1:21). During this time of service, he was used by God to interpret the king's forgotten dream. God gave the king his dream, and God made him forget the content while allowing him to remember that he'd had a dream. In Daniel's prayer of thanksgiving, we get an intimation of the dream's interpretation: "And it is He [God] who changes the times and the epochs; He removes kings and establishes kings" (2:21). Nebuchadnezzar's dream revealed coming times and epochs and future world powers, even to the time of Jesus' worldwide reign. God gave an ancient Babylonian king a dream from which we can still learn about things yet to happen.

1 PETER 3:8-4:6

Persecution gives us an opportunity to demonstrate God's love.

Furthermore, we should always be ready to "give an account for the hope that is within" us, doing so "with gentleness and reverence" (3:15). What some Christians call street witnessing is nothing more than "spiritual mugging." We should present the gospel lovingly, kindly, respectfully.

Two passages in our reading today are somewhat difficult to interpret: 3:19-20 and 4:6. It seems that while the spirit of Jesus was in the heart of the earth, He proclaimed something to some spirits who were disobedient during the time of Noah. But who were they and what did He tell them? Scripture doesn't say. Some interpret this passage to mean that Jesus, through the Holy Spirit's anointing Noah, preached to people who were disobedient in Noah's day and are now in hell. That's a possibility, especially if we take the translation of "Spirit" rather than "spirit" in 3:18. However, that interpretation does take some liberties.

My conviction is that Jesus preached to some spirits "in prison" who were on earth during Noah's time. Possibly they were the spirits of unsaved men, but probably they were fallen angels. I assume Jesus proclaimed to them the news of His great victory.

The other difficult passage, 4:6, states that the gospel has "been preached even to those who are dead, that though they are judged in the flesh as men, they may live in the spirit according to the will of God." Peter might have been referring to people who were dead but who had heard the gospel while alive. Certainly Peter was not teaching that there were a class of people who heard the gospel, believed it, and were born again after they had died. That would be contrary to the rest of Scripture. Another possible interpretation is that Peter was not referring to the *physically dead* hearing the gospel but the *spiritually dead.*

Peter seemed to be saying in 3:21 that we're saved by baptism, making his comparison to Noah's "big baptism." But it was the ark, not the water, that saved Noah. (Actually, it was his faith.) So, too, it's not the water of baptism that saves us; it's Jesus, our "ark of safety."

PSALM 119:65-80

PROVERBS 28:14

NOVEMBER 26

DANIEL 2:24-3:30

Nebuchadnezzar saw in his dream a multi-metallic statue; each metal from top to bottom represented a kingdom that would successively dominate the world.

The head, made of gold, represented Nebuchadnezzar and his kingdom of Babylon. The breast and arms of silver represented the dual empire of the Medes and Persians, which would overthrow Babylon in about seventy years. The belly and thighs of bronze represented the kingdom of Greece, which dominated the world from about 334 B.C. Finally, the legs of iron with feet and toes of iron and clay represented the Roman Empire.

We will learn later that the ten toes represent ten kings of a "revived Roman Empire." During their time, Jesus, "the stone cut out without hands" (2:34), will bring an end to their kingdom and all previous kingdoms and establish His divine, eternal kingdom (see 2:44).

The real mystery of this vision revolves around the statue's feet and toes, signifying a kingdom partly strong and partly brittle; the people of the ten-nation confederacy will intermarry, but they will not "adhere to one another" (2:43). Many think that this ten-nation confederacy is the European common market.

In light of Daniel's interpretation, note that Nebuchadnezzar set up a statue made of all gold (see 3:1). In the dream, though, Nebuchadnezzar was only the head of gold. This impressive statue stood about as tall as the Statue of Liberty.

Who was the fourth man in the fiery furnace? It might have been an angel, but I like to think it was Jesus. Nebuchadnezzar said the fourth man looked like a "son of the gods" (3:25), but he had no knowledge of Jesus' being the Son of God. Though the king was astonished by the deliverance of Daniel's three friends, apparently all he gained at that time was a greater respect for their God (see 3:29).

1 PETER 4:7-5:14

All of us have received some gift from God, and we should employ those gifts in serving one another (see 4:10). You don't earn your gift; it comes because of God's grace. Have you discovered your special gift? Peter listed two possibilities (see 4:11): speaking the Word of God and physically serving in some way (by relying on God's strength). Other ministries and gifts are mentioned elsewhere, including those in Romans 12:6-8. Because we're stewards of those gifts (see 4:10), we will someday have to give an account.

When Peter talked about our sharing "the sufferings of Christ" (v. 13), he was referring to persecution from the world, not suffering sickness or disease.

What should we do in times of trial or persecution? Peter said what James said: to the degree we suffer, to that same degree we should rejoice (see 4:13). When we're persecuted, we're blessed, because it proves that God's Spirit rests upon us (see 4:14).

Does suffering and persecution perfect us? No, God perfects us (see 5:10), but God can use the suffering we experience to bring spiritual growth if we'll do what the Word of God says in the midst of our suffering. Peter's readers were being tempted by the devil to forsake Jesus, but Peter admonished them to resist Satan by faith. Peter reminded them that their fellow Christians in other cities were experiencing the same persecutions (see 5:9).

Do you think these Christians had reason to worry? Peter instructed them to cast all their anxiety on God, because He cared for them (see 5:7). God cares about you more than you care about yourself. Be faithful, and rest in His love; trust that He will do what He said He would. You couldn't be in better hands.

PSALM 119:81-96

PROVERBS 28:15-16

NOVEMBER 27

DANIEL 4:1-37

This incident occurred in the latter years of Nebuchadnezzar's rule. Other historical sources record that he suffered some great malady beginning in the forty-third year of his reign.

Considering archaeological evidence, it's not hard to imagine Nebuchadnezzar's pride over his great city of Babylon. The Greek historian Herodotus described the city's wall as being sixty miles long, three hundred feet high and eighty feet wide. It had one hundred gates of brass. The city's magnificent hanging gardens were among the seven wonders of the ancient world. Archaeologists discovered one of Nebuchadnezzar's inscriptions in the city's ruins that attest to his pride: "The fortifications of Esagila and Babylon I strengthened, and established the name of my reign forever."

The lesson of this chapter? God humbles the proud; God exalts the humble. The greatest miracle of this story is Nebuchadnezzar's restoration to his original powerful position—after such humiliation. This story is another testimony to God's great mercy!

2 PETER 1:1-21

We don't have much background information on Peter's second letter. We assume it was addressed to the same people as was his first letter, and apparently it was written near the end of his life. It serves as a warning against accepting heresies and departing from the faith, which isn't surprising, as we know it was written during a time of intense persecution against the church. Also not surprisingly, Peter assured the church of the certainty of Jesus' return and the blessedness of the future kingdom.

This chapter refers to incidents recalled from the three years Peter spent traveling with Jesus. Because of what Peter saw on the Mount of Transfiguration (see vv. 16-18; Matt. 17:1-13), he could speak with great confidence of the Lord's second coming; Peter actually *saw* Jesus as He will look in His glory. It more firmly confirmed the Old Testament predictions of Christ's glorious return (see v. 19). This in turn gives further credence for all the prophetic predictions of the Old Testament. Those ancient men were "moved by the Holy Spirit;" they spoke "from God" (v.21).

Notice that God has granted to us "everything pertaining to life and godliness," but that we experience only the benefits of what He has granted us "through the true knowledge of Him" (v. 3). Only through believing His "precious and magnificent promises" (v. 4) can we become partakers of God's divine nature. All of us, at least to some degree, are partakers. Because we're born of His Spirit, He lives in us. Yet we all still have room to grow, as we continue to possess all our inheritance and walk in the fullness of what God has provided through His Word.

We have "escaped the corruption that is in the world by lust" (v. 4). Peter was referring to our deliverance from the realm and dominion of spiritual death. Thank God we are free!

Verses 5-7 list what some refer to as "steps to spiritual growth." However, Peter wasn't suggesting we take those steps one at a time, but that we diligently strive to excel in all the areas: faith, moral excellence, knowledge, self-control, perseverance, godliness, brotherly kindness (Greek *phileo*) and Christian love (Greek *agape). Every believer should be displaying all these traits.*

PSALM 119:97-112

PROVERBS 28:17-18

NOVEMBER 28

DANIEL 5:1-31

This chapter is set about twenty-six years after chapter 4. Five kings reigned in Babylon after Nebuchadnezzar, and Belshazzar was the final one. He disregarded the things of God, using the temple vessels during his drunken party, which wound up being crashed by God. You can see where we get the expression "The handwriting is on the wall."

Daniel, here at least eighty years old, was no different now from ever before. He related that Belshazzar knew only too well how God had revealed Himself to his grandfather Nebuchadnezzar, but that he himself had not turned to the living God as his grandfather had. So, just as Daniel had predicted to Nebuchadnezzar years before, the 150-year-old golden kingdom of Babylon was replaced by the silver kingdom of the Medes and Persians. That very night Daniel's prophecy was fulfilled; Belshazzar was slain in the invasion of Babylon. The Chaldeans had boasted that their great city was impregnable, but Cyrus the Persian diverted the Euphrates River that flowed under the wall of Babylon; troops entered into the city via the dry riverbed and let the remaining army in.

2 PETER 2:1-22

Isn't it amazing that today's text was penned by a man who, when he first met Jesus, was an unlearned fisherman? By the time of this letter, he had become an eloquent preacher—with the help of the Holy Spirit, of course.

This chapter serves primarily as a warning against false teachers and *to* false teachers. Their judgment will be swift, as exemplified by God's dealings with former false prophets. These false teachers are characterized by their denial of Jesus, by their greed, sensuality, adultery and resistance to authority. To sum it all up, they can be known "by their fruits." Peter cited three examples of God's past judgment: upon angels that rebelled with Satan (see v. 4), upon the unbelieving world of Noah's day (see v. 5) and upon Sodom and Gomorrah (see v. 6). He cited two examples of God's deliverance of the righteous, Noah and Lot, as proof of how God deals with those who obey Him and those who do not.

Balaam was mentioned as a true prophet to whom money became more important than obedience to God, exemplifying the false teachers of Peter's day (see v. 15). Apparently, these false teachers at one time had known and served the Lord (see vv. 1, 20-22), yet now they were leading others astray.

PSALM 119:113-28

PROVERBS 28:19-20

There is more to financial prosperity than just paying tithes and believing God. Hard work, faithfulness and contentment all work together to bring wealth. Do you know what it means to be faithful? *It means continuing to do what you've been doing even when you want to quit.*

NOVEMBER 29

DANIEL 6:1-28

The first verse of this chapter marks the beginning of the Persian Empire, which lasted for 2,500 years, until the shah of *Iran* (synonymous with Persia) was deposed. Daniel was appointed as one of three commissioners over the kingdom, and even at his age, he was so superior to his peers that they ganged up against him, knowing he was to be promoted. Their scheme to bring down Daniel certainly played on Darius's ego: everyone was required to pray to him. When Daniel learned of the new law, did he stop praying for thirty days or pray secretly? No, he just kept right on praying to the Lord three times a day, facing Jerusalem, as Solomon had directed (see 2 Chron. 6:26). He was a man of no compromise.

Daniel was delivered from the lions because "he had trusted in his God" (v. 23). The men who had maliciously accused Daniel learned the truthfulness of the proverb "He who digs a pit will fall into it, and he who rolls a stone, it will come back on him" (Prov. 26:27). It's unfortunate that the wives and children of those corrupt men were executed as well, but that was common practice in ancient heathen societies. Quite possibly, the wives and adult children were equally guilty in the conspiracy.

Once again God was glorified, and a proclamation was made throughout the world that all men should fear the living God. Remember, the same thing happened when the three Hebrew children were delivered from the fiery furnace. God has had a witness to every generation, and no one is without excuse before Him.

2 PETER 3:1-18

Have you ever been tempted to doubt the Lord will come to judge the earth? God may seem slow, but He *always* keeps His word. To the One who lives in eternity, one day is like a thousand years (see v. 8). So in God's mind, it has been only two days since Jesus ascended into heaven. God's "slowness" reveals His patience; He is allowing people more time to repent (see v. 9).

Peter said that we can "hasten the coming of the day of God" (v. 12), although he didn't say how. I presume we can do so by obeying Him now and doing all we can to spread the gospel.

Finally, notice that even Peter said some of Paul's writings were difficult to understand (see vv. 15-16). I'm so glad he was honest enough to say that. It makes me feel better.

PSALM 119:129-152

PROVERBS 28:21-22

NOVEMBER 30

DANIEL 7:1-28

In this vision, which Daniel had before the fall of Babylon to Darius, he saw four beasts, which most commentators believe represent the same four kingdoms represented in Nebuchadnezzar's dream of the multi-metallic statue. Daniel saw the "four winds of heaven" stirring up the Mediterranean, and four beasts came out of it (see vv. 2-3). The first beast, a lion with wings, represented Babylon, which devoured like a lion and was swift as an eagle in its conquests. The lion standing and being given a human mind could refer to Nebuchadnezzar's losing and regaining his mind.

The second beast, a bear with three ribs in its mouth, represented Medo-Persia. The third, a leopard with four wings and four heads, represented Greece, which was divided into four parcels and given to generals after the early death of Alexander the Great. The fourth beast represented the Roman Empire, which in the last days will be revived in a confederation of ten kings (the ten horns of the beast's head). From among those ten kings will arise another leader, the Antichrist.

God will set up His kingdom after taking away the Antichrist's dominion. The saints will be given into the hand of the Antichrist for "a time, times, and half a time" (v. 25). This is commonly thought to be the last half of the seven-year tribulation, one "time" equaling one year; "a time, times, and a half a time" is three and a half years. The *identical* expression is used in Revelation 12:14.

Why is so much of this prophecy given in symbolic terms? God didn't want us to know perfectly all that was going to happen. Daniel's vision is as clear as

God intended it to be. The important part to understand is that the day is coming when Jesus will defeat the Antichrist and rule all the nations of the world.

Did you notice that Daniel mentioned the same "burning wheels" on God's throne that Ezekiel attempted to describe (see v. 9)? One final note: Jesus quoted verse 13 at His trial before the Sanhedrin. When they asked, "Are you the Christ, the Son of the Blessed One?" He responded, "I am; and you shall see the Son of Man sitting at the right hand of Power, and coming with the clouds of heaven" (Mark 14:61-62).

1 JOHN 1:1-10

This letter, assumed to have been written around A.D. 85 or 90, may have been one of the final New Testament epistles. Christianity was almost sixty years old. Most if not all the original apostles had been martyred, with the exception of the aged apostle John, who reportedly spent the last years of his ministry in Ephesus before being banished to the Isle of Patmos. To what group of Christians was John writing? We don't know, but he obviously wrote to admonish them to love and to correct them from swallowing false teaching. In his day, some had taught a concept of the complete, separate distinction between the physical (impure) and the spiritual (pure); it made no difference what a person did with his body, as long as his spirit was clean. This kind of logic led to the heresy that Jesus came only in the spirit, not in the flesh; it eliminated the truth of Christ's physical death on the cross.

John attacked the heresy right from the start. In verses 1-2, he clearly stated that he knew Jesus personally, had seen Him and even touched Him. Jesus was not just a spirit.

Just as in his Gospel account, John here wrote metaphorically. In verse 5, we have a prime example: "God is light." Light is symbolic of purity; darkness, of sin. We can't say we're walking in fellowship with God, who is pure, if we're sinning. If we're walking in purity, we'll have fellowship with one another (as opposed to the broken fellowship of enmity), and Jesus' blood cleanses us from all sin (see v. 7). If we have enmity with our brother or sister and yet say we have no sin, we're deceiving ourselves (see vv. 8, 10; 2:9-11). However, if we confess our sins, God is faithful to forgive and cleanse us (see v. 9). You may not feel forgiven after you've confessed a sin, but you must take God at His promise and *act* forgiven. The feelings will come after you act on your faith.

PSALM 119:153-76

PROVERBS 28:23-24

DECEMBER 1

DANIEL 8:1-27

At least a portion of this vision is explained, although it does contain mysteries. Let's look first at the obvious.

The ram represented Medo-Persia (see v. 20), which at the time was only about twelve years from conquering Babylon (see 8:1). It had two horns, "but one was longer than the other, with the longer one coming up last" (v. 3). The longer horn last was probably symbolic of Cyrus the Persian.

Daniel then saw a goat coming from

the west "with a conspicuous horn between his eyes" (v. 5). The goat was Greece, and the "conspicuous horn" was Alexander the Great (see v. 21), who conquered Medo-Persia in 331 B.C. Not only that, but he also conquered most of the civilized world, then met his untimely death at age thirty-three. Then "the conspicuous horn" was broken off (see v. 8), and four other horns grew up in its place. Sometime after Alexander died, his conquered territories were divided among his four generals. Those territories were Egypt (including northern Africa), Syria, Greece and Asia Minor (Turkey).

Daniel further saw that out of one of those kingdoms, another little horn would arise, "which grew toward the south, toward the east, and toward the Beautiful Land" (v. 9), which is probably Palestine. This little horn represented a king who would arise in "the latter period of their rule" (v. 23). Commentators differ on whether this man was Antiochus Epiphanes, an evil Syrian ruler who persecuted the Jews in the second century B.C., or the future Antichrist. I believe both views are correct. Just as we've seen in the books of the other major prophets (including Daniel already), there is often a blending of imminent events with similar end-times events. Antiochus Epiphanes certainly foreshadowed the Antichrist. He was an extremely cruel man and a great persecutor of the Jews, reportedly crucifying one hundred thousand of them who refused to worship his gods. He eventually sacrificed a pig on the temple altar in Jerusalem and dedicated the temple to Zeus. However, the Jews revolted, and under the leadership of Judas Maccabee, they threw off the Syrian yoke and then cleansed their holy temple. To this day, Jews celebrate that event, commemorated by the feast of Hanukkah, which takes place during our Christmas.

It's clear from verses 10-14 and 23-26 that this little horn must be the Antichrist. Not all the verses are perfectly clear, but we can see that this "little horn" is a man who arises during the end times (see vv. 17,19,23). This man will probably come from somewhere in the Middle East, out of the territories of Alexander's four generals. He will "remove the regular sacrifice" (v. 11), seemingly concurring with Daniel 9:27, which reveals that the Antichrist will forbid the Jews in Israel to continue making their daily sacrifices after the first three and a half years of the tribulation. The time period of the twenty-three hundred evenings and mornings is a mystery, except that it's equivalent to about three and a quarter years (see v. 14).

The Antichrist will obviously oppose Jesus, the "Commander of the host" (v. 11) and the "Prince of princes" (v. 25), but he will be "broken without human agency" (v. 25). Again, not all is perfectly clear in this section, but we can trust that God made it as clear as He wanted it to be. Even Daniel was somewhat baffled (see v. 27). But the parts we do understand are exciting!

1 JOHN 2:1-17

John's message today is essentially the same message as James's: faith without corresponding actions is dead. We can tell if we have really come to know Jesus by our obedience to His commands (see vv. 3-6), particularly His commandment to love one another (see vv. 9-11). James also stated that if we love the world, it proves our hearts are not turned toward God (see v. 15; compare with James 4:4).

Aren't you glad you have an "Advocate" with the Father (v. 1)? Jesus is our defense attorney, and He will never lose a case for us, because He can present the evidence that the penalty for our crimes has already been paid in full!

Women might be offended that John seemed to be writing only to men in this letter (see vv. 12-14). However, it is likely that the "little children, children, young men and fathers" in these verses are representative of four stages of spiritual growth. You can locate where you are spiritually by examining what John had to say to each group.

What are the "lust of the flesh, the lust of the eyes, and the boastful pride of life" (v. 16)? Many see them as the temptations of sex, money and power, which are the primary temptations to most Christians.

PSALM 120:1-7

PROVERBS 28:25-26

DECEMBER 2

DANIEL 9:1-11:1

Daniel had been in Babylon for almost seventy years; he knew the Jews would soon be permitted to return to their homeland. So why did he offer a prayer of confession for the sins of the people if the seventy-year exile was almost over? Wouldn't God keep His word regardless? Possibly Daniel was praying that God would credit the Jews with seventy years, starting from the first exile, of which he was a part. That exile was in 606 B.C., but there were two more—one in 591 B.C. and one in 586 B.C., when Jerusalem was destroyed. However, you can see that if God was counting seventy years from the final exile, Daniel and his fellow Jews had another twenty years to wait in Babylon.

Regardless of the answer to those questions, Daniel got more than he bargained for when Gabriel arrived from heaven with revelation from God. He told Daniel that "seventy weeks" had been decreed for his people, the Jews, and Jerusalem (see 9:24). We now can say with certainty that Gabriel meant seventy weeks of years rather than seventy weeks of days. Thus, 490 years (7 times 70) had been marked for God's dealing with the Jews and Jerusalem. Within that 490-year period, at least six major things would occur: (1) "to finish the transgression." That could mean the Jewish rebellion against God would run its full course. (2) "to make an end of sin." That could mean Israel's national chastisement would end. (3) "to make atonement for iniquity." That was a reference to Jesus' atoning sacrifice. (4) "to bring in everlasting righteousness." That seems to refer to the start of the millennium. (5) "to seal up vision and prophecy." That either means the fulfillment of all the Old Testament prophecies, or that the final visions and prophecies that are to be given will be given within the 490-year time period. (6) "and to anoint the most holy." That could be referring to the beginning of Christ's reign in the millennial temple in Jerusalem.

When will this 490-year period begin? "From the issuing of a decree to restore and rebuild Jerusalem" (9:25). That decree was made by King Artaxerxes on March 14, 445 B.C., according to *Encyclopedia Britannica* (also see Neh. 2:1-2). Gabriel said that from that decree "until Messiah the Prince there would be seven weeks and sixty-two weeks," or a total of sixty-nine of the seventy weeks, or 483 years. If we count exactly 483 years from 445 B.C., making adjustment for the shorter, 360-day Jewish calendar, we arrive at the date of 32 A.D., the same year that Jesus made His triumphal entry into Jerusalem! Daniel predicted the Messiah would die ("be cut off and have nothing," 9:26) just when

Jesus actually did die!

Gabriel foretold that after the death of Jesus, Jerusalem and the temple would be destroyed by "the people of the prince who is to come" (9:26). Jerusalem was destroyed by the Romans in A.D. 70, and they are the people of "the prince who is to come"—the Antichrist. As we learned in the vision of the four beasts in chapter 7, the Antichrist will come out of the nations of the revived Roman Empire. This revelation from Gabriel confirms that.

Jesus died at the end of the sixty-ninth week (483rd year), and that was when the Jewish time clock stopped for the duration of the church age, in which we're now living. That means there is only one week left on the Jewish time clock, or seven years. That time period is the seven-year tribulation, also referred to as "Daniel's seventieth week." Can you see the parts of the prophetic puzzle coming together?

The final verse of chapter 9 describes that final week, or seven years. At that time, "he" (the prince who is to come—the Antichrist) will make a seven-year covenant with the Jews. But he will break the covenant in the middle of the week, or after three and a half years. He will put an end to the sacrifices and grain offerings of the Jews, and we know from other scriptures that he will display himself in the temple as being God (see 2 Thess. 2:4). However, in the end, a complete destruction will be poured out upon the "one who makes desolate"—that is, the Antichrist. Hallelujah! Then the millennium will begin.

In chapter 10, we read the introduction to a subsequent vision Daniel received a few years after Cyrus made his decree allowing the Jews to return to their homeland. Tomorrow we'll read the actual vision, but notice the struggle in the heavenlies between the angel who delivered the message to Daniel and the "prince of Persia" (10:13). From the day Daniel began fasting and praying, his words were heard (see 10:12), but the answer took twenty-one days to get to him because the "prince of Persia" and the "kings of Persia" withstood the angelic messenger. Then the archangel, Michael, came to assist, and apparently the first angel broke through the heavenlies to get to Daniel. We already know from Paul's revelation in the New Testament of the evil, satanic forces that abide in the atmosphere, but this story makes that revelation come alive. Notice also that the angelic messenger, when leaving Daniel, stated that he must once again fight the prince of Persia, and that soon the "prince of Greece" would be coming (10:20). Greece would be the next dominant world power, but the whole thing was being manipulated in advance by demonic forces in the heavenlies. I wonder what would have happened if Daniel had stopped praying after a few days. It seems as if he played a vital role in the outcome of this heavenly battle, and it ought to make us more aware of how vital our prayers are, especially for our government.

1 JOHN 2:18-3:6

Isn't it interesting that we would be reading about the Antichrist in Daniel's book, and now John brings up the same subject? John stated that there are many "antichrists"—referring to anyone who opposes Jesus. He was speaking of the false teachers who had left the Christian camp and were now denying the Lord (see 2:19), teaching that Jesus was not the Messiah. John said that if they denied the Son, they were also denying the Father. Yet John's hearers shouldn't be alarmed but should hold fast to that which they had from the beginning (see 2:24). They should rely on the "anointing" they each possessed by virtue of the Holy Spirit who lived within them (see 2:20,27). He would witness when they heard false teaching.

Have you ever experienced that "warning anointing" in your spirit when you hear something from some teacher that doesn't seem correct? I know of brand-new Christians who were more sensitive to that "warning anointing" than older Christians who swallowed false teaching hook, line and sinker.

Don't interpret John's statement in 2:27 as meaning that true Christians don't need to listen to any teaching, period. John was referring to false teachers. If John meant that Christians shouldn't listen to any teachers, he wouldn't have written this letter by which he was teaching his hearers.

I love 3:1-3. We are now—actually, really, truly, no doubt about it—children of God Himself, born of His Spirit! John said we don't know what we shall be, referring to how we will be when we're given glorified bodies at the rapture, but we know that "when He appears, we shall be like Him" (3:2).

John also said in 3:6 that "no one who abides in Him sins; no one who sins has seen Him or knows Him." We'll learn tomorrow that John was referring to the person who *habitually* sins as a way of life. John was trying to protect his hearers from false believers who professed to believe in Jesus but denied Him by their actions. True believers are living to please God and are conscious of whether their thoughts, deeds and words please God.

PSALM 121:1-8

PROVERBS 28:27-28

When was the last time you shared something of your own with someone who needed it?

DECEMBER 3

DANIEL 11:2-35

This detailed and confusing passage outlined what was, in Daniel's day, the future of Israel, Egypt and Syria, from 537 B.C. to about 165 B.C. It began by predicting the reign of three more kings in Persia, who were Cambyses, Pseudo-Smerdis and Darius Hystaspes. Then a fourth king would arise in Persia (his name was Xerxes) and arouse his nation against Greece. The "mighty king" of verse 3 was Alexander the Great, who lost his kingdom in verse 4; then it was "parceled out toward the four points of the compass." As previously mentioned, Alexander's kingdom was divided among his four generals after his death. General Ptolemy started a Greek dynasty in Egypt that had eleven successive leaders and lasted until 30 B.C. General Seleucus started a dynasty in Syria that lasted until 65 B.C. Verses 5-35 describe the three hundred years of wars between those two Greek dynasties—Egypt (the "king of the South") and Syria (the "king of the North")—right up until the time of Antiochus Epiphanes (vv. 21-35), the evil persecutor of the Jews in the second century B.C. He's the one who set up "the abomination of desolation" (v. 31) in the temple, sacrificing a pig on the altar and erecting a statue of Zeus there. He prefigured the future Antichrist. And true to prophetic form, this prophecy suddenly blended with future events in verse 36, completely bypassing the church age. From verse 36 to the end of the book is all end-time events.

You're probably not interested in a dissertation on the four-hundred-year history of Syria and Egypt, but their wars were part of God's plan of judgment on the Israelites, who obviously lived between those two nations. Ninety-year-old Daniel did a remarkable job of predicting the details of the future events involving those nations and even mentioned at least one person you'll recognize—Cleopatra! She is mentioned in verse 17, although not by name, and has gone down in history as a wicked woman who betrayed her own father, Antiochus III. She was the sister of Antiochus Epiphanes.

1 JOHN 3:7-24

It should be easy to tell who are and who are not true believers in Jesus by their life-styles. Those who are practice righteous living. Those who are not practice sin (see vv. 7-8). They are, spiritually speaking, children of Satan (see v. 10), because they have his nature in their spirits. True believers have a new nature, and therefore don't have a sinful spiritual nature. They "cannot sin" because they are "born of God" (v. 9). That means a sin nature does not reside in their spirits rather than that true Christians never sin. Jesus came to destroy the works of Satan, the first sinner, so it should be obvious that those who practice sin are not true believers (see v. 8).

Speaking more specifically of sins, John stated that a man who hates his brother is not a true believer and therefore is not really a brother. In fact, we can tell we have "passed from death to life because we love the brethren" (v. 14). I'm sure you have experienced that supernatural love for fellow Christians. Many times while driving, I'm passed by cars that have some kind of Christian bumper sticker. I always sense an immediate love for the people in those cars, even though I don't know their names. I know they're part of the same family!

On the other hand, if a person hates other Christians, it proves he has a satanic nature—that of a murderer. And there is no way a murderer can have eternal life unless he becomes saved (see v. 15).

If we truly love our brothers and sisters in Christ, our love will be manifested in deeds of kindness and consideration, not just words (see vv. 16-18). We can assure our hearts of our salvation by examining our lives (see vv. 19-20).

Are we displaying the true fruit of one who believes in Jesus? Are we obedient to the two commandments listed in verse 23—to believe in Him and love one another? Once our hearts are assured that we are truly children of God, we can have great confidence that He will answer our prayers, because He's our very own Father!

PSALM 122:1-9

PROVERBS 29:1

This ought to motivate anyone to listen to rebuke!

DECEMBER 4

DANIEL 11:36-12:13

We begin today with a prophecy that blended Antiochus Epiphanes (171-65 B.C.) with the man he prefigured—the Antichrist. At this writing, no one has appeared who qualifies for that position, because this man will publicly "exalt and magnify himself above every god and will speak monstrous things against the God of gods" (11:36). The description of him offered in 11:36-39 is not perfectly clear, but in his time, he will be obvious to anyone who studies these scriptures. He will "show no regard for the gods of his fathers or for the desire of women...he will honor a god of fortresses'' (vv. 37-38).

Daniel 11:40-45 describes some of the Antichrist's conflicts during the tribulation with (we assume) Egypt (''the king of the South'') and Syria (''the king of the North''). Some say the ''rumors from the North'' (11:44) are a reference to an invasion by Russia, as supposedly predicted in Ezekiel 38-39.

You can see that we're beginning to get speculative. Regardless, this man will enter Israel (''the Beautiful Land'' of v. 41) and meet his end near Zion (''the beautiful Holy Mountain'' of v. 45). Those conflicts will occur either during the tribulation or at the end of the millennium. Most think this passage refers to the tribulation because of the obvious reference to the Antichrist's demise at Jerusalem. But that's never proof positive, because there are going to be numerous ''antichrists'' who lead their nations to battle Jesus in Jerusalem at the end of the millennium (see Rev. 20:7-10).

It's safer not to be dogmatic about scriptures like these. I think the most embarrassed folks in heaven will be dogmatic end-times preachers!

Chapter 12 contains many mysteries, but we know for certain that we're reading about the last half of the tribulation, called the ''great tribulation,'' in verse 1 (also see 12:7), and about the resurrection of the dead at the end of the tribulation (*and* millennium—see Rev. 20:4-6) in verse 2. God clearly intended this book not to be completely understood until the predicted events began to come to pass, according to the angel's words to Daniel in 12:4 and 9. So there's no sense in our trying to figure it all out.

The angel did reveal that there will be 1,290 days from the time the Antichrist abolishes the sacrifice and sets up the ''abomination of desolation'' in the temple to (we assume) the end of the conflict with God's people. That is exactly 30 days more than three and a half years if we count 360-day years. It's interesting that the book of Revelation states that the two witnesses who appear at that time will prophesy for 1,260 days, and that a number of the people of Israel will be hidden from the Antichrist in the wilderness for 1,260 days (see Rev. 11:3; 12:6). The same time period is mentioned in 12:7 as well: ''a time, times, and half a time.'' Possibly the extra thirty days mentioned here will be for the regathering of all the descendants of Israel from around the world and for setting up the millennial government. The angel also stated in 12:12, ''How blessed is he who keeps waiting and attains to the 1,335 days!'' That's an additional forty-five days after the first period, and we can only speculate what will occur during that month and a half. We know there will be a great judgment, and possibly that's when some of our rewards will be given to us, as well as our positions of authority during the millennium. Daniel was told in 12:13 that he would be resurrected during that time to receive his ''allotted portion.''

I can't explain everything to you, but I can promise that someday it will all be perfectly clear to all of us!

1 JOHN 4:1-21

Continuing with the same themes, chapter 4 begins with a warning against false prophets, and John offered a test whereby they can be judged. Any person who denies that Jesus came in the flesh (see vv. 2-3), and any person who denies that Jesus is the Son of God, is not from God. Actually, John wasn't referring to testing prophets, but rather to testing spirits. In both cases, though, the same rule applies.

If a person was prophesying under the influence of the Holy Spirit, he would never say Jesus did not come in the flesh or that He wasn't the Son of God. It seems that the Corinthian church was having problems determining who was truly speaking under the influence of the Holy Spirit and who was speaking under the influence of a demon in their assembly. Paul wrote them that no one who was speaking under the influence of the Holy Spirit could say "Jesus is accursed." However, no one under the influence of a demon could say "Jesus is Lord" (see 1 Cor. 12:2-3).

We have nothing to fear when it comes to demon spirits, because we have overcome them. Greater is He (the Holy Spirit) who is in us than he (the devil and evil spirits) who is in the world (see v. 4)!

Did you learn from verse 5 that all false ideas about Jesus originate from the evil spirits? The world listens to them. All false religions were actually started by demons who succeeded in getting people to listen to their lies.

The second half of this chapter reveals another way in which people can be tested to see if they're true believers. True Christians display the same unselfish love God displays. God's love was demonstrated by His aggressively reaching out to an undeserving world. If people truly have God living inside them, they will demonstrate God's nature.

Displaying that love for the brethren gives us confidence that we truly are children of God. If people are afraid of standing before God at the judgment, it indicates they're not "perfected in love" (v. 18). That means either that they're not displaying love for the brethren to the degree that it proves they're truly born of God, or that they're not developed enough in their faith in God's love for them.

Keep in mind that John was writing to confused Christians—hated by a group of other "Christians" who were teaching that Jesus was not the Son of God. You probably have never been faced with a similar situation. However, if you know someone who claims to be a Christian yet hates you, that person is not truly born of God. Those who love God will also naturally love God's children.

PSALM 123:1-4

PROVERBS 29:2-4

DECEMBER 5

HOSEA 1:1-3:5

Hosea begins the final section of the Old Testament, referred to as the "minor prophets." We are jumping back more than two hundred years from the last chapter of Daniel to the time of Isaiah. Hosea prophesied during the final fifty years of Israel's (the ten northern tribes) decline, until it fell to Assyria in 722 B.C. So you can probably already predict the dominant themes in this book—imminent judgment and future blessing. During Hosea's ministry, seven kings ascended to the throne of Israel, and four of them were murdered by their successors, just as we read in Proverbs: "By the transgression of a land many are its princes" (28:2). Israel was on the fast track to judgment, and unfortunately it never heeded the warnings of Hosea.

Like Jeremiah, Hosea was required by God to act out in real life God's message to His people by taking a wife who became a harlot, representing God's marriage to a nation that had become unfaithful. Her name was Gomer, and by her Hosea had three children who were each named symbolically according to God's instructions. The firstborn son was named Jezreel, because God is about to repay the house of King Jehu for the blood shed in the city of Jezreel. Hosea's second child, a daughter, was named Loruhumah, meaning "she has not obtained compassion." God would no longer have compassion on Israel. The third child, a son, was named Lo-ammi, which means "not My people."

After having already read the four major prophets, we can immediately recognize that it was really God doing the speaking in this book, because He sounds just as He did in the other four. The warnings of judgment were accompanied by promises of future blessing, as we find in 2:10-3:1, 3:5 and 3:14-23. The day will come when God's people would not be named "Loruhumah" but "Ruhamah," meaning "she has obtained compassion." They will not be named "Lo-ammi" but "Ammi," meaning "My people." Just as we read in Ezekiel, one day Israel and Judah will be reunited under one leader, and they will become the sons of God (see 1:10-11). David was mentioned as being a future king over them, and we must assume the Lord was actually referring to Jesus, descendant of David (see 3:5).

In chapter 2, God called to repentance His wayward people, a nation of spiritual adulterers who had gone after other gods, just as Gomer had now left Hosea to "play the harlot." The Lord will discipline Israel until she decides to return to her first husband, and then He will restore her and bless her (see 2:7). That time will be in the millennium, because God said that He will then abolish war from the land, and nature will be changed (see 2:18).

In chapter 3, we find Hosea purchasing his wife, Gomer, and taking her back, even though she had "played the harlot." His action was symbolic of the Lord's undying love for His people, even though they had gone after other gods (see 3:1), and it was symbolic of the fact that one day they will return to their true husband, the Lord Himself, after He purchased them with His blood (see 2:16). Isn't it amazing that God can promise so many nice things to a group of people who had been so unfaithful!

1 JOHN 5:1-21

If a person believes Jesus is the Messiah, he is born again; and if he loves God the Father, He will love God's children (see v. 1). If he truly loves God, he will obey His commandments (see v. 3). This reiterates what John already said: eternal life comes only through Jesus. If you don't have Jesus, you don't have eternal life (see vv. 11-12). One of the main reasons John wrote this letter was so his hearers would have assurance that they did possess eternal life (see v. 13).

Whoever is born again has "overcome the world" through faith in Jesus (see vv. 4-5). Notice that we're not *going to* overcome; we *have* overcome.

What did John mean when he stated that three things bear witness to Jesus—the Spirit, the water and the blood (see vv. 68)? The Holy Spirit in us bears witness with our spirits that when we believe in Jesus the Messiah, we are children of God (see Rom. 8:16). Possibly the "water" represents Jesus' baptism into water, at which time He was identified as the God/man with whom God was well pleased. When we're baptized in water, it identifies us with Jesus. The blood refers to the shedding of Jesus' blood on the cross, by which our sins have been remitted. That act also marked Him as the Messiah, and when we partake of the Lord's supper, it also marks us as believers. So, the Spirit, the water and the blood identified Jesus as Savior, and the Spirit, the water and the blood mark us as believers.

I like the promise of verses 14-15: if we ask anything according to God's will, we know He hears us. "And if we know that He hears us in whatever we ask, we know that we have the requests which we have asked from Him." Unfortunately, too many Christians have interpreted this to mean that if they pray for something and don't get it, it must not have been God's will. But that's not what John was saying. We don't determine God's will *after* we pray; we determine it *before* we pray. God's will can only be determined by knowing Him through His word. Only when we know His will can we then pray in faith, knowing He has heard us, and knowing "that we have the requests which we have asked from Him." Notice also that "we know we *have*" the requests, not "we know we *are going to get* the requests." Jesus told us that we are to "believe that we have received" when we pray (see Mark 11:24).

What is "the sin leading to death" that John mentioned in verses 16-17? Some think it's a sin leading to *physical* death, but if that were the case, why would John say we shouldn't pray for a brother who had committed a sin that would result in his physical death? John must have been talking about a sin leading to *spiritual* death. From our studies in the book of Hebrews, we know that the only unpardonable sin is one of willfully, deliberately turning your back on Jesus after having reached a certain level of spiritual maturity. To pray for a person who has committed that sin is a waste of time, because "it is impossible to restore [him] again to repentance" (Heb. 6:6). Obviously, there were some in John's day who had committed this sin.

Notice also the positive side of these verses (16-17). We can pray for a Christian who has committed a sin "not unto death," and God "will for him give life" (v. 16). I can't claim to fully understand what John meant, but that won't stop me from praying for Christians who have sinned, asking God to give them life.

PSALM 124:1-8

PROVERBS 29:5-8

DECEMBER 6

HOSEA 4:1-5:15

Here we have a catalogue of Israel's main sins: idolatry, deception, murder, theft, adultery, faithlessness, violence, drunkenness and so on. Devastation by the Assyrian armies was coming (5:8-15).

2 JOHN 1-13

This letter, written by the apostle John, was addressed to "the chosen lady and her children" (v. 1), which was either a Christian woman and her spiritual children or a church and its members. If it was written to a specific woman, this lady probably had a church that met in her house (see v. 10). The letter carries with it the same themes of John's first epistle—love for the brethren and warning against false teachers. Apparently John knew the false teachers would be arriving in the chosen lady's area soon, and he therefore warned her not to let them into her house or even give them a greeting. The same doctrinal error is mentioned here: that of denying Jesus came in the flesh.

Finally, John informed her of his plan to visit personally to share more fully. If the "chosen lady" was actually a church, "the children of your chosen sister" (v. 13) would probably be the members of John's own church in Ephesus.

PSALM 125:1-5

PROVERBS 29:9-11

According to this proverb, you can always tell if you're having a controversy with a fool. His reaction will not be one of careful consideration of your argument. Rather, he will rage—angry that he was wrong but can't admit it—or he will laugh, attempting to cover up the fact that he has no counterargument.

DECEMBER 7

HOSEA 6:1-9:17

In 6:1-3, it seems as if we're reading the words of repenting people—in response to God's rebukes through Hosea—but the words are only shallow promises, according to God's reply in 6:4. The entire nation was corrupt, including priests, kings and princes (see 6:9; 7:3). They may have followed some of the Law's rituals, but they had completely disregarded the ethical standards of God's commandments. Once again, God told them they would be punished by being deported to Assyria (see 8:9; 9:3).

Remember that Ephraim, being the dominant tribe of the northern kingdom, became synonymous with Israel.

3 JOHN 1-14

Gaius, to whom this short letter was addressed, was commended for his hospitality to traveling ministers and missionaries. John stated that we ought to be involved in supporting such men that we may be "fellow workers with the truth" (v. 8). Not all of us can take the gospel to foreign countries, but all of us can help those who can.

On the other hand, Diotrephes, a man of some influence in the church, was marked as a self-seeking individual who had slandered John, who had not "received the brethren" as Gaius had, and whom John would publicly expose when he arrived (see v. 10). Sometimes love does not "cover a multitude of sins," but love must expose sins so that a multitude of people aren't hurt. The Bible teaches that hypocrites, especially those in leadership, should be publicly exposed (see 1 Tim. 5:20).

PSALM 126:1-6

PROVERBS 29:12-14

When a leader is corrupt, those who work for him usually become corrupt as well (see v. 12). If you have people working for you, what kind of example are you setting?

DECEMBER 8

HOSEA 10:1-14:9

God never changes—He calls His wayward people to repentance, showing mercy when none is deserved. God was torn between love and justice, so beautifully stated in 11:8: "How can I give you up, O Ephraim? How can I surrender you, O Israel?...My heart is turned over within Me; all my compassions are kindled." Yet if they would not repent and receive His mercy, terrible judgments awaited them.

And once again the Lord promised eventual restoration and blessing in 11:9-11 and 14:4-7. Someday we will see those precious promises fulfilled in Israel.

JUDE 1-25

Jude's book is very much like Peter's second epistle, and some think that one borrowed material from the other. I prefer to think the Holy Spirit inspired both to write similar letters. The apostle Jude, a younger brother of Jesus and James, wrote his letter to warn of false teachers who were introducing heresy into the churches.

Specifically, those false teachers were turning "the grace of God into licentiousness" (v. 4), which means they had carried the truth of God's grace to an extreme that led to sinful living. "If God is so merciful, sin all you want; He'll forgive you!" was their logic. Also, they were denying that Jesus was the divine Son of God (see v. 4), practicing sexual perversion, rejecting authority, reviling angelic majesties (see v. 8), grumbling, finding faults with others, following their own lusts, speaking arrogantly, flattering people for the sake of gaining an advantage (see v. 16), and mocking and causing divisions (see vv. 18-19). Yet they were in the church (see v. 12)!

These false teachers were not true Christians, and sure judgment awaited them, as clearly stated through Jude's references to Old Testament events. Jude sternly warned the believers about following the false teachers, citing two examples of those who formerly were on God's side but who were judged when they defected: unbelieving Israelites who died in the wilderness, and angels who "abandoned their proper abode," possibly referring to the angels who cohabited with "the daughters of men" before the time of Noah's flood (see vv. 5-6; see Gen. 6:1-4). The destruction of Sodom and Gomorrah was cited to show how God views homosexuality and other sexual perversions practiced by the false teachers.

There was no need for alarm; God foretold that ungodly people would arise in the "last time" (v. 18). We shouldn't be alarmed at the present state of the church as a whole, which denies the power of God, because the Scriptures predicted it long in advance (see 2 Tim. 3:5). We should simply hold fast to that which we have, build ourselves up on our "most holy faith," pray "in the Holy Spirit," keep ourselves in God's love and patiently wait for His coming (see vv. 20-21).

Commentators have debated portions of Jude's epistle where he quoted two apocryphal books—books that have not been accepted as actually inspired by the Holy Spirit and therefore not included in the Bible. They're found in verse 9, where Jude referred to the devil's having a dispute about the body of Moses, and Michael's saying to him, "The Lord rebuke you." This incident was recorded in a book called *The Assumption of Moses,* and in it the devil tried to claim Moses' dead body because he had once killed an Egyptian. Remember that no one knew where Moses' body was buried; God performed the funeral (see Deut. 34:6). Here we learn that Michael did the actual burying of Moses' body.

The other example of quoting an apocryphal book is found in verses 14-15, where Jude quoted from the *Book of Enoch.* Remember that Enoch was the man who "walked with God; and he was not, for God took him" (Gen. 5:24). Enoch prophesied in the book by his name concerning the return of the Lord to execute judgment on the ungodly of the earth.

Why did Jude use material from books that today are considered uninspired? The only answer I can think of is that Jude was not endorsing those apocryphal books; he was simply endorsing two passages as historically true, yet not necessarily inspired by God.

Verse 24 is my favorite in this book: God is able to make us "stand in the presence of His glory blameless with great joy." I don't know of a scripture that more positively affirms our right standing before God. Under the old covenant, nobody could stand in God's glory. When the glory came into the temple, even the priests couldn't stand to minister (see 2 Chron. 5:13-14). But we can!

PSALM 127:1-5

PROVERBS 29:15-17

Here are two good proverbs that plainly teach children need discipline in two forms—verbal reproof and "the rod." But don't forget the positive reinforcements as well, such as praising your children when they give their best effort.

DECEMBER 9

JOEL 1:1-3:21

We don't know for certain when Joel wrote this book, but most conservative scholars date it around the same time as Hosea, possibly around 800 B.C. Apparently his book was written during a plague of locusts in Israel—a result of God's judgment. Like so many other times in the books of the prophets, Joel's prophecy merged current events with end-times events, and in this case the terrible plague of locusts blends with an even more terrible time—the day of the Lord.

Chapter 1 describes the locust plague of Joel's day in graphic terms—everything green was eaten—and man and beast suffered immensely because of it. Then, beginning with verse 14, Joel wrote of the impending day of the Lord, during which time the same sorrows will be suffered, only to a greater degree.

In chapter 2, we read not of an invading army of locusts, but of an invasion of men—the "northern army" of 2:20. Their invasion will be terrifying, leaving complete devastation in their wake (see 2:3-9), and accompanied by cataclysmic signs in the heavens (see 2:10, 30-31). This will occur at the final part of the tribulation period, and the battle of Armageddon is more fully described in chapter 3. Then the restored Jews in Israel will cry out to the Lord, and before it's too late, God will bring a supernatural deliverance to them. He and His great army will appear from heaven (see 2:11), and His victory will be awesome (see Rev. 19:11-21). From then on, after Israel's true repentance and regeneration, the Lord will favor them greatly, showering blessings on them for eternity, having judged the nations, and living among them on Mount Zion (see 2:18-29; 3:18-21).

You may have noticed Joel's famous prophecy in 2:28-29, which Peter quoted in his sermon on the day of Pentecost. Peter recognized that God's promise of pouring out His Spirit upon all mankind was being partially fulfilled the day the 120 disciples spoke in tongues. But after reading Joel's prophecy closely, you'll see that this promise won't be ultimately fulfilled until the future. God will not only pour out His Spirit upon the church, but He will also pour out His Spirit on *all mankind.* The day of Pentecost was just a sampling of what is yet to come.

REVELATION 1:1-20

We'll have a great time exploring Revelation for the final twenty-three days of our Bible study.

Nobody can claim to fully understand everything described in this book. My fundamental premise in interpreting

Revelation is that if God wants something to be clear, He can make it clear. The reason Revelation is sometimes vague is that God intended for it to be vague. He wants us to wonder, so that's what we'll do!

I will divide the book of Revelation into three sections. The first part, which you've just read, is the introduction. The second part, chapters 2-3, contains messages to seven actual churches that existed in Asia Minor in John's day. The third part, from chapter 4 to the end, contains revelation of events that are yet to occur, primarily during the tribulation.

John was on the Isle of Patmos in the Aegean Sea around A.D 95, banished there by the Roman emperor Domitian. In a vision, John saw Jesus in His glorified state, standing in the middle of seven golden lampstands and holding seven stars in His right hand. The lampstands represent the seven churches to whom John was writing, and the seven stars represent the seven angels over those churches, as Jesus explained in verse 20. The word translated "angels" in this verse can also be translated "messengers," and some think that Jesus was not speaking of angels, but of the pastors over each of the seven churches. If that's the case, it sure is nice to hear pastors referred to as angels. Too many times, they're called by other names!

This book is prophetically tied in with the Old Testament books of Daniel and Zechariah. John quoted from both books in verse 7: "Behold, He is coming with the clouds, and every eye will see Him, even those who pierced Him; and all the tribes of the earth will mourn over Him." We will read numerous other references in Revelation to other Old Testament books as well. In fact, there's no way you can hope to understand Revelation without a good knowledge of the Old Testament.

The description of the Lord in verses 13-16 is difficult to understand, but John did his best to describe in earthly terms what he saw. It is next to impossible to describe heavenly things with earthly comparisons, and notice that when John first saw the Lord, his natural reaction was to fall "at His feet like a dead man." But Jesus immediately told him not to be afraid (see v. 17).

PSALM 128:1-6

PROVERBS 29:18

Truly, when people have no revelation of God, they are lawless. If you know anything about God, it has to affect your behavior.

DECEMBER 10

AMOS 1:1-3:15

Amos, a shepherd and farmer from Tekoa, about twelve miles south of Jerusalem, was a contemporary of Hosea and Joel. Although from the southern nation of Judah, he was called by God to prophesy to the northern kingdom of Israel about thirty-five years before its fall to Assyria.

Chapters 1-3 contain messages to Syria, Philistia, Phoenicia, Edom, Ammon, Moab, Judah and Israel. All except Judah and Israel were rebuked for their cruelty to neighboring nations, and God later used the cruel armies of Assyria and Babylon to repay them. Chapter 2 begins a section of God's indictments against all of Israel, and we read in 3:3-6 a list of seven rhetorical questions, all of which demonstrate some cause and effect. For example, a lion doesn't roar unless it has found some prey (see v. 4). A trap doesn't spring unless something springs it (see v. 5). All these causes and effects lead up to God's main point: "If a calamity occurs in a city, has not the Lord done it?" (v. 6). The calamity that was about to come upon Israel would come because the Lord was judging the nation. It wouldn't happen just by chance. And Israel was without excuse because God had warned His people over and again through His prophets (see v. 7).

Those prophecies are really words that testify to God's mercy more than anything else. He warned Israel in hopes that they would repent, and He forestalled His judgment year after year. His words remind us that God's judgment will one day come to the whole earth, and we must do all we can to help people escape that condemnation by turning to the Lord.

REVELATION 2:1-17

This begins the second natural division of Revelation—the things which are (1:19). Why would Jesus send a message to seven particular churches in modern western Turkey out of hundreds that existed at that time—sixty-five years after the day of Pentecost? Several theories have been offered. Some say those seven churches represent seven periods in church history, and that we're presently in the final, or "Laodicean," period, when the church is lukewarm (see 3:16). Another theory speculates that those seven churches represent the seven different kinds of churches that always exist in the body of Christ. I favor the second theory. Regardless, it would be a good idea for most pastors to give a sermon titled "If Jesus sent a message to our church, what would He say?"

Notice that the Lord began each message to the three churches in today's reading by complimenting them. The Lord wants to build us up, not tear us down. One of the tests of a true gift of prophecy is that it edifies (see 1 Cor. 14:3). If you hear a prophecy in church that only condemns and tears down, forget it—it wasn't from the Lord. However, just as in the prophecies we read today, a true prophecy may include admonishment and rebuke.

The first message was to the church at Ephesus. The Lord commended them for their deeds and toil and perseverance, but He held them guilty of "leaving their first love" (v. 4). They weren't as "on fire" as they were at first, and the Lord called them to repentance. If they wouldn't repent, He would come and "remove their lampstand out of its place." Exactly what that meant, I don't know, except we know that John saw seven lampstands around Jesus, and each lampstand represented one of the churches listed here. Possibly Jesus was warning them their church would die if they didn't repent.

The church at Smyrna was a persecuted church, and part of the source of their persecution was a local group of Jews, here referred to as a "synagogue of Satan" (v. 9). The persecution of the believers in Smyrna resulted in financial hardships, but the Lord reminded them that although they were temporarily poor because of their faith, they were spiritually rich and would ultimately be rich in heaven.

Did the Lord promise them He would put an end to their persecution? No, He told them to get ready for even more intense persecution that would last ten days. Some would be thrown into prison; some would die. In verse 10, God helps us understand why He sometimes permits His people to be persecuted: "that you may be *tested*" (italics mine). Notice *the devil* was responsible for imprisoning the saints, not God. But God permitted their faith to be tested. In our studies, we have read numerous examples of God's testing His people, including examples of testing while they were enduring Satan's temptations (see Deut. 13:1-3).

Jesus' word to the church at Pergamum reveals His disapproval of the teaching of the "Nicolaitans" (v. 15). We don't know who the Nicolaitans were; however, we do know that their teaching resulted in immorality and also caused Christians to stumble. In His message to Ephesus, Jesus said that He "hated the deeds of the Nicolaitans" (v. 6). Notice that the Lord didn't hate them, He hated their deeds.

After each message to the churches, Jesus promised a reward to those who overcome. We learned from reading John's epistle that anyone who is born again has overcome the world (see 1 John 5:4-5). From those verses and from closely examining the rewards to overcomers here in Revelation, I think we can say that all those rewards will be ours. We are overcomers!

PSALM 129:1-8

PROVERBS 29:19-20

DECEMBER 11

AMOS 4:1-6:14

After reading most of the Bible, I'm confident you have a balanced understanding of God's character. You know He's love, but also that He is a consuming fire. In chapter 4, the judgment side of God seems to be emphasized the most, and rightfully so, because God's words were addressed to rebellious people. But notice God's great mercy, manifested even in His judgment. Beginning with verse 6, we read of the progressively harsher judgments that came upon Israel. First they experienced lack of food (see 4:6), then lack of rain and lack of water (see 4:7-8). Then "I smote you with scorching wind and mildew; and the caterpillar was devouring your many gardens" (4:9). Next it was a plague, then death of their young men at war (see 4:10). The final judgment was imminent: "Prepare to meet your God" (4:12).

Notice that after each judgment God said, "yet you have not returned to Me." In other words, they could have repented during any of the calamities, and that would have stopped the next one from coming. Can you see God's mercy even during His judgment? He didn't begin with the most severe judgment; He began with the least severe one, hoping Israel would repent.

In chapter 5, God's loving heart cried out to His people for their repentance. If they sought Him, they would live, but if not, the majority would die or be deported to Assyria. God even predicted that the wealthy women of Israel (the "cows of Bashan," 4:1) who grew rich by oppressing the poor would be led away with meat and fish hooks (see 4:2). Their cruel Assyrian captors actually did just that!

Did you notice in 5:8 that God revealed the principle of evaporation and the cycle of rain, hundreds of years before people discovered it? God said that He "calls for the waters of the sea and pours them out on the surface of the earth." How can anyone say the Bible isn't divinely inspired?

REVELATION 2:18-3:6

In most of the churches mentioned in Revelation, problems arose from within, not from outside the church. I can tell you from experience that some of the greatest adversaries to the people of God arise from inside the church. False teaching, strife and division hinder the church more than any persecution from the outside.

The church at Thyatira was doing well spiritually, except that they were "tolerating the woman Jezebel, who calls herself a prophetess." (2:20). It's unlikely that the woman's name was actually Jezebel, but the Lord called her that name symbolically because the Old Testament Jezebel introduced the worship of Baal to Israel (see 1 Kin. 19-21). This Jezebel of Revelation should have been dealt with long before, because she easily could have been recognized as a false prophetess by "her fruits." Specifically, her teaching was leading God's people to "commit acts of immorality and eat things sacrificed to idols" (2:20). We know from Paul's writings that there is nothing innately wrong with eating meat that had been offered to idols, but apparently Jezebel's followers were doing it in devotion to the idols.

The church at Sardis was doing very poorly spiritually, perhaps the worst of the seven. It was almost a dead church, except for a small remnant of believers there who "had not soiled their garments" (3:4). Jesus called them to "wake up" and "repent" (3: 2-3). If not, He would come to them by surprise.

Not one of the seven churches addressed in Revelation was perfect. If you're looking for a perfect church to attend, forget it. Even if it were perfect before you arrived, once you joined it, it wouldn't be perfect anymore!

Five promises are given today to those of us who overcome: (1) we will be given authority over the nations to help Jesus when He reigns during the millennium; (2) we'll be given the "morning star" (Jesus Himself—see 22:16); (3) we will be clothed in white garments, which represents being clothed in Jesus' own righteousness; (4) our names will not be erased from the book of life; and (5) Jesus will confess our names before the Father and His angels (see 3:5).

PSALM 130:1-8

PROVERBS 29:21-22

DECEMBER 12

AMOS 7:1-9:15

Again we see God's mercy revealed by His responses to Amos's intercession on behalf of the people of Israel. God planned for a plague of locusts to devour Israel's crops, but in response to Amos's prayer decided to show mercy (see 7:3). Then judgment was about to fall in the form of a great fire that would burn the farmland, but God changed His mind after Amos prayed (see 7:4-6).

Why would God ever change His plans in response to a person's prayer? I can only assume that when people pray, God has an "excuse" (for lack of a better way to say it) to show mercy a little while longer—His mercy restrains His judgment. God's love motivated Him to give Amos those two visions of devastation, and His love also motivated Amos to intercede.

Like Jeremiah, Amos was persecuted for his predictions by a religious leader, but he refused to compromise. His chief persecutor, Amaziah the priest, eventually suffered severe judgment for his sin; he and his children died, his land was parceled up and his wife became a harlot (see 7:17). Those who fight God's people are fighting God Himself.

In chapter 8, the impending doom is predicted once again, but we see, as in other prophecies, a blending into the events of the end-times. The Assyrian invasion was a foreshadowing of God's final judgment during the tribulation. Then "the sun will go down at noon," and the earth will be made "dark in broad daylight" (8:9).

Chapter 9 continues the dual theme of imminent and future devastation, and it can certainly put the fear of God into anyone. There will be no hiding from Him when judgment arrives (see 9:2-4). However, God will not "totally destroy the house of Jacob" (9:8). Eventually, the surviving remnant will multiply and be restored to the land. The millennial temple will be rebuilt, as well as the ruined cities Jesus, the Davidic king, will reign, and true Israel will experience blessings of abundance and security, dwelling in the promised land forever (see 9:11-15). Aren't you glad this book has a happy ending?

REVELATION 3:7-22

The church at Philadelphia was doing fairly well spiritually. Because of their faithfulness, God had opened a "door which no one can shut" (v. 8). But they were a persecuted group, and apparently the source of their persecution was a local group of Jews whom Jesus called "a synagogue of Satan" (v. 9). Those Jews hated the Messiah. Jesus promised His faithful followers in Philadelphia that He would cause those Jews to come and bow down at their feet. We don't know if that happened in their day or if it will be fulfilled after the resurrection.

God promised the Philadelphian Christians that because they had persevered, He would keep them from the "hour of testing...which is about to come upon the whole world, to test those who dwell upon the earth" (v. 10). We don't know for sure what God was speaking about here, but it's definitely a worldwide holocaust. I think He was speaking of the tribulation.

The church at Laodicea was a lukewarm church that Jesus said He would "spit out of My mouth" (v. 16). That doesn't necessarily mean they would lose their salvation; it means they gave Jesus no pleasure and would be disciplined in some manner. The materialistic Christians thought they needed nothing but riches, but Jesus said that spiritually speaking, they were "wretched and miserable and poor and blind and naked" (v. 17). Jesus rebuked them severely, but He did it because He loved them. He rebukes and disciplines those He loves (see v. 19). His rebuke is full of appropriate symbols. Laodicea's water was channelled from distant hotsprings and arrived in the city lukewarm; it was a wealthy city whose commerce was based on banking and woolen clothing production; and it had a medical school renowned for producing an ointment for diseased eyes. He advises them to purchase things money can't buy—knowledge of His Word, holiness and enlightenment of God's ways (see v. 18).

A verse we usually apply to non-Christians is really addressed to believers: "Behold, I stand at the door and knock; if anyone hears My voice and opens the door, I will come in to him, and will dine with him, and he with Me" (v. 20). Jesus wants to have intimate fellowship with all of us, but when a person is a lukewarm Christian, Jesus is just like an "outsider." Have you ever seen that famous painting of Jesus knocking at the door? If you look closely, you'll see that the artist who painted it, Holman Hunt, did not put a doorknob on Christ's side. It can only be opened by the person inside.

The final promises to overcomers are wonderful, although a few are hard for our finite minds to comprehend. We will be pillars in God's temple (this has to be figurative), and the name of the Father, the name of the city of God (the new Jerusalem that will come down from heaven) and Jesus' new name will be written upon us (see v. 12). I think this symbolically means that we will be permanently marked as God's own and citizens of His kingdom. We'll also have the opportunity to sit with Jesus on His throne ruling the world (see v. 21)!

PSALM 131:1-3

PROVERBS 29:23

DECEMBER 13

OBADIAH 1:1-21

This shortest book of the Old Testament is directed toward the descendants of Esau (Edom), who were a neighboring nation to Israel located in modern Jordan. Remember that Esau and Jacob (Israel) were twin brothers born to Isaac and Rebekah. Therefore, the people of Israel and Edom were, in a sense, "brothers," as they're called in verse 10. Because Edom rejoiced at and greatly added to the calamity of Israel during an enemy invasion, they would be judged and "cut off forever" (v. 10). There is no promise of restoration for them.

Of course, what God said came to pass. Isaiah, Jeremiah and Ezekiel had all prophesied Edom's demise, and in the fifth century B.C., Arabs took the country.

With verse 15, we merge into the time of future judgment during the tribulation, and Edom is representative of all nations who have oppressed God's people. Israel will be triumphant over all her enemies (see vv. 18-21), and "the kingdom will be the Lord's" (v. 21).

REVELATION 4:1-11

This chapter begins the third section of Revelation—the things that shall take place "after these things" (compare 4:1 with 1:19). John was suddenly transported right up to heaven after hearing a voice "like a trumpet." Some view John's "rapture" into heaven as symbolic of the church's pretribulational rapture at the sound of "the last trumpet" (see 1 Cor. 15:52). Also, we will discover that the church, after being mentioned so many times in the first three chapters, is not mentioned again until chapter 22. Thus, I believe that John was about to foresee events that will take place during "Daniel's seventieth week," the seven-year tribulation. The church would then be in heaven, and some see the twenty-four elders as symbolic of the raptured church.

John did his best to describe the scene around the throne of God, and it's wise just to take his words literally, as someone who was trying to describe a sight that was almost indescribable to earthly minds. Can you imagine a primitive man from the jungles of Borneo visiting America and then trying to describe what he saw when he returned to his friends?

Some try to find symbolism in every detail, but that seems pointless. There were actually twenty-four elders seated on thrones around the throne of God. There were actually four living creatures who were very similar to the cherubim Ezekiel saw (see Ezek. 1,10) and the seraphim Isaiah saw (see Is. 6).

John also saw "seven lamps of fire burning before the throne" and said that they are the "seven Spirits of God" (v. 5). Those seven fires might be representative of the sevenfold nature of the Holy Spirit, listed in Isaiah 11:1-6: "And the

Spirit of the Lord will rest on Him, the Spirit of wisdom and understanding, the Spirit of counsel and strength, the Spirit of knowledge and the fear of the Lord."

Won't it be wonderful when we see it just as John did? I hope no one will be saying, "Boy, David Kirkwood really messed up interpreting those scriptures!" That's why I'm not going to be dogmatic—I don't want to be too embarrassed!

The best way to read this chapter is by simply being awestruck rather than trying to understand it completely. It should move us to worship the great God of heaven and earth.

PSALM 132:1-18

PROVERBS 29:24-25

When we're afraid of people, we're bound to disobey God. But when we trust God in spite of other's criticisms and persecutions, we will be exalted. It doesn't always happen instantly, but it does ultimately.

DECEMBER 14

JONAH 1:1-4:11

Jonah is my favorite book of the minor prophets, probably because I like stories the best. This story is easy to follow and easy to relate to.

Jonah was divinely commissioned to proclaim imminent judgment upon Nineveh, the capital of Assyria and the largest city of the world at that time. However, Jonah didn't want to proclaim God's message to the people of Nineveh, because He didn't want them to repent; he wanted them to be judged. Why? The Bible doesn't exactly say, but I think we can make a good guess. The people of Assyria had a reputation of being extremely cruel warriors. We know they had to be very wicked people, because God was going to have their great city destroyed in forty days. For that reason, Jonah didn't want God to show them mercy—he wanted God to give them what they deserved. Consequently, he headed in the opposite direction of Nineveh, taking passage on a boat for Tarshish, in modern Spain.

However, God "hurled a great wind upon the sea" that placed the ship and all its passengers' lives in jeopardy. God did it to get Jonah to repent. He first had to get Jonah to repent before He could get Nineveh to repent.

God overrode a pagan ritual of casting lots to expose Jonah to the crew members, and although they tried desperately to get safely to land, they were finally exasperated and threw Jonah overboard at his request. All the men who a few minutes before were "each praying to his god" were now praying to Jonah's God (see 1:14). They became instant converts, especially when they saw the winds immediately calmed as Jonah touched the water and then possibly saw a huge fish swallow the man! They probably turned to one another and said, "Hey—this Jehovah—you don't wanna mess with Him!" God can even use a disobedient prophet to lead some heathen sailors to Himself!

Isn't it amazing that Jonah didn't repent on the boat? He demonstrated that he would rather die than go preach to the Ninevites. But God has a way of bringing people to repentance, and Jonah's discomfort was increased considerably inside the stomach of the fish. Some don't believe this actually happened, but Jesus referred to the story as being authentic (see Matt. 12:40), and certainly God can do anything He wants. But can you imagine what Jonah suffered wallowing in the digestive juices of that fish? It must have been terrible. So Jonah finally repented, the fish swam to dry land after three days, and Jonah was vomited out.

To Jonah's displeasure, the 120,000 citizens of Nineveh sincerely repented of their wickedness, fearing the Lord. Jonah complained and asked God to kill him. But God asked, "Do you have good reason to be angry?" (4:4). The answer, of course, is that he didn't. We never have a right to be angry when God chooses to show mercy to undeserving people. We should remember that we ourselves have been shown undeserved mercy.

But the story isn't over yet. Jonah hoped that either God would change His mind or the Ninevites would go back to their sinful ways so God could judge them. He set up camp outside the city walls to see what would happen. God supernaturally caused a plant to grow overnight to shade Jonah from the heat of the day, and then He sent a worm the next day to cause the plant to die. Jonah was angry about the plant, and it now becomes clear that God had a lesson in mind. Jonah had more compassion for that plant than he did for the people of Nineveh. He didn't want the plant to die, but he didn't care if 120,000 people died. It wasn't a perfect object lesson, because Jonah was only concerned about the plant for selfish reasons, whereas God was concerned for the Ninevites for unselfish reasons. Nevertheless, God got His message across.

Did Jonah ever learn his lesson? The Bible doesn't say. The most important question is, have we learned our lesson? We're commanded to be merciful just as our heavenly Father is merciful (see Luke 6:36).

REVELATION 5:1-14

My rule of interpretation is to take what I read literally unless doing so is obviously absurd, or unless the scripture itself claims to speak symbolically. In chapter 5, at least three things are symbolic. First, the twenty-four elders and four living creatures each have golden bowls full of incense, which "are the prayers of the saints" (v. 8). Second, the Lamb who is worthy to open the seven-sealed book is symbolic of Jesus (see v. 6). Third, the seven horns and eyes on the symbolic Lamb represent "the seven Spirits of God, sent out to all the earth" (v. 6). All the rest I take literally.

The scene that John witnessed is self-explanatory. No one was found who was worthy to open the seven-sealed book except "the Lion of the tribe of Judah, the Root of David." He then appeared as a "Lamb...as if slain" (v. 6) and took the book. The rest of the chapter details the worship that followed from the elders, the four living creatures, the myriads of angels, and "every created thing which is in heaven and on the earth and under the earth and on the sea" (v. 13). Obviously, the opening of this seven-sealed book will be a momentous occasion in history, and we'll learn that the opening of the first seal marks the beginning of the seven-year tribulation.

Think for a moment about all those angels mentioned in verse 11: "the number of them was myriads and myriads, and thousands and thousands." That's a lot of angels! What were they all doing up in heaven? Some say that because the church is in heaven at this point in the narrative, all the guardian angels are there in heaven, too. That's an interesting thought. The important point is that angels are working now on our behalf, and we've got quite a few on our team. Won't it be great to see angels all the time?

Verse 9 is of utmost importance: "for Thou wast slain, and didst purchase for God with Thy blood men from *every tribe and tongue and people and nation*" (italics mine). When we started our study almost a year ago, we learned of God's ultimate plan in calling Abraham. God told him that through him, "all the families of the earth would be blessed" (Gen. 12:3). We know it was through Abraham's seed (Jesus) that God's blessing would come, and now we learn from Revelation that God's plan will be fulfilled. There will be representatives from every tribe, tongue, people and nation in heaven! But we must obey Jesus' command to take the gospel to every *ethnos* (see Matt. 28:19). If Jesus came back today, as many as 12,000 people groups would have no representatives in heaven.

Finally, notice that those redeemed ones of verse 9 have been made "priests to our God; and they will reign upon the earth" (v. 10). That's us!

PSALM 133:1-3

PROVERBS 29:26-27

If you feel you haven't gotten justice from someone over you, appeal to the highest authority! "Justice for man comes from the Lord" (v. 26).

DECEMBER 15

MICAH 1:1-4:13

Micah prophesied during the same time period as Isaiah, the eighth century B.C., and he was also a contemporary of Amos and Hosea. His words were directed to the capital cities of divided Israel—Jerusalem of Judah and Samaria of the ten northern tribes (see 1:1). He was alive during the fall of Samaria to the Assyrians. Micah's message was the same as that of the other prophets; and not surprisingly, since it was the Holy Spirit speaking through him as the others.

Chapter 4 is the most interesting, because the majority of its promises are yet to be fulfilled in the millennium. Then Mount Zion will be "established as the chief of the mountains" (4:1), and Jerusalem will become the religious and political capital of the world. The people of the world will journey there to learn the ways of God, and Jesus will "render decisions for mighty, distant nations" (4:3). Then there will be nothing to fear; there will be no more wars (see 4:3). If you think you've read something similar to those words of Micah before, you have; Isaiah said the identical words in Isaiah 2:2-4.

Finally, in 4:11-13, we get a glimpse of the gathering of the nations for the battle of Armageddon, where Israel will experience its greatest deliverance and victory at the end of the tribulation.

REVELATION 6:1-17

Now the scene changes from heaven to earth, and when we read of the "seal judgments," it is generally thought that we're reading about the beginning of the seven-year tribulation. The first four "seal judgments" will release four horsemen (who are obviously symbolic) upon the earth. Most commentators think the first rider on the white horse symbolizes the revelation of the Antichrist, because as an impostor of the Messiah, he will ride a white horse, just as Jesus clearly will in 19:11-14. This Antichrist "went out conquering, and to conquer" (v. 2). We know from Daniel's visions that the Antichrist will rise up from a ten-nation confederacy and subdue three of those nations (see Dan. 7:8,20-24), so that could also be what John witnessed.

The second rider of the red horse is clearly symbolic of a war or wars. Some expositors correlate this second rider with the war described in Ezekiel 38-39—Russia's supposed invasion of Israel. However, as I stated before, the war described there could be the final uprising at the end of the millennium. Regardless, there will be a war or wars on the earth then, and Jesus predicted the same (see Matt. 24:6-7).

The third seal will release a rider with a pair of scales in his hand, riding a black horse. He is representative of famine; food will become so scarce that its price will skyrocket (see v. 6). It's interesting that Jesus predicted the same three initial judgments during the end-times in Matthew 24:5-7—false messiah(s), wars and famines: "For many will come in My name, saying, 'I am the Christ,' and will mislead many. And you will be hearing of wars and rumors of wars...for nation will rise against nation, and in various places there will be famines and earthquakes."

The fourth seal will release a rider named "Death" on an ashen horse, and "Hades was following with him" (v. 8). This rider will be given authority over one-fourth of the earth, to kill by war, famine, pestilence and wild beasts. This doesn't necessarily mean that one-fourth of the world's population will be killed at that time, but that this rider will have authority over only one-fourth of the earth, to kill a certain percentage of that one-fourth.

The fifth seal will reveal a group of martyrs in heaven who will cry out for their blood to be avenged. These may be the faithful martyrs of all the ages, or more possibly those who will be killed during the first part of the tribulation. If so, this suggests there will be people saved on the earth during the tribulation. They will be told to wait a little while longer, until future martyrs arrive in heaven (see v. 11).

The sixth seal will release cataclysmic events upon the earth—great earthquake tremors, the sun will be darkened, the moon will become blood red, and the stars will fall from the sky to the earth (possibly meteorites). Every mountain and island will be moved from its place (see v. 14). All the earth will cower in terror from the wrath of the Lamb and Him who sits on the throne (see vv. 15-16).

I don't think we can say for certain that these six "seal judgments" will all take place during the first three and a half years of the tribulation, as some think. From other scriptures, we learn that the sun will be darkened and stars will fall from the sky at the *end* of the tribulation, right before Christ's second advent (see Matt. 24:29-30). My opinion is that John was just given an overview of some of the sorrows of the entire seven-year period. The main point is that it will be a terrible time to live on the earth. We can thank God that we have been saved from His wrath through Jesus' blood (see 1 Thess. 5:9).

PSALM 134:1-3

PROVERBS 30:1-4

This new author, Agur, realized in his wisdom that he didn't really know anything! You know you're getting wiser as you come to understand less. Or I could say it this way: the more you learn, the less you see that you know!

DECEMBER 16

MICAH 5:1-7:20

Micah continued with the same theme set during the end-times in chapter 5, and in verse 2 he predicted—seven hundred years in advance—that the Messiah would be born in Bethlehem! There is no possibility he was speaking of any other ruler in Israel, because this person was one whose "goings forth are from long ago, from the days of eternity" (v. 2). He would "arise and shepherd His flock....at that time He will be great to the ends of the earth. And this One will be our peace" (5:4-5).

In 5:7-15 we find what seems to be a description of the blessed future kingdom age, when Israel will have overcome her enemies and be cleansed by the Lord.

In chapters 6-7 we're back in the present-day situation of Micah, and God called His people "on the carpet" for their sins. Things were so bad that even members of one's own household couldn't be trusted (see 7:5-6). Finally, beginning with 7:7, Micah echoed the prayer of the restored remnant of the end times (see 7:7-10) and predicted the eventual forgiveness, restoration and exaltation of Israel, as well as God's long-promised judgment upon the nations (see 7:11-20).

REVELATION 7:1-17

In this chapter, the scene changes once again, from earth to heaven. (Again, this is not necessarily a chronology of events.) There is an interlude during which 144,000 descendants of Israel are marked with a seal on their foreheads. At least one cult has taught in the past that this passage proves there will be only 144,000 people who make it into heaven, but that's absurd. Those 144,000 are all descended from Israel, 12,000 from each tribe. There is not one Gentile among them. Why are they marked? Some think they will be the only Israelites saved during the tribulation, but that's doubtful in light of the improbability of there being exactly 12,000 from each tribe. Others think that those believing Israelites are specially marked as evangelists to take the gospel to the world during the tribulation.

Then John witnessed a "great multitude...from every nation and all tribes and peoples and tongues, standing before the throne and before the Lamb" (v. 9). This group that John saw will come out of "the great tribulation" (v. 14), which is commonly thought to be the second half of the tribulation period. This also suggests there will be multitudes saved during that terrible period—so there is still hope for your unbelieving friends and relatives!

God's great love for them is described beautifully in verses 15-17. The chapter ends with, "and God shall wipe every tear from their eyes."

PSALM 135:1-21

PROVERBS 30:5-6

God is "a shield to those who take refuge in Him" (v. 5). The only way to take refuge in Him is to trust His Word. When we do, we're protected from anything Satan may bring.

DECEMBER 17

NAHUM 1:1-3:19

Jonah was sent to warn the people of Nineveh, the capital of the Assyrian Empire. The short book of Nahum was aimed at the same people, only about 150 years later, after God had used them as a tool of His judgment upon Israel and other nearby nations. They had repented at Jonah's preaching, but now, several generations later, they were ripe for judgment again. But this time they didn't repent. Nineveh fell in 612 B.C. to the Medes and Chaldeans, and today the city is only a mound of dirt.

God told Nineveh that she would reap exactly what she had sown. He asked her in 3:19, "For on whom has not your evil passed continually?" History records that the Assyrians were unmercifully cruel people who plagued the ancient world from 850 B.C. to the fall of Nineveh. God said in chapter 1 that He is slow to anger, but He will by no means leave the guilty unpunished (see 1:3). He is "a stronghold in a day of trouble," and "He knows those who take refuge in Him," but He is also jealous, avenging and wrathful upon His enemies (see 1:2).

Just as in most of the other books of prophecy, Nahum's predictions of coming doom prefigure God's terrible judgment that will come to the whole world. Nineveh's fall was representative of the fall of all the enemies of Israel during the end times, because from then on God promises that "never again will the wicked one pass through you; he is cut off completely" (1:15). Then "the Lord will restore the splendor of Jacob" (2:2).

In chapters 2-3, Nahum graphically described the siege and devastation of Nineveh, comparing her to a den of lions (see 2:11-12) and a harlot, "the mistress of sorceries" (3:4). History records that the Tigris River providentially overflowed its banks, which washed away a portion of the palace and the two-hundred-foot-high wall of the city, giving the Babylonian army easy access into the "impregnable" city. Nahum predicted this as well, "But with an overflowing flood He will make a complete end to its [Nineveh's] site....The gates of the river are opened, and the palace is dissolved" (1:8; 2:6).

Finally, the prophet brought to remembrance Assyria's conquest of the Egyptian city of Thebes (see 3:8), reminding her of her cruel treatment of Thebes's citizens. They had "dashed to pieces her small children" (3:10). God warned them that they would have no escape from His wrath; He certainly couldn't let them off the hook if He didn't let Thebes off the hook. It would soon be done to them as they had done to others.

REVELATION 8:1-13

It seems that the opening of the seventh seal brings no judgment but only results in a half hour of silence in heaven. However, the seventh "seal judgment" actually releases seven "trumpet judgments" upon the earth, and the silence in heaven may be an indication of the gravity of what is about to happen. The judgments are preceded by thunder, lightning and an earthquake (see v. 5) and are precipitated by the prayers of the saints—possibly the persecuted believers on earth (see vv. 3-4).

The first four "trumpet judgments" need little explanation—they will result in a third of earth—trees, grass, sea creatures, ships, rivers and springs—being either burnt up, polluted, destroyed or killed. Furthermore, many men will die from drinking the polluted waters, and a third of the sun, moon and stars will be smitten. I take all these judgments as literal except where impossible. The thought may have crossed your mind how similar those judgments are to the plagues Egypt experienced when she wouldn't let God's people go. Those judgments were literal, too.

When will those "trumpet judgments" take place? Some place them during the "second quarter" of the tribulation, and some place them during the second half. My guess would be during the second half, but only because of their intensity.

PSALM 136:1-26

PROVERBS 30:7-9

This is a wise prayer. The Scripture plainly teaches that both poverty and riches can cause men to stumble. God will entrust with riches only those who have proved themselves trustworthy by their faithful stewardship. Agur, the author of this proverb, knew he couldn't trust himself.

DECEMBER 18

HABAKKUK 1:1-3:19

Habakkuk lived during the time of Jeremiah, Zephaniah and Nahum, right before the fall of Jerusalem to Babylon. God explicitly revealed to Habakkuk that He was going to use the Chaldeans to bring His judgment on Judah, but Habakkuk couldn't understand how God could discipline His people by using a nation even more wicked (see 1:13). It didn't seem right—almost as if God wasn't righteous in His dealings.

God's reply in chapter 2 was beautiful. He always does right. The only reason people question God's dealings is that they can't see the end from the beginning as He can. God promises to bring judgment upon all evil, and we must wait for the appointed time. "Though it tarries, wait for it; for it will certainly come, it will not delay" (2:3). Every evil deed that temporarily succeeds will be brought to judgment: pride, drunkenness, oppression, violence, murder, sexual immorality, idolatry. That means the Babylonians would one day be judged for their evil. Of course, you and I know it as history.

Finally, now that Habakkuk had a fuller understanding of God's faithfulness and overall plan, he could rejoice before the Lord—even as he witnessed the beginnings of Judah's sorrows that would culminate in the certain dreaded invasion from Babylon (see 3:16-19). We, too, can rejoice no matter what our present circumstances—because we know God is ultimately in control over the past, present and future. We are the "righteous who live by our faith" (2:4), and we will one day enjoy that time when all "the earth will be filled with the knowledge of the glory of the Lord, as the waters cover the sea" (2:14).

REVELATION 9:1-21

When the fifth trumpet is sounded, a star (we assume an angel) is seen falling from heaven to earth. He is given a key that allows him to open a bottomless pit from which smoke and locusts pour out (see v. 3). From their description in verses 5-11, we learn these are not ordinary locusts. Therefore, many commentators, including myself, see them as demon spirits, invisible to the naked eye. Their leader is a demon named "Abaddon" or "Apollyon" (v. 11). Regardless of whether they're physical or spiritual, they will grievously torment people for five months, except those who have been sealed on their foreheads by God (see 7:3-8).

Notice that those stinging locusts are permitted to harm anyone who doesn't have the seal of God on his forehead (see v. 4). The only ones who have God's seal are the 144,000 descendants of Israel. This strongly suggests the church will not be on earth at that time, because the majority of us could never qualify to receive the seal of God by virtue of our not being physical descendants of Israel. If we're still on earth at the time of the fifth trumpet, we will be tormented by locusts. That's not even a remote possibility.

The sixth trumpet brings greater woe—four angels who were bound at the Euphrates River are loosed so that one-third of mankind might be killed (see v. 15). Apparently those angels have control over 200 million horsemen, and once again there is debate about the physical or spiritual nature of those horsemen. Some think John was describing a Chinese army of 200 million men (based upon 16:12) and tanks equipped with flame throwers and machine guns; others, like myself, believe those horses and horsemen are demon spirits. The main point is that even though a terrible holocaust results, the surviving people on the earth still don't repent of their wickedness (see vv. 20-21).

PSALM 137:1-9

PROVERBS 30:10

A slanderer is in great danger because once he is discovered, he'll look much worse than the person he slandered.

DECEMBER 19

ZEPHANIAH 1:1-3:20

Zephaniah prophesied about the same time Jeremiah's ministry was getting underway. The first chapter blends imminent events with future events. Zephaniah prophesied concerning the future judgment of the world (the "day of the Lord") and the soon-coming judgment of Judah. In fact, the entire book follows the same pattern of blending the near future with the far. Judah's judgment will be a "mini day of the Lord."

In chapter 2, the Lord called Judah, as well as numerous other surrounding nations, to repentance, that judgment might be avoided. The Lord predicted the downfall of Philistia, Moab, Ammon, Ethiopia and Assyria (see 2:4-13). He also foretold the destruction of Nineveh (see 2:13-15), as Nahum prophesied.

Chapter 3 begins with a woe to Jerusalem (see 3:1-7) and a woe to all future kingdoms of the time of the end (see 3:8). The final result of God's judgments will be a purified world and people (see 3:9-13). That will happen during the time of the millennium, when the Lord Himself will dwell on Mount Zion, and "the Israel of God" will have everlasting peace and prosperity, exalted as chief of the nations of all the earth (see 3:14-20). Have you noticed that Hosea, Joel, Amos, Obadiah, Micah, Habakkuk and Zephaniah all end happily? Almost every one of them ends with promises of great future blessing! Isn't that just like God?

One final note: did you notice the description of Jesus (during the millennium) in 3:17? "The Lord your God is in your midst, a victorious warrior. He will exult over you with joy, He will be quiet in His love, *He will rejoice over you with shouts of joy*" (italics mine). People who think it's not appropriate to shout in church should read this verse. The Lord is excited enough about us to shout over us! Shouldn't we be at least as excited about Him?

REVELATION 10:1-11

God doesn't want us to understand everything that takes place in this chapter, because John was *forbidden to write down what the "seven peals of thunder" said* (v. 4). This chapter is parenthetical between the sixth and seventh trumpets.

This chapter signifies the end of a delay and the finishing of the "mystery of God." It will occur "in the days of the voice of the seventh angel" (v. 7). I interpret that to mean that everything predicted about "the day of the Lord" and all the mysteries surrounding that final time will begin to come to pass when that angel makes his proclamation. In other words, this is the beginning of the end. Some think this marks the beginning of the second half of the tribulation.

The book that John ate is apparently symbolic of the words that he would prophesy concerning the final part of the tribulation, contained in the remainder of this book. It may also be the same book previously sealed with seven seals (see chapter 5).

PSALM 138:1-8

PROVERBS 30:11-14

DECEMBER 20

HAGGAI 1:1-2:23

We read several months ago, in Ezra 5:1-2 (set during the return of the Jews to Jerusalem after the seventy-year captivity), "When the prophets, Haggai the prophet and Zechariah the son of Iddo, prophesied to the Jews who were in Judah and Jerusalem," they "arose and began to rebuild the house of God which is in Jerusalem; and the prophets of God were with them supporting them." So it was through the encouragement of Haggai and Zechariah that the discouraged Jews began to rebuild the temple after a ten- to fifteen-year standstill. The final three books of the Old Testament are the only ones set after the time of the exile.

Apparently the repatriated Jews used the excuse that it was not God's timing for the temple to be rebuilt (see 1:2). They determined God's will by the circumstances rather than by His clearly revealed word. They figured that because they had adversaries who were trying to discourage them, it must not be the Lord's will for the temple to be rebuilt. They were wrong. God "called them on the carpet" for hypocrisy—they had found the time and energy to build their own houses, so why couldn't they build His? Consequently, God permitted them to experience the afflictions listed in 1:5-11. We have heard many times of the blessings of obedience, but here we have a listing of the cursings of disobedience. Those people were not "seeking first the kingdom of God" and suffered lack as a result. Their priorities were all wrong. But Israel repented after hearing the word of the Lord (see 1:12-15).

About a month after the first prophecy, Haggai received a second word from the Lord to encourage the builders of the temple. It would not compare with Solomon's temple, but God promised: "Once more in a little while, I am going to shake the heavens and the earth....And I will shake all the nations; and they will come with the wealth of the nations; and I will fill this house with glory....The latter glory of this house will be greater than the former." (2:6-9). This prophecy will have its complete fulfillment in the millennium, when the temple of Ezekiel 40-48 will be built. Truly then the glory of that "house" will far surpass the glory of Solomon's temple.

Haggai also received two more greatly encouraging prophecies concerning God's blessings on the remnant of Judah who returned to Jerusalem. The first prophecy apparently came on the day the actual construction resumed on the temple, and God promised to bless them from then on; their time of discipline was over, because they had finally begun to obey (see 2:18-19).

The second prophecy came specifically for Zerubbabel, governor of Judah. God promised him that someday all the kingdoms of the world would be overthrown in one great battle (Armageddon), and that Zerubbabel would be "like a signet ring" then. Quite probably, because Zerubbabel was a descendant of David, this promise is ultimately directed to his descendant, Jesus.

REVELATION 11:1-19

You may be surprised to discover how many times the Bible makes reference to the coming kingdom age, when Jesus rules from Jerusalem. We have always been taught to look forward to being in heaven, but we should really be looking forward to "heaven on earth"! In both Old and New Testament readings today, we've read about the blessings of that coming kingdom.

Today we learn that during the last half of the tribulation, Jerusalem will be trodden by the Gentiles. Verse 2 states a time period of forty-two months, which is exactly three and a half years, half of Daniel's seventieth week. Remember that Daniel said that at the midpoint of the tribulation, the Antichrist will break his covenant with Israel (see Dan. 9:27). That event marks the beginning of the "great tribulation."

During that final half of the tribulation, God will anoint "two witnesses"—actually prophets—who will prophesy for exactly 1,260 days, clothed in sackcloth (see v. 3). If we divide 1,260 by the number of days in a Jewish year, 360, we discover that 1,260 days is exactly equal to three and a half years. God calls those two prophets the "two olive trees and two lampstands that stand before the Lord of the earth" (v. 4). We find almost the same expression in the book of Zechariah. We don't know who those two prophets are. Some think Moses and Enoch; some think Moses and Elijah; some think Joshua and Zerubbabel. Nothing is said, however, about their being Old Testament characters.

God gives those two prophets tremendous power to kill those who oppose them. Fire comes from their mouths; they stop rain and smite the earth with plagues. They will be killed at the end of their ministries by the Antichrist ("the beast" of v. 7) and will lie dead in the streets of Jerusalem (see v. 8) for three and a half days (see v. 9). Apparently the whole world will view their dead bodies and celebrate their deaths by sending gifts to each other (see v. 10)! This gives you an idea of how wicked the world will be at that time.

God will resurrect the two dead bodies of His prophets after three and a half days, right in front of everyone, and will immediately rapture them to heaven (see vv. 11-12). Then there will be an earthquake in Jerusalem, during which a tenth of the city will fall and seven thousand people will die.

Those events will probably occur during the last half of the tribulation. Right after the two prophets are raptured, loud voices arise in heaven saying, "The kingdom of the world has become the kingdom of our Lord" (v. 15). The twenty-four elders also worship God at that time, saying, "Thou hast taken Thy great power and hast begun to reign... and the time came...to destroy those who destroy the earth."

Verse 18 sums up the final events of the tribulation and the interim period before the actual start of the millennium. God's wrath comes upon the nations at Armageddon, the dead are judged, and the righteous are rewarded. John will have more details concerning those events later in his book.

Finally, John saw another great scene in heaven: the ark of the covenant appears, which hasn't been seen since the days of the Babylonian exile. That is probably not the ark Moses made, but rather the actual heavenly ark of which Moses made a copy. This could be symbolic of the end of the "times of the Gentiles" (Luke 21:24) and the consummation of God's covenant with Israel, when the believing remnant will be restored and exalted to the land promised the descendants of Abraham, Isaac and Jacob.

PSALM 139:1-24

PROVERBS 30:15-16

DECEMBER 21

ZECHARIAH 1:1-21

For the next eight days, we're in for a doubleheader—reading both Zechariah and Revelation at the same time. The prophet Zechariah had some amazing visions like John, and in fact John referred to some of Zechariah's words.

Zechariah prophesied during the same time as Haggai (520 B.C.), and the prophecies you're about to read helped encourage the fifty thousand repatriated Jews to rebuild what would be known as Zerubbabel's temple. Herod would later dismantle it and rebuild another to court the favor of the Jews; it stood during the time of Jesus and was destroyed by the Romans in A.D. 70. Although not always perfectly clear, this is an amazing book. It has been called the most messianic book of the minor prophets, and it's quoted in the New Testament more than any Old Testament book.

Like Haggai, Zechariah first called the returned exiles to repentance (see vv. 2-6), and they heeded his words. Then, about two months after Haggai had received his last prophecy, Zechariah received eight visions in the night. In the first one, he saw what was probably a number of horsemen and horses who had been patrolling the earth, finding it peaceful and quiet (see v. 11). He also saw an angel who asked God how long He would be indignant toward Judah and Jerusalem (see v. 12). God's reply was reassuring; He promised that Jerusalem and the temple would be rebuilt, He will bring prosperity to His restored people, and He was angry with the nations that oppressed Judah (see vv. 14-17).

In the next vision, Zechariah saw four horns that represented earthly kings or nations. The angel explained that those four horns were those that had scattered Israel and Judah. Most commentators identify the four horns as Babylon, Medo-Persia, Greece and Rome. The four craftsmen who threw down the four horns (see vv. 20-21) would have to be Medo-Persia, Greece, Rome and Jesus Christ, who will one day bring down the restored Roman Empire, as we learned studying Daniel 2 and 7. I'm so glad God is sovereign over history!

REVELATION 12:1-13:1a

This chapter is not a part of any chronological order that may have already been established in John's Revelation. It symbolically covers the history of Israel from (at least) the time of Jesus' birth to the midpoint of the tribulation.

John first saw a woman who was with child and in labor. The best interpretation is that the woman represents Israel and the twelve stars on her head represent the twelve tribes. Jesus was born as a descendant of Israel. He is portrayed in 12:5—the one who will "rule all the nations with a rod of iron" and who was caught up to the throne of God after His resurrection. Satan, the dragon of 12:4, tried to kill Jesus from His birth.

The symbolism surrounding Satan is difficult to interpret. The dragon has seven heads and ten horns, and "on his heads were seven diadems" (12:3). Many have speculated about what these horns and heads represent; they are most likely governments and leaders. The dragon's tail sweeping away a third of the stars in heaven and throwing them to earth possibly represents a third of the angels joining Satan's original rebellion against God.

The woman (Israel) fled into the wilderness where she found a place prepared by God, to be nurtured there for 1,260 days, or for the last half of the tribulation. Remember that Jesus instructed His followers to "flee to the mountains" (Matt. 24:15-18) when they saw the "abomination of desolation" standing in the holy place (spoken of by Daniel)—namely, when the Antichrist sets himself up in the temple as being God. Jesus said that event would mark the beginning of a "great tribulation" (Matt. 24:21). Many believe that hiding place in the wilderness will be the ancient rock fortress of Petra, located across Israel's eastern border in modern Jordan.

Notice that the woman was protected in the wilderness for "a time, times, and half a time" (12:14)—the identical expression found in Daniel 7:25 and 12:7 as the time that the saints would be given into the hand of the Antichrist. Comparing 12:14 with 12:6 ("1,260 days"), we can say that "a time, times, and half a time" is equal to three and a half years.

Apparently it is during the midpoint of the tribulation that Satan and his angels will be cast out of heaven down to earth. When that happens, a voice in heaven will proclaim woe to the earth and its inhabitants, because Satan has "great wrath, knowing that he has only a short time" (12:12). He will persecute Israel, the woman, who then is supernaturally protected and transported to the wilderness. Unable to persecute her any longer, he will then persecute "her offspring," who are believing Jews. Why these Jews have not also fled to the wilderness is a mystery.

PSALM 140:1-13

PROVERBS 30:17

DECEMBER 22

ZECHARIAH 2:1-3:10

Zechariah's third of eight night visions contained within it some glorious promises for the complete restoration of Israel—when "Jerusalem will be inhabited without walls," because there will be "a wall of fire around her" and "the Lord will be the glory in her midst" (2:4-5). This is a clear reference to the time of the millennium, and the Lord also promised to recompense Israel's enemies and foretold that "many nations will join themselves to the Lord in that day" and become God's people (2:11). Zechariah received those night visions during the time of the rebuilding of the temple after the return of the Jews from Babylon, so those promises would have been great encouragement to them. They needed to hear that God would be a wall to their city, because the present walls were heaps of rubble and wouldn't be rebuilt until Nehemiah's time, about seventy-five years later.

Notice also in this passage that God called for the return of all His people from Babylon (see 2:6-7). Less than fifty thousand actually returned after Cyrus's decree allowing it. Those who remained in Babylon were in danger, because God was going to judge Babylon. During the millennium, all the scattered twelve tribes will be regathered to Palestine.

Chapter 3, the fourth vision, is somewhat foggy, but it seems to carry with it two valid interpretations. Joshua was actually the high priest during Zechariah's time (see Hag. 1:1). This vision of him standing before God's throne and having his filthy garments removed and replaced with festal robes could have been a great encouragement to his contemporary Jews, symbolizing that God had ordained and sanctified him to be their high priest. The other interpretation is that Joshua, whose name means "Jehovah saves," represents Jesus, who took upon Himself the sins (filthy garments) of the world, but who was declared to be our righteous high priest before God. There is no doubt that Jesus is "the Branch" referred to in 3:8, just as He is referred to in Isaiah 11:1,53:2; Jeremiah 33:15 and Zechariah 6:12. "The Branch" is the one who "will remove the iniquity of that land in one day" (3:9), either a reference to Jesus' death on the cross or to His cleansing the earth of sin at His second advent (or both). He will initiate a time of universal peace, idiomatically described by the expression "everyone will invite his neighbor to sit under his vine and under his fig tree" (3:10).

REVELATION 13:1b-18

There are many differing interpretations. Two beasts are introduced, and commentators disagree about who they are. In other places of Scripture, beasts represent either kingdoms or kings. In my opinion, the first beast represents both the Antichrist personally and the revived Roman Empire that he heads.

The beast had characteristics of a leopard, bear and lion. That reminds us of one of Daniel's visions in which he saw four beasts come out of the sea, the first three of which successively looked like a lion, bear and leopard. The fourth beast Daniel saw (the indescribable one, revived Rome), like John's first beast, also had ten horns, each representing a king who would come under the domination of the Antichrist. John's beast had seven heads, which either Daniel's fourth beast didn't have or else Daniel didn't mention. Again, I believe this beast represents the Antichrist and the Roman Empire he dominates. He was given his power and authority by Satan (see v. 2). Notice that Satan was also described as having ten horns and seven heads in 12:3.

John saw one of the heads of the first beast receive a fatal wound, but then the fatal wound was healed, and it caused the world to be amazed and worship both Satan and the beast (see vv. 3-4). This one head on the beast that was miraculously healed was possibly the Antichrist. This head was described as "speaking arrogant words and blasphemies" (v. 5), just as Daniel's "little horn" did who was clearly the person of the Antichrist (see Dan. 7). Also, just as Daniel's "little horn," this seventh head of the first beast made war with the saints, and John said that he had authority to act for forty-two months—exactly three and a half years (see v. 5). If this seventh head was the Antichrist, he was truly a false christ, due to the fact that he was raised from the dead after being fatally wounded. It's easy to see why the world began to worship him.

Some think that the resurrection of the fatally wounded head represents the reviving of the old Roman Empire under the Antichrist's leadership, which is certainly also a possibility, except that 17:10 makes it clear that each head of the beast represents an individual king.

The second beast, called "the false prophet" in 16:13 and 19:20, was also connected to Satan, the dragon (see v. 11). He was the leader of the new religion of beast worshippers, and he even performed signs to deceive his followers. Jesus foretold that "false christs and false prophets will arise and will show great signs and wonders, so as to mislead, if possible, even the elect" (Matt. 24:24). This false prophet instructed his disciples to make some kind of an image of the beast, to which he was able to "give breath," cause to speak, and cause to kill "as many as do not worship the image of the beast" (v. 15).

This false prophet was also the one who forced people to be given a mark on their hand or forehead without which no one could buy or sell. Some see the advent of what is called the "UPC code," which is used to mark products and can be read by the scanning eye of a computer, as the way this prophecy will be fulfilled. There will be no need of cash and no worry of stolen credit cards, because almost everyone will have an identifying mark on him by which his bank account can be automatically credited or debited. However, this interpretation has its opponents, because John clearly said that the mark would be the name or number of the beast, indicating the mark would symbolize allegiance to the beast.

PSALM 141:1-10

PROVERBS 30:18-20

DECEMBER 23

ZECHARIAH 4:1-5:11

Zechariah's fifth vision of the golden lampstand and two olive trees contains a few mysteries. We have already read what may be a reference to this vision in the book of Revelation, and there we learned that the two witnesses of the great tribulation are referred to as two lampstands and two olive trees (see Rev. 11:3-4). Because Zechariah seemed to be indicating that Zerubbabel, governor of Judah, and Joshua, the high priest, were the two olive trees on either side of the lampstand (see 4:14), some commentators think they will be the two witnesses of Revelation. But that's speculative.

Although details of what Zechariah saw in this vision are not completely clear, the message behind the vision is very clear. It contained great encouragement for Joshua, and especially for Zerubbabel. First the angel explained the meaning of the lampstand. It seems that once again, the lampstand represented the Holy Spirit. Zerubbabel would not finish the huge task of completing the temple by his own might or power, but only through the help of the Holy Spirit (see 4:6). That's a good promise for us to memorize as well. The task set before him seemed impossible; it looked like an immovable mountain (see 4:7). Possibly the Lord was referring to the ruins of the former temple—the mountain of stones and rubble he would use to build this temple. But the Lord promised to turn the mountain into a plain—as sure as Zerubbabel had laid the foundation stones, he would place the capstone on the temple (see 4:7-9). We, like Zerubbabel, shouldn't "despise the day of small things" (v. 10). Mountains are climbed by starting with a few small, seemingly insignificant steps.

Zechariah's sixth vision of the huge flying scroll is self-explanatory. It represents a curse that will purge the earth of all evildoers. This will come during Jesus' reign.

The seventh vision, a woman sitting in a bushel basket (ephah), isn't as easy to interpret. The woman, representative of wickedness, is cast into an ephah and covered with lead, then carried off by two other women to the "land of Shinar" (5:11), or Babylon. Whatever the details of this vision signify, the general meaning is that the sin in Israel would be removed and carried far away. I'm sure there is greater significance to this vision than we realize now, but we'll have to wait to understand its end-time application.

REVELATION 14:1-20

This chapter seems to be a foresight of the end of the tribulation. We first find Jesus and the 144,000 sealed Israelites standing on Mount Zion, and then they sing a new song before the throne of God. Possibly this indicates that they have been raptured to heaven after meeting Jesus on Mount Zion.

Next, three angels are seen flying through mid-heaven. One preaches the gospel and admonishes the earth dwellers to worship God, the next announces the fall of Babylon, and the last warns the people on earth of the terrible consequences that will result for those who worship the beast or take his mark: they will be tormented forever (see 14:10-11).

We have to wonder how the fall of Babylon could be announced at the end of the tribulation in light of the fact that it was destroyed centuries ago and is no longer a city. Either Babylon will be rebuilt, or else Babylon represents something else. It's described as having "made all the nations drink of the wine of the passion of her immorality" (v. 8). Some suggest Rome, others Jerusalem. Some say it is the unnamed capital of the Antichrist, and some think Babylon represents the entire satanic world system. We'll look at the subject more closely when we read of Babylon again in chapters 17-18.

In verses 14-20, the great reaping of the wicked from the earth is viewed, and I assume it's a description of the battle of Armageddon, when Jesus comes to wage war with the armies of the Antichrist outside Jerusalem. The carnage is so great that blood is described as coming up to the horses' bridles for a distance of two hundred miles (see v. 20). I certainly hope for their sake that he was talking about dead horses lying in the ground!

Zechariah described the way Jesus will destroy that great horde of millions of the Antichrist's followers: "Now this will be the plague with which the Lord will strike all the peoples who have gone to war against Jerusalem; their flesh will rot while they stand on their feet, and their eyes will rot in their sockets, and their tongue will rot in their mouth" (Zech. 14:12).

PSALM 142:1-7

PROVERBS 30:21-23

DECEMBER 24

ZECHARIAH 6:1-7:14

Remember that Zechariah had these eight visions all during the same night. His final vision of the four chariots reminds us of the "four horsemen of the apocalypse" that John saw and recorded in Revelation 6:1-8. The horses John saw were white, red, black and ashen; Zechariah's were white, red, black and dappled. It seems that in both cases the horses represent different judgments on nations, with Zechariah's vision emphasizing judgment on the "north country" (6:6,8). Again it seems that Zechariah's vision had application both to the Jews of his day and also to the end times when God will judge the whole earth.

Also during Zechariah's eighth vision, he was instructed to make a crown of silver and gold from an offering that had been brought from three Jews who had just arrived from Babylon (see 6:10). He was to set that crown upon the head of Joshua, who was the high priest in Zechariah's day. This vision has great significance, as we learn from 6:12, where the Lord informed Zechariah that a man "whose name is Branch" will branch out from where He is and build the temple of the Lord. "The Branch" is obviously Jesus. It was unheard of for one man to fill both roles of priest and king, as Joshua's coronation represented. But Jesus, of course, will fill both those offices in the millennium (see 6:13). Remember we have previously learned that Jesus has been made a high priest after the order of Melchizedek, who was king of Jerusalem and priest of God Most High. Zechariah was instructed by the Lord to place that crown in the new temple as a reminder of the coming king and high priest who will one day rule from that very spot (see 6:14).

Chapter 7 takes place two years after the first chapters. Construction of the temple had been progressing. The ruined cities of Judah were beginning to be rebuilt and repopulated, and some men from Bethel (a few miles from Jerusalem) arrived to inquire if they should continue to keep the fast of the fifth month. That fast had been practiced since the destruction of the temple in Jerusalem, in commemoration of that event. Now that the temple was being rebuilt, it seemed that possibly it was time to end this more than seventy-year-old tradition. The fast of the seventh month (mentioned by the Lord in 7:5) was practiced in memory of their murdered governor, Gedaliah (see 2 Kin. 25:25). God responded by questioning their true motives when they fasted—it had become a self-promoting ritual, just as in Isaiah's day (see Is. 58). God desired that they honor the moral and ethical requirements of His law.

REVELATION 15:1-8

Although not everything in Revelation is clear to us, we can certainly understand the major messages of the book. We know generally how this age will end—with the greatest display of

God's wrath the earth has ever seen. And we know in general what will happen when Jesus returns in His glory. It seems clear that God doesn't intend for us to understand every detail of Revelation, but He has designed the book so that we can understand what He wants us to. Don't be concerned about all the mysteries; they will be revealed in their time.

This chapter prepares us for the final seven plagues of God's wrath upon the earth during the last days of the tribulation. They're known as the "bowl judgments." Some commentators place this chapter at the midpoint of the tribulation, while others say that at this point there is only one month remaining of the seven years. I would place the last seven plagues at the very end of the tribulation.

In verses 2-4, we probably have a scene of the martyred tribulational saints before the throne of God in heaven. They refused to take the mark of the beast or worship his image and were either killed or "raptured" off the earth. It seems that at this point in the tribulation, there are no longer any believers in Jesus on the earth, and now the fullest measure of God's wrath is about to be poured out.

Notice also, in verses 5-8, the temple in heaven, where God's throne is located. The tabernacle of Moses and the temple of Solomon were both patterned after the temple in heaven (see Ex. 25:9,40; 1 Chron. 28:11-19; Heb. 8:5, 9:23).

PSALM 143:1-12

PROVERBS 30:24-28

DECEMBER 25

ZECHARIAH 8:1-23

Merry Christmas! I'm glad we know that Jesus is the reason for the season.

Zechariah 8 is a great chapter. You may have recognized the law of double reference at work once again. This chapter was probably a great encouragement to the repatriated Jews in Judah during Zechariah's time, but it has fuller application to the millennium. We learn that natural people will be living on the earth (see vv. 4-5), and as we learned from Isaiah, longevity will be restored (see Is. 65:20). The normal fasts will be turned into feasts (see v. 19). And once more we see the theme of Israel exalted among the nations, "Many peoples and mighty nations will come to seek the Lord of hosts in Jerusalem and to entreat the favor of the Lord....In those days ten men from all the nations will grasp the garment of a Jew saying, 'Let us go with you, for we have heard that God is with you' " (see vv. 22-23).

Incidentally, there are those who believe that God's plan no longer includes the physical descendants of Israel, but that all of Israel's promises apply now to the church because the majority of the Jews have rejected Jesus. They say we are now the "Israel of God." However, this type of thinking is hardly supported by Scripture. The apostle Paul plainly taught that God still has a plan for the physical descendants of Israel, and that one day there will be a great many Jews who confess faith in Jesus (see Rom. 11). He made it obvious that the many promises in the Old Testament that refer to the regeneration of the nation of Israel do in fact apply to the physical descendants of Israel.

Some believe that those of Anglo-

Saxon descent are actually the physical descendants of the ten lost tribes of Israel. This is referred to as "British Israelism," and its adherents have even tried to prove that the king of England is a direct descendant of David, ruling over the ten lost tribes who live in the British Isles! Such a belief has no support in Scripture.

REVELATION 16:1-21

The seven "bowl judgments" are clearly the worst yet. During those final judgments of the tribulation, everyone who has taken the mark of the beast will be plagued with malignant sores, the entire sea turns into coagulated blood, and the rivers and springs will become blood as well, creating an unbearable stench. That is a just recompense upon the wicked people of the earth, because they've poured out the innocent blood of God's children during the previous years (see vv. 5-6). Furthermore, the sun will increase its intensity and scorch people with "fierce heat" (see vv. 8-9). Notice that even after all these judgments, the earth's inhabitants still won't repent of their wickedness, but rather blaspheme God (see v. 9). The implication of verse 9 is that the earth's inhabitants could repent at that stage and be saved, but they will choose not to.

During the fifth bowl judgment, the beast's kingdom will be "darkened," and earth's inhabitants will experience great pain to the degree that they gnaw their tongues in anguish (see v. 10). Amos, Nahum and Zephaniah all foretold the time of darkness during the "day of the Lord" (Amos 5:18; Nah. 1:6,8; Zeph. 1:15). And still people don't repent!

The sixth bowl judgment results in the drying up of the Euphrates River "that the way might be prepared for the kings from the east" (v. 12). This is a preparation for the battle of Armageddon, at which the nations gather in Israel for one final battle. When the 1,780-mile Euphrates River is dried up, it will give easier access for any nation east or north of Israel.

Finally, we see that the nations will gather through the influence of demon spirits to "Har-Magedon" (Armageddon), a wide valley in central Israel that has been the site of numerous other battles throughout history (see vv. 13-16). Napoleon is said to have stated that the valley of Har-Magedon is the ideal battleground for all the armies of the world. Little did he realize that his words would one day come to pass! When they do, the final "bowl judgment" will be poured out, resulting in the world's greatest earthquake and a rain of huge hailstones. Zechariah, Haggai, Joel and Isaiah all spoke of a great earthquake during the time of God's wrath (see Zech. 14:4-5; Hag. 2:6-7; Joel 3:1-16; Is. 24:18-20). The Bible makes it plain that these judgments are falling upon extremely evil people (v. 21). Babylon is again mentioned as drinking the cup of God's wrath (v. 19). We'll discuss what Babylon represents during the next two days.

Those final plagues mainly affect that which unsaved people take for granted, things that are truly gifts from God—health, pure water, the gentle warmth of the sun, firm ground to walk upon. Let us thank God for the wonderful blessings we experience every day of our lives.

PSALM 144:1-15

PROVERBS 30:29-31

The implication here is that the king doesn't strut so stately when he is all by himself. Without his army, he's like any other man.

DECEMBER 26

ZECHARIAH 9:1-17

The first seven verses of this chapter are a foretelling (in Zechariah's day) of Alexander the Great's conquests of Syria, Phoenicia and Philistia, fulfilled in the early part of the fourth century B.C.

I'm sure you recognized the messianic prophecy of verses 9-10. Notice that there is no mention of the church age, but it appears that Jesus will reign as king of the earth during His first appearance. However, we know that verse 9 describes His triumphal entry into Jerusalem during His earthly ministry (see John 12:15), and verse 10 describes His reign of peace that is yet to come.

Verses 11-17 had initial fulfillment in the return of the Jews from Babylonian-Persian captivity and the limited freedom from Greece that they later experienced. The verses will ultimately be fulfilled by the return of all Israel's exiles from the nations, by their deliverance from the Antichrist, and by the blessings that will result.

REVELATION 17:1-18

In this chapter another strange character is introduced: a woman clothed in purple and scarlet who sits on a scarlet beast—a beast that seems to be the same as the first one we read about in chapter 13, who also had seven heads and ten horns.

Of what or whom is this woman symbolic? Verse 18 says she is "the great city which reigns over the kings of the earth," and she is described in verse 5 as having a name written on her forehead: "Babylon the great, the mother of harlots and of the abominations of the earth." So she is referred to as a city, and that city is called Babylon. She is a harlot, which from many Old Testament passages we understand can refer to a spiritual apostasy. It certainly must in this harlot's case, because she is not a literal woman but a city. She has "committed acts of immorality" with the kings of the earth, and the inhabitants of the earth were "made drunk with the wine of her immorality" (v. 2). In other words, this city served the kings of the earth rather than God and influenced many people to also commit spiritual adultery.

Further, this woman is very wealthy, adorned with gold and precious stones and pearls. She holds a gold cup that hides abominations and "the unclean things of her immorality" (v. 4). She is seen as "drunk with the blood of the saints," indicating she is responsible for the martyrdom of Christians. She has a worldwide influence, because she is seen sitting "on many waters" (v. 1), which are later explained to be "peoples and multitudes and nations and tongues" (v. 15). And she is seen sitting on the seven heads of the beast, which are explained as being seven mountains and seven kings (vs. 9-10).

Now let's look at the beast on which the harlot rides. As I've already stated, this seven-headed, ten-horned beast is probably the same one as in chapter 13, which apparently is the Antichrist and the revived Roman Empire he leads. This beast that John saw "was and is not, and is about to come up out of the abyss and to go to destruction" (v. 8). I assume this refers to the fall of imperial Rome in the fifth century and its resurrection in the end. Don't laugh at the idea of a revived Roman Empire—Europe is becoming more unified all the time. In 1992, twelve European nations will be abolishing all remaining trade barriers between themselves, providing an unrestricted flow of goods and services across their borders.

Someday soon there will be a "United States of Europe." The birth of the E.E.C. (European Economic Community) is just the beginning.

The ten horns are explained as being ten kings who give their power and authority to the Antichrist for "one hour" (v. 12). Those ten horns correspond to the ten toes on Nebuchadnezzar's statue (see Dan. 2:31-45) and the ten horns on Daniel's indescribable beast (see Dan. 7:7,20-24).

The seven heads of the beast are a little more difficult to understand. John said the seven heads represent seven mountains and seven kings (see vv. 9-10). Of those seven kings, "five have fallen, one is, the other has not yet come; and when he comes, he must remain a little while" (v. 10). Commentators differ on the interpretation of that explanation. Some say they represent Roman emperors of John's day. Others say those seven heads represent the great Gentile kingdoms of the Bible—Egypt, Assyria, Babylon, Persia, Greece, Rome, revived Rome and then "ultimate Rome" under the Antichrist.

It's important to remember that the beast is doomed for destruction, and Jesus will defeat the armies of the Antichrist at His coming (see v. 14). That much is very clear. The best chapters of Revelation are yet to come!

PSALM 145:1-21

PROVERBS 30:32

Don't ever deal with your sin by sinning more! Stop it and confess it to the Lord.

DECEMBER 27

ZECHARIAH 10:1-11:17

Chapter 10 continues yesterday's theme of the blessings of Judah and Ephraim during the kingdom age. First the Lord will deal with the false shepherds and corrupt leaders ("male goats"—10:3) of His people. He will make His people victorious over their enemies (see 10:3b,5,11) and restore them to their land once more (see 10:6,8-10) where they will multiply greatly (see 10:10). Those promises have greater application than only to Judah's return from Babylonian captivity. They will ultimately be fulfilled by Israel's descendants during the millennium.

Chapter 11 doesn't paint such a nice picture. It symbolically recounts Israel's rejection of God to the extent of rejecting His Shepherd/Messiah, who was valued and sold for thirty pieces of silver (see 11:12). Zechariah even foretold that the money used to pay for Jesus' betrayal would go to a potter; Matthew revealed that it was used to buy a potter's field (compare 11:13 with Matt. 26:15; 27:3-10).

The destruction of the land and people that was forthcoming was graphically foretold in 11:1-6. This prediction was either fulfilled during the destruction of Jerusalem by Titus in A.D. 70, will be fulfilled during the tribulation, or possibly both. Although not every detail of this chapter is clear, it is obvious that God was saying He no longer favored Israel when they broke His covenant, and that as a result of His judgment, Israel was divided. Their ultimate rejection of the Messiah would lead to ultimate judgment. Zechariah 11:15-17 seems to apply to the future Antichrist, a false shepherd of Israel, whom the Jews will look to during the first half of the tribulation as their great protector, until his true character is revealed when he breaks his covenant with them after three and a half years. Zechariah indicated that after God has used this false shepherd to judge Israel, He will then judge the false shepherd.

REVELATION 18:1-24

Expositors generally interpret this chapter as the destruction of "commercial Babylon." Some do not view this Babylon as the same Babylon the great harlot represented in chapter 17. They refer to the two Babylons as "ecclesiastical Babylon" and "commercial Babylon." Some say this second Babylon is New York City. Some say that Babylon will actually be rebuilt on its ruins in Iraq. I disagree with the premise that the Babylons of chapters 17-18 are not the same. I think they both represent the same city. Chapter 17 simply emphasizes the religious aspects, and chapter 18 emphasizes the commercial aspects of Babylon.

In both chapters, Babylon is described using identical terms. John seemed to be speaking here of a literal seaport city that will be a great center of world commerce. Therefore, this Babylon is not just representative of the world's commercial system, as some think. Also keep in mind that this book was not written with chapter divisions; they were added later.

The main point of this chapter is that this Babylon will be ruined "in one hour" (v. 10), and her political and commercial friends who profited by her will lament her destruction (see vv. 9-19). On the other hand, heaven will rejoice at the demise of this wicked city, especially the millions who were murdered through her influence down through the centuries.

PSALM 146:1-10

PROVERBS 30:33

DECEMBER 28

ZECHARIAH 12:1-13:9

It's interesting that we're reading in both Revelation and Zechariah about the same time period—the final days of the tribulation. In this chapter, Zechariah described the final battle, when all the nations gather to attack Jerusalem. They will meet with some degree of success in their campaign, as we will see in chapter 14. However, God will first deliver the surrounding cities of Jerusalem and then Jerusalem itself (see 12:6-7), and He will grant the Israelites supernatural ability to fight (see 12:6,8).

The most significant aspect of this time is that apparently the Israelites will see Jesus personally return to defend them, and then they will realize He is the Messiah whom they rejected, as He said in 12:10: "they will look on Me whom they have pierced; and they will mourn for Him." They will weep in repentance for their previous rejection of Him (see 12:11-14). I'm sure the "Jews for Jesus" ministry people will be thrilled to see so many Jews being born again!

Chapter 13 first describes some of the results of the national conversion—there will no longer be any idolatry, and false prophets will not be tolerated. Believing Israel will be cleansed in the blood of the Lamb (see 13:1).

Possibly 13:6 describes Jesus, the one who was "pierced." He is asked by one, "What are those wounds between your arms?" His reply demonstrates the same gracious love He showed from the cross as He asked God to forgive the ones who crucified Him: "Those with which I was wounded in the house *of my friends*" (italics mine).

Zechariah 13:7 foretells the Roman garrison that arrested Jesus in the Garden of Gethsemane and the subsequent scattering of His disciples, as explained by Jesus in Matthew 26:31. Verses 8-9 are somewhat unclear, but I would guess they refer again to the time of the tribulation, which only a third of the Israelites will survive. They will be the ones who come to believe in the Lord Jesus after being refined and tested in the trials of the tribulation.

REVELATION 19:1-21

Now we're into the best part of Revelation! Notice that it begins with a stupendous worship service, as the heavenly multitude rejoice over the judgment of the harlot and the beginning of the kingdom age (see vv. 1-6). Notice also that the worship is very loud (see vv. 1,6)! If you don't like loud worship now, you need to change, because you'll be with this heavenly multitude!

The "marriage supper of the Lamb" will occur sometime near the end of the tribulation or the beginning of the millennium. We, the church, are the Lamb's bride, so you will definitely be invited to that supper. We'll be clothed in fine linen to symbolize the "righteous acts of the saints" (v. 8). Possibly this marriage supper was what Isaiah spoke of: "And the Lord of hosts will prepare a lavish banquet for all peoples on this mountain; a banquet of aged wine, choice pieces of marrow..." (Is. 25:6).

Poor John, probably the most spiritual man alive in his day, was so overwhelmed that he made the mistake of worshipping an angel (see v. 10). That should make us feel better about our mistakes!

There is no doubt who the main character of this chapter is; nobody but Jesus fits John's description. When He returns at the end of the tribulation, He comes to wage war, and the Antichrist, the kings of the earth and their armies assemble to fight Him as He returns with His army. This makes it clear that those supporting the Antichrist are under the deluding influence of the devil. This is the battle of Armageddon.

Jesus makes short work of them all, throwing the Antichrist and the false prophet into the lake of fire and killing the rest with a sword "that comes out of His mouth" (v. 21). This could be symbolic of the fact that He kills them with just a word, which is no trouble for the One who created the world with His words! Paul wrote concerning the Antichrist: "And then the lawless one will be revealed whom the Lord will slay with the breath of His mouth and bring to an end by the appearance of His coming." (2 Thess. 2:8). We also learn that the Antichrist's armies become bird food (see vv. 17-18,21). Jesus mentioned this "feast of the fowl" at His return in Matthew 24:27-28, "For just as the lightning comes from the east and flashes even to the west, so shall the coming of the Son of man be. Wherever the corpse is, there the vultures will gather."

You'll be right in on the action of this battle, because it's clear from verse 14 that we come back with Jesus, also riding on white horses as part of His army.

Tomorrow we will read Zechariah's added details of this same event.

PSALM 147:1-20

PROVERBS 31:1-7

This begins the final section of Proverbs, written by a gentleman named King Lemuel, who opened with a word of wisdom from his mother, who wisely warned him against the evils of alcohol. She stated that wine clouds a person's thinking, and in the case of a king, a clouded mind could have disastrous results.

DECEMBER 29

ZECHARIAH 14:1-21

This battle Zechariah described must be the same one we've been reading about in Revelation, the battle of Armageddon, because it centers on the valley of Megiddo in Israel. We learn from Zechariah that when the nations gather against Jerusalem, they will experience a certain degree of success (see v. 2). But then the Lord will go forth to fight Jerusalem's enemies, actually descending upon the Mount of Olives (see v. 4), which sits right beside Jerusalem and Mount Zion. Remember that it was from the Mount of Olives that Jesus ascended, and as His disciples watched Him go, two angels appeared and said to them, "Men of Galilee, why do you stand looking into the sky? This Jesus, who has been taken up from you into heaven, will come in just the same way as you have watched Him go into heaven" (Acts 1:11). Not only will He come in the same way, but He will also arrive on the same spot!

When Jesus' feet touch the Mount of Olives, there will be another great earthquake, and the mountain will be split in half, east to west. The new valley it creates will somehow provide an escape route for some of the inhabitants of Jerusalem (see v. 5). Furthermore, this new valley will become the riverbed for the living waters that will flow from Jerusalem, about which we have already read in Ezekiel 47:1-12. Those living waters will flow in two directions, half toward the Mediterranean and half toward the Dead Sea (see v. 8). As Ezekiel explained, the result will be that the Dead Sea will no longer be dead, but rather a fisherman's hot spot!

The topography will be further altered by the flattening of the land from a point six miles north of Jerusalem to a point thirty-five miles southwest of Jerusalem. And just as Isaiah prophesied, Mount Zion (upon which Jerusalem sits) will be elevated even higher than it is now (see v. 10; Is. 2:2).

Finally, we see that there will be some who survive the tribulation and the battle of Armageddon and are permitted to enter into the millennium (see v. 16). They will be required to travel to Jerusalem annually to worship Jesus during the Feast of Booths. If they don't, they'll be judged (see vv. 17-18). Along with other nations, Egypt is specifically mentioned, and this passage proves that not everybody living during Christ's millennial rule will be serving Him from the heart. People will serve Him only because of His "iron rule." At the end of the millennium, when Satan is loosed for the final time, the rebellious of the earth will gather once again at Jerusalem to overthrow Jesus. But they will be consumed with fire from heaven. Isn't it amazing that some people, who will be living when Jesus is ruling the earth, will actually rebel against Him? That fact reveals the awful condition of unregenerate people's hearts.

REVELATION 20:1-15

At the onset of the millennium, Satan will be bound by a great chain and cast into the abyss for one thousand years, which will restrain him from deceiving the nations (see vv. 1-3). Then we'll be granted our positions of authority based on our faithfulness while on earth, as we reign with Christ during the millennium. The bodies of the martyred tribulational saints will also be resurrected and joined with their spirits that have come from heaven (see v. 4). They will help Jesus rule as well. The Scripture makes it clear that the bodies of the unsaved dead will not be resurrected until after the millennium (see v. 5). However, they are very much in existence all during that time, as disembodied spirits in hell (literally, "Hades").

After one thousand years, Satan will be loosed "for a short time" (v. 3) to deceive the nations, obviously misleading only those who have been offering Jesus feigned obedience. Up until then they never rebel openly against the Lord, but once Satan is loosed, he will deceive them into imagining they can actually overthrow Christ's government! As difficult as it is to imagine, there will be multitudes who come to make war against Jesus in Jerusalem. Notice that they come up "on the *broad plain* of the earth" and surround the "beloved city" (v. 9, italics mine). That agrees perfectly with what Zechariah stated about the hills around Jerusalem becoming a forty-mile-long plain during the millennium. This will be a short battle, just like the one a thousand years before; fire will come down from heaven and consume them all. And finally, Satan will join the Antichrist and the false prophet in the lake of fire, where "they will be tormented day and night forever and ever" (v. 10).

We need to realize that the "lake of fire" and "Hades" are two different places. The lake of fire is the "Gehenna" of which Jesus spoke—people will be cast into it bodily, after they've been resurrected (see Matt. 5:29-30). Presently, unsaved people go to Hades, which is located in the heart of the earth. They go there as spirits, awaiting their bodily resurrection and their final judgment at the end of the millennium, after which they will be cast into the lake of fire for eternity.

John described this final judgment, called "the great white throne of judgment," before which all unbelievers will stand. Words can hardly describe the awesomeness of the scene as the book of life is searched for the names of the ones who are standing before the very throne of God. Other books, which describe the deeds of their lives, are searched as well. They will have no argument of defense before their Maker, as their deeds will testify to the unbelief that has always been in their hearts.

Aren't you glad you've come to know Jesus? Isn't it wonderful to be able to read passages like this one without any fear? Do you now feel a greater urgency to spread the gospel to the whole world?

PSALM 148:1-14

PROVERBS 31:8-9

DECEMBER 30

MALACHI 1:1-2:16

Malachi is appropriately placed as the final book of the Old Testament, as it was the last book to be written—about 430 years before Jesus' incarnation. The temple had been rebuilt more than 50 years before through the encouraging prophecies of Haggai and Zechariah, and we are now at the time that corresponds to the book of Nehemiah, the man who mobilized the Jews to rebuild Jerusalem's walls. Malachi addressed some of the same problems that both Ezra and Nehemiah did. It's obvious from this book that the original zeal of the returned Jews had worn off, and they had grown slack in their devotion to the Lord. Their religion was mere formality, and they even questioned

God's love and justice.

You may question God's statement that He loved Jacob but hated Esau (see 1:2-3). God was not talking here about the *individual men* Jacob and Esau, but rather about the nations that stemmed from their progeny. God was saying He loves the people to whom Malachi's prophecy was directed—Israel, the sons of Jacob. But He hates the descendents of Esau, the nation of Edom. We have read prophecies in other books that were directed at Edom, and you might remember the little book of Obadiah was written primarily to condemn that evil nation and predict its demise, fulfilled during the Babylonian invasion. Now God said through Malachi that even though Edom claimed that it would rebuild its ruined nation, He would tear down anything they build (see 1:4). The main point of this passage seems to be that the repatriated Jews were questioning God's love for them (see 1:2), and God was pointing out how blessed they are to have a second chance—something that wasn't offered to the Edomites.

From reading the second part of chapter 1, we learn that the people, following the example of the priests, were bringing unacceptable sacrifices to the Lord—animals that were basically worthless because of some defect. That was forbidden under the Law of Moses. This portion of Scripture always reminds me of the many missionaries who have told me about some of the so-called care packages they've received from the States. People send them all the clothes they no longer wear because they're worn out or out of style. What kind of "sacrifice" for the gospel is that? We should give God our best. Otherwise, our shoddy giving shows how cold our hearts have grown toward Him.

Notice the promise of 1:11, which indicates that one day all the earth will serve the Lord wholeheartedly: "For from the rising of the sun, even to its setting, My name will be great among the nations, and in every place incense is going to be offered to My name."

Chapter 2 is first directed to the priests, who were probably the ones most guilty of offering the defective sacrifices. They were also corrupting God's covenant with their father, Levi, by leading people astray and dishonoring the Lord through their halfhearted service. This was a true message of "repent or else!"

The second half of chapter 2 addressed the same problem Nehemiah had to deal with—some of the men of Judah had divorced their wives to marry non-Jewish women. Yet those same men were covering the altar of the Lord with tears and complaining that He didn't answer their prayers (see 2:13). God doesn't answer the prayers of those who don't obey Him. Their sin would be the equivalent of a Christian man's divorcing his Christian wife and marrying a non-Christian.

REVELATION 21:1-27

Peter declared in his second epistle that one day "the heavens will pass away with a roar and the elements will be destroyed with intense heat, and the earth and its works will be burned up" (2 Pet. 3:10). Jesus also foretold that "heaven and earth will pass away." (Matt. 24:35). That won't be the end of everything; God will just be cleaning up the results of Satan's earthly reign, thousands of years of humanity's sins, and the mess that is left after the tribulation. John saw the new heaven and earth that God will create at that time (and which Isaiah predicted—Is. 65:17).

John also saw the New Jerusalem coming down from heaven to earth, and it is almost beyond description. It's quite a huge city—1,500 miles by 1,500 miles, and is even 1,500 miles in height! Apparently the main material used in its construction is gold so pure that it appears transparent (see v. 18). It's a good thing the city is transparent, because the whole city has one light source—the glory that emanates from God (see v. 23). Somehow it will illumine the entire earth, and all the nations will be subservient to our Father God and the Lord Jesus Christ, who live there (see vv. 22-24). Now won't that be something? I realize there are many questions that could be raised about those future glories, but we'll just have to wait to have them answered. The point is, if your name is recorded in the Lamb's book of life, you'll be there! There will no longer be any death, crying or pain (see v. 4).

One more promise to those who "overcome" was added to the promises of the early part of this book—God said that those who overcome shall "inherit these things, and I will be his God and he will be My son" (v. 7). This is the final proof that the expression "he who overcomes" refers to all those who have been born again through faith in Jesus Christ, and not just to an elite group of supersaints who obtained perfection on earth. We are the overcomers!

PSALM 149:1-9

PROVERBS 31:10-24

If you want to be a good wife, here are the virtues for which to strive. Notice that most emphasized is her devotion to her husband and children, her compassion on the less fortunate, and her ability to earn money.

DECEMBER 31

MALACHI 2:17-4:6

This reading opens with Israel questioning God's justice, and God's reply in chapter 3 was that He was sending One who would bring true justice to light and who eventually will purify Israel and eliminate all evildoers. John the Baptist was also mentioned as "the messenger of the covenant" (3:1).

The Lord then called those backslidden people to return to Him, but they innocently asked, "How shall we return?" (3:7). In response, God called them thieves who had robbed Him by not paying their tithes or giving Him their offerings. As a result, they had been cursed financially (see 3:9), just as will any Christian who withholds what is God's due.

God also indicted those who had brazenly stated that it was vain to serve Him and who had called the wicked people more blessed than those who obeyed God. Those observers made the mistake that many others have—interpreting God's mercy and patience as a sign of His approval.

Apparently, there was a group of people who repented at God's words through Malachi, and God took notice and wrote their names down in a book (see 3:16-17). Possibly it was one of the books that will be opened at the great white throne of judgment we read about in Revelation.

Finally, God warned once more of the coming terrifying "day of the Lord," when the wicked will be burned in God's consuming fire (see 4:1-3). And the Lord promised to send Elijah the prophet "before the coming of the great and terrible day of the Lord" (4:5). We know from the New Testament that this promise was partially fulfilled by John the Baptist, and we'll have to wait to see its complete fulfillment in someone else (see Matt. 17:10-13).

After Malachi was written, there were four hundred silent years until the birth of Jesus in Bethlehem. One notable event that occurred between the Old and New Testaments was the translation of the Hebrew Old Testament for the first time. It was translated into the Greek language, which came to be called the Septuagint. That was the version used by the first Christians.

P.S.: Congratulations! You have just completed something that has not been done by most Christians. You've read the entire Old Testament! It seems like a wonderful day for ice cream!

REVELATION 22:1-21

The river of life mentioned in this chapter is similar to the one Ezekiel and Zechariah saw (see Ezek. 47:1-12; Zech. 14:8). The main difference is that Ezekiel and Zechariah saw the river of life during the millennium, whereas John saw it in the "eternal state." Ezekiel saw the tree of life as well, but the idea of its leaves being for the healing of the nations is a mystery. It is interesting that we read about this tree on the first day of our Bible study (see Gen. 2:9), and now we're reading about it again on the final day. Someday, when we're permitted to eat from it, we will better understand its significance (see v. 14).

We also read that there will no longer be any night (see v. 5). That's a good thing, because I assume that our resurrected, glorified bodies will have no need for sleep. John said there will be no need for the sun or moon (see 21:23; 22:5) because of the brilliance of God's glory that will shine throughout the city.

It's interesting that the angel told John that the things he saw "must shortly take place" (v. 6), and that "the time is near" (v. 10), in light of the fact that it has now been almost two thousand years since John had his vision. Of course, we know that a thousand years to us is like one day to God (see 2 Pet. 3:8), so from His standpoint, the things John saw *would* take place shortly.

Also in today's reading is a theme prevalent throughout the Bible: everyone reaps what he has sown. Jesus said in verse 12, "Behold, I am coming quickly, and My reward is with Me, to render to every man *according to what he has done*" (italics mine). Thank God that in our case, Jesus has already reaped what we have sown as far as our sins are concerned, but we will still reap reward or loss of reward in heaven based on what we've done as Christians (see Rom. 14:10-12; 1 Cor. 3:12-15). That should be a most sobering thought to us, one that guides the affairs of our lives and charts the course of our remaining years here on earth.

Maranatha!

PSALM 150:1-6

PROVERBS 31:25-31

This virtuous woman is also a woman of faith—"she smiles at the future" (v. 25). Why? Because she "fears the Lord" (v. 30) and knows He will always keep His promises.

Last Words

I can't help being a little sentimental as we finish our journey through the Bible today. We've come a long way, haven't we? There has never been a year of my life in which I spent so much time studying God's Word, as well as numerous other commentaries and biblical resources. Thanks for reading with me!

It has been my sincere prayer that this commentary would help you to grow in the grace and knowledge of our Lord Jesus Christ, for His greater glory. Just as important, I hope you have formed a daily habit of reading God's Word that will continue until you see Jesus. For that reason, I include a daily reading plan for you to follow, beginning tomorrow! You'll notice that this plan will guide you through the New Testament only, which I think will be best for you during the next year. If you follow this plan, you'll read through the New Testament twice in one year. You'll also notice that your reading time each day will be shorter, allowing you more time for reflection, meditation and prayer. May the Lord bless you as you draw closer to Him.

You may feel as if you know me pretty well now that we've spent a year together, and I probably know a few things about you, too. You're probably a person dedicated to serving God, and you're seeking first His kingdom, just as I am. My highest desire is to see the gospel go to the ends of the earth. Because of that, I have founded ETHNOS Ministries. You'll remember that *ethnos* is the Greek word for "nations," but for us, it is also an acronym that stands for "Equipping, Teaching, Helping National Overseas Servants." We are working in places around the world to equip God-called servants of Christ to take the gospel to their own culture and other nearby cultures. I've written a book titled *The Christian Disciple's Manual* that we're giving to pastors in other nations. It's filled with fundamental Bible teaching, and through it, national Christian workers are able to learn life-changing truths that you and I might take for granted but that they've never heard. We're looking for people like you who will help us put this *Disciple's Manual* into the hands of more pastors in other nations. We need people who will sponsor sending one *Disciple's Manual* per month to a dedicated pastor or Christian worker somewhere in the world. If you're interested, I would love to send you more information about how God can use you in this important ministry. You can write to me at the following address: ETHNOS Ministries, P.O. Box 0446, Library, PA 15129.

Finally, if you're a pastor or Christian leader in a nation other than the United States or Canada and would like a copy of *The Christian Disciple's Manual*, please write to me at the above address. Thank you, and God bless you.

New Testament Bible Reading Plan

Matt. 1:1 - 3:6
Matt. 3:7 - 4:25
Matt. 5:1-48
Matt. 6:1 - 7:14
Matt. 7:15 - 8:17
Matt. 8:18 - 9:17
Matt. 9:18 - 10:25
Matt. 10:26 - 11:30
Matt. 12:1-45
Matt. 12:46 - 13:46
Matt. 13:47 - 14:36
Matt. 15:1 - 16:12
Matt. 16:13 - 17:27
Matt. 18:1 - 19:12
Matt. 19:13 - 20:28
Matt. 20:29 - 21:46
Matt. 22:1 - 23:12
Matt. 23:13 - 24:28
Matt. 24:29 - 25:30
Matt. 25:31 - 26:46
Matt. 26:47 - 27:14
Matt. 27:15-66
Matt. 28; Rom. 1:1-17
Rom. 1:18 - 2:24
Rom. 2:25 - 3:31
Rom. 4:1 - 5:5
Rom. 5:6 - 6:23
Rom. 7:1 - 8:8
Rom. 8:9-39
Rom. 9:1 - 10:13
Rom. 10:14 - 11:36
Rom. 12:1 - 13:14
Rom. 14:1 - 15:22
Rom 15:23 - 16:27
1 Cor. 1:1 - 2:5
1 Cor. 2:6 - 3:23
1 Cor. 4:1 - 5:13
1 Cor. 6:1 - 7:24
1 Cor. 7:25 - 8:13
1 Cor. 9:1 - 10:13
1 Cor. 10:14 - 11:16
1 Cor. 11:17 - 12:26
1 Cor. 12:27 - 14:17
1 Cor. 14:18 - 15:28
1 Cor. 15:29 - 16:24
Mark 1:1 - 2:12
Mark 2:13 - 3:30
Mark 3:31 - 5:20
Mark 5:21 - 6:29
Mark 6:30 - 7:23
Mark 7:24 - 8:38
Mark 9:1 - 10:12
Mark 10:13-52
Mark 11:1 - 12:17
Mark 12:18 - 13:13
Mark 13:14 - 14:21
Mark 14:22-72
Mark 15:1 - 16:20
2 Cor. 1:1 - 2:11
2 Cor. 2:12 - 3:18
2 Cor. 4:1 - 5:10
2 Cor. 5:11 - 6:13
2 Cor. 6:14 - 7:16
2 Cor. 8:1-24
2 Cor. 9:1 - 10:18
2 Cor. 11:1-33

2 Cor. 12:1-21
2 Cor. 13; Gal. 1
Gal. 2:1 - 3:9
Gal. 3:10 - 4:31
Gal. 5:1-26
Gal. 6; Eph. 1
Eph. 2:1 - 3:21
Eph. 4:1-32
Eph. 5:1 - 6:24
Phil. 1:1 - 2:18
Phil. 2:19 - 3:21
Phil. 4; Luke 1:1-25
Luke 1:26-80
Luke 2:1-52
Luke 3:1-38
Luke 4:1 - 5:11
Luke 5:12 - 6:11
Luke 6:12 - 7:10
Luke 7:11 - 8:3
Luke 8:4-39
Luke 8:40 - 9:27
Luke 9:28 - 10:12
Luke 10:13 - 11:13
Luke 11:14 - 12:7
Luke 12:8-59
Luke 13:1 - 14:6
Luke 14:7 - 15:32
Luke 16:1 - 17:10
Luke 17:11 - 18:17
Luke 18:18 - 19:27
Luke 19:28 - 20:26
Luke 20:27 - 21:28
Luke 21:29 - 22:34
Luke 22:35 - 23:12
Luke 23:13 - 24:12
Luke 24:13-53; Col. 1:1-20
Col. 1:21 - 2:23
Col. 3:1 - 4:18
1 Thess. 1:1 - 3:13
1 Thess. 4:1 - 5:28
2 Thess. 1:1 - 2:17
2 Thess. 3; 1 Tim. 1
1 Tim. 2:1 - 3:16
1 Tim. 4:1 - 5:25
1 Tim. 6; 2 Tim. 1
2 Tim. 2:1 - 3:17
2 Tim. 4; Titus 1
Titus 2:1 - 3:15
Philem. 1; John 1:1-28
John 1:29 - 2:25
John 3:1 - 4:3
John 4:4-54
John 5:1-47
John 6:1-42
John 6:43 - 7:29
John 7:30 - 8:20
John 8:21-59
John 9:1 - 10:21
John 10:22 - 11:53
John 11:54 - 12:50
John 13:1 - 14:14
John 14:15 - 15:27
John 16:1 - 17:26
John 18:1 - 19:22
John 19:23 - 20:31
John 21; Heb. 1
Heb. 2:1 - 3:19
Heb. 4:1 - 5:14
Heb. 6:1 - 7:17
Heb. 7:18 - 8:13
Heb. 9:1-28
Heb. 10:1-39
Heb. 11:1-31
Heb. 11:32 - 12:29

Heb. 13; James 1:1-18
James 1:19 - 3:18
James 4:1 - 5:20
1 Pet. 1:1 - 2:10
1 Pet. 2:11 - 4:6
1 Pet. 4:7 - 5:14; 2 Pet. 1
2 Pet. 2:1 - 3:18
1 John 1:1 - 2:17
1 John 2:18 - 3:24
1 John 4:1 - 5:21
Acts 1:1 - 2:47
Acts 3:1 - 4:37
Acts 5:1 - 6:15
Acts 7:1-50
Acts 7:51 - 8:40
Acts 9:1-43
Acts 10:1-48
Acts 11:1 - 12:23
Acts 12:24 - 13:41
Acts 13:42 - 14:28
Acts 15:1 - 16:15
Acts 16:16 - 17:34
Acts 18:1 - 19:12
Acts 19:13 - 20:38
Acts 21:1-36
Acts 21:37 - 23:10
Acts 23:11 - 24:17
Acts 25:1 - 26:13
Acts 27:1-44
Acts 28; 2 John 1
3 John 1; Jude 1
Rev. 1:1 - 2:17
Rev. 2:18 - 3:22
Rev. 4:1 - 5:14
Rev. 6:1 - 7:17
Rev. 8:1 - 9:21
Rev. 10:1 - 11:19
Rev. 12:1 - 13:18
Rev. 14:1 - 15:8
Rev. 16:1 - 17:18
Rev. 18:1 - 19:21
Rev. 20:1 - 21:27
Rev. 22:1-21

Notes